940.53
E45
1988
c.3

ISR
Circulating

ECHOES FROM THE

Philosophical Reflections on a Dark Time

D1227253

6/97 Repl.

ECHOES FROM THE

Edited by Alan Rosenberg
and Gerald E. Myers

HOLOCAUST

Philosophical Reflections on a Dark Time

Temple University Press
Philadelphia

Temple University Press, Philadelphia 19122
Copyright © 1988 by Temple University.
  All rights reserved
Published 1988
Printed in the United States of America

The paper used in this publication meets the
minimum requirements of American National
Standard for Information Sciences—Permanence of
Paper for Printed Library Materials, ANSI Z39.48-1984

Library of Congress Cataloging-in-Publication Data

Echoes from the Holocaust.

  Includes index.
    1. Holocaust, Jewish (1939–1945)—Moral and
ethical aspects.   2. Indifferentism (Ethics)
I. Rosenberg, Alan, 1939–   .   II. Myers, Gerald E.
(Gerald Eugene), 1923–   .
D810.J4E217   1988   940.53′15′03924   87-18109
ISBN 0-87722-539-7 (alk. paper)

*To all those who seek to understand the Holocaust
in order to protect the future*

CONTENTS

PREFACE

The murder of six million Jewish men, women, and children during World War II was an act of such barbarity that it constitutes one of the central events of our time; yet a list of the major concerns of professional philosophers since 1945 would exclude the Holocaust. Compared to their output on the mind-body problem or on the merits of utilitarianism, philosophers' contributions to discussions of the Holocaust have been scanty. The editors' collaboration began when Alan Rosenberg, having worked mostly alone on the philosophical ramifications of the Holocaust, called his colleagues' attention to the paucity of relevant writings by members of philosophy departments. With Dr. Ernest Schwarcz, dean of the School of General Studies and professor of philosophy at Queens College, we organized a conference of philosophers at Queens College, City University of New York, in May 1985 to discuss the significance of the Holocaust for philosophy.

The complexities of approaching the Holocaust philosophically became evident during the conference sessions. There are hazards in philosophizing about the Holocaust, but there are also hazards in not doing so. The former include issues of sensitivity and taste as well as those of fact and meaning, whereas ignorance and forgetfulness are obviously among the latter. Respect for the victims of Auschwitz and Treblinka makes everything said appear somehow inadequate, yet that same respect makes intelligent responses imperative. To write about the Holocaust is to live with this conflict unresolved.

In undertaking this volume, we encountered further complexities. Some philosophers doubt that the Holocaust is particularly relevant for academic philosophy; others explicitly deny its relevance, arguing that its special impact is not upon philosophy but theology. Some find the subject too intimidating, while others, because their lives or those of relatives have been severely affected by the catastrophe, find it too distressing to write about. A few colleagues, who were surprised that members of the profession had not taken up the issue of the Holocaust and thought such a volume was an excellent idea, nevertheless declined our invitation to participate in this project because they felt they knew too little about the subject.

There are, of course, members of the profession who do declare an interest in the Holocaust, some of them contributing here. There are philosophers who think, like John Dewey (in his *Problems of Men* [New York: Philosophical Library, 1946], pp. 11–12), that some events "in their production of good and evil . . . are so central, so strategic in position, that their urgency" demands "the most systematic reflective attention that can be given." Like Dewey, they believe that philosophy can relate interpretively to such events, not only for recalling or understanding them, but also for transforming culture and intellect by defining the enduring significance of those events. Or, like Hegel, who viewed the French Revolution's excesses as abstract formulations gone amok, some philosophers hold that, until the Holocaust is framed in its global philosophical dimensions, its meanings will elude us.

But, as the Queens College Conference revealed and as was reinforced by the postconference deliberations leading to the preparation of this book, an agreement that philosophy ought to reflect systematically and urgently on the Holocaust can end in disagreement about philosophy's proper role and goal in this endeavor. How should philosophy approach the Holocaust? Inevitably, this itself becomes a philosophical question. Appreciating this, we submit, should stimulate rather than inhibit philosophers' interest in the subject.

Although professional philosophy has been overly reticent about the Holocaust, other intellectual disciplines have been more vocal. Novelists, historians, psychologists, and theologians have presented the chilling facts and the kinds of questions and interpretations that those facts provoke. Films such as *Shoah* have helped to connect contemporary sensitivities to the incredible realities of the Nazi death camps. Holocaust memorials, victims' stories of horrors, and media attention to newly identified Nazi criminals have created a post-Holocaust culture. To this, as well as to the Holocaust itself, philosophy needs to give its attention and to ask where, in all of it, the discipline has an important part to play.

It can be argued that philosophy discharges a duty to itself in being responsive to the implications of the Holocaust, as well as thoroughly critiquing itself in the light of it. The idea must be faced, as it was briefly at the Queens College Conference, and as it is in some of the essays in this volume, that aspects of modern philosophy as well as the tradition of German philosophy were among the villains in the Nazi rise to power. For example, from Fichte to Martin Heidegger, the suggestion runs, there is an intellectual streak that George Santayana called the egotism of German philosophy, which may have insinuated into the culture the perverse assumption that power is the supreme value. The suggestion may be unfair, a more accurate reading of German philosophy may be at hand, but in our post-Holocaust theorizing we cannot afford to leave it unscrutinized.

What cannot be left unexamined is the notion that a culture constructs its identity from multiple forces, including the philosophies taught in its universities, and that those philosophies, accordingly, are to be held responsible for their diffused effects beyond the campuses. The eyewitness report of a Nazi soldier, from whose pocket Kant's *Critique of Pure Reason* could be seen protruding, smashing a Jewish infant to death, is only one of the sickening instances of how a rich culture failed to abort the nihilism of National Socialism in Germany. Philosophy thus conducts an obligatory self-examination in asking, in our post-Holocaust culture, what part the philosophical climate played in allowing Hitlerism its temporary triumph? What is the philosophical climate today and what are its probable cultural effects? Can philosophy help our culture to become a bulwark against future agents of evil?

This volume represents but a small step toward the desired consideration of such questions; for the most part, they are treated here indirectly and suggestively. Until philosophers become more familiar with the facts and problematics of the Holocaust, their ways of relating it to their discipline will betray a first-approach kind of tentativeness. Philosophy's self-examination in the light of the Holocaust, therefore, has barely begun.

We regard this book, together with the few philosophical efforts already made by others, as a beginning of what needs to be done. Our hope is that the essays in this volume will help to identify problems and directions that philosophers can fruitfully investigate. As our planning developed subsequent to the Queens College Conference, it became apparent that a volume of essays by a multidisciplinary authorship, including philosophically minded representatives of other disciplines, would be more effective than one by professional philosophers exclusively. A context for philosophizing is needed, a context in which the Holocaust is approachable for searching its meanings. Philosophy's inquiry about its relationship to the Holocaust requires the assistance of other disciplines such as history, sociology, political science, and religious studies. We also decided, for this reason, to incorporate previously published papers among the ones written expressly for this book.

Temple University Press reviewers of our original prospectus recommended various important revisions, one of them being a historical overview of the Holocaust at the outset. Part One, "The Historical Impact," consisting of George M. Kren's essay on the Holocaust as history, provides the historical perspective from which the book's other essays can be studied, as it also provides a concrete context in which the meanings of the historical events can be looked for. Kren's overview presents certain themes that reappear in the papers that follow—the uniqueness of the Holocaust, the special features of the Nazi mentality, the technology and death machinery of the concentration camps, and the widespread moral indifference in Europe and America that was shown toward the destruction of the Jews.

The papers collected in Part Two, "Assault on Morality," address specific moral themes. Rainer C. Baum develops the thesis that reflecting upon the Holocaust reveals the major form of modern evil to be moral indifference. Not ideology but passivity and indifference sentenced six million Jews to death, and, unless modern moral consciousness transcends mere conventionalism, the eruption of evil from banal sources is likely to happen again. The Holocaust leads Martin P. Golding to a consideration of a concept of moral pathology that can be applied to societies as well as to individuals. Golding's paper demonstrates the importance of such a concept for developing different ways of approaching the Holocaust, connecting it, for instance, with what may be called the legal pathology of the Nazi system, its use of law as a mystification device.

Lawrence L. Langer, upon reading accounts of existence in the death camps, asks in his essay whether it makes sense to speak of moral choices in such contexts. Langer challenges the attempts made by some to see the Holocaust as a kind of continuum in man's spiritual history or to equate morality with the resolution to survive. Like Langer, Abigail L. Rosenthal questions whether the morality of the Holocaust's victims has been correctly depicted. Her essay is directed toward the question of whether the Jewish victims were guilty of passivity and even complicity. Her analyses converge on a negative answer to this, thus allowing us, as she asserts, to draw firm moral lines between those who commit evil and those who suffer it.

Taking the suicide of a death-camp survivor as an example, John K. Roth views the Holocaust as having caused a traumatizing loss of trust in the world. His paper explores what this loss of trust means. This leads him to ask what if anything emerges in our understanding of the Holocaust that can restore, in some measure, the lost trust. The key concept of trust is also addressed by Laurence Thomas who wonders, given the evil and the moral indifference that characterized the Holocaust, whether Jews will have any good reason for trusting fellow human beings in a future catastrophe. At some point he refers to current relations between Jews and blacks, concluding that in a world whose unreliability is all too obvious it is yet possible to discern an important potential basis of trust.

While disturbed by the silence of academic philosophy on the Holocaust, Kenneth Seeskin stresses the problems met by philosophy in trying to say something significant—for example, about the nature of evil. Saddened by the fact that the Holocaust seems not to have effected more changes in the world's consciousness, that evil seems to defy comprehensibility, Seeskin proposes that we not concentrate on the theoretical question of how the Holocaust can be understood but rather upon the practical one of how its recurrence can be prevented. The nature of evil is also the topic of Warren K. Thompson's paper. He asserts that the philosopher is blocked by a variety of obstacles in seeking a deeper insight into the evil of the Holocaust, one of them being its alleged irrationality; for if it is consigned to the irrational, then nothing deeper in the way of knowledge can be hoped for. Perhaps all that philosophy can conclude, Thompson suggests, is that the crisis of ethics and values created by the Holocaust is still very much with us, and that recognizing this crisis must precede any effort toward its resolution.

Part Three, "Echoes from the Death Camps," contains a group of papers that, while focusing on quite different topics, share an urgent concern for what the Holocaust's reverberations may teach us regarding significant aspects of Western culture. Edith Wyschogrod's essay, employing the concepts of life world and death world, illuminates what it is about our everyday world that is taken for granted and is put into question by the nature of life in the concentration camps. An important conclusion of her essay is that no matter how desperate the circumstances, as long as one can recognize someone else as a site of value, one can keep the ethical dimension alive, though everything in the surroundings threatens to extinguish it. Alan Rosenberg and Paul Marcus demonstrate the ways in which the Holocaust is a major challenge to the foundations of our civilization, and at the same time a test of philosophy's ability to meet and explore that challenge, by constructing a conceptual framework within which the meanings of the Holocaust can begin to be unraveled. The purpose of Ronald Aronson's essay is to explore what the Holocaust has to tell us about the idea and reality of progress. He is also concerned with examining various efforts at relating the Holocaust to progress and asking whether they help us in making sense of our world after Auschwitz.

Berel Lang points to the unusual features of the Nazis' use of language that developed with the Holocaust. Lang's essay explains in depth why the language of genocide is a challenge to our understanding of the use of language in the present as well as in the past. Steven T. Katz, while also concerned with matters of language, devotes his paper to an analysis of the technology of destruction. Katz shows that the technology of destruction was part of a larger cultural–ideological process that must be understood if we are to comprehend the dehumanization of the death camps, and if we are to realize the potential monstrousness of a mechanistic environment.

George Kren's second essay analyzes the inability of moral theory to deal with individuals and groups willing to commit unspeakable atrocities in the service of the state. Ethical theory, he notes, needs to study the issue of the individual acting as an agent of the state and how it is that a sense of transcendence can move people to inhumane behavior. Hans Jonas, in reflecting upon the Holocaust's horrors, asks a different question in his essay: Can the Jews remain unaffected in their faith? Jonas immediately answers in the negative. In rethinking the Jewish theological heritage and in returning to Job's question, Jonas outlines a post-Holocaust theology that neither quite deserts nor wholly preserves the traditional faith. The echoes of the death camps resound also in Gerald E. Myers's paper which, in surveying the psychology of man since the Holocaust, holds that post-Holocaust psychology has justifiably replaced the concept of human nature with that of the human condition, and that this becomes an object of interdisciplinary investigation. Myers identifies the militarized consciousness as one of the factors responsible for the Nazi mentality and its senseless destructiveness.

Another set of philosophical concerns is assembled in Part Four, "Challenges to the Understanding." Hannah Arendt, in her (virtually forgotten) paper, argues that the unprecedented nature of the Holocaust forces social scientists and historical scholars to reconsider their fundamental preconceptions about the course of human behavior. Nazi destructiveness challenges our understanding. How can we render intelligible those insane actions that were motivated neither by passion nor by utility, and how can we morally come to grips with crimes unanticipated by the Ten Commandments?

Alice L. and A. Roy Eckardt share Arendt's worries about comprehensibility and suggest a number of difficulties that one must face in trying to answer the questions Arendt poses. For example, they raise the issue as to whether calling what happened to the Jews "The Holocaust" does justice to the event. Alan Rosenberg is also concerned with the difficulties of coming to terms with the Holocaust and suggests a number of reasons for this problem, some of which result from our own mystification of the events. Dan Magurshak focuses on the claim that the Holocaust is incomprehensible and shows how this view blocks our very ability to understand what we must understand. He agrees that at present the Holocaust is largely uncomprehended, but this hardly disproves the possibility of a more coherent and complete account of the events and factors that caused it. Indeed, it must be possible; it is not enough merely to remember Auschwitz and Treblinka, for unless we critically and compassionately analyze and explain them, we remain impotent to prevent such future hells.

Attempting to understand the Holocaust includes an appreciation of what its meanings do and do not imply. The Holocaust looms over ongoing debates in contemporary ethics, and it can be used for taking one side in such debates by accusing the other side of starting down a slippery slope to another Holocaust. Peter H. Hare, in his discussion of how this can happen in debates about mercy killing, warns of the need to distinguish between use and abuse of Holocaust studies. Manfred Henningsen is justly troubled in his essay by the failure of certain German historians to see the Holocaust accurately and in full glare. Their failure can be linked to Chancellor Helmut Kohl's taking President Ronald Reagan to Bitburg Cemetery in May 1985 in order, as Henningsen views it, to secure a historical legitimation for the West German state. Consequently, the world is still challenged to locate Nazi Germany in the context of German history so that apologies will never be allowed to replace our stunned realization of what the Holocaust's realities were.

In conclusion, let us agree that the Holocaust will never cease to challenge our understanding and our sensitivities. The Holocaust raises some of the most profound and disturbing questions ever to confront the philosophically minded. The profoundest questions have a way of remaining perennial ones, and philosophy, as is often said, is perennial because of the questions it asks. It is not surprising, then, that philosophy and the Holocaust do seem joined henceforth.

ACKNOWLEDGMENTS

Completion of this book would not have been possible without the support of our many colleagues and friends.

First and foremost, we are indebted to our colleagues in the Philosophy Department of Queens College for their enthusiasm for our project. Especially helpful were Professors Eugene Fontinell, Peter Manicas, R. W. Sleeper, and Edith Wyschogrod. And our appreciation to the secretarial staff, Joan Lesnoy, Gladys Passoa, and Barbara Pauker, and the staff of the Word Processing Center, Arlene Diamond, Muriel Finkelstein, and Julia Kwartler, who managed to meet our impossible deadlines. Without proper sources little can be accomplished. It was through the persistence of the staff of the Paul Klapper Library that we were able to obtain the necessary materials.

A special debt is owed to Morris Rabinowitz, Branch Librarian, Dedham Public Library, who read the entire book more than once and provided invaluable suggestions.

We are especially grateful to Mary Chiffriller for her expert assistance in the final phase of the manuscript.

Others who contributed in large ways were Professor John J. McDermott, Texas A&M, Dr. Paul Marcus, a practicing psychotherapist, and Doris Katz, whose continued devotion to the project was appreciated—especially when the going got tough.

And, of course, our gratitude and appreciation to Jane Cullen and Mary Capouya, Temple University Press, who made our idea of a book into a reality.

PART ONE
The Historical Impact

1

THE HOLOCAUST AS HISTORY

George M. Kren

Before interpreting the Holocaust, what happened must be established. Such a task corresponds to the primary charge given by Leopold von Ranke, that the historian's purpose is the recreation of the past as it really happened. For Ranke this was essentially a simple matter: The professional historian would bring back the facts from hitherto unexamined records. He held to an implicit faith that these facts would speak for themselves. Their enumeration, usually in a chronological order would present a true picture of the past. The meaning of the events would be self-evident. This faith has ceased to be tenable, since we know that the act of recreating the past involves decisive subjective moments, and that a gulf separates fact from meaning.

ON WRITING ABOUT THE HOLOCAUST: EPISTEMOLOGICAL CONSIDERATIONS AND CONSTRAINTS

Venerable treatises on historical methodology have examined the means used by historians to validate their sources, how through elaborate external and internal criticism it becomes possible to establish that an event took place and describe that event in detail, with a high degree of certainty that the description accurately corresponds to the historical reality. That mass killings of Jews, Gypsies and others were carried out by the Germans in a systematic way, that a complex infrastructure for killing was evolved can be established beyond doubt.[1] The Germans[2] left behind voluminous documentation of their acts, and it is not difficult to establish *wie es eigentlich gewesen war*. Indeed the evidence available—testimonies from victims and perpetrators, documents, still and moving-picture photographs—at times threaten to become overwhelming and inundate the researchers with more materials than can be handled. Decades after the events detailed monographs of what happened in Greece or Romania still appear. Yet though some details of the Nazi actions still need to be filled in, the evidence for documenting in precise detail who did what to whom, who

3

supported it, who profited from it is readily available.[3] There is no difficulty in establishing the date on which Himmler gave the order to build Auschwitz—or finding which firms did the work. Numerous works describing the Nazi mass murder have appeared.[4] These generally well documented books accurately present the facts. The seeming objectivity—the belief that the words, paragraphs, and chapters hold up a mirror to that most recent past, in which it reflects itself—disguises the fact that the presentation of facts and events is filtered through the perspective of the author. The failure to recognize the subjective component of all historical presentations fundamentally misconstrues the nature of historical knowledge.

Contemporary analysis of historical writings has replaced nineteenth-century epistemological optimism with a radical pessimism that doubts the possibility of the recreation of the past.[5] In photography, advancing technology has created lenses that do not distort, that are able to create a true picture of the external reality. Historians do not possess such lenses. Nor is this a matter of correcting erroneous conclusions to achieve an ever-increasing accuracy. Physicists are able to increase the accuracy of constants. Historians view the same events from different premises and perspectives, but the later ones are not necessarily more accurate than the early accounts. The reason for critiquing the use of these metaphors of lenses and mirrors is that the past described by historians never happened, but is a construct of their minds. The evidence that permits description of concrete events is usually—at least for modern history—more than complete; however, the historian's task has never been primarily the discovery of the lost fact, but the imposition of a structure upon discrete past events in order to create an ordered meaningful image of the past.

What the so abundant evidence cannot show, what necessarily is inaccessible to direct observations, are the connections that have led to the creation of the concept "Holocaust." How "Holocaust" is defined is a matter of judgment dependent on values as much as facts. A recent work describing the brutal killing of Poles by the Germans used the deliberately provocative title *The Forgotten Holocaust*.[6] The word Holocaust does not refer to an event, but is a generalization that unites a variety of discrete events under one rubric: the killing of the mentally ill in Germany, the mass shootings of Jews by the *Einsatzgruppen*, the *Kommissarbefehl* (commissar order) that resulted in the killing of Communist functionaries, and the establishment of death camps. The unity between these events is a historical judgment, never self-evident, and in the case of the Holocaust always subject to polemical arguments. Should the (strikingly unreported) systematic mass starvation of Soviet prisoners of war be included in the Holocaust?[7] These killings were grounded, as was the killing of Jews, in Nazi racial theory and in their ideal of a Europe in which Jews did not exist and Slavs and other ethnic groups were to be completely subservient. Gypsies were exterminated in Auschwitz for racial reasons. The opposition to William Styron's *Sophie's Choice* and the film made from it was that the heroine who survived Auschwitz was not Jewish and was the daughter of a Polish anti-Semite.[8] Lucy Dawidowicz is not alone in arguing that the central fact of the Holocaust was that its victims were Jewish, and that it was the intent of the Nazi leadership to kill all Jews within the Nazi sphere of influence.[9]

Some recent writers have strongly connected the commissar order that authorized killing Russian Communists and the killing of Jews. Hitler's bitter and longstanding hatred of Jews is more than adequately documented. How significant was the identification of Jews and Bolsheviks in Hitler's mind? Was it this that led from an anti-Semitism whose aim was the expulsion of Jews from Germany, a policy implemented until 1941, to one committed to mass killings? The commissar order unequivocally contemplated the killing of Soviet Communist functionaries.[10] The text of the order demonstrates the perceived connection between Jews and bolshevism, yet it would be erroneous to interpret the order for the killing of Russian "commissars" and Communists as a euphemism for the killing of Jews. The Holocaust literature has largely avoided drawing connections between the killing of Jews and Communists, and indeed accounts may be read in a way that (indirectly) suggests that the killing of Communists appeared to some authors, if not legitimate, then a far lesser crime than the killing of Jews. While Himmler recognized some Gypsies as belonging to a special racial group and permitted them to live, his view clearly contemplated the total extermination of all Jews in German territory. Groups within the SS argued as to whether the extermination should take place immediately or whether Jewish labor power should first be exploited, but there appears little doubt that all Jews within the territory controlled by Germany were ticketed for death.

The language of history frequently models itself on that of the natural sciences, concerned with finding causes. The Holocaust had antecedents. Anti-Semitism, racism, eugenics, existed in the nineteenth century and earlier. Nationalism in the nineteenth century became ever more xenophobic. The years between World War I and World War II saw the erosion of liberalism and the disenchantment with liberal and democratic values. The European Right adopted anti-Semitism as a fundamental program. Although fascism and anti-Semitism were general phenomena of the interwar years, only Germany established the killing of Jews as a program possessing the highest priorities. Is the

Holocaust to be perceived primarily as a German or as a Euopean phenomenon? Clearly Hitler's role in the decision to kill Europe's Jews was important. Is Hitler's individual development to be accorded a primary focus—and since feelings toward other groups are rooted in subconscious tendencies what accord is to be given to Hitler's psychosexual development? Several historians have thought to analyze Hitler's psychology and in different ways concluded that his murderous hatred toward the Jews was rooted in unique patterns of personal development.[11] More recently some historians (labeled not altogether appropriately functionalists) have attempted to minimize Hitler's role in the Holocaust.[12] At what juncture did the Holocaust become "inevitable"? Clearly anti-Semitism and racism had prevailed in many countries in Europe without leading to mass killings. Karl A. Schleunes titled his examination of Nazi anti-Semitic legislation as "the twisted road to Auschwitz,"[13] suggesting that though there was no grand design, they "stumbled toward something resembling a Final Solution to the Jewish problem."[14] Certainly mass killing was not in the minds of the Germans when they passed the Nuremberg Laws. When was the decision to kill all the Jews made and by whom? Almost anyone looking at Europe in the summer of 1939 could not help but see the war coming. Its outbreak caused no surprise. Although the German anti-Semitism of the 1930s could be understood from its antecedents, the Holocaust did not appear inevitable in 1939, or even in 1941. The Nazis came into power because of disillusionment with the Versailles treaty, because of unemployment, because of Hitler's magnetic personality, but no convincing evidence exists for the view that the Nazis had always intended to kill all the Jews. Had that been in their minds, they would not have done everything in their power to expel the Jews from Germany. The difficulty for the Jews was not that the Germans sought to keep them in, but that few countries were willing to take them.

A difficulty, a limitation of the power to know historical events that must be faced, is that as soon as the historical task has shifted from describing what happened to providing an explanation of why it has happened, one *necessarily* enters the realm of the subjective. One mode of explaining historical events is to assign causal meaning to previous ones. The negative image of the Jew in German and European culture, the long history of the perception of the Jew as "culture destroying" certainly may be assigned causal significance in the evolution of anti-Semitism. But it is important to recognize that the connection between these and the Holocaust is always a subjective judgment, never the result of direct observation. In contrast to the physical sciences, in history a mode of explanation requires attributing motives to individual historical actors. Prior to the invasion of Russia, Napoleon decided to do this. From the evidence we may *infer* Napoleon's thought processes. These are never available for direct examination. The various decisions by the Nazi establishment concerning the Jews permit some inferences (though many are remarkably ambiguous) as to what the leadership wished to accomplish and what ideas moved it, but it is imperative to recognize that the best that the historian can do is to make inferences, and that motives and motivations cannot be established with the certainty that permits stating that a given event took place. And the introduction of psychological concepts suggesting that expressed motives and wishes may be disguises for other, unexpressed ones certainly complicates this.

In explaining why the Holocaust took place historians can show a compelling set of reasons, but never a demonstrated certainty. Analysis requires intepretations about the meaning of individual actions. The manner in which a judgment is made, the mode of explanation used, frequently depends on the value commitments of the historians. Historians writing at an early period, in which religious faith had a greater acceptance than it does now, would explain an event as the consequence of some divine intervention. As views changed, divine intervention as an explanation disappeared from historical writing. But value commitment and mode of interpretation are still joined together. A Marxist may interpret anti-Semitism as a defense of a capitalistic class, seeking to focus proletarian discontent on Jews rather than on themselves. Marxists have sought to explain anti-Semitism by focusing on the role of Jews as traders and middlemen in Eastern Europe or court financiers in the West. Liberals have sought to explain it on the basis of "prejudice," to be overcome by efforts of education in tolerance, while those on the political right have found explanations in the conduct attributed to Jews.

Any analysis requires that the event also be seen through the eyes of the participants. It is evident that the motives of those who engaged in the murder of Jews were "sincere," that is, the killings were not undertaken to gain political support or even to steal the property of the Jews, but because of their "honest" feeling that this was required to create a better world. Frequently analogies from surgery were used to legitimize acts. Just as a surgeon amputates a gangrenous leg, so the "gangrenous" Jews, whose presence would poison the body, must be eradicated.

Historical accounts designate some events as important, others as unimportant. The meaning of these judgments requires explication. In the first and most frequently used manner the concern is with a loosely quantitative designation of how causally significant any event was. The murder of Ernst von Rath in 1938 is designated as important because it triggered massive anti-Semitic actions in Germany. Here the future consequences define the importance of an event. An event may manifest some major dissonance with accepted values. The Holocaust has been labeled important because it violated values that, with the triumph of the Enlightenment and democracy, had come to be taken more and more for granted as a pillar of modern civilization. One notes a radical dissonance between writers on the Holocaust who regard it as a focal point of history, a *novum* that requires a change in the manner in which the world and human nature are perceived, and other historians who view it as only another example of human destructiveness of a kind that appears to have been a constant throughout history. Histories of Europe in the twentieth century assign little space to it, and many textbooks of "Western civilization" all but ignore it. At best it stands as another example that history has always produced victims, and Nazism is seen only as another example of a recurrent "inhumanity of man to man." Contemporary historians of the twentieth century have tended to see the Holocaust as one of the many brutalities of Nazism, proof of the dangers of racism, but hardly as a focal point of modern history. Its consequences were minimal, and, in contrast to other events that have become significant components in philosophical, historical, literary, or theological discourse, it is the subject of few serious discussions. The argument of its centrality must then rest upon reasons other than that it produced visible consequences. Most historians writing on the twentieth century perceive the killing of a substantial portion of Europe's Jews and the destruction of Eastern Europe's Yiddish culture as events of no great significance. An examination of historical accounts documents the thesis that most historians do not regard the Holocaust as particularly important.[15]

THE EVOLUTION OF ANTI-SEMITISM

The commitment of the Nazi leadership to the killing of all Jews within its sphere of influence did not come out of the void; neither, however, is it a logical extension of previous modes of anti-Semitism. It resulted from the unique amalgamation of several traditions and ideas—anti-Semitism, racism (the two are by no means identical), eugenics—within the context of a political and institutional framework.

Anti-Semitism has a long history, going back to the pre-Christian era. It changed and adapted itself to political and social changes, and different modes of anti-Semitism have evolved over time, with older forms, however, not necessarily dying out but coexisting with modern ones. In pre-Christian antiquity, it was based on "certain peculiarities of morals and behavior expressly imposed by the Old Testament,"[16] a result of the "social consequences of Jewish religious law."[17] Rosemary Ruether has pointed to a special Egyptian strain in anti-Semitism. The Egyptian myth of the Exodus differs from the Old Testament account by depicting the Jews in negative terms and arguing that it was the Egyptians who sought to get rid of the Jews as an unacceptable leprous people.[18] The Greek view of Jews was ambivalent. On the one hand, Greek culture saw everything non-Greek as barbarian and perceived Jewish dietary rituals or circumcision negatively; on the other hand, some Greek thinkers viewed Jewish monotheism positively. Ruether notes that

> their exclusiveness was decried as an absurd misanthropy and a pretension to superiority in a foreign people whom the educated Greek regarded as superstitious "barbarians." Their various customs, such as circumcision, abstinence from pork, and Sabbath leisure, were regarded with amused contempt, rather than hatred. [But] there was the traditional Greek philosophical curiosity and Roman political practicality that created cultural assimilation and administrative accommodation.[19]

Christianity developed from Judaism. Their connection has been the single most significant fact in defining the relationship between Jews and Christians. Erich Kahler (inter alia) interpreted Jesus as the culmination of the Jewish prophetic tradition. The two primary components of that tradition were the transformation of a tribal, jealous, and vengeful God into a universal one who is God not to a particular people but to all of humanity, and the redefinition of justice from one that called for an eye for an eye and a tooth for a tooth into one that stated that God demanded love of one's neighbor. Although the prophets believed ethical conduct to be of greater significance than the literal fulfillment of ritualistic law, none rejected law and none sought to found a new religion. God and ethics were on the way to becoming universalized, but the context remained that of Israel as specially chosen with the task of bringing the "light," that is, the message of a universal God, the message of the essential human community to the Gentiles. Viewed in this manner the teachings of Jesus only continue the evolution of the prophetic tradition from Elijah to Hosea:

> All the aspects of the life and teachings of Jesus are the result of a long development of Jewish history, of the Jewish world in which Jesus arose. . . . Jesus was the sum of sufferings of many past generations, the epic of a whole people in one simple, beautiful personal story, lived at a turning point in the history of man, and so he became the redeeming symbol of all human suffering to come.

His personal story became the symbol and nucleus of human history.[20]

The basic step that created a new world religion occurred when Jesus' disciples defined him as the previously much prophesied Messiah and joined that to a belief that he had risen from the tomb. Here is the beginning of the deification of Jesus. Paul, after a conversion experience, founded what came to be a new church which replaced a no longer normative Jewish law with a belief in Christ. A new covenant replaced the old, and the chosen people, most favored of God, became despised for having rejected Him, and indeed held guilty of the crime of deicide, the murder of God. This would become a fountain for future anti-Semitism.[21]

In a psychoanalytic interpretation of anti-Semitism, Richard Rubenstein argues that the Jews' claim to being God's chosen people had produced feelings analogous to the envy a favorite child evokes.[22] Jews, he holds, fulfilled a dual role in Christian thought: "They provide *both* the incarnate Deity *and* his murderers."[23] He then cites Freud's view that both civilization and religion began with a "primal crime," the murder of the father by the tribe of the sons, who then out of guilt transform the father into a heavenly father. Freud perceived the sacrificial death of Christ as a "return of the repressed." Those cannibalistic aspects of the primal crime (the sons ate the father) are repeated in the Mass which Freud viewed as a symbolic repetition of the original crime.[24]

In *Moses and Monotheism,* Freud argued that the Jews murdered Moses, and that Christ became his substitute and successor. Jews, in contrast to Christians, continue to deny the murder: They heard the reproach "you killed our God" rightly interpreted as "you won't admit that you murdered God, . . . we admitted it, and since then have been purified." Freud added other explanations for anti-Semitism, but concluded with the view that anti-Semitism is also a hatred of Christianity:

> The peoples who now excel in the practice of anti-Semitism became Christians only in relatively recent times, sometimes forced to it by bloody compulsion. One might say that they are "badly christend" under the thin veneer of Christianity they have remained . . . barbarically polytheistic. . . . They have not yet overcome their grudge against the new religion. . . . The hatred for Judaism is at bottom hatred for Christianity.[25]

The religious dimensions were primary in defining the relationship between Jews and Christians in medieval Europe.[26] They provided the legitimization for a variety of discriminatory acts against Jews. At the same time (in contrast to heretics, witches, etc.), Jews were permitted to live in medieval Europe as Jews.[27] Popes and princes frequently protected Jews against popular anti-Semitism, which reached a peak during the Crusades.

Joshua Trachtenberg has collected popular manifestations, including cartoons, illustrating medieval anti-Semitism.[28] These include images of Jews stabbing the host, a barely disguised reenactment of their killing of Christ, as well as the Jew as a disguised Satan. The perception of the Jew as "Christ killer" has been central for anti-Semitism throughout most of its history. A second major component of anti-Semitism is the association of Jews with usurious practices. One picture by Trachtenberg shows Satan wearing a Jewish badge, participating in financial activities. Bernard of Clairvaux used the term "to Jew" as a synonym for moneylending.[29] This view has become immortalized in Shakespeare's Shylock. The German romantic writer Achim von Arnim has a Jewish character, *Halle und Jerusalem*, who, upon learning that he has lost his money, drops dead, signifying the view that a Jew without money has nothing to live for.[30] Charles Dickens's Fagin in *Oliver Twist* embodies a similar Jewish stereotype. *Debit and Credit*, one of the most famous nineteenth-century German novels, shows how the Jewish business house of Ehrenthal engages in dubious practices, and contrasts it with the honest German way of doing business.[31] Benjamin Nelson, in an important, though strangely neglected work, has traced the connection between Jews and usury from biblical times to the present.[32] Since Christians were prohibited from lending at usury (interest) to "brothers" during the medieval period, Jews served as moneylenders.

Martin Luther accepted and indeed intensified the medieval stereotypes of the Jew. At first sympathetic—he hoped that Jews would convert to Christianity now that it had been purified—in the bitter diatribe of 1543, *On the Jews and Their Lies*, which still serves as a viable anti-Semitic publication, Luther spoke of Jews as "bloodthirsty, believing itself to be God's people. . . . Know Christians, that next to the devil thou hast no enemy more cruel, more venomous and violent than a true Jew."[33]

The Western European intellectual elites of the eighteenth century attempted to replace the biblical view with one based on science and reason. Enlightenment thinkers viewed Christianity as a medieval superstition, and strongly attacked religious persecution.[34] Their attitude toward Jews was ambivalent. They favored eliminating restrictions on Jews, but also demanded that Jews abandon Judaism, a religion as superstitious as Christianity. Voltaire, as Peter Gay has succinctly shown, continued to perpetuate the old stereotype of Jews as usurious and greedy, iniquitous, clever, and ruthless. He also loudly trumpets the theme of Jewish sexuality.

What shall I say to my brother the Jew? Shall I give him dinner? Yes, provided that during the meal Balaam's ass doesn't take it into its head to bray; that Ezekiel doesn't mix his breakfast with our dinner; that a fish doesn't come to swallow one of the guests and keep him in his belly three days; that a serpent doesn't mix into the conversation to seduce my wife; that a prophet doesn't take it into his head to sleep with her after dinner, as that good fellow Hoseah did for fifteen francs and a bushel of barley.[35]

Anticipating Nietzsche, Voltaire also held the Jews guilty of fathering Christianity: "When I see Christians cursing Jews, methinks I see children beating their fathers."[36]

The development of nationalism in the nineteenth century coincided in Western Europe with the elimination of Jewish ghettos and the assimilation of Jews to the nation. Jews identified themselves as Frenchmen and Germans who differed from their compatriots only in minor ways. However, many of their compatriots refused to accept this. The most frequently voiced theme in France during the Dreyfus crisis was that Jews were not really loyal to France. They were accused of not being good Germans or good Frenchmen. In Germany and Austria anti-Semitic parties, largely grounded in resentments of the lower middle classes, whose position came under increasing threat with the expansion of capitalism, sought to blame the Jews for all economic misfortunes. Many continued to define Jews on the basis of religion. Heinrich von Treitschke, a leading nineteenth-century historian and anti-Semite, argued that Jews should convert to Christianity as a way of becoming good Germans. But while many anti-Semites still held that the Jewish character was caused by religion,[37] and affirmed that conversion would mean that Jews could escape their condition, a new doctrine of race was developing.[38] German Jews perceived themselves as Germans, and indeed were proud of the contributions they made to German culture, blindly failing to realize that many Germans did not accept them as members of the nation.[39]

Anthropological concepts of race became wedded to anti-Semitic ideas to create a new definition of the Jew.[40] The essence of racist doctrine is that racially flawed individuals cannot change their nature by conversion and therefore present a constant danger to the nation. Count Arthur de Gobineau's mid-nineteenth-century *Essay on the Inequality of Human Races* not only differentiated between the quality of races, but posited that race provided the clue to human history: Racial purity produced cultural creativity, whereas cultural decline and decadence were produced by racial intermixing.

The myth of a Jewish world conspiracy represents a modern adaptation of an ancient demonological tradition. According to this myth there exists a secret Jewish government which through a worldwide network of camouflaged agencies and organizations controls political parties and governments, the press and public opinion, banks and economic development. All actions are in pursuance of an age-old plan and with the single aim of achieving Jewish dominion over the entire world. Sir John Retcliffe in the novel *Biarritz* (1868) describes a meeting in the Prague cemetery. Representatives of the twelve tribes of Israel meet with the son of Satan. They report that the earth will again belong to Jews.[41] Soon this fictionalized document ceased to be regarded as fiction. The various speeches were consolidated in a single speech which was labeled historically authentic.[42]

Osman Bey, in his *World Conquest by the Jews* (1840), wrote that

> a Jewish parliament was summoned at Cracow. It was a sort of Ecumenical Council, where the most eminent leaders of the Chosen People met to convene. The purpose of summoning them was to determine the most suitable means to ensure that Judaism should spread from the North Pole to the south. . . . Suddenly a clear voice rang out. . . . It was the voice of recognized authority; people saw that an oracle had spoken, that a new illumination had dawned upon their minds, to give firm directions to their efforts.[43]

The nineteenth-century transmitters of the myth of the Jewish world conspiracy are a varied crew. They prepared the way for the famous Russian forgery, *The Protocols of the Elders of Zion*, which was to survive long after their own writings had disappeared. This document circulated widely in the 1920s and 1930s.[44] A consistent theme is the identification of Jews with postures of modern liberalism. The protocols appeared first in Russia in 1903 and have had an extraordinary career. They are still sold as a contemporary anti-Semitic document. They identify ideas of liberalism and democracy as part of a Jewish plot to gain control of a country by undermining authority. Here the connection of anti-Semitism with the political Right is systematically expressed. All Jewish political commitment is only a device to gain power. Both capitalism and communism are means to the identical end—hence the logic of Hitler in speaking of a Jewish bolshevik Wall Street conspiracy.

An examination of the evolution of anti-Semitism shows that it has retained a basic core of ideas, yet adapted itself to divergent conditions; there appears a certain integral logic to its development. It is important to note that older stages of anti-Semitism do not always die out but are at times combined with newer ones. What is evident is that these ideas were taken seriously and informed Nazi genocidal policy.

GERMAN ANTI-SEMITISM TO THE OUTBREAK
OF WORLD WAR II

Through the eighteenth century anti-Semitism had been a religious, intellectual, or social viewpoint. By the second half of the nineteenth century it had also become political. In Germany and in the Habsburg monarchy political parties were formed whose primary object was the eradication of Jewish influence. Most political parties of the Right in the nineteenth and twentieth centuries to the end of World War II included anti-Semitism as a major component of their political programs. Fascist parties in the twentieth century sought the destruction of liberal values of pluralism and toleration and advocated an integral nationalism. Jews were not regarded as eligible for membership in the nation.[45] Anti-Semitism was adopted as a platform by the Nazi party from its beginning in 1920, and the party went on to absorb specific anti-Semitic ideas and expressions from the varied *völkisch* movements that eventually joined it.[46]

Nazi policies toward Jews sought two primary goals: The first was to eliminate the influence of Jews in Germany by removing them from positions within the civil service, universities, and cultural and economic institutions. The second was to force Jews to leave Germany. There is no evidence of any plan for killing Jews before the outbreak of the Second World War.

Hitler's radical followers expected immediate and dramatic actions against the Jews; they only received partial satisfaction.[47] Shortly after Hitler had become chancellor the Nazi party declared an official boycott of Jewish businesses, which led to individual acts of violence. The Nazi leadership gradually learned that popular mob actions would be self-defeating—closing a Jewish department store also meant increasing unemployment. Increasingly the realization that simple solutions would not work led to the implementation of anti-Semitic policies through legal and formal means. A law of April 7, 1933, "For the restoration of the Professional Civil Service" achieved the firing of Jews from governmental service. It was followed by laws limiting attendance of Jews in schools and universities, and in July and August by laws that revoked the citizenship previously granted to "undesirables"—a law that affected mostly Poles, and was a prelude to their expulsion.

At the 1935 Nazi party congress the Nuremberg Laws were proclaimed. Drawn up in haste, they also expressed the conflict between moderate and radical elements on the question of how much Jewish blood would be required to label a person as a Jew. Individuals with three full Jewish grandparents were defined as "full" Jews, followed by *Mischlinge* (mongrels) of the first degree (two Jewish grandparents); one Jewish grandparent created a *Mischling* of the second degree. Different liabilities were attached to these definitions. Jewish refugees sought to leave Germany, only to encounter resistance almost everywhere they attempted to flee. At the same time, until 1939 many German Jews had faith that tolerable arrangements between Jews and Nazis would develop, and made no effort to leave Germany. Some who had left under the impact of the events of 1933, finding émigré life unsatisfactory and assuming that the radical phase of Nazism had passed returned to Germany. The level of actions against Jews remained stable for the next several years, with the government and the party realizing that a variety of unintended consequences went with anti-Semitic actions. In their attempt to further emigration the Nazis favored German Zionist associations over assimilationist ones, and even entered into discussions with representatives of Haganah to establish programs that would retrain Jews for agricultural occupations, which would help them settle in Palestine.[48]

In March 1938 Germany annexed Austria and created Groβdeutschland (Greater Germany).[49] Immediately anti-Semitic actions and violence against Jews took place in Austria, caused at least in part by the intense enthusiasm for anti-Semitism and National Socialism there. Yehuda Bauer succinctly summarizes this:

> When the Nazis marched into Austria . . . the Austrian population . . . rallied to them with great enthusiasm . . . The process of degradation, terror and expropriation that had taken five years in Germany was completed—indeed surpassed—in a few months in Austria. Men and women were forced to scrub streets on their knees, while crowds of Viennese stood by and cheered. Shops were invaded, robbed, and their owners beaten.[50]

Adolf Eichmann centralized Jewish emigration by establishing a *Judenauswanderungszentralle* (Jewish Emigration Office), which made wealthy Jews pay for the costs of emigration of poor ones. The two issues that had plagued previous efforts to further the rapid emigration of Jews were not solved: Germany was not willing to allow Jews access to foreign currency, and increasingly other countries closed their doors to Jews.

Poland had promulgated a law in March 1938 that required Poles living abroad to have their passports and thereby their Polish citizenship validated. Jewish passports were not validated. At the same time Germany sought to deport Polish Jews. It took several days before the German and Polish governments reached a compromise solution, but not before the unlucky individuals had been miserably shuffled back and forth. Seventeen-year-old Herschl Grynszpan heard from his father what happened, and went to the embassy in Paris, bent on revenge.

He shot a third secretary, Ernst von Rath. This triggered massive violence in Germany, the *Reichskristallnacht* orchestrated by Joseph Goebbels and the SA (*Sturmabteilung*). Synagogues were burned, and the windows of Jewish stores smashed. Some 30,000 Jewish males were sent to concentration camps.[51] *Kristallnacht* produced unfavorable consequences for the Nazis—and was a major factor in the decision to eliminate popular actions from anti-Semitic policies. The pressure to emigrate increased sharply. The process of Aryanization and exclusion of Jews from the economy accelerated rapidly, but no evidence of any plan except forced emigration is evident at this time.

FROM APPEASEMENT TO WAR

Nazism was firmly committed to anti-Semitism. The increasing intensity of an anti-Semitic policy paralleled not only domestic but also foreign policy successes. Both domestically and in foreign policy no significant and effective opposition to Hitler's anti-Semitic policies developed; the Nazi leadership correctly recognized that the implementation of these policies would not entail any actions against it.

Hitler had announced even before coming to power his aim to revise the Versailles settlement. He soon implemented this, and Germany's foreign policy went from one success to another. The violation of Versailles began with the breaking of the limitation on rearmament, which evoked no opposition from the other powers (March 16, 1935). When the German army marched into the Rhineland in March 1936, even the French, who were most affected, were unwilling to engage in military action. The annexation of Austria (which was strongly desired by the Austrian people) in March 1938 only produced mild statements that territorial changes in Europe should not be undertaken unilaterally. When Hitler in the fall of 1938 made territorial demands on Czechoslovakia, France and England met at Munich and forced Czechoslovakia to cede the Sudetenland—the part of Czechoslovakia inhabited by Germans—to Germany (September 29, 1938). Six months later Hitler, who before Munich had stated that "he had no more territorial demands in Europe," annexed the rump Czech state. Germany felt invincible, its leadership convinced that it was riding the wave of the future. *"Und heute gehört uns Deutschland, und morgen die ganze Welt"* ("Today Germany belongs to us, tomorrow the whole world") had become more than a popular Hitler Youth song.

Why did the Western democracies "appease" Germany? The destructive experiences of World War I had created a strong pacifism, a conviction that that kind of destruction ought never to happen again. This conviction was joined, particularly in a politically divided France, to a spirit of defeatism, to the sense that democracy and liberalism were weak and that in a conflict with a virile Germany, France would lose. D. H. Lawrence documented this defeatism when he remarked after World War I that all the great ideas were dead. William Butler Yeats even more explicitly noted that the "best lack all conviction."

It was evident that the price for stopping German aggression would be collaboration with the Soviet Union in a system of collective security. This was anathema to many conservatives in France and England. In France the slogan "better Hitler than Stalin" could be heard. In some circles there was much admiration for the vigor shown by Germany, and many would have liked to have seen Hitler's anti-Semitic policies applied to France. The opinion that French and English statesmen secretly hoped that Nazi Germany and the USSR would fight and destroy each other has surfaced frequently. Some may indeed have held such a view, but it is unsupported by any statement or documentary evidence.

The announcement of a German–Soviet pact in August 1939 stunned the rest of the world. Stalin's motives were clearly based on a perception of Russian unpreparedness and the need for security, while Germany wished to avoid a two-front war.

Hitler expected that France and England would not fight for Poland. The declarations of war on Germany by France and England (September 3, 1939) following Germany's attack on Poland could in no way stop its rapid conquest; no military aid was extended to Poland. The Soviet Union, on the basis of a prior accord reached with Germany, invaded Poland from the east. After having fought against numerically and technically superior forces Poland surrendered (September 27). Portions of Poland were directly annexed to Germany, others organized as a protectorate, governed by Hans Frank, former German minister of justice.

The next few years witnessed one major German military failure and numerous successes. Although for a time the German *Luftwaffe* bombed British cities, including London, in one of the decisive events of the war the RAF (Royal Air Force) was successful—in what is now called the Battle of Britain—in wresting control of the sky from Germany, thereby interdicting the contemplated German invasion of Britain.

It was different on the continent of Europe. Belgium and Holland quickly fell to Germany, while the famed Maginot line was unable to stop the German Blitzkrieg into France. Denmark was conquered without any resistance, while the Norwegian resistance was soon crushed. Mussolini's forces were unsuccessful in Greece; Germany came to the rescue and conquered and occupied Greece. Yugoslavia was unsuccessful in resisting the German forces. Then to the surprise of the Soviet government, which had expected Germany to live up to its accord, German armies on June 22, 1941, invaded the Soviet Union. Germany occupied vast territories in the Soviet Union, but, contrary to the predictions by experts, the Germans were unable to defeat Russia. The Battle of Stalingrad in 1943 was the turning point of the war. Soviet armies began pushing German armies back, until two years later they reached Berlin. Allied armies invaded Europe on June 6, 1944, and overcoming continued German resistance made their way into Germany, which signed a surrender agreement in April 1945.

OCCUPIED POLAND

Poles were expelled from those territories Germany wished to annex. Germany unleashed a regime of terror against Poles and Jews, predicated on the premise that both were inferior human beings (though not to the same extent). Almost immediately a mass destruction of the Polish intellectual elite was attempted. Members of Reinhard Heydrich's *Einsatzkommandos* (special SS squads whose primary task was killing) rounded up Polish teachers, doctors, officials, and priests, and herded them to collection points where they were usually shot. The plan was to "liquidate" the radical (i.e., Polish nationalistic) elements.[52] Himmler also arranged to have Polish children of "good" racial heritage kidnapped and brought to Germany. No collaboration on the pattern of France or Norway took place, because of the Germans' low estimation of the Poles. Yet Jews were in a different class from the Poles.

Even before the fall of Warsaw, Heydrich had given orders to the *Einsatzgruppen* leaders that the Jews of Poland were to be segregated:

I refer to the conference held in Berlin today and once more point out that the planned *overall measures* (i.e. the final aim) are to be kept *strictly secret.* Distinction must be made between

1. The final aim (which will require an extended period of time), and
2. The stages leading to the fulfillment of this final aim (which will be carried out in short terms)

For the time being the first prerequisite for the final aim is the concentration of the Jews from the countryside into the larger cities. This is to be carried out with all speed. [The document then differentiates between territories which are to be made a permanent part of Germany and other occupied territories.]

As far as possible the area mentioned in item 1 is to be cleared of Jews; at least the aim should be to establish only a few cities of concentration.

In the areas mentioned in item 2, as few concentration points as possible are to be set up, so as to facilitate subsequent measures. In this connection, it is to be borne in mind that only cities which are rail junctions, or at least are located along railroad lines are to be designated as concentration points.

On principle, Jewish communities of fewer than 500 persons are to be dissolved and to be transferred to the nearest city of concentration.[53]

This order provided the foundation for the establishment of ghettos in Poland. These included not only Polish Jews, but also some who had been expelled from Germany and Czechoslovakia.[54]

Substantial documentation of ghetto life is available.[55] The Germans even made a propaganda film attempting to show how well the Jews were treated, which despite the intent of its makers gives dramatic glimpses into ghetto life. Although the history of different ghettos varied in detail, there exists a striking similarity, which permits speaking of almost a "natural history" of the life and death of the ghettos.

The central fact of the ghettos was their radical isolation from the rest of the population. Photographs of the wall of the Warsaw ghetto illustrate this. Association with individuals outside the walls of the ghetto was increasingly difficult, though smuggling and other contact did take place. There were cases of individual acts of help extended by some Poles; however, the Jews in the ghettos could not count on sympathy, much less help, from the Poles. Poland has its own long history of anti-Semitism; the Nazi occupation did not change this, and many Poles were pleased that the Germans were solving their Jewish problem. The one area of agreement between many Poles and Germans was that the Jews ought to be eliminated. Anti-Semitism had been an explicit platform of the Polish Right; the Roman Catholic church was a significant element in legitimizing anti-Semitism. Contemporary Polish Communist historiography now tends to suggest that the Communists and their allies on the left really cooperated with the Jews in the ghettos. Certainly the Polish Left was less hostile than the nationalistic Right.

The basic defensive strategy of the ghettos was survival through work. The ghettos provided slave labor for the Nazi war machine; Polish Jews worked in German offices, installations, and workshops. The belief existed that the Germans were rational enough not to destroy the ghettos so long as these were producing items that furthered the German war effort. Though this tactic failed, some ghettos were able through work to postpone their destruction. Work also differentiated those who could stay and those who were deported, and competition for jobs and cards documenting those jobs was fierce. The policy, explicitly stated by some *Judenrat* (Jewish council) leaders, was that work could achieve survival, and that if not all could be saved, that it was legitimate to save some.[56] The Germans made some efforts to dissemble that their intent was the killing of all Jews; a pattern of denial as a way of coping with this reality characterized many in the ghettos, who had hopes that at least some would survive. The at times heroic efforts in some of the ghettos to maintain cultural activities, to educate children, to maintain a religious life also served as a denial mechanism. Some Jewish leaders such as Leo Baeck, when they learned of the fate of those deported, took it upon themselves to hide this from others, believing that such knowledge would only create greater agony and despair among the victims.[57]

The Germans demanded the establishment of a *Judenrat*, creating an institution through which they transmitted orders to the ghetto.[58] Hannah Arendt not only indicts the *Judenrat* leaders,[59] but also concludes that whatever their intent, they helped German policy. Raul Hilberg views them negatively;[60] Isaiah Trunk arrives at a less unfavorable judgment.

As a matter of policy the Germans dealt through the *Judenrat*. It was required to carry out all German orders. The individuals who made up the *Judenrat* were usually drawn from the leadership of the prewar Jewish community. The *Judenrat* became the de facto government of a new society. Most accounts and memoirs emphasize the personal dedication and integrity of the *Judenrat* leaders (though examples of corruption could be found). The primary aims of the leaders of the *Judenrat* were negotiating with the Germans, gaining concessions, bribing individuals, and attempting to regulate a new kind of society. Since it could decide who was to be deported, who was to work for it, who was to be given access to jobs that entailed better food rations, the *Judenrat* had, in effect, a power of life and death.

Food shortages were chronic and devastating. The food allocations by the Jewish council created a new class system. In December 1941 in the Warsaw ghetto the highest food consumption—1,665 calories—went to council employees, as against 1,407 to independent artisans and 1,229 to shopworkers. In Lodz the population was divided into two segments. On top were those who received a supplemental food allowance. These included members of the council and high functionaries of the ghetto administration. The councils in their allocations of limited resources tended to favor the old Jewish elites at the expense of the ordinary poor. It does not require a Marxist analysis to show that the *Judenrat* protected those who had achieved economic success in the prewar world at the expense of the poor, that it held the life of a worker to be of less value than the life of a former wealthy businessman. Nor does it require any complex sociological analysis to note that the *Judenrat* bureaucracy developed a stake in its own existence and policies. That policy held that the best road to survival was cooperation with the Germans, making oneself useful, and offering no armed resistance. Hence (though there are a few exceptions to this) the *Judenräte* were opposed to resistance and held that the road to saving a maximum number was to be found in the traditional Jewish response to persecution: Lie low, cooperate with some powerful individual among the oppressor, petition, bribe. It was a policy that had worked in the past. It failed here because the Germans were committed to the destruction of the Jews. The effect of the *Judenrat* as an institution was to inhibit resistance activities.

The Jewish police was a unique ghetto institution.[61] Judgments about these policemen are consistently negative. They enforced regulations of the *Judenrat* and of the Germans, including participation in the rounding up of individuals for deportation. Corruption among them, in contrast to the *Judenrat*, was substantial. More and more the police became an organ of the German administration engaging in systematic collaboration with the Germans.[62] The film *Warsaw Ghetto*, using German footage, shows a devastating picture of the Jewish ghetto police beating children and rounding up people. Trunk notes that the police included some former criminal elements and that its position "rendered them most vulnerable and submissive to the negative influence of life in the ghetto, and of the destructive, nihilistic, German morality. . . . Penetrated as it was by a number of low, asocial elements [it] faced difficult ethical tests which not all passed unblemished."[63] Its behavior, however, is to be explained not primarily on the basis of a failure of individual morality, but as implicit in its structure and tasks. The premise that some had to be sacrificed so that others could be saved opened up an incredible abyss. Their tasks transformed them into direct servants of SS policies. Zelig Kalamanovitch has attempted to justify their actions:

> Our policemen were sent there with passes to be distributed among the remaining workers, and to turn over the rest of the people, "the superfluous," to the hands of the authorities to do with them what is customary these days. The young took upon themselves this difficult task. They donned their official caps, with the "Star of David" upon them, went there and did what they were supposed to do. The result was that more than 400 people perished; the aged, the infirm, the sick and retarded children. Thus 1500 women and children were saved. Had outsiders, God forbid, carried out this action, 2000 people would have perished. The commandant [of the

Jewish police] said, "To be sure, our hands are stained with the blood of our brethren, but we had to take upon ourselves this dreadful task. We are clean before the bar of history."[64]

JEWISH RESISTANCE

In order to answer "charges" that Jews have been passive and did not know how to fight, Reuben Ainsztein begins his detailed history of Jewish resistance to the Nazis by showing that in the past Jews had demonstrated their ability to fight heroically.[65] The word "resistance" has acquired a romantic tinge; partisan activities took place in many countries occupied by the Germans, from France to the Soviet Union; the issue of Jewish passivity has been raised frequently, joined to the accusation that the Jews went to their death "like sheep to slaughter." (The phrase stems from Abba Kovner, who appealed to Jews *not* to go like sheep to slaughter.)

Wherever resistance movements existed that did not reject Jews, they became actively involved. In France, beginning with the French Revolution, Jews had become integrated with the nation; they perceived themselves as French citizens and (except for the political Right) were accepted. The greater acceptance of Jews in France was one reason why a greater percentage survived there.

The issue of Jewish resistance, using that term as it became defined in World War II, is only applicable to Eastern Europe. In Eastern Europe there were resistance movements, but not a Jewish resistance. Jews attempted survival through work as their first tactic. The overall strategy, accepted by a majority, was to make themselves useful in production to the German war effort so that at least some might survive. And indeed work kept ghettos going for a time. Few Jews realized the primacy the Nazis attached to their extermination.

Two issues dominated the question of resistance in the ghettos. The first, strongly advocated by the various *Judenrat* leaders, was that through cooperation the ghetto could survive. When the Germans threatened to destroy the Vilna ghetto unless a resistance leader, Itzik Wittenberg, who had escaped, was handed over to them, the ghetto inhabitants clashed with the partisan organization FPO (United Fighting Organization). The head of the ghetto, Jacob Gens, actively tried to capture Wittenberg so that he could be handed over to the Germans. Wittenberg's Communist cell, aware of the opposition of the population, urged him to turn himself in to the Gestapo. Apparently he had the opportunity to commit suicide before his interrogation.[66]

Armed resistance took place in most ghettos. The revolt of the Warsaw ghetto is the most dramatic. Under the leadership of Mordecai

Anielewicz the ghetto resisted, and was destroyed only after a major German military commitment under SS General Stroop.[67] Yisrael Gutman cites some very limited support activities by the Polish underground, both by the AK (*Armia Krajowa*, or Home Army) and the left-wing AL (*Armia Ludowa*, or People's Army).

An organ of the intelligence branch of the AK commented on the revolt:

> If the overwhelming majority of Europe's Jews were murdered as they remained completely passive, the remnant, in their racial materialism, lacked any motivation to resist. Only a tiny proportion of the few thousand Jews remaining in Warsaw (about 10 percent) engaged in the struggle—and with support from the Communist camp at that. . . . The resistance . . . was organized and effected by the Bund and the Communists. It is precisely among that element that a mood of hostility toward the Poles has been evident throughout the occupation, and they have trained themselves in the framework of Communist organizations for a bloody battle against the Poles during the decisive transition period.[68]

The Polish Right viewed the Warsaw ghetto revolt as instigated and carried out primarily by Communists. During the attacks the Polish population watched. Sympathy was with the Germans:

> During Easter week Christ was tortured by the Jews, [and] during Easter week the Jews were tortured by the Germans.

> A seventy-year old priest: It is a good thing. The Jews had a large military force in the ghetto. If they hadn't turned it on the Germans, they would have turned it on us.[69]

The attitude of partisans toward Jews varied. Many Polish partisan units, themselves anti-Semitic, were unwilling to accept Jews, while Soviet partisans were more sympathetic. Even where partisans in the woods were sympathetic, resistance would have involved abandoning the families, the aged, the infirm, and the children, and most were unwilling to do this.

The situation in Poland for Jews in the ghettos was defined not only by the ruthless commitment on the part of the Germans to kill them, but also the fact that the major Polish resistance group was also explicitly anti-Semitic. Jews were not perceived as Poles, and their identification with communism further exacerbated relations.

Revolts also took place in the death camps, most dramatically in Treblinka and Sobibor. However, at no time in Eastern Europe were Jews able to establish a united infrastructure. The separate resistance organizations never could develop coordination. The Germans had achieved complete success in isolating the ghettos and camps. The absence of a sympathetic population was decisive in limiting options.

The evidence clearly does not support charges of Jewish passivity. What is clear is that only certain social and political conditions permit the development of partisan organizations and that these conditions rarely existed for Jews in Nazi-occupied Europe.

FROM DEPORTATIONS TO MASS KILLINGS

In July 1941 Göring charged *Obergruppenführer* (SS rank comparable to lieutenant general) Reinhard Heydrich "with making all necessary organizational, functional and material preparations for a complete solution of the Jewish question in the German sphere of influence in Europe."[70] The Wannsee Conference, held January 1, 1942, discussed some of the problems that would arise. This much quoted protocol foresaw using Jews for forced labor,

> in the course of which action, a great part will undoubtedly be eliminated by natural causes. The possible final remnant will, as it must undoubtedly consist of the toughest, have to be treated accordingly, as it is the product of natural selection, and would, if liberated, act as a bud cell of a Jewish reconstruction (see historical experience).[71]

Killings of Jews and Poles by *Einsatzgruppen* had already taken place in Poland. It came to be part of a systematic policy after the attack on the Soviet Union in June 1941. The conjunction of these events was not fortuitous. It rested upon the connection between Jews and bolshevism that existed within Hitler's mind specifically and within Nazi ideology more generally. Nazi ideology perceived bolshevism—Nazi documents prefer using the term bolshevism to that of communism—not only as an evil in its own right, but primarily as a Jewish device to gain power. The Commissar order, which authorized the immediate killing of Communist functionaries, spelled out the ideological nature of the war, while establishing an identity between Jews and Bolsheviks.[72] An army directive of June 1941 stated that

1. *Bolshevism is the mortal enemy of the National Socialist German people. Germany's struggle is directed against this destructive ideology and its carriers.*
2. This struggle demands ruthless and energetic measures against *Bolshevik agitators, guerrillas, saboteurs, Jews,* and the complete elimination of every active or passive resistance.[73]

A directive by General von Reichenau noted that

> The most essential aim of the campaign against the Jewish-Bolshevist system is the complete crushing of its means of power and the extermination of Asiatic influences in the European region. Therefore the soldier must have *full* understanding for the necessity of a severe but just atonement on Jewish subhumanity. An additional aim in this is to nip in the bud any revolts in the rear of the army which, as experience proves, have always been instigated by Jews.[74]

A massive killing operation against Jews was conducted by the *Einsatzgruppen*.[75] Numerous detailed accounts of these killings exist. It was essentially a handicraft method of murder. Individuals were collected, a tank ditch was dug, and the people were shot down by machine guns.

Major Rösler, the commander of an infantry regiment, heard fire and went out to look and saw "a picture of such barbaric horror that the effect upon anyone coming upon it unawares was both shattering and repellent." In a pit were bodies of Jews of all ages and sexes.

> In this grave lay, among others, an old man with a white beard clutching a cane in his left hand. Since this man, judging by his sporadic breathing showed signs of life, I ordered one of the policemen to kill him. He smilingly replied: "I have already shot him seven times in the stomach. He can die on his own now."[76]

The final solution was a component of a systematic social policy.[77] At the same time the constant gratuitous cruelties, the casual ease with which individuals engaged in unchecked violent behavior command attention: A woman refused to reveal a hiding place and one of the men gripped her baby and smashed its head against a door. An SS man who observed it commented that "it went off with a bang like a bursting motor tyre. I shall never forget that sound as long as I live."[78] Examples could be given ad infinitum. (Similar "surplus sadism" was also characteristic in the various camps.) That the victims were Jews does not appear to have been a significant component in inducing this kind of behavior.[79]

The role of the army varied. Some commanders were appalled and protested, others thought that the SS was helpful in taking the burden of antipartisan warfare from them. The special squads were attached to army units.[80] Many of its leaders were academics, some had doctoral degrees. Opposition to participation in the killing operations does not seem to have existed. The common experience of fighting the war in Russia had brought the SS and the army closer together. Army commanders praised the *Einsatzgruppen*: "These people are worth their weight in gold to us."[81] Much of the actual killing was done by non-Germans, particularly Ukrainians, White Russians, Letts, and Lithuanians whom the Germans employed. There was no dearth of volunteers.

The Jews of Russia were unprepared and allowed themselves to be rounded up. The toll the *Einsatzgruppen* took was immense. By the winter of 1941-42 *Einsatzgruppe* A reported 249,420 Jews killed; *Einsatzgruppe* B, 45,467; *Einsatzgruppe* C, 95,000; and *Einsatzgruppe* D, 92,000.[82] The *Einsatzgruppen* were followed by groups from the *Ordnungspolizei* (regular police) who killed those who had been missed in previous operations.

These massive killings took their toll among the killers, with some having difficulties in coping. Himmler suggested that the men engaged in this were performing heroically in the service of a great mission:

> Most of you will know what it means to see a hundred corpses, five hundred, a thousand, lying there. But seeing this thing through and nevertheless apart from certain exceptions due to human infirmity remaining decent, that is what has made us hard. This is a never recorded and never to be recorded page of glory in our history.[83]

There were psychic costs—nightmares, nervous breakdowns, at least one suicide, and an increasing reluctance on the part of the commanders to continue. After the war Paul Blobel remarked that "the nervous strain was far heavier in the case of our men who carried out the executions than in that of their victims. From the psychological point of view they had a terrible time" (pp. 412-13; page references here and in the next paragraph are to Höhne's *The Order*).

Himmler wished his minions to receive no personal gratification from the killing, to be appalled by it, but to sublimate their horror and do it as a service for Germany:

> I can tell you that it is hideous and frightful for a German to have to see such things. It is so, and if we had not felt it to be hideous and frightful, we should not have been Germans. However hideous it may be, it has been necessary for us to do it and it will be necessary in many other cases (p. 414).

That the massive killings, with a nearly direct confrontation between executioners and victims—who included women, children, and babies—created psychological difficulties in some individuals who could not deal with the horror, should not disguise the fact that the vast majority kept on in their grisly task, and with only a few exceptions, the psychic costs of the killings did not decrease efficiency.

THE INDUSTRIALIZATION OF DEATH

Hermann Langbein, discussing the shift toward gassings as an alternative to shootings, posits that the change was not only based on its increased efficiency but because it "humanized" the killings for the killers.[84] Otto Ohlendorf, leader of an *Einsatzgruppe*, at his trial spoke of this humanizing of mass murder.[85] What was meant by this was that it was psychologically easier to kill in this way than with previous methods, which had involved a direct confrontation of perpetrator and victim.

The major transformation that took place in the extermination program was the shift from handicraft production to an unprecedented industrialized mode of death production. From relatively small beginnings within Germany with the euthanasia program, the equivalent of an industrial revolution in the manufacturing of death, using modern techniques of mass production, took place, leading to the building of gigantic factories of death comparable to Detroit's River Rouge plant. Here the means used fundamentally redefine the nature of the act.

Romantic eugenic ideas about perfecting the race, a component of Nazi ideology of particular importance to Himmler and his circle, came to be joined to a wish not to have to feed "useless" mouths.[86] These ideas were translated into a program that permitted the killing of patients who were mentally ill or defined as incurably ill. Whatever the merits of euthanasia—the word means "good death"—now usually interpreted to mean the right of a person with an incurable disease to die without having life prolonged against his or her wishes, these had almost nothing to do with the program as practiced. The Nazi formula "suppression of lives unworthy of being lived" permitted broad interpretations. Hitler hesitated a long time, and the decree activating the program was backdated September 1, 1939, the day war began. The program was directed primarily at the feebleminded and incurably insane, with the definition of incurable being rather loose. In the two years that the program was operative, more than 50,000 persons were killed—the numbers cited vary from 50,000 and "between 80,000 and 100,000."[87] Neither the victims nor the families were consulted. Many techniques, such as disguising the room in which patients were killed as a shower, were later adopted in death camps. Personnel who had worked in the T4 program, a code name for the euthanasia program, were transferred to the death camps in Poland. Victims were selected from concentration camps, which were combed for physically or mentally unfit individuals who were chosen for killing. Other considerations also played a part. Dr. Fritz Mennecke described it in a letter to his wife:

I examined 105 patients, Müller 78, so that 183 questionnaires were filled out. Our second batch consisted of 1,200 Jews who do not have to be "examined"; for them it was enough to pull from their files . . . the reason for their arrest. . . . After the Jews will come 300 Aryans who have to be "examined." We shall be busy up the end of next week.[88]

Despite attempted secrecy, knowledge of the euthanasia programs leaked out and met with protests from both the Protestant and the Roman Catholic clergy, most notably from Bishop Theophil Wurm, Bishop Preysing, Bishop Galen, and Cardinal Faulhaber. Lutheran Pastor Braune sent a memorandum to the Reich Chancellery, protesting the killings. He was arrested a few days later for "irresponsible sabotage of government measures."[89] The program was discontinued in the summer of 1941. Gitta Sereny questions whether, as most of the literature has suggested, this was the result of the protest of the churches.[90] Almost every study notes that no comparable protest against the mass killing of Jews came from any of the churches. Rolf Hochhuth's play *The Deputy* dramatized the Vatican's silence and has generated a voluminous polemical literature.[91]

The experience gained with the euthanasia program was applied to the creation of killing apparatuses in special camps. The Nazi system created a wide variety of camps.[92] Lessons from one were applied to others and led to the development of an increasingly more efficient technique. Efficiency meant, as it does for any industrial enterprise, increased production with fewer individuals required for the work. Second, as in industrial production, the specialization of labor led to an alienation of the worker from his product—everything was done to ensure that no one would feel that he was killing anybody. Four camps were devoted almost exclusively to killing: Chelmno (Kulmhof), Belzec, Sobibor, and Treblinka. Odilo Globocnik was in charge of these camps and used personnel with experience in the euthanasia program—most notably Christian Wirth, Belzec's first commander.

The use of gas for systematic killing began in Chelmno, near Lodz, in December 1941. Chelmno was the first camp exclusively designed for killing. Only 10 people out of some 300,000 brought there for extermination escaped. Killing was done by primitive gas vans, which had already been used in the Soviet Union, using the carbon monoxide from the exhaust of the engine. Eichmann described the operation:

I followed the van and then came the most horrifying sight I've ever seen in my life. The van drew up along side a long pit, the doors were opened and the bodies thrown out; the limbs were still supple, as if they were still alive. They were thrown into the pit. I saw a civilian pulling out teeth with a pair of pliers and then I took off. I rushed to my car and departed and said no more. I was through. I had had it. A white-coated doctor said I ought to look through the peephole and see what went on inside the vans. I refused. I couldn't, I couldn't speak. I had to get away. Frightful, I tell you. An inferno. Can't do it, I can't do it. That's what I told him (Müller).[93]

Belzec was the first camp to use permanent gas chambers. At first exhaust gases were used—the Nazis used the term Heckholt Institute to describe the operation, after the mechanic who ran the diesel,[94] but, in a process that involved a professional rivalry between Belzec's commander Wirth and Rudolf Höss, Zyklon B was substituted. Kurt Gerstein, who had joined the SS after his sister-in-law was killed in the euthanasia program to find out what happened, had gained a reputation for his technical expertise in delousing troops and prisoners of war. He delivered some experimental gas to Belzec. Witnessing an "action" he tried to communicate it to the papal nuncio, who refused to talk to him, but succeeded in passing information about what he had seen to Baron Gorran von Otter, from the Swedish embassy, whom he met on the train from Warsaw to Berlin.[95]

Sobibor camp existed between May 1942 and October 1943, its existence terminated by a prisoner revolt, led by Alexander Pechersky, a former political commissar of the Red Army.[96]

Franz Stangl, who had commanded Sobibor, replaced Irmfried Eberle as commandant of Treblinka, technically the most advanced camp.[97] Stangl's assistant, Kurt Franz, did most of the running of the camp. He created a near perfect genocidal society where, at the price of a brief extension of life, the victims participated in its running. Here Jews not only from Warsaw, but also from Austria, Greece, Germany, the Low Countries, and Czechoslovakia were killed. As in Sobibor, the prisoners revolted, and the revolt, which produced a few survivors, led to the closing of Treblinka. From then on the killing was to be centered on a much larger scale in Auschwitz.

AUSCHWITZ

Survivors' accounts of life in the camps say that only prisoners who had lived through it could know what it was really like. David Rousset speaks of it as a different universe.[98] All express the position that the experience was so totally without references to a normal situation as to make communication barely possible. There is a danger of mystification here, but an equally great one of not listening to what former prisoners are saying. Auschwitz was not hell, the SS were not devils;

Auschwitz was a modern institution created by the German state; the SS was an official organization of Germany.

Hermann Langbein begins his history of Auschwitz with a quotation from Martin Walser, a former inmate:

> Only inmates can know what Auschwitz was; no one else. Because we can not empathize with the situation of the prisoners, because the degree of suffering exceeded every previous concept, and because therefore we cannot create a true picture of the perpetrators Auschwitz is called Hell and the perpetrators devils. . . . However Auschwitz was not hell but a German concentration camp.[99]

During the Nazi period, and particularly in its last years, numerous and varied camps dotted Europe's landscape like poisonous mushrooms: Dachau, Buchenwald, Dora, Mauthausen, Treblinka. They all have their unique history, but it is Auschwitz that is identified with the "Final Solution." Auschwitz was not a "pure" extermination camp. It was a labor camp and provided labor for a variety of enterprises, including the I.G. Farben factories, which were set up to utilize the available labor. German industries were quite willing to participate in the exploitation of the available labor.

There is a voluminous survivor literature, primarily from those who had become the permanent cadres of the camp. The majority of arrivals passed immediately from the trains to the gas chambers. Criteria for selection were age and physical condition.

Authority was always totally arbitrary. It was exercised not only by the SS but also by Kapos—the origin of the word is in doubt—foremen, trustees of the prisoners who received certain privileges and who exercised their authority in various ways, while themselves being responsible to the SS. The authority of the Kapos included the de facto right to kill. If a Kapo reported someone departed by death, no one asked how. Every prisoner had a colored triangle sewn on a sleeve. Red was for political prisoners and green for criminals, and in all the camps a struggle between the greens and the reds for control of the camp infrastructure took place. "Asocial" prisoners, that is, people who refused to work and the like, wore black; Jews had a yellow star of David; nationality was also indicated—P for Polish, F for French, and so on.

The range of behavior of prisoners who could exercise power varied greatly. Some used their authority to gain privileges for themselves and mistreat those over whom they had control. Others, particularly among the political prisoners, used it as a means of resistance and to improve the lot of prisoners. Langbein cites specific cases where prisoners had opportunities to modify their situation.[100] His own relationship with the chief camp doctor, Dr. Eduard Wirths, had a major impact in reducing the number of ill prisoners who were killed.

Trains would bring prisoners in from all of Europe. A selection at the ramp would separate those marked for immediate killing from those who were to be used as slave labor. At the same time constant selections in the camp destroyed those who could not maintain their health and physical strength.

The rationalization and industrialization of mass killing were here developed further than anywhere else. Originally the killing apparatus consisted of several relatively small gas chambers. With the support of a number of German business firms, new installations were begun in the summer of 1942 and completed in 1943 with larger capacities both for killing and, what had been a major bottleneck at other camps, for the destruction of bodies. Konnilyn Feig notes that

> leaders of the Third Reich and industrialists had the opportunity to view the entire operation on the formal inauguration day, a bright March morning in 1943. . . . The program consisted of the gassing and burning of 8,000 Cracow Jews. The guests . . . were extremely satisfied with the results and the special peephole fitted into the door of the gas chamber was in constant use. They were lavish in their praise of this newly erected installation.[101]

The camp grew rapidly, taking in more and more prisoners. Satellite camps, which used prisoners for labor, were built. As experience in running the death technology increased, output also increased. The exact number of killed can not be accurately determined, but estimates range between two and four million.[102] Rudolf Höss commented on how easy mass killings were: "One did not even need guards to drive them into the gas chambers; they simply went in, because they assumed that they would shower there, and instead of water we turned on poison gas. It went very quickly [*Das Ganze ging schnell*].[103] The mass killings in Auschwitz differ from previous mass killings by their duration. In contrast to the Spanish fury or Drogheda or Bangladesh, the requirements for industrial efficiency largely eliminated expressions of passion. Killing became a routinized activity. It was a logical plan, a carefully orchestrated program of mass murder. It required cooperation between killers, scientists, bureaucrats—Raul Hilberg has noted the importance of the German railroads in the killings. As in a slaughterhouse the attempt was made to use all by-products. The property of those killed was collected; the extracted gold teeth supported the currency; ashes were used as fertilizer; hair was cut and collected for further industrial use.

A unique position was occupied by the *Sonderkommando*—the name applies to those who handled the bodies of those who had been gassed.

These prisoners received some special privileges, were allowed to use alcohol. They ate the food that had been brought by victims of the transports. The psychological costs defy description. One member of the *Sonderkommando* commented that, "if in our work one does not go insane the first day, one gets used to it. . . . I do not wish to survive for the sake of life, I no longer have any one, all my relatives have been gassed, but I want to live to bear witness and take revenge."[104] The men of the *Sonderkommando* were regularly killed every six months and replaced by new ones.

Filip Müller survived the *Sonderkommando*. His memoirs provide one of the most important documents about these events, and the description of his attempted suicide is unique.

> Now, when I watched my fellow countrymen walk into the gas chamber, brave, proud and determined, I asked myself what sort of life it would be for me in the unlikely event of my getting out of the camp alive. . . . I had never yet contemplated the possibility of taking my own life, but now I was determined to share the fate of my countrymen.
>
> I managed to mingle with the pushing and shoving crowd of people who were being driven into the gas chamber. . . . I was overcome by a feeling of indifference: everything had become meaningless. Even the thought of a painful death from Zyclon B gas, whose effect I of all people knew only too well, no longer filled me with fear and horror. I faced my fate with composure.
>
> The atmosphere in the dimly lit gas chamber was tense and depressing. Death had come menacingly close. It was only minutes away. No memory, no trace of any of us would remain. Once more people embraced. Parents were hugging their children so violently that it almost broke my heart. Suddenly a few girls naked and in the full bloom of youth, came up to me. They stood in front of me, without a word, gazing at me deep in thought and shaking their heads uncomprehendingly. At last one of them plucked up courage and spoke to me: "We understand that you have chosen to die of your own free will, and we have come to tell you that we think your decision pointless: for it helps no one." She went on, "*We* must die, but you still have a chance to save your life. You have to return to the camp and tell everybody about our last hours. . . . As for you, perhaps you'll survive this terrible tragedy and then you must tell everybody what happened to you. . . . The girls took hold of me and dragged me protesting to the door of the gas chamber. There they gave me a quick push which made me land bang in the middle of the group of SS men. Kurschuss was the first to recognize me and at once set about me with his truncheon. [He] yelled at me:

"You bloody shit, get it in your stupid head: *we* decide how long you stay alive and when you die, not you. Now piss off, to the ovens!"[105]

In October 1944 the *Sonderkommando* attempted a revolt, which blew up one crematorium. None of those who had participated in the action survived.[106]

Killing was only one of the activities at Auschwitz. As the material situation for Germany worsened, German industry, most notably I.G. Farben, took advantage of the availability of cheap labor to build factories for the production of synthetics. Prisoners were literally worked to death; it provided some, who possessed special skills, the opportunity to survive.[107]

Medical experiments using prisoners as subjects were carried on by some SS doctors. Josef Mengele, perhaps the best known physician of Auschwitz, was interested in Noma, a disease that attacked the cheeks of children. He had a prisoner physician, a Dr. Epstein, do research on it and write a scholarly paper for him. He was also interested in research on twins, which frequently involved killing both at the same time to compare the organs. He injected children in the eyes to change their eye color. Mengele's teacher, Professor Freiherr von Verschuer, worked at the Kaiser Wilhelm Institute and remarked that Mengele had been responsible for presenting many interesting eyes with differentiated colors. These had come from Gypsies whom Mengele had ordered killed, in order to possess their eyes. Professor Verschuer had never asked where the specimens came from.[108]

Dr. Carl Clauberg asked Himmler to transfer him to Auschwitz so that he would have "materials" for experimentation. He attempted to find a cheap method of sterilizing women without an operation. Himmler had an interest in matters of this sort, which would permit exploiting the labor of conquered people while at the same time ensuring their destruction. A block was made available for him in Auschwitz, in which women—called "rabbits" (*Kanninche*) in camp parlance—were injected with experimental substances to test their efficacy.[109]

No account of Auschwitz would be complete without reference to the memoirs of its commander, Rudolf Höss.[110] Höss wrote his memoirs in a Polish prison prior to his execution. Originally destined for the priesthood, he was brought up by a stereotypical German family (a strong, domineering father, use of corporal punishment, etc.). He abandoned his commitment to religion following an episode in which he believed that the priest had betrayed the secret of the confessional to his father. Psychohistorians have singled out the statement that he was unable to connect emotionally to his sisters (and others) as indicative of his general difficulty in forming warm human relations.

The relationship between my parents was one of loving respect and mutual understanding. Yet I never remember any display of tenderness; . . . I had always, from my earliest years, fought shy of any sign of tenderness, much to the regret of my mother and of all my aunts and other relatives. . . . Although both my parents were devoted to me, I was never able to confide in them the many big and little worries that from time to time beset a child's heart. My sole confidant was my pony, and I was certain that he understood me. My two sisters were very attached to me, and were perpetually trying to establish a loving and sisterly relationship. But I never wished to have much to do with them. . . . I was never able to have any warm feelings for them. They have always been strangers to me. I had the greatest respect, however, for both my parents. . . . But love, the kind of love that other children have for their parents, . . . I was never able to give them.[111]

Describing his first sexual experience he notes that "at first I was distressed by her tender caresses. . . . For, ever since my earliest childhood, I had shunned all demonstration of affection."[112]

In 1914, underage, he enlisted in the army. In 1918 he ended up in Damascus and with his men made his way back home through Bulgaria, Romania, and Hungary. He joined the *Freikorps* (the volunteer corps) and participated in a *Vehmegericht* (secret kangaroo court) which led to his conviction and imprisonment. He served six years until released by an amnesty of July 1928. He joined the SS in the fall of 1933 and quickly ended up in the concentration camp service, in which he rose rapidly. In his autobiography he portrays himself as sensitive—he states that he considered trying to leave the concentration camp service because he felt too much pity for the prisoners.

Höss was appointed commandant of Auschwitz in April 1940. He built it from small beginnings into the largest camp. Nothing indicates any sadistic inclinations. Höss was intensely loyal to Himmler and believed that all orders, no matter how difficult, had to be obeyed.

When in the summer of 1941 he [Himmler] himself gave me the order to prepare installations in Auschwitz where mass exterminations could take place, and personally to carry out these exterminations, I did not have the slightest idea of their scale or consequences. It was certainly an extraordinary and monstrous order. Nevertheless the reasons behind the extermination program seemed to me right. I did not reflect on it at the time: I had been given an order, and I had to carry it out.[113]

Throughout the autobiography Höss expresses self-pity because of the tasks he had to carry out, taking satisfaction in praise from Himmler, who, on seeing the extermination, commented that "these are battles, which future generations will no longer have to fight."[114] Before his execution he doubted his commitment to National Socialism, admitted errors, but never condemned himself: "Let the public continue to regard me as the bloodthirsty beast, the cruel sadist, and the mass murderer; for the masses could never imagine the commandant in Auschwitz in any other light. They could never understand that he, too, had a heart and that he was not evil."[115]

THE HOLOCAUST IN OCCUPIED EUROPE

Between 1939 and 1945 Germany had established, either through conquest or through an alliance system, control of most of the continent of Europe. In some of the satellites the indigenous governments were able to maintain some autonomy. The German sphere of influence included major portions of the Soviet Union, Austria, Poland, Lithuania, Latvia, Estonia, Belgium, Holland, France, Czechoslovakia, Denmark, Hungary, Croatia, Serbia, Yugoslavia, Italy, Norway, Slovakia, Romania, and Bulgaria. (Obviously some of these designations overlap—Slovakia only became an independent state after the destruction of the Czech state.) German success in destroying Jews varied among countries. Ninety percent of Poland's Jews were annihilated, 75 percent of the Netherlands', 20 percent of Italy's, while none of Denmark's Jews was killed. (Fifty-one died of natural causes in the Theresienstadt ghetto.) No Jews from Finland were deported.[116]

The primary, but not the only significant element accounting for the divergent survival rate of Jews in different countries within the German sphere of influence, is the extent of SS control. Without extensive SS control, if the government of the country did not support the Final Solution, German killing efforts were unsuccessful. During the period of their alliance with Finland, the Germans requested that the Finns deport their Jews to Germany. The Finnish government refused and that was the end of it. Italy was Germany's oldest and closest ally, but Italian Jews were shipped to Auschwitz only after the Germans had occupied Italy. At times the Italian army protected Jews in territory it occupied. The population of Holland was sympathetic to the Jews, and in a unique action even called a general strike, which was brutally broken by the Germans. Most Dutch were opposed to the Germans—though a small Dutch Nazi movement existed, but the Dutch resistance movement was unable to prevent the deportation of Jews to the East.

In Denmark the Germans sought to create a model administration. The country had been overrun without resistance, and the Germans permitted the indigenous government to continue to function. Georg Duckwitz, a German shipping expert in Copenhagen, had informed Hans Hedthof of the impending plan to deport the Jews; Hedthof then warned the Jewish community. The Danish army was unwilling to cooperate in the planned roundup. In a unique show of solidarity, Danes hid Jews and helped ship them to Sweden, which was willing to accept them.

Where the SS was in complete control it could round up Jews for deportation even amid a population sympathetic to the Jews. But in many countries elements of the population approved the German actions against Jews, and in some supported it.

Poland had no neo-Nazi party, but a longstanding tradition of intense anti-Semitism. Collaboration was not an issue (the Germans were not willing to accept a Polish puppet government), but elements of the population willingly helped the Germans in their actions against the Jews. Jews who escaped the ghetto were denounced and turned over to the Germans. The resistance movement, the AK, refused to support the revolt of the Warsaw ghetto or other Jewish resistance attempts with any seriousness, not only because of its anti-Semitic tradition, but also because the nationalistic Polish underground identified Jews with communism and support of the Soviet Union. Though the issue of Polish–Jewish relations during World War II is still debated—the widespread showing of the film *Shoah* has contributed to the revival of this debate—that many in Poland approved of the German extermination of Jews is beyond dispute.

Anti-Semitism was prevalent and popular in many, probably most European countries. Jews in hiding were frequently betrayed to the Germans: the betrayal of Anne Frank in Holland is the best known instance, but numerous other examples may readily be documented from France to Hungary to Poland. The Germans had no difficulty in recruiting auxiliaries from the Ukraine, Latvia, Lithuania, and other countries to serve in concentration and death camps, and local police forces were available in many countries to help the Germans.

Marxism has always been viewed as an international movement, in contrast to National Socialism, which has been interpreted primarily as an intense expression of German nationalism. This ignores the international dimension that National Socialism and the SS in particular acquired during the war. Himmler transformed the *Waffen* SS, the militarized branch of the SS, into an international fighting force committed to an anti-Bolshevik ideology. It included volunteers from France, Denmark, Flanders, Holland, Norway, and other countries. After the war its commander, General Paul Hausser, was to speak of the group as a forerunner of NATO, a European armed force committed to opposing the Soviet Union.[117]

Just as the Russians could count on the support of the Communist parties when they liberated a country, so in many countries the support for the Germans was organized by proto-Nazi movements, which identified with the ideology of the new order, including agreeing with the Germans that the Jews were a mortal danger. The Ustashi in Croatia, the Nationaal-Socialistische Beweging (N.S.B.) under Anton Mussert in the Netherlands, Norway's Nasjonal Samling under Vidkun Quisling, the Green Arrow in Hungary, the Hlinka Guard in Slovakia, and similar movements supportive (always with some local variations) of Germany's new order, existed in many countries. In most (but not all) countries allied with or occupied by Germany, willing helpers were available to send Jews to their death. In some cases the government or the population took advantage of the political situation to kill Jews even in the absence of any German initiative.

The Romanians actively engaged in mass killing of Jews, and some Romanian Jews were deliberately pushed into German-occupied territory where they were killed by *Einsatzgruppe* D. So many were pushed across that the Germans attempted to call a halt. The Germans also protested that the Romanians were killing Jews in an undisciplined manner. An *Einsatzgruppen* report of July 25, 1944, notes that "there would be nothing to say against numerous executions of Jews if it were not that the technical preparation and the method of execution is defective. The Romanians leave the executed people where they have fallen without burying them.[118] In Slovakia the government purposefully cooperated with the Germans in arranging for Jewish deportations. The Holocaust as a systematic social policy was originated by the German government, but most accounts minimize the resonance and support this policy found in most European countries.

It was not only that the proto-Nazi movements shared the Nazi views of the Jews. Equally significant is that much of the population of Europe, even when not actively anti-Semitic, was willing to go along with and on occasion profit from the situation. In Holland, which was not pro-German, one Jewish physician noted that his colleagues "swooped on my practice like vultures on carrion. The Aryans. They all wanted to take it over. . . . The Medical Association completely let me down. At no time did I ever receive any help from it."[119] In France the French police rounded up stateless Jews and Jewish children for deportation.[120] Rainer Baum has attempted to understand the bystander who did nothing (his study is restricted to Germany, but its concepts have general significance).[121] Many Germans—Baum is primarily concerned with analyzing the German elites—were not rabid anti-Semites; some were even out of sympathy with the Nazis or their program, but were willing to permit the Nazis a free hand to do to the Jews what they wished in return for other rewards. Many Germans unsympathetic to Hitler's radical anti-Semitism supported his attempt to revise the terms of the Versailles treaty, to regain for Germany a new, powerful position in Europe. Though Jews had for a century become increasingly integrated into the national communities of Central and Western Europe, had felt themselves to be Frenchmen, Germans, or Dutch, their acceptance by the non-Jewish national community was rarely complete, and the fate of Jews was not a primary concern of their compatriots. (The exceptional behavior of the Danes in this regard has already been cited.) In a classic late nineteenth-century work, Ferdinand Tönnies characterized modernity as a shift from *Gemeinschaft* to *Gesellschaft*, from community to society.[122] This involved a shift from personal to contractual obligation; Benjamin Nelson's history of the idea of usury used the phrase "From Tribal Brotherhood to Universal Otherhood" as a subtitle. Both writers suggest the development of a society where everyone is a stranger to everyone else and where there are few bonds between people. Arthur Koestler addressed this reality when he wrote:

> There is a dream which keeps coming back to me at almost regular intervals; it is dark, and I am being murdered in some kind of thicket or brushwood. There is a busy road at no more than ten yards distance; I scream for help but nobody hears me, the crowd walks past laughing and chatting.[123]

Because of anti-Semitism, the fact that the victims were Jews very likely made concern with their fate of lesser importance than it would have been for other victims; however, the killing of gypsies, or the mass starvation of Russian prisoners of war also evoked little sympathy and concern. News of mass killings in the postwar world in Cambodia and elsewhere also did not create any concern. The indifference that much of the population of Europe (and the United States, among others) showed to the fate of the Jew is grounded in the general atomization within modern society, where the victimization of strangers evokes few or no responses. The "Kitty Genovese" phenomenon—a woman was attacked in New York, called for help, and not one of the forty people who heard her cries bothered to do anything about it—appears characteristic of modern urban societies. The indifference to the fate of Jews rests upon the disappearance of sympathy and concern for others in the modern world.

When, particularly after the *Kristallnacht*, the position of Austrian and German Jews became more and more untenable, they generally found that other countries were unwilling to give them refuge. The specific reasons have been spelled out in detail in the literature—the fear of offending the Arabs caused Britain to place severe limits on emigration to Palestine. The existence of unemployment and the fear that further emigration would lead to an increase of anti-Semitism were elements that led to the United States not opening its doors. After the Nazi assumption of power many establishments in Germany posted signs saying *Juden unerwünscht!* (Jews not wanted). This was also the view of most neutrals and most of the Allies.

During the war there were studied efforts by both England and the United States not to address the problem of the German killing of Jews. The American State Department systematically attempted to minimize awareness of the killings, for fear that this might raise a demand for rescue efforts. Suggestions by Jewish leaders that railroad tracks to Auschwitz be bombed were rejected with patently false excuses of technical infeasibility. Several opportunities for rescuing Jews existed; they were consistently rejected.

Yet though the overwhelming response of neutral countries and the Allies was one of indifference, there were individuals who, at the risk of their lives, protected Jews. Jews survived in Berlin, hidden by Germans who shared meager rations with them. Jewish children were hidden in monasteries and nunneries, and by individual families in Holland, in France, in Poland, and elsewhere. Raoul Wallenberg's heroic efforts were responsible for saving untold numbers in Hungary—and the price he paid for this was lifelong imprisonment in the Soviet penal system.[124]

UNRESOLVED ISSUES

This essay began with a quotation from Leopold von Ranke that the task of the historian was to show how it really happened. Four decades of research have reconstructed a detailed record. Yet expressions that the meaning of the Holocaust cannot be grasped from the historical record appear in many accounts of survivors and others who write about it.[125] On one level statements such as that by Elie Wiesel that "we shall never understand how Auschwitz was possible" are false.[126] The motives of those who created Auschwitz, the mechanics of its establishment, the way it was run may clearly be explained with the same epistemology as is used to comprehend the origins of the Crimean War or the Athenian conquest of Melos. In this context, frequent recourse is had to juxtaposing knowing and understanding. There is a difference between reading statistics of a few thousand killed and seeing a thousand bodies. What is meant by those statements about failure to understand the Holocaust is that reason can describe a horror to which feeling cannot do justice.

The magnitude of the Holocaust not only in numbers but in scope, in its unprecedented union of sadistic fantasies and rational action, has produced a loss of innocence. For those who have experienced the Holocaust, for those who have examined the events, the world appears different. This is not only manifested by a sense of disquietude that creates insecurity because the Holocaust has revealed a hitherto un-fathomed level of human actions, but the knowledge that ordinary people have the capability of doing what was done raises questions about the meaning of being human.

Although it has not penetrated modern consciousness, the Holocaust has destroyed the Enlightenment view of fundamental human good-ness and potential perfectability. Even though few recognize it as such, the Holocaust was a transformational event that has radically altered the world.[127] The demonstration that what was hitherto regarded as unthinkable could happen has eroded trust. The old image of human nature has been basically altered, though most continue as if nothing had happened.[128]

The Holocaust has had a traumatic effect on Jews, who were its primary, but not its only victims. It has led to numerous discussions that argue the uniqueness of the Holocaust.[129] In most of these discus-sions the intent is to differentiate Jewish victimization from that of other victims of Nazism, as in the following examples:

To deny Jewish uniqueness is to allow oneself to be limited by the anti-Semitic imagination. Shall we stop speaking of the Holocaust because Arab, Neo-Nazi, and Communist propagandists all claim that Jews are using the Holocaust to garner good will for Israel?[130]

The fact that all Jewish babies and children were to be murdered along with all adults, discloses ... the unique uniqueness of the Holocaust: not a single Jew was to remain upon earth. Such an eschatological decision and hope contrasts sharply with Nazi policy towards the gypsies, as it does with the earlier Turkish slaughter of the Armenians.[131]

What underlies the attempt to deprive the Jews, as it were of their terrible unique experience as a people marked for annihilation? ... By subsuming the Jewish losses under a universal or ecumenical classification of human suffering, one can blur the distinctiveness of Jewish fate and consequently one can disclaim the presence of anti-Semitism. ... In denying the uniqueness of the fate the Jews experienced as the chosen victims of mass murder, the univer-salizers of Auschwitz do not necessarily deny the uniqueness of the mass murders. At least they understand that the mass murder which the National Socialist state perpetrated stands alone in the annals of human murderousness, that something new in human history happened when Hitler's Germany arrogated to itself the right to decide who was entitled to live in the world and who was not. But all too often the necessary and essential distinction between the murder of the 6 million Jews and the accelerating violence and terror of our time is blurred. . . . By denying the particularity of the Jewish experience under the German dictatorship and, still more, the enormity of the Jewish losses, by equating the destruction of the European Jews with other events, they succeed in obscuring the role of anti-Semitism in accomplishing that murder.[132]

Jews were the preeminent victims of Nazi hatred, and occupied the central role in the Nazi extermination program. They were not the only victims of Nazi hubris. Other victims included Poles, Russian prisoners of war, Russian Communists, and most Gypsies. The Nazis clearly attempted to kill all Jews within the territory they controlled, while not all Gypsies or Poles were targeted for death. Yet some of the above remarks, whatever the intent of their authors, are open to the interpretation that the death of Jews is a greater tragedy than the death of other persons.

The Holocaust had a traumatic impact on Jews. Germany engaged in a process of seeking to kill all the Jews it could lay its hands on; some of the rest of the world applauded, many were indifferent, and few wished to oppose this mass murder. One response to the Holocaust has been to connect the Holocaust to the establishment of the state of Israel.

The event [the Holocaust] therefore resists explanation—the historical kind that seeks causes, and the theological kind that seeks meaning and purpose. . . . What holds true of the Holocaust, holds true also of its connection with the state of Israel. Here too, the explaining mind suffers ultimate failure. *Yet it is necessary, not only to perceive a bond between the two events, but also to make it unbreakable.*[133]

Emil Fackenheim clearly perceives the birth of the state of Israel as a monumental event in Jewish sacred history, and connects it dialectically with the Holocaust.[134] A consequence of this position is that those Jews who do not identify with Israel or are opposed to its policies are defined as unauthentic. Opposition to Zionism or to the policies of the state of Israel is a political judgment. Though anti-Zionism may indeed mask anti-Semitism in some, the automatic identification of opposition to Israeli policies with anti-Semitism is both fallacious and dangerous.

In Fackenheim's search for authentic responses one senses his view that to abandon Judaism is to give Hitler a posthumous victory. Hitler wished to destroy Jews, as defined by "racial," not religious, criteria. To identify Jewishness with Judaism is to deny the authenticity of anti-religious Jews such as Sigmund Freud, who saw religion as a regressive infantilism, or nonpracticing Jews such as Albert Einstein, or the many Jews who, remaining Jews, identified with a universalist ethic such as socialism or Marxism.

The centrality of the memory of the Holocaust for Jews cannot be overstated. Just as the mass murder of Jews in Europe evoked few serious responses, so the impact of the Holocaust on the non-Jewish consciousness has been minimal. More than a decade ago, Gerd Korman examined American textbooks and found that the Holocaust was barely mentioned.[135] Studies of ethics by philosophers examine medical issues from abortion to surrogate motherhood, but the philosophical and ethical issues created by the Holocaust—under what conditions should orders be disobeyed, when is resistance required—are not mentioned. Philippe Ariès's monumental history of death and dying never mentions gas chambers.[136] A few Christian theologians have reexamined the Christian foundations of anti-Semitism, but in no sense has the Holocaust had an impact on Christian theology.

Those who have experienced the Holocaust, those who have studied it, have, whatever their different interpretations, perceived it as having fundamentally altered the human condition. Yet they are unable to share their vision with the rest of the human community, for which the Holocaust has been only a historical episode.

NOTES

1. Within the last several years in the United States, Germany, and France, publications have appeared arguing that the gassing of Jews did not take place—a view advanced by the *Journal of Historical Review*—or that Hitler did not know that Jews were being gassed (David Irving), or that the number of Jews killed has been vastly exaggerated. A listing of some of these publications is in George M. Kren's "The Holocaust: Some Unresolved Issues," *Annals of Scholarship* 3, no. 2 (1985): 35–61. Some of these publications appear to be financed and supported by extreme right-wing groups. The perception of these groups as belonging to a "lunatic fringe" may be the reason a much-needed, detailed analysis of the groups and their publications has not yet been undertaken.

2. The use of the term "German" rather than "Nazi" or "SS" already suggests an interpretation—in this case, that others besides the SS or Nazis share responsibility.

3. This statement applies to the action of the Germans and their supporters. The Jewish evidence is much more incomplete. Since there were *no* survivors from some of the smaller camps and since the Germans who ran the killing apparatus will be silent, what has happened has been erased from human memory. This applies in varying degrees to knowledge of ghetto life, particularly its end phases, and to resistance groups, many of which perished, leaving no records behind.

4. The single best work is the revised edition of Raul Hilberg, *The Destruction of the European Jews: Revised and Definitive Edition*, 3 vols. (New York: Holmes and Meier, 1985).

5. The literature on this issue is voluminous. The classic statement is Charles A. Beard, "That Noble Dream," *American Historical Review* 41 (October 1935): 74–87.

6. Richard C. Lukas, *The Forgotten Holocaust: The Poles under German Occupation 1939–1944* (Lexington: University Press of Kentucky, 1986).

7. The literature on the Holocaust has consistently avoided dealing with the mass killings of Russian prisoners of war, which was also grounded in racial theory and in the identity that Hitler and other Nazis perceived between Jews and bolshevism. One cannot help but be astounded at the seeming lack of concern over the killing of Russian Communist functionaries in the Holocaust literature. It is as if the German killing of Communists possessed some kind of rationality, if not legitimacy, as if being a Communist was a crime deserving punishment, in contrast to the case of the Jews who were killed not for any act of their choice—even renouncing Judaism would have done them no good—but only because of what they were. Similarly the killing of Russian prisoners of war is rarely mentioned. Is it that the German army, now a mainstay of NATO, was as much involved as the SS in this, so that this must be regarded only as a *"Schönheitsfehler"* ("minor lapse") on their part, and that contemporary cold war realities make it impolitic to speak about the German army's extensive involvement in mass murder? Is there a perception that killing done by acts of omission—many prisoners were simply permitted to starve to death (although some of the installations in Auschwitz were first tried out on Russian POWs)— rather than active killing is less culpable? See Christian Streit, "The German Army and the Policies of Genocide," in *The Politics of Genocide: Jews and Soviet Prisoners of War in Nazi Germany*, ed. Gerhard Hirschfeld (London: Allen and Unwin and the German Historical Institute, 1986). Streit has written a detailed and strangely ignored work on this matter: Christian Streit, *Keine Kameraden: Die Wehrmacht und die sowjetischen Kriegsgefangen 1941–1945* (Stuttgart: Deutsche Verlagsanstalt, 1978).

8. Baruch Hochman in a review of William Styron's *Sophie's Choice* and D. M. Thomas's *The White Hotel* writes: "With regard to the Holocaust, it was striking that two gentiles, of very different moral and literary complexions, and writing in very different novelistic modes, had chosen to convey the experience of the horror through women, and that both of them had chosen women who, for all intents and purposes, were not Jewish: that is, were not even 'proper' members of the chief target community of Hitler's extermination machine." (I believe that this statement is dubious as far as *The White Hotel* is concerned.) Baruch Hochman, "Doomsday as Gang Bang, or Dodging the Reality of the Holocaust," *Tikkun* 2 (1987): 103–7.

9. Lucy S. Dawidowicz, *The War against the Jews, 1933–1945* (New York: Holt Rinehart & Winston, 1975) and Lucy S. Dawidowicz, *The Holocaust and the Historians* (Cambridge, Mass.: Harvard University Press, 1981). Henry Feingold writes that the Holocaust was a unique event because "its primary victims, the European Jews, were a unique people in the context of European history." Henry L. Feingold, "How Unique Is the Holocaust?" in *Genocide, Critical Issues of the Holocaust: A Companion to the Film Genocide*, ed. Alex Grobman and Daniel Landes (Los Angeles: Simon Wiesenthal Center and Chappaqua, N.Y.: Rossel Books, 1983), pp. 397–401.

10. Cf. Hirschfeld, *The Politics of Genocide.*

11. The psychohistorical literature on Hitler and Nazi Germany is vast. For a bibliographical introduction see Terry Mensch, "Psychohistory of the Third Reich: A Library Pathfinder and Topical Bibliography of English Language Publications," *Journal of Psychohistory* 7 (Winter 1978–80): 331–54, and George M. Kren, "Psychohistorical Interpretations of National Socialism," *German Studies Review* 6 (Fall 1978). The major works are Rudolph Binion, *Hitler among the Germans* (New York: Elsevier, 1976); Gertrud M. Kurth, "The Jew and Adolf Hitler," *Psychoanalytic Quarterly* 26 (1947): 11–32; Walter C. Langer, *The Mind of Adolf Hitler: The Secret Wartime Report* (New York: Basic

Books, 1972); Helm Stierlin, *Adolf Hitler: A Family Perspective* (New York: Psychohistory Press, 1976); Robert G. L. Waite, *The Psychopathic God: Adolf Hitler* (New York: Basic Books, 1977); Norman Bromberg and Verna Volz Small, *Hitler's Psychopathology* (New York: International Universities Press, 1983).

12. Ian Kershaw, *The Nazi Dictatorship: Problems and Perspectives of Interpretation* (Baltimore: Edward Arnold, 1985), provides a succinct summary and a useful bibliographic introduction.

13. Karl A. Schleunes, *The Twisted Road to Auschwitz: Nazi Policy toward German Jews 1933-1939* (Urbana: University of Illinois Press, 1970).

14. Ibid., p. ii.

15. For a documentation of this point, see Gerd Korman, "The Holocaust in Historical Writing," *Societas* 2 (Summer 1971); Henry Friedlander, *On the Holocaust: A Critique of the Treatment of the Holocaust in History Textbooks* (New York: Anti-Defamation League, 1972); Dawidowicz, *The Holocaust*; Kren, "The Holocaust," pp. 39-61.

16. Léon Poliakov, *The History of Anti-Semitism* (London: Elek, 1965), p. 11.

17. Rosemary Ruether, *Faith and Fratricide: The Theological Roots of Anti-Semitism* (New York: Seabury, 1979), p. 24.

18. Ibid.

19. Ibid., pp. 27-28.

20. Erich Kahler, *Man the Measure: A New Approach to History* (New York: George Braziller, 1943), p. 144.

21. Following popular usage I use the term "anti-Semitism" to designate hostility toward Jews. Technically others besides Jews are included in the term "Semite." It appears to have first been used by William Marr in Germany about 1879. Alexander Bein, "Der Moderne Antisemitismus and seine Bedeutung für die Judenfrage," *Vierteljahrshefte für Zeitgeschichte* 7, no. 4 (October 1958): 340. Many have addressed the question, Who is a Jew? Cf. George M. Kren, "Race and Ideology," *Phylon: The Atlanta University Review of Race and Culture* (Second Quarter 1962): 167-77 and George M. Kren, "The Jews: The Image as Reality," *Journal of Psychohistory* 6 (Fall 1978); 285-99.

22. Richard L. Rubenstein, "Religion and the Origins of the Death Camps," in *After Auschwitz: Radical Theology and Contemporary Judaism* (Indianapolis: Bobbs-Merrill, 1966), pp. 1- 44.

23. Ibid., p. 9.

24. Ibid., p. 11.

25. *Moses and Monotheism* (New York: Vintage Books, 1955), pp. 114-15.

26. Among the most recent discussions are Robert Chazan, "Medieval Anti-Semitism," and Jeremy Cohen, "Robert Chazan's 'Medieval Anti-Semitism,'" both in *History and Hate: The Dimensions of Anti-Semitism*, ed. David Berger (Philadelphia: Jewish Publication Society, 1986), pp. 49-72.

27. An important article having a bearing on this is Israel Shahak and Timothy Garton Ash, "'The Life of Death': An Exchange," *New York Review of Books* 34, no. 1 (January 29, 1987): 35-49 (a response by Shahak to a previous article by Ash and the latter's response).

28. Joshua Trachtenberg, *The Devil and the Jews: The Medieval Conception of the Jew and Its Relation to Modern Anti-Semitism* (New Haven: Yale University Press, 1943).

29. Chazan, "Medieval Anti-Semitism," p. 57.

30. Achim von Arnim, *Halle und Jerusalem: Studentenspiel und Pilgerabentheuer* (Heidelberg, 1811).

31. Gustav Freytag, *Soll und Haben: Roman in sechs Büchern*, original ed. 1855. The work has been reprinted numerous times. On Freytag see George L. Mosse, "Culture, Civilization and German anti-Semitism," and "The Image of the Jew in German Popular Literature: Felix Dahn and Gustav Freytag," in George L. Mosse, *Germans*

and Jews (New York: Grosset & Dunlap, 1970); George M. Kren, "Gustav Freytag and the Assimilation of the German Middle Class," *American Journal of Economics and Sociology* 22 (October 1963): 483–94.

32. Benjamin N. Nelson, *The Idea of Usury: From Tribal Brotherhood to Universal Otherhood* (Princeton: Princeton University Press, 1949).

33. Cited in George M. Kren, "Race and Ideology," *Phylon* 13 (Summer 1962): 168.

34. The basic thrust of the Enlightenment was its rejection of religion, identified as a harmful superstition. The philosophes attacked the church as an institution and Christianity as a doctrine. Gotthold Lessing appears as one of the very few advocates of toleration who also believed that religions embodied some truth. *Nathan the Wise* argues for religious toleration on the ground that the three major religions are of equal value and essentially identical to each other. There is no suggestion that all three are to be viewed as superstitions.

35. Quoted in Peter Gay, *Voltaire's Politics: The Poet as a Realist* (New York: Vintage Books, 1965), pp. 351–52.

36. Cited in ibid., p. 353.

37. In Freytag's *Debit and Credit*, the one good Jew (and until the emergence of racism many anti-Semitic novels contained at least one good Jew) explains the dishonest behavior of other Jews on the basis of their religion. The Talmud is frequently cited as a source for dishonest business practices.

38. Uri Tal, *Christians and Jews in Germany: Religion, Politics, and Ideology in the Second Reich, 1870–1914* (Ithaca, N.Y.: Cornell University Press, 1975), an important study which also contains an excellent bibliography.

39. Sidney M. Bolkosky, *The Distorted Image: German Jewish Perceptions of Germans and Germany, 1918–1935* (New York: Elsevier, 1975).

40. The basic work is George L. Mosse, *Toward the Final Solution: A History of European Racism* (New York: Howard Fertig, 1978); also Leon Poliakov, *The Aryan Myth: A History of Racist and Nationalist Ideas in Europe* (New York: Basic Books, 1974).

41. Norman Cohn, *Warrant for Genocide: The Myth of the Jewish World-Conspiracy and the Protocols of the Elders of Zion* (New York: Harper & Row, 1969), p. 34.

42. Cohn, in ibid., reproduces some of this material in the appendix.

43. Ibid., p. 60.

44. Cohn's *Warrant for Genocide* is definitive.

45. Anti-Semitism was an important component of right-wing and Fascist parties in Romania, Poland, Hungary, France, Austria, and Germany, but not in Italy or Spain.

46. From a vast literature on National Socialist ideology I single out Eberhard Jäckel, *Hitler's Weltanschauung: Entwurf einer Herrschaft* (Tübingen: Rainer Wunderlich Verlag Hermann Leims, 1969). An English edition has been published by Wesleyan University Press, 1972.

47. An excellent detailed account of German anti-Semitic actions is in Schleunes, *The Twisted Road to Auschwitz.*

48. The complex Nazi attitudes toward Palestine are discussed in Frances Nicosia, *The Third Reich and the Palestine Question* (Austin: University of Texas Press, 1986).

49. Austria was not "conquered" by Germany, as the majority of Austrians welcomed annexation to Germany. By 1938 most Austrians strongly disliked Schuschnigg's clerical fascism and many had committed themselves to National Socialism.

50. Yehuda Bauer, *A History of the Holocaust* (New York: Franklin Watts, 1982), p. 106.

51. Ibid., p. 108.

52. Heinz Höhne, *The Order of the Death's Head: The Story of Hitler's SS* (New York: Ballantine Books, 1971), p. 339; cf. Martin Broszat, *Nationalsozialistische Polenpolitik, 1939-1945* (Stuttgart: Deutsche Verlags Anstalt, 1961).

53. The document is reproduced in Bauer, *A History of the Holocaust*, pp. 147-51. Cf. the discussion in Isaiah Trunk, *Judenrat: The Jewish Councils in Eastern Europe under Nazi Occupation* (New York: Macmillan, 1972); Yisrael Gutman, *The Jews of Warsaw 1939-1943: Ghetto, Underground, Revolt* (Bloomington: Indiana University Press, 1982). Yehuda Bauer and Nathan Rotenstreich, eds., *The Holocaust as Historical Experience* (New York: Holmes and Meier, 1981), contains an important discussion of Trunk's book *Judenrat* and a discussion of the institution of the *Judenrat* by Yehuda Bauer. A substantial literature, consisting of diaries, memoirs, and studies of the ghetto is now available.

54. Trunk, *Judenrat*, p. xxvii, notes that Jews did not object to segregation, because they feared the attitude of the local population. Lukas's *The Forgotten Holocaust* suggests that after the invasion a sense of community existed between Poles and Jews, but the evidence against that interpretation is overwhelming. An important study written during that time by a Jewish historian (who did not survive) is Emmanuel Ringelblum, *Polish-Jewish Relations during the Second World War*, ed. Joseph Kermish and Shmuel Krakowski (New York: Howard Fertig, 1976).

55. Of particular importance are Raul Hilberg, Stanislaw Staron, and Joseph Kernisz eds., *The Warsaw Diary of Adam Czerniakow: Prelude to Doom* (New York: Stein & Day, 1982); Lucjan Dobroszycki, ed., *The Chronicle of the Lodz Ghetto 1941-1944* (New Haven: Yale University Press, 1984); Emmanuel Ringelblum, *Notes from the Warsaw Ghetto: The Journal of Emmanuel Ringelblum*, ed. Jacob Sloan (New York: Schocken, 1974). The book published by the International Center for Holocaust Studies, Anti-Defamation League of B'nai Brith, *The Holocaust in Books and Films: A Selected, Annotated List* (New York: Hippocrene Books, 1966), contains a useful list of works in English.

56. Many discussions of this issue refer to Maimonides' injunction that "if pagans should tell them [the Jews] 'Give us one of yours and we shall kill him, otherwise we shall kill all of you,' they should all be killed and not a single Jewish soul should be delivered." Trunk, *Judenrat*, p. 422.

57. There is a brief discussion of this in Jacob Robinson's introduction to Trunk's *Judenrat*. Leo Baeck's statement deserves quoting. After having been informed of the gassings in Auschwitz (while he was in Theresienstadt) he wrote: "I went through a hard struggle debating whether it was my duty to convince Grünberg that he must repeat what he had heard before the Council of Elders. . . . I finally decided that no one should know it. If the Council of Elders were informed, the whole camp would know within a few hours. Living in the expectation of death by gassing would only be harder. And this death was not certain for all: there was selection for slave labor; perhaps not all transports went to Auschwitz. So I came to the grave decision to tell no one." Thus, Baeck, whose personal integrity is beyond question, nevertheless given the logic of events, collaborated with the Nazis in rounding up Jews for deportation. "I made it a principle to accept no appointments from the Nazis and to do nothing which might help them. But later, when the question arose whether Jewish orderlies should help pick up Jews for deportation, I took the position that it would be better for them to do it, because they could at least be more gentle and helpful than the Gestapo and make the ordeal easier. It was scarcely in our power to oppose the order effectively." Leo Baeck, "A People Stands before Its God," in *We Survived: Fourteen Histories of the Hidden and Hunted of Nazi Germany*, ed. Eric Boehm (Santa Barbara, Calif.: Clio Press, 1966), pp. 288, 293.

58. Trunk, *Judenrat*, pp. 2-3.

59. Hannah Arendt, *Eichmann in Jerusalem: A Report on the Banality of Evil* (New York: Viking, 1965).

60. "An Analysis of Isaiah Trunk's *Judenrat*" in Bauer and Rotenstreich, *The Holocaust as Historical Experience*, pp. 155-71.

61. Trunk, *Judenrat*, provides a detailed discussion.

62. Ibid., p. 500.

63. Ibid., p. 499.

64. Zelig Kalamanovitch, "A Diary of the Nazi Ghetto in Vilna," *YIVO Annual of Jewish Social Science* 8 (1953): 31; George M. Kren and Leon Rappoport, *The Holocaust and the Crisis of Human Behavior* (New York: Holmes and Meier, 1980), pp. 119-21.

65. Reuben Ainsztein, *Jewish Resistance in Nazi-Occupied Eastern Europe* (New York: Barnes and Noble, 1974).

66. Bauer, *A History of the Holocaust*, pp. 252-53.

67. Gutman, *The Jews of Warsaw*. The Polish police assisted the Germans. Ibid., pp. 369, 380. The report of General Stroop to Hitler has been published in an English translation and provides a valuable source: Sybil Milton, ed. and trans., *The Stroop Report: The Jewish Quarter of Warsaw Is No More!* (New York: Pantheon, 1979).

68. Cited in Gutman, *The Jews of Warsaw*, p. 409.

69. Cited in ibid., p. 412.

70. The text of the document is in John Mendelsohn, ed., *The Holocaust: Selected Documents in Eighteen Volumes* (New York: Garland Publishing Company, 1982), vol. 11, pp. 39-40.

71. The text of the document, with the English translation used in the Nuremberg trials, is in ibid., pp. 1-32.

72. It deserves to be noted again that the moral indignations in the Western world against German behavior never extended to the Communists murdered by the Germans. One senses—it is never spelled out—that the killing of Communists as such appears to be perceived by some as a lesser crime than the killing of Jews. See note 7.

73. Quoted in Dawidowicz, *War against the Jews*, p. 124.

74. Ibid., pp. 124-25.

75. Höhne, *The Order*, has a good account.

76. Ibid., p. 409.

77. See Kren and Rappoport, *The Holocaust*, pp. 8-12.

78. Höhne, *The Order*, p. 409.

79. The term "sadism," which appears frequently in the literature, is inappropriate. Sadism designates behavior in which the individual derives significant, normally sexual gratification by inflicting pain on others. What is more typical, however, than compulsive sadistic behavior is a casualness—as one person might squash a mosquito, so here a person is shot because he blocks the view. The cruelties were rarely even goal oriented. There were always individuals who in a situation in which they were free (including the absence of any peer opposition) to kill or inflict pain on others did so because they found it amusing. Anti-Semitism appears to have played no role in this; it was simply that victims were available to whom one could do things without any sanctions.

80. Robert L. Koehl, *The Black Corps: The Structure and Power Struggles of the Nazi SS* (Madison: University of Wisconsin Press, 1983), p. 177.

81. Ibid., p. 417.

82. Höhne, *The Order*, p. 410.

83. Ibid., p. 413.

84. Hermann Langbein, *Menschen in Auschwitz* (Vienna: Europaverlag, 1972), p. 37.

85. "Diese Humanisierung bezug sich freilich nicht auf die Opfer, sondern auf die Täter, denen man die mit Erschießungen am laufenden Band verbundene Nervenbelastung ersparen wollte." Ibid., p. 37.

86. Cf. Hedwig Contrad-Martius, *Utopien der Menschenzüchtung: Der Sozialdarwinismus und seine Folgen* (Munich: Kosel, 1953); Loren R. Graham, "Science and Values: The Eugenics Movement in Germany and Russia in the 1920's." *American Historical Review* 82 (1977): 1133–64.

87. Dawidowicz, *War against the Jews*, p. 134. Most works on the Holocaust discuss the euthanasia program and its relationship to the use of gas. Nora Levin, *The Holocaust: The Destruction of European Jewry 1933–1945* (New York: Schocken, 1973); Dawidowicz, *The War against the Jews*; Léon Poliakov, *Harvest of Hate: The Nazi Program for the Destruction of the Jews of Europe* (New York: Holocaust Library, 1979). The research on this issue of Gitta Sereny, *Into That Darkness: An Examination of Conscience* (New York: Vintage Books, 1983), among the best works on the Holocaust, deserves greater attention than it has hitherto received in the literature. There is a detailed study by Lothar Gruchmann, *Euthanasie und Justiz im Dritten Reich* (Stuttgart: Deutsche Verlags-Ansalt, 1972).

88. Cited in Poliakov, *Harvest of Hate*, p. 185.

89. Ibid., p. 190.

90. Sereny, *Into That Darkness*, pp. 48–90.

91. Rolf Hochhuth. *The Deputy* (New York: Grove Press, 1964).

92. See Konnilyn G. Feig, *Hitler's Death Camps: The Sanity of Madness* (New York: Holmes and Meier, 1979), which provides a classificatory scheme.

93. Höhne, *The Order*, p. 424.

94. Feig, *Hitler's Death Camps*, p. 277.

95. Gerstein's actions are dramatized in Hochhuth's *Deputy*. After the war Gerstein turned over documents to the French occupying forces; he was arrested and died in a French military prison, officially a suicide. The likelihood that he was killed by other SS men in the prison is substantial. On Gerstein (whose testimony is cited in almost all studies of the Holocaust) see Saul Friedländer, *Kurt Gerstein: The Ambiguity of Good* (New York: Knopf, 1969) and Pierre Joffroy, *A Spy for God: The Ordeal of Kurt Gerstein* (New York: Harcourt Brace, 1971).

96. Alexander Pechersky, "Revolt in Sobibor," in *They Fought Back*, ed. Yuri Suhl (New York: Schocken, 1975), pp. 7–50.

97. Jean-François Steiner, *Treblinka* (New York: New American Library, 1979), is an important, controversial novel. The Sereny biography of Stangl, *Into That Darkness*, is invaluable.

98. David Rousset, *A World Apart* (London: Secker and Warburg, 1951).

99. Langbein, *Menschen*, p. 17.

100. Ibid.

101. Feig, *Hitler's Death Camps*, p. 357.

102. Langbein's chapter *"Zahlen"* (Numbers), *Menschen*, pp. 70–80.

103. Ibid., p. 79.

104. Ibid., pp. 223–24.

105. Filip Müller, *Auschwitz Inferno: The Testimony of a Sonderkommando* (London: Routledge and Kegan Paul, 1979), pp. 111–14.

106. Langbein, *Menschen*, pp. 229–34.

107. Primo Levi, *Survival in Auschwitz: The Nazi Assault on Humanity*, trans. Stuart Woolf (New York: Collier, 1961), is an important account.

108. Langbein, *Menschen*, pp. 383–84.

109. Ibid., pp. 385–86.

110. Institut für Zeitgeschichte, *Kommandant in Auschwitz: Autobiographische Aufzeich-nungen von Rudolf Höß*, eingeleitet und kommentiert von Martin Broszat, (Stuttgart: Deutsche Verlags-Anstalt, 1958); *Commandant of Auschwitz: The Autobiography of Rudolf Hoess* (Cleveland and New York: World Publishing, 1959); the American edition includes some material which for reasons of tact was cut from the German one. Hoss's name is variously spelled Hoess, Höss, and Höß .

111. Höss, *Commandant of Auschwitz*, p. 33.

112. Ibid., p. 41.

113. Ibid., p. 160.

114. Langbein, *Menschen*, p. 348.

115. Hoess, *Commandant of Auschwitz*, p. 202.

116. Helen Fein, *Accounting for Genocide: National Responses and Jewish Victimization during the Holocaust* (New York: Free Press, 1979), attempts to account for the different success the Germans had in implementing the genocide programs in different countries. Her study also contains a detailed bibliography on the fate of Jews country by country. Lucy S. Dawidowicz provides a useful summary of the fate of Jews country by country, concluding with a statistical summary that estimates the number killed in each country and the percentage of the Jewish population that was killed. Dawidowicz, *War against the Jews*, pp. 483–544.

117. After President Reagan's visit to the Bitburg cemetery, one fully expected him to define the SS as "premature anti-Communists."

118. Cited in Levin, *The Holocaust*, p. 572.

119. Feig, *Hitler's Death Camps*, p. 266.

120. Jews not only fought in the French resistance movement, but special Jewish units existed. Many French men and women risked their lives to protect Jews. In contrast to most of the clergy of Eastern Europe, the French clergy generally opposed Nazi anti-Semitic acts. A unique example of help extended is described by Phillip Hallie, *Lest Innocent Blood Be Shed: The Story of the Village of Le Chambon and How Goodness Happened There* (New York: Harper & Row, 1979). The basic work on the complex situation in France is Michael Marrus and Robert O. Paxton, *Vichy France and the Jews* (New York: Basic Books, 1981).

121. Rainer C. Baum, *The Holocaust and the German Elite: Genocide and National Suicide in Germany, 1871–1945* (Totowa, N.J.: Rowman and Littlefield, 1981). This important study is strangely neglected in the literature.

122. Ferdinand Tönnies, *Community and Society: Gemeinschaft und Gesellschaft*, trans. Charles P. Loomis (1887; New York: Harper Torchbooks, 1963).

123. Arthur Koestler, "On Disbelieving Atrocities," in *The Yogi and the Commissar and Other Essays* (New York: Macmillan, 1945), pp. 88–93.

124. Several excellent biographies have been published, among them Per Anger, *With Raoul Wallenberg in Budapest: Memories of the War Years in Hungary* (New York: Holocaust Library, 1981); Elenore Lester, *Wallenberg: The Man in the Iron Web* (Englewood Cliffs: Prentice-Hall, 1982). Wallenberg had gone to Budapest with Swedish diplomatic status to rescue Jews. Thanks to indomitable courage he was eminently successful. He went to see the Russian command on January 17, 1945, and was arrested by the Russians. Conflicting reports by individuals who are reported to have seen him in the Russian prison system have surfaced. Efforts by Sweden and the Allies to put pressure on the Soviet Union for information and for his release have been ineffectual.

125. Alan Rosenberg provides a philosophical analysis of this in Chapter 19, "The Crisis in Knowing and Understanding the Holocaust."

126. Elie Wiesel, *One Generation After* (New York: Avon, 1970), p. 167.

127. The labeling of the Holocaust as a transformational event is a thesis in Kren and Rappoport, *The Holocaust*. Cf. Alan Rosenberg and Alexander Bardosh, "The Holocaust and Historical Crisis: A Review Essay," *Modern Judaism* 3 (December 1981): 337–46. Also Rosenberg, Chapter 19, "The Crisis in Knowing and Understanding the Holocaust."

128. Experiments by Stanley Milgram showed how individuals found it easy to obey an order to harm others. P. Zimbardo had individuals play roles as prisoners and jailers and found that those playing jailers acted with such enthusiasm that the experiment had to be terminated. Except for Bruno Bettelheim, few in the analytic tradition have addressed the issue of perceptions of human character and human nature after the Holocaust. See Bruno Bettelheim, *The Informed Heart: Autonomy in a Mass Age* (New York: Free Press, 1960); Stanley Milgram, *Obedience to Authority: An Experimental View* (New York: Harper & Row, 1975). The Zimbardo studies are discussed by Erich Fromm, *The Anatomy of Human Destructiveness* (New York: Holt, Rinehart & Winston, 1973), pp. 52–61.

129. Examples in Kren, "The Holocaust," pp. 39–61; Alan Rosenberg, "Was the Holocaust Unique? A Peculiar Question," in Isidor Wallimann and Michael Dobkowski, eds., *Genocide and the Modern World: Ideology and Case Studies of Mass Death* (Westport, Conn.: Greenwood Press, 1987), pp. 145–61.

130. Feingold, "How Unique Is the Holocaust?" p. 398.

131. "The Holocaust and the Enigma of Uniqueness: A Philosophical Effort at Practical Clarification," *Annals of the American Academy of Political and Social Science* 45 (July 1980): 165–78.

132. Dawidowicz, *The Holocaust*, pp. 15–16.

133. Emil Fackenheim, *The Jewish Return into History: Reflections in the Age of Auschwitz and a New Jerusalem* (New York: Schocken, 1978), p. 279. Elsewhere Fackenheim writes: "What is more, that state [Israel] has become a moral necessity, not only for the Jews of Israel but for all Jews throughout the world, . . . For no matter where they live, *it has become a duty for Jews in this century not to tolerate 'moral discrimination' any longer.* However, they shall find the strength to fulfill this duty only because of the heroic example of the state of Israel." Ibid., p. 198.

134. See the study on Fackenheim by Irving Louis Horowitz, "Many Genocides, One Holocaust?: The Limits of the Rights of State and the Obligation of Individuals," *Modern Judaism* 1, no. 1 (May 1981): 74–89.

135. Korman, "The Holocaust in Historical Writing"; see also Friedlander, *On the Holocaust*. Kren, "The Holocaust," reviews textbooks dealing with twentieth-century history that, with a few exceptions minimize the Holocaust or connect it with a variety of other events.

136. Philippe Ariès, *The Hour of Our Death*, trans. Helen Weaver (New York: Knopf, 1981).

PART TWO
Assault on Morality

2

HOLOCAUST: Moral Indifference as *the* Form of Modern Evil

Rainer C. Baum

> that the destruction of the Jews would one day pose a threat to himself and the existence of his "thousand-year Reich" was evidently not a possibility foreseen by Hitler—otherwise he would have avoided it.
>
> *Krausnick and Wilhelm*[1]

> Bayard: You're an intelligent man, Prince. Are you seriously telling me that five, ten, a thousand, ten thousand decent people of integrity are all that stand between us and the end of everything? You mean this whole world is going to hang on that thread?
>
> *Arthur Miller (1966)*

Two voices address us here. The first is that of social science, the second that of poetry. The former sounds assertive, the latter interrogative. The first contributes to explanation, the second to moral meaning. The former is a quotation from the definitive history of the *Einsatzgruppen* (mobile extermination squads), the latter one from the play *Incident at Vichy*. Yet these differences notwithstanding, they seem to suggest the same idea: that a little more thoughtfulness among the principal perpetrators and a little less moral indifference among the bystanders were all that stood between life and death for millions of victims in *the* crime of our time. Could it be true? What of it?

But how does one deal with such questions? One answer, as strikingly honest as it is deceptively simple, is: "One doesn't; not well, not finally. No degree of scope or care can equal the enormity of such events or suffice for the sorrow they encompass."[2] Two issues confront us in this concern with how one can cope with such questions. One derives from the recency of these events. Some of the survivors are still alive and through them we, the readers and writers of Holocaust history and philosophy, are still tied to the dead. That bond demands, insistently, some language of profound respect. This is not merely a question of taste, however much that too is involved. This is, above all else, a question of faith, of remembering in order to commemorate in that universal religious sense that seeks to transpose suffering injustice into sources of life. Yet I have no such language.

The other and related issue concerns historical truth itself. If all historical work tries to describe and explain a past reality, the issue here is to find a mode of representation that adequately captures it. And on this point the impact of the television series "Holocaust" proved highly instructive. In West Germany it was cathartic. The network had set up phone-in centers. There, historians stood ready to provide a little extra education. But in fact, priests and therapists were in far higher demand. Phone lines were jammed until all hours of the morning and not with learned explanations but with descriptive realization, stammering, voices that broke, weeping. The reality of the past had dawned, and, very evidently for the first time, for many thousands of callers.[3] This constitutes a serious indictment of the failure of academic scholarship as well as newspaper reporting. After all, an enormous amount of historical writing, stretching over decades, had preceded the broadcast. Similarly, many trial proceedings had filled the pages of newspapers. Yet it was a movie, and so not the pursuit of truth but that of profit, that brought home the truth, or rather the morally compelling aspect of the truth. Thus we know how this aspect can be captured from the past and brought forward into the present. It is by selecting characters the viewer can identify with and by depicting the nature of suffering. Certainly, movies simplify. But it is not complexity that turns historical scholarship or newspaper reportage into failure. It is rather the relative inability of the historian and the reporter to portray what concrete historical subjects *felt*. It is a matter of the medium. The language of the historian and the reporter tends to repress emotion, the movie does not. In the name of a far too simplistic understanding of the requirements of objectivity, both academic scholarship and professional reporting have adopted styles that systematically hide from us the emotional reality of past experience. And since we experience moral relevance through our emotional attachment to standards of judgment, an emotionally sanitized rendition of past events excludes that part of history from what has moral relevance in the present. Where Clio has been left behind, Minerva's vision has been dimmed.[4] In fine, to a disturbing extent contemporary scholarship and the physicians at Auschwitz who made the selections have one feature in common, mechanisms of numbing.

Let us try for however brief a moment, to be different. Let us try to remember as concretely and vividly as possible, in terms of phase-representative occurrences, the emotional reality that was this complex of *definition, concentration, confiscation,* and *annihilation* now labeled Holocaust. And focusing on the victim in this task, to begin with, let us imagine the realities of finding oneself recategorized by law as unwanted and deprived of citizenship, robbed of accustomed ways of making a living, socially isolated and uprooted, dispossessed of valuables, deported and imprisoned, and, finally, destroyed, starved to death, worked to death, executed, asphyxiated. And only after having stood there at the gates of hell may we turn to the comforts of abstraction involved in modern learning.

THE SIGNIFICANCE OF THE QUESTIONS

But if the problem of how one should deal with such questions has no satisfactory answer, their significance seems clearer. Here the issue is nothing less than the nature of modern evil. Hannah Arendt's famous formulation of its banality keeps haunting us. By this she meant of course an utterly unprecedented disproportionality between the evil committed and the motivation leading to it. Eichmann, so she argued,[5] was a normal person, essentially no different from most of us. And that, so goes the implication, was not just true of this official but of Germany's "writing desk murderers" more generally. We are wont to react to extraordinary evil from two partly competing, partly complementary perspectives, psychopathology and ideology. And so we regard the mass murderer as mad, as a zealot driven by some vision, or both. Yet therein lies false comfort. The critical perpetrators who made the implementation decisions were not mad.[6] Nor, excepting a tiny minority involving Hitler and some of his friends, were they "true believers."[7] Therefore, we are *not* confronted with just another instance of the all too familiar, the unleashing of massive violence in the name of virtue.

We are confronted instead with a new page in history. We have always known about the violent nature of man. We are war-making creatures. But unlike the warrior ant, we never before lacked copious reasons, ample justification, and, more often than not, very elaborate legitimations for visiting violence and death upon each other. From the Christian Children's Crusades to the more recent wars "to save democracy," one finds one unbroken universal allegiance to a synthesis: Among humans, collective violence and its legitimation form a meaningful whole. The Holocaust shattered it. It brought a new and radically frightening reality. Contrary to the experience of history, the modern division of labor permits participation in state-administered mass murder on the part of people who are ordinary as regards mental health and the beliefs they hold without transforming them into demonic or other extraordinary characters in any lasting way. Here again Eichmann remains representative. After the war, they led, often enough, utterly ordinary lives. Historically, a third factor also made extreme violence plausible, the temptation of extraordinary gain. But the Holocaust did not advance Germany's war aims.[8] Thus with the figure of Adolf Eichmann, a person who was not sick, or an ideologue of racism, or, finally, ever rewarded commensurately with the enormity of the deed, but just an ordinary official, Arendt admonished us to acknowledge what we resist: the realization that the Holocaust constitutes a step beyond the human condition.

That the modern division of labor altered and even fundamentally threatened the moral nature of man was a concern of the founding fathers of sociology. Emile Durkheim devoted his life to this problem; so, in their different ways, did Max Weber and Karl Marx. But among contemporary scholars one searches in vain for figures of a similar stature who care as deeply about the precarious nature of morality under conditions of modernity.[9] Moreover, if by amoralism one understands failure to connect and legitimate fidelity to particular conduct norms institutionalized in some niche of society with, and in terms of, supravening ethical standards expected to encompass and regulate all social life, then one needs no Ph.D. in sociology to see that the opportunities for amoralism expand in direct proportion to the division of labor. Conscientiousness can take the place of conscience very easily. Everybody working in an office knows it. The paycheck is a reward for conscientiousness. But the occasional Sunday confessional aside, and that only for church attenders, life in modern society simply generates no demand for conscience. And it is this that is the source of that fundamental moral indifference that, in Germany, led to the Holocaust. For we must not only ask, Why did the Germans kill the Jews? We must ask as well the more important question, Why did they permit mass murder of the Jews, and of millions of Russian prisoners of war, and thousands of Poles, and thousands of Gypsies?

Why, then, did we not care and simply let it happen? That question demands clarification in two respects. One, treated here in commonsense terms because I am not a philosopher, concerns the meaning of moral indifference or not caring. The other, as behooves a sociologist, turns on some critical characteristics of our modern way of life that generate moral indifference.

First and briefly stated, moral indifference is the opposite of taking moral responsibility for one's actions and beliefs. Beliefs deserve emphasis because they shape our orientations to our fellow human beings and influence the extent to which we are ready to accept personal accountability for our conduct. Exercising moral responsibility is, then, first, one part of decision making manifest in a caring concern with all the foreseeable consequences of our action for others; but shaped by our beliefs, it also includes a similarly caring concern with relating to all these others whose lives our conduct will likely affect as objects of fundamental respect rather than viewing them as merely means to other ends, such as "the solvency of the company," or "national security," ends that in practice are for most individuals not freely chosen by themselves but simply givens of the conditions under which they live. Moral indifference, in turn, is the absence of these two kinds of caring concern.

Next, a propensity toward moral indifference is deeply woven into the social fabric of modern life, particularly in the sphere of work. There the modern division of labor generates moral indifference in at least two specific ways. One of these concerns the extremely segmentalized nature of the social bonds; the other derives from the impersonal nature of authority.

By definition, modern society is characterized by a high division of social labor. This is evident in a plethora of specialized roles and organizations touching on virtually all aspects of life from education to problems of integration managed by the legal and other professions, and from production to administration in the private and public spheres. All such organizations are specialized for managing some particular aspect of life. None, however, is left to address in a comprehensive fashion that fundamental ambiguity and ambivalence that give uniqueness to humans, the need to confront the moral imperative. Instead of coping with this chunk of the moral burden which makes us human, from the point of view of the specialized roles involved, we address issues in the form of smaller, seemingly more manageable bits, bits for which specialized knowledge and skills exist. Moral failure, which once was called sin, is scarcely a popular idea. The comprehensiveness of its historical meaning has been lost. We deal with components of it, calling on a variety of specialists. Crime is managed by the police and the legal complex, problems of social adjustment by social workers, motivational problems by therapists, purely religious concerns where they still exist by clerics, and illness by the medical complex. Except for sensitive areas involving public support, such as research with human subjects where we call on medical ethicists, moral problems, also specialized, have been socially tamed by relegation to the college curriculum.

In everyday life, as long as one has no need for any of these specialists one may afford the sense of being safe and sound, all around. Such specialization not only maintains a complex social order, it also gives us freedom. But its underside deserves attention. Everyday life organized in specialized roles simply generates no effective demand for exercising moral responsibility. Normally, we are not asked to concern ourselves with consequences of action that reverberate beyond our specific sphere of competence and control. In a complex social order the presumption is that such reverberating consequences will be taken care of by other relevant experts. Whether they actually take care and how well are not our concern. Such concerns would overtax us. But that this arrangement systematically reduces the opportunity and even the need to exercise moral responsibility in a personal and therefore meaningful way is not recognized. Just how much modernity restricts our capacity for the two kinds of caring concern identified above as the essence of morally responsible conduct is most evident in the sphere of work. In turn, this is directly relevant for comprehending the nature of modern evil. The Holocaust was a state-administered destruction of politically designated surplus populations. And, after initial fumbling, an inevitable accompaniment of truly new forms of social action, this mass murder was accomplished as work. Hence, understanding how the modern organization of work systematically numbs us into moral insensitivity is important.

Everywhere modern work is regulated by the norms of specificity, performance, and universalism. Specificity means that only the work-related skills and attitudes are relevant. Everything else about human nature belongs to the private sphere. In case of doubt about the relevance of some concern at work, the burden of proof rests on the person wishing to include it. This burden of proof keeps the work sphere insulated from many consequences of work. That leaves us free, unconcerned, and thereby amoral. Performance standards involve rules regarding punctuality, and reliability regarding quantity and quality of output. Universalism is a norm calling for the impartial application of the yardsticks of specificity and performance just mentioned, regardless, as the saying goes, of age and sex, of color or creed. These are the official norms. Obeying them guarantees getting along and, often, getting ahead. Conformity is rewarded. Conscientiousness pays, literally, and figuratively in enhanced self-esteem. Nonconformity earns us deprivation. But conformity here is action with moral indifference. Considered jointly, action in accord with specificity and performance systematically hides the full person in the manifold of roles and obligations. Only the employee-self enters the halls of labor. Such a highly selected portion of a social self does not deserve a caring concern with fundamental respect because the appropriate object for it, the unique person with all the ambiguity and ambivalence that make us human, is not there. Present is only an employee, one factor of production, subject to cost considerations like all others. Universalism, in turn, removes a reasonable basis for a caring concern with all foreseeable consequences of our work that go beyond the doors of factory or office. It prohibits us from taking account of the fact that our associate at work is also a father, burdened by parenthood, and involved with many other roles and competing obligations. To illustrate, when an executive decides to meet a profit requirement with a layoff because that happens to be the most effective and efficient means at his disposal, he is supposed to sleep well even when aware of the potentially devastating consequences on the families affected. In theory, such consequences are the responsibility of the welfare complex. But the all too often visible inadequacy of such safety-net agencies does not entitle the executive in his role as a businessman to alter his decision merely because of houses without heat, ill-clad children, and despair. However foreseeable the consequences of his decision, the executive remains conscientious to the extent that he disregards them. Only a violation of the work norms would yield a different result. One would have to be an impractical dreamer to act with the above-mentioned caring concerns that make conduct moral. However, impractical dreamers do not become executives. In short, in modern society, and regardless of who owns the means of production, the division of labor rewards conscientiousness in following the dictates of specialized work norms. Also, not only does it fail, absolutely, to generate demand for the exercise of conscience, calling forth those two caring concerns that make us morally responsible, the modern division of labor systematically discourages any such inclination. From all we know about him, Eichmann was a conscientious official. Apparently, he never listened to the voice of his conscience. Whatever else may have contributed to the moral silence that characterized that life, just being a conscientious official created that utter stillness that disregards and therefore endangers the human condition.

Turning now to the nature of authority, in modern societies, democratic or not, the authority that prevails in formal organizations is impersonal. It is always some "it" in the name of which we make ourselves and each other toe the line. In political life one obeys "the law." Elsewhere one follows "regulations," regulations more or less formal, but impersonal nonetheless. Whether we dance to the tune of "the bottom line" or exact compliance from self and other in the name of "national interest," the very impersonality of the voice of authority contributes its share to suppress that double-caring concern that constitutes a personally felt and therefore genuine moral responsibility. In deference to some "it," at whatever level in an organization, we also treat each other and ourselves not as persons deserving fundamental respect and accountable for all foreseeable consequences of our action but merely as agents of impersonal purposes, which are imposed upon us by the division of labor. In effect, agenthood turns us all, self and other alike, into some kind of statistics, and, as someone said, statistics are people with their tears wiped off. And so, "the administration of things" has become a reality for all of us in a way never intended by Saint-Simon. This too has direct relevance for our topic. The Holocaust was a divided labor of destruction. Many participated in the exercise of authority in many organizations involved in it. Whether they administered definitions concerning victims, concentration, confiscation, or annihilation, there can be little doubt that the sense of abstract agenthood involved in the exercise of authority facilitated their work and the cooperation among the agencies involved. Agents busy with paper work tend to forget about the concrete consequences of their delimited duties. Hence the majority of participants in mass murder were already habituated not to inquire about the concrete end results of their action, while the same habituation to impersonal authority contributed to the numbing among the minority actually living in the midst of mass dying.

To avoid misunderstanding, I am *not* suggesting that anti-Semitism was irrelevant for the Holocaust, nor that among the many victims of National Socialism the Jews were the only group for whom a politically determined artificial race criterion sufficed for annihilation. Of course, the Holocaust remains unthinkable without Hitler and his small coterie of racial ideologues. What I am suggesting is indeed equally well established historical fact but, to a very large extent, not acknowledged. The Holocaust served no discernible political need in Germany, and it was accomplished with the indispensable aid of many normal people, neither zealots of a racial myth or indeed any theoretically coherent *Weltanschauung,* nor rewarded commensurately with the atrocity of their deed.

Three illustrations should suffice to show how much effort is taken to evade facing up to the role of moral indifference. First, in Helen Fein's explanation of the Jewish victimization rate, anti-Semitism plays a central role.[10] She sees National Socialism as an integralist movement that had to kill the Jews in order to legitimate its rule. As will be seen below, this is erroneous. Second, Robert J. Lifton constructs a "biocratic vision" to interpret the prominent role of physicians in the selections at Auschwitz. But he ignores his own evidence that most of them were not ideologues.[11] Third, despite his primary concern with the facts rather than their interpretation, Raul Hilberg employs a kind of standard formula. One recalls the painful and shameful history of anti-Semitism all the way back to the middle ages; one quotes Martin Luther, selects a quotation from a *Reichstag* speech of some member of the tiny anti-Semitic parties of Wilhelmine Germany, and ends with a selection from an anti-Semitic outburst of Hitler. And so, a line of seemingly inevitable historical progression from conversion, to expulsion, to annihilation is constructed, as if the whole history of the German people had to culminate in a war against the Jews. That view is reinforced by focusing on the cooperation between the ministerial bureaucracy, the army, industry, and the party, where "one may truly speak of their fusion into a machinery of destruction,"[12] rather than on the many conflicts, and above all on the language of bureaucrats which hid the reality of the destruction they administered from their own eyes, as evident in the protocol of the Wannsee Conference.[13]

However significant the findings such perspectives produce, they nonetheless do harm by omission. They hide instead of revealing the role that moral indifference played in the Holocaust. That this role was large will be demonstrated here. Since however, historical events have many causes, the skeptic might still ask, so what? My response is fourfold.

First, in a deliberately selective fashion I have indicated above how the modern organization of work engenders moral indifference. How far this can go is, as will be seen below, evident in the Holocaust. Thus in the Holocaust we confront, for the first time in history, the modern form of evil. Second, some of the intended victims in Eastern Europe sensed something of the radically new nature of the evil confronting them. In that milieu many had looked for generations to Germany as a Western beacon of modernity and rationality, and so the place whence would come the forces for liberating oppressed minorities in the comparatively backward East. They apprehended that the opposite was upon them, a bureaucratized efficiency of destruction, death *sine ira et studio*. They made themselves survive to let us know. We owe it to them and all who died to comprehend this truth. Third, for Germans this means getting rid of the false alibi created at the Nuremberg trials where the SS (*Schutzstaffel*) was declared a criminal organization. The awesome suffering and death was not primarily brought about by the few of us driven by a racial ideology; it was realized because we, the vast majority, simply did not care. That deepens the stain on our history. How to live with it in some constructive way, I cannot say. Fourth, and for all who now live as citizens of nuclear powers or countries allied with them, the fact of the Holocaust to be revealed here makes quite clear that it is not enough to disdain the rhetoric of pride and hate. Instead we must learn to keep the technologically feasible, a global nuclear winter, constantly before our eyes. It can bring a truly final solution to all human problems. And we must realize, more than we care to, our personal responsibility in having placed the survival of humanity at risk, if only by our role as taxpayers. And having grasped just how much sheer moral indifference contributed to the Holocaust, we must train ourselves to become afraid of our accustomed ways of getting along at work and getting ahead, these daily experiences of the segmentalized other and self as statistics that seduce us into moral indifference.

ON SOURCES AND THE NATURE OF THE ARGUMENT

Our central question is: Was anti-Semitism central enough in the legitimation of the National Socialist regime to require the Holocaust such that state-administered genocide filled a systemic need? The evidence available varies from indirect and inferential to direct forms. Among the former is the social composition of the voters for and the members of the National Socialist party. Insofar as these people belonged to socioeconomic groups seemingly threatened in their way of life by economic modernization, they may have been attracted by political anti-Semitism. This rests on the assumption that a perceived threat to be squeezed out of existence by "big labor," on the one hand, and "big business," on the other, lent itself to effective symbolic concentration on the figure of the "rootless Jew" as the incarnation of the evils of modernity. Motivated in this fashion, a vote could have had charismatic character. Born of distress, it could have been simultaneously an expression of anger and hope, a deep resentment against the forces of change as well as an expectation that a much feared fate could be delayed or perhaps averted entirely. More direct evidence on the prominence of anti-Semitism can be obtained from studies of Nazi propaganda as well as estimates of public opinion. Finally, the most direct evidence is to be found in biographical and autobiographical materials.

For the convenience of the reader, presentation of this evidence is organized by distinguishing external and internal legitimation. The former refers to the grounds on and extent to which a party or movement finds acceptability among the general population. The latter refers to the party's acceptability among its followers and the members of its affiliated organizations, most notably the SA and SS.

Proceeding in this fashion, I shall demonstrate that anti-Semitism did *not* play an important role in external or internal legitimation. Then, knowing already that neither psychopathology nor greed was involved at any imaginable level commensurate with the deed, this leaves moral indifference as a residual factor. Hence, there may be others. Therefore, also, this line of investigation is like a journey that has just begun.

THE EVIDENCE: EXTERNAL LEGITIMATION

A first sign of the marginal role of anti-Semitic extremism was already evident early in Hitler's rise to power. After the abortive beer-hall *Putsch* of 1923 he adopted the tactic of "the legal revolution." Sensitive to the evidently powerful presence of commitments to law, Hitler swore at his trial that he would abide by the constitutional rules in his pursuit of power only in order to change them once in power. That was a correct comprehension of the constitution.[14] It was also shrewd. For the out-sider, or the general public, reliance on legality meant protection against the implications of radicalism, probably particularly those concerning private property. But for his following, the insiders, the attention could remain focused on the revolutionary implications of the phrase "legal revolution." The compromise was crucial in establishing National Socialists as credible contenders for power. Revolutionary charisma had never brought decisive change in modern German history. Such change had always rested on following procedure *and* personalized bonds of trust involved in traditional authority. The democratic revolution of 1848 had been a failure; but Bismarck's engineered contract among sovereigns had established the modern nation in 1871; the 1918 revolu-tion had been a failure, but the compact between the army and Social Democracy had established Weimar democracy; the rightist authoritarian Kapp *Putsch* of 1920 had failed just like Hitler's 1923 episode. *Only* observing the niceties of legality and the appearance of traditional authority through the support of notables could get you anywhere in Germany.[15] Hitler understood that. Thus, insofar as the physical destruction of the Jews would have had to be legitimated by an anti-Semitic doctrine of charismatic character, had it been legitimated at all, Hitler's adoption of the "legal path" to power tells us that his rise to power did not build up the requisite charismatic resources.

In turning now to the question of how many and who voted for Hitler in free elections, two facts have to be kept in mind. First, at the height of their electoral success in the presidential and parliamentary elections of April and July 1932, the National Socialists gained about 37 percent of the popular vote.[16] Second, the possible appeal of anti-Semitism has to be seen in light of the fact that there were scarcely any Jews in Germany. In 1871 Jews made up 1 percent of the population; by 1939, and so about two years before the deportations "to the East," and to death, began, this figure had shrunk to 0.33 percent.[17] Thus, two or three large cities with some Jewish presence aside, in Germany Jews had no visibility. This means that for most people all the traditional varieties of anti-Semitism, whether religious, economic, or social, simply lacked an object. Consequently, only the modern variant, political anti-Semitism with the figure of the "rootless Jew" representing all the evils of modernity, could have played a role, if, that is, an ideology of anti-Semitism did legitimate National Socialist rule as Fein maintains.

The connection between political anti-Semitism and Hitler's support has traditionally been examined from the point of view of social groups particularly threatened in their accustomed ways of life by economic modernization. This is the basis for the interpretation of the Nazi vote as a manifestation of "extremism at the center" in contrast to the extremisms of Left and Right.[18] Accordingly, Hitler drew his primary support from the "old" lower middle class in small towns and the countryside, and therefore from people who made their living as independent small shopkeepers, artisans, and farmers. They, so one believed, had rational grounds to vote for Hitler. For the rhetoric about "Blood and Soil" and Jewish department stores seemed to promise that National Socialism might provide some relief from the relentless modernizing pressures of big business and big labor that appeared to herald the doomsday of a cherished and centuries-old way of life. But this "centrist thesis" of the Nazi vote as one against modernity is an academic myth, something partly true and partly false, and, therefore, just like all effective propaganda, a dangerously misleading article of faith.

One fact never compatible with this antimodern, lower-middle-class thesis has always been the religious cleavage. The Catholic lower middle class, just like Catholics in general, did not support Hitler to any notable degree. However, all this tells us is that socioeconomic susceptibility to National Socialism in general and charismatic anti-Semitism in particular might have been offset by other factors. Hence, as in the case of Germany's organized working class, a longstanding political tradition fortified by a rich organizational infrastructure involving unions, educational societies, credit unions, sports organizations, and of course one's very own political party, made members of these political milieus impressively resistant against the appeals of National Socialism.[19] The case of significant working-class resistance is relevant here. Charisma, so it is widely held, is a product of crisis. By 1932 the German economy was in a crisis. For example, the unemployment rate stood at 44 percent, more than twice that of Britain and Sweden, and almost double the rate in the United States.[20]

Yet whatever the connection between economic distress and support of the Nazi party, it could not have been simple and direct. While there was a strong positive correlation between the electoral support of National Socialism and the unemployment rate at the national, aggregate level, once one controls for religious affiliation and urbanization in that relationship, it turns negative: the higher the unemployment rate of an electoral district, the lower the percentage of the total vote gained by the National Socialists.[21] If one surmises that the primary victims of unemployment were members of the working class, their relative immunity to National Socialist propaganda should make us very cautious about inferring any direct relationship between economic misery and the actual effectiveness of Hitler as a self-proclaimed charismatic leader. A serious challenge to the "lower middle class thesis" of National Socialist support also came from "above," as it were. Germany's urban upper and upper middle classes voted for Hitler at a rate above their representation in a city's population.[22] Constituting the leading cadres of bureaucratic organization in modern life, they could not have been motivated by socioeconomically grounded fears of modernity. Finally, the work done by Jürgen Falter and his associates has also challenged the lower-middle-class thesis from "below."[23] After 1928, of all the Nazi party votes, about 40 percent came from members of the working class. While this amounts to underrepresentation when one calculates that the working class made up 45 percent of the voting population, the socialist part of National Socialism must have made Hitler's party at least acceptable to significant numbers of workers. Alternatively, if these workers were similar in outlook to Britain's Tory workers, then a well-established fact from community studies becomes critical. It was local notables who made Hitler acceptable.[24] Here the well-publicized joint Harzburg Front rally of Hitler's SA and Germany's Soldiers' League might have played a similar role even though the incident was anything but harmonious.[25] After all, Marshall von Hindenburg, also president of the Republic, was a member of the Soldiers' League. General Seeckt, the army's chief, a Prussian Crown Prince, and other luminaries of Prussia–Germany had been in attendance at this rally. To the extent that ties of this kind made Hitler a credible contender, the appeal rested on respect for tradition and trust in legality. But above all, the religious cleavage proved decisive. In July 1932 only 15 percent of Catholic voters cast their ballot for Hitler, but 39 percent of the Protestant ones did so.[26]

Thus the differential National Socialist appeal to the self-employed in small-town and rural milieus remains a fact. But without the legitimating support from Germany's urban upper and upper middle classes on the one hand, and appreciable working-class support, on the other, the NSDAP could not have gained the 37 percent of the national vote it did in the spring and summer of 1932. And thus also, in terms of the sociodemographic makeup of its voters, the NSDAP was in fact, what it proclaimed so loudly, a *Volkspartei* (people's party). Given this class mixture of electoral support, seeing the Nazi vote as one against modernity and therefore evidence of political anti-Semitism is no longer tenable.

Keeping in mind that Hitler did not gain executive power through the ballot box but through negotiation further diminishes the relevance of "the Jewish question" in his rise to power. Representatives of the army, big business, and President von Hindenburg gave Hitler the chancellorship. Following in the grooves of rule without parliamentary support and on the basis of emergency decrees already in force for about two years, these groups could not have cared less about anti-Jewish propaganda. Their aim was the establishment of an authoritarian regime. They believed they could use Hitler toward that end and get rid of him later. In this the army pursued its institutional interest, rearmament; big business had a stake in controlling unions, reversing some of the social legislation, and getting rid of restrictions imposed by the Versailles treaty.[27]

Yet, if a sociodemographic basis for political anti-Semitism played no role in Hitler's rise to power and if we cannot argue an "authoritarian personality" syndrome in any empirically respectable way,[28] what about possible cultural sources for despair about modernity? After all, anti-Semitic literature was no stranger to the German scene.[29] Let us turn, then, to analyses of National Socialist propaganda and the themes around which the critical elections of 1930 and 1932 were contested.

To begin with, in contrast to anti-Semitic popular writing, politically organized anti-Semitism in Germany had always been minuscule in modern times. In Wilhelmine Germany very small anti-Semitic parties appeared, only to disappear quickly again. For a long time, Hitler's movement seemed to follow the same pattern.[30] Further, during the critical elections, particularly the presidential one, the main campaign slogans did not refer to Jews. Quite clearly, these were campaigns fought about the fate of democracy. Its defenders threatened the electorate with the specter of a revolution from the Left; the advocates of an alternative to Weimar democracy threatened voters with an otherwise inevitable continuity of economic misery and of the shameful acceptance of the Versailles peace treaty. In effect, one voted either for or against democracy and little else. The socialists intoned that "a vote for Thälmann [of the Communists] is a vote for Hitler"; the conservative right (DNVP, German-National People's party) "argued" that "a vote for Hitler is a vote for Thälmann"; the Communists cried "a vote for Hitler is a vote for Hindenburg," thus Weimar democracy; and the Nazis shouted "a vote for Thälmann is a vote for Hindenburg."[31]

But even more direct evidence exists. As shown by Ian Kershaw's analysis, throughout the period 1923–33, Hitler's struggle for power, anti-Semitism was *not* among the central themes of his propaganda.[32] The main themes were instead sovereignty of the German people (which served to legitimate imperialist claims);[33] a national community without class conflict; militant anti-Marxism; the leadership principle; a frank espousal of meritocratic principles whereby, as in contemporary Western societies, rank was to be attained by achievement and talent rather than by birth; chauvinism and the glorification of war; and, of course, the antidemocratic stance. This set was, in effect, reducible to what one may call modern collectivism. It did promise upward mobility to all men (true, not women) on the basis of proven ability. But it legitimated such ambitions not in the name of individual happiness but in the service of setting the putative interests of the German people "above all else," in a strikingly literal sense of that word with regard to both domestic and international affairs. Therefore, National Socialist propaganda was utterly continuous with the nationalism of the Wilhelmine period, only, and this does remain significant for the moral indifference thesis proposed here, it was much more extreme or militantly strident in tone. Nonetheless, without this historical continuity, the urban upper- and upper-middle-class support would have been unthinkable.

Still following Kershaw, there were but two points in National Socialist propaganda that did set the party apart from the conservative Right. Aspects of Hitler's "leadership principle," the first was "struggle." This theme too was a celebration of Max Weber's occidental "world domination." But the Nazi version of this value complex had a collectivist *and* militarist character. The image of the good person and the good society revolved around *Leistungskampf,* a struggle for competitive achievement. For individuals, this meant striving for socioeconomic advancement and for the advancement of the interests of the group they worked for; for Germany as a people, it meant a forthright commitment to enter into the so-called Darwinian struggle among nations. As to the leadership principle, two features remain important. On the one hand, that phrase evoked an image of the ideal society as a set of dynamic teams in ceaseless competitive struggle for achievement in the service of the good for all. On the other hand, the fundamental social bond was an authority relation in which the ends were unquestioned, as in the relation between coach and team, and leadership a reward for winning. Yet this militarist image of the ideal society never found much resonance in the population, not even at the height of success after the fall of France.[34] The second distinctive feature was a cult of leadership concentrated on Hitler. He was portrayed as *the* leader of the Germans and *not* as just another party leader. In his own eyes, he was the ideology, the movement, and in him, and him alone, there was a clear linkage between anti-Semitism, war, and *Lebensraum*. However, and this remains the significant fact about external legitimation, neither anti-Semitism, nor foreign policy in general and *Lebensraum* in particular figured prominently in Nazi electoral appeals. As Kershaw puts it, "more remarkable than the unimportance of *Lebensraum* as a main motivating force is the limited role played by anti-Semitism—the central plank in Hitler's *Weltanschauung*—in activating support for the NSDAP."[35] And in light of suffering and death on a scale so difficult to visualize, I would add, yet more remarkable remains Hitler's nonsocial vision of domination itself. Hitler appreciated his anticipated great empire in terms of technological images where bigger was better. For him the New Order was a vision of huge buildings, trunk roads, double-decker railroad trains connecting Munich with Rostov on the Don at speeds of 120 miles per hour, the world's largest harbor at Trondheim with huge naval vessels that would dwarf the Japanese giants of World War II, and even recreational bigness with the Isle of Rügen, the world's largest tourist resort, with 45 miles of beach, a main building, 6 miles long, serving fourteen million tourists a season.[36] In all of this human beings provided at best a kind of statistical backdrop to represent the products of technology and the affect-laden idea of bigness. But one always finds exceptions. In some regions in Germany, anti-Semitism did play a role in Nazi propaganda, even if only as background music to emphasize economic issues. This was true in some of the elections in lower Franconia, Hesse, Westphalia, and parts of the Rhineland.

And what about anti-Semitic themes in the regime's propaganda effort after 1933 when, now in power, Hitler could draw on a newly created Ministry of Propaganda? Significantly, anti-Semitic slogans became more prominent, but this agitation did not succeed in turning the population around to a hatred of Jews. Widespread negative reactions to the one engineered pogrom, the *Kristallnacht*, clearly marked Goebbels's efforts as a failure.[37] The main propaganda aims were the maintenance of commitments to the *Volksgemeinschaft* (populist idea of community), the need for racial purity, the fanning of hatred for enemies within and without, and trust in leadership. All these were of instrumental significance in the regime's effort at the psychological mobilization of the people for war. By and large propaganda succeeded as long as it fed on existing predispositions to believe, as with themes like anti-Marxism, hostility to Weimar democracy, and "the wrong" of Versailles. But while loyalty to the Führer could be maintained until 1942, the psychological mobilization for war was a failure, as was the generation of the desired level of enthusiasm after its onset. The *Untermenschen* (inferior races) rhetoric proved wholly ineffectual as soon as actual combat experience in the eastern theater of operations accumulated and the casualty list became daily fare in the newspapers. No amount of exhortation could cover up the failure of the air force to protect German cities against bombing, the serious food shortage, and the realization that the fall of Stalingrad signaled the irreversible end to the prospect of winning the war. By late 1942 when the press still predicted victory at Stalingrad, a massive loss of confidence in Hitler's leadership had set in. It was never repaired. Henceforth, for news the BBC had become a substitute for Goebbels's ministry. Finally, and of central importance for our purpose here, the effort to generate support for anti-Semitic policies during the war had almost completely failed. While National Socialist propaganda did succeed in establishing the perception that a "Jewish question" had existed for some time, it failed to turn it into hatred of Jews, and it also failed in keeping it alive as an issue.

But what is known about the public reaction to organized mass murder? With thousands of soldiers in Eastern Europe existing in a milieu in which the Holocaust was not a successfully kept secret at all,[38] how did the people at home react? The only available answer comes from the closest approximation to public opinion polling in the Third Reich, the public morale estimates (*Stimmungsberichte*) of the domestic branch of the SS intelligence service.[39] That source tells us that very few noticed anything. As to the exclusion of the Jews from social life, popular reaction to the introduction of the segregation badge (the Star of David Jews were forced to wear) in September 1941 was reported as indifferent to mildly supportive.[40] Some people seemed surprised at the number of Jews still in Germany; some expressed worry about retaliation against Germans abroad; most did not care. Thus one finds precisely the kinds of public concerns one would expect of a people who had not been turned into a charismatic community with anti-Semitic zeal: worry about bombing raids, about getting enough to eat, about the outcome of the war. As to knowledge about systematic mass murder, while that was common in Eastern Europe by 1942, it was scarcely evident among the German people.[41] In the public morale estimates the only exception to this general picture of indifference was a few reports about quite explicit references to "going up in smoke," getting gassed, and the like, in some lower-class neighborhoods. But among the German public in general, the euphemisms employed by the administrators of genocide veiled the fate of their victims.[42] Thus the available evidence shows that the Holocaust did not serve the external legitimation of National Socialism.

THE EVIDENCE: INTERNAL LEGITIMATION

But did the mass murder of European Jewry perhaps serve the internal legitimation requirements of the regime? Was it necessary to keep the loyalty of members of the party, the SS, and the SA, groups conceivably committed to a doctrine of anti-Semitism? A first sign that no such requirements existed is to be seen in the fact that it remains almost impossible to say anything meaningful about the social demography of the members of political organizations during the Weimar period. The dropout rate of the Nazi party during that time was about 50 percent. We have no techniques to correct for its possible effect when estimating the social class composition of the party in our efforts to use it as an index of, or at least a resource for, political anti-Semitism as an expression of antimodernism.[43] Still, this tells us something important. Whatever their bases, Hitler's leadership cult and proclaimed charisma were not very powerful; they could not keep the faith of half the membership.

Keeping in mind this severe limitation of available data, are we to think that the party attracted primarily those threatened by modernizing economic change, the "old" lower middle class, small shopkeepers, artisans, and farmers? The answer is yes, but it was also so attractive to members of other classes, most notably the German elite, that, like its voters, NSDAP membership had considerable *Volkspartei* character. Following Michael Kater, let us distinguish four periods, the early 1920s before Hitler took "the legal route," the later 1920s, the early 1930s before Hitler became chancellor, and the period of the Third Reich.[44] This reveals the relative *Volkspartei* character of the NSDAP membership as follows: First, relative to its representation in the population (54 percent), the lower class was consistently underrepresented; however, it always made up over one-third of all party members (approximately 36–39 percent). Second, while the "old" lower middle class was always overrepresented in the party relative to its representation in the population (25 percent), it never made up more than 40 percent of all party members, and it constituted a paltry 29 percent of those who joined the party after 1933. Third, and in contradiction to the thesis of antimodernism with the symbol of the Jew as the evil of modernity, during two of the four periods the "new" lower middle class was overrepresented in the party relative to its representation in the population (18 percent). It made up about 23 percent and 28 percent of all party members during the later 1920s and after 1933, respectively. Fourth, Germany's elite, here calculated as representing 3 percent of the population, was consistently overrepresented among party members. In the early 1920s it constituted 12 percent of all party members, in subsequent periods probably between 7 and 9 percent which is still very impressive, given the mass character of the party. Thus the relative *Volkspartei* character of the party reduces the thesis of "centrist extremism," as did the sociodemographic profile of its voters. In party membership one cannot find that kind of social basis that presumably generates political anti-Semitism.

In turning now to the SS, let us begin with those directly involved in murder. Sociodemographically, the commanders of the *Einsatzgruppen* were among the most modern leadership cadres conceivable. In terms of education, they belonged to Kater's upper 3 percent of society. Products of German universities, 43 percent with a doctorate, they were among the most highly educated of all the leaders of the Third Reich.[45] Their fundamental moral indifference is best exemplified by Otto Ohlendorf, commander of *Einsatzgruppe* D and otherwise chief of domestic SS intelligence (*SD* [*Sicherheitsdienst*] *Inland*). As best as one can ascertain, he "volunteered" for mass murder for no other reason than concern that refusal might jeopardize his career, a fear that was unfounded, as we know from the subsequent fate of other SD intellectuals who evaded this demand of loyalty to the Führer's wish.[46] There is no convincing evidence of a sociodemographic basis of anti-Semitism among the leading officials of SS State Security (*SS-Reichssicherheitshauptamt*), the agency in charge of the Final Solution. Even though the author of its sociodemographic profile simply surmises that they must have been anti-Semites, their social characteristics suggest nothing of the kind, and direct evidence is lacking. Like their first boss, Reinhard Heydrich (of whom more below), they were predominantly of upper-middle- and middle-middle-class background, at least one-third university educated, and the majority was very young (35 or under in 1939). Two facts stand out. They point to moral indifference rather than anti-Semitism. Ideological convictions played no role in their recruitment, and only one-quarter joined the party before 1933.[47] At this time adequate social demography to serve as the basis for an inference concerning anti-Semitism for the SS as a whole is not available.

In concluding our sociodemographic estimates of anti-Semitism, let us note that the SA was heavily recruited from the working class, particularly in the early 1930s, and an escape from unemployment rather than ideological concerns was the main motive for joining up.[48]

If a case for a sociodemographic basis of political anti-Semitism cannot be made, what about alternative sources of some "cultural despair?" While interesting work on general intellectual currents in Germany seems to suggest cultural sources for hatred of the Jews,[49] an answer to the question about the internal legitimation requirements of genocide calls for information concerning the ideological beliefs of the members of the party, the SA, and the SS.

In the case of early party members, we have the most reliable information, autobiography. Remarkably, even among Hitler's old fighters anti-Semitism was a distinct minority phenomenon. According to Peter Merkl's classification of Theodore Abel's 581 autobiographical vitae of early party members, no more than 13.6 percent could be classified as ideological anti-Semites. Instead, the primary ideological concerns focused on the *Volksgemeinschaft* (31.7 percent), superpatriotic nationalism (22.5 percent), and the Hitler cult (18.1 percent). What is more, when they indicated their expectations of the gain of power in 1934 after years of struggle and fervent hopes, less than 5 percent looked forward to liberating Europe from Jews and Marxists. A bare majority (50.7 percent) expected a domestic national renaissance, while a national resurgence of Germany abroad was expected by very few (6.4 percent). Remarkable as well is the fact that this group simply did not share expectations of what was to be gained with power. With the exception of a domestic renaissance, making Germany proud again, all expectation categories fail to capture even 10 percent of the Abel sample.[50]

If the early party members showed no interest in the Jewish question, the same picture emerges later from a small private "opinion survey" conducted in 1942, estimating the level of support for the Final Solution among sixty-two individuals, mostly party members and of upper-middle-class standing. Of these, 5 percent registered enthusiastic approval, 5 percent categorical disapproval, and 90 percent indifference or confusion.[51] And we can safely disregard the issue of ideological training in the party more generally. Whatever its nature, we know not only that no significant demand for mass murder came from that quarter; we know that the Reich leadership feared that knowledge of the fate of European Jewry would undermine support of the regime. When returning soldiers from the East spread the news about the activities of *Einsatzgruppen*, managing the truth became an official task of the party. Here Martin Bormann's turnabout in issuing the pertinent language regulations provides the evidence. The first, issued in October 1942, ordered that the truth be told, confidentially and within the party, of course. But only six months later that order was reversed. The discussion of the extermination of the Jews inside the party was forbidden. Instead, one was to admit to no more than that "a complete mobilization of Jewish labor for the war effort" was under way.[52] Apparently, Hitler had concluded much earlier that the imposition of mass death on civilians was simply unacceptable in Germany. The euthanasia program for the mentally ill had brought forth protest. From this he learned that the Jews would have to be destroyed outside Germany, under more effective camouflage, and in a manner that would hide his own involvement.[53]

The SA receded from power after the alleged Ernst Röhm *Putsch* of 1934, which Hitler struck down with the aid of the army and a few SS loyalists.[54] It never recovered its status as an important actor and, as shown above, ideology was of little concern. In stark contrast, the SS rose to a major power complex in the Third Reich. It was executor of the Final Solution. Yet it was anything but a charismatic community fired by anti-Semitic zeal.

To begin with, the SS was the only official voice in National Socialist Germany ever to denounce publicly so "crude, primitive, and emotional an anti-Semitism" as one that demands the physical destruction of the Jews.[55] A self-declared aristocracy of the New Order, the SS, in utterly modern fashion maintained an ideological commitment to the end of all ideology. But while Hannah Arendt still believed that a genuine commitment to unbelief required careful indoctrination, it is known that ideological training was despised, and a simple middle-class idolatry of "getting ahead" produced obedience to orders. When Heydrich had his *Einsatzgruppen* trained, he made sure that the aim of the mission was released only after their departure. None of the principal leaders of these murder squads was an ideological zealot. Neither were the commanders of the most notorious death factories "true believer" anti-Semites.[56]

As best we know today, then, the main National Socialist organizations exerted no pressure for a Final Solution. This seems to hold as well for the Hitler Youth. If the leadership of the Hamburg Hitler Youth was not completely misrepresentative of others, and that is "the big if" of all community studies, the values propagated in the Third Reich were so devoid of doctrinaire character that not even idealistic youth had an ideology. Remarkably, just like their elders, they devoted their energies to the never-ending struggle for position. They displayed no interest in clarifying and comprehending what National Socialist convictions might mean; their energies were absorbed in "making it."[57]

Unconcern, if not indeed genuine boredom, with questions of ideology also characterized leading figures of the Reich intimately involved with the Holocaust. This is evident from biographical material.

Reinhard Heydrich, chief of SS State Security, was not the initiator of the Holocaust but its principal architect. Assassinated in May 1942, he was not to see much of what the division of labor in mass murder wrought. Yet from his biographer and the memoir of his wife we know that he was certainly not an ideologue.[58] From an archetypical family of Germany's cultural middle class, he was, in 1929, completely indifferent to Hitler and politics in general. Three accidents led him to those who would come to rule Germany: (1) he was unexpectedly discharged from the navy, his first career choice, (2) his Uncle Karl, then SA brigadier and later SS general, obtained a job interview for the young unemployed man with Heinrich Himmler through Röhm, and (3) Himmler confused the navy's signals corps, Heydrich's assignment, with intelligence work for which he had an opening. Heydrich was exceptionally bright and ambitious. He was also a cultivated person with diverse interests, a violinist of competence, and a fencing champion, among other accomplishments. Above all else, a classic "workaholic," he cared only to rise to the top, not for reasons of economic gain and social prestige, the chief preoccupations of his wife, but for leadership, hence domination, as an expression of self-realization. If he had cared about a philosophy of life in the sense not of a felt one (which he had) but of an articulated world view (which he had no need for), it would have been a Nietzschean vitalist philosophy. More important, his only object of passionate rejection was the Catholic church, and not because of matters of creed, but because of the power and organizational skill he attributed to the church.[59] According to his wife, who showed no hesitation about expressing her anti-Semitic prejudice, Heydrich was not preoccupied with Jews, either politically or socially, but he did take it for granted that they would have to disappear. In his eyes, so she said after the war, Jews were "rootless, homeless, booty hunters [*hergelaufene, heimatlose Beutemacher*], only out to gain advantages for themselves, attaching themselves like bloodsuckers onto host bodies" (*um schliesslich wie Blutsauger am fremden Volkskörper zu kleben*). Still, she recalled, as they discovered in a conversation with Hjalmar Schacht, "they personally, that is, in any extraordinary aversive sense, felt nothing at all against social contact with Jews" (*dass sie persönlich, d.h. gewissermassen ausserordentlich, durchaus nichts gegen den Umgang mit Juden hatten*).[60] This is clearly no more than simple anti-Semitic prejudice. We also know its source. Heydrich's father, director of the Conservatory of Music in Halle, had Jewish students and patrons, and as a child Heydrich had been taunted and called a "Jew boy," allegations that later some competitors for power tried to use against him, unsuccessfully as it turned out.[61] The point here is that simple prejudice sufficed him for the organization of mass murder. A self-declared Zionist in 1938, Heydrich talked about a territorial solution until February 1942, although he had already started the organization of the Final Solution in May 1940. Without any inner convictions of a doctrinaire kind, and feeling no qualms whatever about the physical destruction of any who *actively resisted* National Socialist rule, at least once he said that "bumping off" all Jews actually got him down. But he accepted this, like other "hard duties," as the necessary cost of his rise to a top leadership position in the Third Reich, one he gained as *Reichsprotektor* (of the Czech portion of Czechoslovakia) when his sole superior was Adolf Hitler himself.[62] A product of the technological era, he regarded society and self as objects to be fashioned, to be manipulated by human willpower, but neither meant more than office accumulation and power expansion. And because this achiever with an ascetic life style was buried with pomp and circumstance of "religious" proportions that pushed the news from the front off the front pages, we can recognize in Reinhard Heydrich the quintessential National Socialist.

Ernst Kaltenbrunner, Heydrich's successor, does not fit my indifference thesis as well. An Austrian, like others so deeply involved in the Holocaust, he did grow up in a milieu of political anti-Semitism. There was, however, nothing in his social background to predispose him toward antimodernism. His family of origin was impeccably middle class and one unusually well off in post–World War I Austria. Not at all a marginal man in modern society but a lawyer working for a company, he sacrificed work well integrated into modernity for the more exciting prospects of public life in the Third Reich. As regards ascetic drivenness, he was the opposite of Heydrich, a man given to womanizing and drink. More significant, his main motives in accepting the position were simple boredom with ideological work and frustration over a stalled SS career far from the seat of power. When he took over, the machinery of destruction was in place. The provisioning of the victims to the camps was managed by the Gestapo Office, Section IV of SS State Security and so under his supervision; but the actual killing of Jews transported by his men was under the jurisdiction of the Concentration Camp Directorate. During most of Kaltenbrunner's tenure, this was Oswald Pohl's Economic and Administrative Head Office SS (*SS-WVHA*). Kaltenbrunner signed death sentences only for specific individuals. By and large Section IV ran the deportations so well that he only had to get involved on comparatively rare occasions. And there is no evidence that he did his work out of any doctrinaire or ideological convictions; instead, advancing and preserving the powers of his office were the reasons.[63]

This brings us to Heinrich Müller, Gestapo chief in charge of Section IV, and thus directly responsible for the removal of Jews and other categories of so-called state enemies from society. A noncommissioned officer and fighter pilot in the First World War, this official of the political department of the Munich police was in charge of the surveillance of Communists during the Weimar period. Known as a professional anti-Communist, he did not shy away from legally questionable means. However, in the eyes of the Munich NSDAP this had little to do with his beliefs. The party deemed him equally capable of violating the law to suppress the political Right, had this been his task, for he was a man "of immense ambition," out to gain recognition regardless of the system he served. And while the local National Socialists therefore saw little future for this pious church attender in the Third Reich, his dedication to duty and ambition were precisely what led Heydrich to secure his services. Anticommunism aside, Müller's ill-concealed cynical contempt for ideology was well known. His rise to SS general and his role as Gestapo chief demonstrate well that what counted in the Third Reich was action, not conviction.[64]

A distinctive lack of interest in doctrine characterized Heinrich Himmler, chief of the SS and later head of the Ministry of Interior, as well. In the posthumous publication of his confidential orations to insiders one finds that it was the rare occasion indeed when he spoke about the Final Solution explicitly at all. On one of these, his speech to party leaders in Posen in 1943, we can use his own voice as testimony concerning the absence of internal legitimation pressure as a factor in the Final Solution. Said Himmler, "I dare to claim that if you take the number of applications for exceptions [from deportation and death] as an index of prevailing opinion, more 'decent' Jews must live in Germany than the total number enumerated. . . . I mention this only because you know yourself from your experience in your districts that each respectable National Socialist knows his 'decent' Jew."[65] In another speech to SS leaders, also in Posen in 1943, Himmler expressed his utter indifference to the fate of the conquered humanity in Eastern Europe: "Whether other nations live well or starve to death is of interest to me only insofar as we need them for slaves for our culture; otherwise it does not interest me. Whether ten thousand Russian women collapse in constructing a tank trench interests me only with respect to whether or not the trench gets done."[66] Neither the decimation of Poles nor the extermination of Jews was a question of ideology for Himmler. He considered them surplus populations because Hitler desired their removal. But we also know from his masseur and intimate Felix Kersten that Himmler constantly engaged in attempts to decriminalize and miniaturize his work of death.[67] Evidently Himmler too lacked the convictions one attributes to zealots.

Remarkably, as best we know, even Hitler himself paid scarcely the kind of detailed attention to the progress in making Europe free of Jews (*judenrein*) that we would expect of someone who did attempt the historically unprecedented, the physical destruction of a people. When Joachim Fest looked in the mountain of Hitler's surviving verbalizations for evidence of his concern and interest, he found scarcely any.[68] We also know that Hitler's orientation to ideology was very instrumental. His party, a latecomer on the map of German party politics, could only gain a respectable plurality of the national vote if it managed to attract the support of all those whose party attachment was weak, regardless of their views. Hitler knew this and acted on it with success. Nonetheless, his political testament attests clearly to his deeply felt anti-

Semitism. However much his eye, day to day, was fixed on the main show, Germany's drive to supremacy in Europe, his anti-Semitic commitment was, apparently, important to his self-concept as a missionary figure. Acting on his emotions, the extermination of Jews seemed to reassure him in his view of human life as a ceaseless Darwinian struggle among societies (*Völker*). The imposition of mass death on civilian populations more generally convinced him, so it would appear, of what he wished to feel, that he, and to a large extent he alone, was indeed ruthless enough in his convictions to deserve unabridged power to make his contribution to world history.[69] But since very few others even among the "old fighters" cared about this aspect of the Führer, we have to acknowledge, whether we want to or not, that the role of doctrine in the suffering and death of millions was minuscule.

Thus the Holocaust served neither the external nor the internal legitimation requirements of National Socialist rule. It was not anti-Semitic zealotry but massive moral indifference backed, if at all, by simple prejudice that sufficed for the destruction of millions of lives designated by political authority as worthless surplus populations. This is particularly evident in the case of non-Jewish victims. The principal groups here were Gypsies, Russian prisoners of war (POWs), Russian conscript labor, and Italian conscript labor. If these groups shared anything in their status as victims, it was either a prejudice directed against those who refused to join the majority in the bureaucratized work routines of everyday modern life, the Gypsies, or prejudice against those from less developed countries which, in Europe, fell into an arch stretching from the east, over the Balkans, to Italy.

About one-quarter of a million Gypsies perished. Their death rates varied from 1 percent of the resident population in Slovakia to 100 percent in Holland, Luxembourg, Estonia, and Lithuania. About three-quarters of Germany's Gypsies were destroyed. Prejudice against Gypsies was a Europeanwide phenomenon. Without beating any "anti-Gypsy" drum, Germany deprived the Gypsies of their citizenship in 1935. Their public employment was prohibited, and they were shipped off first to special camps, later to concentration camps to perish, first by starvation, then by gas. The fact that a bureaucratic solution of a social problem proceeds more easily the fewer exceptions you make, sufficed for the demobilization of Gypsy soldiers in the army and the air force, and their subsequent shipment to camps and death, regardless of their proven utility as servicemen. If you were a Gypsy, war decorations did not save your life.[70]

As best we know, 5.7 million Russian POWs perished; 3.3 million of hunger, disease, and by execution. This constitutes a death rate of 57.8 percent for all Russians captured during World War II, more than ten times the comparable figure for World War I (5.4 percent). During the Third Reich many were left to die in POW camps under army administration. To appreciate the depth of the moral indifference among the army high command at issue here, one has to keep Hitler's priorities in mind. The removal of the SA as a contender for power in 1934 had made that clear. Hitler needed the army. Had the army high command opposed his "Guidelines for the Campaign in the East," the Russian POW death rate would have been normal. If we ask why the high command complied so willingly, three reasons stand out. First, these officers subordinated all considerations of human rights to the goal of blitzkrieg victory in the East. That simply meant there were insufficient resources either to keep prisoners alive, or to feed the population in occupied areas. Second, they decided to "outhitler" Hitler in their radical commitment to conquest at any price in order to retain the Army's position as a credible power contender after the war. Third, in 1941 when the critical decisions concerning logistics were made, they did anticipate speedy victory. Furthermore, it was neither the party nor the SS, but officials of the Food Ministry who acted as the relevant experts. They pointed out quite clearly to the high command that the decision to let the armies supply themselves with food in the field to avoid an otherwise critical food shortage at home meant that "tens of millions" would have to starve to death. Prejudice, on the one hand, and anticipated retaliatory action from the prisoners' home country, on the other, led to the following nationalities' hierarchy in the treatment of POWs: The British, and later the Americans, were at the top with the best in food and housing; next came prisoners from Western Europe, then southeastern Europe, with Poles and Russians at the bottom.[71]

By trying to save as much manpower as feasible and yet exploit Poland as much as possible, the German occupation imposed anomie on Polish society. Terror reduced the social fabric to the nuclear family. Dislocation in conjunction with German settlement policies, hunger, and typhus ravaged the Polish people. To say that Germany brought hell to them is not to say too much; to say, however, that this hell constitutes "the forgotten Holocaust" is misleading because, in contrast to being designated Jewish, Polish nationality did not automatically schedule the bearer for destruction.[72] And while the eastern border regions of Germany had generated negative stereotyping of Poles, that never hindered, in fact, it probably helped, their significant participation as guest labor in Germany's industrialization during the nineteenth and early twentieth centuries. In short, no evidence of a doctrinaire ideology of "anti-Polishness" exists. During the Third Reich prejudice against people from economically underdeveloped countries was one factor in an otherwise cold calculus of political domination. That, and not ideology, governed occupation and exploitation policies eventuating in mass death.

The same phenomenon is perhaps most evident in the use of conscript foreign labor during the Second World War. In contrast to the Treblinka phenomenon, for many OST workers (from the Soviet Union) death by work was the rule. Furthermore, these workers were present in practically all the larger cities in the Reich, and visible there in abject misery as the ill clad, ill fed, and ill housed; no one today who lived then in Germany can say he did not know. There had been no intention to capture labor power. Dependency on foreign labor arose from the manpower shortage of war. By 1944 over seven million foreign laborers worked in Germany. Three-quarters of these were civilian conscripts, one-quarter POWs. Of the total, 37 percent were from the Soviet Union and marked with the mandatory OST badge, 2 percent were Poles, mostly employed in agriculture, and 17 percent were French. One-half of the labor force in the armaments industries was foreign, as was that of agriculture.[73]

National Socialist policies and practices showed continuity with those pertaining to foreign guest labor before and conscripts during the First World War, as well as a drastic increase in exploitation and control. Policies regarding pay, food rations, housing, off-duty fraternization with Germans, and restrictions of access to public transport and recreational facilities reflected the west–east, north–south ethnic hierarchy of prejudice. In practice, and if only in terms of food, Poles working in agriculture fared best. The Russian POWs were the worst off. At Krupp and other armaments factories where success in training them adequately would have consigned their teacher, the German skilled worker, to front-line duty, a tacit mutuality of interest developed that made life in the plant tolerable. In contrast, in mining where Germans were exempted from military duty, the Russians fell victim to officials who deemed their supply infinite, the built-in brutality of that particular occupational subculture, and the fact that supervising foreigners constituted an upward-mobility channel for German workers. Nothing like fraternization among the allegedly Communist-prone on both sides, much feared in party circles, developed at all. On the contrary, Russians were excessively maltreated. In the camps, off the plant premises, they were shortchanged on already meager food rations and clothing allowances, a fate they shared with civilian OST workers. On the job, they were ruthlessly exploited.[74]

Most significant as an indication of complete moral indifference to the fate of strangers remain three facts. First, regardless of variation in on-the-job treatment of foreign laborers, German workers did not care at all about their fate off the plant premises. Second, a prejudice-driven exploitation of foreign labor assumed autodynamic character that could not be altered by policy changes at the top. Reflecting a switch in war propaganda to "the defense of Europe against bolshevism," the presumed "racial" policies against Easterners were explicitly reversed by Hitler at least three times (in October 1941; October 1942; and more comprehensively again in 1943). But this did little to alter significantly a brutal exploitation of OST workers characterized by long hours, barbed-wire enclosed housing, inadequate food, clothing, shelter, medical care, and physical abuse. Third, and perhaps dramatically making the point, given their low standing as relatively despised Southerners, the Italians were never in fact treated as well as official policy dictated for workers from an ally. Additionally, after the fall of Italy, the fate of the Italians in Germany became the same as that of the Russians. Henceforth, the Italians starved, and froze, and died just like the presumed "Slavic *Untermenschen.*"[75] But I have never encountered an ideology of anti-Italianism in German political history. Thus the history of foreign labor in the Third Reich also attests to massive moral indifference rather than a doctrinaire racist ideology.

CONCLUSION: LEARNING FROM A CRIMINAL PAST

Was it, then, moral indifference among many banal people that permitted the few a heretofore unknown indulgence in political anti-Semitism? Was it an ample presence of passive bystanders and a scarcity of men and women with integrity that stood between life and the end of everything for millions? Unless facts yet to be discovered alter the meaning of those listed above, the answer is a truly frightening yes. Not ideology, nor any belief commensurate with the deed brought us Treblinka. This is a truth we do not wish to face. How much more bearable to believe that this page in our history is not really new after all, that death in Treblinka too was imposed in the name of some virtue. But the truth, however unwelcome a guest particularly among us Germans, will not go away. Even within the limits of a sociological approach, the causes of this awesome moral indifference, that truth we do not want, are complex enough to fill a book.[76] In summary fashion, they indicate that what Max Weber called our occidental "ethos of world domination" had been driven, in Germany, beyond the human condition as customarily understood. But while highly specific historical conditions may make plausible how we could become so morally indifferent, their legacy does not simply disappear when a war is lost, a nation is divided, and one has, once again in one part, democracy. For if we cannot blame zealots, we must accept that this crime was committed *not* by some "in the name of Germany," as polite convention has it, but by the uncaring cooperation of all in each one of the principal institutions of Germany. And we have to confront the unsettling fact that we, the descendants, were shaped by these same institutions.

It is human to kill with justification. Potentially, our religious heritage permits us to forgive Hitler. But the banal, the indifferent man who organized mass murder, or simply followed orders placed himself beyond the reach of the categories of sin and atonement. We know at least how this was done, by giving conscientiousness its due and forgetting conscience. And that is a temptation built into the fabric of our modern Western division of labor. That is why the Holocaust invites us not to carry on with our accustomed image of man. And therefore, too, we should cease focusing on political anti-Semitism as the critical factor in its history. Now that we are nuclear armed and thus able to end the human condition, the continued evasion of the truth is as much a disregard of the dead and the message the survivors left us as would be remaining indifferent to the fact that not even Treblinka brought an end to political anti-Semitism.[77]

Hannah Arendt alerted us to the dream world in which the German leadership existed. Let us recall one concrete example. At the Wannsee Conference where the Final Solution was coordinated among representatives of several ministries, a target population of eleven million was mentioned. But the greatest effort was spent on the problem of definition. Everyone present knew that the applicable laws used religious affiliation as a basis for a presumed racial classification. And since all present had at least enough education to realize what every high school child knew, that religious affiliation cannot serve as a biological measure, one can safely infer that these officials did not care. Theirs was not the task of making law, theirs was to apply it.[78] What we need to realize, more than we want, is how easy it is not to care, and how much we are wont to go along with a situation, once defined, even if that demands abandoning common sense. I shall draw on some American research to make that point. Probably, most readers are already familiar with it. That does not matter. The respective experimental findings deserve the constant attention of all those who believe, as I do, that while the Holocaust was committed by Germans, we Germans hold no monopoly over the capacity to perpetrate such crime. And trusting that this is a reasonable belief, one that can be shared, when I refer to "we" below, I invite you, my reader, to join me.

Experimental social psychology tells us that we are creatures of "group think," amazingly able and willing to deny the reality our senses perceive. This is quite evident in Asch experiments, where a rigged majority opinion about the length of lines on a screen can seduce a surprising number of people to go along with false reality perceptions. The only comfort here is that supplying the hapless victim even with one companion reduces joining the false majority dramatically.[79] Similarly, Philip Zimbardo's prisoner experiments alert us to the enormous and truly cruel extent to which we are wont to fall into stereotyped role play. Zimbardo assigned participants randomly to the roles of prisoner and guard, but the experiment had to be discontinued much sooner than anticipated simply to avoid serious harm.[80] Further, Stanley Milgram's experiments tell us of an unsettling degree of willingness, on the part of utterly normal people from all walks of life, to obey "scientific authority" in rigged learning experiments asking participants to inflict electroshock pain, similarly rigged, on others acting as learners. Here the experimenter's "assistant" found himself very audibly, and in some versions of the experiment even visibly, exposed to the apparent pain he was inflicting on his fellow human beings who begged to be spared further torture. Yet a shocking percentage of participants continued to obey authority, and only, as they believed, in the name of the advancement of science. Here, the small comfort one is tempted to take from a small minority who refused to obey is significantly diminished again by another minority who proved only too eager to continue in their "work."[81] Finally concerning this sobering news about our human nature, whatever the controversy about the ethnocentric and gender bias in the work of Lawrence Kohlberg, it seems rather unlikely that the major finding according to which most adults remain at a conventional level of moral development, one originally thought appropriate for adolescents, can be attributed to methodological flaws alone.[82] If so, we must accept that, unless we change ourselves, most of us are and remain, throughout our lives, morally comparative simpletons. As such, we are able to conform to rules, as institutionalized in a given social setting, but we are unable to transcend them. Thus we can act with conscientiousness in a given role but remain unable to obey the imperatives of a postconventional conscience.

However, it was only when I connected all of the above findings with the answers found to two questions that I began to see their importance. The two questions were, How many SS men refused orders to murder? What happened to them? As far as Hans Buchheim can tell us, very few refused, despite the fact that refusal and evasion were possible.[83] That point was more dramatically revealed by one of the former Auschwitz physicians. He had simply refused to participate in selections. Nothing happened to him. He even had a chance to leave. He did not take it because, as he recalled so many years later, his prisoner-doctors begged him to stay. The Auschwitz doctors took to drinking at night, for about a week after their arrival. That was all the "training" they needed for their new assignments. Afterward, they never again even talked about the meaning of "such work."[84] The human ability to normalize the abnormal is frightening indeed. The day before the Treblinka camp was dissolved, the guards and their surviving inmate-workers had a party, drinking together, celebrating a solidarity created by sheer cooperation. How awesome those forces of conformity, forces no more extraordinary than habituation to respect peer opinion, to fall into the grooves of established roles, and to obey authority.

And what are we to do with such findings? We ought not suspect that underneath everybody is German, save for the historical opportunity to demonstrate it. Certainly, such a suspicion, were it but lasting and nagging, could be more useful than the escape into false comfort evident in seeing in the Holocaust little more than another instance of anti-Semitism. Very likely though, the suspicion cannot be lasting, nor sufficiently nagging. We may infer that shortcoming from the way we cope with a possible opportunity of a relevant kind. The latter is not difficult to imagine. It would be nuclear war with Russia. And in light of this possibility, every day that passes without public debate over our policy of M.A.D., Mutual Assured Destruction, is a day calling to our attention our moral indifference, among other deficiencies of our imagination. But therein lies the catch. The alert remains too cerebral. Arrested at an adolescent, conventional stage of moral development, we cannot really see ourselves reflected in the face of a Soviet apparatchik, and that is why we tend to forget about his wife, possibly a teacher like myself, and his children whose eyes, brimming with the joys or expressing the sorrows of childhood, are absolutely indistinguishable from those of my neighbor's children. Fixated, as we seem to be, at a juvenile level of morality, we can, perhaps, grasp the idea that no institutional arrangement invented by man to order the ambiguity and ambivalence of human existence is worth risking a nuclear winter. Ideas have their consequences. They have given us nuclear arms and heart transplants, the possibility of final death, and the reality of the gift of more life. But as every sociologist knows, mere ideas have never altered the psychosocial nature of man. Therefore, we must, to begin with, use these findings to remember. With our minds clearly focused on Germany's desk murderers, the primary source of evil, we should with all the strength of heart and mind recall the "Muselmann," the victim of the camps, just before death, and a person then already beyond the ability of communicative response. In that life, at that moment and a few days before, we confront the nature of true hell, which is meaningless suffering and dying, in unmitigated solitude, where pain serves no role, affirms no identity. And in remembrance we should strive to break that solitude of suffering, that hell imposed by indifference, and the spell it casts over life now. And we should remember in this way in order to find the strength necessary to change ourselves so that we may, eventually, mitigate those extremes of our ethos of "world domination" that yesterday through German agency created hell, extremes that remain for us today a threat to all our existence. Of the many possible first steps on this long journey, three perhaps deserve brief mention.

First, and foremost in Germany, but elsewhere too where the Holocaust reality encountered so much indifference,[85] let us help each other find ways of public mourning so that we can hope to learn, eventually, the nature of our loss. Second, let us use memory to realize just how deeply we have woven the opportunities for amoral conduct into the social fabric of modern life, how easy we have made it for ourselves to adopt the role of the passive bystander. Let us acknowledge that our lives are compartmentalized, that we follow one set of rules at work and obey another in kinship. But let us objectify our discontent with the fact that we are always rewarded for conformity to such antithetical norms, yet rarely rewarded and rarely reward others for that which must remain our aspiration, striving to integrate these inescapable normative antitheses through commitments to more general values which alone, when shared and felt in the sharing, can bind us into a community of responsible citizenship. And last, and aware of the fact that explaining past events is one thing, attributing significance to them so that they deserve explanation another, let us acknowledge our ambivalence in wanting to learn and come to understand. For here, as nowhere else in confronting the past, the need to comprehend stands in irreconcilable tension with the need, and indeed the duty, to condemn. No one knows yet how to satisfy both without letting success in one come at the cost of the other. Yet where so much evil has been wrought by such ordinary, banal people, we have no choice but to bear the tension and seek our way in the dark. Let us continue learning, knowing too that more knowledge and more memory will serve diverse ends. If we are to learn from Treblinka, as we must, analogies are inevitable. But in remembrance, in standing there in hell, as best we can in our imagination, with mind trained on the victimizer and heart and mind on the victim, seeing his pain yet deepening it so that some of it can be shared across time and space, we can hope not to pursue the false analogy, the one that trivializes and contributes confusion, but the right one that clarifies further what we wish to mourn and therefore can nourish us in our effort to change.

NOTES

Acknowledgments: The editors supplied helpful suggestions that are acknowledged here with gratitude, as is the patient counsel of my colleague John Marx.

1. Helmut Krausnick and H. H. Wilhelm, *Die Truppe des Weltanschauungskrieges* (Stuttgart: Deutsche Verlagsanstalt, 1981), p. 625.

2. Terrence Des Pres, *The Survivor* (New York: Oxford University Press, 1976), p. v.

3. Peter Märthesheimer and I. Frenzel eds., *Im Kreuzfeuer: Der Fernsehfilm "Holocaust": Eine Nation ist betroffen* (Frankfurt: Fischer Taschenbuch, 1979).

4. Of course facing up to a criminal history has many determinants. Also, historical scholarship varies considerably in recapturing so immense a suffering. Partly a function of the sources used, if you draw on German bureaucratic memoranda of the time, you confront the milieu of the writing-desk murderers. Cf. Raul Hilberg, *The Destruction of the European Jews: Revised and Definitive Edition*, 3 vols. (New York: Holmes and Meier, 1985). If you draw on sources from survivors, you confront a different reality, one of suffering so intense that you may not read more than fifty pages at a time lest you become numbed and fail to take in what you seek to apprehend. Cf. Martin Gilbert, *The Holocaust: The Jewish Tragedy* (New York: Holt, Rinehart & Winston, 1985).

5. Hannah Arendt, *Eichmann in Jerusalem: A Report on the Banality of Evil* (New York: Viking, 1963).

6. George M. Kren and Leon Rappoport, *The Holocaust and the Crisis of Human Behavior* (New York: Holmes and Meier, 1980).

7. Heinz Höhne, *Der Orden unter dem Totenkopf* (Gütersloh: Sigbert Mohn, 1967), pp. 303ff.

8. Hilberg, *Destruction*, pp. 94–144, 947–61.

9. The work of Lawrence Kohlberg and Stanley Milgram comes to mind. Neither has become a cult figure comparable to the founding fathers of sociological thought. See Lawrence Kohlberg, *The Philosophy of Moral Development* (San Francisco: Harper and Row, 1981); Stanley Milgram, *Obedience to Authority: An Experimental View* (New York: Harper and Row, 1974).

10. Helen Fein, *Accounting for Genocide: National Responses and Jewish Victimization during the Holocaust* (New York: Free Press, 1979), pp. 29–30.

11. Robert J. Lifton, *The Nazi Doctors: Medical Killing and the Psychology of Genocide* (New York: Basic Books, 1986), pp. 434–42; "Unlike most SS doctors, Mengele was a true ideologue" (p. 377).

12. Hilberg, *Destruction*, pp. 5–9, 393. The quotation is on p. 56. Of course, Hilberg's invaluable work sheds considerable doubt on the inevitability of the Holocaust. For example, he reminds us of the critical role of secrecy (pp. 962–67); of the fact that the "Jews were not killed before the emigration policy was exhausted" (p. 394); that even so trivial an event as pique about German arrogance could save 30,000 Jewish lives (pp. 784–87); and that this "machinery of destruction" disintegrated into quarrelsome impotence when Danish officials refused to cooperate (pp. 558–68).

13. See the full text, treated as a state secret (*Geheime Reichssache*), which was read by 200 persons, in Lina Heydrich, *Leben mit einem Kriegsverbrecher* (Pfaffenhofen: Verlag Ludwig, 1976), pp. 184–96.

14. Karl Bracher, *Die deutsche Diktatur* (Cologne: Kiepenheuer & Witsch, 1970), p. 211.

15. Ibid., pp. 209–18.

16. Ibid. p. 208; Rainer Lepsius, "From Fragmental Party Democracy to Government by Emergency Decree and National Socialist Takeover: Germany," in *The Breakdown of Democratic Regimes: Europe* ed. J. J. and A Stepan Linz (Baltimore: Johns Hopkins University Press, 1978), pp. 34–79; quotation, p. 70.

17. Marlis G. Steinert, *Hitler's War and the Germans* (Athens: Ohio University Press, 1977), p. 133.

18. Seymour M. Lipset, *Political Man* (New York: Doubleday, 1959), esp. pp. 131–76.

19. Ibid.; Emil Ritter, *Die Katholisch Soziale Bewegung und der Volksverein* (Cologne: Bachem, 1954); Günther Roth, *The Social Democrats in Imperial Germany* (Totowa, N.J.: Bedminster Press, 1963).

20. Furthermore, in Germany, relative to 1929, total industrial production in 1932 was down by 42 percent, the GNP showed a decline of 38 percent, wage and salary income declined by 39 percent, and public transfer payments increased only 9 percent. See Lepsius, "From Fragmented Party Democracy," pp. 52–59.

21. Werner Kaltefleiter, *Wirtschaft und Politik in Deutschland* (Cologne: Westdeutscher Verlag, 1968), p. 37; for the negative correlation, cf. Jürgen Falter et al., "Arbeitslosigkeit und Nationalsozialismus," *Kölner Zeitschrift für Soziologie und Sozialpsychologie* 35, no. 3 (1983): 525–54.

22. Richard Hamilton, *Who Voted for Hitler?* (Princeton: Princeton University Press, 1982).

23. Jürgen Falter, "Die Wähler der N.S.D.A.P. 1928–1933: Sozialstruktur und parteipolitische Herkunft," in *Die nationalsozialistische Machtergreifung,* ed. Wolfgang Michalka (Paderborn: Ferdinand Schönigh, 1984), pp. 47–59; Jürgen Falter, "Politische Konsequenzen von Massenarbeitslosigkeit," *Politische Vierteljahresschrift* 25, no. 3 (1984): 275–95; Jürgen Falter and R. Zintl, "The Economic Crisis of the 1930s and the Nazi Vote" (Paper read at the Annual Conference of the Midwest Political Science Association, Chicago, April 19, 1985); Jürgen Falter, "Die erste moderne Integrationspartie?" *Frankfurter Allgemeine Zeitung* 66, March 19, 1986.

24. Sheridan Allen, *The Nazi Seizure of Power* (Chicago: Quadrangle Books, 1965).

25. Volker R. Berghahn, *Der Stahlhelm: Bund der Frontsoldaten* (Düsseldorf: Droste, 1966), pp. 185–86.

26. Falter, 1984. "Die Wähler der N.S.D.A.P. 1928–1933," p. 53.

27. Bracher, *Die deutsche Diktatur,* pp. 184–218; Lepsius, "From Fragmented Party Democracy," pp. 71–74.

28. See T. W. Adorno, Else Frenkel-Brunswik, Daniel J. Levinson, R. Nevitt Sanford, *The Authoritarian Personality* (New York: Harper & Brothers, 1950); and remember that authoritarian attitudes are not, by themselves, related to behavior; see P. L. Heaven, "Do Authoritarians Hold Authoritarian Attitudes?" *Journal of Psychology* 95 (1977): 169–71.

29. George L. Mosse, *The Crisis of German Ideology* (New York: Grosset & Dunlap, 1964); George L. Mosse, *Germans and Jews* (New York: Howard Fertig, 1970); George L. Mosse, *Toward the Final Solution: A History of European Racism* (New York: Howard Fertig, 1978).

30. Bracher, *Die Deutsche Diktatur,* pp. 35–52; Dietrich Orlow, *The History of the Nazi Party* (Pittsburgh: Pittsburgh University Press, 1969).

31. Hannah Arendt, *The Origins of Totalitarianism* (New York: Harcourt Brace, 1951), pp. 264–65.

32. Ian Kershaw, "Ideology, Propaganda, and the Rise of the Nazi Party," in *The Nazi Machtergreifung,* ed. Peter D. Stachura (London: Allen and Unwin, 1983), pp. 162–81.

33. Kershaw, "Ideology," p. 163, translates *Volk* as "racial people." While this does

capture the ascriptive, communal aspect, it suggests an erroneous biological one. See note 63, this chapter, for further comment.

34. Stephen Salter, "Structures of Consensus and Coercion," in David Welch, ed., *Nazi Propaganda*, (London: Croom Helm, 1983), pp. 86-116, esp. p. 91.

35. Kershaw, "Ideology," p. 167.

36. Jochen Thies, "Nazi Architecture—A Blueprint for World Domination: The Last Aims of Adolf Hitler," in Welch, *Nazi Propaganda*, pp. 45-64.

37. On this and the following assessment of the effectiveness of National Socialist propaganda after 1933, cf. Ian Kershaw, "How Effective Was Nazi Propaganda?" in Welch, *Nazi Propaganda*, pp. 180-221.

38. Hilberg, *Destruction*, pp. 301-26.

39. Heinz Boberach, *Meldungen aus dem Reich: Auswahl aus den geheimen Lageberichten des Sicherheitsdienstes der SS* (Düsseldorf: H. Luchterhand, 1965).

40. Steinert, *Hitler's War*, p. 135.

41. Boberach, *Meldungen aus dem Reich*; H. G. Adler, *Der Verwaltete Mensch: Studien zur Deportation der Juden aus Deutschland* (Tübingen: J.C.B. Mohr, 1974), pp. 473-85; Sarah Gordon, *Hitler, Germans, and the "Jewish Question"* (Princeton: Princeton University Press, 1984), p. 186.

42. Boberach, *Meldungen aus dem Reich*, p. 63; for a list of some of the euphemisms see Hilberg, *Destruction*, p. 328. A report about Mrs. Schirach, wife of a Hitler Youth leader and Gauleiter, illustrates the veil. When in Amsterdam, she witnessed a roundup of Jews at night. Shocked by the brutality, she told her husband. He suggested telling Hitler directly since, surely, the Führer would not tolerate such conduct. During their next visit, Mrs. Schirach complained but Hitler responded ungraciously that she ought not to be so sentimental. The scene was experienced as embarrassing, and the couple left the gathering; see ibid., p. 1015. Evident as well is that the Gestapo assumed that German Jews remained ignorant of the fact that death was the reward for compliance with deportation orders; cf. Adler, *Der Verwaltete Mensch*.

43. Michael Kater, *The Nazi Party: A Social Profile of Members and Leaders, 1919-1945* (Cambridge, Mass.: Harvard University Press, 1983), p. 34.

44. The table on the next page is based on figures in ibid., Tables 1, 2, 3, 6, 7, pp. 241, 243, 244-45, 250, 252-53. I separated out the "old" and "new" lower-middle classes and calculated averages across various estimates, giving the range of percentages in parentheses below where applicable.

45. Krausnick and Wilhelm, *Die Truppe*, pp. 622-36; 6 of 14 had earned a doctorate, p. 644.

46. Michael A. Musmanno, *The Eichmann Kommandos* (Philadelphia: Macrae Smith, 1961); Höhne, *Der Orden*, pp. 197-209, 315, 327.

47. Friedrich Zipfel, "Gestapo and the SD: A Sociographic Profile of the Organization of Terror," in *Who Were the Fascists?* ed. S. Larsen, Stein, et al. (Bergen: Universitetforlaget, 1980), pp. 301-11.

48. Conan Fischer, *Stormtroopers: A Social, Economic, and Ideological Analysis, 1929-1935* (London: Allen and Unwin, 1983).

49. Fritz Stern, *The Politics of Cultural Despair* (New York: Doubleday, 1961); Mosse, *Crisis of German Ideology*.

50. Peter H. Merkl, *Political Violence under the Swastika* (Princeton: Princeton University Press, 1975), pp. 453, 469.

51. Léon Poliakov, *Harvest of Hate* (New York: Syracuse University Press, 1954), p. 282.

52. Steinert, *Hitler's War*, pp. 141, 144.

NSDAP JOINERS BY SOCIAL CLASS

	1933 Percentage total of population	Membership (in %)		
		Fall 1923 Reich	1925–1930 average (range)	1930–1932[c]	1933–1944[d] average (range)
Lower class	54	36	39[a] (32–46)	36	36 (31–43)
"Old" lower-middle class	25	40	31[b] (26–38)	39	29 (24–35)
"New" lower-middle class	18	12	23[b] (19–33)	16	28 (22–23)
Elite	3	12	7[b] (6–9)	9	7 (3–12)

[a] average based on 11 estimates; range of these estimates in parentheses below
[b] average based on six estimates; range of these estimates in parentheses below
[c] column A, p. 250;
[d] columns A–G average based on seven estimates; range of these estimates in parenthesis below.

53. Gerald Fleming, *Hitler und die Endlösung: Es ist des Führers Wunsch"* (Wiesbaden: Limes, 1982).

54. Heinz Höhne, *Mordsache Röhm* (Reinbek: Spiegel, 1984).

55. Hohne, *Der Orden*, p. 301.

56. Arendt, *Origins*, p. 385; Höhne, *Der Orden*, pp. 146–49, 328–30, 313, 327, 307; Musmanno, *Eichmann Kommandos*; Arendt, *Eichmann*; Gitta Sereny, *Into That Darkness: From Mercy Killing to Mass Murder* (New York: McGraw-Hill, 1974); Rudolf Höss, *Commandant of Auschwitz: The Autobiography of Rudolf Höss* (Cleveland and New York: World Publishing, 1959).

57. Geoffrey J. Giles, *Students and National Socialism* (Princeton: Princeton University Press, 1985).

58. Günther Deschner, *Reinhard Heydrich: A Biography* (New York: Stein & Day, 1981); Heydrich, *Leben*.

59. Deschner, *Heydrich*, pp. 35–42, 97–107.

60. Heydrich, *Leben*, pp. 42–43, 97.

61. Deschner, *Heydrich*, pp. 20, 60–68.

62. Ibid., pp. 151, 167, 176, 181–86.

63. Peter R. Black, *Ernst Kaltenbrunner: Ideological Soldier of the Third Reich* (Princeton: Princeton University Press, 1984). The subtitle here is very misleading, as any reader will discover, provided only there is willingness to learn that the administration of mass death from a desk in Germany required neither pathology nor theology. Acceptance of the war as a means to establish a New Order made members of the upper-middle class extremists in their commitment to "modern collectivism." And that made them completely indifferent about other lives. When Kaltenbrunner wrote a memoir in prison to explain himself to his children, he did refer to what I have called this collectivist version of the modern achievement ethos; see ibid., pp. 267–76, particularly p. 269. A *"völkische Gemeinschaft,"* however, refers to a "people as com-

munity," in contrast to *Gesellschaft* based on the market model of man as a utilitarian rationalist engaged in exchange with others, not to a "racial community." When the Nazis meant race, they said race, as in SS Race and Settlement Head Office (*SS-Rasse und Siedlungshauptamt*). Such mistranslations do not advance our comprehension of historical truth, though they may well make us sleep more comfortably.

64. Ibid., pp. 127, 198; Höhne, *Der Orden*, pp. 166ff.

65. B. F. Smith and A. F. Peterson, *Himmler Geheimreden, 1933–1945* (Frankfurt: Propyläen, 1974), p. 169.

66. Heinrich Fraenkel and R. Manvell, *Himmler* (Frankfurt: Ullstein, 1965), p. 131.

67. Felix Kersten, *Totenkopf und Treue* (Hamburg: Robert Möhlich, 1952).

68. Joachim C. Fest, *Hitler* (Munich: Propyläen, 1973).

69. Whether anti-Semitism had even this much importance to Hitler cannot be definitively established. On January 23, 1942, hence three days after the Wannsee Conference, he declared to his associates that, as far as he was concerned, he only told the Jews to get lost. If they broke a few ribs on the way, he could not help that; but if they refused, he saw but one possibility: their destruction. "Why should I regard a Jew as in any way different from a Russian POW? Many die in POW camps. That is not my fault. I wanted neither war nor POW camps. Why did the Jew provoke the war?" Krausnick and Wilhelm, *Die Truppe*, p. 630. From the study of the *Einsatzgruppen* we do know this much: Not acting "on the Führer's wish" was far easier than we care to believe. On the problem of establishing a new party in an already well established party system, see Juan J. Linz, "Political Space and Fascism as a Late-Comer," in Larsen, Stein, et al., *Who Were the Fascists?*, pp. 153–89.

70. Donald Kenrick and G. Puxton, *The Destiny of Europe's Gypsies* (New York: Basic Books, 1972), esp. pp. 18, 73–79, 183–84. For an "ambivalence hypothesis" that helps explain the persistence of the "Gypsy problem" see Werner Cohn, *The Gypsies* (Reading, Mass.: Addison-Wesley, 1973).

71. Christian Streit, *Keine Kameraden: Die Wehrmacht und die sowjetischen Kriegsgefangenen 1941–1945* (Stuttgart: Deutsche Verlagsanstalt, 1978), esp. pp. 10, 15, 25–32, 50–59, 69–70.

72. Jan T. Gross, "A Society under Occupation: Poland 1939–1944" (Ann Arbor, Mich.: University Microfilms, 1975); Richard C. Lukas, *The Forgotten Holocaust: The Poles under German Occupation 1939–1944* (Lexington: University Press of Kentucky, 1986).

73. Ulrich Herbert, *Fremdarbeiter: Politik und Praxis des "Aüslander-Einsatzes" in der Kriegswirtschaft des Dritten Reiches* (Berlin: Verlag Dietz Nachf., 1985), p. 11.

74. Ibid., pp. 96–131, 207–11, 218–20, 225–27.

75. Ibid., pp. 141, 148, 175–77, 238–40, 260–61, 288. We should not call these laborers slaves as suggested by Albert Speer's *Der Sklavenstaat* (Stuttgart: Deutsche Verlagsanstalt, 1981). Given the fact that the German labor force had been subject to temporary conscription since 1935 and had been completely governed by conscript regulations since 1943 (see Herbert, *Fremdarbeiter*, pp. 45, 47, 238), using the label "slave labor" could serve to suggest that the Third Reich enslaved its own people just like others, which, once you go beyond restrictions on occupational choice, is simply untrue.

76. Rainer C. Baum, *The Holocaust and the German Elite: Genocide and National Suicide in Germany, 1871–1945* (Totowa, N.J.: Rowman and Littlefield, 1981).

77. See for example "The New KKK," *Common Cause Magazine*, November-December 1986, pp. 32–38.

78. On the law see Hilberg, *Destruction*, pp. 66–67; on the conference, note 13 above.

79. See the description of Asch experiments in Caroline Hodges-Persell, *Understanding Society* (New York: Harper & Row, 1984), pp. 157–58.

80. See the description of Zimbardo's findings in ibid., pp. 206-7.

81. Milgram, *Obedience*; using Milgram's work as well as that of Asch and Zimbardo is not to be construed as approval of the questionable ethics they had to use to generate these discoveries. Today scarcely any university ethics committee would allow so crass a manipulation of others as subjects. While I have to admit not having thought the issue through, I trust that an acceptable case can be made for the use of knowledge once in existence, regardless of the immoral means by which it was obtained.

82. See the discussion of Kohlberg's work in William Damon, *Social and Personality Development* (New York: Norton, 1983), pp. 272-99, esp. pp. 278-79.

83. Hans Buchheim, et al., *Anatomie des SS-Staates* (Freiburg in Breisgau: Walter Verlag, 1965), vol. 1, pp. 314-80.

84. Lifton, *The Nazi Doctors*, pp. 303-36, 195-97.

85. David S. Wyman, *The Abandonment of the Jews: America and the Holocaust, 1941-1945* (New York: Pantheon, 1984); Martin Gilbert, *Auschwitz and the Allies* (New York: Holt, Rinehart & Winston, 1981); Michael Marrus and Robert O. Paxton, *Vichy France and the Jews* (New York: Basic Books, 1981).

3

WHAT PHILOSOPHY CAN AND CANNOT SAY ABOUT EVIL

Kenneth Seeskin

With few exceptions, academic philosophers have had little to say about the Holocaust. There was a time when I considered this outrageous. How could a discipline that examines human values and aspirations ignore one of the most significant, if not *the* most significant, events of the century? We are rightly disdainful of the scientists and professors in Germany who continued their studies amid some of the most fiendish evil ever imagined. How can we criticize them if the present philosophical community sees nothing in the Holocaust worth discussing? Unless we entertain the dubious proposition that philosophy has nothing to do with the historical circumstances in which it is written, we must ask how the events in Germany force a reexamination of philosophical categories.

I say *there was a time* when I considered philosophy's silence outrageous because at present the whole issue seems more complicated than it once did. It is not that I have given up the conviction that philosophy reflects the historical context in which it is written. Nor have I come to doubt that the Holocaust is critical for understanding the history of the twentieth century. But it is one thing to say that an event like the Holocaust demands philosophic reflection and another to identify the philosophic issues it raises.

There is an obvious respect in which genocide and mass murder are beyond the scope of philosophic analysis. As the late Arthur Cohen put it: "There is something in the nature of thought—its patient deliberateness and care for logical order—that is alien to the enormity of the death camps."[1] If, as Cohen and others have argued, reason is overwhelmed by evil on this scale, it is unclear what philosophy can contribute to the discussion. It can clarify terms like *genocide, murder,* or *intention.* For example, unlike mass murder, genocide is directed to a specific group. It seeks the destruction of every member of the group without regard for individual differences. It may be said, therefore, that the "crime" that genocide attempts to punish is not what a person has done but what a person is. How large the group must be for the killing to count as genocide, and whether the group must constitute a biological division, are open to question. I believe, however, that when people ask philosophers to think about the Holocaust, what they want is not sharper-edged concepts. Rather than wishing us to claim that we have a firmer grasp of the categories at our disposal, they want to claim that these categories have somehow broken down. Thus Cohen speaks of a caesura, Emil Fackenheim of a rupture. In both cases, there is an underlying conviction that the philosophic paradigms of the Enlightenment are no longer valid. We cannot talk about reason, history, evil, or the liberal state in the way our forebears did. According to Fackenheim, the Holocaust poses radical "countertestimony" to traditional philosophy.[2] He concludes that "where the Holocaust is, *no* thought can be, and where there is thought it is in flight from the event."[3]

Behind this talk of conceptual breakdown is the assumption that the Holocaust constitutes a unique form of evil and is without precedent in human history. For many writers, uniqueness is the central issue. Affirm it and you force people to take the Holocaust seriously. Deny it and you relegate the Holocaust to the back burners of the modern intellectual's agenda. Unfortunately there are no available criteria for deciding what makes a complex event unique. As Alan Rosenberg has argued, the whole question of uniqueness is a peculiar one.[4] Decisive events like the Peloponnesian War, the Renaissance, or the Protestant Reformation are unique in the sense that they involved specific people acting in unrepeatable circumstances. No one doubts that they changed the course of history. But any historian will admit that there were precedents and contributing factors. Although they may be unrepeatable in a strict sense, events like these are not anomalous. So if a person were to press us on the question of their uniqueness, the obvious response would be that the question has to be reformulated. To a religious believer, Sinai and Calvary were unique because they involved special cases of divine intervention. In secular events, like the Peloponnesian War, however, the participants are subject to general laws or at least some type of observable regularity. We would therefore have to ask: unique in respect to what?

It is also worth noting that some events that could be called unique do not require categorial revision, for example, the first moon launch. Some events that do require categorial revision are part of recurrent patterns. The massacre of the civilian population of Melos in 416 B.C. exposed the ruthlessness of Athenian imperialism in a shocking way. In one respect, the massacre was unique—it was a turning point in the war and the ultimate expression of Athenian hubris. But to an astute observer, the Melian massacre was the outcome of policies in effect since the time of Pericles. According to Thucydides, the importance of the Melian massacre is not that it was a one-time-only event outside the course of history but exactly the opposite: It is indicative of patterns that will repeat themselves as long as human behavior remains the same.

What all of this goes to show is that uniqueness and importance are not the same—at least not if uniqueness means that nothing comparable to the event has ever happened before. On the other hand, if uniqueness means that an event is strange or alien, that it pushes our sensibilities to the limits, then a unique event can be an important one. In this sense, we can say, with Berel Lang, that genocide is *always* unique—even if there have been or could be multiple instances.[5] It is unique because we cannot respond to it in the way we respond to murder, lying, promise breaking, or other normal varieties of evil. I do not think people have paid sufficient attention to this distinction; as a result, much of what is said about the uniqueness of the Holocaust is beside the point. Genocide poses philosophic questions. The frequency with which it occurs does not. The questions posed by genocide amount to this, Is there a rational way of responding to the *irrational*? Can we devise a strategy for preventing future occurrences or must we simply recoil in horror? Notice, however, that these questions are practical in nature. They do not call for another attempt at theodicy, for a general account of why people are attracted to the demonic, or for a rupture of the philosophic paradigms we inherit from the Enlightenment. Some authors assume that unless one calls for sweeping revision of our moral vocabulary, one is not taking the six million deaths seriously. I believe this is a terrible mistake.

THE LIMITS OF MORAL DISCOURSE

I repeat: The Holocaust is unique in the sense that thought is overwhelmed by evil on this scale. But for precisely that reason, the practice of comparing the Holocaust to other instances of mass murder is suspect. Mass murder is always overwhelming. We can compare the historical context in which one instance of it occurs to the contexts in which other instances occur. But can we say that one instance is unique in respect to evil—that it is somehow worse than the others?

I submit that the answer is no. Moral reason is not infinitely extendible. It reaches a threshold at which comparisons of this sort either make no sense or are reprehensible in their own right. In the *Nicomachean Ethics* (7.5), Aristotle refers to incomprehensible evil as *bestiality* and claims it falls beyond the limit of vice or any other human shortcoming. To continue with his insight, we can distinguish murder from manslaughter, and murder without remorse from murder simpliciter; but when murder is indiscriminate, when it takes on the dimensions of a sacrament, a work of art, or a national purpose, our capacity to understand, to see nuances, breaks down. Unless we adopt the crudest sort of utilitarianism and look to body count or units of pain, the Western moral tradition offers no principle according to which "better" or "worse" have any meaning here. The loss of even one innocent life is outrageous. It does not follow, however, that lives are additive. Hitler's actions would be no more bearable if he had killed "only" five million Jews rather than six. By the same token, I do not think anything would be changed if he had killed his victims with swords or permitted some to live if they espoused Nazism. There would still be a Holocaust to talk about and a debate over its implications.

Let me be more specific, even graphic. What follows are three accounts of mass murder. The historical contexts in which they occur are quite different. The issue is whether one raises moral questions not raised by the others. The first is Thucydides' account of the massacre at Mycalessus. In reading it, keep in mind that the invaders were never in physical danger and that taking the town served no military objective.[6]

> The night he [Diitrephes] passed unobserved near the temple of Hermes, not quite two miles from Mycalessus, and at daybreak assaulted and took the town, which is not a large one; the inhabitants being off their guard and not expecting that any one would ever come up so far from the sea to molest them, the wall too being weak, and in some places having tumbled down, while in others it had not been built to any height, and the gates also being left open through their feeling of security. The Thracians bursting into Mycalessus scaled the houses and temples, and butchered the inhabitants, sparing neither youth or age, but killing all they fell in with, one after the other, children and women, and even beasts of burden, and whatever other living creatures they saw; the Thracian race, like the bloodiest of the barbarians, being ever most so when it has nothing to fear. Everywhere confusion reigned and death in all its shapes; and in particular they attacked a boys' school, the largest that there was in the place, into which the children had just gone, and massacred them all. In short, the disaster falling upon the whole town was unsurpassed in magnitude, and unapproached by any in suddenness and in horror.

The second is taken from *The Brothers Karamazov* by Dostoevsky.[7]

> "By the way, a Bulgarian I met lately in Moscow," Ivan went on, seeming not to hear his brother's words, "told me about the crimes

committed by Turks and Circassians in all parts of Bulgaria through fear of a general rising of the Slavs. They burn villages, murder, outrage women and children, they nail their prisoners by the ears to the fences, leave them so till morning, and in the morning they hand them all—all sorts of things you can't imagine. People talk sometimes of bestial cruelty, but that's a great injustice and insult to the beasts; a beast can never be so cruel as a man, so artistically cruel. The tiger only tears and gnaws, that's all he can do. He would never think of nailing people by the ears; even if he were able to do it. These Turks took pleasure in torturing children too, cutting the unborn child from the mother's womb, and tossing babies up in the air and catching them on the points of their bayonets before their mother's eyes. Doing it before the mother's eyes was what gave zest to the amusement. Here is another scene that I thought very interesting. Imagine a trembling mother with her baby in her arms, a circle of invading Turks around her. They've planned a diversion; they pet the baby, laugh to make it laugh. They succeed, the baby laughs. At that moment a Turk points a pistol four inches from the baby's face. The baby laughs with glee, holds out its little hands to the pistol, and he pulls the trigger in the baby's face and blows out its brains. Artistic, wasn't it? By the way, Turks are particularly fond of sweet things, they say."

The third is an eyewitness account of a Polish guard at Auschwitz and is part of the official record of the Nuremberg trials.[8]

WITNESS: . . . women carrying children were [always] sent with them to the crematorium. [Children were of no labor value so they were killed. The mothers were sent along, too, because separation might lead to panic, hysteria—which might slow up the destruction process, and this could not be afforded. It was simpler to condemn the mothers too and keep things quiet and smooth.] The children were then torn from their parents outside the crematorium and sent to the gas chambers separately. [At that point, crowding more people into the gas chambers became the most urgent consideration. Separating meant that more children could be packed in separately, or they could be thrown in over the heads of adults once the chamber was packed.] When the extermination of the Jews in the gas chambers was at its height, orders were issued that children were to be thrown straight into the crematorium furnaces, or into a pit near the crematorium without being gassed first.

SMIRNOV: (Russian prosecutor): How am I to understand this? Did they throw them into the fire alive, or did they kill them first?

WITNESS: They threw them in alive. Their screams could be heard at the camp. It is difficult to say how many children were destroyed this way.

SMIRNOV: Why did they do this?

WITNESS: It's very difficult to say. We don't know whether they wanted to economize on gas, or if it was because there was not enough room in the gas chambers.

Clearly there are historical differences between these events. My point is that there are no grounds for making moral comparisons. In a recent article, the historian Charles S. Maier tells us that numbers *are* important.[9] This remark occurs in a context in which Hitler is compared to Stalin and the Khmer Rouge. The question is whether extermination based on class is fundamentally different from extermination based on race. When confronted by the fact that Stalin killed several times more than Hitler, and by his own criterion should be a "worse" case of evil, Maier quotes Raymond Aron as follows: "Hostility based on the class struggle has taken on no less extreme or monstrous forms than that based on the incompatibility of race. . . . But if we wish to 'save the concepts,' there is a difference between a philosophy whose logic is monstrous, and one which can be given a monstrous interpretation." I do not know what "concept" is being saved or what relevant difference there is between a monstrous philosophy and a monstrous interpretation of an otherwise acceptable philosophy. There is no question that extermination based on class has often taken on racial overtones so that, in the last analysis, it is difficult to say whether we have the theory or its interpretation. Racial murder is confined to a specific group and is therefore easier to administer than an effort to kill the entire bourgeoisie. Yet why should that make a difference? Indeed, why did this discussion ever get started? When one considers the moral implications of such comparisons and recognizes the awful details of what is involved in exterminating any group of people, the mind simply boggles.

In this respect, I am in agreement with Elie Wiesel: Tragedies do not cancel each other out as they succeed one another.[10] The evil of the Holocaust does not make the massacre of Bulgarians any less detestable or any more understandable. Nor does the evil of the Bulgarian massacre make the Holocaust any less important from a philosophic standpoint. To the degree that Jewish tradition is relevant, radical evil in the person of Amalek has been with us since the Exodus and has reared its ugly head in century after century. If what people expect from philosophers is a way of distinguishing one encounter from another, then disappointment is inevitable. This does not mean that, to use Maier's term, I am "relativizing" the Holocaust. On the contrary, extermination based on race, class, or just plain fun is still extermination. It is supremely evil. If relativizing the moral depravity of the Nazis is objectionable—and it is—so is relativizing the depravity of Stalin, the Khmer Rouge, and anyone else who undertakes the systematic murder of innocent human life.

EVIL AND EVILDOERS

It will be objected that we can compare instances of mass murder by considering the intentions of the perpetrators. Intentionality is a moral category, and if there are important differences in what the murderers are trying to do, there are grounds for making philosophic distinctions. On this issue, there is important work by Steven Katz arguing that the intentionality of the Nazis has no precedent in human history, that the Holocaust was, indeed, a *novum*.[11] To establish the unique intentionality of Nazi genocide, he compares the policies and official propaganda of the Nazis to those of other groups. This strategy is informative up to a point. As one would imagine, the Nazis' justification for killing Jews was based on a particular ideology. For all I know, it was unprecedented. But propaganda is not always a reliable way of establishing intentionality. Sometimes propaganda is nothing but hyperbole, sometimes it obscures well-established facts. In the case of Hitler, there is an extended debate on when a consistent policy of extermination was formulated, whether it was the result of a single set of factors, and whether there was an unbroken continuity from Hitler's anti-Semitism to the construction of the gas chambers.[12] I refer to this debate not to pronounce on the historical evidence but to point out that however difficult it may be to ascribe intentionality to a single agent, these problems are nothing compared to those of ascribing it to an entire nation.

We do talk about the will of the German people or their national purpose. There is, however, a great risk in talking about *the* intentionality of the Holocaust—as if it were a single act or isolatable phenomenon. Did the bureaucrats who ordered the gas have the same intention as the people who turned it on? Did either have the same intention as the officers who designed ingenious methods of torture, or the citizens who looked the other way? As long as intentionality is the deciding factor, there is no reason why the circle should not include people in occupied countries who did not participate in the extermination of Jews but wished they could—or those in previous ages who tried to exterminate the Jews but lacked the physical means. All would agree that Jews should be disposed of. But can we really speak of a single intention?

For my part, the horror of the Nazi death machine does not become visible until we move from intention to action. We can talk all about abstractions like, "All Jews should be exterminated"—but there is a gap between proposing such a policy and the day-to-day activity of taking human life. We are told that even virulent anti-Semites became ill upon seeing the piles of charred bodies. It is the people who actually turned on the gas, killed the babies, and operated the crematoria who push our moral sensibilities to the limit. But when we move from intention to action, the claim of unprecedented evil weakens. A case in point is the fate of Gypsies. We can accept the arguments that show that Nazi policy regarding Gypsies did not call for total extermination. Some Gypsies were permitted to live. Yet surely the action of killing the hundreds of thousands slated for death is as loathsome and as incomprehensible as that of killing Jews. The same can be said for homosexuals, Marxists, intellectuals, "decadent" artists, and all other enemies of the Reich. Whether their deaths fall within the technical meaning of *genocide* is irrelevant. Moral reason shudders the second killing of this sort begins.

To his credit, Katz tries to avoid ethical or theological conclusions. He admits that numbers alone do not tell the full story. In his survey of mass murder, he refrains from judgments of better or worse. Unlike Maier and Aron, he does not get tangled in distinctions between an ideology and its interpretation. His thesis is simply that the uniqueness of the Holocaust consists in its "genocidal intent against the Jewish people." The question is whether he can employ a concept like *genocidal intent* without falling victim to moral comparisons he does not want to make. If the Nazi extermination of Jews is the first and only case of genocidal intent in history, how can we not conclude that it unleashed a new and previously unimagined form of evil? One cannot refer to a term like *genocidal intent* without expecting the audience to draw moral inferences for itself—particularly when writing on the Holocaust. So while Katz is anxious to stay clear of these inferences, his language gives him away. This is more than a verbal dispute. Even if Katz were to replace a charged word like *intentionality* with a neutral one like *policy,* the same problems would arise. Nazi policy regarding the Jews may have no precedent in history, but it is the evil of carrying out that policy that matters. And if we look at the action of killing Jews, it is neither better nor worse than that of killing other peoples. In fact, it is neither better nor worse than the actions described by Thucydides and Dostoevsky. All of these actions are unique in the sense of being radically alien.

UNIQUENESS AND IMPORTANCE

Many people will balk at this conclusion and regard it as a form of heresy. They are adamant that the Holocaust not be seen as "just another massacre." But the powerful emotions that accompany this issue suggest that for many people uniqueness is a cover for importance. The extermination of six million Jews can never be forgotten and demands some kind of adequate response. It will not do to look at the smokestacks or mass graves and return to business as usual. The Holocaust must be given the same attention we give events like the French Revolution or the First World War.

Nowhere is this more evident than in the work of Lucy Dawidowicz. In the foreword to *The Holocaust and the Historians*, she explains how she came to write the book:

> While I was working on *The War against the Jews 1933–1945* and *A Holocaust Reader*, I was dismayed to find how inadequately the murder of the European Jews had been recorded in history books. I became haunted by the fear that the history of 6 million murdered Jews would vanish from the earth as they themselves and their civilization had vanished.[13]

And a legitimate fear it was. The resulting study is a shocking account of how contemporary historians have ignored, distorted, or undercut an event of such magnitude. Some books on the history of Europe do not mention it at all, some mention it only in passing, some discuss Nazi genocide without mentioning that it was directed against the Jews, some suggest, in not very subtle ways, that the Jews were responsible for their own fate. The reasons are various but they boil down to two factors: (1) in the Eastern bloc, state-sponsored anti-Semitism is so prevalent that the facts of Jewish suffering under Hitler must be covered up or presented in such a way that the Jews are transformed from victims to victimizers; (2) in the West, there seems to be an unwritten rule according to which anti-Semitism is a Jewish problem best left to Jewish authors. The result is that research on the Holocaust is sketchy and heavily biased. Although Dawidowicz's book was published in 1981, four years before Reagan visited Bitburg cemetery, the rise of revisionist history in Germany underscores her point.

Yet her way of arguing for more research and greater rigor is to insist on the lack of historical precedent, and her way of arguing for that is to fall back on the notion of intention.[14] Here she opens herself to the same problems that beset Katz. Her case would be strengthened if she put uniqueness aside. To return to Thucydides, an event may be important because it reveals tendencies in human behavior that were always present but never displayed in such a stark way. To the degree that the Holocaust reveals such tendencies and forces us to look at history from the standpoint of the victim, it would constitute a turning point. Serious reflection on it would affect our understanding not only of the events of 1933–45 but of prior and subsequent events as well.

We could no longer look at centuries of officially sponsored anti-Semitism in Europe without seeing them as a contributing factor nor discuss absolute forms of government without looking into the fate of "undesirables." Put otherwise, the importance of the Holocaust would derive from the fact that it is *not* an anomaly. That is why no competent historian can ignore it.

If, on the other hand, historians have ignored the concentration camps, there is reason to suspect they have ignored other atrocities as well—or used them for blatantly political purposes. How extensive is our evidence on the Gulag or the Khmer Rouge? I suspect that like our evidence on the Holocaust, it is sketchy. The feeling that the Holocaust not become "just another massacre" is legitimate in the sense that we cannot shrug our shoulders at the loss of six million people. To the degree that it is a turning point, we can no longer regard it or other events like it as aberrations—no matter how unpleasant it is to discuss them nor how damaging to one's cherished ideology. History must reflect the dark side of human behavior as well as its high spots. Notice, however, that all of this can be said, and the importance of the Holocaust affirmed, without claiming that nothing like it happened before.

CONSEQUENCES AND IMPLICATIONS

If historical studies on the Holocaust are rare, then, in the words of Dawidowicz, "its theological implications have proliferated." The event is so wrenching and leaves such an indelible impression on one's memory that any number of people have tried to appropriate it. The Holocaust refutes moral relativism by showing that at least one judgment is absolute. The Holocaust refutes moral absolutism by showing what can happen when people do not question orders. The Holocaust shows that the traditional understanding of God is bankrupt. The Holocaust shows that the traditional understanding of God is needed now more than ever before. The Holocaust shows that the theory of the liberal state is unacceptable because it has nothing to guarantee that such a catastrophe will not be repeated. The Holocaust shows that the absolute state is an abomination. The Holocaust shows that many of the dominant notions of rationality are false. The Holocaust shows that irrationality is too dangerous to contemplate. The Holocaust reveals the inherent evil in modernism, capitalism, fascism, nationalism, industrial technology, or refutes the theories of Hegel, Nietzsche, and Heidegger. The Holocaust proves once and for all the truth of Zionism, atheism, socialism, or liberal democracy.

Enough. People predisposed to anti-Semitism still find ways to hate and oppress Jews. Mass murder is still an option for world governments. Those who are suspicious of science, modernity, and technological progress would be so even if the Holocaust had never occurred. Those who are committed to the ideals of the Enlightenment and the theory of the liberal state will see in the Holocaust another reason for affirming them. It is only by putting our faith in these ideals that we have any chance of avoiding another catastrophe. Those who think the Holocaust proves the futility of capitalist production have said this about a thousand and one other things. To see how easily the Holocaust can be appropriated by people of all descriptions, one has only to consider the title of Andreas Hillgruber's book *Two Sorts of Destruction: Shattering of the German Reich and the End of European Jewry*. This work, which transforms victimizers into victims, is a good example of the revisionist history now popular with conservative movements in Germany.[15] It is, in fact, nothing but the mirror image of the Marxist interpretation which cites Jewish compliance with the Nazis to transform victims into victimizers. According to Saul Friedländer: "Three decades have increased our knowledge of the events as such, but not our understanding of them. There is no clearer perspective today, no deeper comprehension than immediately after the war."[16]

Even the people arguing for conceptual upheaval have reached a stalemate, as evidenced by Fackenheim's *To Mend the World*. Having mantained for hundreds of pages that the Holocaust constitutes a rupture in the fabric of rationality and a break with traditional philosophy, he finds near the end of the book that he must invoke the very concepts he earlier rejected in order to make sense of the heroism of concentration camp victims, the idea that resistance to evil is an ontological category, and the faith that the world can, in fact, be mended. By his own admission, he is faced with the dilemma that he can neither accept the traditional categories nor get along without them.[17] If we accept them, there is no rupture; if we get along without them, there is no repair. According to Fackenheim, there is little choice but to dwell between the extremes of this dilemma and endure the tension to which it gives rise.

My own suspicion is that the Holocaust leaves much of traditional philosophy intact. Even if Cohen is right, and the enormity of the death camps is alien to the deliberateness of philosophic reflection, the traditional philosopher still has a reply: Our inability to appropriate evil of this magnitude does not mean there is something wrong with our normal categories. We can still talk about freedom, virtue, and rationality even though there are people whose actions put them outside the boundaries of these determinations. If the traditional philosophers are right, we *have* to talk about freedom, virtue, and rationality or we will have no grounds for saying why events like the Holocaust terrify us. Try reading the historical passages cited above without thinking about the dignity of human life.

It is no accident, therefore, that Fackenheim cannot get along without the conceptual machinery he earlier repudiated. The old categories are still adequate for the situations they were meant to describe. They tell us what sort of actions can be praised or blamed and for what reasons. They offer principles on the basis of which one can make rational decisions. The fact that they cannot describe the universe of the mass murderer or enable us to understand why he does what he does does not mean that the categories themselves are at fault. If there were categories to explain this universe, if we could understand what makes people throw babies into a fire, then the Holocaust would no longer be alien. Thought would have a purchase on it. From a moral perspective, this is an impossibility. We *ought* to be overwhelmed by evil on this scale. If so, the old categories do exactly what we want them to: permit us to be rational when rationality is indicated and prevent us from thinking we understand what is too horrible to contemplate. There is, I submit, no "countertestimony" to them.

On the other hand, the *existence* of something that the old categories cannot explain may be philosophically significant. If we cannot comprehend evil on this scale, if mass murder is so alien that our mind boggles, then there are things that reason cannot penetrate, things that will remain forever absurd. These things are not supersensible realities or secrets of nature; they are human actions. The human mind can create a world that is orderly and efficient but irredeemably evil. Is this not a sufficient ground for revision?

In one respect, the answer is yes. According to the Neo-Platonic tradition, evil has no reality of its own: it is a lack or privation of goodness. On this view, it is impossible to have order where goodness is lacking. A completely evil society would soon destroy itself. If this tradition is wrong about the metaphysical status of evil, it is importantly right about the epistemological. Irredeemable evil may exist, but it is not comprehensible. We cannot compare one instance to another. We do not know why people are attracted to it, let alone a whole nation of people. To the degree that there is nothing about it of which we can approve, there is nothing about it that we can understand.

Kant defines the ultimate evil as a case where a rational agent chooses to undermine the grounds of rationality.[18] But this evil, which he terms *radical*, is at bottom a mystery. Unlike the Neo-Platonists, Kant does not deny its existence; in fact, he emphasizes how prevalent it is. But he insists that no explanation of it will ever be forthcoming. If so, we cannot use evil as the foundation of a world view. Unlike the

Exodus from Egypt, the Renaissance, or the French Revolution, the Holocaust is not a formative event. It does not disclose a new set of values or give rise to a new set of aspirations. The only thing it "reveals" is its own radical negativity, which is to say that it does not reveal anything. It does not follow that historians are justified in ignoring it. The point is that we cannot expect new philosophic paradigms to emerge as a result. Once we admit the incomprehensibility of this kind of evil, there is little we can do except turn to the question of how to oppose it—a point that Fackenheim concedes as one of the horns of his dilemma.

The question then becomes, How can reason oppose something it cannot understand? Can we forgive mass murder? Should we extend legal protections to those who advocate it? Can we ally ourselves with someone who is considering it? Should we risk everything to prevent it? In true philosophic fashion, I have raised questions but not answered them. My point is that *these* are the questions we should be asking, not the ones that require comparisons between one atrocity and another. If we are going to take the Holocaust seriously, at least let us do so in a way that informs the choices we have to make in the future. We can then hope that the relative silence that has characterized the philosophic community up till now will give way to open discussion.

NOTES

1. Arthur A. Cohen, *The Tremendum* (New York: Crossroad, 1981), p. 1. The claim of incomprehensibility is common in the literature. It is challenged by Dan Magurshak in "The 'Incomprehensibility' of the Holocaust: Tightening up Some Loose Usage," *Judaism* 29 (1980): 233–42, reprinted here as Chapter 22. Space limitations prevent me from taking up the claim of incomprehensibility in greater detail. I address this issue in an as yet unpublished paper entitled, "Coming to Terms with Failure: A Philosophic Dilemma."

2. Emil L. Fackenheim, *To Mend the World: Foundations of Future Jewish Thought* (New York: Schocken, 1982), p. 13.

3. Ibid., p. 200.

4. Alan Rosenberg, "Was the Holocaust Unique? A Peculiar Question?" in Isidor Wallimann and Michael Dobkowski, eds., *Genocide and the Modern World: Ideology and Case Studies of Mass Death* (Westport, Conn.: Greenwood Press, 1987), pp. 145–61.

5. Berel Lang, "The Concept of Genocide," *Philosophical Forum* 16 (1984–85): 1–18.

6. Thucydides, *The Peloponnesian War*, trans. Crawley (New York: Random House, 1951), 6.21.29.

7. Feodor Dostoevsky, *The Brothers Karamazov*, trans. Constance Garnett (New York: Random House, 1950), p. 283.

8. Taken from Irving Greenberg, "Cloud of Smoke, Pillar of Fire: Judaism, Christianity, and Modernity after the Holocaust," in *Auschwitz: Beginning of a New Era? Reflections on the Holocaust*, ed. Eva Fleischner (New York: KTAV, 1977), pp. 9–10.

9. Charles S. Maier, "Immoral Equivalence," *New Republic*, December 1, 1986, pp. 36–41.

10. Elie Wiesel, "Job: Our Contemporary," in *Messengers of God* (New York: Random House, 1976), p. 221.

11. Steven T. Katz, "The 'Unique' Intentionality of the Holocaust," in *Post Holocaust Dialogues* (New York: New York University Press, 1983), pp. 287–317.

12. For a discussion of this issue, see Michael R. Marrus, "The History of the Holocaust: A Survey of Recent Literature," *Journal of Modern History* 59 (1987): 114–60.

13. Lucy S. Dawidowicz, *The Holocaust and the Historians* (Cambridge, Mass.: Harvard University Press, 1981), p. 1.

14. Ibid., p. 14.

15. For further comment, see Jürgen Habermas, "Defusing the Past: A Politico-Cultural Tract," in *Bitburg in Moral and Political Perspective*, ed. Robert Hartmann (Bloomington: Indiana University Press, 1986), pp. 43–49.

16. Saul Friedländer, "Some Aspects of the Historical Significance of the Holocaust," *Jerusalem Quarterly* 1 (1976): 137.

17. Fackenheim, *To Mend the World*, pp. 309–10.

18. Immanuel Kant, *Religion within the Limits of Reason Alone*, trans. with introduction and notes by T. H. Greene and H. H. Hudson (1934; rpt. New York: Harper & Row, 1960), pp. 20, 25, 27–29. Note Kant's conclusion (p. 38): "But the rational origin of this perversion of our will whereby it makes lower incentives supreme among its maxims, that is, of the propensity to evil, remains inscrutable to us."

4

LIBERALISM AND THE HOLOCAUST: An Essay on Trust and the Black–Jewish Relationship

Laurence Thomas

> In Germany the Nazis first came for the Communists, and I didn't speak up because I wasn't a Communist. Then they came for the Jews, and I didn't speak up because I wasn't a Jew. Then they came for the trade unionists, and I didn't speak up because I wasn't a trade unionist. Then they came for the Catholics, and I didn't speak up because I was a Protestant. Then they came for me, and by that time, there was no one left to speak for me.
>
> — *Pastor Martin Niemöller*

After one has managed, as best one can, to come to grips with the fact that the Holocaust occurred, the next most shocking matter that one has to confront is the fact that so many did so little to prevent the Jews from being taken to the furnaces, to prevent the genocide of a people—although much assistance could have been offered that would not have seriously jeopardized anyone's safety.[1] Whatever the causes of anti-Semitism might be, this much is clear: It exercised a most tenacious grip upon the will of so many who could have helped. First, it blinded people to the reality of the moral horror that was occurring; then when the evidence made it utterly impossible to deny that the Nazis were determined to exterminate the Jews, anti-Semitism enabled people to refrain from helping. It cast upon the minds of most non-Jews a pall of indifference to the plight of the Jews.

Willful genocide and willful indifference to it—two sins of the most grievous kind. I do not believe that either is forgivable.[2] Be that as it may, it should be clear that anti-Semitism hardly explains the moral horror of the Holocaust; for precisely what one wants to understand is just how such a virulent strain of anti-Semitism could have come about.

Evil is deplorable. Yet we can often make sense of evil behavior. The evil done out of jealousy, grudge bearing, greed, envy, and even

105

insecurity is understandable; that is, we can make sense of why it happened, though we find it utterly deplorable. Indeed, we even have a deep grasp of how these sentiments come about. One major exception to this is the Holocaust. Nothing remotely resembling a satisfactory explanation is available.

Not even the most heinous charge that members of a Christian culture, as were the Nazis, could conceivably bring against the Jews, namely that they killed Christ, makes sense of the Holocaust. For, as the biblical account goes, the world is immeasurably better off for Christ's death; in fact, the death and resurrection of Christ are said to be the cornerstone of Christian salvation. Thus, conceptually, the killing of Christ simply cannot be a reason for any Christian to hold a grudge against anyone, including Jews, because Christ's death cannot, in the final analysis, be regarded by any Christian as a loss. It constitutes an extraordinary gain, instead. Since the Holocaust was committed and tolerated by members of a Christian culture, this point cannot be overemphasized. Presumably, Christians ought not to hold grudges, anyhow, given the commandment to love one's enemies. This conceptual point, however, does the commandment one better in that in the case at hand a grudge is ruled conceptually out of court. The argument here is meant from a temporal standpoint: No one in modern times can rightly hold a grudge against the Jews who were Christ's contemporaries on account of their supposed killing of him.

I shall call an evil of which no sense can be made a cognitively impenetrable evil. Between an evil of which sense can be made and a cognitively impenetrable evil, the latter is the worse of the two, where the harm or the wrong done is the same.

Now, I do not deny that stories can be told that purport to explain what motivated the Nazis' attempt to exterminate the Jews; nor do I deny that those who did next to nothing to help the Jews escape proffered explanations for their behavior. What I deny, rather, is that we can make sense of these explanations. We should note that it is in this light that every Jew can rightly ask whether he or she can trust that history will not repeat itself.

Trust involves making ourselves vulnerable. When we trust another we put our fate in his hands to some extent in that the person whom one trusts could indeed cause one harm. But trust can be reasonable or unreasonable. Trust is reasonable only if it is based upon a positive assessment of a person's character as to the way in which he will behave given the item(s) with which he has been entrusted—a secret, a person's life, money, or whatever. Otherwise it is not. Of course, a person's character may change—though not just like that, and there can be weak points that go undetected. Infallibility, however, is not a prerequisite for reasonable trust. I amplify this account somewhat below.

The question, then, is, Given the character of individuals, can Jews trust that history will not repeat itself? There are two questions here. Can the Jews trust that there will not be another attempt to exterminate them? Can, in any case, they trust that assistance would be offered on a more widespread basis should there be another attempt to exterminate them (the Jews)? I think not, in either case. However, I shall address only the second question in what follows.

The reason for this is straightforward enough. The very nature of cognitively impenetrable evil defies rational assessment. It would seem to be impossible to be clear about when the seeds for such evil would spring up. Thus for me, at any rate, the more interesting question becomes not whether the world will ever witness such evil again, but how the world responds to it. After all, even if the world should at any given time be full of morally good people, it is possible that some segment of the population will become evil. The intuitive idea here is this. Accidents will happen no matter how many safeguards are taken. In view of this reality, there is not much to be said for dwelling upon whether or not an accident will happen, in spite of the proper safeguards having been taken. The more interesting concern has to do with how others will respond should an accident occur. An event like the Holocaust is rather like a morally evil "accident," since its cognitive impenetrability rules out the possibility of making a rational assessment as to its occurrence. It is an evil "accident" of the worst kind. So, as I have said, the question I shall consider is, Can, in any case, the Jews trust that assistance would be offered on a more widespread basis should there be another attempt to exterminate them?

Consider a crude account of the morally decent person, one that the ordinary person subscribes to, and to which various philosophers have been wont to give a philosophical underpinning.[3] This conception of the morally decent person, as ordinarily conceived, is anchored in a liberal conception of society, which would seem to rail against an objective conception of the good and the idea of the good of persons as being tied to their participation in such an objective good—hence, its relentless insistence upon pluralism. Liberalism does not insist or even invite the members of society to identify with an objective good; indeed, it often denies that a satisfactory case can be made for such a good. Moreover, it denies that there is an objective reason why individuals should identify with the good of others. Accordingly, individuals are encouraged to pursue their good as they conceive of it, provided that they do not harm others. Consider the dearth of good samaritan laws, at least in the United States. Liberalism thus conceived does not inspire moral courage. For courage is born of the conviction that there is something out there worth risking one's life or well-being for, that there are objective reasons for taking seriously the good of others. Courage is at odds with the view that all goods in life are anchored in the self-interests of persons. The struggle to live can itself be courageous if it exemplifies the ideal that life itself is a good. Some such struggles do; others do not. Liberalism does not inspire courage because it is hard pressed to offer an account of the good that, in the end, is not anchored in the tastes and preferences of individuals; for it wishes to remain shorn of any metaphysical baggage.[4] Needless to say, champions of liberalism, such as John Stuart Mill and Thomas Jefferson, have been individuals of great courage. However, I have not claimed that liberalism is incompatible with moral courage, but only that it fails to inspire such courage.

Implicit in the preceding argument is the following psychological principle. The ideological foundation upon which a society is built profoundly influences the moral sensibilities of its members. The ideal of liberalism is harmonious noninterference. And it is this ideal that makes it so easy to rationalize indifference or failing to offer assistance as justified noninterference.[5] As I have characterized it, the liberal conception of society tends to deaden the moral senses.

To begin with, then, it is primarily in terms of acting in accordance with negative, rather than positive, duties that we conceive of the morally decent person. A morally decent person does not do certain things to others, such as kill them or steal from them or lie to them, and so on. There are positive duties that apply to persons, but these are generally thought to be less stringent than negative ones. Hence, even if a person has done a wrong in not helping someone who dies as a result, the wrong he has done is not as great as it would have been if he had actually killed the person. Though one would expect the morally decent person to make an occasional charitable donation, a morally decent human being need not be a good samaritan. On this view such an individual may even have some untoward thoughts (from time to time) regarding others just so long as she or he does not act on them. Finally, being a decent human being is about the most that we actually expect from others, at least under normal moral circumstances. It is not just that we do not require people to be good samaritans, we do not even expect this of people.

Now, what the Holocaust shows all too painfully, I am afraid, is that the so-called morally decent individual is quite capable of tolerating moral atrocities,[6] and that being such an individual does not entail having vast moral reserves that can be called upon under extraordinary moral circumstances. Instead, being a morally decent individual would seem to be quite compatible with leading a kind of low-level moral life, as it were: One's manifest intentions might not ever be to harm others; yet, one does not see it as morally incumbent upon one to put oneself out on behalf of others—which is what one would expect of a person with low moral reserves. This is significant for the obvious reason that being a morally decent person would seem to be compatible with allowing others to suffer great harm.

But there is also this. An individual's sense of the extent to which a community will tolerate or be indifferent to evil behavior performed against others plays a pivotal role in his assessment of whether or not he can get away with the performance of evil action. As writers like Adam Smith (*The Theory of Moral Sentiments,* 1759) and John Stuart Mill (*Utilitarianism,* 1863) rightly maintained, moral disapprobation is a formidable factor in preventing a person from acting on the desire to do evil. After all, few people are willing, and fewer still can afford, to run the risk of widespread moral disapprobation, and the alienation that it can give rise to. However, if my characterization of the so-called morally decent individual is sound, then being a morally decent person is compatible with failing to respond with moral disapprobation, even in the face of evil of the worst sort. Sometimes all that one can do is display moral outrage. Better that, however, than deafening silence.

Now, the very idea that there could be another Holocaust is anything but comforting. But just the thought that such an event might not immediately and spontaneously give rise to widespread moral outrage and disapproval is deeply unsettling, to say the least. For although evils cannot always be prevented, it would seem that there can be no excuse, let alone justification, for worldwide toleration of evil. The thought that another Holocaust would not immediately and spontaneously give rise to widespread moral outrage and disapproval does not and should not incline Jews to trust others. And there is nothing about the morally decent individual, as I have characterized him, that would suggest that it is unreasonable for Jews to have such a thought as this. Quite the contrary, for some would say that the morally decent individual of today has a less robust moral character than the morally decent individual of years gone by.[7] If that is so, then the concern over the possibility of there being another Holocaust is ever the more justified.[8] Trust, I have said, is reasonable only if it is based upon a positive assessment of a person's character as to the way in which he will behave given the item(s) with which he has been entrusted; otherwise, it is not.

On the strength of the account I have given of the so-called morally decent individual, I do not believe that Jews are warranted in making a positive assessment of non-Jews regarding the willingness of the non-Jews to come to the aid of Jews should another Holocaust occur. What is particularly poignant here is that according to the characterization I have given of the morally decent person, such an individual cannot even be counted on to display the appropriate emotional response to evil, let alone the appropriate moral behavior.

Jews who do not identify with being Jewish might be able to have such trust, but not those who do so identify. However, I should think it is a mistake for Jews not to identify with their heritage—if for no other reason than that anti-Semitism, like racism, hardly discriminates between those Jews who do and those who do not identify with being Jewish.[9]

It is agreed by all but the ideologically warped that for their desire and efforts to exterminate the Jews the Nazis are rightly regarded as wicked. But their actions did not take place in a vacuum. A great many people did far too little to help the Jews, failing even to express moral outrage. These people are not normally regarded as wicked; indeed, they rarely come to mind when we think of the wicked then. Is it not revealing, startling, and frightening that those who could tolerate so much evil can pass for being morally decent individuals? This consideration alone would suggest that our view of the morally decent stands in need of serious upgrading, as does the liberalism that gives rise to it.[10]

The implications of what has been said for the present situation in the Middle East is too obvious for words. As I have said, trust is reasonable only if it is based on a positive assessment of a person's character. But our assessment of the firmness of a person's character in this regard is sometimes tied to our general sense of what the moral community will tolerate. It is much easier to trust a member of one's community not to steal from one if one believes that there would be widespread moral outrage in the community were a theft to be reported than if one believes that the community would turn a deaf ear to one's complaint. Likewise, it is easier for group A to trust group B in political matters if group A believes that there would be widespread moral outrage among many members of the moral community if group B were to violate the trust of group A. It clearly follows from what I have said that Jews in the Middle East have no reason to believe that there would be such moral outrage were their trust in others to be violated. None of this is to deny that the same may hold for Palestinians. At present the moral outrage, if one can call it that, which the violation of trust by parties in the Middle East occasions, is clearly tied to preexisting loyalties, as opposed to the moral significance of groups failing to keep their word.

Things are somewhat more distressing than one might surmise

given my remarks thus far. For even if the morally decent are capable of sympathetically identifying with the concerns and fears of Jews, it does not thereby follow that they could be trusted to display moral outrage over an attempt to exterminate the Jews. Consider blacks in this regard. As with Jews, blacks know what it is like to have the machinery of an entire state pressed into service against them. Furthermore, in view of the following, the idea that whites took black slaves to be less than fully human is absolutely mind boggling: (1) slave masters kept black women as mistresses; (2) the wives of slave masters were sometimes jealous of black female slaves; (3) slaves cared for and suckled the children of whites; and (4) slaves were speakers of the language. With regard to being victims of oppression that is extremely difficult to fathom, blacks and Jews are emotional siblings.

So one would have thought that if any two groups can sympathetically identify with one another's concerns and, therefore, trust one another, it would be Jews and blacks. But anti-Semitism is no stranger to blacks,[11] just as racism is no stranger to Jews. It is true that Jews have been remarkably supportive of a pluralistic society, and this has benefited blacks enormously. This support, however, need not entail that Jews trust blacks with regard to the concern that I have been addressing in this essay. For one thing, there is no logical incompatibility between supporting or deeply caring for another and not trusting that person. For another, it is only under the umbrella of pluralism that many Jews feel they are protected from the hailstones of anti-Semitism, understandably holding that a conservative Moral Majority type society, which would just as soon see Christian prayers held in all public institutions, is inimical to the flourishing of Jews.

But if, as I have claimed, the liberal conception of society does not inspire moral courage, then Jews pay a heavy price for their commitment to it. For such a conception readily fosters indifference to the plight of others or, in any case, enables people to rationalize their doing nothing in the name of not interfering. Hence, built into the very liberalism that Jews support are strong tendencies that could permit the occurrence of another Holocaust. Liberalism, as I have explicated it, is not, and cannot be, the firm source of security that Jews would like it to be. If sound, this observation could have some explanatory power. If Jews are less trusting of or comfortable among non-Jews than one would have thought appropriate given a liberal society, one reason might very well lie in the observation I have just made.

In any case, if Jews cannot believe that in the event of another Holocaust they could trust morally decent individuals (as ordinarily conceived), who have had quite parallel experiences of oppression, to offer assistance or just to express moral outrage, then it is just plain, isn't it, that trust of this sort really is not an option for Jews? But this truth also gives us a sense of just how low the moral reserves are of what I have characterized as the morally decent individual. The existence of anti-Semitism among blacks and racism among Jews, assuming morally decent individuals in either case, is deeply disconcerting. The depth of society's influence is hereby revealed. Being a morally decent individual, along with being a member of a group that has been the victim of evil in its most virulent form, would not seem to give individuals quite the immunity to the sentiments of anti-Semitism and racism that one would have hoped for.

Now how can it be that there is so little harmony and, therefore, trust between blacks and Jews? I shall not say any more than I have already said as to why Jews may not be trusting of blacks. It suffices surely that anti-Semitism persists in America and that blacks, in spite of having suffered in sufficiently similar ways, would not seem to have any immunity from anti-Semitism. In what follows, I attempt a brief answer as to why blacks are not disposed to act in harmony with and trust Jews.

Let me begin by introducing the notion of group autonomy. A group has such autonomy precisely when by and large it is regarded by other groups as the foremost interpreter of its own history and experiences. So, while there can be nonmembers of a group that has group autonomy who contribute to the group's grasp of its history and experiences, such is far from being the norm. Nowadays, at any rate, women have come to have considerable group autonomy.[12]

As I have characterized the notion, Jews have group autonomy, whereas blacks do not. Or, in any case, Jews have considerably more group autonomy than blacks. Jews are regarded as the foremost interpreters of their history and experiences. To be sure, there are non-Jews who are regarded as authorities on the Jewish experience, but there are very few of them, and it is interesting that there would seem to be very few black scholars who have studied any aspect of the Jewish experience.[13] The overwhelming majority of writers on the Jewish experience are themselves Jewish. The very idea of attempting to understand the Jewish experience without reading what Jews have written about that experience is unthinkable. By contrast, much of black history and experience has been interpreted by nonblacks, including many Jews: Roger Abrahams, Stanley Elkins, Herbert Gutman, Bruce Jackson, Lawrence Levine, Gilbert Osofsky, and Theodore Rosengarten.[14] A reasonable person setting out to learn about the black experience can find a wealth of information, facts, and stories pertaining to the black experience that have been collected, edited, and interpreted by a great many people who are not black.

To see that the lack of group autonomy can be a problem, notice that on an individual level the most significant indication that others take us seriously is that they regard us as the foremost interpreters of who we are: our desires, aims, values, beliefs, and so on. Suppose only as a matter of courtesy that another inquired of your aims and so on, having actually satisfied himself as to what you are about by having consulted someone else. If one has any self-respect at all, this should leave one feeling insulted, as well as resentful and angry. Imagine, then, what it is like for an entire ethnic group to live with the realization that few, if any, regard them as the foremost interpreters of their own experience, to live in a society where for the most part a person's turning to a black for an assessment of blacks has the air of simply being a courtesy.[15]

I contend that the interaction between blacks and Jews has been made problematic by just this difference between them. While the depth of evil constitutive of American slavery may not have equaled that of the Holocaust,[16] the Holocaust left Jews relatively intact with respect to group autonomy, whereas American slavery virtually devastated blacks in this regard. And if, as I believe, there is a fundamental connection between a group's having autonomy and its being master of its destiny, the Jews survived the Holocaust as masters of their destiny, whereas blacks did not so survive American slavery. I suspect that the explanation for this difference does not reflect positively or negatively upon either Jews or blacks. Lest there be any misunderstanding, in claiming that the Holocaust left Jews relatively intact with respect to group autonomy, I am not in any way denying the profound evil of the Holocaust. The explanation for why the Jews survived the Holocaust with group autonomy need hardly be exculpatory. If a person sets out to suffocate me, and mistakenly leaves me for dead, my survival in no way reflects positively upon that individual's moral character.

Resentment born of envy[17] is how I would characterize the negative attitude toward Jews that is specific to blacks and that explains why blacks are not disposed to interact harmoniously with Jews.[18] The envy is over the fact that Jews have, whereas blacks lack, group autonomy. The resentment is due to the disparity between blacks and Jews brought on by this difference between them. Matters are aggravated by the fact that in addition to having group autonomy, Jews have been among the foremost interpreters of the black experience. One need not attribute questionable motives to Jews here in order to suppose that this gesture on the part of Jews has served to deepen the resentment and envy that blacks may feel toward Jews. After all, deep gestures of good will can be morally painful when the circumstances surrounding them make it impossible for the gestures not to be an affront to one's self-respect and dignity.

Now, while I hardly wish to claim that there are no other relevant factors (wealth often comes readily to mind), I should like to think that the explanation proffered here is central to any understanding of the negative attitude of blacks toward Jews. It is true that Jews have been racist and blacks have been anti-Semitic in ways that are characteristic of American racism and anti-Semitism generally, but I do not think that this explains the special tensions between Jews and blacks. For one might have thought that both groups could have easily acknowledged that they have been unwitting accomplices in the other's suffering in the United States, and then have gotten on with living in harmony with one another. Nothing of the sort has come about, and that needs to be explained. I have offered an argument that can go some way toward explaining this. Some of the negative attitudes that blacks have toward Jews are surely anti-Semitic, but I have argued that not all of it can be thus characterized. It is of the utmost importance that both Jew and black alike realize this. It is most unfortunate that liberalism, with its relentless insistence upon individualism, has been a formidable obstacle to our appreciation of the importance of group autonomy.

A final comment concerning this matter: It should be observed that the point that blacks have resentment born of envy toward Jews—as a result of Jews having considerably more group autonomy than blacks—in no way diminishes the suffering that Jews have experienced or are presently experiencing in the world; for as I have defined it, group autonomy does not render individuals invulnerable to any and all forms of heinous injustices at the hands of others. In particular, then, from this point nothing whatsoever follows about who, blacks or Jews, have suffered or are suffering more. Hitler was out to exterminate the Jews. In no way does the notion of group autonomy suggest otherwise.

Total despair is not in order, however. For there are interpersonal relationships characterized by love and friendship. Deep bonds abound here. These ties constitute a commitment to and identification with one another's good that is altogether incompatible with tolerating harm to the other. And nothing I have said entails that there can be no love and friendship between Jews and non-Jews or, for that matter, between any two people whatever their ethnic background may be—though what I have said would seem to suggest that in the absence of ties of this sort, trust of the sort being addressed in this essay is totally unwarranted. So, there is a way out. And that is good. For it should be clear that what I have said surely does suggest that trust is not just a problem for Jews (vis-à-vis non-Jews), but for any identifiable ethnic group whose circumstances make it an easy target for oppression. As

Elie Wiesel put it "[the Holocaust] means to mankind that whatever happens to us may happen to everybody."[19]

Is it reasonable, then, to have secular moral faith? I believe so—but not because the alternative of no faith at all is devastatingly grim, though that is certainly true, but because evil, in spite of all of its manifestations, has failed to extinguish the flame of love, which is capable of forging a bond of trust between individuals that can overcome even the perverse myopia of ethnic chauvinism and the threat of cognitively impenetrable evil.[20] That is to say, if we can have hope at all it is because it is plain that love knows no boundaries.

NOTES

Acknowledgments: In writing this essay, I owe an inestimable debt of gratitude to Naomi Galtz, an Oberlin College student. An ever so intense conversation we had regarding Jews and blacks was instrumental in my being motivated to write this essay. Lawrence Blum, Alasdair MacIntyre, Thomas Nagel, Charles Silberman, and Judith Jarvis Thomson were encouraging at various junctures along the way. In the final stages of this essay, Ira Yankwitt, also an Oberlin College student, was a constant source of support; his familiarity with my philosophical views was pivotal in my getting clearer about what I wanted to say. The final draft owes much to Norman Care's perceptive comments. Finally, I would like to thank Alan Rosenberg for bringing several references to my attention. Support from the Earhart Foundation is gratefully acknowledged.

1. For instance, many countries could have opened their doors to Jews. The United States, e.g., far from being galvanized by righteous indignation to help the Jews, was embarrassingly and shamefully slow to come to their assistance, contrary to the myth. For a definitive account of this and related matters, see David S. Wyman, *The Abandonment of the Jews: America and the Holocaust, 1941–1945* (New York: Pantheon, 1984). Wyman observes that "to kill the Jews, the Nazis were willing to weaken their capacity to fight the war. *The United States and its Allies, however, were willing to attempt almost nothing to save them*" (p. 5, emphasis added). Later he writes: "Two or three clear statements from Franklin Roosevelt would have moved this news into public view and kept it there for some time. But the President was not so inclined, nor did Washington reporters press him. In retrospect, it seems almost unbelievable that in Roosevelt's press conferences (normally held twice a week) not one word was spoken about the mass killing of European Jews until almost a year later. The President had nothing to say to reporters on the matter, and no correspondent asked him about it" (p. 62).

2. Here I am indebted to Martin P. Golding, "Forgiveness and Regret," *Philosophical Forum* 16 (1984–85), and Jeffrie G. Murphy, "Forgiveness and Resentment," *Midwest Studies in Philosophy* 7 (1982), though I do not claim that the view I have expressed is attributable to either author.

3. See, e.g., Jean Blumenfield, "Causing Harm and Bringing Aid," *American Philosophical Quarterly* 18 (1981); Philippa Foot, "The Problem of Abortion and the Doctrine of the Double Effect," *Oxford Review*, no. 5 (1967); and Richard Trammel, "Saving Life and Taking Life," *Journal of Philosophy* 72 (1975). Indeed, John Rawls (*A Theory of Justice* [Cambridge, Mass.: Harvard University Press, 1971]) himself thinks

that there is something to be said for the distinction between positive and negative duties, claiming that there are positive and negative natural duties (p. 114). However, he does make the following disclaimer: "The distinction between positive and negative duties is intuitively clear in many cases, but often gives way. I shall not put any stress upon it" (p. 114).

4. Thus, we find John Rawls, surely a champion of liberal political theory, at pains to show that his theory is relatively free of any metaphysical claims. See John Rawls, "Justice as Fairness: Political not Metaphysical," *Philosophy and Public Affairs* 14 (1985). I believe that libertarianism is open to the same or very similar criticism here. In connection with this matter, see Bernard Boxill's eloquent essay, "How Injustice Pays," *Philosophy and Public Affairs* 9 (1981). Finally, I should mention that Vinit Haksar, *Equality, Liberty, and Perfectionism* (New York: Oxford University Press, 1979), objects to liberalism on grounds similar to the ones that I have raised and attempts to shore up the conception. I was reminded of this by Norman Care.

5. Support for this line of thought may come from the work of Melvin J. Lerner, "The Desire for Justice and Reactions to Victims," in *Altruism and Helping Behavior*, ed. J. Macaulay and L. Berkowitz (New York: Academic Press, 1970) and "The Justice Motive: Some Hypotheses as to Its Origins," *Journal of Personality* 45 (1977). He suggests that in order to be able to go on maintaining that we ourselves are just in spite of all that is unjust in the world, we sometimes see the world in a more positive light than is warranted.

6. See Stanley Milgram, *Obedience to Authority: An Experimental View* (New York: Harper Colophon Books, 1975).

7. See Robert N. Bellah, *Habits of the Heart* (Berkeley: University of California Press, 1985).

8. In a comment to the text, Charles B. Silberman, *A Certain People* (New York: Summit Books, 1985), writes: "Jewish religious schools, which once ignored the Holocaust for fear that it would be too upsetting to young students, now make its study an important part of their curricula, and there are well over 700 courses on the history and literature of the Holocaust in secular American colleges and universities; these courses attract more students than any other Judaic studies" (p. 198).

9. Jean-Paul Sartre made the same observation in *Reflexions sur la question juive* (1946), trans. George J. Becker as *Anti-Semite and Jew* (New York: Schocken, 1965), p. 75.

10. For a serious attempt at this sort of upgrading, see Joel Feinberg, *Harm to Others* (New York: Oxford University Press, 1984). For an account of social interaction to which I am very sympathetic, see Norman Care, *On Sharing Fate* (Philadelphia: Temple University Press, 1987).

11. Indeed, anti-Semitism is thought to be on the rise among blacks. See Silberman, *A Certain People*, pp. 353–55.

12. It is thus no accident that a recent essay by Annette Baier, "What Do Women Want in a Moral Theory," *Nous* 19 (1985), has received the attention that it has. It is a powerful exercise in group autonomy for women, by a leading member of the profession who is a woman.

13. In a letter (to me) confirming my suspicions in this regard, Charles Silberman writes: "Although students of the Jewish experience are predominantly Jewish, there are some notable exceptions. A number of white Christian theologians have written about the Holocaust. . . . I know of no Black scholar who has studied any aspect of the Jewish experience."

14. I am grateful to Charles Silberman for speaking to the ethnic identity of these individuals. His name should also be added to the list.

15. Thomas Nagel has suggested (in conversation) a reason for this. Because American slavery took place on American soil, it is thus a part of American history.

Hence the "right" to interpret American history yields the "right" to interpret the black experience. The Holocaust did not take place on American soil; more generally, the history of the Jews very much predates the very existence of the United States (as well as modern Europe); consequently, Americans do not feel that the history of Jews is theirs to interpret. I accept this, as my remarks later in the text would suggest, for I do not think that the fact that Jews have group autonomy and blacks do not reflects negatively upon either Jews or blacks.

16. For a discussion of this, see Stanley Elkins, *Slavery: A Problem in American Institutional and Intellectual Life,* 3d ed. (Chicago: University of Chicago Press, 1976).

17. As Rawls acknowledges, the existence of envy need not be the result of wrongdoing on anyone's part. See sect. 80 of *A Theory of Justice.*

18. See Bat-Ami Zucker, "Black Americans' Reaction to the Persecution of European Jews," *Simon Wiesenthal Center Annual* 3 (1986).

19. As quoted by Michael Freeman, "Can Social Science Explain Genocide?" *Patterns of Prejudice* 20 (1986): 10.

20. This is a response, albeit an oblique one, to Annette Baier's essay "Secular Faith," in her *Postures of the Mind* (Minneapolis: University of Minnesota Press, 1985). She writes: "One of the chief arguments for the moral faith I shall present is the great unreasonableness of any alternative to it" (p. 294).

5

THE DILEMMA OF CHOICE
IN THE DEATHCAMPS

Lawrence L. Langer

Do you know how one says *never* in camp slang? *Morgen früh:* tomorrow morning.

—*Primo Levi*

Suppose Dante's pilgrim in the *Divine Comedy* had arrived at the exit from the Inferno to find the way barred by a barbed wire fence, posted with warnings reading "No trespassing. Violators will be annihilated." When the spiritual and psychological equivalents of Purgatory and Paradise are excluded from human possibility, to be replaced by the daily threat of death in the gas chamber, then we glimpse the negative implications of survival, especially for the Jews, in the Nazi extermination camps. After we peel from the surface of the survivor ordeal the veneer of dignified behavior, hope, mutual support, and the inner resolve to resist humiliation, we find beneath a raw and quivering anatomy of human existence resembling no society we have ever encountered before. When such an existence transforms the life instinct and forces men and women who would remain alive to suspend the golden rule and embrace the iron one of "do unto others before it is done unto you," we must expect some moral rust to flake from the individual soul. We are left with a spectacle of reality that few would choose to celebrate, *if* they could tolerate a world where words like dignity and choice had temporarily lost their traditional meaning because Nazi brutality had eliminated the human supports that usually sustain them. But such a world so threatens our sense of spiritual continuity that it is agonizing to imagine or consent to its features without introducing some affirmative values to mitigate the gloom.

For those like Viktor Frankl who see life as a challenge to give meaning to being, the notion that the *situation* in Auschwitz deprived

This article originally appeared in *Centerpoint: A Journal of Interdisciplinary Studies* 1, no. 1 (Fall 1980): 53–59. It is reprinted here with the permission of the author and *Centerpoint.*

being of meaning is the highest form of impiety. He speaks of the deathcamp as a "living laboratory" or "testing ground" where he witnessed how "some of our comrades behave like swine while others behaved like saints." But this arbitrary division into heroes and villains is misleading, since it totally ignores the even more arbitrary environment that shaped human conduct in Auschwitz. Frankl cannot resist the temptation to incorporate the deathcamp experience into his world view, to make events serve his theory of behavior: "Man has both potentialities within himself: which one is actualized depends on decisions but not on conditions."[1] This may be an accurate description of human character in a Dostoevski novel: We shall see how much evidence Frankl was required to ignore to protect his image of man in the deathcamps as a self-determining creature, no matter how humiliating his surroundings. Auschwitz was indeed a laboratory and testing ground, but if we contemplate the "experiment" without rigid moral preconceptions, we discover that men could not be divided simply into saints and swine, and that self-actualization as a concept evaporates when impossible conditions obliterate the possible decisions we have been trained to applaud. To speak of survival in Auschwitz as a form of self-actualization is to mock language and men, especially those who did not survive.

If we pursue the proposition that some stains on the soul of history—and the Holocaust is such a stain—are indelible, where will it lead us? It will lead us certainly to an unfamiliar version of survival, to the conclusion that after Auschwitz the idea of human dignity could never be the same again. It will force us to reexamine the language of value that we used before the event, and to admit that at least when describing the Holocaust, if not its consequences, such language may betray the spirit and the facts of the ordeal. Perhaps this is what Primo Levi, himself a survivor, was trying to say in *Survival in Auschwitz* when he wrote:

> Just as our hunger is not that feeling of missing a meal, so our way of being cold has need of a new word. We say "hunger," we say "tiredness," "fear," "pain," we say "winter" and they are different things. They are free words, created and used by free men who lived in comfort and suffering in their homes. If the Lagers [camps] had lasted longer a new, harsh language would have been born; and only this language could express what it means to toil the whole day in the wind, with the temperature below freezing, and wearing only a shirt, underpants, cloth jacket and trousers, and in one's body nothing but weakness, hunger and knowledge of the end drawing near.[2]

This crucial observation leaves us with a profound dilemma, since no one has yet invented a vocabulary of annihilation to modify the language of transcendence employed by Frankl and similar commentators. For this reason we must bring to every "reading" of the Holocaust experience a wary consciousness of the way in which "free words" and their associations may distort the facts or alter them into more manageable events.

The consequences of this predicament may seem threatening to the conservative ethical intelligence, but they are nonetheless unavoidable. They illuminate a version of survival less flattering to the human creature than more traditional accounts, but their spokesmen and spokeswomen deserve a hearing if only to clarify our vision of how utterly the Nazi mentality corrupted moral reality for the victims. Moreover, this complementary vision may enable us to comprehend better how little discredit falls to these victims, who were plunged into a crisis of what one might call "choiceless choice," where critical decisions did not reflect options between life and death, but between one form of "abnormal" response and another, both imposed by a situation that was in no way of the victim's own choosing. Consider this brief episode narrated by Judith Sternberg Newman, a nurse by profession, who was deported to Auschwitz from Breslau with 197 other Jewish women; three weeks later, only 18 of them were still alive.

> Two days after Christmas, a Jewish child was born on our block. How happy I was when I saw this tiny baby. It was a boy, and the mother had been told that he would be taken care of. Three hours later, I saw a small package wrapped in cheese cloth lying on a wooden bench. Suddenly it moved. A Jewish girl employed as a clerk came over, carrying a pan of cold water. She whispered to me "Hush! Quiet! Go away!" But I remained, for I could not understand what she had in mind. She picked up the little package—it was the baby of course—and it started to cry with a thin little voice. She took the infant and submerged its little body in the cold water. My heart beat wildly in agitation. I wanted to shout "Murderess!" but I had to keep quiet and could not tell anyone. The baby swallowed and gurgled, its little voice chittering like a small bird, until its breath became shorter and shorter. The woman held its head in the water. After about eight minutes the breathing stopped. The woman picked it up, wrapped it up again, and put it with the other corpses. Then she said to me, "We had to save the mother, otherwise she would have gone to the gas chamber." This girl had learned well from the SS and had become a murderess herself."[3]

How is one to pass judgment on such an episode, or relate it to the inner freedom celebrated by other commentators on the deathcamp experience? Does moral choice have any meaning here? The drama involves the helpless infant, whose fate is entirely in someone else's hands (and the fate of the infant Oedipus only reminds us of how far life in Auschwitz had drifted from the moral order, to say nothing of the moral ironies, of art); the absent mother, who may or may not have approved of the action; the "agent" who coolly sacrifices one life to preserve another, as a deed of naked necessity, without appeal, not of moral choice; and the author, sole witness to a crime that is simultaneously an act of charity and perhaps of literal secular salvation to the mother. Conventional vocabulary limps through a situation that allows no heroic response, no acceptable gesture of protest, no mode of action to permit *any* of the participants, including the absent mother, to retain a core of human dignity. The *situation* itself forbids it, together with the Nazi "law" stating that mothers who refuse to surrender their newborn infants to death must accompany them to the gas chamber. This predatory profile of survival, when fear of such death, not affirmation of a basic human dignity, drives men and women to behavior they would not consider under normal circumstances, confirms another moment when reality defeats both a language of judgment and a mode of moral behavior: "I wanted to shout 'Murderess!' but I had to keep quiet and could not tell anyone."

In the absence of humanly significant alternatives—that is, alternatives enabling an individual to make a decision, act on it, and accept the consequences, all within a framework that supports personal integrity and self-esteem—one is plunged into a moral turmoil that may silence judgment, as in the above example, but cannot paralyze all action, if one still wishes to remain alive. Ella Lingens-Reiner, another Auschwitz survivor, offers a crude but critical instance of how effectively the optionless anguish of the deathcamp could alienate dignity from choice. In her barracks there was a single limited source of water for washing and for draining excrement from the latrine. If the women took the water for washing, the primitive sewage system would be blocked, creating an intolerably offensive (and unhealthy) situation. Outside the camp, there would be various options to solve this dilemma: Complain to the landlord or health department, call a plumber or find a new source of water—or simply change your residence. In Auschwitz they were of course excluded. Lingens-Reiner lucidly sums up the condition of choiceless choice, where the only alternatives are between two indignities: "It is dreadful to be without water; it is impossible to let people take away all the water while feces are piling up in the ditches!"[4] As one wavers between the "dreadful" and the "impossible," one begins to glimpse a deeper level of reality in the deathcamps, where moral choice as we know it was superfluous, and inmates were left with the futile task of redefining decency in an atmosphere that could not support it.

In contradiction to those who argue that the only way of surviving was to cling to the values of civilized living despite the corrupting influence of the deathcamps, Lingens-Reiner insists that those who tried to salvage such moral luggage imposed fatal burdens on themselves. She tells of her own difficulty in ridding herself of such inclinations: Shortly after arriving, she says,

> I was still under the impression that it was advisable for people in our situation to behave with exemplary correctness. To the very last I could not get rid of this notion, although it was quite absurd. In reality only those prisoners had a chance to survive in the camp—if they were not privileged on account of their profession, beauty, or other specially favorable circumstances—who were determined to do the exact opposite of what they were told to do, on principle to break every rule governing civilian life.[5]

This harshly practical view flatters no one, neither the author nor her companions nor the reader, all of whom are confronted by conditions that with very few exceptions *prohibit* the exercise of uncontaminated moral freedom and hence the achievement of a tragic dignity to temper the austerity of human doom in Auschwitz.

We have seen how the sharing that represents a social ideal in normal societies was not necessarily the most effective, and certainly not always the most possible form of behavior in the deathcamps. Even less accessible in that degrading environment was the moral idea that celebrates the dignity of the self through conscious choice. Suppose we suspend our need to discover an ethics of survival, whether based on moral values or social imperatives, and approach the camp ordeal as one from which no familiar or generally acceptable system of cause-and-effect behavior can be derived. The implications reach far beyond moral ideology to the role of time and history in human destiny, to the structure of character and the very unity of our lives in the twentieth century. History assures us that man is superior to time when retrospectively he can explain the unexpected, account, in this instance, for the extermination of a people, uncover a system for surviving and thus reduce the event to a partial intellectual order that somehow theoretically balances the price in human lives paid for that order. But from the perspective of the victims, who of course far outnumbered the survivors, the disorder of meaningless death contradicts the ordering impulses of time. Those who died for nothing during the Holocaust left the living with the paralyzing dilemma of facing a perpetually present grief. To the puzzled inquiry why interest in the Holocaust seems to grow as the event recedes in time, one answer may be that there is no inner space to bury it in.

Lingens-Reiner helps to illuminate this paradox. As time passed, she says, the sense of the world outside (*our* world still) blurred, and the inner life of people who endured months and years in the camps atrophied. Such people "transferred their ambitions and emotions to the life inside the camp. Therefore they would fight for positions not only because they intended to survive, but also for their own sake, because it satisfied their need to win power, recognition and a following within the precincts. Some of them invested their whole being in these matters, and so lost much of their intellectual and even moral standards." She writes not with contempt, but with compassion, with an effort to convey how subtly a deathcamp-inspired behavior could infiltrate a common sense of dignity and triumph over the victim's vision of decency. After praising the tremendous achievement of some women for preserving "their personal integrity in spite of everything," she adds with utter frankness: "the truly frightening thing was that women who had striven for that integrity, who still took life and ethics seriously, proved in the end too small for their overwhelming destiny, and never noticed when they acted on principles which were in reality those of National Socialism."[6] She speaks not of habitual criminals, or self-serving collaborators, but of individual women who believe in integrity but find their response to reality determined by a "destiny" that admits no meaningful moral opposition: the threat of death in Auschwitz.

Such a destiny created a situation beyond good and evil that even a Nietzsche could not imagine. How are we to portray or apply ethical measures to that prototypical example of choiceless choice, the mother of three children who reputedly was told by the Nazis that she might save *one* of them from execution? She was free to "choose," but what civilized mind could consider this an exercise of moral choice, or discover in modern history or Jewish tradition a myth to dignify her dilemma? The alternatives are not difficult, they are *impossible,* and we are left with the revelation of a terrifying question posed by a universe that lacks a vision to contain it. How is character to survive *any* decision in such a situation, and retain a semblance of human dignity? The human need *outside* the deathcamps to see the Holocaust as some kind of continuum in the spiritual history of man repeatedly stumbles over the limits of language, to say nothing of the limits of traditional moral theory. An entire ethical vocabulary, which for generations furnished a sanctuary for motive and character, no matter how terrible the external details, has been corrupted by the facts of *this* event.

Against the natural longing for a Moment of Truth in the death-camps, when the human will asserted itself and a reborn dignity prevailed, we must measure moments of truth like the following, narrated by Hermann Langbein in *Menschen in Auschwitz* from a report by David Rousset, who was describing a group of "selectees" being escorted to the gas chamber:

> An old man, who could hardly move his legs any more, sat down along the way. An accompanying guard roared at him. "Get moving, or I'll beat you within an inch of your life!" Quickly the old man exclaimed: "No, don't kill me, I'm going, I'm going!" and rejoined the procession to the gas chamber.[7]

Once again the choice is not between life and death, resistance and submission, courage and cowardice, but between two forms of humiliation, in this instance each leading to the extinction of a life. By shielding himself instinctively from an immediate threat, the victim inadvertently consigns himself to a consequent one. Once one's ultimate fate had been decided by the murderers—and for the Jews, extermination was their fate from the moment they entered the camps—freedom of moral decision vanished because the antagonist was in total control of the means of supporting life and the manner of imposing death. One could not escape one's enfolding doom, even temporarily, by pretending that responses from the normal world would be heard with sympathetic ears. Langbein's example dramatically ratifies that. Perhaps this is what one survivor meant when he wrote bitterly: "Only to survive, to survive, everything consists in that, and the forms of survival are extreme and loathsome [*ekelhaft*], they are not worth the price of a life."[8]

The illusion that under the worst of circumstances—and in Auschwitz, for the Jews and Soviet prisoners of war in particular, all but a few of the circumstances were of the "worst"—men and women could meaningfully distinguish between what they did (or suffered) and the attitude they adopted toward their deeds is supported more easily by language than by events. The relation between deed and motive, fate and intent (so vital to familiar moral discourse) collapsed so often in the deathcamps that it ceased to represent an ethical bulwark for the victims. "I lived better than many of my comrades," confessed one of the prisoner functionaries, "without feeling that it was immoral. In the concentration camp, no one has the right to judge himself according to moral rules that would be valid in normal times."[9] This survivor is not *proud* of his behavior, nor is he particularly happy about the suspension of values that dominated the general struggle to survive in the world of Auschwitz. Imagine the desolation of Salmen Lewental, whose diary was literally unearthed from the ashes of Auschwitz in 1962, as he tries to describe what the will to survive has done to prisoners who were forced to live "ill" beyond conception by the daily routine of destruction:

> Why do you do such ignoble work, what do you live for, what is your aim in life, what do you desire . . . what would you like to achieve living this kind of life. . . . And here is the crux . . . of our Kommando, which I have no intention to defend as a whole. I must speak the truth here, that some of that group have in the course of time so entirely lost themselves that we ourselves were simply ashamed. They simply forgot what they were doing . . . and with time . . . they got so used to it that it was even strange [that one wanted] to weep and to complain; that . . . such normal, average . . . simple and unassuming men . . . of necessity got used to everything so that these happenings make no more impression on them. Day after day they stand and look on how tens of thousands of people are perishing and [do] nothing.[10]

This is description, not judgment: Man is a creature who adapts. Lewental's shame does not presume blame, nor do his questions about purpose and goal expect replies. He had already answered his questions in an earlier fragment of the diary: "one wants to live because one lives, because the whole world lives." Members of the *Sonderkommando* did not choose degradation, any more than the luckier kitchen workers or medical orderlies "chose" decency. Reduced to the condition of choiceless choice, the human creature exists from hour to hour, often from minute to minute. "Do you think, perhaps, that I *volunteered* for this work?" rings out the desperate voice of another *Sonderkommando* member, who like Lewental did not survive. "What should I have done? . . . You think the members of the *Sonderkommando* are monsters? I tell you, they're like the others only more unfortunate."[11]

Tadeusz Borowski in *This Way for the Gas, Ladies and Gentlemen*, tells the story of a smaller concentration camp where new prisoners arrived daily. The camp had a limited quantity of supplies, and the commandant disliked seeing the prisoners starve to death. But every day the camp seemed to have a few dozen more men than it could feed. "So every evening," he says, "a ballot, using cards or matches, was held in every block, and the following morning the losers did not go to work. At noon they were led out behind the barbed-wire fence and shot."[12] Few examples could illustrate more effectively the notion of choiceless choice. The victims are offered an option that is no option, since the results of a lottery are governed by chance, not choice. And obviously, anyone who refused to participate in the macabre game certified his execution the next day. Refusal to participate in the ritual of extermination was not a meaningful alternative for the victim because he shared no responsibility for the situation that condemned him to such an existence. He lacked the power to act physically in behalf of his own survival, and without this power (which through luck or collaboration or good connections might be *bestowed* on him), no mere control of attitude or feeling of spiritual inviolability could salvage his moral self. Since the deathcamp universe eliminated conditions that support worth, the victim could not "choose" extermination and remain human, while the survivor could not "choose" life and remain human. He could strive for life and, if lucky, remain *alive*, but this was a struggle between states of being, not competing values.

After having "witnessed" some of the agonizing dilemmas confronting prisoners in the deathcamps, we should be less persuaded by comforting half-truths like the following, from Viktor Frankl's version of survival: "Psychological observations of the prisoners have shown that only men who allowed their inner hold on their moral and spiritual selves to subside eventually fell victim to the camp's degenerating influences."[13] How do we present this sanctimonious view to the woman who was forced to drown an infant to save the mother, or the other woman who could only stand by in silence? We have seen that when the environment in Auschwitz supported one person's life, it was often at the cost of another's death—not because victims made wrong choices, or no choices, but because dying was the "purpose" of living in this particular environment: It was the nature of Auschwitz. The need to equate moral activity with continued existence and moral passivity with death reflects a desperate desire to retain some ethical coherence in a chaotic universe. But the "decision to survive" is contradicted by the condition of "choiceless choice," and may betray nothing more than a misuse of what Primo Levi called "free words"; using language to create value where none exists. The real challenge before us is to invent a vocabulary of annihilation appropriate to the deathcamp experience: In its absence, we should at least be prepared to redefine the terminology of transcendence—"dignity," "choice," "suffering," and "spirit"—so that it conforms more closely to the way of being in places like Auschwitz, where the situation that consumed so many millions imposed *impossible* decisions on victims not free to embrace the luxury of the heroic life.

NOTES

1. Viktor E. Frankl, *Man's Search for Meaning* (New York: Pocket Books, 1963), pp. 212–13.

2. Primo Levi, *Survival in Auschwitz: The Nazi Assault on Humanity*, trans. Stuart Woolf (New York: Collier, 1969), pp. 112–13.

3. Judith Sternberg Newman, *In the Hell of Auschwitz* (New York: Exposition Press, 1963), pp. 42–43.

4. Ella Lingens-Reiner, *Prisoners of Fear* (London: Victor Gollancz, 1948), p. 29.

5. Ibid., p. 22.

6. Ibid., p. 91.

7. Hermann Langbein, *Menschen in Auschwitz* (Vienna: Europaverlag, 1972), p. 134. Translation mine.

8. Ibid., p. 112.

9. Ibid., p. 166.

10. Jadwiga Bezwinska, ed., *Amidst a Nightmare of Crime: Manuscripts of Members of Sonderkommando,* trans. Krystyna Michalik (State Museum of Oswiecim, 1973), p. 139.

11. Langbein, *Menschen,* p. 225.

12. Tadeusz Borowski, *This Way for the Gas, Ladies and Gentlemen,* trans. Barbara Vedder (New York: Penguin Books, 1976), p. 119.

13. Frankl, *Man's Search,* p. 110.

6

ON THE IDEA OF MORAL PATHOLOGY

Martin P. Golding

In November 1942 Jan Karski, a member of the Polish underground and delegate of the Polish government, made his way from Warsaw to London. Although his main mission was to report on general conditions, he was able to provide extensive information on the situation of the Jews in Poland and about the Warsaw ghetto, which he had visited a number of times. Subsequent to his sessions in Britain, Karski met with American officials and leading Jewish figures. His conversation with Felix Frankfurter is described in Walter Laqueur's book *The Terrible Secret*:

> Karski told Justice Frankfurter everything he knew about [the mass slaughter of] the Jews, and when he finished the Justice said some complimentary things and then, "I can't believe you." Ciechanowski, who was again with him, told Frankfurter that Karski had come under the authority of the Polish Government and that there was no possibility in the world that he was not telling the unadorned truth. Frankfurter: "I did not say this young man is lying. I said I cannot believe him. There is a difference."[1]

As Laqueur's book amply documents, Frankfurter's reaction was characteristic of very many people, including Jews in Poland itself. For instance, the underground newspaper *Der Vecker* had been one of the first to carry information about the liquidation of Jews who had been transported to Chelmno, but its next issue (February 15, 1942) attacked "alarmists and panicmongers" who were spreading the news that deportations would soon start from the Warsaw ghetto.[2] "After all," people argued, "this is Europe, not the jungle."

If today we have no difficulty in accepting the facts about the destruction of the Jews, it seems nevertheless that we find it hard to explain them or to understand their significance. Our difficulty is perhaps related in part to the horror that contemplation of the facts evokes. We feel horror when we read about the lone mass murderer whose

128

victims number in the tens, say, or even fewer in the case of particularly gruesome murders such as those committed by the Manson Family. How much more so, then, when we contemplate the destruction of the Jews!

Horrifying events are more than realities (actual or imagined) that evoke fear. Horror is evoked by dangerously threatening situations that are imbued with the weird and unnatural, uncanny departures from the usual. It is not suprising, then, if one "can't believe" an account of some horror; nor is it surprising if we find it difficult to comprehend horrifying facts whose existence we are finally prepared to accept. Departures from the usual often strike us as unintelligible in some sense; our difficulties in explaining or understanding horrifying departures seem to be compounded.

The horrifying nature of the Nazis' destruction of the Jews has suggested to many that this behavior was pathological. The term is not inappropriate, for pathology is not the same as everyday deviance. The term "pathology," however, does not have an obvious meaning. In fact, there is a large literature that debates the meaning of the concepts of pathology, disease, and illness. In the case of the individuals we call psychopaths, it is at any rate clear that we are unable to empathize with them; and to that extent their behavior seems unintelligible to us. To the extent, however, that the psychopath and his behavior fall under recognized medical categories, and to the extent that we are able to understand the genesis of his affliction, the unintelligibility is diminished. Psychopathic behavior, moreover, seems related to unusual world views and, again, when it is understood in those terms, the behavior gains in intelligibility, notwithstanding our difficulty in empathizing with it.

In this paper I want to explore the idea of "moral pathology." Although this exploration will not be comprehensive or final, it may prove useful in our attempt to understand—if only in part—the *hurban* (destruction) of European Jewry. The notion of moral pathology, it may be suggested, pushes the concept of morality to its limits, and is therefore appropriate to an event of such extremes as the Holocaust. This suggestion, in fact, is an ingredient of our exploration. Though I am concerned principally with forms of moral pathology at the societal level, with social moralities that may prove useful in understanding pathological cases, moralities that have "gone wrong," it will not be possible, of course, entirely to avoid consideration of individual moral pathology.

Since this exploration of the idea of moral pathology is prompted by the Nazis' destruction of European Jewry, it is hardly necessary to state that there is no pretension, here, of displacing other sorts of inquiries and analyses: psychological, sociological, cultural, historical, or theological. Plainly, many different factors entered into the event and are relevant to the understanding of it. These remarks, however, lead immediately to questions about the status of the notion.

Assuming that the idea of moral pathology is viable at all, does it have the sort of explanatory power that historical factors, say, are presumed to have in contributing to an explanation of the *hurban* of European Jewry? Or does it at best only provide a way of characterizing or describing the event or some of its aspects, whose explanation must come from elsewhere? Putting aside the issue of the nature of historical explanation and causation, it may be noted that the general concept of pathology or disease is in itself not an explanatory idea. It is instead, apparently, a methodological notion. Any particular disease concept, on the other hand, does involve a nomological structure and a theory about the given disease's causation. But this is to speak in ideal terms. Many diseases were identified and described long before it was possible to supply causal explanations of their occurrence. A treatment of whether the idea of moral pathology has explanatory power, in one or another respect, cannot be fully undertaken here.

Although this exploration is prompted by the Nazi case, it is also important to note that there is no presumption that the idea of moral pathology is applicable only to it—quite the opposite. Let us first ask, however, why there is a temptation to regard the Nazi and other cases (e.g., gruesome murders) as instances of pathology of some sort. There seem to be two reasons. First of all, we may wish to distance ourselves from these cases. We might, at times, be bad but we are not mad. (But suppose one is bad all the time. How would the case be characterized?) The mere thought that one may be like a Nazi or a serial murderer in some morally significant respect is decidedly unpleasant.

Second, the judgment that some person, behavior, or society is pathological, diseased, or sick—in contrast to the judgment that it is (merely) immoral—appears to be "scientific" or "objective." The former judgment, which borrows from the terminology of medicine, seems to be factual, while the latter seems a matter of variable taste and opinion which is at worst purely subjective and at best culturally relative. We therefore feel that the designation of some case as pathological rests on a secure basis. These considerations, however, raise complex issues. Is the judgment that some condition is pathological entirely value neutral? Isn't it also culturally relative in a vital sense? These questions have been much discussed, and they cannot be gone into here beyond the minimum necessary for our exploration. It may in fact be conceded that pathology is not an entirely value-neutral concept. Certainly, to call some condition pathological is to "condemn" it in some respect or at least to designate it as unwanted or even undesirable. But this concession does not exclude the possibility that the concept's elements include some factual (objective) criteria or conditions by reference to which the judgment is made.

The question of moral relativism may also be bypassed, I believe. The mass murder of the Jews (20,000 a day at Auschwitz when it was in full operation) is not something about which one can sit on the fence or be indifferent. I am not making this claim because I think that the Holocaust was unique. Perhaps it was in many of its aspects, but it makes no difference for my point. If it wasn't truly evil, then nothing is. (I do not mean to suggest that all aspects of the philosophical problem of moral relativism are settled by this example. In general, I think, philosophy tends to go wrong when it focuses on extreme cases, but such a focus is unavoidable in this exploration.)

On the other hand, if the slaughter of the Jews was truly evil, it may seem rather paradoxical to view it as a paradigm case of moral pathology. For the designation of some act or person as pathological usually excuses the agent from responsibility and blame; he is mad, not bad. And the characterization of Nazi morality as pathological would seem to cut the ground from under ascriptions of responsibility. In the case of "ordinary" crimes and wrongs, the distinction between being mad and being bad, whose workability depends on having relatively narrow criteria of madness, is one that is important to keep. Merely because somebody did something wrong, it does not follow that there is something wrong with him. But perhaps it does follow in some cases of wrongdoing, when the wrongful act is indicative of a moral defect, and both the act and the agent may be deemed blameworthy.

The Nazis' destruction of the Jews, at any rate, may be just the sort of case in which the pathological and the wicked come together. (Compare the identification of psychopathy and character disorder.) And it is for this reason that it pushes the concept of morality to its limits. The social morality of Nazism might be so defective as a morality, that it would be proper to view it as both mad and bad, as it were. This issue, however, is one that we should leave open for the moment. It might be mentioned, though, that being party to the social morality of Nazism would not of itself excuse the individual Nazi from responsibility and blame. The purpose of this inquiry is not to find a way of excusing Nazi wickedness.

As mentioned earlier, the concept of pathology (or disease) is not unproblematic, and neither is the notion of morality. It may seem only foolhardy to want to conjoin such notions, but I shall press on in any case. Clearly, there is much that can be said about these terms, much more than can be said in this paper. Since the focus, here, is social morality, let us begin with it.

Although there has been some debate in the philosophical literature on whether morality is inherently social or inherently personal, we do not need to enter into it.³ I think it would be conceded by all hands that it makes sense to speak of the morality of a society or social group. Some philosophers have in fact maintained that a society is to be defined in terms of rules and standards of conduct that are held in common. We do not need to go quite that far. It is enough to maintain that a group of people who engage in social intercourse and social transactions, and who share a set of rules and standards about how they should behave toward each other, has a social morality. And this morality will also include rules and standards of conduct on how members of the group should behave toward individuals who fall outside of it. (Admittedly, the notion of "the group" is something that deserves analysis.) A social morality, furthermore, may contain commonly held values and ideals as well as rules. It is a neat question whether a pluralistic society, taken as a totality, has a uniquely specifiable social morality. As it has been characterized thus far, I don't think it can be denied that the Nazis (if not the Germans as a whole) had a social morality.

It still remains to consider whether all this is enough to characterize a social morality. Must the rules and standards, the values and ideals, also have a distinctive content in order for them to comprise a *morality?* And what is the relationship between law and social morality? Only the first question can be taken up at this point. It has an obvious importance for the topic of moral pathology, and we shall have occasion to return to it.

In order to put the matter briefly, I shall, with some modification, follow the lead of H. L. A. Hart.⁴ Among any other rules and standards of conduct that a social morality might contain, it must include rules of the following *kinds:* rules that provide for the protection of the person and property of members of the group, rules that guarantee a degree of mutual forbearance and respect for the interests of other members of the group, and (astoundingly, a point unmentioned by Hart) rules governing, for members of the group, relations between the sexes. So characterized, a social morality is, in a respect, much of an in-group affair; it is left open whether or not the group regards itself as bound by the same rules in its dealings with outsiders. Also left open is the specific content of the different kinds of rules. No doubt, though, the content of the rules will be shaped partly by what is required for the group to survive as a group, other things being equal.

Any individual might reject some constituents of a social morality, although such rejection would raise a question as to whether he should be regarded as a member of the group. However this issue is to be decided, it is plain that there will be some mechanisms for the enforcement of a social morality against deviations and threatened deviations. Putting aside obvious complications, we can recognize two such mechanisms: external and internal. The former involves the use of force and expressions of disapproval. The latter involves a process of "socialization" whereby the norms of the group are "internalized."

Despite the years of research on this process, it may not be fully known how socialization takes place. We do have some idea of its outcome, however: The individual acquires a conscience, which may be nothing more than an ability to look at oneself from the perspective of the rules, values, and ideals of the shared morality and to feel the "moral emotions" of guilt and shame in accordance with it. But conscience, guilt feelings, and a sense of shame may not be the whole story of internal enforcement mechanisms. A desire for social approval, a commitment to the group's values and ideals, and feelings of good will toward the members of one's group may also be operative. It should be noticed that these last remarks begin to connect social morality with individual morality in one of its forms.

An individual who has been socialized in the described manner may be said to have acquired a "social self" and a "moral self." I do not think it is necessary to maintain, as some theorists have done, that these two selves are identical; we need acknowledge only that there is a very close relationship between them. Nor is it being maintained that the moral self, as described here, is the complete story about moral selves. In any case it is important to recognize that the Nazis had a moral self—a Nazi moral self.

I take all the above to be a correct enough account of the notion of a social morality. There is, of course, nothing novel in it. (I want to emphasize, however, that I am not advancing it as an account of all of morality.) It is now time to turn to the second term in the idea we are exploring, "pathology."

It would be impossible for us to survey, here, the literature on the concept of pathology, or disease, illness, mental illness, sickness, and so on. There is no denying that these terms are problematic; as noted earlier, their meaning, and even their meaningfulness, have been the subject of much debate. I would like instead to develop an account of moral pathology based on a feature that seems to be common to many uses of the term. I then develop an account suggested by the theory of "general pathology" propounded by a founder of the science of cell pathology, Rudolph Virchow (1821– 1902).[5]

Despite the problematic character of the above-mentioned terms, few authors seem to take the trouble of offering a definition of them. For instance, Freud's famous book *The Psychopathology of Everyday Life* contains fascinating discussions of slips of the pen, slips of the tongue, bungled actions, and the like. The continuity of everyday behavior with the symptomatic behavior of neurotics is thereby shown. But an explicit definition of "psychopathology" is not supplied. (At least I couldn't find one.) Books that deal with "social pathology" often turn out to be books on juvenile delinquency, alcoholism, divorce, and the like that do not offer any definition or analysis of the concept. Examples could be multiplied from other fields.

It seems to me that the rarity of explicit definitions—to interpret the situation in a charitable light—reflects a widely held assumption that pathologies of all sorts have a common characteristic, namely, that pathological conditions are *dysfunctional*. This assumption probably is clearest in the area of the "mental illnesses," where, as might be expected, the notion of illness has received its most vigorous challenge.

The proposition that health has to do with proper functioning and illness with dysfunction is of course quite ancient. Its *locus classicus* is Plato's *Republic*. Because Plato is so anxious to connect morality and the health of the soul (to put it quaintly) or mental health (to put it in modern terms), it is worth our while to dwell on the *Republic* a bit. It would not be inappropriate to regard Plato as having presented the classical model of moral pathology. The dominating question of the *Republic*, why should one be just, leads to an elaborate treatment of what justice is in the *polis* and in the soul of the just man.

In Books VIII and IX of the *Republic*, as is well known, Socrates nails down his response to Thrasymachus and his other interlocutors on whether it pays to be just. Socrates traces the devolution of a society and the soul from a condition of justice and health to one of injustice and "mental illness." The account correlates structural changes in a society and the individual psyche with the course of a pathological condition. In society and in the individual there is a transition from rule by the best element to rule by the worst: from aristocratic rule through timocratic, oligarchic, and democratic rule, to tyrannic; from the rule of reason to rule by the basest impulses. It is in Plato that we find the first suggestion of the longstanding view that immorality and mental illness are kinds of irrationality.

In form, Plato's model of moral pathology is similar to that of the anatomical pathologist's. It relates structure and function, certain structural changes to dysfunction; the structural changes are, as it were, social or psychological lesions; pathological conditions, further, are nomologically patterned.

As R. L. Nettleship pointed out years ago, Plato's treatment of social and individual moral disintegration does not purport to be historical; it is rather a "logical" picture of the progress of evil. It is a picture in which there appears a progressive fracturing of the *unity* of the society or the soul, a unity conceived virtually as a good in itself. (Aristotole's criticism of the *Republic* turns on its evaluation of unity and on its institutional arrangements for achieving unity; see *Politics* 1263b29–1264a1.) The comparison of the tyrannical to the just-souled man thus clinches the argument that justice pays: The tyrannical man cannot want or choose what is good for himself as a *whole* because his soul is divided against itself, while the soul of the just man is unified under the rule of reason, and he can choose what is good for himself as a whole rather than what gratifies a particular impulse. A parallel argument is made at the societal level. At each stage of the described structural changes the pursuit of the good of the whole becomes increasingly impossible.

The dysfunctional character of a pathological condition, on the above account, is clear. It is the inability to choose or act for the good of the whole, of the society or the individual, as the case may be. Because the whole, society or self, is in greater or lesser degree divided against itself, it is unable to choose what the whole judges to be good or right. This inability *is* unhealth and injustice; and it is a moral defect. For all the difficulties that one might find in Plato's account, something like it seems to be assumed in many contemporary discussions of social pathology and mental disorder. (The tradition that regards social conflict as a condition to be overcome thus has hoary roots; few social theorists have found merit in social conflict.)

While Plato helps us to get a grasp on the feature of dysfunction, especially in a way that appears to have a bearing on the idea of moral pathology, the concept of the good of the whole may still leave one with the feeling that the problematic nature of the idea has not been removed. For it is plain that the notion of moral pathology is not, under this analysis, value neutral. The moral for us, however, may be that the search for a value-neutral understanding should be given up.

It is now time to try to bring together the strands of the above discussions: social morality, the social and moral selves, and dysfunction, the inability to choose for the sake of the good of the whole. I shall be beginning to consider the question of Nazi morality: If, as claimed earlier, it makes sense to speak of a Nazi social morality and a Nazi social and moral self, how does the idea of dysfunction fit in?

Since we are following a line of thought suggested by Plato, it is important to take note of an item that was insufficiently stressed earlier in the exposition. This is the correlation he makes between the stages of social and moral disintegration and changes in the *ends* that are sought in choice and action. Thus, in the tyrannical condition of the state and the soul, the end is the satisfaction of the basest impulses; in the democratic condition, by contrast, no end or desire is recognized as any better, or any worse for that matter, than any other. The democratic condition might be described as one of total amorality, and rational choice and action are possible only to the extent that there is, as it were, a temporary "coalition" among social or individual interests.

But this notion of rational choice and action employs too "thin" a conception of rationality. For it is the point of the above remarks that a condition of society or self cannot be deemed nonpathological merely because the social or individual agent selects means that are appropriate to whatever ends one happens to have. In order to determine the condition of a society or self, it is important to look to the motives for choice and action and to the beliefs on which choices are based. It is important, furthermore, to determine the extent to which choice and action involve reflexive deception regarding societal and personal motives.

I do not have the competence to examine in detail the gamut of motives supplied by Nazi social morality and their institutional setting or, correspondingly, the motives of the moral self of individual Nazis. Certainly, the motives that were often overtly asserted by Nazi leaders and officers after the war rarely ring true. Eichmann's claim, for example, that he was merely doing his duty, following the Categorical Imperative, hardly seems adequate to what he did. Despite the complexity of the topic of Nazi motives, though, an examination of them is necessary here. This examination, conducted in general terms, is far from complete.

The callousness and indifference to the interests of others that the Nazis displayed in their conduct have frequently been noted, especially the callousness and indifference shown in acts of killing and torture. This absence of affect surely is a sign of a defective personality, and one might be tempted to view it as a sort of amoralism. The accuracy of such a view is, however, questionable in the Nazi case. Amoralism was characterized above in terms of the notion of a "democratic" social or individual morality, a morality that in effect recognizes all values as equal, which is tantamount to a lack of values. A moral self of this sort would truly be in a pathological moral condition, a highly dysfunctional condition. But it does not seem to have been the case that Nazi callousness and indifference stemmed from a "democratic" morality; the underlying motivations were quite different. Moreover, the indifference might have been a "defense mechanism" of sorts.

But consider the last point. Callousness and indifference are attitudes that may well have to be adopted in order to function in situations of "tragic choice," choice between evils. Such attitudes seem frequently to be adopted by soldiers in wartime, for otherwise the burden of guilt in doing acts that the agent recognizes as evil would be too heavy to bear. In a situation of psychic conflict, callousness and indifference, therefore, seem to be what the psychoanalytic theorist Charles Brenner calls "compromise formations." According to Brenner, a compromise formation can be pathological. As he says, "A compromise formation is pathological when it is characterized by any combination of the following features: too much restriction of gratification of drive derivatives, too much anxiety or depressive affect, too much inhibition of functional capacity, too great a tendency to injure or destroy oneself, or too great conflict with one's environment."[6] One should note both the vaguenesses—"too much"—and the connection between pathology and dysfunction in this statement.

As difficult as it is to interpret the motives of individuals, though, there seems little doubt that for *some* individuals who participated in Nazi mass murder callousness and indifference were defense mechanisms in circumstances of "tragic choice," as they saw it. This proposition, I believe, is well documented in Robert J. Lifton's morbidly fascinating book *The Nazi Doctors*.[7] These people, however, tended to be incomplete Nazis, as we may call them; their social and moral selves were engaged in internal battle. They suffered from psychic conflict, conflict of motives. For many of them, the compromise formations were dysfunctional and pathological.

These considerations invite the suggestion that a pathological social morality is one that contains a large potential for conflicts of motives and which, therefore, socializes selves with such a potential. Or to put it in other terms, the ends of action that a pathological social morality mandates or legitimates are ends that will be in conflict in a manner that promotes dysfunctional adjustments in the individual, though how far such adjustments are actualized will depend on the individual's constitution. A pathological social morality is one that produces defective moral selves, selves with a divided conscience.

As plausible as this possibility is as an account of moral pathology—and it would take a great deal of spelling out, admittedly—it would only cover part of the ground. It would not adequately characterize the fully committed Nazi. Individuals of this type were not, from their own perspective, making tragic choices. Their actions were readily facilitated for them, without much self-consciousness. There was no feeling of guilt because there was no need for it in the situation as they saw it. (Eichmann was a good example.) For the Nazi who viewed National Socialism as nothing but "applied biology," as Rudolph Hess put it in 1934, genocide was a necessity; there was a disease that had to be cured. The choices that had to be made would not be tragic, for the Final Solution would eliminate evil. In the case of the fully committed Nazi, the person who fully accepted Nazi ideology and values and had a Nazi moral self, then, the above suggestion about the nature of moral pathology may not be adequate.

I am not sure, however, that this conclusion would be accepted by Lifton, whose position is influenced by Otto Rank's idea of the "shadow self."[8] This idea is similar to the ancient (Jewish) notion of an evil inclination, an inclination as innate to man as an inclination for good; it recognizes that human beings have malevolent and destructive motives as well as good-willed and creative ones.

In an extension of Rank's idea, Lifton's study of Nazi doctors employs the notion of "doubling" to explain the behavior of the physicians who ran the mass killing program at Auschwitz. The phenomenon of doubling is more extreme than the "divided self" that was attributed, above, to the incomplete Nazi. According to Lifton, even the most extreme of Nazi doctors developed a "double self" in order to carry through their program. Doubling involves a division of the self into two functioning wholes, so that part of the self acts as the entire self, each part acting in a different context. The doubling process resulted in a change in moral consciousness wherein guilt feelings could be avoided in the situation of mass killing.[9] Lifton, as I understand him, sees this process as occurring to some extent even in the incomplete Nazi.

According to this view, it appears, the social and moral self of the completely committed Nazi would be in a pathological, dysfunctional, condition. For a "doubled" self cannot choose for the good of the whole self or choose what the whole self regards as good or right. Its motives exist in two separate realms, and it can function at all only when one of the realms is completely dominant, so to speak.

But why should doubling occur at all in the case of the fully committed Nazi? With regard to Nazi *doctors*, it is Lifton's view that doubling was necessitated because of a conflict between the healing ethic of medicine and the Nazi ideology of death. (The symbolism of death pervades much of Nazi rhetoric.) Doubling was necessary to resolve the "healing–killing" paradox, that killing cures. Assuming that Lifton is correct, however, it still remains to ask whether something like doubling also obtained with regard to fully committed nonmedical Nazis.

Lifton's account, it should be noted, supposes that Nazi physicians in effect were subject to two moralities and that they therefore had two social and moral selves, which clearly is a dysfunctional state. Could a similar condition have held for other Nazis?

The fact that the Nazis engaged in bureaucratic mystification in carrying out their "hygienic" program, especially in its earlier phases, suggests that this was the case. In the prewar "euthanasia" program, death certificates were falsified so as to attribute the deaths to natural causes rather than direct homicide, and at its start Auschwitz was labeled a "public health venture." (Another mystification device, to be discussed later, was the retroactive legalization of criminal and other illegal acts.) Why all this deception? Part of the explanation may be that it was a public relations effort directed to the not fully committed. But might it not have also been a kind of *self-deception?* If the committed Nazi was subject to two competing social moralities and therefore felt the psychic conflict of incompatible ends and motives, these deceptive practices would bring relief if they also operated self-deceptively.

A bit more is said about this point below. But before we turn to it, we should notice that the above discussion has supplied us with an account of the moral pathology of the individual Nazi. It has not answered the question of whether Nazi social morality, as such, was pathological because it is not clear that it was, of itself, dysfunctional. And one may even doubt that the account really works for the fully committed Nazi. We should consider, therefore, whether there might be some conception of pathology other than one that so strongly emphasizes the idea of dysfunction.

Such a conception in fact is suggested by Rudolph Virchow's theory of "general pathology," propounded in the 1850s. General pathology is concerned to describe abnormal processes such as atrophy, inflammation, necrosis, calcification, and the like; it studies disease in general, not any particular disease. According to this approach all pathological formations are degenerations, transformations, or repetitions of normal (i.e., typical) physiological structures. As Virchow put it, pathology is nothing but physiology with obstacles; diseased life is nothing but healthy life interfered with by all manner of external and internal influences. Diseases thus are functions of the general laws of physiology, particular departures from general physiological norms. Virchow did not deny that diseases are reflected in deranged function; what he did stress was that diseases are "orderly manifestations of definite phenomena of life (normal in themselves) under unusual conditions which are simply quantitative."[10]

Virchow's "physiologic" view is meant to contrast with an "ontological" conception. According to this latter conception diseases are *entia* that have real existence as such, discrete entities with their own laws of development; the disease process is a lower life form that manifests itself in a characteristic picture. According to some versions of this conception, a disease is a real type that exists apart from its particular instantiations, which themselves may be atypical—a kind of platonism in medicine. Virchow's physiological view sees disease as a quantitative deviation from the normal course of bodily function. (In later years Virchow became reconciled with the ontological conception by taking the deranged cell, an altered body part, as the disease entity.)

Let us now see what idea of moral pathology, applied specifically to social morality, is suggested by Virchow's view of disease as normal life under abnormal conditions. It should be obvious that the idea of a pathological social morality will not be perfectly congruent with Virchow's conception of disease. In particular, it will not employ the idea of quantitative deviation from the normal. It is concerned with "normal moralities" and moralities that deviate from them because of extraneous, abnormal conditions. This means that it will be concerned with the *content* of a social morality.

The conception of a morality that is suggested by this approach may be developed as follows. Let us assume, first, that every social morality has two components: a high-level component of abstract rules and principles (the "core" of a morality) and a lower-level, more concrete component that is derived from the former in conjunction with nonmoral statements. (The idea of derivative moral rules, principles, or beliefs is used by many writers. My discussion draws on Ronald D. Milo's suggestive book *Immorality*, without endorsing its substantive theses.)[11] The second assumption is that every morality has the selfsame core of abstract rules and principles, so that we may speak of the "normal core" of social moralities. It contains such elements as the following: Peace is a good; don't harm your neighbor; pursue your own interests but respect the rights of others; cruelty is a vice; honesty is a virtue; be fair in your dealings; and so on. This normal core makes up part of the content of any set of commonly held rules, ideals, and standards that deserves to be called a morality. In other words, the normal core contains as its elements the sort of rules and standards that are recognized in the great moral traditions. It is not the case that any abstract rule or principle, as long as it is commonly accepted in a society, may be an element in the normal core.

The operative morality of a society, however, also includes lower-level derived rules and standards that are more concretely action guiding or action prescribing. At this level, *alternative moralities* become possible, for the second component of a social morality is a function of both the normal core, which is common to all social moralities, and nonmoral beliefs about the world. As is often argued by ethical theorists, disagreements in moral judgment, whether they be disagreements between cultures, societies, or individuals, are traceable to differences in nonmoral belief.

It is at this point that we can introduce the notion of moral pathology by analogy to Virchow's conception of disease as normal life under abnormal conditions. Moral pathology is expressed at the concrete level of derived moral rules and principles that are based upon the normal core plus *false* nonmoral beliefs. The assumption here is that there is just one "healthy" morality, namely, a morality whose derived rules and principles are based on true nonmoral beliefs. But there may be many degrees and kinds of moral pathology, depending on such factors as the number of morally effective false nonmoral beliefs or their bizarreness. Essentially, then, false nonmoral beliefs constitute the "abnormal conditions" that generate deviations from normal, healthy morality. At its extreme, this conception is concomitant with the apparent fact that psychopathic behavior is connected with highly unusual and irrational world views.

The two-level conception of social morality offers an initially plausible approach to understanding the morality of Nazism and how it could mandate the destruction of European Jewry as well as other nefarious deeds. The Nazis, we may now suppose, had no qualms over initiating a war for territorial expansion, no qualms over incarcerating, torturing, or killing German enemies of the regime, no qualms over the brutal mass slaughter of Jews—and all not because they did not believe that torture and murder are wrong. Quite the contrary: At its core their morality was the same as everyone else's. What justified or even mandated these deeds was the Nazis' derivative moral rules and principles, which were based on the normal core and a particular set of nonmoral beliefs. These deeds were not merely the product of indifference to the interests of others or of indifference to their perceived wrongfulness. Rather, the deeds were held to be morally justified. If Nazi morality was pathological it was so because false nonmoral beliefs (e.g., "racial science") were used in deriving concrete prescriptions.

It is important, however, to add something about false nonmoral beliefs, for one may hold such beliefs for many reasons. A person may be mistaken as to the truth of some belief, and his mistake could be a reasonable mistake. Furthermore, because of ordinary human limitations, all of us probably have many false beliefs. Here is the true "banality of evil": actions prompted by derivative rules and principles based on garden-variety nonmoral falsehoods. But there also are false beliefs that result from unreasonable mistakes, willful ignorance, and self-deception. It is also because of the variety of the sources of false nonmoral belief that we can speak of kinds of moral pathology, and it seems clear that some social moralities might be judged to be worse cases than others.

How satisfactory is this conception of moral pathology? Can nonmoral beliefs always be easily distinguished from values, ideals, and standards? Can the derivative elements of a given social morality always be distinguished from its core?

Putting aside the problem of how beliefs are to be individuated, let us note, first of all, that just one belief can make a big difference to conduct, for example, the belief that animals have souls. (Perhaps this is equivalent to three beliefs: There are souls, there are animals, and animals have souls.) In some cultures, it appears, this belief gives animals a moral status equal to that of humans. Because this belief is so morally fertile, one may well hesitate to classify it as a nonmoral belief. It is quite plain, at any rate, that some beliefs are extraordinarily complex, and it may be difficult to disentangle their moral and nonmoral components.

Consider, for instance, the assertion "Every Jew active in Europe represents a danger to European culture," which was made by Baldur von Schirach, leader of the Hitler Youth and Gauleiter of Vienna. He used this belief to justify the claim that transportation of Jews from Vienna to the ghettos in the East would be a "positive contribution to European culture." Schirach's statement may be equivalent to a complex of moral and nonmoral assertions that would be hard to disentangle. More important than this sort of consideration, however, is the very plausible point that the distinction between moral and nonmoral beliefs is not easy to draw because (recognizably?) moral principles, standards, and values influence the way one looks at the world and how one describes it. It can hardly be claimed that the so-called racial science of the Germans (which antedated Nazism) was simply a conglomeration of nonmoral beliefs that, in combination with the normal core, justified the derivative moral rules and principles that mandated the destruction of European Jewry.

Related to the above considerations is a legitimate doubt as to whether disagreement over derivative moral principles is always traceable to differences in nonmoral belief. Consider a dispute over whether animals have rights or, if they do have rights, the weight that should be assigned to them. The parties to this dispute do not disagree over nonmoral facts, such as whether animals feel pain. Their disagreement seems to turn on more abstract concerns: what a right is, why anyone has rights, the weight carried by certain moral considerations as opposed to others, and so on. It would not be unreasonable to conclude that there is, at best, a hazy borderline between what is core and what is derivative in a given social morality. In Hitler's Germany beliefs about the *moral* inferiority of the Jews, and the belief that the Jews were a disease from which Europe needed to be cured, were very close to the hard core, at the very least.

In my earlier discussion of the "Virchowian" conception of moral pathology, I remarked that the nefarious deeds of the Nazis were not merely the product of indifference to the interests of others or indifference to their perceived wrongfulness. Putting aside the criticisms just made, according to this conception we may regard, as part of the normal core, the moral proposition that causing death or pain to someone is a reason for not doing it and, as derivative, the proposition that death or pain may (or should) be caused to Jews. A possible explanation of how the Nazis could hold both propositions at once is that through an act of willful self-deception they made up or bought a story about the Jews that enabled them to rationalize a preexistent hatred, a story about the Jews as a danger to European civilization or about racial inferiority, which we will now assume to be comprised of purely nonmoral statements. Acceptance of such a story might explain the behavior of the Nazis, both incomplete and fully committed, without having to suppose a divided self or doubling.

I frankly do not know how to evaluate this hypothesis. There is evidence that some of this story deliberately was "made up." The evidence was presented in detail as early as 1946 in Max Weinreich's neglected book, *Hitler's Professors: The Part of Scholarship in Germany's Crimes against the Jewish People.*[12] On the other hand, it is quite clear that many Germans sincerely believed the story. Are sincerity and willful self-deception compatible? I am not sure. I don't understand how the mechanism of self-deception works. Perhaps, in the end, we do need to suppose something like a divided self (e.g., conscious and unconscious forces) in order to understand self-deception.

But there is another explanation of Nazi behavior, a more satanic and, I think, a more plausible explanation. It is that the Nazis held the proposition that causing death or pain to someone is a reason for not doing it *unless* that person is a Jew, and that for them this was as fundamental and underived as the proposition without the unless clause is for others. What we have, then, is a core of moral principles that invert the values of the normal core. Viewing the matter in this way would help explain how the Nazis could continue to pursue a policy of mass slaughter even after it was clear that the war was lost. It would also help explain Auschwitz. As has been said, "Auschwitz was a world unlike any other because it was created and governed according to the principles of absolute evil. Its only function was death."[13] The explanation is terrifying. One gazes on in horror.

In adopting the sort of explanation just suggested, I think that we have in effect abandoned the idea of moral pathology just developed. If we wish to retain the term "moral pathology" with regard to the Nazis, we should take it to mean that their social morality was straightforwardly immoral. The magnitude of the evils that their morality mandated and the malevolent motives that it supported are confirmation of this judgment.

Finally, I want to consider not so much the idea of moral pathology (or another conception of it) but rather a "fault" that is potential, and in some degree even actual, in every social morality. This fault has to do with the stance that a social morality may take toward obedience to law and authority. As Stanley Milgram's studies in the 1960s showed, obedience to authority can lead otherwise ordinary people to inflict pain on innocent victims.[14] And a recent study of men who commit torture as a matter of occupational routine (e.g., in military regimes) suggests that such people are selected for their total obedience to authority.[15] That a consideration of this issue is germane to our subject is obvious.

The fault I have in mind is connected to a sort of pathology, namely, the pathology of legal systems. Legal pathology is concerned with how a legal system might "break down" and decline eventually into nonexistence. Although the phenomenon is discussed by a variety of writers, the most interesting and relevant approach is found in the late Lon L. Fuller's *The Morality of Law*.[16]

In this book Fuller considers the qualities that law must have in order to elicit the citizen's obligation to obey it, and he examines how legal pathology affects the obligation. In contrast to traditional substantive natural-law doctrine, Fuller propounds a "procedural" conception of natural law. Before there can be good law there must be law, and success in the enterprise of lawmaking presupposes conformity to the ideal of legality, to the "inner morality" of law. The fact is, according to Fuller, that all legal systems, even the most exemplary, have a degree of legal pathology and therefore raise the question of obligation. Fuller is much concerned with whether the "law" of Hitler's Germany suffered from legal pathology.

On Fuller's view, lawmaking is the enterprise of governing conduct by means of rules, and there are eight ways in which this enterprise may fail: (1) failure to make rules at all, so that every issue must be decided on an ad hoc basis, (2) failure to publicize the rules to the affected party, (3) abuse of retroactive legislation, (4) failure to make the rules understandable, (5) enactment of contradictory rules, (6) enactment of rules that require conduct beyond the power of the affected party, (7) introduction of such frequent changes in the rules that the subject cannot orient his actions by them, and (8) lack of congruence between the rules as announced and their actual administration. Failures in these respects are failures in adherence to an inner morality of law by which laws are required to be general, public, prospective, and so on. Each failure is a symptom of legal pathology, a way in which a legal system can go wrong and fail to achieve the status of law, which happens when its failures are persistent in any one of these respects or relatively pervasive in a few. Every legal system, as Fuller demonstrates, fails in some degree.

Plainly, the inner morality of law describes the idea (or ideal) of the rule of law. Its underlying thought is that lawmaking and governance must themselves be subject to rules that are not legal rules, rules internal to the very idea of governing by rule. As Fuller points out, law is not the same as managerial direction; contrary to the tendency of legal positivism, law is not a one-way projection of authority. Law depends for its existence on a reciprocity of expectations between the governed and the governors, expectations that survive only when there is adherence to the rule of law. It is fairly clear, I think, why Fuller holds that the quality of the citizen's obligation to obey the law is much affected by whether officials have adhered to the inner morality of law, even before we come to the question of whether some particular law is a good law.

We are now in a position to begin to bring the above discussion to bear on the "fault" that a social morality may exhibit in its stance on the question of obedience to law and authority. I think it is plain that every social morality, except perhaps the morality of specialized groups, generally will include an obligation to obey the law and official authority. And for a very good reason. As Fuller says, law provides a base line for a manifold of social interactions. Does a social morality condemn marital infidelity? Does a social morality condemn theft? If it does, it does so within a legal framework that defines what marriage and private property are. The point is that there is an interplay between law and social morality, and not just in the respect that legal positivists admit, namely, that the social morality influences the law. Rather, the law penetrates into the interstices of the morality at innumerable points. An obligation to obey the law and, it should be added, to obey officials, therefore, is salient for a social morality. But what is the citizen's obligation when the lawmaker and other authorities fail to adhere to the inner morality of the law? What should a social morality require of a citizen under a regime that is affected by legal pathology?

Here it is relevant to turn to law in Hitler's Germany. The fact is that the regime had a curious view of law. In its early stages everything it did was "legalized," and done under the color of law. Thus, in 1933, shortly after Hitler came to power, the Reichstag passed the so-called Enabling Law, the *Gesetz zur Behebung der Not von Volk und Reich*, which gave him power to govern by decree, in effect a law that permitted him to ignore the law, thus destroying the constitutional state. In the Röhm Purge of 1934, Hitler took care of his rivals in the Nazi party by having nearly one hundred persons murdered. These murders were turned into lawful executions by the prompt enactment of a retroactive statute. The great German legal codes of the turn of the century were never abolished by the regime, but were ignored when it was found expedient to do so. In 1936, Dr. Hans Frank, the minister of justice, let the courts know that whenever the codes might require a decision against the sound interests of the German people, the judges should turn to him and he would provide them with a new law that would do the right job. Frank was thinking of decisions that might favor Jews.

What we find, then, is the use of law as a mystification device, along the lines mentioned earlier in connection with bureaucratic mystification in the "euthanasia" program. Altogether, the Nazis had a rather curious view of law. The system suffered, of course, from a severe case of legal pathology, a case that lasted throughout its existence.

Fuller's own words on Nazi law are instructive. Their context is a reply to a possible objection to his notion of law as an "enterprise," which implies that both rules of law and a legal system can "half exist":

> It is truly astounding to what an extent there runs through modern thinking in legal philosophy the assumption that law is like a piece of inert matter—it is there or not there. It is only such an assumption that could lead legal scholars to assume, for example, that the "laws" enacted by the Nazis in their closing years, considered as laws and in abstraction from their evil aims, were just as much laws of those of England and Switzerland. An even more grotesque outcropping of this assumption is the notion that the moral obligation of the decent German citizen to obey these laws was in no way affected by the fact that they were in part kept from his knowledge, that some of them retroactively "cured" wholesale murder, that they contained wide delegations of administrative discretion to redefine the crimes they proscribed, and that, in any event, their actual terms were largely disregarded when it suited the convenience of the military courts appointed to apply them.[17]

What in fact was "the moral obligation of the decent German citizen to obey these laws"? What I now wish to suggest is that a *fault*, a serious moral fault, exists in a social morality that continues to endorse an obligation to obey the law and obedience to authority in the presence of a legal system infected with the sort of pathological condition I have been describing. One effect of such a fault, and it was a highly significant one for German society at large, is that it permits the citizen to turn a blind eye to what is actually going on in the society.

It is in the context of such a morality that we should understand the extensive use of the defense of superior orders against war crimes charges, a defense raised by Eichmann. When Eichmann was asked by a Christian minister to repent his sins shortly before his execution, he replied that Hans Frank (who had become governor general for Poland) needed to repent, but he (Eichmann) had done nothing wrong; he was only following orders. The usual rationale for the defense of superior orders is that the individual is not offered the genuine option of disobeying, for failure to comply may result in his own death or harsh punishment. But if we could perform an "autopsy" on the mind of Adolf Eichmann and discover the "source of the evil sickness," as is suggested by the Christian minister just referred to,[18] I suspect that we would find the traces of the fault I have been describing.

It is of course necessary to be cautious. I am not asserting that all of Nazi behavior can be attributed to the presence of this fault in German social morality. The assertion would no more be true than claims that the First World War was attributable to Kant and Hegel, as seems to have been suggested respectively by Santayana and Hobhouse.[19] But perhaps there is some truth to the claims, since (as I believe) philosophy has consequences for practice.

It is also easy to exaggerate the extent to which Nazi officers and subordinates did "follow orders." The situation in the death camps seems often to have approached one of corruption and anarchy, and there were endless protestations about orders from higher authority. Otto Friedrich reports the testimony given in Frankfort in 1964 by Ella Lingens, a Viennese physician sent to Auschwitz in 1943 for helping Jews escape from Austria: "Judge: Do you wish to say that everyone could decide for himself to be either good or bad in Auschwitz? Dr. Lingens: That is exactly what I wish to say."[20]

I am hardly maintaining, however, that the existence of this fault in a social morality excuses the commission of evil deeds. It can be argued with plausibility, I think, that the fault is a necessary element in any social morality, as paradoxical as that sounds. It exists wherever there is legal pathology. So it exists in every society. But both legal pathology and the extent of the fault are matters of degree. In the German case, they were severe, and the fault immeasurably contributed to the slaughter of European Jewry. We may even hold that the social morality was a pathological case.

This complex event needs to be studied from a variety of perspectives if we can ever hope to understand it. We also need to understand the *hurban* in the perspective of Jewish history. Hitler was not Haman, and Germany was not the Persian Empire. The destruction of the Jews came in the wake of the Enlightenment, a period of Jewish expectations of equality and the rights of citizenship. It is not surprising if the Jews could not believe that mass slaughter would occur. After all, this was Europe, not the jungle.

NOTES

1. Walter Laqueur, *The Terrible Secret* (New York: Penguin Books, 1982), p. 237.

2. Ibid., p. 130.

3. See W. K. Frankena, "The Concept of Morality," in *Perspectives on Morality* (Notre Dame, Ind.: University of Notre Dame Press, 1976), chap. 10.

4. H. L. A. Hart, *The Concept of Law* (Oxford: Oxford University Press, 1961), pp. 189–95.

5. Rudolph Virchow, *Disease, Life and Man: Selected Essays*, trans. Lelland J. Rather (Stanford: Stanford University Press, 1958).

6. Charles Brenner, *The Mind in Conflict* (New York: International Universities Press, 1982), p. 161.

7. Robert J. Lifton, *The Nazi Doctors: Medical Killing and the Psychology of Genocide* (New York: Basic Books, 1986).

8. See also Ernest Becker, *Escape from Evil* (New York: Free Press, 1975) and Mary Midgley, *Wickedness* (London: Routledge & Kegan Paul, 1984).

9. Lifton, *Nazi Doctors*, pp. 481ff.

10. Virchow, *Disease*, p. 59.

11. Ronald D. Milo, *Immorality* (Princeton: Princeton University Press, 1984).

12. Max Weinreich, *Hitler's Professors: The Part of Scholarship in Germany's Crimes against the Jewish People* (New York: Yiddish Scientific Institute–YIVO, 1946).

13. Otto Friedrich, *The End of the World* (New York: Coward, McCann and Geoghegan, 1982), p. 333.

14. Stanley Milgram, *Obedience to Authority: An Experimental View* (New York: Harper & Row, 1974).

15. Reported in *New York Times* (national edition), May 14, 1986, p. 19, in "The Torturer's Mind: Complex View Emerges."

16. Lon L. Fuller, *The Morality of Law*, rev. ed. (New Haven: Yale University Press, 1969).

17. Ibid., p. 123.

18. William L. Hull, *The Struggle for a Soul* (Garden City, N.Y.: Doubleday, 1963), p. xii.

19. See A. L. Rowse's foreword to George Santayana's *The German Mind: A Philosophical Diagnosis* (New York: Thomas Y. Crowell, 1968) and Leonard Trelawny Hobhouse's dedication in his *The Metaphysical Theory of the State* (London: George Allen & Unwin, 1918).

20. Friedrich, *End of the World*, p. 291.

7

THE RIGHT WAY TO ACT:
Indicting the Victims

Abigail L. Rosenthal

It is clear that our moral and dramatic landscape, the narrative look of the twentieth century, would be far different if we could imaginatively erase the Nazi from that landscape. He occupies it with us. He is a kind of measuring rod of our relation to the category of evil. But the Nazi's outstandingness in that department has also been challenged. One of the challenges to the consensus about Nazi villainy has involved redirecting a part of it to the Jew, as the victim who obviously suffers the fullest impact of that villainy. Questions of the most serious kind have been raised about the integrity of the Jewish victims, or the "purity" of their victimization. Holocaust victims have been charged with various kinds of moral default, ranging from passivity to complicity, charges that make it hard to see them clear, for the purposes of the whole moral analysis.

If the Nazi's victim *is* in complicity, then we get instead the picture of an odd sort of morbid human interaction, a shared sickness, an epidemic if you like, where clear lines between poisoners, carriers, and felled members of the healthy population can no longer be drawn. A responsible physician would withhold praise and blame alike from his patients. But the task of a responsible moral being is rather different. It belongs to the latter to bestow praise and blame, whether on oneself or on another, in the right way. If we do not know where the victim as victim begins, we will not be able to make out sufficiently clearly where his victimizer in turn begins. It will then become a tricky thing, theoretically and practically, to make any use at all of the category of evil in what is generally held to be its most salient context. Accordingly, my task in this essay will be to help make the category of evil serviceable again in this context by pointing out that the Jewish Holocaust had approximately six million genuine victims, victims in the pure sense of the term. Said that way, it sounds almost too obvious to be worth saying. How, then, did the point get to be so inobvious?

In May 1960, in Buenos Aires, Israeli agents seized SS Lieutenant Colonel Adolf Eichmann, head of the variously initialed and named

Gestapo Section IV D4, B4, and IV A4, on "Jewish Affairs and Deportations," and removed him clandestinely to Jerusalem to stand trial before the District Court of Jerusalem for, among other charges, five counts of "Crimes against the Jewish People." It was the first time that the Holocaust had been brought to the attention of the world as a single, planned crime of immense scope, with many stages. That there had been slaughters of terrifying magnitude and thoroughness was a fact that had sunk into consciousness with the liberation of the camps. Evidences of these mass murders had figured prominently in the Nuremberg trials, but always among others. But here a case that the planning and carrying out of *this particular project of genocide* in all its broad ramifications and details had occurred was to be made in a court of law, with the kind of evidence acceptable in a proper court of law, original documentary evidence or attested copies and eyewitness testimony, and safeguarding the right of the accused to hear the charges against him, to defend himself, and to introduce evidence that he did not do it—or evidence of an exculpatory nature.

It was one of those moments of contemporary history where the opportunity to see justice done that was opened by a court proceeding also opened a channel to conscience and stock taking in the world. Into that moment stepped Hannah Arendt, with a report on the Jerusalem trial that—more than any other report—captured the moral imagination of the intellectual community. The thesis of Arendt's *Eichmann in Jerusalem* was threefold: (1) Eichmann was administratively subordinate and psychologically free of malevolence, or "ordinary"—a sort of boring clerk or mailman; (2) *the Jewish victims were in crucial ways in complicity with their Nazi executioners;* (3) the jurisdiction of the Jerusalem court and its findings were legally and morally questionable. Arendt's case against the Jews (point 2 above) is the one that will be reexamined here.[1]

Arendt's case against the Jews was not a report of the trial at all—which incidentally gave quite a different picture. It was largely a condensation of Raul Hilberg's far more carefully worked through evidence, as presented in his historic work, *The Destruction of the European Jews,* which came out in 1961, after the conclusion of the trial.[2] The case for Jewish complicity (popularized by Arendt) is one that I will accordingly try to evaluate in Arendt's source, working from Hilberg's revised and expanded three-volume 1985 edition, and comparing that study with some other materials, including testimony given at the Eichmann trial. My purpose, in evaluating Hilberg's case, will not be to counter it with empirical evidences of Jewish noncooperation and resistance. I am not a historian. I have opinions here, but the dispute is not exactly on my territory. My purpose will be rather to get clearer about how moral judgments ought to work in such a case, what factors are relevant, what factors irrelevant, and what standards ought to guide the moral thinker.

The problem of Jewish complicity needs, I think, now to be viewed in the widest possible context, that of "world history." I have said elsewhere (in *A Good Look at Evil*) that there is no such thing as "world history," if by that is meant a single, universally agreed-upon narrative making collective sense of the stories of all individuals in their respective *genē* (plural of the Greek *genos*, meaning tribe or race), and of all *genē* together. The myth of such a common narrative, already emplaced, is what gives ideologues their spurious authorization to overthrow real stories, of real people and of real *genē*. Nevertheless, such a universally agreed-upon story is not logically impossible. It is what happens, writ small, when any two individuals, who have lived a certain course of experience together, agree as to the factual content of what happened and as to its significance. Such an agreement *can* come about, without any necessary sacrifice of the uniqueness of the parties, or the indissoluble otherness of each one's particular perspective. If individuals can do this (and if doing it is crucial to the ratification of their experiences), and call the doing of it "friendship," then larger groups might in principle also do it. In utopian or millenarian vision, what is at best pictured is all individuals and all *genē* getting a sort of shared (in the Quaker sense) "sense of the meeting," and getting it in an unforced way. This state of universal, unforced friendship, lifted free of empty platitudes, embedded in each person's real story, may be a kind of "regulative ideal," horizoning the goodness of each of us. When one thinks of how difficult it is for any single person to get his own story straight, one has a dim notion of the real obstacles that will delay indefinitely the actualizing of this regulative ideal. But, as long as we know that this ideal is what we are talking about, we *can* talk about "world history."

In the context, then, of "world history," what should we suppose was really happening in the course of the Holocaust, from start to end? At the very least, here was a whole people seeking to erase another people from its history, and from world history altogether. The German people worked as a team to get this done, and to let it get done. They looked away at the right times and they pitched in at the right times. The implementation of Nazi orders affecting Jewry required the active or passive consent of virtually all of the adult German population.[3] Whatever economic gains the targeted people could have voluntarily offered the genocidal people were feared, precisely because they might have deflected the genocidal people from its course.[4] On the other hand, whatever spoils the targeted people could *involuntarily* have yielded up to the genocidal people were relished, precisely because these were evidences that the planned genocide was indeed running its course.[5] Set in the world-historical context of German ambitions with regard to Jewry, plundering the strengthless dead loses its base character. Rather, the fact that one *can* do it becomes proof of the success of the original mission.

In sum, on the German side, everything functioned as if this was indeed, as it was self-styled at the time, an act of the national will—if there ever was such a thing in the world's "history." Orders did not have to be given. Far-reaching interpretations and creative implementations welled up from every stratum of the national life. The omissions and the lookings away, the differentiated (not blanket) failures of empathy, were all functional—as they were intended to be.

To that German context in which, world-historically, alleged Jewish complicity has to be viewed, we should add two other important factors. One concerns the non-German part of the world. The other concerns the internal character of Jewish culture—itself also a factor in world history.

As regards the non-German part of the world, there was the fact that rescue was largely unavailable from the lands and people surrounding the victimized Jews. "Where were we supposed to go," said the guide at the United Nations exhibit on Auschwitz, pointing to a map. "The North Sea?"[6] The distribution of such rescue efforts as were made was largely invidious where Jews were concerned.[7] This seems a point crucial to the correct valuation of the Jewish responses. In Denmark, which might be said to have offered a "control" on the Holocaust experiment where the effectiveness of Jewish leadership is concerned, the Jewish community went smartly to its own aid, full on the mark, having people and lands available for its rescue.[8]

It is hard to get a purchase on Jewish culture, as it affected the beliefs and behavior patterns of individuals caught in the Holocaust. Diffused within the divergent host cultures where Jews lived, the effects of Jewish culture took multiply variegated forms. But Jewish culture has been, for thousands of years, permeated by religious convictions and traditions. So it is appropriate to consult these relatively stable components, even when attempting to guess at the passions of secular Jews.

What is peculiar to Jewish religious culture is the belief that a whole *genos* (as opposed to an individual saint, disciple, or prophet) has been singled out as a vehicle of the Providential purpose. The Providential purpose is to accomplish human redemption in man's physical, national, and international setting.[9] There are no precise eschatalogical blueprints for history, as fundamentalist or secular millenarism has them. There is no militant wing of Judaism, committed to organizing cadres for a Jewish world takeover, as anti-Semitic imagination has it.[10]

The story of history is pictured rather as a hidden story, for God to see as a whole and to unfold, and for man to enact bit by bit as the divine intent becomes clearer.

That being the Jewish religious frame of reference, any live occurrence of anti-Semitism does not merely strike a raw nerve, evoking its antecedents in the long train of such incidents. It also recharges a profound theological anxiety, from which only the most pious are wholly free, an anxiety on behalf of God's purposes. And for the secularized Jew, for whom God's purposes are quite out of it, it remains a given that justice and mercy *must* be done in human history. To take the extraordinarily long view remains second nature. It is not even necessarily a conscious thing. But an urgent sense of concern for mankind, and—in the same breath and by the same token—concern for or about the Jewish people, gets manifested by the secular Jew in all kinds of ways, big and little. Both concerns have a common, theological essence. What the Holocaust struck at, then, was the system of meaning internal to Jewish culture.

That being the world-historical context, German, non-German non-Jewish, and Jewish, how shall we view the alleged "complicity" of the Jewish people in their own destruction?

Hilberg, perhaps the most articulate and historically careful spokesman for this view, cites a number of evidences of Jewish complicity. They vary in scope and moral gravity. Included are fatalism about the end (pp. 841, 969; these and future page references in this paragraph are from Hilberg's *Destruction of the European Jews*) and mass compliance (e.g., with ghettoization) without actual force having to be used (p. 773). They further include giving administrative assistance to the Germans in supplying lists and other information (pp. 187, 434f), and in manufacture and distribution of such instruments in the isolation of the Jewish people as yellow star armbands (p. 216). They include cooperating, often under armed threat, by self-denigrating words and gestures (pp. 456, 471). They include providing assistance in actual roundups (pp. 460, 463f). They include popular opposition to the armed resistance movement (pp. 385, 500, 503 and note 69, p. 504). They include blindly self-deceived reliance on German information (pp. 459, 696, 1040), and blocked awareness or fatal absence of awareness (pp. 314f, 707). They include decisions by Jewish leaders to withhold information from the rank and file on misguidedly humane grounds (pp. 461, 639). They include sectarian divisions between potential resistance groups (p. 385). Included too are instances of self-aggrandizement of the leadership at the expense of the community (pp. 580, 589) or ready use of class and wealth distinctions to favor the privileged in the struggle for survival (pp. 218, 230, 262f, 439, 448f, 577, 778). Of all the accusations, the most grave concern the activity of Jewish leaders in the Selection of successive detachments of Jews for Nazi deportation to the death camps. That Jews were also put to work in the killing centers, in readying the condemned and stripping the dead, is sometimes mentioned, but less often recently, since it has somehow become common knowledge that actual concentration camp inmates were up against overwhelming force.

Let us take these charges one by one, not of course to assess the conduct of individuals (that would be a case-by-case matter, and a matter either for evidence in a court of law or for the God's-eye view), nor certainly to array on the other side the many well-attested instances of Jewish resistance at every point of the Nazi operation and from every stratum of the community. Our purpose is rather to try to see the *moral* sense of these charges, as they are applied to human behaviors of which a moral assessment is due.

Perhaps my own biases should be stated at this point. My childhood was colored by the knowledge that there was a man across the sea named Hitler, who had got under way a project to "kill us all." If he won the war, he would come over here to our walk-up apartment at Park Avenue and 86th Street, and simply finish the job. Since that outcome was by no means unimaginable in Yorkville, many of my preoccupations were horizoned by the question, "Would we all behave well *when that happened?* Would we go through that furnace *in the right way?* Would we die correctly, as one should, rather than incorrectly, as one shouldn't?" It was a childish conviction with me (the conviction seems subsequently to have been shared by many adults) that one had to behave *correctly* during one's Holocaust. Courage is grace under pressure, and all that.

Our question is, then, what is the right way to act during one's Holocaust? Let us take the wrong ways alleged by Hilberg (or some of them), and consider these one by one. The reader will be the Jew, and I will be, if you please, the philosopher.

Fatalism. You are the Jew, standing somewhere on the map of Europe. A whole people, armed and effective, wants to erase you from history. The surrounding peoples, some of them also armed and effective, having some conscious relation to your place in their history, stand by and they let it happen. Fatalism, under the circumstances, strikes *me* as a form of sanity. A preliminary form, to be sure. But you may not get much beyond the preliminaries. Meantime, to be sane, you must see that this is indeed happening, and not deny it. To understand that it "is" happening is also to understand that it "will" happen. That is, there is precious little you can do to stop it. *Except,* of course, hope and expect that the Allies will at last win the war and, by dint of doing that, take you off the back burner.

Anticipatory Compliance. In the somewhat ritualized struggles between male wolves in a pack, it is sometimes found that baring the throat, or making some other gesture of anticipatory compliance, will deter the victor from moving in for the kill. Analogous gestures of disarming submission are met with in other species. The instincts to make such gestures go very deep. There are few among us who, finding ourselves to be weaker in a natural struggle (e.g., between females and males, children and parents, weaker and stronger schoolmates, subordinates and bosses), have made no gestures of anticipatory compliance.

The more ferociously it seems we are menaced, the more we may hope or reason that it is the aggressor's primitive "needs" or "fears" that must have prompted him to threaten us, and that we ought merely to redouble our efforts to allay those needs and fears. After all (in the Nazi case), the aggressor is not merely moving to tear us apart boisterously and laughingly (though he does that too). Overall, he is moving to tear us apart with moral seriousness, with enraged *accusations.* If we can only prove to him that he need not hate us, or fear us, or absolutely despise us by his own moral lights, perhaps, perhaps, he will desist in time. He will not go the whole distance.

Now, in this kind of judgment there is a mixture of animal instinct and the common sense of the species. It is no more than an extension of the judgments we make for our survival every day. (Hannah Arendt, for example, told me of having been menaced by a young mugger in an elevator. Without a second's hesitation, she told him not to be afraid, just to calm down, that he would get his money. He did, got the money, and decamped forthwith. Her survival instincts, for quick compliance, had been sound and sure, and they worked. When I had asked her, earlier in the conversation, how she personally had managed to understand in time that the Nazis would be resistant to normal human appeals, she cited not her instincts but her *political theorist's* grasp of German culture, her educated realization that the Nazis were an element unlike any other.)

If survival is possible and desired, and escape impossible, then ordinarily this judgment (for anticipatory compliance) is the one to make. Nor is the compliance to be understood as gratuitously "anticipatory." The Nazis made no secret of the disproportionate violence of their reprisals. In these situations they always held hostages. Noncooperativeness was interpreted as active resistance and was punished in the same way, namely, by killing a disproportionate number of other Jews.[11] The *morality* of thus indirectly causing their deaths is unclear to me. A split-second practical judgment, hard to make in an armchair, is what is involved.

Administrative and Executive Support. This has the same basic motive as anticipatory compliance, except that often enough it is given in response to even more direct and credible threats.

Popular Opposition to Armed Resistance. This has the same motive as administrative support and anticipatory compliance.

Self-Deception. As a Jew, you want to live the best life you can, in history, in the human theater. That your values have been so patterned that the reach toward the transcendent is rerouted, as it were, toward immanence, is something of which you may or may not be consciously aware. But that patterning is shared by other members of your culture, across the spectrum from extreme orthodoxy to assimilationist humanism. All of a sudden, important numbers of your fellow actors in the human theater, actors within other cultures but on the same stage, want you out of it. Out of it, with all that was Egypt, and with all that was not Egypt. Out of it, without a footstep left on the sandy floor. This desire, to have you out of it, gives evidence of its existence on many hands—but you persist in deceiving yourself as to the real character of these evidences.

Now it is over. You have survived, although a great many of your fellow Jews did not. You survive, having been, it seems, as horribly hated and as callously neglected or disdained by members of brother cultures as it is possible for a human being to be. You are now told that you should not have deceived yourself about this. You should have known that confiscation of goods and jobs, and residential concentration—the ripping out of phones, the prohibition on talking to Gentiles—all that meant that you would be ripped out of the social organism. You should have known that those were death trains, not bound for resettlement areas. You should have known that those were gas chambers, not showers.

But in fact you *did* know. Not quite consciously, it is charged, you knew. And there is your real moral lapse. That you did not bring it all up to consciousness. That you tampered with your fatalism. That you were therefore in bad faith. By contrast, the killers seem models of psychic transparency. They *knew* what they were about. You alone give an unpleasant opacity to this psychic terrain.

As I was penning these lines, in a museum café, two middle-aged women tried persistently to enter and take seats, having been told by the young manager that the café was closed. They did nevertheless sit down at a table, promising him that they would stay only "two minutes," and that they would order nothing. They sat surrounded by other patrons, who were finishing their cups of coffee and so on at a leisurely pace, while the staff cleaned up. I saw the thwarted young manager pause and then gather himself up for a more concerted try. He strode to the women's table and told them that he was *ordering* them out. Unmoved, they smilingly remonstrated with him. In support of the young manager, other waiters came over. A security guard was summoned and added her point. At last the two women left, to the sounds of mimicry from the staff who, from the look of them, were possibly in the arts. What the two women had not been able to believe was that—in that small, diffuse informal community ruled by the café staff—*they were not wanted.*

For good people, the thing is the more implausible as it becomes more global. Good people have a necessary residuum of optimism that enables them, so to speak, to get their goodness done.

Such a thing is conceivable (always presupposing your goodness) only if you believe, being for example religiously a Hassid, or in secular faith a Bundist, or a Zionist, that, as Elisha said, "they that be with us are more than they that be with them" (2 Kings 6:16). Membership in some such outgunning or outnumbering community, supernatural, international, or national, makes it psychologically possible to see clearly that you are not wanted in another, more restricted or eccentric community.[12]

But imagine that, for one reason or another, you are not able psychologically to postulate your membership in that kind of an outnumbering community. (It must be admitted that, in the 1933–45 case, such membership would have had to have been an article of faith, not an evidence of things seen.) What would follow, from your inability to postulate such membership, would be the admission that all your good works and all your affections would come to nothing, would be kept in no human repository.

It is a central contention of this essay that such an admission is radically incompatible with human goodness.

Self-Aggrandizement, Corruption, Class Privilege. "The world," Léo Bronstein used to say, "prefers a murderer to a petty-petty thief," indicating as he said so the aesthetically plausible but morally abysmal "purity" of the murderer.[13] We should perhaps take some care not to share the world's preference. But here again, the context has to be borne in mind for the purpose of a moral analysis. If what you "buy" with your bribe or payment to the extortionist is sufficient food for your own child, while another child starves, and the *fair* result would be that both children got to be equally malnourished, and you have greater natural affection for your own child than for another's—and there is no actual and coherent army of the beleaguered Jews, allocating strictly equal rations and duties, able to enforce its orders and to deliver release from the present state of nature—why, then the claims of natural affection do have some natural right.

It is to be remembered that the Nazi machinery had already broken up the old organizational lines of traditional Jewry and, more significantly, had broken Jewish communication lines with the outside communities, of other Jews and of non-Jews. (This included communication through participation in the wider work of the world, communication by speaking, writing, telephoning, use of public transportation, and the like.) Concomitantly, "Jewish Councils" were formed at gunpoint. In spirit and purpose, these were not "Jewish" and they were not "councils." They were formed as part of the German destruction process, to distribute the inadequate rations and laughable medical provisions to terrified people, recently rendered jobless and crowded into unfamiliar, often walled-off, concentration areas for Jews. The "Jewish Councils" were also to distribute the work cards that were the tormented community's only means of staving off deportation, and to transmit the orders by which that community could learn what its kidnappers wanted of it. We have gone over the point that at every stage noncooperation was interpreted as active resistance and was met by overwhelming force. In these circumstances, personal corruption was probably a sign of some kind of natural health. The organism was fighting back—not by fair means but by any means available. ("Prisoner's dilemma" reasoning doesn't apply here. All the prisoners were going to be killed whatever they did.)

However, there were paths open to those who wanted to escape personal corruption—and we have looked down some of them.[14] There were the partisan groups, dedicated to a political redemption, and you could join them if you were young or able bodied, and if you had no more family being held hostage. There were also the pious, which only a certain prior acculturation would have placed you among, and for them it was forbidden to save your son's life if the life of another's son would be forfeited in consequence.

Both kinds of self-exemption from corruption were *willed* departures from a real and prevailing state of nature, in the light of an unseen "world to come." But even if you were in a position to make such metaphysical wagers, they could not be made at every juncture. If a crust of stolen bread came into your palm, presumably you would want to share it with your best buddy, not crumb it into equal bits for the whole barracks.[15] And given the metaphysical wager, on the coming classless society, or Zion, or God, there could not be Kantian fairness in getting there. If the biological *genos* in whatever future form it would take needed the young and the able, and if God needed whoever best served His Providential purposes, then, even from a standpoint of the "world to come," there was favoritism. There was a selection.

It is not clear to me that the moment-to-moment selection that natural affection performs in favor of those whom it loves is *morally* worse.

Selection. The gravest of the accusations leveled against the so-called Jewish Councils is that, at German gunpoint, they made the actual selections of those who were to be deported from the slower death of the German-made ghettos to the quicker death of the killing centers. Acting in this way, some of them saved some of their own relatives; some saved some of those who were already privileged; some saved groups they thought politically more vital; some saved, or tried to save, some of the children; some (but by no means all) saved themselves. Many who participated in the Selections withheld from the deportees the information or educated guesses they possessed as to what "resettlement in the East" really meant.

It seems to me that the moral objections taken here fail fully to picture the nature and scale of this emergency. Rabbinic casuistry was not unfamiliar with the situation of a whole community taken hostage. The traditional rulings had been to the effect that a *guilty* fugitive may be surrendered by such a community if he is demanded by name (thus absolving the community of the moral taint of making a selection among the innocents). In a still more extreme case, even an innocent fugitive who is named may be surrendered if, failing to surrender him, his death and the community's would otherwise be certain. But if there is any doubt as to the fatality of the outcome, or it is demanded of the community that it make a selection among innocents, then, the rabbis ruled, the whole community must rather perish.[16]

Now let us alter the picture that the rabbis had in view. We no longer have one town, say third-century Lydda threatened by the Romans, or a twelfth-century legally imposed "Jewish Quarter" in the Maghreb, threatened by the dominant Arabs. Without needing to suppose that every "Jewish Council" member participating in a Selection saw clearly the scope of the German program, it will be admitted that what could be seen was, in its thoroughness, rapacity, and brutal orderliness, like nothing that had ever been seen or heard of before. If the "Jewish Council" member was not thinking, "they are going to kill us all," he was at least trying hard *not* to think that.

What were his options? He could save his own honor—but only by suicide. Noncooperation would bring down the full force of the Holocaust on his family and neighbors forthwith. Suicide is honorable—for a Stoic. But it is not usually honorable in Jewish religious thought. It is not even religiously honorable for one individual to offer his life for another single individual, since each person's life is considered to be his on trust, not a personal possession to be disposed of at will. God is not considered to allow any individual to decide that his own life is less valuable than another's.[17]

In sum, the honor that is saved by suicide is pagan honor, not honor as it is understood in the system of meaning internal to Jewish culture. Furthermore, as witness after witness testified in the Eichmann trial, as memoirists and historians have alike recorded, survival was felt to be an obligation in that realm of the Jewish psyche where history and the supernatural "world to come" are indistinguishable. It was felt to be an obligation in the Kantian sense. It overrode personal inclination. The duty was twofold: to preserve some remnant of the biological *genos* considered as a divine vehicle, and to preserve the memory, incorporating the latter into human memory itself, also considered as a divine vehicle.[18]

Now, considering that no escape routes were provided, that the program of liquidation was encompassing and relentless, *it was clear that survival would be an accident.* Whoever could survive, however he could, had however a twofold obligation to do so. He was not to live, in the collapse of his affections and his hopes, because it felt good. He was not to keep a diary, keep his memories intact, be prepared to tell and retell the story, because it was a great pleasure to do so. Rather, he was to do all that because it was the only appropriate rejoinder to a program of erasing his *genos* from what *both he and his liquidators* understood to be world history. (It cannot be said that the Nazis ignored the big picture. It cannot be said that the Jews were, by acculturated temperament, indifferent to it.)

If I am still, according to our earlier literary conceit, the philosopher, and the reader is still the Jew, the reader might at this point want to ask me, indignantly, "Are you recommending that we take part in a *Selection?*" I am not recommending anything, since my recommendations would presuppose that you have been placed, ethically, culturally, and physically, in a genocidal situation. But, if you are put in a genocidal situation, genocidal without remainder, which heaven forfend, then yes, I am recommending that you take part in Selections. It may be that not everyone selected will actually be killed. Some may be used for slave labor and will somehow survive the war. It may be that not everyone whose Selection is thus postponed will eventually be rounded up and deported. It may be that some will outlast the Final

Solution, one way or another. What is virtually certain is that your whole community will be machine-gunned to death in your hundreds of thousands tomorrow morning if you do not "voluntarily" participate. Your neighbors will look on. There are no forests, or, if there are forests, the young who morally *can* get there—perhaps because they have no more families to suffer reprisals—will in large numbers be killed anyway, as a result of peasant informers, or by the bullets of non-Jewish partisans. And your old and your infants cannot make their way to forests. To cooperate in Selections, is—for the *genos* as a whole—to stall. Yes, cooperate. Yes, stall. Do what they tell you. Whoever survives, will survive by accident.

There are those who study Zen Buddhism in order to learn how, appropriately, to peel a potato, or how, appropriately, to succor the homeless. There is also a minutely appropriate way to undergo one's Holocaust. The appropriate way is to survive it, or to try to.

We are of course not trying to find out about the Holocaust victims, or about any other group of people similarly picked up at random (that is to say, picked up without regard to their wishes), how many were sinners, how many saints, how many heroes, sung and unsung, and how all that interesting stuff is to be measured. We were simply trying to figure out whether, in any sense that is morally intelligible, these victims of genocide were in actual complicity with it. We have not found that they were. If our analysis is correct, then it will be possible in this context to draw the moral lines, between those who have done evil and those who have suffered it, without undue ambiguity.

NOTES

1. Hannah Arendt's point 1 about the banality of evil in the Nazi, and her point 3 partly delegitimating that trial and other such trials, are discussed at length in my *A Good Look at Evil* (Philadelphia: Temple University Press, 1987), Chap. 6, "Banality and Originality," from which this article is adapted. Note, however, that when evil is redefined as "banal," it does not necessarily retain all its usefulness as a moral category. Likewise, only if the trials are legitimate can that moral discourse *proceed* to which the trials have supplied the attested evidence. A foundation of fact, properly come by, must be supplied first. Then one can moralize.

2. Hannah Arendt, *Eichmann in Jerusalem: A Report on the Banality of Evil* (New York: Viking, 1964), p. 282.

3. Raul Hilberg, *The Destruction of the European Jews*, 3 vols. (New York: Holmes and Meier, 1985), pp. 993–1007.

4. Ibid., pp. 1006f.

5. Ibid., pp. 947–61.

6. Mrs. Rosa Goldstein of the International Auschwitz Committee, Brussels, to the author, January 29, 1986. The exhibition, "Auschwitz—A Crime against Mankind," was organized by the International Auschwitz Committee together with the Auschwitz State Museum in Poland.

7. David S. Wyman, *The Abandonment of the Jews: America and the Holocaust, 1941–1945* (New York: Pantheon, 1984), pp. 338ff.

8. Hilberg, *Destruction,* pp. 558–68.

9. See Michael Wyschogrod, *The Body of Faith: Judaism as Corporeal Election* (New York: Seabury, 1983), p. 68.

10. This should go without saying, and would have, had I not noticed that there were more catalogue entries for *The Protocols of the Elders of Zion* in the New York Public Library, in more languages, than for any other text that I came across.

11. For an example of the actual cost to the uninvolved of other people's resistance, see Lucy S. Dawidowicz, *The War against the Jews 1933–1945* (New York: Holt, Rinehart & Winston, 1975), p. 328. For an example of the threatened cost of noncooperation, see pp. 282ff. That such threats were incessantly carried out was made clear by eyewitness after eyewitness at the Eichmann trial. The line between active resistance and passive noncooperation was not respected by the Nazis, despite Arendt's contrary suggestion that Jews should have acted as if it would be; *Eichmann in Jerusalem*, p. 124.

12. See Dawidowicz, *War against the Jews,* chaps. 12 and 13.

13. Quoted in the author's preface to Léo Bronstein, *Kabbalah and Art* (Hanover, N.H.: Brandeis University Press and University Press of New England, 1980).

14. The political paths are explored in chap. 6 of my *A Good Look at Evil,* under the subhead "Sectarian Divisions," where another of Hilberg's charges is reexamined.

15. Cf. Primo Levi, "Last Christmas of the War," *New York Review of Books* 33, no. 1 (January 30, 1986): 5f.

16. See Robert Kirschner, ed. and trans., *Rabbinic Responsa of the Holocaust Era* (New York: Schocken, 1985), pp. 76ff.; and Dawidowicz, *War against the Jews,* pp. 284f.

17. See Kirschner, *Rabbinic Responsa,* pp. 119ff.; and Adin Steinsaltz, *The Essential Talmud,* trans. Chaya Galai (New York: Basic Books, 1976), pp. 203f.

18. "In December 1941, when the German police entered the Riga ghetto to round up the old and sick Jews, Simon Dubnow, the venerable Jewish historian, was said to have called out as he was being taken away: 'Brothers, write down everything you see and hear. Keep a record of it all.'" Lucy S. Dawidowicz, *The Holocaust and the Historians* (Cambridge, Mass.: Harvard University Press, 1981), p. 125. Cf. the testimony of Avraham Aviel, about his thoughts prior to a mass shooting: "Q. What did mother say?" "A. She said, 'Say Shamah Yisrael—die as Jews.' . . . I repeated the words after her but I had inner resistance. . . . Because my thoughts—my thought was always: 'One must survive—*überleben*— . . . and tell what happened.'" Eichmann Trial, *Israel v. Eichmann: The Attorney-General of the Government of Israel v. Adolf, the Son of Adolf Karl Eichmann,* Criminal Case no. 40/61, District Court, Jerusalem (Washington, D.C.: Microcard Editions, 1962), session 29.

8

ON LOSING TRUST IN
THE WORLD

John K. Roth

Jean Améry, lone child of a Catholic mother and a Jewish father, was born in Vienna on October 31, 1912. He fled Nazism by going to Belgium in 1938. There he later joined the Resistance. Captured by the Gestapo in 1943, he was sent to a series of concentration camps, including Auschwitz. Liberated from Bergen-Belsen in 1945, Améry went on to write a series of remarkable essays about his Holocaust experiences. One of them is simply titled "Torture." It drove Améry to the following observation: "The expectation of help, the certainty of help, is indeed one of the fundamental experiences of human beings. . . ." But the gravest loss produced by the Holocaust, he suggested, was that it radically undermined that "element of trust in the world, . . . the certainty that by reason of written or unwritten social contracts the other person will spare me—more precisely stated, that he will respect my physical, and with it also my metaphysical, being."[1] Jean Améry took his own life on October 17, 1978. That fact, along with a host of other particularities generated by the Holocaust, compels one to assess what losing trust in the world can mean.

In the spring of 1942, while Améry resisted Nazism, SS officer Ernst Biberstein went east. He had already been involved in deporting Jews to killing centers, but his new assignment would take him from an administrative post into the field to relieve an officer in *Einsatzgruppe* C. One of four Nazi squadrons charged with eliminating Jews behind the lines of the German advance into Russia, *Einsatzgruppe* C policed the Ukraine. Among its credits was the murder of more than 33,000 Jews at Babi Yar the previous September, a task accomplished in only two days. Biberstein missed Babi Yar, but he did nothing to diminish the record of his unit once he assumed command. It was unnecessary to deport thousands of Jews because Biberstein and his men worked efficiently. This Nazi, however, was not bloodthirsty. No evidence shows that he actively sought to lead a crew of killers or that he relished the operations carried out by those under his command. His is only one example within a spectrum of activity that included not only direct participation in murder but also the many sorts of complicity required to make a process of destruction happen. And yet when we think about losing trust in the world, Biberstein's case makes us wonder. It does so because, prior to his joining the SS in 1936, Biberstein had been a Protestant pastor.

As Biberstein moved from killing by administrative decision to killing by ordering executioners to fire machine guns, a young German soldier reached Munich, following orders that transferred him to the university there for training as a medic. Earlier, his letters alluded to events that had shaken him to the core. "I can't begin to give you the details," he wrote, "it is simply unthinkable that such things exist. . . . The war here in the East leads to things so terrible I would never have thought them possible."[2] Willi Graf referred not to combat against Russian troops but to slaughter by the *Einsatzgruppen*.

In Munich two of Graf's closest friends were Hans and Sophie Scholl, both in their early twenties. Motivated by an understanding of Christianity and a love for Germany that were at odds with Hitler's, the Scholls were determined to do more than ask helplessly, "What can we do?" With Hans in charge, their public dissent began. Although they possessed abundant courage, ingenuity, and high ideals, their power was scant. Nonetheless, along with their philosophy professor, Kurt Huber, fifty-one, and fellow students Alex Schmorell, Christoph Probst, and Willi Graf, leaflets from their resistance movement, The White Rose, attacked Nazism.

German resistance to Hitler remained scattered. It did not land many telling blows, as the Scholls' effort seems to demonstrate. Their group operated for less than a year, its output restricted to several thousand copies of seven different flyers. The war and the death camps churned on for more than two years after the White Rose was crushed. The results seem paltry, but a second glance is in order. The war was still in Hitler's favor when the students' protest began in 1942. By the time the Scholls were caught, that tide had turned at Stalingrad. The White Rose could assume no credit for this reversal, but the Nazis did take its activity seriously, all the more so as Hitler's war plans began to collapse. Nazi justice proceeded quickly. On February 22, 1943, only four days after their arrest, the Scholls and Christoph Probst stood trial. Eight hours later they were beheaded. Again the question, What can anyone do? comes to mind. Sophie Scholl's testimony, documented by the court that convicted her, was that "somebody, after all, had to make a start."[3]

The lives of Jean Améry, Ernst Biberstein, and Hans and Sophie

Scholl unfolded in the midst of modernized economic systems, technological capabilities, and political structures that have produced abundant blessings but also surplus people, unique forms of human domination, and unprecedented quantities of mass murder. As the Holocaust exemplified, the modern political state may not flinch from putting its apparatus of destruction into action. If a ruling elite retains control over this overwhelming power, the more ordinary man or woman seems to fall impotently before it.

The truth about the Holocaust cannot be approached unless one grasps the fact that twentieth-century states may progressively squeeze the individual into obedience devoid of dissent. As people become aware of this reality, however, they are tempted to put the Holocaust into a deterministic framework. What happened seems inescapable, individual responsibility recedes, and, as a consequence, trust in the world suffers. Such a deterministic outlook is as dangerous as it is easy, for it is the stuff of which indifference is made. The truth about the Holocaust cannot be taught unless indifference is resisted, and thus the importance of remembering that, from time to time, courageous resistance did save lives and prevent the Nazis from doing their worst. Many Jews resisted. Some Gentiles did, too, including a few from deep within the German system itself. If Jewish losses did not exceed two-thirds of European Jewry and one-third of the Jewish people worldwide, the credit does not belong entirely to Allied military might. Persons acting as individuals or within small groups made their contributions as well.

The immensity of the Holocaust becomes too impersonal and more inevitable than it really was if one overlooks the fact that individuals did make the decisions and obey the orders that destroyed millions. To drive home that lesson is one of the most important philosophical insights to derive from the Holocaust. By exploring realistically, moreover, what people did or could have done in the midst of the destruction process, perhaps we can glimpse ways to redeem at least some fragments of the trust in the world that the Holocaust destroyed. Consider, therefore, the question put to an imprisoned Franz Stangl, formerly the commandant of Sobibor and Treblinka, on June 27, 1971, by the journalist Gitta Sereny. "Do you think," she asked near the end of a long series of interviews, "that that time in Poland taught you anything?"[4] To be more specific, it is crucial to ask, Could Franz Stangl have left the path that took him to Treblinka where he occupied a middle-management position requiring him to see that others carried out the murderous responsibilities handed to him? And if he could have done so, would it have made any difference if he had?

Simon Wiesenthal, the famed Nazi hunter, was once quoted as

saying that "if I had done nothing else in life but to get this evil man Stangl, then I would not have lived in vain" (p. 351; page references in this and the following paragraph are to Sereny's *Into That Darkness*). At the time, Stangl was on trial in Düsseldorf, Germany, having been extradited from Brazil, where on February 28, 1967, he was arrested in Brooklin, one of the better residential areas of São Paulo. Although Stangl had never flaunted his past, neither was he in hiding. In 1945 American authorities knew about his activity at Treblinka, but Stangl fled to Rome. Assisted by clergy in the Vatican, he obtained a Red Cross passport—it reversed his name from Franz P. to Paul F. Stangl—and then moved on to Damascus, following a route used before and since by his SS peers. Before long he sent for his wife and children, who traveled under their own names and told the Austrian police of their destination. In 1954 the Stangls openly entered Brazil, registering at the Austrian consulate in São Paulo. Eventually employed by Volkswagen, Stangl had made a new beginning.

Although the surprise was less that Stangl had been found than that he had ever been lost, his court appearance brought the darkness of his past to light. On December 22, 1970, he was sentenced by a West German court to life imprisonment. Early in April of the next year, Gitta Sereny met him for the first time. This meeting occurred because Sereny, who had covered Stangl's trial, became convinced that he was "an individual of some intelligence" and that "things had happened to and inside him which had happened to hardly anyone else, ever" (pp. 13, 23). Stangl used the initial interview to rebut accusations made against him, but Sereny was after something more, "some new truth which would contribute to the understanding of things that had never yet been understood" (p. 23). She encouraged Stangl to provide it, promising "to write down exactly what he said, whatever it would be, and that I would try—my own feelings notwithstanding—to understand without prejudice" (pp. 23–24).

After deliberating, Stangl agreed. In fits and starts the layers of his life unfolded in the seventy hours of conversation held in April and June 1971. First published in the *Daily Telegraph Magazine*, these dialogues were later elaborated into book form. In addition to keeping her promise to Stangl, Sereny provides an account more valuable than Rudolf Hoess's autobiographical description of his career as the commandant of Auschwitz.[5] For Sereny went on to interview Stangl's family, many of his associates, and other Holocaust authorities in compiling her narrative. Even after all of the cross-checking, elements of the Stangl story remain open to conjecture, but Sereny's work has the advantage of multiple dimensions missing in Hoess's confession.

Born in 1908 in the small Austrian town of Altmünster, Stangl claimed that he was "scared to death" of his father, a former soldier, who died of malnutrition when his son was eight.[6] Leaving school at fifteen to become an apprentice weaver, he was good at the work and soon supervised others. Music and sailing were his diversions. Looking back, Stangl called these years "my happiest time." In the Austria of the 1930s, however, the young man saw that a lack of higher education would prevent him from further promotions in the textile field. Police work attracted him as an alternative, particularly since it might enable him to assist in checking the turbulence that economic depression had brought to his country. He passed the required entrance examination in 1931 and was notified to report to the Linz barracks for training. Upon announcing his departure, Stangl learned that his textile employer had been planning to send him to Vienna for additional schooling. When Sereny asked whether he still could have seized that opportunity, Stangl responded that his boss "didn't ask me" (pp. 27, 28; page references here and in the following ten paragraphs are to Sereny's *Into That Darkness*).

Stangl's account frequently reveals his passivity, a sense of being conscripted into circumstances beyond his control. A case in point is his early affiliation with the Nazis. It remains unclear whether Stangl was an illegal Nazi in Austria prior to the *Anschluss* (March 1938), but he offered the following story. As a young police officer he was decorated for meritorious service, including special recognition for seizing a Nazi arms cache shortly after Engelbert Dollfuss, the Austrian chancellor, was assassinated in July 1934. That achievement would plague Stangl, but the immediate result was his posting to Wels as a political investigator "to ferret out anti-government activities" (p. 29). Stangl, now married, claims to have had no Nazi sympathies at this time, but in 1938 his situation changed. Early on the National Socialists purged the Austrian police. Among the first victims were three of Stangl's colleagues who had received the same decoration that had come to him for his raid against the Nazis some years before. Out of fear, Stangl told Sereny, he arranged for a friend to enter his name on a list that would certify his having been a Nazi party member for the previous two years.

According to Stangl, the die was cast: "It wasn't a matter of choosing to stay or not stay in our profession. What it had already become, so quickly, was a question of survival" (p. 35). Thus, Stangl remained in police work after his branch was absorbed into the Gestapo in January 1939. Over his wife's objections, he also signed the standard statement that identified him as a *Gottgläubiger*, a believer in God, but severed his ties with the Roman Catholic church. The next decisive step on the path to Treblinka came in November 1940 when Stangl was ordered to Berlin.

These orders, signed by Heinrich Himmler, transferred Stangl to the General Foundation for Institutional Care (Gemeinnützige Stiftung für Heil und Anstaltspflege). This foundation, one unit in the larger network code-named T-4 because its headquarters were at Tiergartenstrasse 4, helped to administer T-4's program of "mercy killing" of the mentally and physically handicapped in Germany and Austria. Stangl was to be a leading security officer in this secret operation. He reports that the assignment was presented to him as a choice, though prudence ruled out the alternatives. Thus, when Stangl returned to Austria, his new post was at a euthanasia center not far from Linz, Schloss Hartheim, which later on would kill Jews from the concentration camp nearby at Mauthausen.

The activities of T-4 were under Hitler's personal control. Moreover, the euthanasia project, which used carbon monoxide gas, had the blessing of influential German scientists and physicians. It lasted many months and claimed some 100,000 lives. Public protest led by prominent German Christians helped stall this death machine in August 1941, but by then the project's goals were virtually achieved. The euthanasia program was probably not consciously devised as a training ground for staff to carry out the Final Solution, but it cannot be sheer coincidence that personnel from Schloss Hartheim and other centers regrouped in Poland to officiate at the death camps. In February 1942, for example, T-4 offered Franz Stangl a new choice: Either report back to Linz, where he would be subject to a superior whom he feared, or take a position in the East near Lublin. This "either or" was no accident either. The Berlin officials were confident that Stangl would choose Poland, and he did. Soon after arriving there, he learned that his commanding officer, SS General Odilo Globocnik, "intended confiding to me the construction of a camp called Sobibor" (p. 103).

Nazi objectives called for much of western Poland to be incorporated into the Reich. Jews from that area would be deported to the Polish interior, an area referred to as the *Generalgouvernement*, where they would be ghettoized with countless other Jews from this region and eventually exterminated. In the *Generalgouvernement*, Globocnik, assisted by Christian Wirth and a team of T-4's euthanasia experts under Wirth's direction, had overall command of "Operation Reinhard," named for its mastermind, Reinhard Heydrich, who had been assassinated in the spring of 1942 by Czech patriots.

The pure death camps opened by Globocnik in the *Generalgouvernement* during 1942—Belzec (March), Sobibor (May), and Treblinka

(July)—were in administrative channels that led directly to Hitler's chancellery. In contrast, Auschwitz and Maidanek, the latter also in this zone, remained under the authority of the Main Office of Economic Administration (WVHA, Wirtschaft-Verwaltungshauptamt) because they were labor installations as well. Himmler often sought to intensify the zeal of his underlings through competition, and thus he had given Hoess sole charge of Auschwitz. Rivalry ensued, but if Globocnik, Wirth, and their associates finished second to Hoess as architects of mass death, they certainly were not failures. Before Belzec, Sobibor and Treblinka were shut down less than two years later, they destroyed nearly two million Jews and thousands of Gypsies, children making up one-third of the total. Sereny reports that the survivors of these camps—"work-Jews" who had to help run them—numbered under one hundred.

Stangl claims not to have known at first the purpose of his construction project at Sobibor, but ignorance vanished when he was taken to Belzec to witness the first large-scale extermination with permanent chambers using exhaust gas. He learned that Sobibor would do likewise and that he would be in charge. Back at Sobibor, Stangl discussed the options with a friend: "We agreed that what they were doing was a crime. We considered deserting—we discussed it for a long time. But how? Where could we go? What about our families?" (p. 113). Stangl applied for a transfer. He got no reply, but in June he did receive a letter from his wife. She wrote that his superiors were arranging for her to bring the Stangl children to Poland for a visit.

Sobibor opened in mid-May 1942 and operated for two months. Then the equipment malfunctioned, and exterminations ceased until October. Meanwhile the Stangl family arrived, lodging at an estate about three miles from the camp. Heretofore Stangl had kept his wife in the dark about the particulars of his work at Schloss Hartheim and in Poland. Now she learned the truth about Sobibor from one of her husband's subordinates. Apparently the possibility of an open confrontation that might lead to his wife's rejection of him was more than Stangl could risk. He not only told her that he had no direct responsibility for any killing but also arranged a speedy departure for his family. By the time they were back home in Austria, Stangl had been transferred to Treblinka.

Franciszek Zabecki, one of the persons interviewed by Gitta Sereny, was a member of the Polish underground. As traffic supervisor at the Treblinka railway station, he tracked German military movements and also became "the only trained observer to be on the spot throughout the whole existence of Treblinka camp" (p. 149). Zabecki counted the extermination transports, recording the figures marked on each car.

"The number of people killed in Treblinka was 1,200,000," he testifies, "and there is no doubt about it whatever" (p. 250).

Dr. Irmfried Eberle, formerly in charge of a euthanasia center at Bernburg near Hanover, was the builder and first commandant of Treblinka. His administration had been wanting in Globocnik's eyes, and thus Stangl replaced him, describing his arrival there as an entry into Dante's Inferno. Stangl rationalized that his major assignment was to care for the riches left behind by those on their way to the gas. "There were enormous—fantastic—sums involved and everybody wanted a piece of it, and everybody wanted control" (p. 162). Indeed, Stangl argued, the main reason for the extermination of the Jews was that the Nazis were after their money. At least one Jewish survivor, Alexander Donat, does not disagree completely. He credits Stangl with being "sober enough to realize that behind the smokescreen of propaganda and racist mystique there was no sacred mission but only naked greed."[7] In any case, Stangl tried to convince himself that his involvement was limited to handling Treblinka's windfall. Actually he headed the entire extermination process, which destroyed five to six thousand Jews per day. The system worked, says Stangl, "and because it worked, it was irreversible." With unintended irony, he reiterates that his work was "a matter of survival—always of survival." "One did become used to it," he adds.[8]

Stangl made "improvements" at Treblinka, among them a fake railroad station to deceive the arriving victims. It was unveiled at Christmas 1942. Meanwhile Stangl was in Austria on furlough. He obtained such leaves every three or four months, but relations with his wife were strained throughout his time at Treblinka. The gassing and burning continued under Stangl's administration during the first half of 1943. However, on August 2, a Monday, which usually was a light working day because transports were less frequently loaded on Sundays, Treblinka's death machine temporarily jammed when a long-planned revolt broke out among the Jewish workers. Although the camp was set ablaze, the gas chambers remained intact. Transports from Bialystok would still end there, the last one arriving on August 19. Thereafter the camp itself was liquidated, disguised with plantings and a small farm "built from the bricks of the dismantled gas chambers" (p. 249; page references here and in the following six paragraphs are to Sereny's *Into That Darkness*). Stangl was reassigned to Trieste.

That same Christmas of 1942, Stangl had become fully assimilated into the SS, and at the war's end his SS uniform led to his arrest by Americans in an Austrian village on the Attersee. Two years later, as Austrian officials investigated Schloss Hartheim's euthanasia campaign, Stangl came to their attention. They requested jurisdiction, which was granted. Interned in an "open" prison at Linz, Stangl walked away as the Hartheim trial proceeded. Twenty years passed before he was brought to justice.

In conversation with Sereny, Stangl never stopped implying that he was himself a victim of the Holocaust. He reckoned that he was caught in a web from which he could not escape. And yet his excuses were less than ironclad, even in his own eyes. Responding to Sereny's question, "Do you think that that time in Poland taught you anything?" Stangl's final words included these: "Yes, that everything human has its origin in human weakness" (p. 363). Not twenty-four hours later, Franz Stangl died of heart failure.

Could anything have strengthened Stangl's heart enough to divert him from the course he took? That issue forms the climax of *Into That Darkness*, and at this point, surprisingly, not Franz but Theresa Stangl takes center stage. In October 1971, Sereny ended her last conversation with Frau Stangl by inquiring:

> Would you tell me what you think would have happened if at any time you had faced your husband with an absolute choice; if you had said to him: "Here it is; I know it's terribly dangerous, but either you get out of this terrible thing, or else the children and I will leave you." What I would like to know is: if you had confronted him with these alternatives, which do you think he would have chosen?

Theresa Stangl contemplated that painful question for a long time. At last she expressed the belief that given the choice—Treblinka or his wife—her husband "would in the final analysis have chosen me" (p. 361).

The next day Sereny received a note from Frau Stangl qualifying her previous statement. Franz Stangl, wrote his wife, "would never have destroyed himself or the family" (p. 362). Sereny, however, believes that the first appraisal contains the greater truth, no matter how difficult it may have been for Frau Stangl to accept it. If Sereny is correct, the web of responsibility, and of human frailty, too, spreads out. Yet one also must ask a second question, Would resistance really have made any difference? Franz Stangl, for one, had his doubts. Quizzed about what might have happened if he had refused his orders, Stangl replied: "If I had sacrificed myself, if I had made public what I felt, and had died . . . it would have made no difference. Not an iota. It would all have gone on just the same, as if it and I had never happened." Sereny accepted the answer but pressed on to ask whether such action might at least have given courage to others. "Not even that," insisted Stangl. "It would have caused a tiny ripple, for a fraction of an instant—that's all" (pp. 231–32).

Such testimony cannot be discounted. Fear and insecurity are never easily dislodged, and even if every SS man had shared Stangl's professed ambivalence about the Final Solution, an isolated defection from the ranks would hardly have halted the destruction process. Those truths, however, detract nothing from others that should be stressed as well. First, Sobibor and Treblinka testify that Stangl's despair, however realistic, does not deserve to be the last word. Second, those death camps, as Theresa Stangl helps to show, also signify that such despair moves closer to self-perpetuation whenever people, especially those nearest and dearest to each other, fail to help one another oppose the weakness that enables those in power to consign defenseless victims to misery and death. Third, had more individuals done for each other what was very much within their power, namely, to call each other to account for their actions, the Holocaust need not have gone on just the same. We are and must be responsible for each other as well as for ourselves. We must be born again as men and women blessed with the capacity to confront each other and care for each other here and now. If those points are obvious, they are anything but trivial. Not to underscore them is to create a silence in which personal responsibility can be too easily shirked and in which helpless people can be too easily found redundant and killed.

Gitta Sereny's encounters with Franz Stangl drove home to her "the fatal interdependence of all human actions" (p. 15). If those actions are to forestall progress that culminates tragically in a paralyzing doom, Theresa Stangl must be taken no less seriously than her husband, his superiors, and their obedient underlings. To discern what she and other individuals, ordinary ones like ourselves, could and could not do, including the ways in which her voice dissolves sanguine illusions about the costs of resistance, contains vital lessons about trust to be learned from that time in Poland.

On October 9, 1974, some three years after Franz Stangl's heart finally failed in a German prison, advanced hardening of the arteries felled a person who played a Holocaust role quite different from the Treblinka commandant's. Black marketeer and bon vivant, Oskar Schindler had a "life of the party" style that frequently made him an unfaithful husband.[9] By some moral conventions, Stangl was a better man than this tall, blond Czech–German who pursued his fortune in the Polish city of Kraków in 1939. Before the war, Schindler joined the Sudeten German party. Wearing its swastika lapel pin proved good for business. Hence, this industrial speculator followed the Wehrmacht into Poland and took over an expropriated enamelware factory. Soon he realized handsome returns by using Jewish labor, which cost him practically nothing—at first. That qualification, however, spells the difference between Schindler's remaining a pleasure-seeking profiteer and his becoming an individual whose personal initiative saved more than a thousand Jews from annihilation.

The tyranny that followed Hitler's seizure of Bohemia and Moravia in March 1939 both surprised and disillusioned Schindler but not completely. Indeed, Schindler would go on to lend his services to Admiral Wilhem Canaris's *Abwehr* (the foreign and counterintelligence department of the German High Command). What decisively changed Schindler's mind was the violence he witnessed as special squads recruited from Heydrich's *Sicherheitsdienst* began to attack Kraków's Jews. Insofar as those tactics targeted productive laborers, Schindler found them utterly counterproductive to the war effort. More than that, this wasting of human life struck him as profoundly morally wrong. Deciding that he could intercede from within the German system itself, Schindler negotiated a daring series of bargains. If his initial purpose was to keep healthy the labor he needed to sustain his factory's productivity, before the war ended Schindler's obsession was more fundamental. He was determined that the hundreds of workers in his care would survive and have a future.

Schindler kept a list. It contained the names of some 1,300 men and women who came to call themselves *Schindlerjuden*. As liberation approached in the spring of 1945, Schindler promised he would "continue doing everything I can for you until five minutes past midnight."[10] His promise was good, just as his word had been for years. During that time in Poland, when his Jewish workers had been forced to live in a slave labor camp under the sadistic Amon Goeth, Schindler spent a fortune in bribes to set up his own subcamp haven at the factory. With the dedicated help of his wife, Emily, that practice continued when Schindler had to relocate his factory in Czechoslovakia as the Red Army advanced. Schindler's efforts even plucked from Auschwitz some of those whose names were written in his list of life.

With the war's end, Oskar and Emily Schindler were refugees. They had lost everything, except that they were not forgotten by the *Schindlerjuden*. Under the leadership of Leopold and Mila Pfefferberg, they rallied to help him when their own recovery permitted. Among many other kindnesses, they saw that Schindler's last wish, a Jerusalem burial, was granted. Today in Jerusalem a tree at Yad Vashem, the Israeli memorial to the Holocaust, grows in honor of Oskar Schindler. It testifies that he took to heart the Talmudic verse he heard in Kraków in 1939 from Yitzhak Stern, a Jewish accountant: "He who saves the life of one man saves the entire world." Even now, however, the *Schindlerjuden* do not know exactly why Oskar Schindler performed his lifesaving missions.

Hoping to revive at least some of the trust that Jean Améry lost, there are social scientists who are trying to determine why people like Schindler helped the defenseless while so many others did not.[11] Just as it is clear that very few of the rescuers regard themselves as moral heroes, it may be that an "altruistic personality" will emerge from these Holocaust studies. Whatever we can learn on that score is important. As another Jewish survivor, Pierre Sauvage, aptly puts the point:

> If we do not learn how it is possible to act well even under the most trying circumstances, we will increasingly doubt our ability to act well even under less trying ones. If we remember solely the horror of the Holocaust, we will pass on no perspective from which meaningfully to confront and learn from that very horror. If we remember solely the horror of the Holocaust, it is we who will bear the responsibility for having created the most dangerous alibi of all: that it was beyond man's capacity to know and care. If Jews do not learn that the whole world did not stand idly by while we were slaughtered, we will undermine our ability to develop the friendships and alliances that we need and deserve. If Christians do not learn that even then there were practicing Christians, they will be deprived of inspiring and essential examples of the nature and requirements of their faith. If the hard and fast evidence of the possibility of good on earth is allowed to slip through our fingers and turn into dust, then future generations will have only dust to build on. If hope is allowed to seem an unrealistic response to the world, if we do not work towards developing confidence in our spiritual resources, we will be responsible for producing in due time a world devoid of humanity—literally.[12]

If we neither deny our century's wounds nor submit meekly to the Holocaust scars that deface humankind, perhaps we can have more than dust to build on. The mending of trust in the world depends on the determination to resist the world's horror with undeceived lucidity. Few have done as well on that score as the winner of the 1986 Nobel Peace Prize, Holocaust survivor Elie Wiesel. Speaking of the Holocaust, Wiesel says, "I'm afraid that the horror of that period is so dark, people are incapable of understanding, incapable of listening."[13] And yet Wiesel's work, including his thirty books, testifies that he does not despair. Hatred, indifference, even history itself, may do their worst, but that outcome does not deserve to be the final word. Such themes permeate Wiesel's writings. In his recent novel, *The Fifth Son*, which he dedicates to his son Elisha, "and all the other children of survivors," those themes take on nuances of special significance for all students and teachers who try to listen and understand more than forty years after Auschwitz.

The story introduces us to Wolfgang Berger, but that is not his name. He should be dead; yet he lives. This man, who is actually Richard Lander, dwells in Reshastadt, a German town. His real home, the place where he became the *Angel*, is farther east. Its name has been Davarowsk as long as anyone can remember. But Davarowsk is not the same place now that it was before. No place is. Nor is any person, whether he knows it or not. *The Fifth Son* shows as much by exploring "an ontological Event" that cannot be reduced to a word: the Holocaust.[14]

Ariel is the fifth son. But who is Ariel? That question makes him wonder. It makes him suffer, too, and not least because the dilemma drives him toward Reshastadt where he intends to be "the bearer of a message." Although Richard Lander is "not aware of either message or messenger," the *Angel* must reverse his customary role and receive both. Whether either reaches him remains unclear. Still, no reader of this novel is likely to be unmoved by Ariel's testimony.

"Was it dawn or dusk? The town of Reshastadt appears crouched and unreal under a steady slow drizzle. . . . Here is the station. In my confusion, I did not know whether I had just arrived or was preparing to leave again. Was I awake?" (p. 13; page references here and in the following paragraphs are to Wiesel's *The Fifth Son*). Linked stylistically to the work of Borges, Camus, and Kafka, this book creates intense personal encounters. Past, present, and future collide within them as the characters interrogate appearance and reality to see what sense life makes during and after the Final Solution. The resulting art—complex and simple at once—transmutes despair into determination by converting revenge into renewal.

At the outset, the author reminds us of the Torah tradition that refers to "four sons: one who is wise and one who is contrary; one who is simple and one who does not even know how to ask a question" (p. 9). But here Wiesel writes to, for, and about the fifth son. This son is different—not because he lacks qualities the others possess but because he is not there. Death explains the absence, and yet it does not because death explains nothing. Besides, even if it has everything to do with death, the fifth son's absence is not a matter of death alone.

The fifth son is Ariel. In a dual sense, he is both dead and alive, for Ariel is not one son but two. The Ariel born in 1949, who seeks and then bears his message by narrating Wiesel's story, is today a professor "in a small university in Connecticut" (p. 218). Raised in New York, a college student during the sixties, he has experienced the tumult of

America during the years of Vietnam. Lisa, his girlfriend, initiates him. Sex, drugs, politics, love—they share them all. But just as "Lisa has left me," though at thirty-five he misses her, so Ariel is shaped less by the American Dream than by the Kingdom of Night he never knew in Davarowsk (p. 217).

Ariel has a brother. That fact was long unknown to him because his brother is also Ariel, the fifth son. If such facts are puzzling, puzzlement only begins to tell the tale. For there is much more to the relationship between Ariel and his brother than questions about a name might suggest. In the case of either of these Ariels, for example, it is an issue whether one or the other is truly the elder or the younger brother.

Though he is eleven years older, the professor's brother will be six forever. That was his age when the *Angel* and his SS cohort hunted Ariel down and took his life in Davarowsk. His Jewish parents, Rachel and Reuven Tamiroff, tried their best for him, although the best was not to be in Davarowsk. Ghettoized with the other Jews, Reuven led the Jewish Council there. He did so fairly, with dignity, and he paid the price. Once he learned the fully murderous intent of Richard Lander and the Nazis, Tamiroff resigned his post and told the ghetto what he knew. The *Angel* allowed Reuven to live but took the lives of six members of the Council and then readied the entire ghetto for deportation to the gas chambers.

The Tamiroffs had to board the death train. Before doing so, they took two other steps. First, Reuven met with Simha Zeligson, Tolka Friedman, and Rabbi Aharon-Asher. He invited them together to share secretly an avenging oath: "'Whoever among us shall survive this ordeal swears on his honor and on the sanctity of our memory to do all he can to kill the killer, even at the cost of his life'" (p. 155). All save the rabbi agreed. Second, Rachel and Reuven located "some good honest people" who would hide Ariel from the killers (p. 184). Then they left him behind. Eventually Reuven learned that Lander, too, took an oath and kept it. Later he also must contend with the realization that his own resolution to kill was no match for the Nazi's.

Lander knew the Tamiroffs too well. When he spied them boarding the train without Ariel, he disbelieved their story that the child had died from ghetto disease. Keeping his word to Rachel and Reuven, the *Angel* found the boy. His vengeance was "terrible and cruel, people spoke of it in all the ghettos near and far." Since learning of it, Ariel's New York brother "cannot tolerate hot milk" (p. 185).

Learning of it—that is what obsesses the American Ariel, the fifth Jewish son who is alive but not there because he is the child of Holocaust survivors whose Ariel did not survive Davarowsk. If Rachel and Reuven endured, reunited, and crossed the ocean, they could not make the new beginnings for which America is famous. Burdened by a past too heavy, they wanted new life, even gave Ariel a second birth to affirm it, and yet they found that a second Ariel might double their sadness more than their joy. For what identity could they give him, and what identity did they give him by naming him Ariel?

No one is better equipped than Elie Wiesel to probe such issues. The two Ariels, their father, and the encounters they have—all are encompassed by his own experience. In the words of Ariel, who in this case seems to speak for Wiesel himself, "I have said 'I' in their stead. Alternately, I have been one or the other" (p. 219). Surviving the extinction of his own childhood in Auschwitz, Wiesel found his way to New York and then to marriage and fatherhood. This book is wrung from his soul. Together they give voice to the silence that threatens to dominate when a life suffers more than anybody's should. Elie Wiesel lives. So does Ariel. And so must *The Fifth Son*, because the tale has to be told. Even Reuven Tamiroff knows as much, although the second Ariel cannot fully extract the story from him until his mother is gone and he discovers the letters that his father has written to the Ariel who is not there. In the discovery, those letters become his as well, and they lead the New York Ariel to strike up a correspondence of his own with the brother in Davarowsk.

Ariel's letters to Ariel are also prompted by discovery of another kind. Part of Reuven Tamiroff's melancholy derives from the conviction that he and Simha Zeligson made good their attempt to assassinate Richard Lander in 1946. For years they meet weekly to study and debate, seeking to determine in retrospect whether their action was indeed just. Their inquiry does little to assuage the guilt whose persistence troubles them in more ways than one. Ariel's discovery goes further. It comes to include the knowledge that the *Angel* lives, prosperous and happy, as Wolfgang Berger, the Reshastadt businessman.

The business Richard Lander started must not remain unfinished. So Ariel Tamiroff, his appointment made with death, heads for Germany to encounter the Herr Direktor. Ariel reaches the station where he must change trains for Reshastadt. It is Graustadt, that gray city where one "can buy anything: a woman for the morning, insurance with a suicide clause or a lifetime ticket on the German Railroad System" (p. 200).

What happened in Graustadt and not long after is not for an article to say. Nor may it be for Elie Wiesel to determine completely. No one but Ariel is Ariel. And yet that is not where we should leave *The Fifth Son*, for the message that Ariel bears in the novel is that he did not kill. The reason he did not, moreover, has everything to do with Ariel's being Jewish, with his being the fifth son, with his being human.

How does that work? Wiesel gives us hints: Ariel, for example, receives advice from his neighbor and friend, Rebbe Zvi-Hersh, who says, " 'To punish a guilty man, to punish him with death, means linking yourself to him forever: is that what you wish?' " (p. 190). In this case, however, the question is just as important as the traditional counsel that precedes it. If "yes" is not the best answer, "no" does not follow without pain. For anyone who cares, as Ariel's "sad summing up" implies, the truth is that a life lived after Auschwitz cannot be one's own alone but instead will be permeated by "the memory of the living and the dreams of the dead" (p. 220).

That fact may account for the name Elie Wiesel bestowed on the two fifth sons. Ariel is a biblical name. It appears more than once in Scripture, and its meanings are diverse. The name can mean "lion of God" and also "light of God," which could explain why a later tradition thought of Ariel as an angel altogether different from the *Angel*. Unfortunately, a darker side haunts the name as well. For instance, in Isaiah's prophecy the following words can be found: "Yet I will distress Ariel, and there shall be moaning and lamentation, and she shall be to me like an Ariel" (Isa. 29:2). The first Ariel signifies Jerusalem; the second suggests that Ariel will become like an altar, a scene of holocaust. But the oracle sees more. In time, "the nations that fight against Ariel" will themselves be quelled by "the flame of devouring fire" (Isa. 29:6-7). Perhaps that is true—or will be—but having met the *Angel*, Ariel Tamiroff remembers an old saying: "The Lord may wish to chastise, that is His prerogative; but it is mine to refuse to be His whip" (p. 213). For both his brother's sake and his own, Ariel, whose American life has also been a scene of holocaust, will identify with his people, with Jerusalem, even though he chooses to live in the Diaspora, and thereby with the well-being of humankind. Thus, he seems most like his namesake in another part of Scripture.

The biblical book of Ezra only mentions Ariel. His name is nonetheless important and vital. For Ariel is called a "leading" man (Ezra 8:16). His leadership urges remembrance and return from exile. It means to respond to devastation and sadness by acts of restoration that rebuild Jerusalem, mend the world, and make trust possible again. Masterfully recounting the history of the Holocaust and its aftermath, *The Fifth Son* leads the same way. It is therefore fitting that Eliezer is also among Ezra's "leading men." His namesake, the author of this book, urges us all to respond by becoming like Ariel—lions, if not angels, of light who resist a losing of trust that Jean Améry equated with arrival at "the end of the world."[15]

These reflections began with the proposition that the Holocaust compels us to assess what losing trust in the world can mean. Jean Améry's testimony warns that, if unreversed, such a loss portends humankind's demise. Just because we may be closer to that outcome than we care to imagine, a crucial point of this essay is that there still can be a mending of the world. That mending, however, will not occur unless we replace the trust-destroying paths of Ernst Biberstein, Franz Stangl, and "the *Angel*" with the trust-creating ways of the Scholls, Oskar Schindler, Elie Wiesel, and *The Fifth Son*. Determination to take those steps—assessing what losing trust in the world can mean deserves nothing less than that conclusion.

NOTES

1. Jean Améry, *At the Mind's Limits: Contemplations by a Survivor on Auschwitz and Its Realities*, trans. Sidney Rosenfeld and Stella P. Rosenfeld (New York: Schocken, 1986), p. 28. See also his *Radical Humanism: Selected Essays*, ed. and trans. Sidney Rosenfeld and Stella P. Rosenfeld (Bloomington: Indiana University Press, 1984).

2. Cited by Richard Hanser, *A Noble Treason: The Revolt of the Munich Students Against Hitler* (New York: G.P. Putnam's Sons, 1979), p. 152. See also Annette E. Dumbach and Jud Newborn, *Shattering the German Night: The Story of the White Rose* (Boston: Little, Brown, 1986).

3. Hanser, *A Noble Treason*, p. 274.

4. Gitta Sereny, *Into That Darkness: An Examination of Conscience* (New York: Vintage Books, 1983), p. 363.

5. See Rudolf Hoess, *Commandant of Auschwitz: The Autobiography of Rudolf Hoess*, trans. Constantine Fitzgibbon (London: Pan Books, 1974).

6. Sereny, *Into That Darkness*, p. 25.

7. Alexander Donat, ed., *The Death Camp Treblinka: A Documentary* (New York: Holocaust Library, 1979), p. 14. Donat's book, which features eyewitness accounts by survivors of Treblinka, is a valuable complement to Sereny's work. See also Claude Lanzmann, *Shoah: An Oral History of the Holocaust* (New York: Pantheon, 1985), which is the complete text from Lanzmann's epic film about the Holocaust.

8. Sereny, *Into That Darkness*, pp. 202, 164, 200. For an important study of Nazi rationalization, especially as it pertained to the euthanasia and death camp enterprises in which Stangl participated, see Robert Jay Lifton, *The Nazi Doctors: Medical Killing and the Psychology of Genocide* (New York: Basic Books, 1986).

9. For more detail on Oskar Schindler, see Thomas Keneally, *Schindler's List* (New York: Penguin Books, 1983). The title of this account is apt, for in addition to referring to Schindler's record about his Jewish workers, the German word *List* means "cunning." Schindler possessed it abundantly and for good ends. Another remarkable story—that of Hermann "Fritz" Graebe—is told by Douglas K. Huneke, *The Moses of Rovno* (New York: Dodd, Mead, 1985). Graebe, the only German citizen who volunteered to testify against the Nazis at Nuremberg, was a structural engineer during World War II. Assigned to the Ukraine by the Railroad Administration of the Third Reich, he was horrified by the murder of nearly 1,500 Jewish men by Nazi killing squads. His response was to build a rescue network that protected hundreds of Jews. At the war's end, he used his own train to bring scores of them across Allied lines to freedom.

10. Keneally, *Schindler's List*, p. 371.

11. Perhaps the most ambitious and promising work of this kind—incomplete at the time of writing—is the Study of the Altruistic Personality Project, which is headed

by Samuel P. Oliner. This sociologist is a Holocaust survivor who was hidden by Polish Catholics during World War II. His important autobiography, *Restless Memories: Recollections of the Holocaust Years* (Berkeley: Judah L. Magnes Museum, 1986), tells that story. Oliner has interviewed hundreds of rescuers and survivors to clarify the factors and motivations that led people to save Jewish lives during the Nazi era. The findings of his study appear in *The Altruistic Personality: The Rescuers of Jews in Nazi Europe* (New York: Free Press, 1988). Although exceptions to them exist, among Oliner's more important discoveries are the following: (1) Rescuers, women and men alike, came from different social classes and diverse occupations. (2) They had learned and deeply internalized values such as helpfulness, responsibility, fairness, justice, compassion, and friendship. (3) They had friends in groups outside of their own family circles or immediate communities. (4) They had high levels of self-confidence and self-esteem and were not afraid to take calculated risks. (5) They knew what was happening around them, and, in addition, benefited from a supportive emotional network—their rescue efforts met with approval from family members or others who could be trusted. Oliner believes that, if he were in trouble and could identify persons with these qualities, his chances of receiving assistance would be excellent.

12. Pierre Sauvage was born during the Holocaust in the French village of Le Chambon, Haute-Loire, where many Jews were hidden and saved. A distinguished filmmaker, he has produced *Weapons of the Spirit* (1987), a documentary about that place. He also heads "The Friend of Le Chambon," an organization that honors those who saved Jews during the Holocaust. His words are quoted by permission.

13. Cited by Richard Zoglin, "Lives of Spirit and Dedication," *Time*, October 27, 1986, p. 66.

14. Elie Wiesel, *The Fifth Son*, trans. Marion Wiesel (New York: Summit Books, 1985), p. 208.

15. Améry, *At the Mind's Limits*, p. 29.

9

ETHICS, EVIL, AND THE FINAL SOLUTION

Warren K. Thompson

Germany's *Endlösung der Judenfrage* is a paradigm of what G.J. Warnock has called a "plain fact" of moral wrong. Philip Hallie, in his account of the French Huguenot village of Le Chambon-sur-Lignon (Haute-Loire), whose citizens shielded Jews during the German occupation, begins by citing Warnock:

> I believe that we all have, and should not let ourselves be bullied out of, the conviction that at least some questions as to what is good or bad for people, what is harmful or beneficial, are not in any serious sense matters of opinion. That it is a bad thing to be tortured or starved, humiliated or hurt, is not an opinion: it is a fact. That it is better for people to be loved and attended to, rather than hated or neglected, is again a plain fact, not a matter of opinion.[1]

One does not have to be a student of ethics to grasp what Warnock calls a "plain fact," namely, that those who care for their fellow human creatures are better people than those who do not.[2]

It is tempting to conclude that these thoughts constitute sufficient philosophical judgment on the Holocaust. In the context of moral "plain facts," what more can be said? Six million and more of Europe's peoples were deliberately done to death from 1939 to 1945 in carrying out a nation–state's official policy. The moral wrongness of this is beyond debate and opinion, without possibility of justification or extenuation.

Yet there is more. And because there is more, philosophers would do well to take a deeper look at the Final Solution. In seeking comprehension, philosophy also looks for and anticipates truth. If this is to be found in the Holocaust, it can be found in the context of ethics and values. The specific philosophical task, then, is an ethical–valuational one. Philosophers will look at the ethical–valuational context within which the Final Solution came to be and limn the moral ramifications of murder on such a scale.

However, dealing with the Final Solution requires attention to a

181

given: Philosophical success, in terms of comprehension and truth, cannot be guaranteed. The tragic reality may be that Germans killed most of Europe's Jews, along with a staggering number of other designated *Staatsfeinden* (enemies of the state), for the simple reason that they wanted to.[3] This disquieting possibility may be one reason why relatively so few philosophers have written about German genocide, leaving the task to historians, theologians, and social and behavioral scientists. Also, some philosophers still see the Holocaust as "too immediate" for genuine philosophical consideration (presumably in another forty-odd years they shall find it sufficiently remote). Others doubtless are overwhelmed by the enormity of the event and find themselves moved only to respectful silence (there is something to be said for this attitude; at the very least it is an understandable one). And there may be those who see philosophy's main, and perhaps only, task as one of constant and continuing debate as to the meaning and interpretation of words and symbols; they likely will see the Holocaust as offering no fruitful areas for study outside of some occasional forays into the more bizarre facets of human behavior. Another troublesome obstacle facing philosophers' attempts to deal with and understand the Final Solution is that the death of so many leads one to see it as a wholly irrational event:

> Common sense emphatically declares that only psychotic and semi-psychotic deviants consumed with apocalyptic visions could possibly conceive of an Auschwitz or a Treblinka and make the vision work. Such commonsense reactions are also seductive because they have the added attraction of allowing the Holocaust to be treated as a historical aberration, an incredible "accident" roughly equivalent to what might be expected if insane inmates were able to take over the operation of a mental institution.[4]

But if the Holocaust is consigned to the irrational, there is nothing left to be said—no interpretation is possible, no lessons to be learned from it. And thus it would be, at best, a mystery or, at worst, a meaningless event.

What should give urgency to a philosophical confrontation with the Holocaust is that it is a startling example of licensed mass indifference to human welfare, an event showing that "none of the achievements of our civilization offers protection against infernal horrors."[5] Not law, or government, or religious institutions, or human good will necessarily protect people who are singled out for abuse by those in power. This too is a moral "plain fact." Philosophy ought to find clear relevance in an event that illuminates so sharply human moral and valuational failure. The Final Solution was a human catastrophe. The primary victims were Jewish, but the Holocaust was also an assault on humanity and the idea of humanity. While the motivation for it was primarily anti-Semitic *at the time*, there is no reason to suppose that Hitler victorious would not have sought additional "solutions" with respect to other "problems." We know his feelings about Poles, Russians, and other racially suspect people, and he did order a "euthanasia program" for the mentally handicapped and those with debilitating diseases, most of whom were Aryan Germans.

The *Endlösung* is a watershed event in history, marking out what can result when people refuse to acknowledge the plain fact that helping others is better than harming them. Hallie's story of how the Chambonnais protected their fellow human beings, not because they were Jews but simply because they were human beings in need of help, is unfortunately the story of a rare happening during the Holocaust years. What these villagers recognized, as others did not, is that moral goodness is "conciliatory" and life celebrating, even though, as Hallie points out,

> goodness does not win wars, does not abolish slavery, and does not destroy concentration camps. It seems that great armies are needed to do these things. Certainly a world full of Chambons would not have defeated Hitler, and Le Chambon itself did nothing to do so. But what it did it did, and the good it did is, to use Warnock's phrase, "a plain fact, not a matter of opinion."[6]

Hallie goes on to say that

> the story of the Holocaust contains many stories of "plain fact," in the sense Warnock uses this phrase—if we do not allow ourselves to be "bullied out of" recognizing them by those who choose to understand ethics *only* in terms of interminably debatable philosophical and counterfactual generalizations. The Holocaust is the story of extreme situations, like Le Chambon and Auschwitz, situations that can display as "plain fact" the "true north"—or the "true south"—of ethics, the clear cases which might help us to take our bearings when we study more problematic cases. Philosophy can affirm plainly as competently as it can affirm argumentatively, and with equal lucidity. If we refuse to see this, philosophy may blind us to what is obvious while offering us only what is recondite.[7]

The Final Solution was conceived, planned, and carried out by "ordinary" people doing uncommon things. Hannah Arendt said this about Adolf Eichmann. Robert J. Lifton concludes much the same in his study of German physicians who served in the euthanasia institutes and later in the death camps. In an interview with an Auschwitz survivor, Lifton maintains that at issue . . . here is the relationship of Nazi doctors to the human species. [An] Auschwitz survivor who knew something about them asked me: "Were they *beasts* when they did what they did? Or were they *human beings?*" He was not surprised by my answer: they were and are men, which is my justification for studying them; and their behavior—Auschwitz itself—was a product of specifically *human* ingenuity and cruelty.[8]

The perpetrators were not the "demonic figures—sadistic, fanatic, lusting to kill—people have often thought them to be" (pp. 4–5; page references in this and the next paragraph are to Lifton's *The Nazi Doctors*). Yet, as a survivor also said, "it is *demonic* that they were not demonic" (p. 5).

Moreover, there is "the disturbing psychological truth that participation in mass murder need not require emotion as extreme or demonic as would seem appropriate for such a malignant project. Or to put the matter another way, ordinary people can commit demonic acts" (p. 5). This is an ancient truth, known to the Greek playwrights and familiar in the Jewish-Christian theological tradition. It is also another "plain fact."

While Arendt's doctrine of the "banality of evil" was never fully developed before her death—and was stringently, though not always honestly, criticized—her portrayal of the ordinariness of Eichmann while he sent thousands to death remains a provocative and disturbing one. There may be good reasons to reject her thesis, yet she has done a service for those who examine the Holocaust. She reminds us that it is ordinary men and women who are capable of doing evil.

Lifton's study makes clear, as do other biographical accounts of the perpetrators, the salient point that an overwhelming majority of those responsible for the Final Solution were ordinary; there were few certifiable psychopaths among them: "With few exceptions [they] were not led to work in the camps by sadistic drives, although most of them participated in acts of extreme brutality."[9]

In accepting Arendt's doctrine of the banality of evil, the sociologist Rainer Baum claims that she has warned us in two important ways:

First, we should not assume that it takes psychopathology to be engaged in mass murder. Completely normal human beings can do it. Second, we can no longer trust that extraordinary action requires extraordinary motivation. Completely ordinary people can do the extraordinary, engage in mass murder, *without* first becoming extraordinary themselves through one or both of the traditional historical mechanisms that always transformed ordinary men and women into unusual characters: (1) conversion to charismatic beliefs legitimating their extraordinary actions or (2) response to an offer of material inducement so tempting as to prove irresistible.[10]

In doing what they did to Europe's Jews and others, the Germans of the Third Reich ignored or broke the "original context" of long-established taboos against killing. As Alasdair MacIntyre points out,

> deprive the taboo rules of their original context and they at once are apt to appear as a set of arbitrary prohibitions, as indeed they characteristically do appear when the initial context is lost, when those background beliefs in the light of which the taboo rules had originally been understood have not only been abandoned but forgotten.[11]

Hitler and what he stood for, as well as what he was able to accomplish as Führer, delimit what is apparent forty-odd years later: Moral prohibitions, once generally accepted and adhered to in society, can be broken with relative ease and impunity once the "original context" is broken. In the case of the Final Solution, the original context was that, while hatred and dislike of others is "allowable"—though not necessarily to be glorified or recommended—extending those sentiments to the logical conclusion of killing the objects of dislike or hatred is forbidden. Killing, and by extension, mass killing is thus "unthinkable" as a legitimate course of action.

Nevertheless, Hitler himself was willing to think "unthinkable" thoughts about some people: Jews, Poles, Russians, and even his fellow Aryans. There were no apparent ameliorating influences in his thinking about those he hated. It is clear that others in Germany and elsewhere similarly were willing to think the "unthinkable" and were thus able to break the context of the taboo against killing.

While it is not accurate to say that National Socialism, as a movement, from its inception desired anyone's extermination (or that a vote for Hitler in 1932 was also a vote for Auschwitz), there were in Germany those for whom such action was a thinkable option, theoretically feasible, and ultimately something to be ventured. The unthinkable for some was thus all too thinkable. As Richard L. Rubenstein points out in *The Cunning of History: Mass Death and the American Future,*

> The passing of time has made it increasingly evident that a hitherto unbreachable moral and political barrier in the history of Western civilization was successfully overcome by the Nazis in World War II and that henceforth the systematic, bureaucratically administered extermination of millions of citizens or subject peoples will forever be one of the capacities and temptations of government.[12]

Any consideration of the Final Solution must accept that it marks a signal human failure, specifically a failure of civilization. It was a failure to resist the doing of clear and immense evil. This too is a plain fact.

That it was done through the authority of a nation-state only sharpens the evil and makes our recognition of it more painful, for it is thereby an "unprecedented form of organized evil."[13]

As a failure of this kind, German genocide demarks a moral crisis in the world, one that has had continuing reverberations since May 9, 1945.

The Holocaust stands as a crucial moral crisis because within the Nazi state, and in most of the territory it eventually came to control, neither traditional law or religion could prevent or comprehend the massive killings. Moreover, those nations allied against the Nazis in the name of law and religion not only failed to act effectively against the Holocaust, but tried for a time to maintain an unofficial awareness that it existed.[14]

A moral crisis of the magnitude of the Final Solution signifies that a society has lost its way. That Germany lost its way under Hitler and National Socialism is beyond doubting; that civilization was also cast adrift as a result is a point worth pondering.

The human failure culminating in Auschwitz was the failure of existing moral and valuational structures: They were insufficient to the task of ensuring human welfare and preventing human harm. In Germany and elsewhere "most of the major social institutions made no special effort to oppose the Holocaust," and those few individual persons who did were easily ignored or removed (p. 130; page references here and in the next paragraph are to Kren and Rappoport's *The Holocaust*).

For George Kren and Leon Rappoport,

the basic explanation for this failure is, at least in principle, not hard to discover. Insofar as Western concepts of morality have evolved in connection with the rise of secular nation-states, these concepts and practices have gradually come to derive their authority from the state rather than any higher force. Both the institutional actions and the traditional values of law and religion are for all practical purposes only allowed to operate in whatever framework is made available to them by the state. By one means or another, the salient interests of the state must be served by law and religion. (p. 130)

In the end, existing social structures did not prevent the Holocaust. Institutions functioning at the time were unable to deal with it, and their impotence was itself a human failure. Government, law, and religion either acquiesced or were indifferent (sometimes both) when those with influence and authority began to think thoughts that previously had been unthinkable. Voices that should have been heard in support of the victims fell silent or spoke for the victimizers. It was a time, so poignantly captured by W. H. Auden, when

In the nightmare of the dark
All the dogs of Europe bark,
And the living nations wait,
Each sequestered in its hate;

Intellectual disgrace
Stares from every human face,
And the seas of pity lie
Locked and frozen in each eye.[15]

The failure of institutions such as government, law, and religion is a particularly unsettling one, for these institutions traditionally supply the standards by which human action can be judged and the guides and inspiration for human attitudes and performance. When they fail, the failure is ramified throughout the whole of society. And in a fundamental way, the failure of government, law, and religion was the failure to keep human welfare as the paramount end (the obverse end here is the prevention of human harm). The Final Solution shows the myriad ways through which government, law, and religion, when weak to the point of failure, can work to produce human harm on a massive scale.

The modern state may do with people as it wishes, given that it has control over them. Consequently, the situation of the individual in the modern state is in principle roughly equivalent to the situation of the prisoner in Auschwitz: Either act in accord with the prevailing standards of conduct enforced by those in authority, or risk whatever consequences they may wish to impose.[16]

Rare is the person who dares challenge the prevailing standards of conduct in the modern state (even rarer is the person whose challenge is successful). There were few such challenges in Hitler's Germany, even well before his power was consolidated, and even fewer once he went to war.

Among the continuing reverberations of the moral crisis that engendered the Final Solution is that murder on such a scale is now a constant potential, and what have been "prior cultural values" (or taboos), supposedly means to prevent it, "were manifestly false."[17] They were made "false" in two tragic ways: Those who were stewards of such values lacked the resolve necessary to defend them when they were attacked; others, particularly those with influence and authority, chose to reject these values and replace them with more expedient ones.

The *Endlösung* stands as an example of what can be accomplished in a world enamored of *Realpolitik* untempered by the humane. It shows the ultimate logical conclusion of "realistic" state policies and attitudes that attach little importance to values and ethical issues in the public, and perhaps not even in the private, realm. It shows, too, the results of moral indifference to the fate of one's fellow human creatures, indifference on both the individual and the societal level (how very convenient it is to be indifferent to one's neighbor when society and state bless this indifference).

Moral indifference has been called, appropriately, the "modern sin," and if we are to understand it we must begin by acknowledging that "moral indifference can carry men to the point where they lose the constraint of commonsense self-interest, a point revealed in modern German history."[18] In a society where the dominant attitude is one of "who's to judge?", where the intellectual constraints on action are lacking for the simple reason that there is no moral *communitas,* indifference serves to construct the prevailing social and individual reality. On this level, indifference also serves as the canon by which the important moral and valuational questions are measured, if they are measured at all. More injuriously, when moral indifference is institutionalized in society, the resulting amorality as good as becomes a virtue.[19]

A society that sees amorality as a virtue has scant reason to draw back from even the most noisome acts, should these acts be seen as warranted, especially for ideological or military considerations. In the Third Reich there was an ideological and military value consensus that otherwise forbidden actions were necessary with respect to certain people (it must be noted that this cannot have been a *moral* consensus, for the actions entailed treating human beings in a clearly immoral fashion; nevertheless, it was a value consensus). While the SS (*Schutzstaffel*) is rightly held responsible for carrying out most of the extermination policies, the German Wehrmacht itself was deeply involved, especially in the East. The claim that regular soldiers had nothing to do with civilian murders, that they indeed opposed it, is mistaken. Army commanders, including some who were later involved in the July 1944 attempt on Hitler's life, were generally agreeable to, and assisted in, the killing operations in Poland and later during the campaign in the Soviet Union. Their support was based on both military and ideological–political considerations.[20]

As Rainer Baum recognizes, there is a direct connection between amorality, impersonality, and bureaucracy.[21] Modern societies are highly bureaucratized, and a bureaucracy functions best when it functions impersonally and "objectively." Things bureaucratic must be done "by the book"—a bureaucracy cannot survive without rules and regulations. There would have been no Final Solution had there not been a German bureaucracy willing to carry out assigned duties without consideration for personal sentiments. The obedience ideal of the Prussian military mind, appropriately stereotyped as *Kadavergehorsam* (as obedient as a corpse), was evident in the German bureaucratic structure and helped make possible a project as immense and complex as the system of concentration and death camps. The bureaucratic valuational attitude necessary to the functioning of the camps was that of "doing one's duty *sine ira et studio* (without anger or zeal)," the identical attitude exhibited by the SS in operating the camps and performing most of the killing.

In modern Germany, even before Hitler, there was an institutionalized "dissensus" of values among the leaders of society, which served, according to Baum, as a prime source of their high level of moral indifference. Moral indifference at the top does not remain at the top; it eventually permeates the whole social structure. In effect, modern Germany was a nation of people who were "ethical strangers" to each other.[22] The value "dissensus"

> pushed you upwards towards an abrogation of morally evaluating your role performance. In his official capacity a reasonable man would not try to be also a moral man. His chances for finding a consensual echo for his caring concern about moral values among critical others were too slim. Given the one more commonly shared value, the work ethic, this particular characteristic pushed you toward overidentification with the work role in a context of profound dissensus on any other values.[23]

Modern Germany is a prototype of what can result when a society idealizes moral indifference and uses it as a governing rubric. Yet to say this is not to give a satisfactory explanation for the Final Solution. While moral indifference is arguably a direct cause, it remains to be shown why the Germans as a nation could be morally indifferent to the fate of so many. Even more vexing is how so many ordinary people were able to involve themselves in the workings of genocide.[24]

These ordinary people ignored the plain facts of human welfare—this much is clear. What is clear, as well, is that plain facts of morality carry little weight with those who make and carry out policy in a modern state. Plain facts of morality do not give a "competitive edge" in a competitive society. (The cynical but incisive question attributed to Stalin, "How many divisions does the Pope have?", was entirely appropriate from a *realpolitische* viewpoint, as were the words of the American officer in Indochina who called in an artillery barrage on a peasant settlement: "We had to destroy the village to save it.")

There is a continuum of functional rationality whose origins can be traced back to the Enlightenment and within which the architects and engineers of German genocide accomplished their ends. It is a continuum that gave birth to and continues to nurture the fact-value divorce, the utilitarian doctrine of "the greatest good for the greatest number," and the separation of public and private morality. Functional rationality provides the dominant metaphor by which modern bureaucratized societies deal with people, whether designing a program of mass extermination or implementing welfare payments. The fabricants of the Final Solution were men and women who knew how to deal with the many problems entailed in mass extermination. Once the leadership had decided on the specific solution, others in the system were prepared, by virtue of their training and experience, and under the prevailing condition of moral indifference, to carry it out in a rational, logical, and expeditious manner, with scrupulous attention to the rules and recommended procedures. When extermination was officially decided upon, the Final Solution became, bureaucratically speaking, mainly a problem of logistics, organization, and personnel administration, a project calling for leadership, managerial competence, and "social engineering" skills.

While philosophers generally have not done much concerning German genocide—or any other kind, for that matter—there are exceptions. Hannah Arendt and Emil Fackenheim are two who have dealt with what Germany did to the "captive peoples" of Europe. A third name should be cited. Alan Rosenberg has written persuasively on the need for a philosophical treatment of the Final Solution.

While acknowledging the difficulties of dealing with the Final Solution, Rosenberg believes they can be resolved. The work of the historian Saul Friedländer provides a frame of reference: The passing of time has "increased our knowledge" of Nazi genocide but not necessarily our "understanding" of it. Rosenberg cites Friedländer to the effect that we have today no clearer perspective or comprehension than we had immediately after the war,[25] and goes on to say

> I believe that unless we undertake a systematic system and analyze what took place we will never be able to comprehend the essential meaning of one of the most important events in history and [will] fail to learn what it says about human conduct and thought, both within the context of its period and for all time to come.[26]

The first step to this end "must be the development of a conceptual framework that will synthesize" the various aspects of the Final Solution and provide them with "a ground in logic" (p. 3; page references here and in the following five paragraphs are to Rosenberg's "Philosophy"). This is necessary, Rosenberg says, for otherwise we shall "never arrive at a significant comprehension of its meaning, reasons and implications" (p. 3). In order to do this, we must presuppose that there is intelligibility in the Holocaust (and other genocidal endeavors).

Rosenberg thus issues a challenge: Examine, in order to understand and make intelligible for others, the organized, state-sponsored extermination of six million and more. This challenge is also a plea to take seriously the ethical ramifications of killing so many people, people killed not for what they did but simply for what they were.

The "logic" *of* Nazi genocide is evident in the rational predictability of exterminating those who were labeled as "plague carriers" (it is tragically ironic that the most cost-effective and efficient means of extermination was found to be a cyanide compound originally used as a pesticide). The "logic" *in* Nazi genocide is that it was a rationally planned and coordinated attempt to do away with an entire group of people. The specific rational objective was to make Germany and ultimately German-occupied Europe *judenrein* (free of Jews), an objective largely attained.

Philosophers should approach the Final Solution from the bias of an ethical and valuational viewpoint untrammeled by the conditional and the contentiously opinionated. "Plain facts" of moral right and wrong form an additional given that must be accepted in considering the Holocaust. We know, beyond doubt and opinion, the plain factual wrongness of what Germany did. Yet what is not plain at all—indeed, what is a refractory problem—is *how* a nation could bring itself to accomplish what Germany did, 1939–45. This is the primal question and is part of the larger fabric of what Germany had become under, and because of, the conditions of modernity.

Whatever the uncertainty as to what precisely led Germany to genocide and to the creation of a literal thanatocracy in occupied Europe, it is clear that an ethical and valuational failure of great magnitude occurred. This failure took the form of a "transformation of values," though not in the configuration that Nietzsche earlier had called for, but one that he assuredly would have scorned. Moreover, it was a valuational metamorphosis afflicting all modern societies.

In looking at what Germany did, Rosenberg concludes that

> it is necessary to see that the whole enterprise of the Nazis presupposes the construction of a "genocidal universe." It can be shown . . . that the genocidal events that make up the Holocaust itself, as well as the associated attempts at genocide, were made possible only after a world had been "made" in which these events could be seen as "necessary"—even, in a sense, as both "normal" and "justifiable." (p. 21)

Philosophy did little to hinder the advent of Adolf Hitler and National Socialism, nor did it have much effect in lessening the excesses once Germany's *Gleichschaltung* (coordination, bringing into line) was established. It can be argued that philosophers should have been astute enough to anticipate what the Nazis would do. It is difficult to confute (by virtue of, admittedly, the clarity and insightfulness that come only with hindsight) that philosophers should have been foremost in opposing Hitler and what his movement represented. Also, to understand how any philosopher could have willingly opted for Nazism and then later, having broken with the regime, remained silent in the face of the plain facts of German wrongdoing, is troublesome in the extreme.

A philosophical examination of the Holocaust is made more difficult because, in looking at what Germany had become in modernity, philosophy should also look at itself. Reflexive scrutiny carries much epistemological risk and uncertainty. The hazards of this are cogently discussed by Fackenheim in his *To Mend the World: Foundations of Future Jewish Thought.* Fackenheim has made some notable criticisms of what philosophers did and did not do concerning the Final Solution, both during the years of killing and afterward. His commentary is a valuable one—and contemporary philosophers could do much worse than to see Germany and Auschwitz through his eyes—for he traces the activities of philosophers, especially in Germany, showing their failures (many) and their successes (few).

The Holocaust is, for Fackenheim, an *Ereignis* (an "event") marking a "rupture" in the continuity of human thought. If one supposes that there has been a kind of philosophical "progress" since Socrates, Plato, and Aristotle, as Fackenheim does, then the Final Solution should be seen as concluding, or at least signifying a pause in, this progress. In fact, according to Fackenheim, not only philosophy but the whole of human thinking was "paralyzed" through Auschwitz.[27]

Since philosophy failed at the very least to mitigate the human abuses of Nazism, it was itself a failure. While this failure was general and widespread, its peculiar locus was in the Third Reich; it was there that the rupture was most glaring. Germany's thinkers bear great responsibility for aiding in this rupture. As Fackenheim points out, the years of Nazism and genocide were a "time of philosophical testing." The testing is exemplified by the thinking of Heidegger and Jean-Paul Sartre:

> Heidegger's thought, though not compelling his 1933 surrender to Nazism, was unable to prevent it; and . . . Sartre, though resisting Nazism, could find no adequate grounds for doing so in his philosophy. To Sartre—if not . . . to Heidegger—this was a source of

philosophical anguish. And philosophers today, were they not forgetful of that time of philosophical testing, might find cause in this failure for uneasiness about philosophy itself in our age.[28]

Fackenheim is concerned that philosophy's legitimacy remains in considerable jeopardy. The kind of failure it experienced with respect to National Socialism fifty years ago is potentially repeatable. If two such then leading thinkers as Heidegger and Sartre could not, in their philosophizing, take a stand against an assault on philosophy's very foundations, what might happen at some future time when a similar attack is mounted?

While Fackenheim remains less than sanguine about the resoluteness of philosophers under siege, he does find comfort in the fact that a genuine mending of philosophy took place in Germany itself during the worst years of death making. At the trial of the White Rose conspirators against the regime, defendant Kurt Huber, an obscure philosophy professor, testified that he had worked against the state from a sense of "responsibility for all Germany," that his actions were an attempt to restore legality, for there were "unwritten as well as written laws." His final statement ends with these words from Fichte's poem: "And act thou as though/The destiny of all things German/ Depended on you and your lonely acting,/And the responsibility were yours" (quoted on p. 267; page references in this and the following two paragraphs are from Fackenheim's *To Mend the World*). Professor Huber and the others from the White Rose were condemned and then beheaded. Appropriately, Huber's act of mending philosophy took place in Munich, the holy shrine of Nazism.

Fackenheim sees Huber's appearance before the *Volksgericht* (people's court) as the "most important trial for philosophy since that of Socrates" (p. 275). While, through the workings of an antihuman outlook, the "idea of man" had been destroyed (because human beings were destroyed), humanity was mended by the deeds of a few men and women, in Munich and those pitifully few other locales of moral rectitude and courage. For this reason, the "idea of man" *can* be mended (p. 276).

Fackenheim concludes his treatment of philosophy and the Final Solution by saying that

> the necessity of somehow rescuing philosophical thought has weighed heavily on us in this exploration, ever since first we cited the dread dictum that Auschwitz does not paralyze this or that philosophical thought but the whole metaphysical capacity. Now that . . . the possibility has emerged, it has come to us not without irony. Fichte's idea of a world-saving mission of the Germans never

had more than fragments of truth, and what little truth it once had was corrupted long before the advent of the Third Reich. It is ironical that its sole unquestionable moment of truth should have occurred when a small band of German men and women took upon itself the responsibility for all things German, brushed aside all thoughts of consequences, and acted in order to save the world, and hence Germany herself, not through but from Germany. However, it was fitting, in the *Volk der Dichter und Denker*, that this [mending] included philosophy, and that the person articulating it was a philosopher. (p. 277)

One hopes that a mending did occur in that Munich courtroom in 1943. Yet, despite the virtually unanimous condemnation of genocide in 1945 and thereafter, the valuational sea change in modern societies has not been rescinded. Though the Final Solution may have been the peak event within a crisis of ethics and values, there is little reason to accept that the crisis has now disappeared. There continues to be ample evidence of a persisting value dissensus, in the midst of which the voice of philosophy, while not unheard, is very distant indeed.

The Final Solution was assayed by a society unclear about civilized values. This unclarity, especially as it touched matters of human welfare, was the social condition enabling some with authority and the ability to convince others to induce an attitudinal acceptance of what was done to Jews and other peoples. The *Endlösung* did not happen in isolation from the major currents of German society, and it was carried out only after significant preparation was undertaken by those with social and political influence. While it may not have been predictable at the beginnings of the Third Reich, or even as late as the onset of war in 1939, intimations of extermination as a realizable possibility were present from 1933 onward for those, in Germany and elsewhere, who wished to accept them.

Thoughtful people in modern societies will find the Final Solution a pungent example of how reason can be used to serve evil ends. Modern societies would not be modern without the pervasive use of "functional rationality," the thinking tool of technologists, managers, business persons, and bureaucrats (but clearly not the reason employed and studied by philosophers and scientists).[29]

Functional reason focuses on ends and consequences and is well suited for tidy and expeditious problem solving. It shuns value questions and ethical considerations, save for accepting as given that they should be shunned, for they only impede solutions. It is an ideal way of thinking for those who wish to "engineer" whole societies, organizations, and individual people in terms of "best" solutions; thus it allows reality to be constructed—or, commonly, reconstructed—to fit desired ends. Functional rationality works equally well in dealing with things *and* people, for in solving problems it makes little distinction between them. It is "objective," goes by the rules, and operates *sine ira et studio*, always in pursuit of the ends.

So it is in any modern society when ethical–valuational questions are banished from the public arena of debate and the process of social engineering and problem solving. And so it was in German society when its leaders took the nation down the road that ended in a solution called Auschwitz. In terms of potential for doing evil through use of reason, no modern society ought to be seen as necessarily different from National Socialist Germany (though clearly in other, more tragic respects Germany under Hitler was much different from most other societies). Given that modernity and functional reason are inseparable, that in order to be modern means a society must give priority to results and lessen its concern for ethical and valuational clarity, it follows that modern nation–states possess the ability to accomplish considerable and often fatal human harm. Unfortunately, it is far from certain in any modern society that development of this ability will, or even can, be aborted.

While it is clear that modernity, seen as "progress" and "betterment," has its price (for one can argue that desirable and beneficial consequences for the many commonly entail some suffering for the few), it ought not be ignored that this kind of reasoning in justification of social policy should be undertaken only with full awareness of its moral risk. While there is no social change without costs, it is also morally necessary to ask "just what the particular costs are, who is asked to pay them, and whether the putative gains make these costs acceptable."[30] The failure to ask such questions signifies moral indifference in a society and the additional failure to be concerned with active support of human welfare. It also follows that failures of this kind indicate that societal priority is given to other, less morally vital issues.

Germans, between 1933 and 1945, and others then and since, failed to ask probing questions about ends, means, and costs with respect to human welfare. The evil of National Socialist Germany's reasoning on the way to a Final Solution was an evil of commission as well as omission, the former for actively engaging in human extermination, the latter for not doing anything to prevent it. (The question persists as to the involvement of other societies in evil by omission for not preventing, or even hindering, what Germany did.)

Thus moral indifference, when it dominates a society or an individual person, is truly the "modern sin," a sinning made easier by the conditions of modernity and legitimized through the "quick-fix" solutions of functional rationality. It remains to be seen if there has in truth been a mending of what was ruptured in human values by the Final Solution and to what extent philosophy may have been a part of it. It is also uncertain what role philosophy might play in militating against the attitudes and thinking that could lead to some future final solutions.

NOTES

1. G. J. Warnock, *Contemporary Moral Philosophy* (New York: St. Martin's Press, 1970), p. 60.

2. Philip Hallie, "Scepticism, Narrative, and Holocaust Ethics," *Philosophical Forum* 16, nos. 1-2 (Fall-Winter 1984-85): 38.

3. Emil L. Fackenheim, *To Mend the World: Foundations of Future Jewish Thought* (New York: Schocken, 1982), pp. 230-40.

4. George M. Kren and Leon Rappoport, *The Holocaust and the Crisis of Human Behavior* (New York: Holmes and Meier, 1980), p. 9.

5. Ibid., p. 142.

6. Hallie, "Scepticism," p. 43.

7. Ibid., pp. 48-49.

8. Robert J. Lifton, *The Nazi Doctors: Medical Killing and the Psychology of Genocide* (New York: Basic Books, 1986), p. 4.

9. Tom Segev, "The Commanders of Nazi Concentration Camps" (Ph.D. diss., Boston University, 1977), p. vii.

10. Rainer C. Baum, *The Holocaust and the German Elite: Genocide and National Suicide in Germany, 1871-1945* (Totowa, N.J.: Rowman and Littlefield, 1981), p. 2.

11. Alasdair MacIntyre, *After Virtue: A Study in Moral Theory,* 2d ed. (Notre Dame, Ind.: University of Notre Dame Press, 1984), p. 112.

12. Richard L. Rubenstein, *The Cunning of History: Mass Death and the American Future* (New York: Harper & Row, 1975), p. 2.

13. Kren and Rappoport, *The Holocaust,* p. 130.

14. Ibid., p. 129.

15. W. H. Auden, "In Memory of W. B. Yeats (d. Jan. 1939)," in *The English Auden: Poems, Essays, and Dramatic Writings, 1927-1939,* ed. Edward Mendelson (New York: Random House, 1977); © 1940, 1968 by W. H. Auden, and reprinted here with permission.

16. On this point see Kren and Rappoport, *The Holocaust,* chap. 6 and Rubenstein, *Cunning of History,* chap. 2.

17. Kren and Rappoport, *The Holocaust,* p. 131.

18. Baum, *The Holocaust,* p. 291.

19. Ibid., p. 295ff.

20. Gerhard Hirschfeld, ed., *The Policies of Genocide: Jews and Soviet Prisoners of War in Nazi Germany* (London: Allen & Unwin and The German Historical Institute, 1986), esp. chaps. 1 and 2.

21. Baum, *The Holocaust,* pp. 295-313 and passim.

22. Ibid., pp. 77-78.

23. Ibid., p. 304.

24. Ibid., p. 7: The "industrialization of killing could not have been done by pathological monsters, seething with inner rage, nor by true believers, charismatically fired up to implement ideals, nor, finally, by men and women tempted by others of status and material advantages they could not afford to turn down. Instead, it

required sober bureaucratic functionaries or technicians. And in their participation, which makes this mass murder different from all others and unique, we find *one* aspect of our history and therefore *one* feature of human potentiality that corresponds to a sociological conception of ultimate hell: the creation of meaningless suffering and the imposition of senseless death. Man's ability to exclude his fellow man from the human realm and to destroy him without any need to explicate to himself his deed, this is what is meant here as the realization of ultimate hell. This is what happened with the aid of the German state. Note that the destruction of German Jewry certainly was *not* the simple elimination of some foreign people under conditions of war. Rather, the Nazis first had to use the tools of a modern nation-state, its rational-legal authority, to exclude German citizens of Jewish ethnic origin *or* religious affiliation . . . from the universe of moral obligations. And only having excluded them could they be led to slaughter. And their death, as well as that of so many others . . . served no institutional purpose. It had very little if anything to do with Hitler's role as a charismatic leader. Millions perished because of a profound moral indifference, one institutionalized in German society and already present long before Hitler appeared."

25. Alan Rosenberg, "Philosophy and the Holocaust: Suggestions for a Systematic Approach to the Genocidal Universe" (Paper read at the American Philosophical Association Convention, December 29, 1979), p. 2.

26. Ibid., p. 3.

27. Fackenheim, *To Mend the World*, pp. 200–201.

28. Ibid., p. 269.

29. Peter L. Berger, *Pyramids of Sacrifice: Political Ethics and Social Change* (New York: Basic Books, 1974), pp. 172–73.

30. Ibid., p. 222.

PART THREE
Echoes from the Death Camps

10

THE HOLOCAUST AS A TEST OF PHILOSOPHY

Alan Rosenberg and Paul Marcus

There are issues in the conduct of human affairs in their production of good and evil which, at a given time and place are so
central, so strategic in position, that their urgency deserves, with
respect to practice, the names ultimate and comprehensive.
These issues demand the most systematic reflective attention
that can be given. It is relatively unimportant whether this
attention be called philosophy or by some other name. It is of
immense human importance that it be given, and that it be given
by means of the best tested resources that inquiry has at command.

—*John Dewey*[1]

Dewey was right. There are such issues that, ". . . in their
production of good and evil . . . are so central, so strategic in position,
that their urgency deserves, with respect to practice, the names ultimate and comprehensive." There can be little doubt that the Holocaust
is such an issue. But Dewey also states, almost casually, that it is
"relatively unimportant whether this attention be called philosophy or
by some other name." Does this imply, as it seems, that it does not
matter that philosophers have paid so little attention to the Holocaust?
Or is it, rather, a matter of considerable importance?

It must be admitted that within Dewey's perspective whether such
an inquiry be called "philosophy" is unimportant. For, so long as such
an examination "be given by means of the best tested resources that
inquiry has at command," what does the name given to the inquiry
matter? Surely philosophers are well accustomed to seeing their "best
tested resources" appropriated by nonphilosophers in the analysis of a
wide range of issues, both trivial and of "immense human importance."
And yet, when it comes to the issues raised by the Holocaust, these
very resources are largely ignored in the vast literature that those issues

have evoked. Accordingly, it may well be argued—and is argued in what follows—that the Holocaust raises issues that do matter to philosophy. The fact is that the issues raised by the events of the Holocaust comprise, in an "ultimate and comprehensive" sense, a critical test of the ability of philosophers to deal with what Dewey has elsewhere called the "problems of men," and which, we are given to understand, are of "immense human importance." It has been clear for some time that the Holocaust is a challenge to the very meaning of our civilization. It is now apparent that it is also a fundamental challenge to philosophy.

We have only to survey the literature that purports to examine the meaning of the Holocaust in order to make explicit the nature of this test of philosophy. The literature presents us with nothing less than a welter of enigmas and paradoxes.[2] On the one hand we are told that we must understand the Holocaust so that we can prevent its recurrence, and yet we are also informed that it is a unique event beyond comprehension.[3] We are told that the Holocaust is an historical aberration, yet we are asked that it be taught as part of history and serve as a warning for the future. We are told that the horrors and violence of the Holocaust have made our conventional language obsolete, yet that same language is regularly employed to press the significance of the events upon us.

The most disconcerting of all the paradoxes and enigmas that surround the Holocaust and the one that we are primarily concerned with in this essay is that although the Holocaust is purported to be an event of profound historical significance that, as such, must have a profound impact on subsequent social, cultural, and political events, at the same time it is recognized that no such profound impact has in fact occurred. In short, it is paradoxical both to hold that the Holocaust is of such great historical significance as to necessarily evoke changes in the values underlying our society, and to recognize at the same time that it has not done so.

The claim that the Holocaust is a profound and significant event constituting a major watershed in world history is often made. Thus Henry Feingold calls it a "central event for our time . . . because what died at Auschwitz was the promise and hope embodied in Western civilization."[4] Emil Fackenheim claims that the Holocaust was epoch making: "The world . . . like the Jewish world . . . can never be the same."[5] Its impact was so momentous that Alvin Rosenfeld and Irving Greenberg state that "the Holocaust . . . like other singular and transforming events . . . has changed our way of being in the world and our way of looking at it."[6] Finally, as Elie Wiesel points out, "At Auschwitz, not only man died, but the idea of man."[7] The message of these statements is that the Holocaust must be understood as an epoch-making event, that it is "transformational" in its historical impact, and yet these same writers confess that no such impact is evident. The "transformational" event has had no "transforming" impact. Thus, for example, Wiesel dramatically writes, "Nothing has been learned, Auschwitz has not served as a warning. For more detailed information, consult your daily newspapers."[8] George Kren and Leon Rappoport are also caught in this paradox. On the one hand they claim that the Holocaust has been the major historical crisis of the twentieth century, a crisis that has radically altered human behavior and values; on the other hand they recognize that this impact has not been widely acknowledged.[9] What follows from this apparent incongruity is that it may be possible for a historical event of overwhelming impact to alter quite radically the prevailing conditions in the objective world without the real significance of the event being absorbed into the historical consciousness. That is, the objective situation may have changed without it having penetrated our "practices," perhaps because we utterly lack categories and concepts for dealing with these conditions? For example, we may still think and act about war in the same way even after nuclear weapons have been used. But for an event to be truly transformational in the sense required for understanding the Holocaust as creating just such a transformational crisis, the event must radically alter the objective reality and the concepts with which we deal with that reality, and it must also be absorbed into the innermost consciousness. As Fackenheim has succinctly stated:

> Only when [the events] are assimilated by the historical consciousness of succeeding generations are they capable of transforming the future and thus becoming historical in the deeper sense . . . The passage of time has brought [the Holocaust] closer rather than moving it farther away, disclosing that the world has thus far shied away from it but must at length confront it with unyielding realism and, if necessary, despair.[10]

Some have hypothesized that the Holocaust's failure of impact can be attributed to its presentation as a horrifying event, or a gruesome historical aberration. Alice and Roy Eckardt, for example, warn of the dangers of reducing the Holocaust to a nightmare, a horrible episode, something from which we have long awakened, part of a unique political tragedy, or the whim of an insane man.[11] And certainly the manner in which the genuinely horrible nature of the Holocaust is presented will affect our ability to go beyond these horrors to some coherent understanding of their implications for the future of humankind.[12]

Beyond this, however, our tendency to see as incomprehensible the horrors that we ourselves, as human beings, have created, reveals a certain tendency to think about our culture and its intellectual tools in a particular way. It is doubtless true that "normal" philosophy, to use a term adapted from Thomas Kuhn, is largely a reflection as well as a critique of "normal" culture. And this culture can be understood partially as a composite of the ways in which we solve the "normal" problems that occur within that culture. Yet Patricia Bender comments that no cultural framework provides us with a way to encompass genocide.[13] It may be that philosophers have concluded that the conceptual frameworks that "normal" philosophy provides are equally incapable of showing the way to encompass genocide. And yet what is needed from philosophy is precisely such a conceptual framework that would illuminate the central paradox of the Holocaust. This is what we take to be the test of philosophy. That is, the test of philosophy is to show in what sense the Holocaust is a transformational event and what that means for our civilization. This task is necessitated by the fact that the Holocaust represents an assault on our civilization that has not been absorbed into either our consciousness or our conscience. Therefore, it demands "the most systematic, reflective, attention that can be given." For it is a dismal fact that philosophy in the years since World War II—very nearly without exception—has been written as if the Holocaust had never occurred. With the exception of Hannah Arendt,[14] none of the major thinkers whose lives were personally touched by the Holocaust has chosen to address the questions of its meaning and significance.

Leaving aside all the major figures of Anglo-American philosophy, from Russell to Rorty, who at least were not intimately involved with the events, we can identify those major philosophers who were: Sartre, Heidegger, Camus, Jaspers, Adorno, and Buber. To be fair, most of these philosophers have, with the obvious exception of Heidegger, dealt with the various aspects of what happened. But they have failed to confront systematically the implications of the Holocaust. None of them has taken the destruction as anything like a major theme or problem in his writings. Heidegger's complete silence with respect to the Holocaust may speak volumes. David Glanz has this to say about Buber's silence:

> It is disturbing to observe how little Martin Buber, a man considered by some as the leading "Jewish" philosopher of the twentieth century, himself an escapee from this modern *mabul*, this Noahidian flood, had to say about it. His inability to grapple with this problem has serious implications for his view of history and of evil. . . . Even in his social and political works after the Nazis, Buber's thought flows on, unperturbed by the Holocaust.[15]

It is not entirely clear why philosophy has so consistently evaded the responsibility of confronting the Holocaust. However, Lewis Feuer has commented on the question of why the Holocaust has evoked so little response from professional philosophers and writers on ethics. He points out that the likely reason that mainstream philosophy has ignored the Holocaust is

> because Western European thought had predominantly arrived at a pervasive pessimistic standpoint long before the Second World War. In empiricist circles at that time the pursuing of one's "values" in logical arguments and critical studies smacked of a desperate effort to obliterate in one's work the meaninglessness of things, an unwritten understanding prevailed that "ultimate" questions were not in good form. What Thomas Henry Huxley called the "nightmare" that had descended upon European intellectuals with the primacy of deterministic convictions still weighs upon Western Thought.[16]

The consequences of this lack of concern about the Holocaust is suggested by Saul Friedländer when he states: "Three decades have increased our knowledge of the events as such, but not our understanding of them. There is no clearer perspective today, no deeper comprehension than immediately after the war."[17]

Does this mean that the events of the Holocaust have bankrupted twentieth-century philosophy? More than one writer has suggested that this must indeed be the case, whether the failure is to be described as moral, metaphysical, or epistemological in nature.[18]

It is not the purpose of this essay to suggest that philosophy is finished. We contend that twentieth-century philosophy does have the tools and methods necessary to begin to confront certain aspects of the Holocaust. However, if other aspects of the Holocaust are shown to resist clarification using those tools and methods, philosophy will be obliged to generate new ways of conceptualizing that will help in understanding the transformational impact of the Holocaust. Or perhaps as John Herman Randall, Jr., says, philosophers must deal with the new and the unknown in concepts that are familiar to them. Human beings, he says,

> can work on only what they have inherited. Fresh experience and novel problems they must understand with the instruments they have learned from those who came before them. New ideas they must grasp in the concepts they already know, for they have no others; new habits they must work slowly into the accustomed pattern of their lives.[19]

Historically, philosophy has long been concerned with the analysis of novel events and phenomena, especially those with alleged "transformational" implications, that challenge the values and direction of cultural change. As John Dewey observed:

> The life of all thought is to effect a junction at some point of the new and old, of deep-sunk customs and unconscious dispositions, that are brought to the light of attention by some conflicts with newly emerged directions of activity. Philosophies which emerge at distinctive periods define the larger patterns of continuity which are woven in, effecting the enduring junctions of a stubborn past and an insistent future.[20]

Moreover, suggesting what are called today the heuristic and hermeneutic functions of philosophy, Dewey goes on to describe the passage of such emergent philosophies as going beyond the merely factual accounts of what happened. Thus:

> Beyond this island of [factual] meanings, which in their own nature are true or false, lies the ocean of meanings to which truth and falsity are irrelevant. . . . In philosophy we are dealing with something comparable to the meaning of Athenian civilization or of a drama or a lyric. Significant history is lived in the imagination of man, and philosophy is a further excursion of the imagination into its prior achievements.[21]

Dewey further specifies the criteria to be employed in such a test of philosophy: "Philosophy marks a change in culture. In forming patterns to be conformed to in future thought and action, it is additive and transforming in its role in the history of civilization."[22]

In sum, then, one response to the test of philosophy in confronting the Holocaust is either to apply the concepts that we already have to what Dewey calls the insistent future in such a manner that the transformational potential of the event is disclosed, or if these well-tried concepts don't adequately illuminate the Holocaust then, as with any anomaly, to invent new concepts. Only then can the potential significance of the Holocaust emerge as actually transforming the accustomed pattern of our lives. Only then will philosophy be performing the role into which it is cast in Dewey's conception of the drama of civilization.

In what follows, an attempt is made to sketch and outline some of the ways in which philosophy can proceed to meet the challenge of the Holocaust, interpret its meaning for our time, and begin the enormous "transforming" work envisaged for it in the conception of philosophy shared by Dewey and Randall. Furthermore, it may also become clear to what extent the conception of philosophy here embraced conforms to that vision.

We must begin with that which is familiar. Our interpretive approach, accordingly, draws upon the insights of a variety of disciplines besides our own. We must place the event within the perspective of the historical process. The search for interpretive signposts involves or incorporates different categories of meaning appropriate to the event, ranging from political and artistic to economic and scientific; from the psychological to the geopolitical. Second, we must analyze the concepts in which the event is articulated, since the reality of the event is only manifested through its language. The confusion over how such terms as "Holocaust," "genocide," "uniqueness," and "resistance" are to be used has helped mystify and obscure the event's meanings. Therefore, as Michael Berenbaum has claimed, "we must . . . establish a common language,"[23] as far as that is possible with the purpose of helping accomplish the task at hand.[24] And finally, and most important, philosophy must examine the Holocaust in relation to the established values and categories that comprise the "taken for granted" character of our civilization.

It is not the intention of this essay to identify and diagnose all the features of the Holocaust that can be said to have a potentially "transformational" effect on our civilization. However, certain features seem to be such likely candidates that they deserve mention as illustrative of the sorts of challenges that any philosophical approach to the meaning of the Holocaust is bound to encounter. Such features of the event we view as "transformational" precisely because they directly force a reexamination of familiar categories and concepts; they demand that we ask ourselves if our assumptions about the world in which we live are, in fact, well grounded. They pose the question as to the very adequacy of our cherished beliefs and customary ideals. The simplest possible answer is, they seem to render ineffectual and impotent certain of our customary habits of thought and action.[25]

If we are to avoid the intellectual trap of dismissing the Holocaust as a mere "aberration" of history, we must look to those social structures and processes that comprise the context of the event itself. We must seek to understand the development of those institutions and predominant modes of thought that established the historical conditions that made such an event as the Holocaust possible.[26] For, as Richard Rubenstein has suggested, "The Holocaust was an expression of some of the most significant political, moral, religious and demographic tendencies of Western civilization in the twentieth century."[27] A complete analysis of such tendencies, while essential for a full critical comprehension of the Holocaust, obviously lies beyond the scope of this essay. However, certain features of Western culture stand out so prominently that they can readily be recognized as paradigmatic. They are central paradigms, or models, of the modern age. They highlight the paramount presuppositions of modernity.

One such paradigm arises from the Enlightenment conviction that science and technology, grounded in functional reason, would inevitably lead to progress.[28] The French Revolution incorporated this paradigm into the fabric of modern history and consciousness in a way that came to dominate our personal and cultural beliefs so completely as to be beyond criticism. As Charles Drekmeier states:

> Technology has invaded our lives to a degree that makes it extremely difficult for us to view it critically. Our basic values have been shaped by a conception of progress rooted deeply in technological development, but in obscuring the very idea of humanity, technology has rendered ambiguous that tradition of enlightened values from which the concept of progress emerged.[29]

From the Industrial Revolution to the First World War, this paradigm was gradually embodied in a culture engaged in colonial expansion and imperial domination. In these "adventures," science and technology, originally conceived as humanizing forces of progress also became dehumanizing instruments of domination. The debilitating consequences of this trend, culminating in the First World War, were scarcely recognized. That war, which might have had transformational consequences, served rather to accelerate the logic of the Enlightenment. The "rationality" of technique became even more firmly rooted in the postwar period. In a world that had been made "safe for democracy," functional reason emerged triumphant.

In this period philosophy came to play its own role in the evolution of the paradigm of modernity. Under the influence of positivism, facts were divorced from values. The language of science and technology alone became the bearer of such "truth" as could be attained by philosophy.[30] The role of mainstream philosophy as critic of culture was abandoned, and this escape from public responsibility was signaled by the increasing professionalization of the discipline on the model of science and technology.[31] The traditional concept of philosophy as the "ground-map of the province of criticism"[32] was given up in favor of a new concept of philosophy as "technique."[33] Thus, philosophy itself becomes part of the paradigm of modernity. By relinquishing its critical role it becomes part of the problem. Insofar as philosophy came to reflect the ascendancy of functional reason and the abandonment of critical reason, it participated in the "logic" that made the Holocaust possible. It would appear, then, that philosophy's failure thus far to meet the test of the Holocaust is no inexplicable aberration. Instead, it is a continuation of a tendency within the discipline since the Enlightenment to abdicate its responsibility for criticism of ethical and cultural matters in favor of more technical pursuits.

What is important for philosophers to recognize and analyze is that the Holocaust has challenged, if not destroyed, the cultural belief that science and technology would lead inevitably to progress. The belief that science is "privileged" and that technologies would always be available to ameliorate, if not to solve, human problems was rooted in the ideal of an earthly paradise, of the fulfillment of human beings on earth, rather than in a transcendental heaven. It is this ideal that was so brutally confronted by the Holocaust.[34]

Most people continue to believe in progress because they have failed to integrate the transformational implications of the Holocaust.[35] "Faith in progress, sorely battered in the traumatic century, still holds its allure for mankind. This generation, which more than most has looked destruction in the face, has no shortage of reformers, manipulators, and utopians who are confident that they know the secret of progress."[36]

However, to sustain a belief in the idea of progress as an inevitability is difficult when we recognize that the Holocaust was made possible largely by both science and technology. We agree with George Iggers when he states that "the Final Solution, which in a sense symbolized the high point of the application of modern science and technology in the service of inhumanity, appears to spell the total absurdity of progress."[37] Irving Greenberg echoes a similar sentiment: "No assessment of modern culture can ignore the fact that science and technology—the accepted flower and glory of modernity— . . . climaxed in the factories of death."[38] This notion was dramatically extended by Max Horkheimer and Theodor Adorno, who reversed the received view of the idea of progress. Because of the Holocaust, they wrote, "history has to mean a progress toward Hell."[39]

Technology and modern science gave us the tools that in the twentieth century made mass destruction possible. The prominent symbol of the idea of progress for humanity is the smokestack, the symbol of Auschwitz. The facilities of modern science and technology helped to generate vast bureaucratic procedures that made the processing of millions for extermination into a relatively orderly routine. Thus, instead of solely aiding humanity in its quest for perfection, science and technology also taught it newer and easier means of murder and destruction of large numbers of people; in the twentieth century the art of mass murder has become the science of mass murder. Killing was made another means of mass production; processing or recycling bodies of the dead was another form of industrial output. As Rubenstein has written, "Bureaucratic mass murder reached its fullest development when gas chambers with the capacity for killing two thousand people at a time were installed at Auschwitz."[40]

Along with the methods of mass killing, science also legitimized the ideological basis, or the motivating cause, for mass murder. The Jews, along with Gypsies, Slavs, and millions of others, were "scientifically" decreed inferior races or designated as "life unworthy of life." The fact that these claims were advanced and even believed in the name of science, and were expounded by scientific authorities, lent a high degree of credence to popular prejudices and made the acceptance of the idea of mass extermination so much easier for a large number of people. After all, under these "scientific" claims, what was taking place was not killing for killing's sake. Rather, it was a deliberate "scientific" undertaking to correct the errors of the past by removal of the causes of these errors, and to improve the best in the racial stock of a nation so that it would become better and stronger in the future. It was a "progressive" effort toward the attainment of the holiest of the Enlightenment ideals: perfection. In recognition of this factor Arendt has written that "there is very little doubt that the perpetrators [of the Holocaust] committed [these crimes] for the sake of their ideology which they believed to be proven by science, experience and the laws of life."[41]

Robert J. Lifton's recent work on medical killing in Nazi Germany further supports the above formulations.[42] He points out that the Nazi "biomedical vision," whereby mass murder was committed in the name of healing the racially "diseased" body of the German Republic, was a central element that made the Holocaust possible. Moreover, it was the Nazi "scientific" notion that dangerous Jewish characteristics could be linked with alleged data of scientific disciplines that made the resulting "racial social biology" a particularly vicious form of anti-Semitism, which had the packaging of intellectual respectability. As Lifton says, "Nazi ruling authority was maintained in the name of the higher biological principle . . . assembling and preserving the most valuable stocks of basic racial elements in this [Aryan] people . . . [and] . . . raising them to a dominant position."[43] Lifton further points out that it was the biological authorities who were called on to articulate and implement "scientific racism," and doctors with their scientific ideology who had a unique place in the killing process at Auschwitz and elsewhere from beginning to end. It was, for example, the doctors who supervised the selections at the death camps—deciding who would live to work, who would die in the gas chambers, and who would become guinea pigs in the cruel experiments. Doctors also cooperated in sterilization and euthanasia programs, counseled patients toward "racially pure" marriages, and expelled Jews from medicine. It is these unforeseen implications of modern science and technology that have not been properly assimilated into our consciousness.

We cannot, of course, indict science and technology as such for the Holocaust. But it is not merely that science and technology were put to horrible use either. Rather, we should notice, first, that industrialized science, tied as it is to the structure of the state, carries with it dangerous potential. Moreover, and critically, there is a distinctive mode of thought that underlies science and technology, what has been called "functional reason." Kren and Rappoport take issue strongly with this mode of thought in *The Holocaust and the Crisis of Human Behavior:*

> The science and technology which had been increasingly celebrated for almost a century as the bastion of Western rationality and had become synonymous with liberal-progressive thought turned out to be a major factor contributing to the feasibility of the Holocaust. . . . In a number of ways the evidence surrounding the Holocaust suggests emphatically that from its origins . . . to its final large-scale industrial actualization at Auschwitz, the scientific mode of thought and the methodology attached to it were intrinsic to the mass killings.[44]

Even allowing for some overstatement by Kren and Rappoport, we have good reason to take their warning seriously. Forty years after the Holocaust, with computers and robotics making possible techniques that would have astounded even the Nazis, we have increasing reason to reassess the role played in our society by science and technology, and we must surely question the mode of thought that it appears to sanction.

It is precisely this mode that has been variously described in the critical literature as "technical reason," "pragmatic reason," and "instrumental reason." Since the term "instrumental reason" suggests Dewey's own "instrumentalism," something far from what we intend here, we have adopted the term "functional reason" to describe the mode of thought referred to by Kren and Rappoport. It is this habit of thought that is at the core of the paradigm of modernity to which we have already referred. It is a way of thinking that can be distinguished by a number of characteristics. It is impersonal. It separates the emotional from the intellectual. It is amoral, concerned with means and not ends. It claims to be value free and outside moral considerations. It is "task oriented," that is, concerned with technique and not substance. It is preoccupied with projecting an image of efficiency; it must be cost effective. To achieve "effectiveness" it quantifies its data; even human subjects are reduced to mere statistics, quantified objects. With functional reason, any qualities of humanness are stripped away, for the humane image of the person interferes with the neat, surgical precision that this mode of reason tries to achieve. Functional reason must treat people as objects, as things to be manipulated and disposed of should the necessity arise. As Lionel Rubinoff has commented, functional reason must dispense with ethics, for ethical considerations merely stand in the way of efficiency.[45] In fact we would claim that functional reason has itself become a form of ethics.

In the context of the Holocaust, functional reason led to a bureaucratic and "scientific-technical" solution to the "Jewish problem." What must be reckoned with here is that the mode of reasoning whose roots are perhaps in Bacon, Descartes, and the Enlightenment ends up finally sanctioning the means whereby enormous numbers of humans are eliminated. Moreover, it is this mode of thought that fundamentally underlies bureaucracy as such; it leads to the treatment of problems by means of bureaucratic solutions. For a great many German officials the "Jewish problem" was merely something that could be solved by finding the right bureaucratic solution. There can be little doubt that were this not the case—were not functional reason in control—the technology of death, which so clearly differentiates the Holocaust from the pogroms of the past, would not have been possible. It is this "scientific-technical-bureaucratic" mentality that comprises one of the necessary conditions for the creation of the giant factories of death used to implement the Final Solution.

The "scientific-technical-bureaucratic" mentality functions to insulate the practitioner from the ethical consequences of his action. "Ends"—in the sense of moral goals—are excluded from deliberation. Focusing on the task at hand as simply a "given" fact, this mentality asks only for the most efficient means of carrying out the task. Because the goal is *not* an appropriate matter for "scientific-technical" analysis, bureaucrats are free to adopt almost *any means necessary* for the efficient accomplishment of their assignments. The question of moral responsibility for the consequences of the adoption of particular means simply does not arise; such questions lie outside the domain of expertise in which the "scientific-technical-bureaucrat" is trained to function. Lifton describes the Nazi medical doctors as having the ability to carry on their scientific "experiments" and "research" with the attitude of professionalism and ordinariness associated with work done at any university laboratory. They had the capacity to focus on their work more or less decontextualized and without any moral awareness or responsibility about the "true" meaning of their murderous behavior.

One of the important factors that fostered this moral evasion was the Nazi use of language. This protected the bureaucrats from comprehending the fact and nature of their crimes. Through what we take to be their distorted language, the Nazis were impeded in their ability to realize why they should never have committed the atrocities they did. The rigid language system of the bureaucrats prevented them from equating their actions with their old "normal moral" knowledge of murder and lies. Such euphemisms as "Final Solution," "evacuation," and "special treatment" were used to help the murderers avoid confrontation with the meaning of their actions. Thus, the moral revulsion that ordinary labels would arouse could be readily suppressed through this "camouflage vocabulary," and the bureaucratic killing could proceed on its routine course.[46] It is, however, also important to appreciate another aspect of the Nazi use of language, namely, that they were attempting to create new meanings for old words, at least in regard to the Final Solution. In this way the new "language rules" fostered a sense in the Nazi that he or she was not murdering innocent people (as we view their actions), but rather that the act of murder had a legitimate therapeutic gain to the individual and to Germany. To the Nazi, murder did not mean murder as we ordinarily use the term, and it is this aspect of genocidal world making that is often not fully appreciated by those who are interested in understanding how the Nazis could do what they did. Without these new language rules the Nazis would not have been able to transform their old ethical world, with its conventional moral vocabulary and conscience, into a new world where mass murder was viewed as an individually and collectively meaningful task to be achieved at all costs. It is within this scientific technical bureaucratic context with its new language rules and tunnel vision that there emerged a new kind of executioner unique to the Holocaust—the "desk killer."[47]

The "desk killer" is an executive type, a functionary in a vast bureaucratic organization, who does his killing from behind a desk without wielding any weapons more lethal than the typewriter and dictaphone with which he deals out orders of death. These are processed along deliberately anonymous channels, through a labyrinth of bureaucratic routines so that the desk killer is isolated from his victims. He never sees the faces of those he consigns to the gas chambers. His concern is merely with numbers. The victims are but numbers of items passed along a conveyor belt by a faceless bureaucracy constructed for the purpose of solving a particular problem. The "desk killer" has mastered the art of functional reason, or it has mastered him, so that the killing of millions of people is an action that is totally devoid of moral responsibility. It is merely a matter of logistics, of carrying out an order given by higher authority in the name of the state.

In the context of the Holocaust, the "desk killer" retains his status and role in society as a normal functionary of the socioeconomic system. Such a person can continue to live a "normal" life as a citizen, family member, husband, father, and respected member of his community. He "need lose no sleep over his victims. He never confronts the results of his distinctive kind of homicidal violence."[48]

For why should he not continue in his normal role? What he does is part of the normal functioning of the society in which he lives. His skill in perfecting the forms of mass murder is a valued asset to the community. Without the development of such skills by thousands of otherwise ordinary men and women, the implementation of the Final Solution could not have taken place; the "desk killer" is but the "organization man"—the "man in the gray flannel suit"—functioning rationally in the context of his society.

In her *Eichmann in Jerusalem*, Arendt describes some of the salient features of the desk killer as she observed them in Eichmann. Arendt was struck by the manifest shallowness of Eichmann, which made it impossible to trace the uncontestable evil of his deeds to any deeper level of motives. She further observed that although Eichmann's deeds were monstrous, he himself was quite ordinary, commonplace, neither demonic nor monstrous—hence the banality of evil. Eichmann, says Arendt, was thoughtless—that is, he handled the world through cliché-ridden language and was thrown into chaos whenever he was not able to apply his stock phrases and clichés at the trial. Eichmann, the paradigmatic desk killer was not "stupid," since he knew how to do what was required of him very well, but he did not understand the reasons, or how such a system that he was part of actually operated and for what purpose—"he never realized what he was doing," observes Arendt.[49]

The desk killer is not only an obedient bureaucrat following orders. As Raul Hilberg has shown, the Nazi bureaucrat was far from a passive functionary in the destruction process. He was constantly innovating, turning the order for the Final Solution into an effective, efficient, disciplined apparatus of destruction. The contract negotiations for Zyklon B, the documents indicating the special handling instructions, the controversy over patents and the economic profits that accrued to the manufacturer—all indicate that the Nazi bureaucrat was not a passive pencil pusher in the destruction process.[50]

Perhaps it is precisely because we find it difficult to consider that any form of rationality could have evil consequences of such vast proportions as the Holocaust that we persistently avoid coming to terms with the implications of the "desk killer." As Ernest Becker has said, we have great difficulty facing the reality of disinterested bureaucratic evil. "It is just too much to believe that simple bureaucratic decision, simple paperwork expediency, can abstractly grind up six million lives."[51]

The work of social psychologists has suggested that "desk killing" is a mode of being that most of us could assume if the powerful situational variables that were in Germany existed today.[52] Stanley Milgram, for example, experimentally studied the conflict between obeying authority and refusing to hurt an innocent person. In these highly publicized experiments an experimenter ordered a subject known as the "teacher" to shock a "learner" each time he or she gave a wrong answer on a learning task. The learner or victim was an actor who actually received no shock at all. As is well known, 65 percent of the subjects obeyed orders and inflicted what they thought was extreme pain on a protesting victim. Says Milgram:

> I must conclude that Arendt's conception of the banality of evil comes closer to the truth than one might dare imagine. The ordinary person who shocked the victim did so out of a sense of obligation—a conception of his duties as a subject—and not from any peculiar aggressive tendencies.
>
> This is, perhaps the most fundamental lesson of our study: ordinary people, simply doing their jobs, and without any particular hostility on their parts, can become agents in a terrible destructive process. Moreover, even when the destructive effects of their work become clear, and they are asked to carry out actions incompatible with fundamental standards of morality, relatively few people have the resources needed to resist authority. A variety of inhibitions against disobeying authority come into play and successfully keep the person in his place.[53]

The phenomenon of the "desk killer," with its frightening implications for the potential evil actions of an ordinary person, is a necessary condition of the Holocaust. As Lionel Rubinoff has observed, "Men acquired the capacity for engaging in evil without experiencing it as such. They learned how to perform evil acts as part of their job description."[54] As Arendt implies, this means that the whole notion of evil as we have conventionally understood it must be radically revised to give it the broadest possible implications. Arendt says that the Holocaust "has brought into the world a radical evil characterized by its divorce from all humanly comprehensible motives of wickedness."[55]

That is, the customary moral and intellectual categories that we use to understand evil are no longer plausible when trying to make sense of the Holocaust. It is this realization rooted in the feeling of being totally overwhelmed by the magnitude of the evil of the event that has fostered a trend in the literature that views the Holocaust as inevitably, fundamentally, and forever incomprehensible. Irving Howe, for example, has written that "Holocaust writings often reveal the helplessness of the mind before an evil that cannot quite be imagined, or the helplessness of the imagination before an evil that cannot quite be understood."[56] It is this "chilling sense of conceptual unpreparedness" that allows philosophers and all those interested in understanding the Holocaust to write as though the Holocaust is incomprehensible.

We believe that it is necessary to evolve new concepts of evil that will help illuminate the Holocaust and give us a language and a sense of moral anchoring in an ethically indifferent universe. It is clear that the old categories of evil are deeply flawed.

In the Enlightenment view, evil is perceived as owing to some kind of intractable ignorance, a "flaw of character" issuing in false pride, hate, envy, or—in the later and more "psychological" phase—as due to "innate" forces of aggression. In its manifest form, overt brutality, evil was simply regarded as the behavior of bullies. But these views of evil fail to explain the systematic, rational, technologically implemented destruction of millions of people in factorylike buildings functioning in a highly cost-effective manner. As Rubenstein comments, "It was only when the bureaucrats took over from the bullies that mass murder became possible."[57] In short, the Holocaust demonstrates the need for a new *conception* of evil, for it has created a new *form* of evil.[58] It is a form that is structured by the calculating ideological rationality of functional reason, practiced by ordinary men and women isolated from both their own consciences and the consequences of their acts by the protective barriers of their executive desks and their bureaucratic agencies. It is a form of evil comprising the ultimate perversion of the Enlightenment ideal of progress.

We believe that the best way to deal with this challenge is to show the relationship between radical and banal evil. This is the crucial dialectic, which needs to be better articulated as a new category of evil. By radical evil we mean evil that cannot be explained by any of the already mentioned conventional human motives nor understood by applying our well-tried modes of analysis and interpretation.[59] Radical evil like the Holocaust is transformative by the very fact that it is viewed as an awesome anomaly and should require a rethinking of our basic assumptions. By banal evil we mean evil that is done by "normal" ordinary people, as part of their everyday routine more or less detached from the overall evil effect of their usual bureaucratic activities. It is the quality of thoughtlessness, says Arendt, that is the important distinguishing feature of banal evil and that helps foster an unawareness in the doer of the effect that such activities have in generating radical evil.

The fact is that the Holocaust has put into sharp focus a terrible irony, namely, ordinary people doing low-level paperwork can foster such horrible events as the murder of millions of innocent people.

Finally, the evil of the Holocaust has also strongly highlighted another issue in need of philosophical analysis, namely, the problem that in a world that is based on the belief that man is a creator of his own values, the judgment of what constitutes evil is ambiguous at best. We do well to remember that Hitler's government can be regarded as legal, at least in terms of how it was instituted. As grotesque as it may be, the truth is that those who abided by the laws of the land committed no blameworthy acts, since what constitutes a criminal act is violation of the law. As Rubenstein has written, "The Nazis committed absolutely no 'crime' in the Holocaust."[60] That is, genocide may be defined as a moral virtue of a given state since there is no universe of moral obligation. The deep problem here, of course, is the problem of ethical relativism. If, as modern man seems to believe, neither God nor Nature can generate for us an unambiguous and coherent set of values and we are left to create them, must we suppose that the moral must yield to the legal?[61]

Eichmann, for example, believed that "what he had done was a crime only in retrospect, and he had always been a law-abiding citizen because Hitler's orders, which he had certainly executed to the best of his ability, had possessed 'The force of law' in The Third Reich."[62] Arendt further points out that Eichmann did not act out of base motives regarding the Jews, "he would have had a bad conscience only if he had not done what he had been ordered to do—to ship millions of men, women and children to their death with great zeal and the most meticulous care."[63] Is the "good person" then but the "good citizen," but in grotesque inversion in which "a good person" is just that person who has no need of a bad conscience just because he is "law abiding"? But indeed, we must then consider the possibility that what any "good person" will do is considerably a measure of the widely shared assumptions of his or her community, of the particular circumstances of his or her life, and of the choices available. And if so, we need to understand how the Nazis were in the process of creating a genocidal society from those historically available materials that are so pervasively features of all modern societies.

Investigating the nature of evil and our ability to make moral judgments that challenge our familiar modes of analysis and interpretation raises the kinds of questions that demand philosophical reflection.

The test that the Holocaust presents to philosophy is substantial. The genocidal universe the Nazis created, the universe of death, the

Final Solution, calls into question our most basic assumptions about the possibilities of the human spirit. The temptation to avoid facing the implications of this event, then, is understandable. Moreover, this exploration is simply one response that philosophy can make to the Holocaust. To move beyond this analysis, to interpret the strategic importance of the Holocaust as a whole so as to "effect a junction of the new and the old," is a staggering task, one requiring great courage and dedication. Yet it is one that we as philosophers dare not shirk. For it is clear that if we do not undertake it, our philosophy becomes irrelevant, and our efforts to capture the meaning of human life and culture in our time will be empty gestures, meaningless postures in the face of history.

We may be aided in this undertaking by recalling what we have already learned about the mentality that led to the Holocaust. Blind faith in the efficacy of functional reason led directly to the horrors of the gas chambers. The "desk killer" mentality, the disjunction of science and technology from ethical and cultural criticism made the Holocaust possible. As philosophers we cannot assume the disjunction between facts and values; we must never again subscribe to the myth of value-free science and technology, or accept that the "mores" of a particular culture can provide an adequate moral justification for whatever practices members of that culture may exhibit.

We must be wary of the hidden implications of vicious cultural relativism, as well as the dangers of moral absolutism.[64] Finally, we can never again allow philosophy to be subsumed under the cultural framework it is meant to consider and critique. Philosophy, if it is ever to truly meet the test of the Holocaust, must dedicate itself to the wider questions of human meaning and worth, not simply to the safer arenas of technique and analysis. As Adorno has said, a philosophical thinking that does not test itself in the light of extremity is comparable to the music by which the SS customarily drowned out the cries of its victims.[65]

Finally, as philosophers, above all else, we must still face the awful possibility that we will, one day, be drawn into another genocidal Holocaust. Indeed, the nuclear threat, laced with the same perilous confidence in technology, may be understood as the genocide to end all genocides. It is to be hoped that philosophy's confrontation with the Holocaust will serve, then, as a truly transformational encounter, one that opens our eyes to questions of the greatest importance, which must be faced if humanity is to survive, and if philosophy is to maintain its basic integrity. As Kren and Rappoport have written "the only visions of the world that can be taken seriously are those that come through their irrevocably ash-darkened prisms of post-Holocaust sense and sensibility."[66]

NOTES

1. John Dewey, *Problems of Men* (New York: Philosophical Library, 1946), pp. 11–12.

2. For analysis of these enigmas and paradoxes, see Alan Rosenberg, "Understanding the Holocaust," *European Judaism* 17, no. 2 (Winter 1983–84): 16–20; and Chapter 19 in this volume, "The Crisis in Knowing and Understanding the Holocaust."

3. See Alan Rosenberg, "Was the Holocaust Unique? A Peculiar Question?" in *Genocide and the Modern Age: Ideology and Case Studies of Mass Death*, ed. Isidor Wallimann and Michael N. Dobkowski (Westport, Conn.: Greenwood Press, 1987), pp. 145–61.

4. Henry Feingold, "Four Days in April: A Review of NCC's Dramatization of the Holocaust," *Shoah* 1, no. 1, 16.

5. Emil Fackenheim, *The Jewish Return into History: Reflections in the Age of Auschwitz and a New Jerusalem* (New York: Schocken, 1978), p. 279.

6. Alvin Rosenfeld and Irving Greenberg, *Confronting the Holocaust: The Impact of Elie Wiesel* (Bloomington: Indiana University Press, 1978), p. xi.

7. Elie Wiesel, *Legends of Our Time* (New York: Holt, Rinehart & Winston, 1968), p. 190.

8. Elie Wiesel, *One Generation After* (New York: Avon, 1970), p. 15.

9. George M. Kren and Leon Rappoport, *The Holocaust and the Crisis of Human Behavior* (New York: Holmes and Meier, 1980), pp. 12–15. For an elaboration of this problem, see Alan Rosenberg and Alexander Bardosh, "The Holocaust and Historical Crisis: A Review Essay," *Modern Judaism* 1, no. 3 (December 1981): 337–46.

10. Fackenheim, *The Jewish Return*, p. 210 and pp. 106–7.

11. Alice L. and A. Roy Eckardt, "Studying the Holocaust's Impact Today: Some Dilemmas of Language and Method," *Judaism* 27, no. 2 (Spring 1978): 227. Reprinted here as Chapter 23.

12. For an interesting approach to this problem, see Ronald Aronson, "Why? Towards a Theory of the Holocaust," *Socialist Review* 11, no. 4 (July–August 1981): 67–68.

13. Patricia Bender, Ethel Roskies, and Richard Lazarus, "Stress and Coping under Extreme Conditions," in *Survivors, Victims, and Perpetrators*, ed. Joel Dimsdale (New York: Hemisphere Publishing, 1980), p. 253.

14. Hannah Arendt, "Social Science Techniques and the Study of Concentration Camps," *Jewish Social Studies* 12, no. 1 (January 1950): 49–64. Reprinted here as Chapter 18. Also, see *Totalitarianism*, pt. 3 of Arendt's *The Origins of Totalitarianism* (New York: Harcourt, Brace and World, 1968).

15. David Glanz, "Buber's Concept of Holocaust and History," *Forum* 30–31 (Spring–Summer 1978): 142. More recently philosophers have begun to grapple with the Holocaust. See "Philosophy and the Holocaust," a special double issue of the *Philosophical Forum* 16, nos. 1–2 (Fall–Winter 1984–85); "A Special Issue on the Holocaust," *Journal of Social Philosophy* 13, no. 3 (September 1982).

16. Lewis S. Feuer, "The Reasoning of Holocaust Theology," *This World*, no. 14 (Spring–Summer 1986): 81.

17. Saul Friedländer, "Some Aspects of the Historical Significance of the Holocaust," *Jerusalem Quarterly* 1, no. 1 (Fall 1976): 36.

18. Jacob Katz makes this point very explicit in his article, "Was the Holocaust Predictable?": "To Auschwitz and Treblinka there was no historical analogy, no philosophical or for that matter, theologic framework in which they might be accommodated. This was an absolute *novum*, unassimilable in any vocabulary at the disposal of the generation that experienced it. And it remains so today, despite the tremendous effort to investigate all its aspects. . . . Given the radically transcendent

nature of the Holocaust, what significance can there be to the mere historical recording of its events, let alone attempting to lay bare their roots in a more or less remote past? What enlightenment may be possibly derived from tracing the history of anti-Semitism, or Jewish-Christian relations in past centuries, if indeed the Holocaust has to be conceived as an absolute *novem*, unparalleled in previous generations? . . . What is the use of rehearsing these horrors in historical retrospect? Is it not a kind of masochism, a form of useless penitence for not having shared the fate of the victims?" *Commentary* 59, no. 5 (May 1975): 45. This kind of an argument, if taken seriously, is an invitation of philosophers and others to continue to ignore the problem. George Steiner raises in part a similar point, but in a more sensible manner. In writing about the Holocaust he states: "We are not—and this is often misunderstood—considering something truly analogous to other cases of massacres, to the murder of the Gypsies or, earlier, of the Armenians. There are parallels in technique and in the idiom of hatred. But not ontologically, not at the level of philosophic intent. That intent takes us to the heart of certain instabilities in the fabric of Western culture, in the relation between instinctual and religious life." *Bluebeard's Castle: Some Notes Towards the Redefinition of Culture* (New Haven: Yale University Press, 1971), p. 36.

19. John Herman Randall, Jr., *The Career of Philosophy* (New York: Columbia University Press, 1962), p. 9.

20. John Dewey, *Philosophy and Civilization* (New York: Capricorn Books, 1963), p. 7.

21. Ibid., p. 5.

22. Ibid., p. 8.

23. Michael Berenbaum, "Reflections on Teaching about the Holocaust," *Conservative Judaism* 34, no. 3 (January–February 1981): 41.

24. For an excellent illustration of how philosophical analysis can aid in clarifying the language used in discussing the Holocaust, see Dan Magurshak, "The 'Incomprehensibility' of the Holocaust: Tightening up Some Loose Usage," *Judaism* 29, no. 2 (Spring 1980): 233–42. Reprinted here as Chapter 22.

25. For a more detailed analysis of the Holocaust as a transformational event, see Kren and Rappoport, *The Holocaust*, and Rosenberg and Bardosh, "The Holocaust."

26. For one of the most significant attempts to establish the conditions that made the Holocaust possible, see Hannah Arendt, *Imperialism*, pt. 2 of *The Origins of Totalitarianism*, esp. pp. 65–101. For a concise summary of Arendt's position, see Henry Feingold, "The Bureaucrat as Mass Killer: Arendt on Eichmann," *Response* 12, no. 3 (Summer 1980): 48–49.

27. Richard L. Rubenstein, *The Cunning of History: Mass Death and the American Future* (New York: Harper and Row, 1975), p. 6.

28. For an exceptionally clear analysis of the development of the idea of progress, see Peter T. Manicas, *A History and Philosophy of the Social Sciences* (London: Blackwell, 1987), pp. 53–72.

29. Charles Drekmeier, "Knowledge as Virtue, Knowledge as Power," in *Sanctions For Evil*, ed. Nevitt Sanford and Craig Comstock and Associates (Boston: Beacon Press, 1971), p. 220.

30. Feuer, "The Reasoning of Holocaust Theology."

31. For a fascinating analysis of this problem, see Alan Janik and Stephen Toulmin, *Wittgenstein's Vienna* (New York: Simon & Schuster, 1973), pp. 26–27 and 239–62.

32. John Dewey, *Experience and Nature* (New York: Dover, 1958), p. 413.

33. For a good review of the significance of this problem, see William Barrett, *The Illusion of Technique: A Search for Meaning in a Technological Civilization* (New York: Anchor Books, 1978), pp. 3–29.

34. Henryk Skolimowski, "The Scientific World View and the Illusions of Progress," *Social Research* 41, no. 1 (Spring 1974):52-53.

35. Robert Nisbet's *History of the Idea of Progress* (New York: Basic Books, 1980) is an excellent example of this omission. Nisbet's book, widely regarded as the most important work on the subject since J. B. Bury's *The Idea of Progress: An Inquiry into Its Origin and Growth* (New York: Dover Publications, 1955) tries very hard to show that progress should continue to be the animating and controlling idea of Western civilization. Yet he makes no mention of the Holocaust's impact on this proposition in his book.

36. Roger Shinn, "Perilous Progress in Genetics," *Social Research* 41, no. 1 (Spring 1974): 83.

37. George Iggers, "The Idea of Progress: A Critical Reassessment," *American Historical Review* 71, no. 1 (October 1965): 15.

38. Irving Greenberg, "Cloud of Smoke, Pillar of Fire," in *Auschwitz: Beginning of a New Era? Reflections on the Holocaust*, ed. Eva Fleischner (New York: KTAV, 1977), p. 15.

39. Michael Landman, in Zoltan Tar, *The Frankfurt School* (New York: Wiley, 1977), p. xvi.

40. Rubenstein, *Cunning of History*, p. 25.

41. Arendt, "Social Science Techniques," p. 62.

42. Robert J. Lifton, *The Nazi Doctors: Medical Killing and the Psychology of Genocide* (New York: Basic Books, 1986).

43. Ibid., p. 17.

44. Kren and Rappoport, *The Holocaust*, p. 133.

45. Lionel Rubinoff, "Auschwitz and the Pathology of Jew-Hatred," in Fleischner, *Auschwitz*, p. 355.

46. Herbert C. Kelman, "Violence without Moral Restraint: Reflections on the Dehumanization of Victims and Victimizers," *Journal of Social Issues* 29, no. 4 (1973): 29-62.

47. It may be that ever since the Industrial Revolution and the increase in technological and bureaucratic means of warfare the "desk killer" has been in existence. What is new in the Holocaust is that this type of killer becomes dominant to such a degree that the whole meaning of murder is altered. Mass murder becomes an "executive" matter—the "executioner as executive."

48. Rubenstein, *Cunning of History*, p. 26. The fact is that both persecutors and victims normalize even the most barbaric of situations, for without this capacity the individual would lose everything that he regards as essentially human. Those who were incarcerated in concentration camps, for example, who witnessed the torture of fellow inmates, eventually created some kind of "normal" experience where the suffering of their fellow inmates did not obsess them and occupy their whole lives. The same point could be and has been made about those who operated the concentration camps.

49. Hannah Arendt, *Eichmann in Jerusalem: A Report on the Banality of Evil* (New York: Viking, 1963). What was new about the Nazi genocide was the preponderance of the bureaucratic desk killer with his keen organizational skills. However, we must not lose sight of the fact that bureaucrats need loyal henchmen to carry out their administrative orders. The Third Reich had a usually plentiful amount of sadists and killers who were only too willing to do the bureaucrat's dirty work. See Leon Wieseltier, "Demjanjuk in Jerusalem," *New Republic*, March 30, 1987, pp. 15-16.

50. See Michael Birenbaum, "The Inner and Outer World of Hell," *Tikkun* 1, no. 2 (1986): 113.

51. Ernest Becker, *Angel in Armor* (New York: Free Press, 1975), p. 140.

52. See Stanley Milgram, *Obedience to Authority: An Experimental View* (New York: Harper Colophon Books, 1975); Kelman, "Violence without Moral Restraint"; Craig Haney, Curtis Banks, and Philip Zimbardo, "Interpersonal Dynamics in a Simulated Prison," *International Journal of Criminology and Penology* 1 (1973): 69–97.

53. Milgram, *Obedience*, p. 6.

54. Rubinoff, "Auschwitz and the Pathology of Jew-Hatred," p. 361.

55. Hannah Arendt, "The History of the Great Crime: A Review of Léon Poliakov's *Harvest of Hate*," *Commentary* 13, no. 3 (March 1952): 300–304. Arendt gave up the notion of "radical evil" because she no longer believed that evil can have depth or demonic dimension. She therefore substitutes the term "extreme evil" as she claims it does not have these characteristics. See her *The Jew as Pariah* (New York: Grove Press, 1978), pp. 250–51.

56. Irving Howe, "Writing and the Holocaust," *New Republic*, October 27, 1986, p. 30.

57. Rubenstein, *Cunning of History*, p. 27.

58. For a provocative analysis of the need for a new understanding of evil in the modern world, see Kurt H. Wolff, "For a Sociology of Evil," *Journal of Social Issues* 24, no. 1, (1969): 111–25.

59. It is worth mentioning in passing that most religious philosophers and theologians generally believe that the Holocaust has radically challenged our classic theodicies, requiring a new framework to comprehend Auschwitz. See Steven T. Katz, *Post-Holocaust Dialogues* (New York: New York University Press, 1983).

60. Richard Rubenstein, "Discussion: The Judenrat and the Jewish Response," in *The Holocaust as Historical Experience*, ed. Yehuda Bauer and Nathan Rotemstreich (New York: Holmes and Meier, 1981), pp. 244–45.

61. For interesting analyses of the problem, see H. L. A. Hart, "Positivism and Separation of Law and Morals," and Lon L. Fuller, "Positivism and Fidelity to Law: A Reply to Professor Hart," in *Society, Law, and Morality*, ed. Frederick A. Olafson (Englewood Cliffs: Prentice-Hall, 1961), pp. 439–505.

62. Arendt, *Eichmann in Jerusalem*, p. 24.

63. Ibid., p. 25.

64. For a provocative analysis of this problem see Michael A. Arbib and Mary B. Hesse, *The Construction of Reality* (New York: Cambridge University Press, 1986), pp. 260–61.

65. See Emil L. Fackenheim, *To Mend the World: Foundations of Future Jewish Thought* (New York: Schocken, 1982) p. 182.

66. Kren and Rappoport, *The Holocaust*, p. 143.

11

THE HOLOCAUST AND HUMAN PROGRESS

Ronald Aronson

> After Auschwitz, our feelings resist any claim of the positivity of existence as sanctimonious, as wronging the victims; they balk at squeezing any kind of sense, however bleached, out of the victims' fate. And these feelings do have an objective side after events that make a mockery of the construction of immanence as endowed with a meaning radiated by an affirmatively posited transcendence.
>
> Theodor W. Adorno[1]

After Auschwitz is absorbed as fact, it must be contemplated as meaning. Philosophy, and other disciplines as well, must paint its gray in gray, setting it alongside what we already know and think about human beings, their actions, the life and world they have created. Language, for example, must be rethought in light of both the massive masking and distorting functions it assumed during the Holocaust,[2] and its weakness in rendering what happened. Is it no more than a desperate rhetorical flourish to say that poetry is impossible after Auschwitz?[3] Furthermore, all disciplines concerned with morality must be rethought in light of both the unexpected human possibilities for evil revealed at Auschwitz and our lack of a moral vocabulary for properly expressing them. The very coldness, system, and deliberateness—the *industrial* character— of the extermination camps reveal human capacities that will forever banish complacency about the human prospect. Our secularized world is left grasping in vain for words both descriptive and condemnatory, of sufficient charge and resonance to carry the weight of events in the extermination camps. Or rather, we are driven to recover such terms as *evil* from our obsolescent theological lexicons. But what else can remain of the theologies? Religions must lose all relevance to human life if they fail adequately to confront the greatest accusation that can be made against any God: that he let millions of innocent children die at the hands of the Nazi executioners.

In other words, long after we have chronicled it, Auschwitz will occupy us for years to come in sifting through its implications. It forces recasting after recasting of our pre-Holocaust knowledge, values, intellectual tools, hopes, and conclusions. Above all, I would suggest that it forces us to ask anew what we, human beings, are doing on this planet. What is the meaning of our history? If history can produce the Holocaust, where, if anywhere, is it headed?

In this essay I focus on the outlook most directly threatened by the Nazis' "Final Solution to the Jewish Problem." Before 1933 most people in the West believed, in J. B. Bury's famous formulation, that the world was slowly advancing in "a definite and desirable direction" leading to a "condition of general happiness" which would "justify the whole process of civilization."[4] And this mood continued long after 1945. Most members of Western society have been raised, in the words of Charles Frankel, "to expect that, short of a cataclysm, their children would live happier and better lives than they. They have supposed that this improvement would be cumulative and continuing and that although temporary setbacks, accidents, and disasters might take place, human knowledge, power, and happiness would increase over the long run."[5]

Frankel's qualification indicates our task. What has become of progress? Do we now walk away from the (surprisingly briefly held) view of steady human betterment and search for new ways to orient ourselves in time? Was the Holocaust a cataclysm exploding progress itself, or was it a limited disaster? On the one hand, the Holocaust was a cataclysm for its millions of victims, but the rest of the world was spared. On the other, it did destroy a world. And in so doing, it revealed the very real possibilities of cataclysm lying in wait for all of us. Although Frankel wrote the above lines after 1945, his own death—at the hands of a robber in New York—proposes an answer as eloquent as his continued hope. After Auschwitz, I would argue, progress as we have come to know it is over. What, then, if any, revised vision of progress is compatible with the Holocaust?

AUSCHWITZ AND THE END OF PROGRESS

First, the Holocaust explodes as myth the popular belief in steady, irreversible progress. Generally this view accepts the existing social order, sees significant development in either (or some combination of) science and technology, education, gradual democratization, or the productivity of capitalism (and, more recently, socialism). It sees an incremental, almost mechanical improvement in human life culminating in general well-being in the near term. This mood was captured well in 1927 by Alexander Mackendrick:

> The remarkable increase in the efficiency of industry through the achievements of science and the multiplication of tools and machinery seems to justify the belief that the age of plenty has dawned. Whatever may have been the case a century ago, it is now fairly certain that the power of production and the means of transport are such that the entire human race might be comfortably housed, clothed and nurtured.... A consciousness of social solidarity has manifested itself that is a new fact in human history.... The daily press and fictional literature have done much to focus the minds of all classes on the subjects of common interest, and to promote that sense of mutuality, of membership one with another, which must form the basis of any just demand for the establishment of rights and recognition of duties.... Such considerations would seem to offer some support to the belief in a natural law of progress, and to strengthen that unquenchable hope that by the gradual evolution of sweeter manners and purer laws, the *Civitas Dei* will ultimately be reached, and the Apocalyptic visions of seers realized.[6]

It is worth noting that this passage makes appeal to natural law. Since Auguste Comte, progress has often involved such a hidden or open appeal, resting itself on pseudoscience or on superhuman forces that crept in through the back door of history just as God was being shown the front door.[7] I call this Progress with a capital P, in order to stress its reified status as a force beyond and acting upon human beings. The onus belongs not only on Comte. Even Marx, archenemy of reification and philosopher of praxis, can sound as if history moves on its own and social contradictions have a life of their own: "What the bourgeoisie therefore produces, above all, is its own grave-diggers. Its fall and the victory of the proletariat are equally inevitable."[8] In the crudest of progressive visions, such as Mackendrick's, history seems to unfold in a positive direction virtually all by itself, carrying us humans along into a promised land of plenty.

It is also worth noting that for Mackendrick, as for so many believers in inevitable progress, the social order remains established, and within it productivity expands, science and technology flourish, and human relations grow sweeter. He foresees significant change without significant change. This illusion should have been dispelled forever by the piles of bodies unearthed in 1945 by Allied bulldozers in the liberated extermination camps.

Why? The argument springs first from a feeling, a sense of the most profound contradiction: nothing fundamentally good can contain such incredible evil as Auschwitz. But how does this conviction become converted into argument? Logically speaking it might be possible to argue that these eleven million murders of Jews and others—indeed, the Second World War of which they were part or even the twentieth century which has so far seen tens of millions more—are not incompatible with a yet more general human advance. The postwar history of both Eastern and Western Europe, for example, sites of the various Nazi camps, can be seen as following underlying prewar trends toward increasing equality, economic rationality, state intervention to ensure meeting basic human needs, and economic plenty. In this long-term perspective World War II and its massive death and destruction are only (perhaps unavoidable) interruptions of the secular trend; indeed, the catastrophe may have had the effect of eliminating obsolescent obstacles to it, such as the old central European aristocracies and lower middle classes.[9]

And so we are scarcely surprised to see politicians of all stripes speaking in common terms of continuing progress as the catastrophic century nears its close. Perhaps the Holocaust has been absorbed in a yet wider arc of human progress, but perhaps it has simply been repressed or ignored. We can think about Auschwitz, and we can think about the expansion of democracy, productivity, human rights, and benevolent science, but hardly in the same sequence of thoughts. Progress remains the dominant public mood, in spite of everything. Catastrophes that have already happened, like the Holocaust, do not puncture the mood, although perhaps more daily problems, such as recession and inflation, or catastrophes in the offing, such as nuclear war, do. In the United States, the exceptional politicians who express doubts, such as Jerry Brown or Jimmy Carter, lose to the true believers whom nothing daunts. Even the remarkably successful German Greens, in becoming the world's only major political party to speak *against* what we have come to know as progress—and indeed in the land of the Final Solution—do not point to catastrophes that have already happened, but to impending ecological, energy, and nuclear crises.

Personal testimony and other forms of historical evidence may be adequate for contradicting the revisionists who would deny that the Holocaust happened. But how can this evidence contradict the belief in progress? Certainly the horrible, irrefutable fact says something about the meaning and direction of human history, but exactly what?

To understand how the Holocaust cancels that popular Western, especially American, sense of progress that verges on natural law, we must first characterize the nature of the claims we have just seen Bury, Frankel, and especially Mackendrick voice. The difficulty, of course, is that there are so many different formulations of progress that we are at a loss to know whose definition to take. Nevertheless, progress is both philosophical idea and public mood, which has long since spread everywhere in the West, assuming the status of a secular religion. The idea of the general, steady improvement of the human lot, as a composite of the main themes that have pervaded the West, includes three kinds of assertions: (1) The growth of human powers and (2) the improvement of human relations will lead (3) to an amelioration in the conditions of human life and so to greater individual happiness.

By the growth of human powers is meant first of all, the continued growth of scientific knowledge, which immediately translates into greater and greater human power over nature. Economically this means greater productivity, and thus a heightened level of consumption. As human beings know more about the secrets of nature, more people will gain access to this knowledge, and will live better and more securely.

Human relations will improve in the direction of greater democracy, equality, and social justice. Science will be applied to the human as well as the natural world, yielding wisdom about how to improve social arrangements. The greater availability of the means to fulfill vital needs will lessen both internal social conflicts and international conflicts. And the general rise in education and political rights will create a further demand for more humane social arrangements and democratically shared political power. And so, concurrent with the rise in productivity, humans will progress politically and morally.

Individuals will become more and more secure from the terrors of the past, both human and natural. At the same time they will gain greater power over all areas of their own lives, and greater freedom to pursue directions of their own choosing. They will be able to satisfy their needs more fully and to discover and develop their capacities. In short, human happiness will become possible as never before for the great mass of people.

Thus does progress, in my composite presentation of it, have a social–political side, a scientific–technological one, and an economic one. And above all, it terminates in the foreseeable future in the appropriate consequence of all these massive social changes: individual well-being.

What the Holocaust explodes immediately is the human side of progress. Anne-Robert-Jacques Turgot, for example, spoke of a "softening" of manners,[10] the Marquis de Condorcet of greater equality, many writers of a greater sense of security in the world resulting both from lessened human conflict and from greater human control over nature. Such thinkers see human beings becoming more civilized, more humane: greater knowledge about ourselves and the world, a higher level of material consumption, and a greater assertion of human dignity would lead us, indeed compel us, to treat each other less oppressively, more humanely, less violently. And the resulting climate of security and peace would further accelerate these trends, which in turn would enhance human well-being and happiness.

The first aspect of progress to be punctured by the Holocaust is its character as quasi-natural law unfolding around and within us. The inevitability of short-term betterment is mocked most cruelly by the gas chambers, as the above epigraph by Adorno testifies. Whatever that Comtean (or other) natural law may be, it is plainly no match for the human capacity for evil. Humans clearly have a capacity for genocide and even mass suicide that confounds all optimistic projections.[11] Second, Auschwitz patently demonstrates that the projected increase in humaneness has *not* taken place, or at least that lying beneath its surface is the ability, about which we have chilling evidence, to regress to incredibly violent forms of behavior. Furthermore, what are we to say of the hope for advances toward equality when the concentration-camp universe treated members of one religion or national group, Jews, as subhumans, for the most racist of reasons—as biological parasites fit only to be exterminated? Indeed, in step after step the Jews' humanity was denied with arguments that might apply to any religious or national minority, their dignity further brutalized, until, no longer regarded as humans, their murder was a logical conclusion. In this operation the main hope of progress, human science, was used for destruction; Nazi "knowledge" about the Jews was bizarre pseudo-science filled with lunacy and fantasy, and covered with a patina of scientism. In other words, genuine science, supposed to herald human advancement, became subjected to and twisted by the Nazis' insane goals.

The degradation of Jews was paralleled by their tormentor's self-degradation. It is not the testimony of the victims, for example, in the great Holocaust literature, that leads us to doubt human dignity (or even the hope of its progress) in the wake of Auschwitz; it is rather the image of the Nazi executioners operating their killing factories, brutalized humans anaesthetized to any meaningful conceptions of morality or humanity, rigorously cut off from human fellow feeling. And it is also the smoothly functioning killing apparatus, its every aspect rooted in a complex division of labor and supported by an entire society.

And what can we say of the hope that progress would lead to increased security? Clearly we are all less secure after the Holocaust then before, utterly certain as never before that human beings can do this because they have already done it. As George Kren and Leon Rappoport note, "If one keeps at the Holocaust long enough, then sooner or later the ultimate personal truth begins to reveal itself: one knows, finally, that one might either do it, or be done to. If it could happen on such a massive scale elsewhere, then it can happen anywhere; it is all within the range of human possibility."[12] The authors stress coming to a sense of "despair over the human species" as a result of contemplating the Holocaust, because of the realization that "human beings can do such things." Human culture is thereby revealed in all its fragility.

Steady, palpable, even inevitable progress? No, it is canceled in a double sense: humans are not only not more humane, but are potentially *less* humane than we had thought. And no, it is canceled in another double sense: not only is the human world not more secure, it is revealed as *less* secure than we had hoped. As Nannerl O. Keohane reflected in a symposium on progress: "The simple faith that things are steadily getting better and, moreover, can be relied on to continue to improve is now vulnerable to powerful opposing evidence and has few professed adherents. We know too much about the human condition to share the naive optimism that characterized the eighteenth-century rationalist or those happy Victorians who flocked to the Crystal Palace in 1851."[13]

To be sure, the world has also seen progress. The resulting picture is not made more confused, and its poignancy is intensified, by our realization of its ironies. The Holocaust occurred during a century in which specific progress was achieved in human relations and in developing capacities for making the human world more secure. Workers, minority groups, women, once-colonial peoples *have* achieved more rights and greater dignity than before; diseases *have* been tamed, many societies *have* come to provide higher levels of well-being for their members—both before and after Auschwitz. It may still be argued, as does Immanuel Wallerstein, that today most of the world's people actually live *worse* off than before,[14] but even this does not deny important areas of advance. This paradox makes our assertion about the Holocaust canceling progress more paradoxical; but this claim gains strength from the fact that the Holocaust was not alone, was only the worst catastrophe in an incredibly catastrophic century, and that even worse disasters beckon. It seems indeed to be part of a more general dehumanization, a general loss of security, a more general fragility. Indeed, we are now accustomed to speaking about the danger of a *nuclear* holocaust!

This setting of the Holocaust in its larger context helps to explain why it is impossible to see it as a momentary aberration, a twelve-year regression in a basically positive forward-looking process. First, it generates insecurities and reminds us of capacities that, now unleashed, will always be present. And second, it is not the only act of mass murder in the century; since 1945 the technology of destruction has been further perfected, just as its human agents and victims have been further habituated to its use. Has the Holocaust itself become a *trend* of history?

PROGRESS INDICTED: THE ADVANCE OF SCIENCE AND SECULARISM

But can we not view it as a local event, attributable to particular historical or cultural perversities, perhaps now eliminated, from which the rest of the world is largely free? This might be plausible if the Holocaust had taken place in one of the world's remote places, far from its revolutionary economic and political developments since 1789 and still under the sway of "traditional" culture. In other words, a society outside of history—or a non-Western one that had not been at the center of the institutional, social, economic, and ideological transformations we commonly think of under the rubric of progress. On the contrary, Germany was in the vanguard of the Western world, one of the most "developed" of societies, a center of progress. Germany was one of the West's great cultural centers, the seat of the Reformation, a major industrial complex, the heartland of belief in the modern state, a center of unresolved class conflict. For these reasons the Holocaust can hardly be seen as a marginal or exceptional event.

But this suggests that the Holocaust can and should be viewed as being tied to, in some sense *stemming from,* progress. Richard Rubenstein argues that "the Holocaust bears witness to *the advance of civilization,* I repeat, to the advance of civilization, to the point at which large scale massacre is no longer a crime and the state's sovereign powers are such that millions can be stripped of their rights and condemned to the world of the living dead."[15]

We have evidence: the "banality of evil" of the killing factories, such details as their use of Zyklon B gas, more and more make it seem beyond doubt that progress itself is directly implicated in the greatest catastrophe of our century and, indeed, is equally guilty of preparing further catastrophes. These realities make the eighteenth- and nineteenth-century predictions of progress appear not only as the gushings of so many innocents, but as some sinister propaganda.

But what is it about progress that must be brought under indictment? Rubenstein has in mind two specific kinds of progress: the development of forms of bureaucratic rationalization and technique unknown to earlier generations, and the advance of secularism to the point where no moral claims can effectively be made against or beyond the modern state.[16] The two are connected and indeed rooted in the

Judeo-Christian tradition itself, which "has produced a secularization of consciousness involving an abstract, dehumanized, calculating rationality that can eradicate every vestige of . . . human dignity in all areas of human interchange."[17] In making their indictment Kren and Rappoport focus directly on a single activity embodying this rationalization and secularization: science. "The scientific mode of thought and the methodology attached to it were intrinsic to the mass killings. Quite apart from the technology, the mentality of modern science is what made the Holocaust possible."[18]

The Holocaust was a product of Western progress because it was rooted in our culture of science and our ability to organize complex human tasks rationally. Certainly there have been massacres all through history, but never carried out with such abstract, industrial detachment, such system, such scientific rigor. Auschwitz was a killing factory, which is why Edmund Stillman and William Pfaff are correct to compare the death camp to the automobile factory:

> There is more than a wholly fortuitous connection between the applied technology of the mass production line, with its vision of universal abundance, and the applied technology of the concentration camp, with its vision of a profusion of death. We may wish to deny the connection, but Buchenwald was of our West as much as Detroit's River Rouge—we cannot deny Buchenwald as a casual aberration of a Western world essentially sane.[19]

At the war's beginning, the mass shooting of over 30,000 Jews at Babi Yar in the Ukraine resembled previous massacres. To all appearances, it might have been carried out at any time since the invention of gunpowder, or at least since the invention of the machine gun. But that was only the beginning. The gas chambers, and the scientific-bureaucratic process they required, were of a new order. Chillingly modern, they absorbed and gave new meaning to the spirit and fruits of rationality extolled ever since the Enlightenment.

Max Horkheimer and Theodor Adorno carry this analysis a step further, although writing in 1944 and without specific reference to the gas chambers. For them Nazism was the natural terminus of the progress of reason. "In the most general sense of progressive thought, the Enlightenment has always aimed at liberating men from fear and establishing their sovereignty. Yet the fully enlightened earth radiates disaster triumphant."[20] Progress creates disaster. This is the underlying reason progress is more and more, in Robert Nisbet's formulation, "at bay," why the skepticism about it "has grown and spread to not merely the large majority of intellectuals in this final quarter of the century, but to many millions of other people in the West."[21]

The analyses we have been pursuing deserve recognition as courageous and important efforts to correct the vague clucking about moods we find in most writings about the decline of progress. By raising the most negative question they go against the grain of official optimism and self-celebration that has survived Auschwitz as well as Hiroshima, Chernobyl as well as Vietnam. If science and technology, reason and systemic organization now make possible the threat of a nuclear Auschwitz and endanger the ozone layer, generate cancers, and poison our lakes, then it is no wonder that people lose faith in our technological civilization. This loss of faith must be given its reasons, made specific, brought down from the level of mood and painted in its true colors. And those who attempt this are breaking new ground.

But precisely for this reason their claims must be examined with stringency. First, we must ask what is being said whenever an aspect of the modern world is blamed for any of its catastrophes. The secular, scientific attitude is one of the great features of Western life since the Enlightenment: it pervades our every activity, indeed, every aspect of our life. It is as much implicated in the Holocaust as in our capacity to talk rationally about the nature and causes of the Holocaust. Certainly it is worth remarking that it entered into the creating and running of Auschwitz, but it enters equally into the creation or running of *every* aspect of our world. It does not thereby *cause*, say, air travel; a specific human, social intention to develop and point this attitude in a specific direction, and the historically achieved technical–productive capacity to realize this intention, are what caused air travel. Everywhere, the secular scientific attitude is therefore also nowhere: it makes our every activity possible, but explains none of the social decisions to pursue them.

I have elsewhere asked about the motivation behind the Holocaust, and have attempted to explain what caused it. My effort was to locate and describe the Nazis' *intention* in slaughtering the Jews: What was the purpose of this plainly mad act, what were the social sources of the decisions?[22] In other words, we must distinguish between efficient and final causes, the conditions without which the Holocaust would have been impossible and the reasons why it happened. If Rubenstein's and Kren and Rappoport's analyses focus on the mental attitudes indispensable for carrying out the extermination of European Jews, they mistakenly treat these attitudes as if they motivated the Holocaust rather than facilitated it. Secularism may have made it possible to carry out the Holocaust (although it might be argued that prior centuries have seen fierce massacres carried out in the name of various gods); this phenomenon common to every contemporary action does not give us its reasons. Bureaucratic rationality may have been one of the tools of the Nazi death machine, but it was not its spring. Science and the scientific attitude were employed in carrying out the Final Solution, but they do not explain it. None of these factors accounts for the Nazis' anti-Semitism or the determination to carry it to its final conclusion. The fact is that for an explanation of why the Germans came to see the Jews, of all people, as a deadly enemy, and so hated them as to destroy them, we must look elsewhere than secularism or bureaucratic rationality or science.[23]

Our explanations seem to presuppose anti-Semitism to the point of mortal hatred. What is new, we are told, is that the means were now available to finally satisfy this hatred. But to blame the Holocaust on science and secular rationality in this way is to leave out its essentially human, *political* character. Historical hatreds, concrete social and political tensions, are not some underlying given, waiting for the right techniques and attitudes to activate them. Such a *need* to murder has itself its own history, its own dynamic origin. Our question must be, What sociohistorical processes generated this need, brought it to *that* point of explosion, so that *those* attitudes and *those* means would be put into play?

PROGRESS DEPOLITICIZED

The first error, I am suggesting, is to stress the scientific–technological and attitudinal core of the question—which, after all, is an important one—as determinative. The second is to ignore its political and social side. But these are common errors where progress is concerned. Ever since the railroads gathered speed and technological progress began dazzling Western man, the political and social components of progress have often been ignored, especially by those who have ceased seeing the political and social realms as continuing to change along with the scientific and technological ones. Above I called this approach that of Progress with a capital P. To critique that reification and stress the social dimension I have entitled this essay "The Holocaust and *Human* Progress."

In the classical exposition of progress Condorcet had stressed the eminently political goal of equality as inseparable from other forms of progress; so had other writers in the French tradition, notably Pierre Leroux and, with ambivalence, Alexis de Tocqueville. Condorcet's fondest hope was for "the abolition of inequality between nations, the progress of equality within each nation, and the true perfection of mankind."[24] In the eyes of Friedrich Engels the progress of the Industrial Revolution terminated in the conditions described in *The Situation of the Working Class in England in 1844*, which led directly to Engels's collaboration with Karl Marx on *The Communist Manifesto*. Scientific, technological, and economic progress lead to proletarian self-organization to incorporate industrial progress within social progress: the demand for *social* democracy.

Auguste Comte, the greatest exponent of reified Progress, suggested a generation later that the major issues for the Western future revolved around a kind of disembodied science creating a brave new world on its own steam within a fixed social and political framework (and, notably, in authoritarian hands). Contemporary writers on progress, such as Gabriel Almond, Marvin Chodorow, and Roy Pearce, essentially accept Comte's version. They domesticate and disfigure what Condorcet knew to be the essentially social and political goal of social equality into matters of "increased political participation" and an "increase in welfare," and instead place science and technology at the center of progress.[25] Keohane follows the same path by consistently thinking about the social side of progress in depoliticized moral terms such as "virtue."[26] Thus do key issues of social relations between human beings and their effect on the world's direction become transmuted—into matters of knowledge, organization, technique, and human "improvement"—and avoid Condorcet's issue: the transformation of human relations from those of privilege, hierarchy, and domination to those of equality, democracy, and freedom.

But this is nothing new. We are all familiar with the two transmutations of progress, of course: into progress in "depoliticized" areas such as expanding knowledge, science, and technology, and into an inhuman juggernaut moving on its own, carrying us along with it. American blacks who participated in the Civil Rights movement will remember otherwise: their progress has come from human struggle. The improvement of human social relations that Condorcet knew to be central to progress, which joined the Industrial Revolution as fully half of Marx's vision of human advancement, has been replaced by large trends rooted in various laws or universal human urges.

The point is that the indictment of progress for the Holocaust unwittingly follows the same path. Like many of the prior and present conceptions of progress, it turns on a depoliticized and, in a key sense, dehumanized progress. When Rubenstein speaks of "the advance of civilization" he operates within, and critiques by showing its results, the scientized conception of progress—without setting it in its larger context. Is it any wonder that destruction of humans using the instruments of this Progress is not identified as *murder*, based on hatreds and even fears, springing from within some of history's most intense, if puzzling, human struggles? Purged from Progress, this conflict and the human social interaction from which it springs have also been purged from efforts to understand the Holocaust as a child of Progress.

PROGRESS INDICTED: DOMINATION AND THE THREAT
OF LIBERATION

The missing question, Why did the Nazis hate Jews enough to destroy them?, leads us away from abstracting one or two strands from a larger historical process to refocus on the complexities of progress itself. The key lines of our corrective are supplied by Horkheimer and Adorno's *Dialectic of Enlightenment*, written before the full story became known about what the Nazis had done to the Jews. As the above quotation indicates, Horkheimer and Adorno place Nazism and the destruction it unleashed squarely within the tradition and development of Western reason. Its instrumental rationality dissolves all particularities before it, makes all individuals into equally manipulable and interchangeable integers. In this sense the Enlightenment is the ideology of a capitalism that subjects everything to the rule of increasingly abstract and over-whelming forces.

In addition to developing intensively this theme of the destructive force of reason, to some extent familiar to us from Rubenstein and Kren and Rappoport, Horkheimer and Adorno stress the dynamic leading to the explosion against the Jews. The domination of reason has not only created an increasingly administered society, but has created immense capabilities for liberation. The tension grows to the breaking point within the dominated, but is successfully shifted by their dominators onto the Jews. There, the subjected classes are set free to do what is prohibited elsewhere in this "rebellion of repressed nature against domination, directly useful to domination."[27]

This analysis is in fact a sustained meditation on progress, asking "why mankind, instead of entering into a truly human condition, is sinking into a new kind of barbarism."[28] On the one hand Horkheimer and Adorno continue to believe that "social freedom is inseparable from enlightened thought" (p. xiii; page references here and in the rest of this section are to Horkheimer and Adorno's *Dialectic of Enlightenment*); on the other, as they write in 1944 they and the world are witnessing "the self-destruction of the Enlightenment." Their starting point is that the conflagration is rooted in both Enlightenment thought and its accompanying social institutions. As believers in progress, they refuse to leave reflection on its destructiveness to its enemies. In such a situation thought, "blindly pragmatized," would be unable to com-prehend what is taking place.

And so, in hoping to "prepare the way for a positive notion of enlightenment which will release it from entanglement in blind domination" (p. xvi), they attempt to develop the self-critique of Enlightenment progress.

The fallen nature of modern man cannot be separated from social progress. On the one hand the growth of economic productivity furnishes the conditions for a world of greater justice; on the other hand it allows the technical apparatus and the social groups which administer it a disproportionate superiority to the rest of the population. The individual is wholly devalued in relation to the economic powers, which at the same time press the control of society over nature to hitherto unsuspected heights. Even though the individual disappears before the apparatus which he serves, that apparatus provides for him as never before. In an unjust state of life, the impotence and pliability of the masses grow with the quantitative increase in commodities allowed them. (pp. xiv–xv)

This remarkable statement encapsulates the vicissitudes of progress that lead us to the gates of Auschwitz. The growth of productivity and social power takes place within relations of domination. Disposition of the fruits and powers of Western civilization is in the hands of a privileged few. Those controlling the fruits of technical progress face pressures to make them universally available and yet tenaciously use their increasing powers to strengthen their position, meeting only the needs they must. "Under existing conditions the gifts of fortune themselves become elements of misfortune" (p. xv). The masses fail to become a social subject with the power to determine themselves and the society as well: "today, because of the enthronement of power-groups as that social subject, it produces the international threat of Fascism: progress becomes regression" (p. xv).

Technological progress within class society leads to human regression: this stands alongside the critique of Enlightenment rationality as a second main theme of the *Dialectic of Enlightenment*. A third appears in a series of connected analyses and aphorisms arguing that the fundamental dialectic of Western civilization leads directly to anti-Semitism. The authors' linchpin is that Jews absorb "the will to destroy born of a false social order" (p. 168). In a situation where economic domination is no longer objectively necessary but is maintained socially, "the Jews are marked out as the absolute object of domination pure and simple" (p. 168). Absolute irrationality, focused as hatred for the Jews, is the response to a social order that simultaneously offers and suppresses the possibility of total liberation.

Manipulated by the rulers, anti-Semitism is at core more than manipulation. Its roots lie in the "dialectical link between enlighten-ment and domination, and the dual relationship of progress to cruelty and liberation" (p. 169). Dominated in the process of production, swindled out of happiness, and blinded about the causes of the swindle, the powerless masses turn against those who seem to enjoy "happiness without power, wages without work, a home without frontiers, religion without myth. These characteristics are hated by the rulers because the ruled secretly long to possess them. The rulers are only safe as long as the people they rule turn their longed-for goals into hated forms of evil" (p. 199). The anti-Semitic masses bow to their authority, but at the same time "gather together to celebrate the moment when authority permits what is usually forbidden, and become a collective only in that common purpose" (p. 184).

Of course this process is fundamentally irrational. In a pathological yet political form of paranoia the masses project onto the Jews their own hatreds and fantasies, "and the mad system becomes the reasonable norm in the world and deviation from it a neurosis" (p. 187). The goal is destruction of the hated object. This social sickness, we are reminded, is no aberration, but remains rooted in the basic attitudes and practices and attitudes of Western civilization: "The unconditional realism of civilized humanity, which culminates in Fascism, is a special case of paranoiac delusion which dehumanizes nature and finally the nations themselves" (p. 193).

I noted above that Horkheimer and Adorno hoped that this critique might free enlightenment "from entanglement in blind domination" (p. xvi). Toward the end of their discussion of anti-Semitism they return to this optimism, briefly envisaging an alternative. "The change depends on whether the ruled see and control themselves in the face of absolute madness and call a halt to it" (p. 199). As we might guess, such a change would amount to a revolution: "If thought is liberated from domination and if violence is abolished, the long absent idea is liable to develop that Jews too are human beings" (p. 199). In this way "the Jewish question would prove in fact to be the turning point of history" (p. 200). Thus would we see a "redemption of the hopes of the past" (p. xv), presumably the Enlightenment hope of an end to domina-tion and privilege, of a democratic and equal society. In fulfilling itself, progress would liberate humanity from the disease of progress.

THE HOLOCAUST AND HUMAN CONFLICT

This last theme was not to be developed by Horkheimer or Adorno, but by their colleague Herbert Marcuse. In fact, the two trends of the *Dialectic of Enlightenment* find their voice in separate projects, those of

Marcuse and Adorno. The divergence will not surprise the reader who has noticed the profound ambivalence of the *Dialectic of Enlightenment.* At best the first and second themes summarized above coexist uneasily; if the essence of reason is or has become domination, where is the basis for transforming the oppressive state of affairs? Anti-Semitism seems to absorb the tensions not only of the current class society, but also of the domination at the heart of Western history. Most of the *Dialectic of Enlightenment* deals with the historical link between reason and domination—in the Enlightenment, in the *Odyssey,* in de Sade's *Juliette,* in the culture industry. In the process Western reason becomes unreason, reveals its essence as domination. The dominant direction of this critique suggests a *negative progress,* and holds little hope for supposing an alternative, nonrepressive conception of reason.

Any hopes that the dialectic will provide an answer are decisively quashed by Adorno's *Negative Dialectics,* published in 1966. Inasmuch as reason has become the basis for a kind of bourgeois privilege in the *Odyssey,* for moral assertions based on faith in Kant, for brutal manipulation and subjugation in de Sade, and for hidden coercion in the culture industry, wherein lies the power of once-revolutionary reason to explode this false state of affairs? *Negative Dialectics* gives us Adorno's final answer: philosophy has missed the moment of its realization. The Marxian revolution, the attempt to change the world in accordance with reason, misfired. And so, today, "Philosophy offers no place from which theory as such might be concretely convicted of the anachronisms it is suspected of, now, as before."[29]

Thus Adorno, mocking Hegel's optimism, had concluded that "permanent catastrophe" was the only world spirit. "After the catastrophes that have happened, and in view of the catastrophes to come, it would be cynical to say that a plan for a better world is manifested in history and unites it."[30] There is indeed a unity in history, drawing together the various strands and moments—"the unity of the control of nature, progressing to rule over men, and finally to that over men's inner nature. No universal history leads from savagery to humanitarianism, but there is one leading from the slingshot to the megaton bomb."[31]

The alternative to this vision of *negative progress* was developed by Herbert Marcuse, who sought to acknowledge the catastrophic character of Western civilization, but in relation to its intertwined potential for liberation. In view of its history, reason may well have to be defined "in terms which include slavery, the Inquisition, child labor, concentration camps, gas chambers, and nuclear preparedness."[32] These horrors "may well have been integral parts of that rationality which has governed the recorded history of mankind." But this reason is thereby false, partial, and demands to be critiqued "by driving Reason itself to recognize the extent to which it is still unreasonable, blind, the victim of unmastered forces."[33]

In other words, the domination of reason discussed by the *Dialectic of Enlightenment* must be evaluated by other historical possibilities, in keeping with yet another conception of reason: precisely those suggested in the more optimistic sections of the *Dialectic of Enlightenment* itself. This, after all, was Marcuse's program.[34] It corresponds to a radically different sense of progress from the one with which Adorno concluded, an explosive conception holding both positive and negative trends, indeed, whose meaning was the conflict between the two. It is a progress that has become deformed by domination and thus become a force of domination even while its potentialities for liberation remain alive and continue to gnaw away at their containment.

"Progress becomes quantitative and tends to delay indefinitely the turn from quantity to quality—that is, the emergence of new modes of existence with new forms of reason and freedom."[35] Marcuse's point is that all scientific, technological, and productive progress occurs within prevailing social, political, and ideological systems that predetermine, direct, and transform it in certain system-serving ways and for certain system-serving reasons. These are, fundamentally, systems of domination: domination of nature, domination of man. Reason and science develop within these systems in keeping with their structures and premises of privilege and domination. This is precisely what we have come to know as progress: scientific and technological transformations within social orders, which only generalize their fruits inasmuch as they serve the dominant interests. Thus certain kinds of progress take place, while others do not. Technological progress and economic progress, we might say, are used to avoid the human progress of which Condorcet spoke.

It should long since have become clear that most progress does not have improving the lot of humanity as its goal, that it brutalizes nature as it moves along cut off from the political and social goals of the Enlightenment, indeed, that its purpose is often to thwart achieving those goals. The fruits of progress become widely available and conform to those political and social goals only after social struggles or when this is in the interests of the rulers. Only then, we might say, does Progress become human progress. As Marcuse said, progress has become quantitative, rather than qualitative, and awaits the social struggles that can transform its direction.

But, as Horkheimer and Adorno have also pointed out, the interests in domination have become immeasurably strengthened through Progress. We might say that struggles for human progress—equality and democracy—will be resisted by those in positions of privilege and power with the full force of their progress proclaimed as everyone's—science, technique, and technology.

ON THE POSSIBILITY OF PROGRESS AFTER AUSCHWITZ

Condorcet's sense of unified social and technological progress has become, in my development of Marcuse's ideas, the promise of Utopia held at bay by the threat (and reality) of catastrophe. Human progress and technological progress both continue, although the latter dominates and contains the former; thus they sometimes develop concurrently, sometimes in the sharpest conflict, sometimes even colliding and mutually canceling each other. I find this approach the most plausible of any we have explored because it suggests the importance of both technique and motivation in explaining the Holocaust, and situates it squarely within the explosive tensions of the modern world.

The purpose of this essay, however, has not been to explain the Holocaust, but to ask what it has to tell us about the idea and reality of progress. Thus I have been concerned with the *plausibility* of the various efforts at relating the Holocaust to progress: Do they attempt to account for what must be accounted for in order to make sense of our world after Auschwitz? What kind of an idea of progress, if any, can survive Auschwitz? What parameters does it bequeath to any meaningful twenty-first-century vision of progress? My conclusions are not intended to prove that progress exists after the Holocaust, but only to say what it must be if it is to be possible.

If it can be sustained, progress after Auschwitz will have to be chastened and humbled. First, it will have to be shorn of any sense of inevitability or even likelihood. The illusion of a benevolent force guiding history died in the gas chambers. The interlinked happy vision of scientific, technological, social, political, and economic betterment is gone forever, an illusion exploded by events. So is the related notion of a single logic governing human development: history is more complex and plural than anyone had dreamed. And contradictory: the destruction of the world is indeed being planned by those who are claiming to defend it. The resulting picture is, to put it simply, terrifying, although not quite as terrifying as Adorno's negative vision that the only historical progress is from "slingshots to megaton bombs."

Second, since progress as a force or trend is dead, any post-Holocaust progress will stress that it is brought about by human beings. There are not really any such things as trends, separate from people, unfolding upon and somehow independent of us. We are more than observers: even progress with a capital P is human power hidden from view. As Lukács made clear, this reification is not just a perceptual or intellectual error, but takes shape in a sociohistorical process. This is as true of evil as of good: if the Holocaust is the victory of a sinister side of progress, that "side" consists of enraged human beings destroying those whom they became convinced were their enemies because they could thereby destroy, using its very tools, the hated modern world.[36]

Third, any future sense of progress will be at best skeptical, and often downright hostile, toward claims of human betterment through the spread of reason, science, and technology. The Holocaust refocuses these various past keys to the future—as so many myths. Indeed, it forces us to sharply distinguish between scientific and technological advances and human progress, and to insist that henceforth human progress be the only meaningful social goal. Thus the blatant positivism of nineteenth-century progress (shared equally by Comte and Marx) will be replaced in the twenty-first century by insistence that value judgments accompany social expectations.

Fourth, those who insist on thinking and talking about progress in the future will be aware of the *dangers* accompanying any form of progress. At the moment I refer not to science and technology going haywire, a real enough threat, but to progress as modernization. Societies and sectors of societies brought within the orbit of the Western technologically developed world undergo a kind of forced progress. In the *Dialectics of Disaster: A Preface to Hope*, I have written about the explosive character of uneven development within and between societies partially modernized and Westernized, partially still traditional. The tensions of uneven development are one of the greatest dangers the world faces today because they propel social classes and leaders into dead-end situations encouraging totally irrational responses. I have argued that the explosive character of Nazi anti-Semitism resulted at least in part from the fact that the deranged masses embracing it began with a sense of the progress of the modern world being a vital threat, carrying no liberation with it but rather endangering all they found precious. An irrational response to progress, perhaps, but was it not equally an irrational progress?

Finally, any further progress will lack an assured sense not only of the future, but of *a* future. It will avoid smugness as a mood and predictions as a habit. Certainly one conceivable future is the liberation projected by Marcuse; alas, it is barely a tendency among others, if that much. Another possible future is the complete destruction of life on earth. And there are many other possibilities, states lying in between. However we imagine it and work toward a better world, we now know for certain what we did not know before Hitler: the world can be destroyed. All thinking about the future will begin with this fact. Does this lead us to the absurdity of absurdities, progress without hope? Any twenty-first-century idea of progress will shift its ground radically, perhaps most radically in its inability to predict anything but continued struggle and continued danger until progress truly becomes human progress.

NOTES

1. Theodor W. Adorno, *Negative Dialectics* (London: Routledge & Kegan Paul, 1973), p. 361.

2. See Hannah Arendt's discussion of "language rules" in *Eichmann in Jerusalem: A Report on the Banality of Evil* (New York: Viking, 1965), pp. 80–82, and George Steiner, "The Hollow Miracle," *Language and Silence* (New York: Atheneum, 1967), as well as Adorno, *Negative Dialectics*.

3. Theodor W. Adorno, *Prisms* (London: Neville Spearman, 1967), p. 34. Adorno actually said "barbaric"; he later conceded that "perennial suffering has as much right to expression as a tortured man has to scream; hence it may have been wrong to say that after Auschwitz you could no longer write poems"; *Negative Dialectics*, p. 362.

4. J. B. Bury, *The Idea of Progress: An Inquiry into Its Origins and Growth* (New York: Dover Publications, 1955), p. 5.

5. Charles Frankel, "The Idea of Progress," in *The Encyclopedia of Philosophy*, ed. Paul Edwards (New York: Macmillan, 1967), vol. 6, p. 483.

6. Quoted in Robert Nisbet, *History of the Idea of Progress* (New York: Basic Books, 1980), pp. 297–98. A recent sketch, "The Logic of the Progress System," was included in the introduction to the colossally mistitled collection by Gabriel A. Almond, Marvin Chodorow, and Roy Harvey Pearce, *Progress and Its Discontents* (Berkeley: University of California Press, 1982), p. 5. These proceedings of a 1979 symposium manage to spend over 500 pages reflecting on the contemporary malaise without a single reference to the Holocaust, Nazism, Hitler, or any of the other catastrophic events of our century.

7. See Ernest Tuveson, *Millennium and Utopia* (Berkeley: University of California Press, 1949), p. 201; quoted in Nannerl O. Keohane, "The Enlightenment Idea of Progress Revisited," in *Progress and Its Discontents*, pp. 25–26. For a discussion of Providence and progress, see Nisbet, *History*; Nisbet is the most recent and most conservative historian of progress. He ties this central idea of Western civilization to a belief in God, regarding those who see progress taking place by human efforts alone, such as Marx or Condorcet, as exceptions to the rule. His emphasis on numbers of believers places these two thinkers in the minority, but surely a substantive evaluation is also needed. The importance of their ideas as well as the power of their analyses places Marx and Condorcet among the major philosophers of progress, and puts their secularism in a central position. (For Nisbet, our loss of faith in progress is not tied to events, such as the catastrophes of our century, but to our loss in religious faith.)

8. Karl Marx, *The Manifesto of the Communist Party, Selected Works*, vol. 2 (Moscow: Foreign Language Publishing House, 1962), p. 45.

9. This view of European history, without however mentioning the Holocaust, can be found in Peter Stearns, *European Society in Upheaval* (New York: Macmillan, 1975), pp. 289–330.

10. *Turgot on Progress, Sociology and Economics*, trans. Ronald L. Meek (Cambridge: Cambridge University Press, 1973), p. 41.

11. Virtually ignored in discussions about Hitler's last months is his decision to let the final period of war lead to the total destruction of Germany.

12. George M. Kren and Leon Rappoport, *The Holocaust and the Crisis of Human Behavior* (New York: Holmes and Meier, 1980), p. 126.

13. Keohane, "The Enlightenment Idea," p. 21.

14. See Immanuel Wallerstein, *Historical Capitalism* (London: Verso, 1983), pp. 97–110.

15. Richard L. Rubenstein, *The Cunning of History: Mass Death and the American Future* (New York: Harper & Row, 1978), p. 91.

16. Ibid., pp. 6, 40–43, 67, 78–97.

17. Ibid., p. 31.

18. Kren and Rappoport, *The Holocaust*, p. 133.

19. Edmund Stillman and William Pfaff, *The Politics of Hysteria* (New York: Harper & Row, 1964), pp. 30–31; quoted in Kren and Rappoport, *The Holocaust*, p. 126.

20. Max Horkheimer and Theodor Adorno, *Dialectic of Enlightenment* (New York: Herder and Herder, 1972), p. 3.

21. Nisbet, *History of the Idea*, p. 317. He typically does not mention lived history as being the root of this malaise, but rather wrong thinking: "The idea has been able to survive a great deal of adversity in its twenty-five hundred years: mass poverty, plagues and famines, devastating wars, economic depressions, eruptions of political and religious tyranny, and so on. But what the idea cannot survive (and this holds true for any complex idea) is *the loss of its crucial premises.*"

22. See Ronald Aronson, *The Dialectics of Disaster: A Preface to Hope* (London: Verso, 1983), pp. 21–63.

23. Rubenstein attempts to do this with his peculiar notion that they were surplus population, and that the "cunning of reason" points to population control. When we examine the realities of German history and the actual social and historical stresses that led to the pseudosolution known as Nazism, and eventually issued in the Final Solution, it is hard to believe that this simplistic suggestion can be meant seriously.

24. Condorcet, *Sketch for a Historical Picture of the Progress of the Human Mind,* trans. June Barraclough (Westport, Conn.: Greenwood Press), p. 173.

25. Almond, Chodorow, and Pearce, *Progress and Its Discontents*, p. 6. Note that their diagram "The Logic of the Progress System" begins with "Development and spread of science and knowledge" which is fed by but moves toward "Development and spread of responsive and efficient organizations and institutions"—their only remotely social or political category. See p. 5. One can only wonder how they would make sense of Condorcet. See Bury, *The Idea of Progress*, pp. 212–13.

26. Keohane, "The Enlightenment Idea," pp. 26, 39. See also her acceptance of Ruth Macklin's similar transformation of social progress into moral progress, p. 24.

27. Horkheimer and Adorno, *Dialectic*, p. 185.

28. Ibid., p. xi.

29. Adorno, *Negative Dialectics*, p. 3.

30. Ibid., p. 320.

31. Ibid.

32. Herbert Marcuse, "A Note on Dialectic," *Reason and Revolution* (Boston: Beacon Press, 1960), p. xii.

33. Ibid., p. xiii.

34. Before writing these lines in 1960, Marcuse had already taken three enormous steps of this journey. First he explored the liberatory character of the Hegelian dialectic as absorbed into Marxian social theory; then he sought to develop, in dialogue with Freudian theory, a nonrepressive conception of reason and society; then he showed how Soviet Marxism had transformed the critical thrust of Marxism

into ideology, in so doing seeking to restore the possibility of a genuine critical theory of society. After his "Note on Dialectic" Marcuse's effort continued to diverge from Adorno's: toward developing the power of negation that holds up—in theory, in language—an alternative to the false rationality of the status quo; then toward finding that alternative embodied in the New Left; then toward seeking it in art. Thus did he preserve the hope, embodied in this "Note on Dialectic," for a fulfillment of progress by its reversal.

35. Ibid., pp. viii–ix.

36. For this explanation, see Aronson, *Dialectics of Disaster*.

12

THE HOLOCAUST: MORAL THEORY AND IMMORAL ACTS

George M. Kren

Susan Sontag writes that "one's first encounter with the photographic inventory of ultimate horror is a kind of revelation, the prototypically modern revelation: a negative epiphany. For me, it was photographs of Bergen-Belsen and Dachau. . . . Nothing I have seen . . . ever cut me as sharply, deeply, instantaneously."[1]

This text may be contrasted with three others: one, by Rudolf Höss, the commandant of Auschwitz, a second by Adolf Eichmann, and finally one by an anonymous railroad official.

Rudolf Höss, while in prison in Poland awaiting his execution, wrote a revealing, self-pitying autobiography. At its conclusion, speaking of himself in the third person, he stated: "He too, had a heart, and . . . was not evil."[2] Adolf Eichmann during his police interrogation in Jerusalem, and later at his trial asserted that "he had lived his whole life according to Kant's moral precepts, and especially according to a Kantian definition of duty."[3] The remarks of both Höss and Eichmann possess a ring of truth; they were not, at least in the obvious sense, self-serving, and express sincerely held views. What does it mean that the commander of the largest death camp in which millions were systematically and deliberately killed, that the person who commanded the machinery of death at Auschwitz, would say about himself that "he was a good man"?

Raul Hilberg, whose *Destruction of the European Jews* is the single most important work on the Holocaust,[4] recounts the following experience:

> In my quest for railroad documents I went to the headquarters of the German railways in Frankfurt on Main. . . . I was directed to an annex building in the heart of the section of the city . . . where the document center was. I stood in the hallway and two gentlemen came by. "What would you be interested in?" they asked. I said

I am indebted to Phil Royster and Robert Linder for helpful discussions of this essay. An earlier version of it was published in the *Journal of Value Inquiry* 21 (1987): 55–64.

"What I'm interested in is a bit of World War II history." "Ah," they said, "Military trains?" "No, civilian passenger traffic on special schedules." "Ah," said one of them, "Auschwitz! Treblinka!" Somewhat astonished by the quick recognition of what I was asking for from my sheer expression of interest in special trains, I asked him how he could know? And he said, "Oh railroad people get around." He had seen ghettos. He had been to Katyn. He was the first one there when the grave, with all those Polish officers shot by the Soviets, was opened.

[After lunch] we came back to the office. . . . He explained to me technical matters pertaining to how trains were routed through timetable zones. . . . And then he said "I have seen Auschwitz." I said to myself: Perhaps this is a German who made a pilgrimage after the war. Aloud I said, "Did you make a pilgrimage?" "Oh no. I was there, then." "What did you do there?" "I put up the signal equipment."[5]

Almost all who have studied the Holocaust speak of it as a radical *novum* which has left an indelible mark upon twentieth-century history. Yet in an odd way that mark is almost invisible, like the latent image of an exposed but undeveloped photographic film. Christian theology has almost completely ignored it, as have philosophers. Though the Holocaust experience raises major ethical issues, students in ethics have shown no interest in dealing with them.[6] Histories of the twentieth century barely mention it.[7] Philippe Ariès, in his monumental history of death, lovingly spent pages on changes in cemetery architecture, on burial customs and charnel houses—but gas chambers are never mentioned.[8] Even in the twentieth century death and dying appear to Ariès as if they were private matters. "The good death," portrayed in many eighteenth- and even nineteenth-century paintings of the dying man— it is always a man—surrounded by many tearful family members to whom he passes on final sage advice, is, after all, not normative for the twentieth century, where death in a prison camp, through bombing or other forms of violence, by execution by left-wing or right-wing death squads, through neglect in jail, through killing because one belongs to the wrong social group—such as in the Soviet Union in the thirties or more recently in Cambodia—has come to be, if not typical, then at least an ever more likely occurrence. If a new edition of Gil Eliot's *Twentieth Century Book of the Dead*,[9] which presents statistical summaries of mass death, were to be published it would show that the number of individuals who have died by violence since 1972 has been substantial, and that deliberately inflicted mass death continues to rise.

Alasdair MacIntyre, the author of a recent highly praised work in ethical theory, provides a detailed analysis of the language that is used to justify or oppose the legitimacy of abortions, but never mentions the ethical issues arising from modern genocide. Is it an accident that works on ethics appear unanimous in not confronting issues about the Holocaust? Is there a moral problem involved in accepting an appointment to command a death camp? Paradoxically the Holocaust is perceived as the essence of radical existential evil, but ethical theory, whether religious or secular, has failed to come to grips with a judgment about the individuals involved.[10] The nature of modern radical mass killings in contrast to individual crimes, does not permit assignment of clear responsibility. In the modern bureaucratized world the view that an individual acting as an agent is not responsible for the act he carries out is universally accepted. Committed opponents of capital punishment criticize the legislature for the passage of such a law and the public for desiring it and vicariously enjoying the killing, but do not fault the executioner for carrying out the sentence. In what sense does this not apply to those who participated in carrying out officially sanctioned mass killings? The judges at Nuremberg argued that the individuals should have known that their action was wrong, as if that proposition were self-evident, and never indicated how they should have known that. It is strange that the perpetrators of what arguably is the most radical horror of this century, while awaiting execution, maintained with obvious sincerity that they had done no wrong. A recurring theme found in all the trial records of individuals who had participated in mass killings and torture is the indignant surprise they express that anyone should blame them for their actions, since they were only doing their duty. (The French who had been involved in the "pacification" in Algiers, which involved a widespread use of torture, used the identical language. The American use of and participation in acts of torture in Vietnam caused few comments. Attempts at mock trials in Sweden, in which Jean-Paul Sartre participated, were simply written off as propaganda.) Adolf Eichmann was no intellectual, yet his definition of the Kantian categorical imperative as "I mean by my remark about Kant that the principle of my will must always be such that it can become the principle of general laws," would certainly get him through Philosophy 100 with a passing grade.[11] Hannah Arendt argues that Eichmann subtly modified and distorted the Kantian principle by making it read that one ought to act as if the principle of your actions were the same as that of the legislator. But even with this distortion, if such it is, this still means that the moral imperative is interpreted so that the individual is called upon to go beyond mere obedience and identify his will with the principle behind the law; Adolf Eichmann certainly did this—enthusiastically. Contrasting Eichmann with the Marquis de Sade makes it apparent that they were different from each other not least in that the marquis sought to legitimize his rather strenuous and perverse sexual athletic activities through a full recognition and affirmation that they were evil, that they represented a violation of nature, because, he held, only in that way could human freedom be asserted.[12] In contrast Eichmann was not plagued by any pangs of conscience, never believed that he was doing anything wrong. Even when facing the gallows he did not express any regret for his actions. Eichmann, as a good Kantian, could have supported the principle that all Jews and indeed all racially inferior people who corrupted the blood of the nation (today we would speak of a genetic pool) ought—no matter how painful and nerve-racking their killing might be to the perpetrators—to be killed for the good of posterity.

Rudolf Höss's statement, in which before his execution he affirmed that he had no sense of wrongdoing, has a remarkable ring of truth to it. Similarly, Franz Stangl, the commandant of Treblinka, stated that his conscience was clear: "I have never hurt anyone myself."[13] When in 1945 individuals who had been involved in the camps were arrested, few denied their actions, but all denied their guilt, showing incredible and genuine surprise that anyone would take them to task for their actions, which they did not believe constituted a crime. In the technical, legal, sense they were certainly right about this. The actions for which they were being tried had not involved a violation of (positive) law at the time that they were committed. These individuals emphasized, and there is no reason to doubt their honesty, that they were carrying out orders and implied, with some justice, that their counterparts in the Allied armies when given orders that violated the dictates of humanity would (and did) carry them out also. Pilots who bombed cities have rarely felt any pangs of conscience, nor have even those who opposed the bombing of cities thought to hold the individual pilots accountable. The officially tolerated (supported?) use of torture by the United States in Vietnam would inter alia suggest that the Germans do not possess a monopoly on carrying out inhumane action within an official context. The individuals who had been involved in the running of the death camps and the murderous *Einsatzgruppen* did not deny their culpability because of any defects of personality or a lack of Kohlbergian moral maturity. Their denial rests above all on the poverty of contemporary ethical theory that is unable to deal with individual acts carried on in the service of the state (and to a lesser extent service to an ideology).

To simplify a complex issue: Morality in Western civilization has two major roots, Christian revelation and the Enlightenment and its successors. From neither one could an ethical theory that would apply to these individuals be derived. Discussion about the nature of good and evil begins with Genesis:

And the Lord God commanded the man, saying, Of every tree of the garden thou mayest freely eat.

But of the tree of knowledge of good and evil, thou shalt not eat of it:

And the serpent said unto the woman, Ye shall surely not die;

For God doth know that in the day ye eat thereof, then your eyes shall be opened, and ye shall be as gods, knowing good and evil.

And the Lord God said, Behold the man is become as one of us, to know good and evil.[14]

This passage has been subject to numerous interpretations; Freudians have had a field day with it.[15] These words referring to the knowledge of good and evil stand in need of explication. Does anyone still dare to maintain that human beings possess inborn concepts of right and wrong? The thrust of contemporary thought is to demonstrate how in the process of socialization individuals internalize moral concepts, and how the needs of a society tend to shape its values. It may be assumed that in the evolution of human beings out of the primeval slime, somewhere along the line the abstract concepts of wrong, right, evil, and sin developed. While it may be possible to infer that animals recognize that they have done "wrong," certainly no abstract concept of wrongness exists for them. Indeed if one were to seek a simple definition of the essential functions of religions, it would be that they attempt to explain how human beings came to be and what is expected of them. It should occasion no great surprise that there is a remarkable similarity between different religious ethical systems. And though stated with different rhetorics, though emphasis may differ here and there, the major moral demands of most world religions appear to be directed toward establishing the legitimacy of some kind of authority from priest to king, and to provide sanctions for restraining appetites and passions so that society may function. Thus the classic seven deadly sins are gluttony, covetousness, avarice, sloth, lust, anger, and pride. The concern is almost exclusively with private conduct. It is the individual who seeks self-gratification in a manner or degree beyond what is considered proper whose behavior is held up for censure. The injunction to resist temptation—above all sexual temptation—is part of an orientation that, particularly on the popular level, tends to equate sin with pleasure. Catholicism and Protestantism (Calvinism is more significant for this than Lutheranism) contain traditions that hold that disobedience to demands of "the magistrate" may be justified under certain circumstances. Some resistance to authority is permitted under certain circumstances; however, except for such groups as Jehovah's Witnesses and in a more limited sphere the "peace churches," such as the Friends, Mennonites, and others; the main thrust has always been that acceptance of authority is a positive good in its own right.[16] Saint Paul spoke about obeying the powers that be since "they are ordained by God," thus giving religious sanction to authority. Nor did the authority have to be legitimate: Thus Luther held that a Christian who had been sold into slavery to the Turks had no right to escape, because to do so would deprive his master of his legal property. Theologians have not condemned Abraham for his contemplated counter-Oedipal infanticide—and indeed Kierkegaard in a brilliant essay affirmed the religious merit of the "suspension of the ethical." There is the very ambiguous and frequently cited statement of Jesus about rendering unto Caesar the things that are Caesar's and unto God those that are God's; the problem is that the line of demarcation has not been defined. In practice the historical record shows that churches throughout time have consistently been willing to give Caesar anything he asked for. Religious bodies have generally held that if the "Prince," to use the generic term, made demands that contradicted the teachings of Christianity, then the individual nevertheless should obey them, since these demands were his responsibility. Actions of the state have usually, by means of at times brilliant casuistry, been legitimized, no matter what their moral content. Machiavelli in *The Prince* argued that the statesman was not bound by Christian morality when he acted for the state—that its preservation legitimized lying, murder, and other acts that, were they done for private gain, would be forbidden. Bismarck, though using a very different kind of language arrived at a similar conclusion. Faced with the question of how one can be a statesman and a Christian at the same time, he had recourse to a Calvinistic doctrine of stewardship from which he derived the conclusion that, as a Christian statesman, his primary duty was to preserve the state, and that therefore any act required to accomplish this, even if it violated dictates of Christian morality, was legitimate.[17]

During the middle ages doctrines of the "just war," and by implication, unjust wars, developed in theological thought. Yet they appear not to have been applied in practice. In the modern period not Italy's invasion of Ethiopia, nor Germany's invasion of Poland, nor the American activities in Vietnam were ever defined by any religious body as unjust wars. Some sects such as Jehovah's Witnesses reject participation in all wars, but no religious group appears to have ever defined any particular war as unjust and enjoined its followers on pain of damnation to participate. No religious body protested Frederick the Great's cynical partition of Poland. Neither religious nor secular ethics has seriously addressed the issue of the moral problems of an individual acting in the service of the state. Indeed a nearly universal consensus appears that all rational activities of violence, even though involving victimization of civilians, if committed in the service of the state during wartime are legitimate.[18] Both religious and secular ethics tend to hold that an individual acting as a servant of the state is not accountable for that action. And indeed a case can be made for this. Should we require of executioners that they personally satisfy themselves of the guilt of the person to be killed? Would one wish to give the right to every soldier to decide whether a given order is moral or not?

Both Protestantism and Catholicism have been most reluctant to suggest that individual conscience should ever be permitted to supersede positive law, a law that is generally religiously sanctioned. Within the Christian tradition there is little that would allow disobeying the state on the basis of conscience.[19] During World War II, Franz Jägerstätter, a simple, pious Austrian peasant about to be inducted into the army, felt that the war was wrong; various church leaders suggested to him that the rightness or wrongness of the war was not his responsibility, since any responsibility for deeds would be with those who had ordered them. He himself remained unconvinced, and was executed. He has not been canonized. Within the Western tradition, anarchy has always been feared more than tyranny. Thomas Hobbes in the *Leviathan* had justified absolute authority on the ground that it prevented anarchy. The historical record contains many appeals to a higher law where individual conscience is used as a legitimization for violating positive law, most frequently when the state demands actions that individuals perceive as violating their religious commitments. This has created martyrs, but the record cannot be read in a manner that would demonstrate that those who opted for disobedience were in any sense right, while those who upheld the law were wrong. Conscience has been used to oppose violence and to call it forth; it offers no valid guide for action.

The paganism of Nazi ideology led to a conflict and at times to persecution of Christian churches, ministers, and priests—although the label *Kirchenkampf*, which some now use, is inappropriate. This has obscured the ambivalent position of Christianity toward anti-Semitism and the Holocaust. The indictment of Jews as "Christ killers" had no significance for Nazi anti-Semitic ideology. However, their racial anti-Semitic policies received support from those who were anti-Semitic out of religious convictions. When Archbishop Kametko of Nietra in Slovakia was approached to intervene to stop deportations he responded:

It is not just a matter of deportation. You will not die there of hunger and disease. They will slaughter all of you there, old and young alike, women and children, at once—it is the punishment that you deserve for the death of our Lord and Redeemer, Jesus Christ—you have only one solution. Come over to our religion and we will work to annul this decree.[20]

Nothing permits holding that such views were not sincerely held, or even that they were un-Christian.[21] Deportations in Slovakia were carried out while the head of its government was a priest (Father Tiso). None of the priests who were members of the Slovak Parliament voted against that body's post hoc authorization of the deportations. No one has been excommunicated for participation in the Holocaust.[22]

Helen Fein, in a work that includes an analysis of the role of the various churches in the Holocaust, writes that in Serbia "priests participated in all aspects of political life, including extermination squads; the Franciscans were especially noted for their leadership. Paris tells us that nearly half of the twenty-two Croatian extermination camps were headed by priests."[23]

Revelation has been one major source for Western morality; another, which became significant in the eighteenth century during the Enlightenment, has been the attempts to define morality on the basis of rationality. Already in antiquity Socrates brilliantly sought to demonstrate that mind could determine knowledge of good and evil, that it did not require the intervention of the gods. Man was to be the measure of all things. This tradition almost disappeared with the triumph of religion and mysticism, only to surface again in Europe during the Renaissance and the Enlightenment. The Enlightenment, in what MacIntyre among others has demonstrated was a logically fallacious way,[24] sought to prove that a jump could be made from knowledge about nature to natural laws which would provide differentiation between good and evil. The attempt failed, but there was a nobility about it, not least because it made no differentiation between nation or race. What was good for the Frenchman was good for the Hottentot. With the triumph of democracy and nationalism the attempt to define universal "laws of nature" was replaced by views that made the national state the fundamental source of definitions of right and justice. Civil rights, derived from and provided by the state, replaced natural rights. The eminent legal theorist Hans Kelsen, in a formulation that still commands much support, essentially identified justice as the codified will of the sovereign power.[25] By this definition the view of the SS as possessing a "criminal superego" suggested by one survivor becomes logically contradictory, since the state by definition can commit no crimes and is the source of all justice beyond which there is no appeal.[26] The attempts to suggest that the identical psychological dynamics that are used to explain individual sadistic or destructive behavior also operate in the commission of legally sanctioned atrocities, remain unconvincing. Sadistic behavior and crimes such as rape involve inadequate ability to handle impulses, a lack of ego control, and suggest that the perpetrators are driven by inner compulsions so that they lack control and could not help themselves. Those who ran the death camps were not acting out some perverse psychological needs. The personality and previous psychosexual history of "perpetrators" in a camp appear to have no relationship to their actions; the attempts to explain them on the basis of psychological evidence are as valid as the attempt to explain a butcher slaughtering an animal as the resolution of a childhood trauma in which an animal played a significant role.

In the wake of the discovery of the camps with their horrifying visual imagery, the question of how people could do these things inevitably arose. How could individuals not only do these things, but do them with an apparently good conscience? Freud showed that conscience, which he labeled superego, was created by authority figures. The child who sticks his or her hands in the cookie jar, gets them slapped several times, and is scolded for this by a parent, very quickly will begin to feel uneasy when contemplating such activity. And the lesson impressed upon the child more than any other is the need for uncritical obedience to authority—parent, teacher, policeman. "You will do this because I tell you and don't ask why." Hence the very fundamental socialization process makes understandable why individuals will obey authority. Shocked by the readiness of people to carry out inhumane orders, the social psychologist Stanley Milgram set up a brilliant experiment in which he had American college students and others administer electric shocks to subjects. Told to increase the dosage, most individuals did so even when the victim was screaming that he was dying or had a heart attack. Milgram concluded from his experiments that "ordinary people, simply doing their jobs, and without any particular hostility on their parts, can become agents in a terrible destructive process."[27]

Yet Milgram should not have been surprised. Viewed from the vantage point of those who carry out the action, the difference between killing defenseless civilians by mass bombing, as was done in Hamburg, Dresden, Hiroshima, Warsaw, Rotterdam, and other cities, as against mass shooting or gassing is after all essentially a matter of style. The psychological requirements for both are similar—a willingness to accept the legitimacy of the authority calling for the act, a belief that the act serves some transcendental and valuable purpose, and probably a conviction that "they" deserve it. The psychological mechanism that internalizes prohibitions against violence for most situations is not operative when a legitimate (now usually bureaucratic) authority calls for it; the military structure of obedience reinforces this.

That the individuals who ordered and carried out mass murder were in no sense pathological is an issue no longer in need of discussion. The attempt to apply medical labels—insane, "criminal superego," pathological—is an attempt to avoid confronting the unpalatable reality that these were ordinary people—that is, they possessed no special qualities, and as the evidence indicates, not only were they replaceable, but every indication exists that most individuals would, if placed in such situations, act in a similar way. Neither political nor ethical theory has even attempted to confront this problem. At the Nuremberg trials prosecutors suggested to accused SS officers that they ought to have known their acts were immoral and unlawful.[28] When members of a new generation sought to use Nuremberg principles to legitimize their refusal to participate in the war in Vietnam, not only did they find themselves frequently in prison, but no legal authority was willing to use the Nuremberg trials as a precedent.

The available political and ethical tradition has difficulty dealing with acts done in the service of the state. Psychiatry, psychology, and psychoanalysis are unable to present any evidence that would permit concluding that individuals who run death camps, torture people day in day out, hang people as a matter of course—if their actions are done legally and are properly authorized—are in any sense a medical problem.

A morality is not derived from logic but socially created. A consensus supports the sovereignty of the nation-state—which means that the state is the final font of justice. States are unwilling to abandon their right to engage in destructive acts, and demand that their citizens will, if ordered to do so, carry those out without consideration of individual conscience. The fabric of modern society rests on this. Executioners are expected to pull the switch on the electric chairs, computer programmers to plot the destructive pattern of a nuclear weapon; the programmers' individual private feelings in this matter are of no relevance. Collectively, modern societies do not permit individuals who are part of a state bureaucracy to decide whether they approve of a given act or not. The bombardier told to destroy a city is not expected to determine the legitimacy of the war, or even of the particular action. In that sense the Nazi individuals who ran the death camps were no different from those who bombed cities. Whatever uniqueness there was to the Holocaust—and a case can be made that it was indeed something radically new—this had no bearing on those individuals who had to implement it. It required individuals who did what they were told, who carried out the intentions of their superiors to the best of their ability (and there never was any dearth of them). Although there were protests against the use of torture (which was usually delegated to South Vietnamese soldiers or officials) during the Vietnam conflict, no one has suggested that those individuals who directly or indirectly participated in it were in any sense morally or legally culpable. Governments in Latin and Central America that engage directly or indirectly in the use of torture and mass killings in the service of counterinsurgency are officially supported by the United States government. Counterinsurgency groups such as the Contras, who have few scruples about the use of murder and torture, are funded by the United States.[29] The decision during World War II to bomb Dresden, which served no useful military purpose, and the nuclear bombing of Hiroshima and Nagasaki have certainly been subject to severe criticism not only on tactical, but also on ethical grounds. Yet the issue of the morality of the individuals who carried out these actions has not been raised—and it would be very dubious to do so. The Holocaust required for its execution not abnormal sadists, but socialized individuals, like the railroad official who had no problem installing the signal equipment for a death camp, persons who were willing to permit others in authority to make ethical decisions for them; it required individuals in authority who were willing to accept responsibility for decisions that they made but that were implemented by others.

Why were individuals, why were collectives, willing to commit so many unspeakable horrors? The previously cited Milgram experiments and others modeled on them demonstrate that moral restraints are suspended in the presence of a legitimizing authority.[30] Indeed it appears that there takes place a suspension of the ethical when actions of the state are involved. Political theorists have attempted to show the moral obligation of the individual to obey legitimate authority. The ability to commit hitherto unimagined horrors and destructive acts (historical reality is ahead of our sadistic fantasies on this) has its source not in human selfishness, greed, or destructive instincts, not in what the Victorians would have labeled man's baser nature. The answer to these questions cannot be found in individual psychology. The primary reason "normal" individuals have so few difficulties in carrying out massive destructive acts of a kind that appear to violate moral and civilized behavior is that these activities are identified with a higher purpose. Placing the Holocaust in a larger context, it is quite clear that in the Western world the primary source of violence is found in the willingness of individuals to be self-sacrificing for an ideal, ideology, or cause. When individuals speak of a willingness to die for a cause, they also mean a willingness to kill. "Give me liberty or give me death" is soon followed by "give me liberty or I will give you death." Arthur Koestler recognized this years ago:

> The crimes of violence committed for selfish, personal motives are historically insignificant compared to those committed *ad majorem*

gloriam Dei, out of a self-sacrificing devotion to a flag, a leader, a religious faith or a political conviction. Man has always been prepared not only to kill but also to die for good, bad or completely futile causes. And what can be a more valid proof of the reality of the self-transcending urge than this readiness to die for an ideal.[31]

The commitment to ideals, the human capacity for transcendence, rather than simple selfishness accounts for most of the horrors of human history. "Immoral" wars for territory or other concrete realizable aims—Frederick the Great's attack on Austria to gain Silesia, or Prussia's attack on Denmark in 1864—involve much less destructiveness than wars carried on for a noble cause. The most destructive acts involve transcendental and millenarial aspirations. These, though not readily apparent, were also present in the Holocaust. The destruction of the Jews was a goal that National Socialism pursued with intensity and commitment, a goal based on the sincere desire on the parts of its architects to create a purer, in their eyes, a better world. The theologian John T. Pawlikowsi writes that the Holocaust "has clearly revealed the dangers inherent in building a society deemed capable of moral excellence without any reference to transcendent ethical norms. . . . A primary task . . . is the development of a sense of transcendence.[32] The opposite is true. It is the human capacity for transcendence, the ability of the human imagination to create an image of the world not as it is, but as it ought to be, that has so frequently been and continues to be the source of the most radical destructive behavior. Christian piety led to the Crusades and the Inquisition, Robespierre's vision of the republic of virtue to the guillotine and the Terror, and Lenin's view of a communal free and classless society to the Gulag. Visions of a national homeland in the minds of Jews and Palestinians have been responsible for the death of thousands. The Nazi image of racial beauty and purity on the one hand, and the sincerely held view that the Jew was the source of corruption, were at the root of the Holocaust. It is difficult to accept the proposition that much of human destructiveness has its roots in utopian visions, in the desire to transform the world into a better, purer, or even more beautiful world. However, these visions almost always require changing real flawed human beings from what they are into what they ought to be, raising them to a new standard of perfection, whether they wish to be perfected or not. And it is in this that a primary source of human destructiveness, from the Crusades to Cambodia may be found. In *The Open Society and Its Enemies*, Karl Popper located the roots of modern totalitarianism in utopian visions; his main culprits are Marx, Hegel, and Plato, who provide ideas that others seek to translate into reality.[33] Modern conservatism, which originated as a response to the French Revolution, condemned universal standards such as the "rights of man" and held that their translation into social reality inevitably led to the terror.[34]

It is certainly possible to read history in a way that argues that nearly every committed attempt to improve the human condition has led to its opposite. Is the conclusion then, as indeed some (Western) Zen Buddhists suggest, that all action in the public realm is futile, and worse, that it only leads to a deterioration of the situation? The French people revolted against the despotism of the ineffectual Louis XVI and ended up with the more despotic and efficient reign of Napoleon Bonaparte. The Russians in 1917 freed themselves from the tyranny of the czar, only to end up with the ruthless dictatorship of Josef Stalin. In the 1930s some liberals defended the totalitarianism and violation of human rights in the Soviet Union by approvingly citing Joseph Stalin's "you can't make an omelet without breaking some eggs" remark.[35] Bertolt Brecht spoke for a Communist mentality when he held that no cost was too high to transform the world:

> With whom would the right-minded man not sit
> To help the right?
> What medicine would taste too bad
> To the dying man?
> What baseness would you not commit
> To root out baseness?
> If, finally, you could change the world
> What task would you be too good for?
> Sink down in the filth
> Embrace the butcher,
> But change the world: it needs it.[36]

Brecht recognized that to carry out the revolutionary task it was at times necessary to commit acts that violated one's sense of right and wrong and made one feel profoundly uncomfortable. He held that sacrificing one's private conscience was at times required to carry out the required task.

> Make it not your goal
> That in the hour of death
> You yourself be better.
> Let it be your goal
> That in the hour of death
> You leave a bettered world.[37]

Explicitly, Brecht, representing what Arthur Koestler has called the mentality of the commissar,[38] emphasizes the legitimacy of violence:

> IT IS A FEARSOME THING TO KILL.
> But we will kill ourselves and not just others, if necessary.

As every living man knows
Only by force can this dying world be changed.
As every living man knows,
It is not granted to us, we said,
Not to kill.[39]

Unlike many others, both Left and Right, for whom the use of violence became an end in itself, Brecht recognized that the use of violence exacted a price.

Do you deny that the use of violence also degrades him who uses it?

Alas, we
Who wished to lay the foundation of kindness
Could not ourselves be kind.[40]

Does all commitment to an improvement of the human condition—and there is of course no consensus as to what constitutes improvement—lead only to destructive behavior? Do attempts to increase the realm of freedom necessarily lead to more tyranny? The historical record certainly may be read this way. Is the alternative then to reject any commitment that requires violence for its realization? Clearly some evils will only respond to change through the use of violence—at the moment one thinks of South Africa and Chile as obvious examples. Are vulgar Yuppies, or individuals whose primary concern is their own psychological or spiritual state, to be preferred to dedicated (frequently suicidal) revolutionaries who wish to change the world?

In contrast to other times, the contemporary world is characterized by an anarchy of values, with no common ground for discourse between them. The sincere desire to make the world conform to ideals frequently leads to ever escalating violence when others (who are then defined as evil) support alternative values. Not only is there no consensus of values, but means of validating one value system against another do not exist. Indeed the thrust of contemporary theory is that in contrast to propositions in science, for which a nearly universally accepted system of verification exists, value propositions, as Max Weber already suggested more than fifty years ago, are in the last analysis only acts of will. Hence force and violence rather than reason will be the arbiter between competing systems.

NOTES

1. Susan Sontag, *On Photography* (New York: Dell, 1977), pp. 19–20.
2. Rudolf Hoess, *Commandant of Auschwitz: The Autobiography of Rudolf Hoess* (Cleveland and New York: World Publishing, 1959), p. 202.

3. Hannah Arendt, *Eichmann in Jerusalem: A Report on the Banality of Evil* (New York: Viking, 1965), p. 135.

4. Raul Hilberg, *The Destruction of the European Jews* (Chicago: Quadrangle Press, 1961).

5. Raul Hilberg, "The Significance of the Holocaust," in *The Holocaust: Ideology, Bureaucracy, and Genocide*, ed. Henry Friedlander and Sybil Milton (Millwood, N.Y.: Kraus International, 1980), pp. 95–102.

6. An alternative reading of the evidence holds that twentieth-century mass death from the trenches of World War I to Hiroshima to Cambodia has made this generation immune, or at least insensitive to human suffering generally. That most victims of the Holocaust were Jews has done much to mitigate its horror for many people.

7. For a discussion of the treatment of the Holocaust by historians, see Gerd Korman, "The Holocaust in Historical Writing," *Societas* 2 (Summer 1971); Henry Friedlander, *On the Holocaust: A Critique of the Treatment of the Holocaust in History Textbooks* (New York: Anti-Defamation League, 1972); Lucy S. Dawidowicz, *The Holocaust and the Historians* (Cambridge, Mass.: Harvard University Press, 1981); George M. Kren, "The Holocaust: Some Unresolved Issues," *Annals of Scholarship* 3, no. 2 (1985): 35–61.

8. Philippe Ariès, *The Hour of Our Death*, trans. Helen Weaver (New York: Knopf, 1981).

9. Gil Eliot, *Twentieth Century Book of the Dead* (New York: Scribner, 1972).

10. Alasdair MacIntyre, *After Virtue: A Study in Moral Theory* (Notre Dame, Ind.: University of Notre Dame Press, 1981). One of my students commented after reading Sereny's study of Franz Stangl that he was as much a victim of the system as the individuals he murdered.

11. Arendt, *Eichmann*, p. 103. During his interrogation in Jerusalem Eichmann stated that "I have taken Kant's categorical imperative as my norm, . . . I have ordered my life by that imperative." Eichmann's interrogator, Captain Avner W. Less, quoted to Eichmann from a *Stern* article: "I was no more than a faithful, decent, correct, conscientious, and enthusiastic member of the SS and of Reich Security Headquarters, inspired solely by idealistic feelings towards the fatherland to which I have the honor of belonging. Despite conscientious self-examination, I must find in my favor that I was neither a murderer nor a mass murderer." Jochen von Lang, ed., *Eichmann Interrogated: Transcripts from the Archives of the Israeli Police* (New York: Farrar, Straus & Giroux, 1983), pp. 288–89.

12. On de Sade see Henry Vyverberg, *Historical Pessimism in the French Enlightenment* (Cambridge, Mass.: Harvard University Press, 1958).

13. Gitta Sereny, *Into That Darkness: An Examination of Conscience* (New York: Vintage Books, 1983), p. 384; Sereny, whose examination of his life and career is one of the most brilliant books in Holocaust literature, believes that as a result of her interviews with him, which came close to being psychoanalytical sessions, Stangl finally came to admit his guilt to himself and, having done that, was ready to die.

14. Gen. 2:16–17, 3:4–5, 22.

15. Thus, Ernest Rappoport, "The Tree of Life: A Psychoanalytic Investigation of the Origin of Mankind," *Psychoanalytic Review* 30, no. 1 (January 1943): 263–72.

16. Significant exception to this appears to be when a rule prohibits the exercise of the "right" religion. Thus John Knox's attack on the improperness of women ruling; generally the Calvinist tradition at least in an ambivalent manner does entertain the idea that there are limits to obedience. This appears almost completely absent in the Lutheran one. There appear to be several coexistent Roman Catholic traditions. The radical sects of the Reformation in the sixteenth century committed themselves to opposing both religious and secular authority, and frequently were

not averse to using violence. They were either destroyed or modified their doctrines to ones of acquiescence to authority.

17. Leonard von Muralt, *Bismarck's Verantwortlichkeit* (Göttingen: Musterschmidt, 1955).

18. Lucy S. Dawidowicz not only argues that the Holocaust was a horror of infinitely greater magnitude than the use of nuclear weapons against Japan and should not be compared to it, but attempted to legitimize the bombing of Hiroshima and Nagasaki: "The purpose of the bombing was to demonstrate America's superior military power and thus convince the Japanese that they had to capitulate, thereby ending the war and further killing" (*The Holocaust and the Historian*, p. 17). Aside from the fact that substantial evidence exists that the intent of the nuclear bombing was not to impress the Japanese, who were already suing for peace, but the Russians, there is a failure to recognize that the victims, who were after all noncombatants in the war, were killed and injured in a particularly horrible way not because of anything they had done, but because they happened to be in the wrong place at the wrong time, and were targeted for death to demonstrate America's new nuclear might.

19. The practice of "conscientious objection," whereby in the United States, England, Germany, and some other countries individuals who find participation in the armed forces a violation of their religious beliefs and are given an exemption from that, to serve in other non-war-related (though almost always very unpleasant) service, does not invalidate this point. On the contrary. The legitimacy of governmental actions is not called into question. A few individuals believing themselves to be "special" make a mutually profitable arrangement with the government—they will not interfere with the war effort, while the government will respect their unique need to maintain moral purity.

20. Cited in Irving Greenberg, "Cloud of Smoke, Pillar of Fire: Judaism, Christianity, and Modernity after the Holocaust," in *Auschwitz: Beginning of a New Era? Reflections on the Holocaust*, ed. Eva Fleischner (New York: KTAV, 1977), pp. 11–12.

21. Similarly, many Nazis sincerely believed in the idea of race and were motivated by a transcendental belief in improving the world through eugenics.

22. Helen Fein, *Accounting for Genocide: National Responses and Jewish Victimization during the Holocaust* (New York: Free Press, 1979), p. 100.

23. Ibid., p. 104; the Paris reference is to Edmond Paris, *Genocide in Satellite Croatia, 1941-1945* (Chicago: American Institute of Balkan Affairs [c. 1960]); Sereny's discussion of the role of the Vatican in protecting war criminals deserves more attention that it has hitherto received; Sereny, *Into That Darkness*.

24. MacIntyre, *After Virtue*.

25. Arnold Brecht, *Political Theory: The Foundations of Twentieth Century Political Thought* (Princeton: Princeton University Press, 1959).

26. Elie A. Cohen, *Human Behavior in the Concentration Camp* (New York: Norton, 1953).

27. Stanley Milgram, *Obedience to Authority: An Experimental View* (New York: Harper & Row, 1974), p. 6.

28. It is doubtful that the killings at the death camps were unlawful.

29. It appears at this time (December 1986) that Israel also participated in supplying the Contras with arms.

30. Milgram, *Obedience*. Using a different kind of experimental procedure, in which individuals acted out roles as jailor or prisoners, P. Zimbardo, "Pathology of Imprisonment," *Transactions* 9 (April 1972): 4–8, reached similar, though considerably more disturbing results.

31. Arthur Koestler, *The Ghost in the Machine* (New York: Macmillan, 1967), p. 234.

32. John T. Pawlikowsi, "Christian Perspective and Moral Implications," in Friedlander and Milton, *The Holocaust*, pp. 298–99.

33. Karl R. Popper, *The Open Society and Its Enemies* (Princeton: Princeton University Press, 1950).

34. See Karl Mannheim, "Conservative Thought," in *From Karl Mannheim*, ed. Kurt H. Wolf (New York: Oxford University Press, 1971), pp. 132–222.

35. The context of this is more complex. The Left viewed fascism and particularly Hitler's National Socialism as the primary danger. Collective security required acceptance of the Soviet Union. The slogan "better Hitler than Stalin" expressed a conservative view and was in effect translated into political reality at Munich. A critical attitude toward the Soviet Union seemed in the polarized context of the 1930s to suggest support of fascism. How could one criticize Stalin when he gave aid to the Loyalists while the democracies supported Franco?

36. Bertolt Brecht, "The Measures Taken," in *The Jewish Wife and Other Short Plays* (New York: Grove Press, 1965), pp. 96–97.

37. *St. Joan of the Stockyards*, cited in Sergey Tretiakov, "Bert Brecht," in *Brecht: A Collection of Critical Essays*, ed. Peter Demetz (Englewood Cliffs, N.J.: Prentice-Hall, 1962), p. 27.

38. Arthur Koestler, "The Yogi and the Commissar," in *The Yogi and the Commissar and Other Essays* (New York: Macmillan, 1945), pp. 3–14.

39. Bertolt Brecht, "The Measures Taken" ("Die Massnahme"), in *The Jewish Wife*, p. 107.

40. Bertolt Brecht, *Selected Poems*, trans. H. R. Hays (New York: Harcourt, Brace, 1947), p. 177.

13

TECHNOLOGY AND GENOCIDE: Technology as a "Form of Life"

Steven T. Katz

Technology is a determinative, metaphysical factor requiring consideration in any analytic probe of the uniqueness of the *Shoah*. Though the technological element has been recognized as repercussive from the inception of the debate over Nazism, it is important for analytic purposes to give it heightened prominence as a "normative" category. The quintessence of this designation lies in the recognition that the dominating reality of technology is not merely a matter of a consuming mechanics, but is tied to a larger uncompromising cultural–ideological process which needs to be described through such modalities as "dehumanization," "rationalization," "disenchantment," bureaucracy, and totalitarianism—all transformative categories that have as one of their seemingly necessary corollaries a growing unconcern with individuals. That is, we need to learn that the role of technology in the mass killings is ontologically significant.

In analyzing the machinery of killing per se, we need to begin by making a distinction between: (1) a given technology per se as representing a "unique" method or technique of killing, and (2) technology as a servant of, a facilitator of, a "unique" goal. Let us examine these two possibilities, beginning with the former; was the technology qua technology used by the Nazis to annihilate Jewry unique? The answer is "no." That is to say, Jewish deaths were caused in three main ways: (1) until 1941 through starvation and the diseases that came in its wake in the ghettos.[1] The death rate in the ghettos was so high that estimates indicate that without any further specific killing operations all Jews would have disappeared in twenty-five years under these conditions. The ghetto inhabitants put it this way: "When we had nothing to eat they gave us a turnip, they gave us a beet—here have some grub, have some fleas, have some typhus, die of disease." (2) At the hands of the *Einsatzgruppen* (murder squads) that accompanied the

Nazi invasion into Russia from late 1941 to 1943.[2] Estimates suggest that these groups killed between 1.5 and 2 million Jews. Their method of execution was simple. The *Einsatzgruppen*

> would enter a village or city and order the prominent Jewish citizens to call together all Jews for the purpose of resettlement. They were requested to hand over their valuables to the leaders of the unit, and shortly before the execution to surrender their outer clothing. The men, women and children were led to a place of execution which in most cases was located next to a more deeply excavated anti-tank ditch. Then they were shot, kneeling or standing, and the corpses thrown into the ditch.[3]

No great technological feat. (3) Through the workings of the death camps, especially the newest, most advanced camp, Auschwitz.[4] In these camps the preferred method of murder was gas. The process has been described by an eyewitness as follows:

> Outside, says Nyiszli, the men on night-shift were handling a convoy of Jews, some 3,000 men, women and children, who had been led from their train into the hall 200 yards long and prominently labelled in various languages, "Baths and Disinfecting Room." Here they had been told to strip, supervised by the S.S. and men of the Sonderkommando. They were then led into a second hall, where the S.S. and Sonderkommando left them. Meanwhile, vans painted with the insignia of the Red Cross had brought up supplies of Cyclon [Zyklon] B crystals. The 3,000 were then sealed in and gassed.
>
> Twenty minutes later the patented mechanical ventilators were turned on to dispel the remaining fumes. Men of the Sonderkommando, wearing gas masks and rubber boots, entered the gas chamber. They found the naked bodies piled in a pyramid that revealed the last collective struggle of the dying to reach clean air near the ceiling; the weakest lay crushed at the bottom while the strongest bestrode the rest at the top. The struggling mass, stilled only by death, lay now inert like some fearful monument to the memory of their suffering. The gas had risen slowly from the floor, forcing the prisoners to climb on each other's bodies in a ruthless endeavor to snatch the last remaining lungfuls of clean air. The corpses were fouled, and the masked men washed them down with hoses before the labour of separating and transporting the entwined bodies could begin. They were dragged to the elevators, lowered to the crematoria, their gold teeth removed with pliers and thrown into buckets filled with acid, and the women's hair shaved from their heads. The desecrated dead were then loaded in batches of three

on carts of sheet metal and fed automatically into one of the fifteen ovens with which each crematorium was equipped. A single crematorium consumed 45 bodies every 20 minutes; the capacity of destruction at Auschwitz was little short of 200 bodies an hour. No wonder Hoess was proud. The ashes were removed and spilled into the swift tide of the river Vistula, a mile or so away. The valuables— clothes, jewels, gold and hair—were sent to Germany, less what the S.S. and the Sonderkommando managed to steal. Nyiszli estimates each crematorium amassed some eighteen to twenty pounds of gold a day. It was melted into small ingots and sent to swell the resources of the Reich in Berlin.[5]

While it is true that the Nazis refined the use of the gas Zyklon B, to do the job more effectively, death by gas was not a major technological advance as compared with, say, the jet engine, radar, and sonar, the Nazis' own V1 and V2 rockets, or, above all else as a qualitative breakthrough, the atomic bomb. Thus, though the Germans were unprecedently disciplined in their application of these methods of mass murder, the technology of death employed by the Nazis already existed, though of course in a less refined state, by the end of the First World War. While Auschwitz may represent a quantum leap in the domain of evil, it has no corresponding significance in the realm of technology in the narrow sense. Technology qua technology does *not* seem an essential mark of Nazi uniqueness.

There is, however, another more sinister side to the consideration of technology, technology in its broader sense as a fundamental transformative category of modern life. That is, though the techniques of murder per se were not unique, the general societal function of technology as employed by the Nazis may well have been. For has there ever been a comparable example of so much disciplined planning and modern technological know-how, so much specialization and concern with efficiency, being harnessed and used solely to murder a noncombatant civil population, where a technology came into being and had as its sole raison d'être the murder of a segment of one's own, and then one's subject (through conquest) population? An entire, sophisticated industry, and much of the energy of the German nation and its allies, were devoted solely to the production of corpses. Everything, from the making of trains to carry the victims, to the making of gas chambers to gas the victims, to ovens to burn the victims, to the communications that controlled the entire process, was the end product of a technologically advanced civilization which decided to turn its economy, as well as its inmost soul, over to manufacturing death.

Still more fundamental is the fact that it was advances in the general state of technology that made the "Kingdom of Night" possible.[6] The sheer size of the European Jewish community and the enormous geographical span of its places of habitation had until the twentieth century been a source of protection, even being often cited in theological discourses as a blessing that preserved the Jewish people "in their sojourn among the nations."[7] Technology, including modern communications, obviated this prophylaxis, though not simply, and not without enormous bureaucratic planning, technological organization, and social manipulation. The large number of Jews to be killed required a novel *plan* (as distinguished from the actual performance of the murderous deeds discussed above, which lacked originality) for it required the efficient "processing" of millions of Jews and the disposal, as well as exploitation, of their remains. An SS officer, it was reported at his trial, "stopped the wild shooting of the Lithuanian auxiliary police, but he substituted for it the routine mechanical slaughter of the Chicago stockyards at the rate of 500 [Jews] a day."[8] Such behavior, in turn, necessarily involved a technological and bureaucratic reconstruction that implicated all segments of German society, all levels of the military–industrial hierarchy.[9]

Raul Hilberg's[10] classic studies of the collusion of German railways, Benjamin Ferencz's[11] and Joseph Borkin's[12] researches into the appalling behavior of German industry, Telford Taylor's study of the complicity of the legal profession,[13] Richard Rubenstein's[14] and Robert J. Lifton's[15] of the ghoulish activities of the medical profession, and the many studies of the eager participation in the slaughter of the churches[16] and academics[17], are all salient cases which collectively represent the totality of the bureaucratic–technological mosaic of the Nazi machine of destruction. The Final Solution required an army of collaborators.

The substantive impact of technology on the murderers can serve as our starting point.[18] To understand it, the most significant factor to grasp is the anesthetizing properties of modern technology. Technology aims to produce more "things" more efficiently, that is, more cheaply and in less time, than other forms of production. In the immediacy of the workplace, it is not concerned, in theory, with the larger metaproductive, ideological issues with which it interconnects, focusing instead on the "object" and its manufacture. In reality, of course, technology is never so pure, never so narrowly situated, for the "objects" produced are, as perceived from the top down, subservient to a larger "good," medical products, for example, to healing as well as profit, and missiles for war and politics as well as profit, but these "ends" do not often intrude into the prosaic elements of the process itself as performed by the technocrats, certainly not the functioning technocrats at lower echelons of control and authority. Their job is meeting schedules, maximizing that particular productive stage in which they are involved. Moreover, larger insidious questions of value, private pieties, *are* irrelevant to the actual task at hand. Murder is not limited by the parameters of passion, death defined by self-interest. Adolf Eichmann could still preen himself in Jerusalem about the smooth operation of his department.[19] Building "a better mousetrap," or gas chamber, is a technical advance into which one can pour all one's energies without either making a moral statement or reflecting on morality. Thus Albert Speer writes to Hitler: "The task which I have to fulfill is an unpolitical one. I felt comfortable in my work as long as my person and also my work were valued solely according to my specialist achievement."[20] Rudolf Höss told his interrogators: "We could only execute orders without thinking about it."[21] The inherently alienated process, and the continual striving to improve the process and its end product, are carried on autonomously and independently of nontechnological normative categories.[22]

A senior SS officer, cited in his trial for exceptional brutality, described a meeting he had attended that had been called to discuss how best to kill several hundred Russian Army political commissars. At the meeting he noted that "there were five SS generals and one civilian, whom he took to be an Army general incognito. . . . The five SS generals vied with each other in ingenuity. Only ways and means were debated; no one expressed any misgivings on the principle of preparing this slaughter."[23] Likewise, Speer defended himself against charges of violence against slave labor not on moral but utilitarian grounds: It would have been imprudent policy counterproductive to productivity goals.[24] If morality means anything in such a setting, it is not a concern with traditional ethical categories, which involve the abuse and harm inflicted on the human victims, but rather issues arising out of the categories of fidelity and obedience, function, and hierarchy. As such, virtue has been reconceptualized as loyalty, loyalty to the system, to one's senior officers who entrusted you with a given task, to the Führer to whom one has sworn ultimate fealty. In this reconstructed environment a selective axiological schizophrenia allows technocrats to kill by day and sleep by night.

Parenthetically, it should be recognized that this extreme alienation at work creates intensifed desires for self-fulfillment and "belonging outside of work" and thus reinforces, for example, that romantic, racial group identity incessantly preached by the Nazi state. Accordingly, the pervasive anomie of one aspect of daily life under the Reich, paradoxically, encouraged heightened self-identification with the Reich on a second, yet more fundamental, level.[25]

These many participants involved themselves in varied and complex ways. On the one hand, there were those who, like Reinhard Heydrich or Martin Heidegger, threw themselves into the fray, while on the other hand many, if not most, of the participants are best understood as manifesting a mode of consciousness that has been instructively described as that of "adaptation," adaptation being understood as "a process whose advance is only in part willed and controlled, and to a much larger extent unconscious."[26] This definition has the virtue of reminding us that the object of the technological modality, of the ideological superstructure, is a transformation of behavior, in the case of the Nazis, murderous, sadistic behavior, such that specific acts are performed "automatically," without reference to the domains of morality and subjective freedom. What Nazism, like all *Weltanschauungen* that aspire to totalitarian absoluteness, seeks to do is to reorient, reconceive, the forms of knowing and acting so that the material content of knowledge and action is "arbitrarily," that is, ideologically, prearranged, though the perception of such knowledge and such action is received as a "given," as a *natural* phenomenon, whose reality and authority is unquestioned. Technology creates, in this broader sense, an a priori form of consciousness analogous to, for example, language, which mediates in fundamental ways our awareness of reality. As a formative epistemic element, it defines not only what we know but how we know, with this mediating effect also, dialectically, in turn, defining what we know—that is, how something is known creates the *what* known. Technology is, in this cognitive, epistemological, manner, an instance of that sort of category that Kant, in his Transcendental Analytic, defined as a "rule for the organization of the manifold of sensibility."[27] Consciousness, at least empirical consciousness, under the form of technology organizes the world into a quite specific, though neither necessary or absolute, unity governed by its own synthesizing, prioritizing awareness, a synthesis operative most elementally on the level of "near instinctive" adaptation, that is, nonreflexively, as an unquestioned regularity. Such a category, even if contingent and alterable (as against Kant's claims for his categories), posits its own rules which establish the order of reality that governs, to the degree to which one's consciousness is such a consciousness, one's individual life. As such, that is, operating under this sort of conceptual structure, its entrepreneurs, including most assuredly those who use it for ideological purposes, intend from the outset that its employment should produce effects, styles of behavior, a hierarchy of values and perceptions, that are predictable, hence exploitable.

"Specific brands of learning," it has been correctly observed, in one application of this epistemological insight, "originate and condition specific modes of thinking, develop and adhere to categories through which they can best express their content and by means of which they can further progress."[28] Applied to technology, this logic suggests that technocrats develop those specific, formidable skills relevant to their immediate, often recalcitrant technical concern, narrowing down, as it were, the wider context of any issue to the particular project they wish to improve. Thus, surveyors concentrate on perfecting accuracy, and civil engineers on durability, and mechanical engineers on efficiency (or other related and overlapping utilitarian values that are content as well as job specific).[29] Hence technology as such helps shape consciousness into a "semi-autonomous cognitive domain."[30] It helps to redirect, to close off, the mind from larger, perennial considerations of the equation of ends and means, of objects and their use. This, in turn, produces a reconditioned mentality that is conventionally amoral (not necessarily immoral) vis-à-vis the composition of the workplace, its operating "system," and its products. In such rites of labor there is an operative rationality that has "goals" but not "ends." Yet it is a ritual not without attraction, for the power and appeal of the "goals" are quite sufficient in their compensatory possibilities to allow the system to operate.[31]

The idiom of means, ends, and "rewards" is repercussive, for it reminds us that technology allows an individual to control singular forms of power (and other human beings subject to that power) while, at the same time being, in turn, an object of manipulation by others elsewhere in the bureaucracy. Thus, the Nazi official uses technology to destroy Jews while he is himself manipulated by the more general, often subliminal, though always coercive technology of Nazi propaganda and fear.[32] In an odd, surprising way, the SS man is no less an abstraction for Nazism than is the Jew.[33]

Technology thus, even paradigmatically, redefines the landscape of the technocrats' reality in terms not improperly described, using Buber's vocabulary, as I-IT.[34] In this living space the concern is with others as "things" not persons, with an impersonal and utilitarian calculus that measures (and sometimes murders!) rather than relates and cares. Through technology the Nazi vis-à-vis Nazism, no less than the Jew vis-à-vis Nazism, is in his or her own concrete, inordinately alternative, ways, turned into objects in relationship to the reigning system. This anonymous, impersonal aspect of technology is not by definition always and everywhere undesirable, for there is much of humane significance accomplished by this manner of organization. But distorted, odiously manifest in the service of a totalitarian dictatorship, exploited as the means of a brutish presentness made into the stuff of daily life, such modes of relationship, such collective exercises in alienation, become the environment in which mass murder, even genocide, becomes realizable.

Technology, moreover, in particular as a consequence of its drive toward efficiency, embodies a modality of abstraction and a calculus of abstract entities that are at variance with the affirmation of individualized, existentially instantiated, human dignity. To be is only to be as a number—at its most diabolical—tattooed on the arm of an Auschwitz inmate. People are translated into *units of production,* values into quantities that can be plotted on a graph. The technocrats' task is to maximize production, not moral value, and in this metamorphosis of the rules governing human intersubjectivity, which transforms moral imperatives into the mathematics of quantity, the humanity of both the technocrat and the "other," now passionlessly understood as a reified "unit," is lost. Viewing the remains of charred Jewish corpses at Treblinka, Christian Wirth asked, "What shall we do with this *garbage?*"[35] Jews were only a problem in the logistics of refuse disposal.

When technology is grounded in an ontological context of freedom, the consequences of its inherent, amoral, mathematical nature are controlled and tempered in, and through, the dialectical mediation exercised by the ruling, constitutive, sociopolitical arrangement. Ecological laws, child-labor laws, union legislation are all examples of such ethical mediation by the body politic. When, however, such countervailing moral tendencies are consciously obliterated and all dialogue between the grammar of compassion and that of "productivity" vehemently sundered, when technology's "unit" mentality is not only exploited but unreservedly exacerbated in the service of a radical totalitarian state, a unique type of human behavior results. An SS sergeant who murdered many in cold blood as part of his "duty" as a camp sick-bay "charge nurse," tells his jury: The murdered "were of no further *use,*" "there were too many *useless* mouths," and, finally, "those aren't people—they have to be handled quite differently." And they were.

> This meant merciless beating of people who were sick or had to be admitted into the over-filled hospital barrack. A particularly cruel incident occurred when 15 young Slovak Resistance fighters were brought to his camp by the Gestapo. All were wounded. GM had them thrown naked into a bare room without windows, their wounds not dressed, and starving. Here he beat them daily until successively they died. He had admitted in court that he had helped a batch of inmates by giving them ropes with which to hang themselves. Eleven had done so, but in three cases he admitted "he had helped a bit" (*nachgeholfen*), by hanging them on bedposts. A young Russian trying to escape had been run down by a pursuit car, and his leg was broken. When sent into the sick bay, GM had thrown him into a cellar among the already dead where the Russian expired.
>
> Some of GM's atrocities, verified in the court, were such that I

hesitate to record them here. Essentially they showed that his greatest venom went to persons who suffered from diarrhoea and were incontinent. His favourite site for beatings were mens' buttocks, but there was much evidence to show that his habitual method of killing was by manual throttling; though he would also use his jack boots to trample prisoners, whom he had floored, to death.[36]

After all this, as a final irony: "A Hungarian physician survivor described in court how the SS 'nurse' had made him draw up the official daily returns of deaths. The doctor was forced to enter fancy diagnoses and even append faked temperature charts that fitted. The monstrous last column entry was 'the body had to be cremated for reasons of hygiene.'"[37]

The sentiment and behavior of the killers who callously operated the death camps in their various phases, and others involved in related stages of the *Endlösung,* provide invaluable evidence of this insistent, yet removed, mentality. Begin with the *Reichsbahn* (railway) workers who had to figure the schedules and also the fee payment for Jews transported to "the East": groups of 400 traveled at 50 percent of third-class rail fare with 50 percent of regular fare for children.[38] This quick, brutal movement of millions of civilians across Europe in the midst of war was a vast undertaking unique to modern technological enterprise. In all 1,400,000 people worked for the *Reichsbahn* in Germany, another 400,000 in Poland and Russia,[39] and all must have known of the palpable cruelty, many of the actual stench of death, inseparable from these journeys. Yet not one *Reichsbahn* official resigned or protested. "All treated the Jewish cattle-car transports as a special business problem that they took pride in solving so well."[40] For the *Reichsbahn* this was a challenge of logistics, not a moral dilemma. Hilberg has cynically, but accurately, summarized the reality: "Despite difficulties and delays, no Jew was left alive for lack of transport."[41] There is in this logic of the transport authorities a consummate utilitarian resolution. It was not their task, as assignments and roles were allocated by the state, to consider the *why* of the project of annihilation as a whole, or even the *why* of their segment of its implementation. In the lived structure in which they made judgments and under which they worked, the concordance between values and facts had been altogether obliterated, and it was not in their self-interest, nor in the interest of the system, nor part of the obligations placed upon them by the public regime in order to reap its rewards, to make such inquiries. Just the reverse: One did one's job best if one did not ask about overriding policy, about where the trains were going and why; one was rewarded, praised, promoted, for allowing the system to run with one's mute collaboration, to operate by making oneself an instrument, a tool, of its design, just as it made Jews into corpses by decree. The profoundest aspect of this relationship between German and Polish workers and the Nazi state is therefore only grasped when one recognizes the contours of the compulsive context in which they operated. The lines of power between individuals and the systemic order need to be read, that is, as flowing from the totality of the political domain downward: the Nazi order runs the *Reichsbahn* officers rather than the reverse.[42] The bureaucratic arrangement[43] of the totality is conceived with just this end in mind. There was no moral collision between individual conscience and state murder because the state had already organized itself through the medium provided by a "rationalized" technological order in just such a way as to usurp all moral autonomy and hence censure while at the same time ensuring the maximum, unobstructed implementation of its grotesque Manichaean prerogatives.

Now move on with the "cargo" to the camps themselves. At least four technological factors and phases of camp operation require deciphering. They are (1) the working of the industrial slave-labor units operated by I.G. Farben and other industrial giants at several of the death camps; (2) the medical experiments on camp inmates; (3) the "efficiency" of the killing operations per se; and (4) the technological exploitation of the dead.

The employment of Jewish labor for industrial production in the slave empire allied to the death camps was predicated on unprecedented, though precise, calculations of a kind possible only in a technological domain operating under Nazi racial principles. Consider the following situation regarding the maltreatment of Jewish slave workers as reported by a Farben agent:

> We have . . . drawn the attention of the officials of the concentration camp to the fact that in the last few weeks the inmates are being severely flogged on the construction site by the Capos in increasing measure, and this always applies to the weakest inmates who really cannot work harder. The exceedingly unpleasant scenes that occur on the construction site because of this are beginning to have a demoralizing effect on the free workers [Poles], as well as on the Germans. We have therefore asked that they should refrain from carrying out this flogging on the construction site and transfer it to . . . the concentration camp.[44]

For the I.G. Farben executive in charge of camp production, the dilemma posed by the sadism of the Capos was not a moral one. His assignment was to guarantee that the construction plans agreed upon by his company and the SS be completed on time and within cost estimates. He had not made these plans, raised the capital, "recruited" the labor, chosen the Capos, or signed any agreements of principle or purpose. His responsibility was that of a good employee seeking to ensure the economic results of his firm's obligations undertaken in "good faith." If the construction work went smoothly, he did his job and was rewarded; at that point his role functions ceased. The atomization of his moral consciousness precedes, as it were, his appointment; it is a requisite component of his technical role to which he acquiesces, usually only tacitly or subconsciously, when he takes up this employment. In time this fragmentation becomes internalized, the technocrat's self-awareness is reshaped to conform to the arrangement of his lived external reality. When he introspectively searches his conscience for guidance, he finds as his primary resource the categories of moral responsibility he had been taught, and assumed, of being a loyal, honest, hard-working employee; of "following orders." His substantive morality has become a "product" of his employment; he has internalized the ethical contradictions of the human tragedy, of technological murder.

Given I.G. Farben's economic interests and its obligation to its shareholders, its imperative was to protect its investment. Yet "I.G. Auschwitz" was, in Joseph Borkin's phrase, "approaching a financial and technical crisis" in 1942.[45] The reasons were obvious: "sickness, malnutrition, the work tempo and sadistic SS guards and Capos also took their toll."[46] What was to be done? The conundrum, as perceived by Farben's board, was technical: how to expropriate more effective labor under death-camp conditions. They had not created Nazism, nor Auschwitz; they only sought to serve their Führer and make a profit as they were obligated to do by the state and encouraged to do by their legal–economic role. Petroleum and rubber, dividends and salaries, were their responsibility, not compassion. Thus they solved their problem in the most rational way open to them: They created their own concentration camp (called Monowitz). In so doing, the board members did not make what can be described as a *personal* decision, an individual choice, nor was their judgment predicated on any moral passion. Rather this conclusion was a further collective, necessarily fragmented, structurally directed step along the prearranged path created by the employment of technology in the service of Hitler's phantasmagoria. From within, from where they sat, given their problems—efficiency, productivity, profit—it was an obvious solution.

> Under the circumstances an I.G. concentration camp had obvious advantages to recommend it. Inmates would not be drained of their already limited energy by the long marches from the main concentration camp to the construction site. Security would improve

and fewer of the scarce S.S. guards would be required. Discipline and punishment would be more effective, and I.G. would also have greater and more immediate control over the use of the inmates. Of no small consequence, costs would be reduced.[47]

A corporate-sponsored slave-labor camp would make it possible for Farben to reach its limited goals; goals that, *ab initio*, systematically did not include moral decisions, for all their fateful ramifications. The ethical equation had already been made at a different, higher, level—the transcendental *Führerprinzip*. What remained was an unreflexive, delimited, merciless, technocratic decision. It was not a matter of who should live and who should die, but given that Hitler had decreed that all must die, how their death could be most usefully arranged. Such a circumstance was not meant to entail agonizing soul searching, to involve questions of guilt and innocence, even good and evil; its only challenge was cost effectiveness within the operating limits permitted by the general death sentence hanging over every Jew.[48] As Hitler told Admiral Horthy: "[Jews] who could not work had to be treated like tuberculosis bacilli."[49] This attitude was nakedly in evidence at Monowitz: R. E. Waitz, a Jewish physician imprisoned there, recalled at Nuremberg: "I heard an SS officer in Monowitz saying to the prisoners: You are all condemned to die, but the execution of your sentence will take a little while."[50] It was preordained, with all the theological implications of this term, that "in the administration of Monowitz, I.G. adopted the principle enunciated by Fritz Sauckel, plenipotentiary for labor allocation in the four-year plan: 'All the inmates must be fed, sheltered and treated in such a way as to exploit them to the highest possible extent, at the lowest conceivable degree of expenditure.' "[51] The results:

> Starvation was a permanent guest at Auschwitz. The diet fed to I.G. Auschwitz inmates, which included the famous "Buna soup"—a nutritional aid not available to other prisoners—resulted in an average weight loss for each individual of about six and a half to nine pounds a week. At the end of a month, the change in the prisoner's appearance was marked; at the end of two months, the immates were not recognizable except as caricatures formed of skin, bones, and practically no flesh; after three months they were either dead or so unfit for work that they were marked for release to the gas chambers at Birkenau. Two physicians who studied the effect of the I.G. diet on the inmates noticed that "the normally nourished prisoner at Buna could make up the deficiency by his own body for a period of three months . . . The prisoners were condemned to burn up their own body weight while working and, providing no infections occurred, finally died of exhaustion."[52]

What is not simple, what is not apparent, is the meaning of such tragedy.

There was, in addition, of course, culpable, gratuitous brutality in the dominion of the technocrats, as there was in that of the SS. No "justification" or "rationality" exists for it in technology *simpliciter*. It was unoriginal, pedestrian sadism on the part of industrial employees:

> During the third week of September 1943, a Director of the Krupp installation at Fuenfteichen, Germany, arrived at the Birkenau quarantine Lager of Auschwitz to select able-bodied inmates of the KZ [concentration camp] to work at his plant. The prisoners, completely naked, were paraded before him . . . I was one of those chosen and thus became separated from my father . . . I was 16 years old . . . I remember very distinctly how . . . at a motion from the Krupp representative the SS man, standing nearby, hit my father across the face with force that broke his eye-glasses. This is how I left my father and made my acquaintance with the Krupp enterprises for which I was destined to work for 15 terrible months . . . I was always hungry, sleepy, filthy, tired beyond any normal human comparison, and most of the time by any normal human standards, seriously ill . . . Whenever a prisoner sneaked closer [to the oven] to warm his stiff hands, he was chased away and usually beaten by the Krupp people. Beating and torture administered by the Krupp charges . . . Hungry, cold, stiff from hard labor, lack of sleep and beating, and in constant fear of our masters we were forced to exert all of our remaining energies to make guns for our oppressors. We worked until we dropped.[53]

Yet even for these acts, if they are to be understood, not exonerated, the ideological norms under which they became possible need to be recalled. The Nazis taught others that Jews were nonpeople upon whom any degradation could be inflicted, in dealing with whom no restraint need be exercised. Sadism was acceptable when its victims were Jews. Thus the camp industrial environments were created to permit, even encourage, through the "signals" emitted in every possible way by the ruling apparatus, such abuse.[54] Moreover, the camp structures emphasized that in the dominant calculus under which the slave-labor industries operated, the only value was production; thus no account of the means taken to achieve such industrial quotas need be given, nor any self-reflection on the inherent, endemic, "spontaneous" brutalities entered into. The liberty of Aryan self-awareness becomes the freedom to immediately disregard, then ignore, the implications of one's behavior. It is the freedom to act without guilt. For the conceptual component that defines authentic autonomous, moral action and its abuses has been removed; Nazism, the Führer, has thought through the *Judenfrage* and offered its, his, devastating resolution, making further critical self-reflection not only unnecessary but even treasonous (for such continued scrutiny and uncertainty implies that the dominant structure may have limitations, even immoral foundations). Thus, in such a matrix, to act aggressively against Jews was not a wholly "individual," that is, a free, action, but the living out of the collective will through a particular agent whose own volition the system hoped to absorb into its collective self. The governing equation is thus not the identification of the individual self with an autonomous moral conscience, but the coalescence of the particular agent with the aims of the state, or in Nazi Europe the will of the Führer mediated through the state apparatus.

The technocrat's behavior thus manifests three criteria: (1) the negation of inherited nontechnological values; (2) a reduction in the status of acts that, under other circumstances, involve autonomy and the requisite ingredients of full moral deeds—would-be moral actions—to the status of technique; (3) an emphasis on the acquisition of high levels of objective knowledge while, simultaneously, eliminating a concern with the effect of such an acquisition on oneself. This is the equivalent phenomenon in the ethical realm of the reduction from policy formulation to procedure in the political–economic sphere. For in both the movement is radically delimited, exorcising the requirements of authentic freedom. In neither domain does the actor transcend the external limits posited by the empirical political gestalt; he or she only *re*acts, and this in ways that are wholly immanent and non-self-reflexive, ways that secure their life and material political well-being at the cost of their human essence. This is the exact inversion of the goal sought by classical theistic and nontheistic moral systems alike. Nor is this turn to be equated with that privatization of conscience that began with the Reformation and Wars of Religion, and that became such a noble virtue in liberal political traditions stemming from Grotius and Locke. What is being advanced in this totalitarian circumstance is the altogether different thesis that there is no valid claim to be made on the public political domain by the individual conscience. The self need not seek, nor the state provide, the means for bringing personal and public, subjective and objective, into line other than to cut through the dilemma by effectively denying or negating one pole of it. Ideally the Nazi technocrat will sense no tension between these alternative, competing, realms; he or she will have abdicated any sense of self-direction, self-valuation, self-criticism, conscience, before the inexorable, uncompromising, objective servitude characteristic of the new order.

After lively competition the contract for the construction of huge crematoria was finally given to J.A. Topf and Sons, manufacturers of heating equipment. On February 12, 1943, Topf wrote to Auschwitz regarding Crematorias Two and Three: "We acknowledge receipt of your order for five triple furnaces, including two electric elevators for raising the corpses and one emergency elevator." Installations for stoking coal and one for transporting ashes were also on order. But other German businessmen continued to compete for the business of corpse disposal. One of the oldest companies in that field offered its drawing for other crematoria. They suggested using a metal fork moving on cylinders to get the bodies into the furnace. Another firm, Kori, seeking the Belgrade business, emphasized its great experience in the field; it had constructed furnaces at Dachau and Majdanek , and given "full satisfaction in practice."[55]

At the very highest level the collaboration between the SS and German industry was more involved and less "mechanical," with many an industrial baron an enthusiastic supporter of Nazi policy, some even sincere devotees of its racial illusions. Yet even at this rarefied remove, the power relationship was wholly asymmetrical, though it did allow, as all bureaucracy allows, for individual initiative to improve the working of that slice of the overall policy that fell to one's lot, at times even straining to the limit the meaning of such initiative.[56] As reflective of the fundamental dynamics involved, consider Dr. Carl Krauch's suggestion to Heinrich Himmler, in a top secret memo sent in July 1943, to establish another synthetic rubber plant "in a similar way as was done at Auschwitz, by making available inmates of your camps, if necessary."[57] Krauch is certainly guilty of flagrant inhumanity and immorality, but is he not still operating within the bounds of that technocratic logic presently of concern, within, in this case, the overriding policy of war production and genocide?[58] Certainly there is one major difference between the situation of these few top Nazi technocrats and most others: They knew the entire plan for the annihilation of Jewry. Thus they could not plead ignorance, nor were they in as totally schizophrenic a position to render moral judgments. But then, alternatively, this knowledge was *after* the fact; that is, it did not generate policy, only procedure in the execution of policy.[59] For the elite, too, was still only an elite within a dynamic, operative, *Weltanschauung* in which its members were, as individuals, dispensable. For example, they had the power to "rationalize" Auschwitz's slave labor by building a more efficient Monowitz camp, but Auschwitz as such did not come into being, continue to operate, or disappear as a result of any intrinsic power residing in I.G. Farben hands.[60] Conversely, any attempt to hinder the existence or operation of Auschwitz would have occasioned great personal risk.[61] In this context the "defense of necessity" plea is not without some truth.[62] This is *not* an exoneration of the behavior of leading German industrialists—the moral issues are extraordinarily difficult in these and related cases—it is rather an attempt to establish a phenomenological deconstruction of their operating matrix, that is, the nature of technocracy's power to influence, even transform, the field of moral vision within the lived reality of a totalitarian technocracy. At a minimum, it can be said with confidence that the character of the problems concerned, their construction, perception, and constellation, are dialectically altered by the power exerted by the medium out of which, in which, and through which, they come to be.

Nowhere is this more evident than in the Nazi perversion of medical science.

Consider first the question of sterilization of Jewish women. The issue, as raised by Himmler, was how to maximize the process, how, that is, to sterilize the greatest number of women in the shortest possible time.[63] Himmler, in presenting the problem to Aryan science, used the arbitrary, not inconsiderable figure of 1,000 Jewish women as the sample case.[64] After a year's experimentation, Carl Clauberg, the SS physician in charge of the project, reported that 1,000 women could be sterilized by one doctor and ten assistants in one day.[65] But Clauberg's was not the only experimental attempt to "perfect" this process. Interest in the logic of the situation created an escalator effect in Nazi scientific circles which drove them to seek a program capable of ever-increasing utility. Thus a competing x-ray sterilization program was begun:

> The experiments were carried out in Auschwitz by Dr. Horst Schumann, on women and men. As Schumann moved into Auschwitz, competition in the experimental blocks was shifted into high gear. Schumann and Clauberg were joined by the chief camp doctor, Wirtz, who started his own experimental series, performing operations on girls seventeen and eighteen and on mothers in their thirties. A Jewish inmate doctor from Germany, Dr. Samuel, was also impressed into the experiments. Another camp doctor, Mengele, confined his studies to twins, for it was his ambition to multiply the German nation. All these experiments, which consumed many hundreds of victims, led to nothing. Not one of the rivals succeeded. One day Brack's deputy, Blankenburg, admitted failure of the experiments conducted on men: the X-rays were less reliable and less speedy than operative castration. In other words, it had taken three years to find out what was known in the beginning.[66]

This is the technological mentality unbridled, the technological consciousness at its purest: technology at the service of an obscene racial doctrine, technology without limits and without parallel in a situation in which the efficiency of murder is *the* only value. The intuitive sense that technology must transcend itself normatively, that it must consider right and wrong, still more good and evil, when in operation has itself been subscended in these experiments. There is no contraposition of facts and values, of inquiry and goals, of data and ideals; there is no juxtaposition of performance and truth. Facts, inquiry, data, performance have become undialectical, supreme. It is also undialectical in yet a second sense: Such acts are premised on the belief that the physician's final, inmost, self-consciousness is not a recognition of human reciprocity between doctor and patient. What takes its place is a mutual, desolate isolation of *things*. Even while alive, the patient–experimentee is dead for the German doctor; the physician's role is already that of coroner, or actuarial interrogator. Technology has created this fateful silence only so it can garner that grim statistical information of which, for no humane reason, it has a desire.

Consider the details of this third experiment related to high altitude research conducted by a Dr. Sigmund Rascher.

> The third experiment developed in such an extraordinary way that, since I was doing these experiments on my own, I called in an S.S. doctor of the camp to witness it. This was a prolonged oxygen-less experiment at an altitude of seven and a half miles on a 37-year-old Jew whose general condition was good. Respiration continued for thirty minutes. After 4 minutes the subject began to perspire and wag his head. After 5 minutes, cramp set in; between 6 and 7 minutes, respiration quickened, the subject lost consciousness; between 11 and 30 minutes, respiration slowed to 3 per minute and then stopped completely. In the meantime a strong cyanosis set in and the subject began to foam at the mouth.[67]

Note the clinical tone, the technical precision, the scientific objectivity, the detachment. Note, too, the categorical absence of any sense of ineradicable evil, the absence of any need for denial. The events were even preserved on film and shown in various quarters.[68]

Again, listen to the aseptic clinical report of the laboratory results of the experiments at "supercooling" in low temperatures: "generally speaking (in 6 cases) death supervenes when the temperature is lowered to between 24.2 deg. and 25.7 deg."[69] One would never suspect by the tone or language that what is being described is the murder of six human beings. There is no horror, no remorse, not a hint of the outrage against all decency that these statistics "report." The very prose conjures an image of unfeeling objects: "6 cases," "death supervenes," "temperature is lowered," "between 24.2 degrees and 25.7 degrees." The vocabulary shields the inmost self of the Nazi scientist as it reduces the Jewish victim to abstractions. It permits the murderer to forget at once that he has murdered, to hide his degeneracy by recasting it as "science." Technocratese is created not least for just this reason. It flattens out the contingent, immediate pain of the victim; it allows a macabre sadism to be called research and thereby legitimates it. This transference from one realm to another also simultaneously shifts the value schemata operative in the mind of the technician–murderer. The norms that are apposite to scientific inquiry are the universal, the mathematical, the dispassionate, the quantitative, all of which measure and describe but do not judge. The Nazi technocrat is required only to perform his studies and report, not to betray himself by leaping into the misplaced syntax of existential communication. To exaggerate, but not to distort, the existence of the coolly disinterested jargon of science makes technological mass murder possible because it facilitates the creation of technological mass murderers.

With some reason, therefore, physicians and other "racial" scientists felt betrayed after the war when they were accused of war crimes. *Rasse und Siedlungs Hauptamt* (Main Office of Race and Settlement) officials, for example, whose judgments on one's racial pedigree actually were a death (or life) sentence, could nonetheless claim that they were not murderers but racial experts merely offering a "scientific" judgment on racial criteria;[70] what became of those classified as *Untermenschen* (inferior races) was neither their idea nor their responsibility. Race, after all, was a biological, not a moral category.[71] Moreover, "the logic of experimental procedure entails that exact cognition already comprises the mastery of effects . . . the cognitive process is, itself, a technical process.[72]

If this implacable instrumental indifference has one especial monument, it is the gas chambers, their conception, creation, and efficient utilization.

To begin with, it is important to recognize the magnitude of the enterprise. Land had to be acquired and cleared,[73] communication and railroad connections established, financing arranged, chains of command formed, a camp hierarchy selected and put in place, and, of course, an efficient machinery of murder and disposal created. At Auschwitz, the greatest of the killing centers, this process involved two "improvements" introduced for the sake of maximizing the facility's utility. The first was the original design of the "killing area," which concentrated in one combined space an anteroom, the gas chambers, and the ovens. The second was the use of Zyklon B gas because it was, in Commandant Höss's words, more "efficient."[74] The use of Zyklon B, in turn, created novel technical problems of manufacture, shipment, and storage because its "useful life" was only three months.[75] These novelties in the manufacture of corpses also set off fierce competition between different camp commanders, a confrontational attitude that continued to exist right through the Nuremberg trials, with each officer vying for the dubious title of "most efficient" mass murderer.[76]

For those not immediately sent to "the showers," the camp managers had made another refined calculation: starvation.

> According to the calculations of the SS chiefs of staff, a prisoner could survive on the daily portion of food he received for about three months. After this time he was supposed to waste away and perish. The calculations of the SS were correct, although in my opinion applied only to young or younger middle-aged prisoners, who arrived in camp well-nourished and in good health. For others it was difficult to survive even the three months, especially in the winter and at hard labor.[77]

The absolute concreteness of this slow, terrible death is "raised" to an abstraction, to categories that effectively and affectively divide the macabre deed from its cognitive conceptualization. The pain of hunger has become a substantively empty, that is, a formal, theoretical determination. The matter is conceived in terms of lawlike sequences and material causality rather than the suffering of people. This is not murder done out of passion or as the result of hubris; the rhetoric of emotion and commitment is inapposite. What he or she is doing is solving an intellectual puzzle rather than responding to visceral, emotional, intuitive, or other human feelings. Genocide has become a logistical challenge; it has ceased being an overwhelming ethical dilemma.

This instrumental, amoral, technological, positivistic mind set did not exhaust itself in its "suggestion" of a "solution" to the challenges presented by gassing and induced starvation. For these "institutions" generated a further, major problem: The bodies of the dead had to be disposed of. An inmate eyewitness recounts the following tale of how experts from Topf and Sons, the builders of the crematoria, experimented with differing loads of lifeless bodies in order to gauge the most efficient way to use the ovens:

> In the course of these experiments corpses were selected according to different criteria and then cremated. Thus the corpses of two *Mussulmans* were cremated together with those of two children or the bodies of two well-nourished men together with that of an emaciated woman, each load consisting of three, or sometimes, four

bodies. Members of these groups were especially interested in the amount of coke required to burn corpses of any particular category, and in the time it took to cremate them. During these macabre experiments different kinds of coke were used and the results carefully recorded.

Afterwards, all corpses were divided into the above-mentioned four categories, the criterion being the amount of coke required to reduce them to ashes. Thus it was decreed that the most economical and fuel-saving procedure would be to burn the bodies of a well-nourished man and an emaciated woman, or vice versa, together with that of a child, because, as the experiments had established, in this combination, once they had caught fire, the dead would continue to burn without any further coke being required.[78]

Mechanics is the issue. The physical laws of weight and force, freed from the immediate material particularity of what is being weighed, lifted, burned, are the focus. There is no recognition of any special normative dimension, no adaptation to the claims of human life and death. For the engineers from Topf and Sons the problematic is divorced from the teleological, or rather what is at issue is a self-contained empirical reality whose decoding is its own, internally justifying, nonreflexive finality. That such normative opacity, with its willed and savage schizophrenia, has become more than an idiosyncratic contingency, is evident in a description regarding the construction of Treblinka, itself a repetition of the Auschwitz account:

In Treblinka, as in other such places, significant advances were made in the science of annihilation, such as the highly original discovery that the bodies of women burned better than those of men.

"Men won't burn without women."

This is not an inelegant joke, a bad pun with a macabre theme. It is an authentic quotation from conversations actually conducted at Treblinka. The statement was based on fact.

It is all very simple. In women the layer of subcutaneous fat is better developed than in men. For this reason, the bodies of women were used to kindle, or, more accurately put, to build the fires among the piles of corpses, much as coals are utilized to get coke to burn. . . . Blood, too, was found to be first-class combustion material.

Another discovery in this field: Young corpses burn up quicker than old ones. Obviously, their flesh is softer. The difference between young humans and older ones is the same as that between veal and beef. But it took the German corpse industry to make us aware of this fact.

It took some time for the technology and terminology of this new industry to reach full development, and for specialists to complete their training in the annihilation of humans, and in the destruction of the dead bodies. One Treblinka document stated: "The burning of corpses received the proper incentive only after an instructor had come down from Auschwitz." The specialists in this new profession were businesslike, practical and conscientious. The instructor in incineration at Treblinka was nicknamed by the Jews as "Tadellos" (perfect); that was his favorite expression. "Thank God, now the fire's perfect," he used to say when, with the help of gasoline and the bodies of the fatter females, the pile of corpses finally burst into flames.[79]

Systematic negation of human worth arising not from betrayal but from annihilatory indifference to the claims of human particularity has now become encoded in the archetypical grammar of the totalitarian technocratic consciousness. The tragic fate of Jewish children under the tyranny of this imperious logic reveals, above all else, the unforgiving, because unconcerned, monstrousness of this mechanistic environment.

Children, too, were often liquidated in the *lazaret* rather than in the gas chambers. These were the toddlers too little to be able to run, children who had no mothers to undress them and lead them by the hand on their "trip to Heaven," or children of large families whose mothers had their hands full. These children were separated from those bound for the gas chambers—in order to "make things easier on the way to the bathhouses." All children of this category were processed in the *lazaret*. If the "caretaker" was kind, he would smash the child's head against the wall before throwing him into the burning ditch; if not, he would toss him straight in alive. There was no danger that small children would climb out of the ditch and would have to be dealt with all over again. Therefore, in Treblinka as in other places, children were often thrown live into the fire, or into the regular mass grave. The most important consideration was to conserve bullets or gas wherever possible. It was also believed that children did not die as easily and quickly from a bullet or from gas as adults did. Doctors had given some thought to this matter, and they had concluded that children have better circulation because their blood vessels were not yet hardened.[80]

And what of the dead? Their "processing" was not yet over. The engineers of Hitler's Reich pushed utilitarianism to its obscene limits, organizing one final stage in their productive program. This entailed the abysmal exploitation of corpses now treated as "raw materials." The procedure was simple, unrestrained, simultaneously dispassionate, "rational," and craven. Before women entered the "showers" their hair was shaved off for blankets and other war needs.[81] Twenty-five carloads of hair packed in balls was sent from Treblinka alone.[82] Hair sold at 50 pfennig a kilogram.[83] After "processing," the victims' still warm bodies were searched for concealed gems and valuables, then their gold teeth were extracted, and their body fat utilized—even their bones, skin, and ashes were used for various "ends." Hilberg has given an appropriately distanced summary of the whole chain:

> Let us examine how the system actually worked. We have said that the confiscations were a catchall operation, but they were more than that. They were a model of conservation. Everything was collected, and nothing was wasted.
>
> How was it possible to be so thorough? The answer lies in the assembly line, a method which was foolproof. Inmate work parties picked up the luggage left in the freight cars of the transports and on the platform. Other inmate Kommandos collected clothes and valuables in the dressing rooms. Women's hair was cut off in the barber shops near the gas chambers. Gold teeth were extracted from the mouths of the corpses, and the human fat escaping from the burning bodies was poured back into the flames to speed the cremations. Thus the two organic processes of the death camp, confiscations and killings, were fused and synchronized into a single procedure which guaranteed the absolute success of both operations.
>
> A corollary to the thoroughness of the collections was the care with which the inventory was conducted. Every item of foreign currency was counted; watches were sorted and valuable ones repaired; unusable clothes and rags were weighed. Receipts were passed back and forth, and everything was accounted for. All this was done in accordance with Himmler's wish for "painstaking exactness" (*die grosste Genauigkeit*). "We cannot be accurate enough."[84]

An intimate participant provides a perhaps yet more informative recollection:

> "Cargo," [Stangl] said tonelessly. "They were cargo." "I think it started the day I first saw the *Totenlager* in Treblinka. I remember Wirth standing there, next to the pits full of blue-black corpses. It had nothing to do with humanity—it couldn't have; it was a mass—a mass of rotting flesh. Wirth said, 'What shall we do with this garbage?' I think unconsciously that started me thinking of them as cargo."[85]

All these instances, while they leave us horror struck, should also inform us of the mode of consciousness operative throughout the Nazi technological universe. In every case we experience that mentality called by German technocrats *Machbarkeit*, the fluid possibility that nothing is given, all is open to novel forms of arrangement, original constellations of relationships, unprecedented usages. Nothing, including Jewish bodies living or dead, has innate worth, only instrumental, extrinsic value. Driven by this original modern technocratic consciousness, the physicians, engineers, builders, scientists seek to discover what is possible when operating without moral restraints in their areas of expertise, to push to the limit their research under the motive of discovery rather than virtue. The method has its own primordial dynamism; its subject matter, its "content," is only a contingency. What the modern planner asks is, Will it work, is it efficient, will it produce the desired effect? If the answer to these queries is affirmative, then the procedure is justified in the regnant axiology. Quantifiable, abstract, measurable, the "end" is the whole. The *Princip der Konzentration auf den Effekt* (the principle of the concentration on the effect), as Arnold Gehlen notes, "exercises a literally compulsive hold upon the men of a technical age."[86] When asked could he "not have stopped the nakedness, the whips, the horror of the cattle pens [areas leading to gas chambers]," Franz Stangl replied with all the integrity he could muster: "No, no no. This was the system. Wirth had invented it. It worked. And because it worked, it was irreversible."[87]

NOTES

1. The literature on life and conditions in the ghettos is vast. Among the more accessible works, see Raul Hilberg, *The Destruction of European Jewry* (Chicago: Quadrangle Books, 1961); Lucy S. Dawidowicz, *The War against the Jews, 1933-1945* (New York: Holt, Rinehart & Winston, 1975); Jacob Apenszlak, ed., *The Black Book of Polish Jewry* (rpt. New York: Howard Fertig, 1982), produced by the World Jewish Congress and other organizations in 1946 and containing important material on these events; Gerald Reitlinger, *The Final Solution* (London: Vallentine & Mitchell, 1968); Philip Friedman, "The Jewish Ghettos of the Nazi Era," in his *Roads to Extinction*, ed. Ada June Friedman, (New York: Conference on Jewish Social Studies, 1980), pp. 59-87. See also in this same volume Friedman's interesting essay in social history relating to life in the ghettos, "Social Conflict in the Ghetto," pp. 131-52; Emil Apfelbaum, ed., *Maladie de famine: recherches cliniques sur la famine executées dans le ghetto de Varsovie en 1942* (Warsaw: American Joint Distribution Committee, 1946); Raul Hilberg, Stanislaw Staron, and Josef Kermisz, eds., *The Warsaw Diary of Adam Czerniakow: Prelude to Doom* (New York: Stein & Day, 1979); Emannuel Ringelblum, *Notes from the Warsaw Ghetto* (New York: McGraw-Hill, 1958); Yisrael Gutman, *The Jews of Warsaw, 1939-1943: Ghetto, Underground, Revolt* (Bloomington: Indiana University Press, 1982); Isaiah Trunk, *Judenrat: The Jewish Councils in Eastern Europe under Nazi Occupation* (New York: Macmillan, 1972). For discussion of Trunk's book and the issue of the *Judenrat* see Yehuda Bauer and Nathan Rotenstreich, eds., *The Holocaust as Historical Experience* (New York: Holmes and Meier, 1981), pt. 3, pp. 155-272. There are also a considerable number of diaries.

See also Lucjan Dobroszycki, ed., *The Chronicle of the Lodz Ghetto, 1941–1944* (New Haven: Yale University Press, 1984).

2. The horrific details of the action of the *Einsatzgruppen* are described in Hilberg, *Destruction*, pp. 182ff.

3. Cited in Dawidowicz, *War against the Jews*, p. 127.

4. The literature on the concentration camps is by now extensive. The most recent and wide-ranging historical review is Konnilyn G. Feig, *Hitler's Death Camps: The Sanity of Madness* (New York: Holmes and Meier, 1979). Feig's volume also contains twenty-five pages of bibliography relating to all aspects of the history and running of the camps both in general and for each camp individually. I would add only one further item too recent to have been included in Feig's bibliography, the essay by Henry Friedlander, "The Nazi Concentration Camps," in *Human Responses to the Holocaust: Perpetrators and Victims, Bystanders and Resisters*, ed. Michael D. Ryan (New York: E. Mellen, 1981), pp. 33–70.

5. Leo Kuper, *Genocide* (New Haven: Yale University Press, 1981), pp. 133–34, quoting Miklos Nyiszli, *Auschwitz: A Doctor's Eyewitness Account* (New York: Frederick Fell, 1960), chap. 7.

6. Many important students of Nazism, since at least Franz Newmann, fail to give due weight to the importance of technology because they one-sidedly overemphasize the romantic, reactionary ideological content of the movement, failing to recognize that Hitler's success lay in his ability to bring together the most advanced technology and the most reactionary, nostalgic axiology. Though for many nineteenth- and even twentieth-century men of the Right, technology was the enemy responsible for the ills of modern society, Hitler and his coterie, e.g., Fritz Todd and especially Speer, adopted a more dialectical, integrationist approach based on the correct recognition that without the power made available by the control and adaptation of technology, Germany would remain forever a weak, second-rate state. Recent German studies have made this fact increasingly evident. See Herbert Mehrtens and Steffen Richter, *Naturwissenschaft, Technik und NS-Ideologie* (Frankfurt: Suhrkamp, 1980); Karl-Heinz Ludwig, *Technik und Ingenieure im Dritten Reich* (Dusseldorf: Droste Verlag, 1979); Timothy Mason, "Zur Enstehung des Gesetzes zur Ordnung der nationalen Arbeit, von 20 Januar 1934 . . . ," in *Industrielles System und politische Entwicklung in der Weimarer Republik*, ed. Hans Mommsen, et al. (Düsseldorf: Droste Verlag, 1974), pp. 323–51. Especially central are the views of Ernst Jünger which have been analyzed in context and data in Karl-Heinz Bohrer's distinguished study, *Die Asthetik des Schreckens: Die pessimestische Romantik und Ernst Jünger Frühwerk* (Vienna: Hanser, 1978). On the political views of Jünger, see also Klaus-Frieder Bastian, *Das Politische für Ernst Jünger: Non Konformismus und Kompromiss der Innerlichter* (Freiburg: Rota-druck, 1962); Hans-Peter Schwartz, *Die Konservative Anarchist: Politik und zeitkritik Ernst Jünger* (Freiburg: Rombach Verlag, 1962). For material in English, see J. P. Stern, *Ernst Jünger: A Writer of Our Time* (New Haven: Yale University Press, 1953); the discussion of Jünger in Walter Struve, *Elites against Democracy* (Princeton: Princeton University Press, 1973); and the chapter on Jünger in Jeffrey Herf, *Reactionary Modernism: Technology, Culture and Politics in Weimar and the Third Reich* (New York: Cambridge University Press, 1984), pp. 70–108.

7. Also suggested by scholars such as Elias Bickerman, *Ezra to the Last of the Maccabees* (New York: Schocken, 1962), p. 3.

8. Cited in H. V. Dicks, *Licensed Mass Murder* (New York: Basic Books, 1972), p. 206.

9. Goring's order to the CSSD of July 31, 1941, issued in his role as chairman of the Ministerial Committee for Defense of the Reich makes this clear: "Make all necessary organizational, technical and material preparations for an overall solution

of the Jewish Problem in Germany's sphere of influence. Other central authorities will co-operate in so far as their responsibilities are affected." This was, in effect, the beginning of the practical translation of the decision earlier arrived at by Hitler and shared with others at the Wannsee Conference of January 1941.

10. Raul Hilberg, *Destruction*, index; and his essay "German Railroads—Jewish Souls," in *Transaction, Social Science and Modern Society* 14 (1976): 60–74.

11. Benjamin Ferencz, *Less Than Slaves* (Cambridge, Mass.: Harvard University Press, 1979).

12. Joseph Borkin, *The Crime and Punishment of I.G. Farben* (New York: Free Press, 1978).

13. Telford Taylor, "The Legal Profession," in *The Holocaust: Ideology, Bureaucracy, and Genocide*, ed. Henry Friedlander and Sybil Milton (New York: Kraus International, 1980), pp. 133–40.

14. See Richard L. Rubenstein's chapter, "The Health Professions and Corporate Enterprise at Auschwitz," in his *The Cunning of History: Mass Death and the American Future* (New York: Harper & Row, 1975); see also Alexander Mitscherlich and Fred Mielke, *The Death Doctors* (London: Elek, 1962).

15. Robert J. Lifton, *Nazi Doctors: Medical Killing and the Psychology of Genocide* (New York: Basic Books, 1986).

16. On this highly controversial issue, see Richard Gutteridge, *Open Thy Mouth for the Dumb: The German Evangelical Church and the Jews 1879–1950* (New York: Barnes & Noble, 1976); Frank Littell and Hubert Locke, eds., *The German Church Struggle and the Holocaust* (Detroit: Wayne State University Press, 1974); Frank Littell, *The Crucifixion of the Jews* (New York: Harper & Row, 1975); Guenther Lewy, *The Catholic Church and Nazi Germany* (New York: McGraw-Hill, 1965); Saul Friedländer, *Pius XII and the Third Reich: A Documentation* (New York: Knopf, 1966); Arthur C. Cochrane, *The Church's Confession under Hitler* (Philadelphia: Westminster Press, 1962); Gordon C. Zahn, *German Catholics and Hitler's Wars: A Study in Social Control* (New York: Sheed & Ward, 1962).

17. One of the most depressing aspects of the Nazi period is the near total capitulation of German (and other European) academics and intellectuals. On this see Fritz K. Ringer, *The Decline of the German Mandarins: The German Academic Communities, 1890–1933* (Cambridge, Mass.: Harvard University Press, 1969); Edward Hartshorne, *The German Universities and National Socialism* (London: Allen & Unwin, 1937); Karl Bracher et al., *Die Nationalsozialistische Machtergreifung: Studien zur Errichtung der totalitären Herrschaftssystems in Deutschland 1933/34* (Cologne: Westdeutscher Verlag, 1960); Alan Beyerchen, *Scientists under Hitler: Politics and Physics Community in the Third Reich* (New Haven: Yale University Press, 1977); Julien Benda, *The Treason of the Intellectuals* (New York: W. Morrow, 1969); Max Weinreich, *Hitler's Professors: The Part of Scholarship in Germany's Crimes against the Jewish People* (New York: Yiddish Scientific Institute-YIVO, 1946). Perhaps the two most famous incidents involve the psychoanalyst Carl Gustav Jung and Martin Heidegger, Germany's greatest philosopher, acclaimed, incorrectly in my view, as the greatest philosopher of the century in many quarters.

On Heidegger, see esp. Emil L. Fackenheim's penetrating critique in his *To Mend the World: Foundations of Future Jewish Thought* (New York: Schocken, 1982). See also Christian Graf von Krockow, *Die Entscheidung eine Untersuchung über Ernst Jünger, Carl Schmitt, Martin Heidegger* (Stuttgart: F. Enke, 1958); George Steiner, *Martin Heidegger* (New York: Viking, 1978); A. Schwan, *Politische Philosophie im Denken Heideggers* (Cologne: Westdeutscher Verlag, 1965); the series of essays by F. Fédier in *Critique*, no. 234 (Paris, 1966), no. 242 (Paris, 1967), no. 251 (Paris, 1967); and David Novak, *Modern Judaism* 5, no. 2 (1985): 125–40. For what this meant in the sciences, see the introduction to Nobel Prize winner [no less] Philipp Lenard's four-volume study entitled *Deutsche Physik in vier Banden* (Munich: J.F. Lehmann, 1938), vol. 1, pp. ix–x. On the growth of anti-Semitism in German universities in the pre-Hitler period, see George L. Mosse, *The Crisis of German Ideology* (New York: Grosset & Dunlap, 1964), pp. 190–203; and Peter G. J. Pulzer, *The Rise of Political Anti-Semitism in Germany and Austria* (New York: Wiley, 1964), pp. 247–58. Ernst Waymar's important study *Das Selbstverständnis der Deutschen: Ein Bericht über den Geist des Geschichtsunterrichts der höheren Schulen im 19. Jahrhundert* (Stuttgart: E. Klett, 1963), is a valuable introduction to still earlier German educational attitudes.

18. What is described in this essay must, of necessity, be cast in the form of an "ideal type," a maximum account, of the technological consciousness. It applies to different individuals, in varying circumstances, in variegated, uneven ways. Also, of course, it is contradicted by other factors at work in the Nazi state that mitigated its actualization.

19. See Eichmann's testimony in Jochen von Lang, ed., *Eichmann Interrogated: Transcripts from the Archives of the Israeli Police* (New York: Farrar, Straus & Giroux, 1983).

20. Cited by Joachim C. Fest, *The Face of the Third Reich: Portraits of the Nazi Leadership* (New York: Pantheon, 1970), p. 198.

21. Cited in ibid., p. 280.

22. By this I mean nonmoral, nonphilosophical, nonaesthetic values relevant particularly to technology, e.g., efficiency, economy, durability, reliability. For more on this see T. Kotarbinski, *Praxiology—An Introduction to the Science of Efficient Action* (Oxford: Pergamon Press, 1965); H. Skolimowski, "Praxiology—The Science of Accomplished Action," *Personalist* (Summer 1965); H. Skolimowski, "The Structure of Thinking in Technology," *Technology and Culture* 7, no.3 (Summer 1966): pp. 371–83.

23. Dick, *Licensed Mass Murder*, p. 102.

24. See *Trial of the Major War Criminals* (Nuremberg: International Military Tribunal, 1948), vol. 16.

25. This seems a general characteristic of technological society. Katherine Archibald's study of blue-collar workers in American shipyards during World War II made the point that the workers organized themselves around, and accentuated, ethnic factors. *Wartime Shipyard: A Study in Social Disunity* (Berkeley: University of California Press, 1947). Thankfully the meaning of ethnicity in 1940s America was not that of 1940s Germany, a decision on life or death.

26. Arnold Gehlen, *Man in the Age of Technology* (New York: Columbia University Press, 1980), pp. 47–48.

27. Immanuel Kant, *Critique of Pure Reason*, sect. II A.

28. Skolimowski, "The Structure of Thinking in Technology," p. 378.

29. I take these examples from ibid., pp. 380–81.

30. Ibid., p. 382.

31. Studies of industrial workers show that they are not dissatisfied with their repetitive jobs even though they are estranged from themselves through its performance. Robert Blauner's study of this phenomenon suggests that between 75 and 90 percent of industrial workers are "reasonably satisfied" with their work. See Robert Blauner, "Work Satisfaction and Industrial Trends in Modern Society," in *Labor and Trade Unionism*, ed. Walter Galenson and Seymour Martin Lipset (New York: Wiley, 1960). See also Blauner's *Alienation and Freedom: The Factory Worker and His Industry* (Chicago: University of Chicago Press, 1964), pp. 24ff.

32. It is not unimportant that there was a hard core of SS officers who manned the death camps throughout the war. For as Robert Koehl has correctly observed, "A kind of common denominator did develop in the war years among a few hundred officers and men who stayed in the camp administration; since preference for

remaining implied disinterest in the front, there was an additional ingredient of ruthlessness in the determination to become indispensable in the productive efforts of the camps." Robert L. Koehl, *The Black Corps: The Structure and Power Struggles of the Nazi SS* (Madison: University of Wisconsin Press, 1983), p. 167.

33. It is notable that Henry Dicks concludes his reflections on his series of interviews with SS murderers with this significant judgment: "The first thing that needs to be said, when we leave the individual predisposition to murder and turn to the conditions of its release or instigation, is to stress the great difference in this regard between the killers investigated by the forensic psychologists cited and my SS men. With the dubious exception of Captain A and KW none of these SS men would have been likely to become common murderers in normal conditions. Their instigatory triggering was not a sudden, solitary experience, but a process extending over time, shared with team mates in a facilitating group setting. It was, as we saw in S2 and the relevant quotation from Hoess's autobiography (Chapter Five) a *conditioning* process which in this context we can term *brutalization*." *Licensed Mass Murder*, pp. 253–54.

34. Martin Buber, *I and Thou*, ed. and trans. Walter Kaufmann (New York: Scribner, 1970).

35. Sereny, *Into That Darkness*, p. 201 (italics added).

36. Dicks, *Licensed Mass Murder*, p. 163.

37. Ibid., p. 164.

38. Hilberg, *Destruction*, pp. 297–98; and Feig, *Hitler's Death Camps*, p. 37. See also Hilberg's pioneering articles "In Search of Special Trains," *Midstream* (October 1979): 32–38; and "German Railroads." See also Adalbert Ruckerl, *NS-Prozesse* (Karlsruhe: C. F. Müller, Verlag, 1972), pp. 112–17.

39. Figures given in Feig, *Hitler's Death Camps*, p. 36.

40. Ibid., p. 37.

41. Hilberg, "In Search of Special Trains," pp. 37–38.

42. I differ here with Raul Hilberg who emphasizes the individual roles of the *Reichsbahn* officials and who stresses, according to his, I believe erroneous, understanding that the power flows upward; The individuals run the system, no more no less. His contention appears to me to lose sight of the unique mechanics of modern technology and bureaucracy.

43. Analyzed more fully by me in a larger two-volume study of the *Shoah* to be published by Harvard University Press in 1989.

44. Borkin, *Crime of I.G. Farben*, pp. 118–19.

45. Ibid., p. 120.

46. Ibid.

47. Ibid.

48. On the especially brutal treatment of Jews at Monowitz, see Ferencz, *Less Than Slaves*, pp. 24–25, and *Trials of War Criminals*, vol. 8, pp. 583, 618. The Nuremberg Tribunal referred to Jews at Monowitz and Buna as "living and laboring under the shadow of experimentation." Ibid., p. 1184.

49. Cited in *Nazi Conspiracy and Aggression* (Washington, D.C.: U.S. Government Printing Office, 1946), vol. 7, p. 190. See also the report of the *Judenreferenten* (Jewish experts) group meeting held at Krummhübel on April 3–4, 1944, at which no minutes were taken because the Nazi goal was still the total elimination of Jewry. Ibid., vol. 6, pp. 4–38.

50. NI-12373, cited in Borkin, *Crime of I.G. Farben*, p. 143.

51. Ibid., p. 121. Saukel's order is found in *Trials of the Major War Criminals*, vol. 1, p. 245, and *Nazi Conspiracy*, vol. 3, p. 57.

52. Borkin, *Crime of I.G. Farben*, p. 125. Quote of physician from *Trials of War Criminals*, Preliminary Brief, pt. 3, p. 97, NI 4830.

53. Ferencz, *Less Than Slaves*, pp. 24–25, 77–78.

54. Koehl's observation regarding SS sadism and abuses in the death camps applies, *pari passu*, to the industrial technocrats as well: "It was not the kind of SS man which was decisive; it was the situation SS bureaucrats had created in the camps which made these excesses possible. Indeed the excesses were more "normal" than the *fact* of the death factories itself." *Black Corps*, p. 176. See also Hilberg, *Destruction*, pp. 575ff.

55. Feig, *Hitler's Death Camps*, p. 356.

56. The taking of initiative is a somewhat more "autonomous" act, though it is, as a rule, still action taken within the highly circumscribed limits of the whole. However, on rare occasions the Nuremberg Court, for example, found otherwise, as when it found Ter Meer guilty of the crime of mass murder for "taking the initiative." *Trials of War Criminals*, vol. 8, pp. 1191–92.

57. Ibid., p. 532. Krauch was chairman of I.G. Krupp at this time.

58. The Nuremberg court was certainly correct to find Krauch guilty of count three, "slavery and mass murder," in his indictment. Ibid., p. 1190.

59. Krauch's actions are still, in my sense, procedural for the war policy requiring synthetic rubber, and its consequent charge to Krupp to produce such rubber, was not caused by Krauch or his industrial superiors. But given the synthetic-rubber mandate, Krauch sought to maximize Krupp's (and his own) role in meeting the national need.

60. I.G. Farben and other industrial giants undoubtedly supported Hitler's rise to power, but this is *not* yet support for his actual murderous activity against Jewry. Few (Germans or Jews) envisioned this would be the actual end of Hitler's anti-Semitic rhetoric. Thus, I.G. board members such as Carl Bosch actively sought to deter Hitler from his anti-Semitic policies, though without success, while a Jew, Carl von Weinberg, deputy chairman of I.G. Farben's supervisory board, was at least publicly, an enthusiastic supporter of Hitler on nationalist and economic grounds. For details of this complex story, see Borkin, *Crime of I.G. Farben*, pp. 53–75; the fate of the Weinbergs under the Nazis is described on pp. 145–46. On the larger, complex issue of big business support for Hitler, see also the recent important study by Henry Ashby Turner, Jr., *German Big Business and the Rise of Hitler* (New York: Oxford University Press, 1985).

61. The Nuremberg Tribunal accepted the defense contention that its defendents in conforming to the slave-labor program, had "no other choice than to comply with the mandate of the Hitler government." And the court went on, "The defiant refusal of a Farben executive to carry out the Reich production schedule or to use slave labor to achieve that end would have been treated as treasonous sabotage and would have resulted in prompt and drastic retaliation." *Trials of War Criminals*, vol. 8, p. 1175.

62. See ibid., vol. 7, pp. 414ff., as introduced by the defense counsels for I.G. Farben officials at Nuremberg. On the court's evaluation of this plea, see ibid., vol. 8, pp. 1179ff.

63. Feig, *Hitler's Death Camps*, pp. 356–57.

64. Hilberg, *Destruction*, p. 606.

65. Letter of Clauberg to Himmler of June 7, 1943, cited in Hilberg, *Destruction*, p. 606.

66. Ibid., p. 607.

67. P. Berben, *Dachau 1933–1945* (London: Norfolk Press, 1975), p. 128.

68. Ibid., pp. 129–30.

69. Ibid., p. 131.

70. One should also include here the medical experts from the *Gemeinnützige Stiftung für Heil und Anstaltspflege* (General Foundation for Institutional Care), which carried out the earlier euthanasia program.

71. On the work of the *RuSha, Rasse-und Siedlungs-Hauptamt* (Main Office of Race and Settlement), see Koehl, *Black Corps*, pp. 188–89; and his more extended study of the RFKDV System, *Reichskommissariat für die Festung Deutschen* (Reich Commission for the Strengthening of Germandom), concerned with German settlement in the East, *RFKDV: German Resettlement and Population Policy 1939–1945* (Cambridge, Mass.: Harvard University Press, 1957).

72. Gehlen, *Man*, p. 70.

73. This proved to be considerably more complicated than one might think. For details see Hilberg, *Destruction*, pp. 564ff.

74. This summary follows Hilberg's description, *Destruction*, p. 565. The following quotation from Höss's affidavit of April 5, 1946, is also cited by Hilberg, ibid., p. 627: "The gassing was a short process in Auschwitz. As soon as the victims were trapped in the Badeanstalt or Leichenkeller, they recognized in a flash the whole pattern of the destruction process. The imitation shower facilities did not work. Outside, a central switch was thrown to turn off the lights. A Red Cross car drove up with the Zyklon, and a masked SS-man lifted the glass shutter over the lattice, emptying one can after another into the gas chamber. Untersturmführer Grabner, political chief of the camp, stood ready with stop watch in hand. As the first pellets subliminated on the floor of the chamber, the law of the jungle took over. To escape from the rapidly rising gas, the stronger knocked down the weaker, stepping on the prostrate victims in order to prolong their life by reaching the gas-free layers of air. The agony lasted for about two minutes; then the shrieking subsided, the dying men slumping over. Within four minutes everybody in the gas chamber was dead. The gas was now allowed to escape, and after about a half-hour the doors were opened. The bodies were found in tower-like heaps, some in sitting or half-sitting positions under the doors. The corpses were pink in color, with green spots. Some had foam on their lips; others bled through the nose."

75. Dawidowicz has described the use of gas in early Nazi euthanasia programs in detail in *War against the Jews*, pp. 132–34. On the difficult technical aspects involved in the production of Zyklon B, see Borkin, *Crime of I.G. Farben*, pp. 122–23. Borkin's review includes the following detail (p. 123), apposite to a close scrutiny of the technological (and bureaucratic) character of the Nazi onslaught: "There was still another episode that gave the officials of Degesch more than a hint of the dread purpose to which their Zyklon B was being put by the S.S. When manufactured as a pesticide Zyklon B contained a special odor, or indicator, to warn human beings of its lethal presence. The inclusion of such a warning odor was required by German law. When the S.S. demanded that the new, large order of Zyklon B omit the indicator, no one familiar with the workings of the S.S. could have failed to realize the purpose behind the strange request. The Degesch executives at first were unwilling to comply. But compassion was not behind their refusal. What troubled them was the fact that the S.S. request endangered Degesch's monopoly position. The patent on Zyklon B had long since expired. However, Degesch retained its monopoly by a patent on the warning odor. To remove the indicator was bad business, opening up the possibility of unwelcome competition. The S.S. made short shrift of this objection and the company removed the warning odor. Now the doomed would not even know it was Degesch's Zyklon B."

76. Note in this context, Höss's comment: "Another improvement we made over Treblinka was that we built our gas chambers to accommodate 2,000 people at one

time whereas at Treblinka their ten gas chambers only accommodated 200 people each." *Trial of the Major War Criminals,* vol. 11, p. 417. See also the account of the acrimonious competition between Höss and Wirth recounted in Hilberg, *Destruction,* pp. 571–72.

77. Anna Pawelczyńska, *Values and Violence in Auschwitz: A Sociological Analysis* (Berkeley: University of California Press, 1979), p. 76.

78. Filip Müller, *Eyewitness to Auschwitz: Three Years in the Gas Chambers* (New York: Stein & Day, 1979), pp. 99–100.

79. Alexander Donat, ed., *The Death Camp Treblinka: A Documentary* (New York: Holocaust Library, 1979), pp. 38–39.

80. Ibid., pp. 37–38.

81. See ibid., pp. 51ff.

82. Ibid., p. 57.

83. Feig, *Hitler's Death Camps,* p. 351. Seven thousand kilos of hair were still at Auschwitz awaiting shipment when Auschwitz was liberated.

84. Hilberg, *Destruction,* pp. 611–12. See also Borkin, *Crime of Farben,* pp. 186ff., for another description of the entire process.

85. Sereny, *Into That Darkness,* p. 201.

86. Gehlen, *Man,* p. 45.

87. Sereny, *Into That Darkness,* p. 202. Let me end by noting that the description of the role of technology in this essay is highly schematized. In these reflections I have attempted to pursue the logic of technology as, what one might call, in "ideal type." Obviously, in the reality of the *Shoah,* in the context of Nazism more generally, technology was inseparably linked to a host of interrelated factors such as bureaucracy, totalitarian politics, the *Führerprinzip,* and the ideological imperatives that drove the entire system. The required, more comprehensive, analysis of all these issues will be found in my forthcoming two-volume study of the Holocaust, to be published in 1989 by Harvard University Press.

14

THE CONCEPT OF GOD AFTER AUSCHWITZ: A Jewish Voice

Hans Jonas

After Auschwitz, that is to say, after the Holocaust for whose widely dispersed reality that single name serves as a blindingly concentrating lens, the Jew can no longer simply hold on to the time-honored theology of his faith that has been shattered by it. Nor, if he wills Judaism to continue, can he simply discard his theological heritage and be left with nothing. "Auschwitz" marks a divide between a "before" and an "after," where the latter will be forever different from the former. For the sake of this after, and in the somber light of the dividing event, we must rethink the concept of God entrusted to us from the past. And even if not to the future, do we owe it to the fast-receding shadows of the victims that their long-gone cry to a silent God be not left without some sort of an answer if we can possibly find one for them and for us.[1] So we must try.

What I have to offer is a piece of frankly speculative theology. Whether this behooves a philosopher is a question I leave open. Immanuel Kant has banished everything of the kind from the territory of theoretical reason and hence from the business of philosophy; and

With the exception of the first paragraph, this is my English version of the German speech with which I accepted the 1984 Dr. Leopold Lucas Prize at Tübingen University. The piece in its present form has a lengthy genesis which bears recounting. In 1961 I gave the Ingersoll Lecture at Harvard University, "Immortality and the Modern Temper" (see note 2). Major parts of this lecture appeared in "The Concept of God after Auschwitz," my contribution to a Holocaust reader (*Out of the Whirlwind*, ed. A. H. Friedlander [New York: Union of American Hebrew Congregations, 1968]). This was further developed and expanded in the Tübingen Lecture of 1984, "Der Gottesbegriff nach Auschwitz: Eine jüdische Stimme," subsequently published in Fritz Stern and Hans Jonas, *Reflexionen finsterer Zeit* (Tübingen: J.C.B. Mohr, 1984), Stern being the other recipient of the Dr. Leopold Lucas Prize in 1984. Shortly thereafter the *Journal of Religion* asked me for an English version, which it took me some time to prepare and see through the press: It appeared in its January 1987 issue (vol. 67) and is here reprinted (unchanged except for the first paragraph and a few single words) by permission of *The Journal of Religion*. © 1987 by The University of Chicago. All rights reserved.

the logical positivism of our century, the entire dominant analytical creed, even denies to the linguistic expressions such reasonings employ for their purported subject matters this very object-significance itself, that is, any conceptual meaning at all, declaring already—prior to questions of truth and verification—the mere speech about them to be nonsensical. At this, to be sure, old Kant himself would have been utterly astounded. For he, to the contrary, held these alleged nonobjects to be the highest objects of all, about which reason can never cease to be concerned, although it cannot hope ever to obtain a knowledge of them and in their pursuit is necessarily doomed to failure by the impassable limits of human cognition. But this cognitive veto, given the yet justified concern, leaves another way open besides that of complete abstention: Bowing to the decree that "knowledge" eludes us here, nay, even waiving this very goal from the outset, one may yet meditate on things of this nature in terms of sense and meaning. For the contention—this fashionable contention—that not even sense and meaning pertain to them is easily disposed of as a circular, tautological inference from first having defined "sense" as that which in the end is verifiable by sense data or from generally equating "meaningful" with "knowable." To this axiomatic fiat by definition only he is bound who has first consented to it. He who has not is free, therefore, to work at the *concept* of God, even knowing that there is no *proof* of God, as a task of understanding, not of knowledge; and such working is philosophical when it keeps to the rigor of concept and its connection with the universe of concepts.

But of course, this epistemological laissez-passer is much too general and impersonal for the matter at hand. As Kant granted to the practical reason what he denied to the theoretical, so may *we* allow the force of a unique and shattering experience a voice in the question of what "is the matter" with God. And there, right away, arises the question, What did Auschwitz add to that which one could always have known about the extent of the terrible and horrendous things that humans can do to humans and from times immemorial have done? And what has it added in particular to what is familiar to us Jews from a millennial history of suffering and forms so essential a part of our collective memory? The *question of Job* has always been the main question of theodicy—of general theodicy because of the existence of evil as such in the world, and of particular theodicy in its sharpening by the riddle of election, of the purported covenant between Israel and its God. As to this sharpening, under which our present question also falls, one could at first invoke—as the prophets did—the covenant itself for an explanation of what befell the human party to it: The "people of the covenant" had been unfaithful to it. In the long ages of faithfulness thereafter, guilt and retribution no longer furnished the explanation but the idea of "witness" did instead—this creation of the Maccabean age, which bequeathed to posterity the concept of the martyr. It is of its very meaning that precisely the innocent and the just suffer the worst. In deference to the idea of witness, whole communities in the Middle Ages met their death by sword and fire with the *Sh'ma Jisrael*, the avowal of God's Oneness, on their lips. The Hebrew name for this is *Kiddush-hashem*, "sanctification of the Name," and the slaughtered were called "saints." Through their sacrifice shone the light of promise, of the final redemption by the Messiah to come.

Nothing of this will still serve us in dealing with the event for which "Auschwitz" has become the symbol. Not fidelity or infidelity, belief or unbelief, not guilt and punishment, not trial, witness, and messianic hope, nay, not even strength or weakness, heroism or cowardice, defiance or submission had a place there. Of all this, Auschwitz, which also devoured the infants and babes, knew nothing; to none of it (with rarest exceptions) did the factorylike working of its machine give room. Not for the *sake* of faith did the victims die (as did, after all, "Jehovah's Witnesses"), nor *because* of their faith or any self-affirmed bend of their being as persons were they murdered. Dehumanization by utter degradation and deprivation preceded their dying, no glimmer of dignity was left to the freights bound for the Final Solution, hardly a trace of it was found in the surviving skeleton specters of the liberated camps. And yet, paradox of paradoxes: It *was* the ancient people of the "covenant," no longer believed in by those involved, killers and victims alike, but nevertheless just this and no other people, who under the fiction of race had been chosen for this wholesale annihilation—the most monstrous inversion of election into curse, which defied all possible endowment with meaning. There does, then, in spite of all, exist a connection—of a wholly perverse kind—with the god seekers and prophets of yore, whose descendants were thus collected out of the dispersion and gathered into the unity of joint death. And God let it happen. What God could let it happen?

Here we must note that on this question the Jew is in greater theoretical difficulty than the Christian. To the Christian (of the stern variety) the world is anyway largely of the devil and always an object of suspicion—the human world in particular because of original sin. But to the Jew, who sees in "this" world the locus of divine creation, justice, and redemption, God is eminently the Lord of *History*, and in this respect "Auschwitz" calls, even for the believer, the whole traditional concept of God into question. It has, indeed, as I have just tried to show, added to the Jewish historical experience something unprecedented and of a nature no longer assimilable by the old theological categories. Accordingly, one who will not thereupon just give up the concept of God altogether—and even the philosopher has a right to such an unwillingness—must rethink it so that it still remains thinkable; and that means seeking a new answer to the old question of (and about) Job. The Lord of History, we suspect, will have to go by the board in this quest. To repeat then, What God could let it happen?

For a possible, if groping, answer, I fall back on a speculative attempt with which I once ventured to meet the different question of immortality but in which also the specter of Auschwitz already played its part. On that occasion, I resorted to a *myth* of my own invention—that vehicle of imaginative but credible conjecture that Plato allowed for the sphere beyond the knowable. Allow me to repeat it here:

In the beginning, for unknowable reasons, the ground of being, or the Divine, chose to give itself over to the chance and risk and endless variety of becoming. And wholly so: entering into the adventure of space and time, the deity held back nothing of itself; no uncommitted or unimpaired part remained to direct, correct, and ultimately guarantee the devious working-out of its destiny in creation. On this unconditional immanence the modern temper insists. It is its courage or despair, in any case its bitter honesty, to take our being-in-the-world seriously: to view the world as left to itself, its laws as brooking no interference, and the rigor of our belonging to it as not softened by extramundane providence. The same our myth postulates for God's being in the world. Not, however, in the sense of pantheistic immanence: if world and God are simply the same, the world at each moment and in each state represents his fullness, and God can neither lose nor gain. Rather, in order that the world might be, and be for itself, God renounced his being, divesting himself of his deity—to receive it back from the Odyssey of time weighted with the chance harvest of unforeseeable temporal experience: transfigured or possibly even disfigured by it. In such self-forfeiture of divine integrity for the sake of unprejudiced becoming, no other foreknowledge can be admitted than that of *possibilities* which cosmic being offers in its own terms: to these, God committed his cause in effacing himself for the world.

And for aeons his cause is safe in the slow hands of cosmic chance and probability—while all the time we may surmise a patient memory of the gyrations of matter to accumulate into an ever more expectant accompaniment of eternity to the labors of time—a hesitant emergence of transcendence from the opaqueness of immanence.

And then the first stirring of life—a new language of the world: and with it a tremendous quickening of concern in the eternal realm and a sudden leap in its growth toward recovery of its plenitude. It is the world-accident for which becoming deity had waited and with which its prodigal stake begins to show signs of being redeemed. From the infinite swell of feeling, sensing, striving, and acting, which ever more varied and intense rises above the mute eddyings of matter, eternity gains strength, filling with content after content of self-affirmation, and the awakening God can first pronounce creation to be good.

But note that with life together came death, and that mortality is the price which the new possibility of being called "life" had to pay for itself. If permanence were the point, life should not have started out in the first place, for in no possible form can it match the durability of inorganic bodies. It is essentially precarious and corruptible being, an adventure in mortality, obtaining from long-lasting matter on its terms—the short terms of metabolizing organism—the borrowed, finite careers of individual selves. Yet it is precisely through the briefly snatched self-feeling, doing, and suffering of *finite* individuals, with the pitch of awareness heightened by the very press of finitude, that the divine landscape bursts into color and the deity comes to experience itself. . . .

Note also this that with life's innocence before the advent of knowledge God's cause cannot go wrong. Whatever variety evolution brings forth adds to the possibilities of feeling and acting, and thus enriches the self-experiencing of the ground of being. Every new dimension of world-response opened up in its course means another modality for God's trying out his hidden essence and discovering himself through the surprises of the world-adventure. And all its harvest of anxious toil, whether bright or dark, swells the transcendent treasure of temporally lived eternity. If this is true for the broadening spectrum of diversity as such, it is even truer for the heightening pitch and passion of life that go with the twin rise of perception and motility in animals. The ever more sharpened keenness of appetite and fear, pleasure and pain, triumph and anguish, love and even cruelty—their very edge is the deity's gain. Their countless, yet never blunted incidence—hence the necessity of death and new birth—supplies the tempered essence from which the Godhead reconstitutes itself. All this, evolution provides in the mere lavishness of its play and the sternness of its spur. Its creatures, by merely fulfilling themselves in pursuit of their lives, vindicate the divine venture. Even their suffering deepens the fullness of the symphony. Thus, this side of good and evil, God cannot lose in the great evolutionary game.

Nor yet can he fully win in the shelter of its innocence, and a new expectancy grows in him in answer to the direction which the unconscious drift of immanence gradually takes.

And then he trembles as the thrust of evolution, carried by its own momentum, passes the threshold where innocence ceases and an entirely new criterion of success and failure takes hold of the divine stake. The advent of man means the advent of knowledge and freedom, and with this supremely double-edged gift the innocence of the mere subject of self-fulfilling life has given way to the charge of responsibility under the disjunction of good and evil. To the promise and risk of this agency the divine cause, revealed at last, henceforth finds itself committed; and its issue trembles in the balance. The image of God, haltingly begun by the universe, for so long worked upon—and left undecided—in the wide and then narrowing spirals of prehuman life, passes with this last twist, and with a dramatic quickening of the movement, into man's precarious trust, to be completed, saved, or spoiled by what he will do to himself and the world. And in this awesome impact of his deeds on God's destiny, on the very complexion of eternal being, lies the immortality of man.

With the appearance of man, transcendence awakened to itself and henceforth accompanies his doings with the bated breath of suspense, hoping and beckoning, rejoicing and grieving, approving and frowning—and, I daresay, making itself felt to him even while not intervening in the dynamics of his worldly scene: For can it not be that by the reflection of its own state as it wavers with the record of man, the transcendent casts light and shadow over the human landscape?[2]

Such is the tentative myth I once proposed for consideration in a different context. It has theological implications that only later unfolded to me. Of these I shall develop here some of the more obvious ones—hoping that this translation from image into concept will somehow connect what so far must seem a strange and rather willful private fantasy with the more responsible tradition of Jewish religious thought. In this manner I try to redeem the poetic liberties of my earlier, roving attempt.

First, and most obviously, I have been speaking of a *suffering God*—which immediately seems to clash with the biblical conception of divine majesty. There is, of course, a Christian connotation of the term "suffering God" with which my myth must not be confounded; it does not speak, as does the former, of a special act by which the deity at one time, and for the special purpose of saving man, sends part of itself into a particular situation of suffering (the incarnation and crucifixion). If anything in what I said makes sense, then the sense is that the relation of God to the world *from the moment of creation*, and certainly from the creation of man on, involves suffering on the part of God. It involves, to be sure, suffering on the part of the creature too, but this truism has always been recognized in every theology. Not so the idea of God's suffering with creation, and of this I said that, prima facie, it clashes with the biblical conception of divine majesty. But does it really clash as extremely as it seems at first glance? Do not we also in the Bible encounter God as slighted and rejected by man and grieving over him? Do not we encounter him as ruing that he created man, and suffering from the disappointment he experiences with him—and with his chosen people in particular? We remember the prophet Hosea, and God's love lamenting over Israel, his unfaithful wife.

Then, second, the myth suggests the picture of a *becoming God*. It is a God emerging in time instead of possessing a completed being that remains identical with itself throughout eternity. Such an idea of divine becoming is surely at variance with the Greek, Platonic–Aristotelian tradition of philosophical theology that, since its medieval incorporation into the Jewish and Christian theological tradition, has somehow usurped for itself an authority to which it is not at all entitled by authentic Jewish (and also Christian) standards. Transtemporality, impassibility, and immutability have been taken to be necessary attributes of God. And the ontological distinction that classical thought made between "being" and "becoming," with the latter characteristic of the lower, sensible world, excluded every shadow of becoming from the pure, absolute being of the Godhead. But this Hellenic concept has never accorded well with the spirit and language of the Bible, and the concept of divine becoming can actually be better reconciled with it.

For what does the becoming God mean? Even if we do not go so far as our myth suggests, that much at least we must concede of "becoming" in God as lies in the mere fact that he is affected by what happens in the world, and "affected" means altered, made different. Even apart from the fact that creation as such—the act itself and the lasting result thereof—was after all a decisive change in God's own state, insofar as he is now no longer alone, his continual *relation* to the creation, once this exists and moves in the flux of becoming, means that he experiences something with the world, that his own being is affected by what goes on in it. This holds already for the mere relation of accompanying knowledge, let alone that of caring interest. Thus if God is in any relation to the world—which is the cardinal assumption of religion—then by that token alone the Eternal has "temporalized" himself and progressively becomes different through the actualizations of the world process.

One incidental consequence of the idea of the becoming God is that it destroys the idea of an eternal recurrence of the same. This was Nietzsche's alternative to Christian metaphysics, which in this case is the same as Jewish metaphysics. It is indeed the extreme symbol of the turn to unconditional temporality and of the complete negation of any transcendence that could keep a memory of what happens in time, to assume that, by the mere exhaustion of the possible combinations and recombinations of material elements, it must come to pass that an "initial" configuration recurs and the whole cycle starts over again, and if once, then innumerable times—Nietzsche's "ring of rings, the ring of eternal recurrence." However, if we assume that eternity is not unaffected by what happens in time, there can never be a recurrence of the same because God will not be the same after he has gone through the experience of a world process. Any new world coming after the end of one will carry, as it were, in its own heritage the memory of what has gone before; or, in other words, there will not be an indifferent and dead eternity but an eternity that grows with the accumulating harvest of time.

Bound up with the concepts of a suffering and a becoming God is that of a *caring God*—a God not remote and detached and self-contained but involved with what he cares for. Whatever the "primordial" condition of the Godhead, he ceased to be self-contained once he let himself in for the existence of a world by creating such a world or letting it come to be. God's caring about his creatures is, of course, among the most familiar tenets of Jewish faith. But my myth stresses the less familiar aspect that this caring God is not a sorcerer who in the act of caring also provides the fulfillment of his concern: He has left something for other agents to do and thereby has made his care dependent on them. He is therefore also an endangered God, a God who runs a risk. Clearly that must be so, or else the world would be in a condition of permanent perfection. The fact that it is not bespeaks one of two things: that either the One God does not exist (though more than one may), or that the One has given to an agency other than himself, though created by him, a power and a right to act on its own and therewith a scope for at least codetermining that which is a concern of his. This is why I said that the caring God is not a sorcerer. Somehow he has, by an act of inscrutable wisdom or love or whatever else the divine motive may have been, forgone the guaranteeing of his self-satisfaction by his own power, after he has first, by the act of creation itself, forgone being "all in all."

And therewith we come to what is perhaps the most critical point in our speculative, theological venture: This is not an omnipotent God. We argue indeed that, for the sake of our image of God and our whole relation to the divine, for the sake of any viable theology, we cannot uphold the time-honored (medieval) doctrine of absolute, unlimited divine power. Let me argue this first, on a purely logical plane, by pointing out the paradox in the idea of absolute power. The logical situation indeed is by no means that divine omnipotence is the rationally plausible and somehow self-recommending doctrine, while that of its limitation is wayward and in need of defense. Quite the opposite.

From the very concept of power, it follows that omnipotence is a self-contradictory, self-destructive, indeed, senseless concept. The situation is similar to that of freedom in the human realm: Far from beginning where necessity ends, freedom consists of and lives in pitting itself against necessity. Separated from it, freedom loses its object and becomes as void as force without resistance. Absolute freedom would be empty freedom that cancels itself out. So, too, does empty power, and absolute, exclusive power would be just that. Absolute, total power means power not limited by anything, not even by the mere existence of something other than the possessor of that power; for the very existence of such another would already constitute a limitation, and the one would have to annihilate it so as to save its absoluteness. Absolute power then, in its solitude, has no object on which to act. But as objectless power it is a powerless power, canceling itself out: "All" equals "zero" here. In order for it to act, there must be something else, and as soon as there is, the one is not all-powerful anymore, even though in any comparison its power may be superior by any degree you please to imagine. The existence of another object limits the power of the most powerful agent at the same time that it allows it to be an agent. In brief, power as such is a *relational* concept and requires relation.

Again, power meeting no *resistance* in its relatum is equal to no power at all: Power is exercised only in relation to something that itself has power. Power, unless otiose, consists in the capacity to overcome something; and something's existence as such is enough to provide this condition. For existence means resistance and thus opposing force. Just as, in physics, force without resistance—that is counterforce—remains empty, so in metaphysics does power without counterpower, unequal as the latter may be. That, therefore, on which power acts must have a power of its own, even if that power derives from the first and was initially granted to it, as one with its existence, by a self-renunciation of limitless power—that is, in the act of creation.

In short, it cannot be that all power is on the side of one agent only. Power must be divided so that there be any power at all.

But besides this logical and ontological objection, there is a more theological, genuinely religious objection to the idea of absolute and unlimited divine omnipotence. We can have divine omnipotence together with divine goodness only at the price of complete divine inscrutability. Seeing the existence of evil in the world, we must sacrifice intelligibility in God to the combination of the other two attributes. Only a completely unintelligible God can be said to be absolutely good and absolutely powerful, yet tolerate the world as it is. Put more generally, the three attributes at stake—absolute goodness, absolute power, and intelligibility—stand in such a logical relation to one another that the conjunction of any two of them excludes the third. The question then is, Which are truly integral to our concept of God, and which, being of lesser force, must give way to their superior claim? Now, surely, goodness is inalienable from the concept of God and not open to qualification. Intelligibility, conditional on both God's nature and man's capacity, is on the latter count indeed subject to qualification but on no account to complete elimination. The *Deus absconditus,* the hidden God (not to speak of an absurd God) is a profoundly un-Jewish conception. Our teaching, the Torah, rests on the premise and insists that we can understand God, not completely, to be sure, but something of him—of his will, intentions, and even nature—because he has told us. There has been revelation, we have his commandments and his law, and he has directly communicated with some—his prophets—as his mouth for all men in the language of men and their times: refracted thus in this limiting medium but not veiled in dark mystery. A completely hidden God is not an acceptable concept by Jewish norms.

But he would have to be precisely that if together with being good he were conceived as all powerful. After Auschwitz, we can assert with greater force than ever before that an omnipotent deity would have to be either not good or (in his world rule, in which alone we can "observe" him) totally unintelligible. But if God is to be intelligible in some manner and to some extent (and to this we must hold), then his goodness must be compatible with the existence of evil, and this it is only if he is not *all* powerful. Only then can we uphold that he is intelligible and good, and there is yet evil in the world. And since we have found the concept of omnipotence to be dubious anyway, it is this that has to give way.

So far, our argument about omnipotence has done no more than lay it down as a principle for any acceptable theology continuous with the Jewish heritage that God's power be seen as limited by something whose being in its own right and whose power to act on its own authority he himself acknowledges.[3] Admittedly, we have the choice to interpret this as a voluntary concession on God's part, which he is free to revoke at will—that is, as the restraint of a power that he still and always possesses in full but, for the sake of creation's own autonomous right, chooses not fully to employ. To devout believers, this is probably the most palatable choice. But it will not suffice. For in view of the enormity of what, among the bearers of his image in creation, some of them time and again, and wholly unilaterally, inflict on innocent others, one would expect the good God at times to break his own, however stringent, rule of restraint and intervene with a saving miracle.[4] But no saving miracle occurred. Through the years that "Auschwitz" raged

God remained silent. The miracles that did occur came forth from man alone: The deeds of those solitary, mostly unknown "just of the nations" who did not shrink from utter sacrifice in order to help, to save, to mitigate—even, when nothing else was left, unto sharing Israel's lot. Of them I shall speak again. But God was silent. And there I say, or my myth says, not because he chose not to, but because he *could* not intervene did he fail to intervene. For reasons decisively prompted by contemporary experience, I entertain the idea of a God who for a time—the time of the ongoing world process—has divested himself of any power to interfere with the physical course of things; and who responds to the impact on his being by worldly events, not "with a mighty hand and outstretched arm," as we Jews on every Passover recite in remembering the exodus from Egypt, but with the mutely insistent appeal of his unfulfilled goal.

In this, assuredly, my speculation strays far from oldest Judaic teaching. Several of Maimonides' Thirteen Articles of Faith, which we solemnly chant in our services, fall away with the "mighty hand": the assertions about God ruling the universe, his rewarding the good and punishing the wicked, even about the coming of the promised Messiah. Not, however, those about his call to the souls,[5] his inspiration of the prophets and the Torah, thus also not the idea of election: For only to the physical realm does the impotence of God refer. Most of all, the *Oneness* of God stands unabated and with it the "Hear, O Israel!" No Manichaean dualism is enlisted to explain evil; from the hearts of men alone does it arise and gain power in the world. The mere permitting, indeed, of human freedom involved a renouncing of sole divine power henceforth. And our discussion of power as such has already led us to deny divine omnipotence, anyway.

The elimination of divine omnipotence leaves the theoretical choice between the alternatives of either some preexistent—theological or ontological—*dualism*, or of God's *self*-limitation through the creation from nothing. The dualistic alternative in turn might take the Manichaean form of an active force of evil forever opposing the divine purpose in the universal scheme of things: A two-god theology; or the Platonic form of a passive medium imposing, no less universally, imperfection on the embodiment of the ideal in the world: A form–matter dualism. The first is plainly unacceptable to Judaism. The second answers at best the problem of imperfection and natural necessity but not that of positive evil, which implies a freedom empowered by its own authority independent of that of God; and it is the fact and success of deliberate evil rather than the inflictions of blind, natural causality—the use of the latter in the hands of responsible agents (Auschwitz rather than the earthquake of Lisbon)—with which Jewish theology has to contend at this hour. Only with creation from nothing do we have the oneness of the divine principle combined with that self-limitation that then permits (gives "room" to) the existence and autonomy of a world. Creation was that act of absolute sovereignty with which it consented, for the sake of self-determined finitude, to be absolute no more—an act, therefore, of divine self-restriction.

And here let us remember that Jewish tradition itself is really not quite so monolithic in the matter of divine sovereignty as official doctrine makes it appear. The mighty undercurrent of the Kabbalah, which Gershom Scholem in our days has brought to light anew, knows about a divine fate bound up with the coming-to-be of a world. There we meet highly original, very unorthodox speculations in whose company mine would not appear so wayward after all. Thus, for example, my myth at bottom only pushes further the idea of the *tzimtzum*, that cosmogonic center concept of the Lurianic Kabbalah.[6] *Tzimtzum* means contraction, withdrawal, self-limitation. To make room for the world, the *En-Sof* (Infinite; literally, No-End) of the beginning had to contract himself so that, vacated by him, empty space could expand outside of him: the "Nothing" in which and from which God could then create the world. Without this retreat into himself, there could be no "other" outside God, and only his continued holding-himself-in preserves the finite things from losing their separate being again into the divine "all in all."

My myth goes farther still. The contraction is total as far as power is concerned; as a whole has the Infinite ceded his power to the finite and thereby wholly delivered his cause into its hands. Does that still leave anything for a relation to God?

Let me answer this question with a last quotation from the earlier writing. By forgoing its own inviolateness, the eternal ground allowed the world to be. To this self-denial all creation owes its existence and with it has received all there is to receive from beyond. Having given himself whole to the becoming world, God has no more to give: It is man's now to give to him. And he may give by seeing to it in the ways of his life that it does not happen or happen too often, and not on his account, that it "repented the Lord"[7] to have made the world. This may well be the secret of the "thirty-six righteous ones" whom, according to Jewish lore, the world shall never lack[8] and of whose number in our time were possibly some of those "just of the nations" I have mentioned before: Their guessed-at secret being that, with the superior valency of good over evil, which (we hope) obtains in the noncausal logic of things there, their hidden holiness can outweigh countless guilt, redress the balance of a generation, and secure the peace of the invisible realm.[9]

All this, let it be said at the end, is but stammering. Even the words of the great seers and adorers—the prophets and the psalmists—which stand beyond comparison, were stammers before the eternal mystery. Every mortal answer to Job's question, too, cannot be more than that. Mine is the opposite to the one given by the Book of Job: This, for an answer, invoked the plenitude of God's power; mine, his chosen voidance of it. And yet, strange to say, both are in praise. For the divine renunciation was made so that we, the mortals, could be. This, too, so it seems to me, is an answer to Job: That in him God himself suffers. Which is true, if any, we can know of none of the answers ever tried. Of my poor word thereto I can only hope that it be not wholly excluded from what Goethe, in "Testament of Old Persian Faith," thus put into Zarathustra's mouth:

> All that ever stammers praising the Most High
> Is in circles there assembled far and nigh.[10]

NOTES

1. In the opening paragraph of the German address, I had noted that Dorothea Lucas, mother of the endower of the prize, perished in Auschwitz as did my mother, and that this fact moved me irresistibly to the choice of my topic.

2. Hans Jonas, "Immortality and the Modern Temper," first printed in *Harvard Theological Review* 55 (1962): 1-20; now in H. Jonas, *The Phenomenon of Life* (Chicago: University of Chicago Press, 1982), pp. 262-81.

3. The same principle has been argued, with a slightly different reasoning, by Rabbi Jack Bemporad, "Toward a New Jewish Theology," *American Judaism* (Winter 1964-65): 9ff.

4. An occasional miracle, i.e., extramundane intervention in the closed causality of the physical realm, is not incompatible with the general validity of the laws of nature (rare exceptions do not void empirical rules) and might even, by all appearances, perfectly conform to them—on this question, see H. Jonas, *Philosophical Essays* (Chicago: University of Chicago Press, 1980), pp. 66-67, and, more extensively, my Rudolf Bultmann Memorial address of 1976 at Marburg University, "Is Faith Still Possible? Memories of Rudolf Bultmann and Reflections on the Philosophical Aspects of His Work" *Harvard Theological Review* 75, no. 1 (January 1982): 1-25, esp. 9-15; see also pp. 17-18 of this address for a statement of the religious objection against thinking of God as "Lord of History."

5. For more about this inalienable postulate of revealed religion—the possibility of revelation itself, i.e., of God's speaking to human *minds* even if debarred from intervening in physical *things*—see Jonas, "Is Faith Still Possible?" pp. 18-20.

6. Originated by Isaac Luria (born 1534-died 1572).

7. Gen. 6:6-7.

8. Sanhedrin 97 b; Sukkah 45 b.

9. The idea that it is we who can help God rather than God helping us I have since found movingly expressed by one of the Auschwitz victims herself, a young Dutch Jew, who validated it by acting on it unto death. It is found in Etty Hillesum, *An Interrupted Life: The Diaries of Etty Hillesum, 1941-1943* (New York: Pantheon, 1983).

When the deportations in Holland began, in 1942, she came forward and volunteered for the Westerbork concentration camp, there to help in the hospital and to share in the fate of her people. In September 1943 she was shipped, in one of the usual mass transports, to Auschwitz and "died" there on November 30, 1943. Her diaries have survived but were only recently published. I quote from Neal Ascherson ("In Hell," *New York Review of Books* 31, no. 13 [July 19, 1984]: 8–12, esp. 9): "She does not exactly 'find God,' but rather constructs one for herself. The theme of the diaries becomes increasingly religious, and many of the entries are prayers. Her God is someone to whom she makes promises, but of whom she expects and asks nothing. 'I shall try to help you, God, to stop my strength ebbing away, though I cannot vouch for it in advance. But one thing is becoming increasingly clear to me: that You cannot help us, that we must help You to help ourselves. . . . Alas, there does not seem to be much You Yourself can do about our circumstances, about our lives. Neither do I hold You responsible. You cannot help us, but we must help You and define Your dwelling place in us to the last.'" Reading this was to me a stunning confirmation, by a true witness, of my so much later and sheltered musings—and a consoling correction of my sweeping statement that we had no martyrs there.

10. "Und was nur am Lob des Höchsten stammelt, / Ist in Kreis' um Kreise dort versammelt"; Goethe, "Vermächtnis altpersischen Glaubens."

15

THE PSYCHOLOGY OF MAN AFTER AUSCHWITZ

Gerald E. Myers

For some people, Auschwitz was an ordinary term, but now the word has taken on a completely new set of meanings. An unusually interesting psychological study might result if someone could demonstrate the way in which meanings passed beyond the accepted boundaries of conventional significance. Why a psychological study? Because the new set of meanings provided the best evidence of the devastation that Auschwitz created in the psyche of every human being. No one was able to resist totally the criminal, amoral logic of everyday life in the concentration camp. To some extent, all of us were drawn into a bizarre transformation of reality. We knew what those innocent words meant, such words as "gas," "selection," but we uttered them, nevertheless, as though there was nothing hidden behind them.

Sara Nomberg-Przytyk[1]

Auschwitz symbolizes, in the words of Sara Nomberg-Przytyk, the devastation "in the psyche of every human being," and it symbolizes, we may add, the devastation of traditional concepts of the human psyche. No Auschwitz was needed to confirm the grimmer verdicts of human nature passed down from Plato through Freud, yet so incredible are the Holocaust and its death camps that today incomprehensibility and despair replace those pessimistically tinged theories of man. Philosophers anxious to understand, somewhat better, the "bizarre transformation of reality" that Auschwitz wrought, must ponder the question, What can psychology tell us about it?

Primo Levi, an Auschwitz survivor, declares that it is "foolish" to suppose that future gestures at justice can ever repair the crimes of Auschwitz, and Irving Howe adds: "Foolish, also, to think that any theorizing can find a point either of rest or satisfaction in trying to grasp it."[2] Philosophical and psychological reflections about the Holocaust do indeed become foolish if such caveats are ignored, but, as my colleague Alan Rosenberg has repeatedly emphasized, to avoid such reflections altogether is to behave irresponsibly. We are obliged not to avert our eyes from monumental evil but rather to see what we can, however much it surmounts our understanding, in the hope that partial vision is more effective than total blindness for the triumph of humanity over bestiality. As modest as our insights must be about the *why* of Auschwitz, the *why* of the Holocaust, through pondering the question of what psychology can tell us about it, they may afford us some sensitivity to the imminence of evil and some opportunity of eradicating it.

What, then, does psychology tell us about human nature, and does this clarify our vision of the conditions that led to Auschwitz? The Freudian picture of the human being forced a gloomy prediction in the early 1930s, Freud writing to Einstein that "there is no likelihood of our being able to suppress humanity's aggressive tendencies."[3] This was hardly surprising, given the Freudian analysis of how id, ego, and superego relate to each other and of the eventual surrender of the entire system to its own death instinct. True enough, in *Why War?* (1932) Freud entertained the hypothesis that acculturation, with its strengthening of the intellect over instincts and its internalization of aggressive impulses, might terminate warfare. But, as he contemplated the troops of communism and fascism marching into the 1930s, that hypothesis had to look increasingly illusory. His own theory of human nature, after all, showed social catastrophe to be but the individual "writ large"; there are no ultimately self-protective devices in human nature, certainly no processes of inherent goodness or decency to redirect an Adolf Eichmann or a Heinrich Himmler so as to protect them as well as their victims from themselves.

The Freudian psychology of man, in broad outline anyway, has been confirmed by the events of the Holocaust. That aggressive impulses require suppression if civilization is to endure was of course appreciated before the advent of Freudian theory, but what psychoanalysis has dramatized is the depth and universality of human aggression as well as the depressing difficulties that beset the management of aggression. When some death-camp survivors encountered something like Hannah Arendt's "banality of evil" in seeing Eichmann at his trial, in seeing an out-of-uniform ordinariness rather than a satanic superman, in suddenly seeming to see in Eichmann possibly even a reflection of their own submerged impulses, they gave added and chilling credibility to Freudian theory. All attempts to formulate a psychology of man in the wake of the Holocaust bear the Freudian influence in one way or another.

Theorists might reject minor or even major features of classical psychoanalysis while retaining the idea that life is an encounter, both cooperative and competitive, between two monolithic structures—human nature and the environment. Kurt Goldstein was one such theorist who also sought, as Auschwitz approached, the role of psychological explanation in political and social interpretation. In his William James lectures delivered at Harvard in the late 1930s and published in 1940 as *Human Nature: In the Light of Psychopathology,* Goldstein attributed twentieth-century cataclysms to the failure of social and political institutions to harmonize with an antecedent human nature. Moreover, that failure brought the character of human nature itself into doubt, making homo sapiens hauntingly problematic, thus intensifying the atmosphere of anxiety and insecurity that prevailed at about the time Hitler would invade Czechoslovakia. Like Freud previously and the sociobiologist E. O. Wilson subsequently, Goldstein believed that social upheavals are determined by the interactions between human nature, at one pole, and the environment (including, of course, human institutions), at the other.

Advocating the need for a "holistic" concept of human nature that would make use of the combined resources of ethnology, sociology, philosophy, psychology, pathology, and physical anthropology, Goldstein drew his own contributions from psychopathology. While concurring with Freud's claim that abnormal psychology is also indispensable for understanding the organization of normal personality, Goldstein rejected essential Freudian principles. The "fatal mistake of psychoanalysis," he wrote, is to couch in adult language the ideas, which get expressed in free association, that allude to the alleged attitudes and needs of infancy; the content of such ideas can hardly have survived since infancy in the unconscious, as Freudianism stipulates, for the simple reason that much of that content, as its very formulation indicates, could have originated only in adulthood.[4] Based on psychopathological research, including studies of the effects of brain lesions on a person's total personality, Goldstein's analysis of what it is in human nature that is especially relevant to sociobiological interpretation diverges, therefore, from Freud's.

His analysis distinguishes two kinds of human performance, "concrete" and "abstract." Concrete behavior is elicited directly by a stimulus and is comparatively "passive" in being determined by what the individual perceives. In "abstract" performances an action is not determined directly and immediately by a stimulus configuration but by the account of the situation which the individual gives to himself. This performance is thus more a primary action than a mere reaction, and it is a totally different way of coming to terms with the outside world.[5] Psychopathology indicates the dependence of concrete performance on the integrity of abstract performance (and the integrity of relevant brain physiology). This leads to the conjecture that disruption of abstract performance, which represents the highest human capacity, disturbs the total personality. Evidence that the abstract attitude is especially vulnerable to anxiety explains why all forms of fascism deliberately incite anxiety. Inherent also in this evidence is the claim that there is one supreme motivation, namely, the tendency to actualize oneself. The conclusion: "Ultimately all failures in social organization are caused by an underestimation of the significance of the abstract attitude and by a misjudgment of the detrimental influence which can emanate from human traits if one changes them through artificial isolation."[6]

Goldstein's analysis of what he called abstract performance and attitude is important and adumbrates a suggestion of Hannah Arendt's that I examine below. But his attempt to understand the paroxysms of German National Socialism through a global connecting of human nature and societal environment appears mostly unhelpful in retrospect. Save for sociobiology, which is more *Weltanschauung* than scientific theory, contemporary thinking recognizes the uselessness of concepts of "human nature" for explanation and prediction. The very particularities that we seek to explain fall between the cracks and remain untouched by global theories of human nature. Such theories are inevitably modified when attention is trained on problematic specifics. Consequently, what we now find are psychological studies of specific groups and personality types in the effort to move closer to the meanings of the Holocaust. The literature presents research on the psychology of death-camp prisoners, of death-camp survivors, of SA (*Sturmabteilung*) and SS (*Schutzstaffel*) personnel, of Nazi doctors, of heroic types.[7]

Two studies—on aggression and obedience—which enjoy landmark status in the literature relevant to our topic, deserve comment. The first, dating from the late 1930s and marking a significant effort by the psychology profession to explain and thus prevent the kind of violence that Nazism brought, was done by J. Dollard, N. E. Miller, and others. These researchers supplied experimental evidence for the hypothesis that frustration of some sort is a necessary if not a sufficient condition for aggressive behavior, and a surprising number of colleagues accepted the findings. Although critics eventually qualified the original sweeping significance and power of the hypothesis, notably by arguing that frustration can elicit responses other than aggression, that noxious stimuli besides frustration can produce aggressive behavior, and that the concept of frustration itself needs serious refinement, the hypothesis has been recently employed by Alan Hughes in his theorizing about the relevance of psychology for politics.

The frustration–aggression theory, according to Hughes, points to the mechanism that connects alienation with ethnocentrism. This is illustrated, for example, by the person who, after striving aggressively for certain goals but for whatever reasons fails, withdraws perhaps into relative isolation to vent his aggressive impulses, if only verbally, against minority groups that are typically too powerless to retaliate.[8] While by no means the only mechanism connecting alienation with ethnocentrism, it is an important one that enables us, Hughes thinks, to understand certain aspects of Nazi psychology. What we must grasp, he suggests, is that the ethnocentrism of the Nazis caused them to hate not the *actuality* but their *idea* of the Jew. "What the Nazis were arguing was for the German people to abandon a conception of the Jew based on the logic of ordinary experience, and to put in its place a stereotype which bore no relation to reality, indeed contradicted it. *But it was one in which they themselves believed.* . . . Hitler [epitomized] those dispositions apparently possessing the audience to whom he addressed . . . authoritarianism, alienation and ethnocentrism."[9]

In illuminating the connections between alienation and ethnocentrism and between these and the frustration–aggression theory, Hughes, it will be noted, also refers to "authoritarianism." The second landmark study alluded to earlier is concerned with that concept, and it was done by Stanley Milgram. Milgram's well-known experiments, conducted at Yale in the early 1960s, showed how (surprisingly) obedient people are, being willing to inflict harm on others if ordered, even though doing so violates their own conscience and normal modes of behavior. The subjects of the experiments, believing (though falsely) that they were administering painful electric shocks to other persons, were prepared to go to almost any lengths if commanded by an authority to do so, and this, said Milgram, was the chief finding of his experiments. This demonstrated also that persons who seriously injure others need not be sadists or monsters, prompting Milgram to come to the defense of Hannah Arendt who had been reprimanded for characterizing Eichmann as a dull bureaucrat rather than a sadistic monster. Arendt's critics assumed that nothing less than the personification of "evil incarnate" could have committed Eichmann's deeds. "After witnessing hundreds of ordinary people submit to the authority in our own experiments," Milgram writes, "I must conclude that Arendt's conception of the *banality of evil* comes closer to the truth than one might dare imagine. The ordinary person who shocked the victim did so out of a sense of obligation—a conception of his duties as a subject—and not from any peculiarly aggressive tendencies."[10]

Milgram's experiments show, at the very least, that more people are more obedient to authority figures than is usually assumed and that more of us underestimate our own subservience to authority than is usually assumed. When Milgram's psychology of obedience is juxtaposed with the psychology of authoritarianism, with such earlier work, say, as T. W. Adorno's *The Authoritarian Personality* (1950),[11] it is hard not to say, in reflecting upon the episodes of the Holocaust, where obedience and authority blended savagely and tragically, "What else could one expect!" The moral and philosophical consequences of this, taken as an unqualified psychology of man, are so ominous that we are obliged to monitor carefully extrapolations from Milgram's experiments.

Erich Fromm's monitoring of the extrapolations is valuable, since anyone, after reading his *The Anatomy of Destructiveness* (1973), should be disinclined to conclude that Milgram's research establishes "obedience at all costs" as an innate feature of human nature. Fromm's critique of theories holding that aggression and destructiveness are instinctual in the human being, including the later Freud's and those enjoying popularity in the 1960s, such as Konrad Lorenz's, applies as well as to the inference that the willingness to be cruel, if authority orders it, is inborn in all of us. Not that we need Fromm to shield us from such an inference, since we are already aware of too many exceptions of courage and heroism outside the laboratory, including behaviors in the death camps that have increasingly been described in Holocaust literature, to permit an experimental, statistical result to become a formulation of human nature. Moreover, even in Milgram's laboratory, as Fromm notes, 35 percent of the experimental subjects reached a point where they refused to obey.[12]

Fromm is especially instructive, however, in his "reading" of Milgram's experiments and in cautioning against using them for facile conclusions about most real-life situations. When one considers that Milgram's experimental subjects were participating in the name of Science and under the auspices of Yale University, that therefore they were in a very special setting indeed, Fromm argues, what can be judged "surprising" is that more than one-third of them exhibited disobedience. Quick analogies between the Yale behavioral laboratory and the situations of German generals, death-camp behaviors, and certain American actions in Vietnam, are clearly inimical to the attempt to locate actual motivations and their determining conditions. On Fromm's reading of Milgram's data, what emerges as most significant is the strength of the subjects' reactions *against* acting cruelly. They experienced high stress and tension while obeying, most of them displaying considerable horror or indignation about what they were ordered to do.

The main result of Milgram's study seems to be one he does not stress: the presence of conscience in most subjects, and their pain when disobedience made them act against their conscience. Thus, while the experiment can be interpreted as another proof of the easy dehumanization of man, the subjects' reactions show rather the contrary—the presence of intense forces within them that find cruel behavior intolerable. This suggests an important approach to the study of cruelty in real life: to consider not only cruel *behavior* but the—often unconscious—guilty conscience of those who obey authority. (The Nazis had to use an elaborate system of camouflage of atrocities in order to cope with the conscience of the average man.)[13]

For his own part, Fromm develops a psychology of man freed from the taint of original destructiveness, a psychology based on man's "love of life" rather than an alleged bent for cruelty, a psychology that offers hope for society despite the pessimism inspired by laboratory experiments and real-life catastrophes such as Auschwitz. The climax of his study is a psychoanalytic diagnosis of Adolph Hitler. Having analyzed Heinrich Himmler as "the typical anal-hoarding, sadistic, authoritarian" personality (p. 321; this and the following page references are to Fromm's *Anatomy*) and identifying some of the conditions for this in Himmler's youth, Fromm moves to a protracted study of Hitler. Taking the word from psychiatry but giving it a twist inspired by Miguel de Unamuno's use of it in 1936, Fromm diagnoses Hitler's malignant aggressiveness as a case of "necrophilia" (p. 325 and passim). The twist in usage is to make the word refer to a character trait rather than a perverse act. Necrophilia as a personality characteristic is a fascination with death and destruction and is the opposite of biophilia or the love of life. Fromm points to facets of Hitler's early career, some of which have become familiar through other studies of Hitler, that one can sensibly infer contributed to his necrophilous character. Episodes in Hitler's youth, revealing a defectiveness of will and a defective sense of reality, are emphasized in building the diagnosis.

Psychoanalytic studies of Hitler and his cohorts exemplify a goodly part of what psychology has done, as was mentioned earlier, in theorizing about how human motivation affects human destiny by trying at the same time to "stare through" the oven smoke of Auschwitz. Global theories of human nature are replaced by diagnoses of specific groups or specific personalities or personality types that were conspicuously present in the Holocaust. A substantial amount of interpretation of the psychological meanings of the Holocaust comes from clinical psychology. Certainly, this diversity of approach is an enormous improvement over one that pits a monolithic "human nature" against an equally monolithic thing called "the environment." It allows a more accurate picture of the events that define the Holocaust through seeing more intimately the kinds of personalities, and their encounters, that were involved. It also permits a more adequate grasp of the causes of the Holocaust. Conjecture about the workings of a putative human nature is totally unpromising in seeking the causes of the destruction of six million Jews, compared to what may be learned through information about the character of a primary cause, the Führer himself.

Oddly enough, according to Milton Himmelfarb, analyses of the Holocaust's causes tend to lose sight of Hitler. The literature, he thinks, concentrates on such factors as tendencies, ideas, traditions, myths, on what can be dug out of the cultural context in which Nazism developed. And it is of course true, all sorts of candidates have been pointed to as the culprit. German philosophy, romantic mysticism, anti-Semitism, the "stab in the back" argument aimed at the Weimar Republic, German big business, the German economy in the wake of the Versailles treaty, the Prussian tradition, insidious occultism associated with "ariosophy," and the threat of Stalinist communism are some of the nominees. (In the welter of such explanations the question inevitably arises, What role can psychological theory play in all of this? It is a question I return to.) An ironic consequence of the "search for causes," Himmelfarb asserts, is that Hitler "disappears" in the literature, becomes an abstraction or is treated like a metaphor. This may in part result from fear of the "great man" approach to historical explanation, but such fear is unjustified if one but recognizes the plain fact that just as Lenin was responsible for the Bolshevik Revolution so was Hitler for the Holocaust. Anti-Semitism without Hitler would not have caused it, for, in Himmelfarb's words, "Hitler willed and ordered the Holocaust, and was obeyed," and "Hitler made the Holocaust because he wanted to make it. Anti-Semitism did not make him make it."[14]

How could anyone, in possession of the basic evidence, deny this? Who does not sigh with relief in having Himmelfarb's blunt statement of the facts to hold after wandering dazed through a literature that piles perplexity upon perplexity, doubt upon doubt, so that one comes away empty handed in searching for the causes of the Holocaust? He seems so absolutely right when one looks back at E.O. Lorimer's small book *What Hitler Wants*, published in 1939, poignantly dedicated "In Sorrow and Mourning to the Memory of the Democratic Republic of Czechoslovakia," and intended to arouse British awareness of Hitler's intentions.[15] Lorimer's presentation of what was said in *Mein Kampf*, what it meant and what it forecast, so clearly appreciated then what Himmelfarb feels it is necessary to assert now—no Hitler, no Holocaust. If ever there were a *historical* fact, it certainly is that Hitler was a necessary if not sufficient condition for the Holocaust.

Without denying this last statement, suppose, however, we ask an odd-sounding question. Is it a *psychological* fact that Hitler made the Holocaust happen? One raises the question heuristically, for instance, when confronted by Heinz Kohut, who has often placed Hitler center stage in his psychological studies:

> I am not, in the Tolstoyean mode, assigning primacy to the role of Hitler among the causes and motivations that led to the historical events in question. My attention is focused on certain aspects of the condition of the German nation. I believe that, in doing so, I am focusing on the crucial psychological condition—however diverse the influences that were responsible for the German state of mind at that time . . . The primary psychological cause of the historical events under scrutiny was a serious disturbance in the strength and cohesion of the German group self.[16]

Kohut would presumably grant that from a narrow perspective it is a historical fact that Hitler was the primary cause of the Holocaust; but, from a broader base of psychological interpretation, it may not be a fact that Hitler, rather than anti-Semitism, say, in conjunction with other currents in German culture, was the Holocaust's primary source. A sketch of Kohut's analysis brings to light issues that are important both methodologically and substantively.

Roughly summarized, Kohut's "Self Psychology" abandons frameworks of biological drives and mental apparatuses, positing instead a primary self and its experiences of "*self*object greatness (assertiveness; ambitions), on the one hand, and self*object* perfection (idealization of one's goals; enthusiasm for one's ideals), on the other" (p. 74; page references here and in the following two paragraphs are to Kohut's *Self Psychology*). Depth psychological inquiry assumes the primacy of the ideals and ambitions of the primary, cohesive self, and in so doing resurrects the tools of empathy and introspection. The data yielded by empathic and introspective observations are both identified and interpreted through theoretical constructions that characterize the empirical sciences, and a prominent concept emerging in Kohut's "Self Psychology" is that of narcissism and its derivative "narcissistic rage."

Drawing upon clinical experience, the self psychologist envisages Hitler as a narcissistic personality who suffered narcissistic injuries (which can be documented biographically) that produced a chronic rage that led to pathological destructiveness. But it is a peculiar truth, if Kohut is right, that the narcissistically wounded can have an uncanny sense of the same thing, when it exists, echoing back from the ranks of society. Extending the pioneering work of Gustave LeBon and Freud on the psychology of groups, Kohut conceives a "group self" analogous to the individual, a conception that facilitates the analysis of how individuals and groups bond, and in particular of how a leader like Hitler bonded with a German group self. Groups display a psychological cohesiveness not unlike that of individuals, and fruitful methods of interpreting the dynamics of leader-and-group relations are generated by deploying the same psychoanalytic concepts to groups as to individuals.

For example, the unconscious fantasies, the psychological needs, the special tensions, and the use of leaders can be interpretively related to the self-selfobject relation of mother and child, and they bestow upon a group a selflike identify (pp. xxix, 51, and passim). "The unconscious fantasies of the group's grandiose self, expressed in the transference upon the image of an appropriate leader figure, thus can play at times a crucial role in its cohesion. The leader of such a group is not primarily the focal point of shared values, as Freud suggested, but self-righteously expresses the group's ambitions and extols its greatness and power" (p. 57). In Germany, after World War I, the loss of national prestige (injury to self-group pride), the loss of self-esteem for millions of people because of unemployment and inflation, decreased social status for the civil service and much of the middle class, and the corrosion of both Christian and traditional values such as were represented by the aristocratic officer caste—these plus other such factors impress Kohut as amounting to narcissistic wounds, with an accompanying narcissistic rage, in the German group self that disposed it to bond instinctively with its Führer's similar but also charismatic character (p. 64). Ultimately, the leader as the expression not of shared values but of the group-self's grandiose fantasies that characterize narcissistic rage, is more dependent upon the group than conversely, for when his psychological function ceases, as happened to Winston Churchill after World War II, the group discarded him (pp. 198–99).

Kohut's application of self psychology or his own psychoanalytic theory to history and to the Holocaust thus assigns importance, of course, to Hitler's personality, but it assigns even greater significance to the psychological constitution of a society that, despite its being a European center of culture, bonded enthusiastically with the likes of Hitler. The historical dimensions of what occurred in Europe between the two World Wars could be achieved only by a grandiose group self that was lying in wait, so to speak, for a leader, similar in self, with whom to bond and act out the fantasies of destruction and self-aggrandizement. So we return to the possibility that, from a narrower but more manageable perspective, it is simple historical fact that Hitler was the Holocaust's primary cause, whereas from a larger psychological vantage point it was rather a society amounting to a kind of group self. Without debating the respective merits of the two perspectives, or the substantive issues involved, and, while clearly appreciating how the narrower historical one is free to examine the contributions to Nazi crimes made by the cultural context, it seems evident that the Kohutian perspective resurrects questions about anti-Semitism and collective guilt with a certain urgency and with at least the hint that a kind of psychological understanding is available that might just help in preventing future resemblances to Nazism.[17]

The foregoing also points up methodological considerations of philosophical significance. The first to be mentioned concerns the nature of historical explanation. The narrower the historical perspective the closer we approach both the straightforward "matter of fact" assertions out of which natural science develops and the causal explanations that science seeks. The more tightly delineated the subject to be explained, the more susceptible it generally is to techniques of investigation of the sort used in science. It should be easier, for instance, to confirm hypotheses about what caused a district of Boston to threaten to secede than about what produced the Civil War. Historical accounting is revisionary, being subject to subsequent changes of perspective, whereas scientific accounting is correctible because it is subject to subsequent changes in prediction. But (since this is familiar enough) the point to notice here is that as psychological explanation is woven into historical accounting the difference between historical and scientific theorizing increases drastically.

Stuart Hampshire has written instructively on the difference that occurs once the concept of "unconscious motives," for instance, is inserted into psychohistorical explanations. The idea that unconscious motives occur is persuasive because of the evidence that unconscious memories exist and that these, as the residues of past experiences, can function as unconscious motives. Motives are to be distinguished from intentions which are ordinarily conscious, so that while motives are often elusive and may be revealed only through psychoanalytic sleuthing, one's intentions are typically transparent. Unconscious motives, when discovered, help to explain present behavior as being an attempt to affect the past that is in some respect unconsciously remembered. An example would be the woman who behaves toward her spouse as she did toward her father, and the unconscious motive for her adult behavior is, by hypothesis, describable as an attempt to alter the past, namely, to win the paternal approval that was never granted.

Motive explanations, however, are not like explanations in physics or the natural sciences, because they have the character of genetical, historical explanations in being retrospective.

Of motives, it can indeed be said that they explain retrospectively, and that they do not provide a corresponding basis for prediction of future behaviour. In my stating that it was so-and-so that moved me to laugh or protest, I have not so far committed myself to any general proposition which justifies a prediction of my behaviour on future occasions; and least of all is there a basis for prediction when the transition may be made from an unconscious motive to the conscious recognition of it [because the conscious recognition may transform what was habitual and unconscious into conscious, controllable behavior].[18]

The second methodological consideration to be noticed is the interdisciplinary nature of explanation that is both historical and psychological. A case can be made, I believe, for the claim that the Holocaust, crying out for some penetration of its apparent incomprehensibility, motivated the contemporary specialties of psychohistory and psychobiography. Strict compartmentalization of academic disciplines blocks all reasonable approaches to the Holocaust, and the influence of that realization in historical accounting must be extensive. Psychologists such as Fromm and Kohut in search of an improved framework within which to interpret man's past and his chances ahead, in the aftermath of the Holocaust, look for assistance from history, political science, medicine, anthropology, philosophy, neurophysiology, literature, the arts, and further. Systematic psychological theory is surely developed, but, unlike Skinnerian behaviorism (which, when applied beyond strictly limited experimental conditions, is more philosophy than science), it collects as supporting evidence what is uttered on the therapist's couch, or startling events that attract public attention, historical figures and episodes, classical examples from abnormal psychology, and illustrations from drama, fiction, and mythology. Kohut's comparison of Hitler with Hamlet in his *Self Psychology and the Humanities* is a case in point. Quite often, it more resembles dramatic narrative plus commentary than scientific theory, but because of and not despite this it casts its own kind of illumination.

The interdisciplinary bent of much current psychology, due in part to the traumatic reverberations of the Holocaust, encourages a common pursuit of topics and themes without undue concern about their place of origin. This is a welcome change from the policy that refuses a subject matter because it crosses artificial academic property lines. Accordingly, a historian or political scientist may seize on an idea originated by a psychologist, and of course the converse also occurs. Although the value of this process, so far as anything like a "psychology of man" is concerned, can be really appreciated only by surveying the whole sweep of research literature, a single example of a cooperative inquiry indicates what can be gained.

The racist ideology of Nazism, as is too well known, vilified Jews and others as threats to Aryan purity. Nazi declarations compared the Jews to deadly bacteria or bacilli, thus propagandizing the notion that their apparent innocence belied their true nature. The viciousness of those declarations, when revisited, never ceases to stun one's sensitivities. It is impossible not to wonder about the psychology of Hitler and the other authors of such declarations and about the need to expose that psychology for our future protection. Consider Hitler's statement:

> That is why within a certain time all of Western Europe must be totally emptied of the Jews. . . . But one must not deport the Jews to Siberia for, given their capacity of adaptation to climates, they will become still much more hardened. . . . It is much better [to deport them] to Africa to expose them to a climate which harms any man having our force of resistance.[19]

The perverse notion of Jews as bacilli is amplified here, it seems, by referring to their capacity to survive. One assumes that Hitler had in mind the remarkable stamina displayed by Jews through a history of persecution, an endurance record he must have resented and not only resented but feared. And this is a thought worth pursuing, especially when a certain Hitlerian characteristic is brought to our attention by Fromm: "It is not altogether far-fetched to assume that the insatiable hate operating within him [Hitler] was connected in unconscious parts of his being with the veiled but always present certainty that the end would be marked by the most horrible failure and by personal extinction, as, in fact, happened in the Reichschancellery on April 30, 1945."[20] Following this and other clues, including Albert Speer's report that he intuited Hitler's subconscious realization that his architectural plans, so enthusiastically expressed to Speer, would never materialize, Fromm pictures the Führer as (unconsciously) never actually wanting his stated goals and the *constructive* work involved.

Data supplied by historians have stimulated a hypothesis of psychological significance that is explored and systematized by Fromm with his theory of necrophilic personality and Hitler as its instantiation, a hypothesis that incites us now to take a further philosophical and psychological step and join an interdisciplinary process of interpretation. The next step is to characterize Hitler as someone uniquely self-destructive, whose destructiveness of others was a function of that, and a major (unconscious) motive behind his brooding over his own conceptions of the Jewish will to live and ability to survive, I conjecture, was the need to crush a basic impulse that so unforgivably contradicted his own self-destructive counterpart. The need in Hitler's self-destructive personality to eradicate inner remnants of self-preservation became objectified through attacking its outer manifestations in others, especially the Jews who symbolized for him a baffling kind of indestructibility.

From this psychological portrait some philosophical lessons are learned. The philosophies of politics, psychology, and culture should enlarge upon the theme of self-destructiveness and its implications. Care should be taken to ensure that it is not mainly compartmentalized in psychology alone. The fact that self-destructiveness can become the orgiastic destruction of millions deserves to become a societal watchword in examining a society's leadership. The concept is prima facie psychological, but its full meaning, since Auschwitz, can be adequately articulated and communicated only by a multiplicity of cooperating disciplines.

Another lesson learned is the requirement to scrutinize political rhetoric for the sort of personality clues that post-Holocaust psychology has brought to light. What "lies behind" the rhetoric, we now know or ought to know, may differ vastly from its manifest content. Consequently, the philosophical examination of arguments offered in the sociopolitical arena cannot afford to be nonpsychological, as it tends to be in following an established policy. That policy cautions against rebuttals that can be viewed as ad hominen. It enjoins an argument's critic to rebut the argument's content, to refute its alleged arrival at a true conclusion via sound reasoning.

At the same time, the policy holds that the motives, conscious or unconscious, that may lie behind a person's argument are no part of the content to be critically or philosophically examined. But this is to identify the philosopher with the "pure" logician, and purely logical responses to sociopolitical arguments are in some contexts obviously inadequate and inappropriate. Yet the bias persists, especially since the divorce of philosophy and psychology as academic disciplines, that questions of motive and intent are alien to the process of assessing arguments. Since the Holocaust, however, that bias is a visibly disastrous one. Confronted by outrageous, vicious, and inflammatory arguments, the philosophical critic must employ all available tools for discovering the clues to motives of self-destructiveness and the like. Learning to be sensitive to the "psychological atmosphere" of arguments should be a standard part of informal logic.

The goal that has been posited for interdisciplinary research in the foregoing discussion is the discovery of psychohistorical (with the emphasis on the psychological) causes behind the symptoms. Narcissism, necrophilia, self-destructiveness, and leader and group self relationships are the kinds of things that may be uncovered in places where they lay hidden too long and from too many eyes. A different though related type of inquiry found in contemporary psychological literature, which has been stimulated by efforts to understand the human condition in the post-Holocaust era, is less concerned to expose the causes behind the symptoms than it is to expand our conceptual awareness of the symptoms themselves. This concern, we may say, is directed toward developing enriched symptomological descriptions.

A vast literature exists, interdisciplinary in nature, on the personalities of Hitler's immediate subordinates and the structures of his power system. Collecting for notice certain strands from this literature also provides opportunities for making further contributions to it. One such strand is the reported slavishness of individuals like Heinrich Himmler, described by one close observer as being more sinister than Hitler because of "his degree of concentrated subordination, of hidebound conscientiousness, something in-humanly methodical with an element of the automatic."[21] This and similar perceptions of Hitler's associates and the echelons of lesser subordinates make Milgram's research all the more relevant, if not to global theorizing about human nature, to analyzing some of the personality types who obeyed the Führer's orders. Part of the same strand are Hannah Arendt's later reflections on what she had said about Adolf Eichmann and the banality of evil in *Eichmann in Jerusalem.*

Looking back a decade later at what she had written in that book, she confesses that the phrase "banality of evil" had contained no special doctrine or thesis for her and that she was only "dimly aware" of its implications. But in her later reflections the same Eichmann traits stood out, shallowness and mediocrity; his evil seemed rooted not in deep but shallow soil. At the Jerusalem trial he displayed a lack even of strong ideological commitments. For Arendt, he exhibited

> something entirely negative; it was not stupidity but *thoughtlessness* . . . It was this absence of thinking . . . that awakened my interest . . . Could the activity of thinking as such, the habit of examining whatever happens to come to pass or to attract attention, regardless of results and specific content, could this activity be among the conditions that make men abstain from evil-doing or even actually "condition" them against it?[22]

A good part of her two-volume *The Life of the Mind* follows the leads contained in this question.

Some prominent Nazi personality symptoms, then, that observers report include excessive subservience, automatism, and thoughtlessness. Each of these, let us note, while immediately understandable in certain respects, is susceptible to an interdisciplinary analysis capable of eliciting its fuller psychoanalytic, philosophical, historical, and sociopolitical meanings. The analysis may explore, for instance, the possible connections between those symptoms and the ways in which the Nazi power system worked. Holocaust scholars have puzzled over the fact that, despite their certainty of Hitler's role in it, apparently no document ordering Jewish destruction has been found that explicitly bears his signature. Raul Hilberg, author of the monumental *The Destruction of the European Jews*, which has received renewed attention upon the publication of its new edition in three volumes, and which tells in massive detail how Nazi bureaucracy and technology were mobilized for genocide, commented on the topic in an interview. Hilberg once believed that Hermann Göring wrote a letter on July 31, 1941, to Reinhard Heydrich, deputy chief of the Gestapo, authorizing Heydrich to launch the Final Solution. But Hilberg subsequently discovered that Eichmann drafted the 1941 letter, thus ruling out its being Hitler's order.

Hilberg's comment in the interview is that the Nazi decision-making process was more complicated than had been assumed, stating: "Adolph Hitler did give any order he wanted, but it's also true that no one man decides everything. Even under a totalitarian regime, any number of people make decisions."[23] Gustave Gilbert, who was the psychologist studying the Nazi war criminals at the Nuremberg trials, in seeking information about the decision-making process and Hitler's precise role in it regarding the Final Solution, reported Göring's reaction to the hypothesis that Gilbert offered him for comment, as follows:

> I shall suggest the following tableau: Hitler, obsessed by anti-Semitism and incapable of tolerating opposition or advice advocating moderation, saying finally to Himmler: "Get rid of them—it little matters how—I don't want to hear about them anymore." Göring reflected a moment, seeming to visualize the scene; then he declared that it was probably like that that it happened.[24]

In remarking upon recent discussions of the difficulty of associating Hitler with any documents ordering the killing, something so easily done in the cases of Himmler, Heydrich, and Eichmann, Lawrence L. Langer asks:

> Did Hitler hope that the legend of his achievements as Führer would outlive the infamy of his crime as a man? Monuments were built to Napoleon long after his ruthlessness had been forgotten. Was Hitler's careful refusal to append his name to documents of destruction a gesture of contempt for future historians, who sometimes substitute a safe faith in archives for the unsettling complexities of human intention? What clairvoyance could have possessed him to conclude that later generations might hesitate to believe that one person could authorize such atrocities?[25]

The Nazi power system seems to have allowed for some initiative at various links in the chain of command, a flexibility of choice consistent with subservience, automatism, and thoughtlessness. But what sort of initiative, necessarily so minimal, is this? How should it be conceptualized? And how does it fit into the bureaucratic mentality that was essential to managing the awesome technology that implemented the Holocaust? R. K. Angress, herself an Auschwitz survivor, objects in her review of Martin Gilbert's *The Holocaust* to his dwelling on instances of death-camp brutality: "Enthusiasm for killing Jews was surely unnecessary for the success of the Final Solution and probably not always available. A willingness to carry out orders, even a reluctant willingness, was just as effective."[26] Angress sees this, not sadism, as the "truly chilling" feature of the Nazis' destruction of European Jewry. A similar sentiment is expressed by Alan Rosenberg in his description of the perpetrators in the chain of command as "desk killers."[27]

The initiative exercised by links in the power system, though severely constricted, was nevertheless a form of voluntary action that cannot be dismissed as being only subservience. The evidence does not warrant our concluding that most "desk killers" acted because duty triumphed over a chronic reluctance to participate in the destruction. Subsuming them under some such appellation as "bureaucratic mentality," in trying to identify more thoroughly the symptoms of people who voluntarily join, with neither enthusiasm nor reluctance, mass-murder programs, at least keeps the bureaucratic character of Nazi destruction in plain sight. It may also assist in connecting other symptoms such as "denial" and "doubling." Insofar as bureaucratic membership requires subservience, we can appreciate how the bureaucratic mentality encourages denial defenses. But we must also bear in mind Milgram's finding that "most frequently among obedient subjects, we find not a denial of events but a denial of responsibility for them," with all that this implies for a post-Holocaust psychology.[28]

The other symptom mentioned—"doubling"—is under discussion because of its use by Robert J. Lifton in his major study *The Nazi Doctors: Medical Killing and the Psychology of Genocide* (1986). In investigating how it happened that doctors became Nazi killers, how doctors lived with themselves while hideously violating the Hippocratic oath, Lifton attributes their behavior to their capacity for "doubling." This is the ability, if we interpret Lifton correctly, to permit a part of oneself (the genocidal doctor) to assume a total self-structure; this structure, by absorbing the genocidal part, gives it the sort of justificatory strength that it could not receive while remaining fragmentary and in active conflict with its original self. This is not the place for a proper formulation or analysis of Lifton's idea, but it deserves at least mention since it points to an important personality symptom of doctors functioning as links in the chain of command. Moreover, one might find that "doubling" is significantly facilitated in a personality that is already imbued with the bureaucratic mentality.

But it is quickly apparent that, while the term "bureaucratic mentality" serves to keep the "truly chilling" feature of Nazi destructiveness in mind, it is too vague, inviting unwarranted indictments of bureaucracy in general. It is inconceivable that any and all hierarchical organizations could be converted overnight into what the Nazis created, despite whatever reservations we may have about the sociopolitical potentialities of such organizations. The symptoms that post-Holocaust psychology has presented for us thus far include subservience, automatism, thoughtlessness, denial, doubling, and an initiative so inhibited that it is always disposed to transfer responsibility to higher authorities. And obviously the list can and ought to be expanded if the Nazi personality is to be understood sufficiently to prevent its recurrence.

The personality syndrome that has emerged here is an integral part of what I call the *militarized consciousness.* The sort of mentality referred to is regimented in a permanent posture of aggression, is dutiful in a typical mood of indifference, is assured that some cause couched in slogans is being served, and is satisfied that power equals a kind of superior, occult knowledge which in one's own subordinacy one has no motive whatever for calling into question. Something of this sort, I believe, was what Hitler created with his speeches, parades, swastikas, uniforms, salutes.

The consciousness that Hitler helped to create is not describable simply as a case of "group psychology" or a collective, bureaucratic mentality. It was rather a militarized consciousness that extended beyond the SS, the Gestapo, and the troops. People from all walks of life were drawn into it. This concept of the militarized consciousness may help in yielding an enriched description of the personality symptoms that require societal monitoring, for it may be the symptoms, rather than their causes, that society will have to work with in order to keep civilized forces in control.

Since Auschwitz, the psychology of man has changed from being a global theory of human nature to an interdisciplinary collection of efforts to understand the human condition. The Holocaust forever proved how fragile the human condition is, and an essential aspect of that fragility, I suspect, is our susceptibility to the proselytizing powers of the militarized consciousness. Elie Wiesel once said of the Eichmann trial that "it will demonstrate that the Holocaust was not unavoidable; that rescue was possible; that Eichmann is the name not of an individual but of a disease that infected many nations."[29] One must concur. One must also hope that the psychology of the human condition has isolated at least the identifying symptoms or warning signals of the disease to which Wiesel refers.

NOTES

1. Sara Nomberg-Przytyk, *Auschwitz: True Tales from a Grotesque Land* (Chapel Hill: University of North Carolina Press, 1985), p. 72.

2. Irving Howe, "How to Write about the Holocaust," *New York Review*, March 28, 1985, p. 16.

3. Quoted by Ronald W. Clark in his *Einstein: The Life and Times* (New York and Cleveland: World Publishing, 1971), p. 366.

4. Kurt Goldstein, *Human Nature: In the Light of Psychopathology* (Cambridge, Mass.: Harvard University Press, 1940), p. 161.

5. Ibid., pp. 59–60.

6. Ibid., p. 223.

7. A few examples of the vast number of such studies, autobiographical accounts, and reports, include Bruno Bettelheim's *The Informed Heart* (New York: Free Press, 1960) and *Surviving, and Other Essays* (New York: Knopf, 1979); Martin Gilbert, *The Holocaust: The Jewish Tragedy* (New York: Holt, Rinehart & Winston, 1985); S. Luel and P. Marcus, eds., *Psychoanalytic Reflections on the Holocaust* (New York: KTAV and University of Denver, 1984); Robert J. Lifton, *The Nazi Doctors: Medical Killing and the Psychology of Genocide* (New York: Basic Books, 1986); Lucy S. Dawidowicz, *The War against the Jews, 1933–1945* (New York: Holt, Rinehart & Winston, 1975); Walter Laqueur and Richard Breitman, *Breaking the Silence* (New York: Simon and Schuster, 1986); Primo Levi's *If Not Now, When* (New York: Summit, 1985), *The Periodic Table* (New York: Schocken, 1984), and *Survival in Auschwitz: The Nazi Assault on Humanity* (New York: Collier, 1971); Frances G. Grossman, "A Psychological Study of Gentiles Who Saved the Lives of Jews during the Holocaust," in *Toward the Understanding and Prevention of Genocide*, ed. Israel W. Charny (Boulder: Westview Press, 1984), pp. 202–16. Note, also, the following films: *Shoah*, produced by Claude Lanzmann and released by New York Films; *The Liberation of Auschwitz*, produced by Irmgard von zur Muhlen, released by the National Center for Jewish Film, Brandeis University, 1986; and *Partisans of Vilna*, European Classics, as well as Claude Lanzmann, *Shoah: An Oral History of the Holocaust* (New York, Pantheon, 1985).

8. Alan Hughes, *Psychology and the Political Experience* (London: Cambridge University Press, 1975), p. 74.

9. Ibid., pp. 168–69. For more on the frustration–aggression hypothesis, see J. Dollard, N. E. Miller, et al., *Frustration and Aggression* (New Haven: Yale University Press, 1939). For criticisms of the hypothesis, see A. H. Buss, *The Psychology of Aggression* (New York: Wiley, 1961) and Erich Fromm, *The Anatomy of Destructiveness* (New York: Holt, Rinehart & Winston, 1973). For a helpful review, see H. T. Himmelweit, "Frustration and Aggression: A Review of Recent Experimental Work," in *The Psychological Factors of Peace and War*, ed. T. H. Pear (London: Hutchinson, 1950), pp. 159–91.

10. Stanley Milgram, *Obedience to Authority: An Experimental View* (New York: Harper and Row, 1974), p. 6. Milgram also writes (p. 180): "I am forever astonished that when lecturing on the obedience experiments in colleges across the country, I faced young men who were aghast at the behavior of experimental subjects and proclaimed they would never behave in such a way, but who, in a matter of months, were brought

into the military and performed without compunction actions that made shocking the victim seem pallid. In this respect, they are no better and no worse than human beings of any other era who lend themselves to the purpose of authority and become instruments in its destructive processes."

11. T. W. Adorno, Else Frenkel-Brunswik, Daniel J. Levinson, R. Nevitt Sanford, *The Authoritarian Personality* (New York: Harper Brothers, 1950).

12. Fromm, *Anatomy of Destructiveness*, p. 51.

13. Ibid., p. 52.

14. Milton Himmelfarb, "No Hitler, No Holocaust," *Commentary* 77, no. 3 (March 1984): 37–43. Himmelfarb's argument goes much further than my discussion, and the controversies it provoked are indicated by the replies in *Commentary* 78, no. 1 (July 1984).

15. E. O. Lorimer, *What Hitler Wants* (Harmondsworth, England: Penguin, 1939).

16. Heinz Kohut, *Self Psychology and the Humanities: Reflections on a New Psychoanalytic Approach* (New York: Norton, 1985), pp. 80–81.

17. Kohut is sensitive to the charge that he may be in danger of trying to make the incomprehensible intelligible. "The inclination is strong to restrict oneself to staying within the limits of a morally buttressed rejection of the evil leaders and their followers. . . . But the depth psychologist knows the task which is assigned to him. . . . Even in the arena of historical action—and perhaps especially here—he must not only judge but also examine, understand, explain. He will envy, but he must not share the philosopher's attitude exemplified by Martin Buber . . . who in accepting the Frankfurt Peace Prize said this about the Nazi evildoers: 'I am sharing only in appearance the dimensions of human existence with those who have participated in those misdeeds.'" Ibid., p. 65.

As but one recent example of the continuing interest in why the Holocaust originated in Germany and whether there is collective responsibility for its occurrence, see Istvan Deak's "How Guilty Were the Germans?" a discussion and review of eleven books relevant to the topic, *New York Review*, 31, no. 9 (May 31, 1984): 37–42.

18. Stuart Hampshire, "Disposition and Memory," in *Philosophical Essays on Freud*, ed. Richard Wollheim and James Hopkins (Cambridge: Cambridge University Press, 1984), p. 88.

19. Quoted in Joseph Billig and George Wellers, *The Holocaust and the Neo-Nazi Mythomania* (New York: Beate Klarsfeld Foundation, 1978), p. 42. See also, as but two examples of an extensive literature on Nazi ideology, George L. Mosse, *Nazi Culture* (New York: Grosset & Dunlap, 1966); and Norman Cohn, *Warrant for Genocide* (New York: Harper and Row, 1967).

20. This was an observation made by Carl Jacob Burckhardt and is quoted by Fromm, *Anatomy of Destructiveness*, p. 430.

21. This observation by Burckhardt is quoted by Karl D. Bracher, *The German Dictatorship* (New York: Praeger, 1970), p. 283.

22. Hannah Arendt, *The Life of the Mind: Thinking* (New York: Harcourt Brace Jovanovich, 1977), pp. 4–5. On the matter of Eichmann's mentality, particularly his responses to moral questions, see A. Zvie Bar-On, "Measuring Responsibility," *Philosophical Forum* 16, nos. 1–2 (Fall–Winter 1984–85): 95–109.

23. Interview reported by Edwin McDowell in *The New York Times*, May 30, 1985.

24. Gustave Gilbert, *The Psychology of Dictatorship: Based on the Examination of the Leaders of Nazi Germany* (New York: Ronald, 1950). An especially valuable article is Israel W. Charny's "Genocide and Mass Destruction: A Missing Dimension in Psychopathology," in Charney, *Toward Understanding*, pp. 154–74.

25. Lawrence L. Langer, "Will the Real Adolf Hitler Please Step Forward?" *Michigan Quarterly Review* 25, no. 1 (winter 1986); 127–35. Langer's review article

focuses on Gerald Fleming's *Hitler and the Final Solution* (Berkeley: University of California Press, 1984) and Alvin Rosenfeld's *Imagining Hitler* (Bloomington: Indiana University Press, 1985).

26. R. K. Angress, "The Weight of Testimony," *Times Literary Supplement*, no. 4, 338 (May 23, 1986): 566.

27. See Chapter 10 in this volume.

28. Milgram, *Obedience*, p. 159.

29. Elie Wiesel's statement appeared in the *Jewish Daily Forward*, April 11, 1961, and is reproduced in a brochure used as part of the Jewish Museum's public program "Justice in Jerusalem Revisited: The Eichmann Trial 25 Years Later," held in New York City, March 30–May 11, 1986.

16

CONCENTRATION CAMPS AND THE END OF THE LIFE-WORLD

Edith Wyschogrod

The fact that the life-world of the concentration camps is radically different from that of ordinary experience is incontestable.[1] But how and in what sense are we to understand this difference? Are the structures of human existence changed merely in regard to this or that component of experience: work, sexuality, habitation, or, even more fundamentally, modes of eating and sleeping, so that a quantitative shrinkage of the life-world is the end result? Or, does the world of the camps present so radical an alteration in the structure of experience that the term "life-world" is inapplicable and we are justified in protecting the ultimacy of this difference by designating the new order, the "death-world." I shall try to show that the concentration camp as a concrete actuality emerges as the consequence of a systematic effort to deconstruct the life-world itself and not merely as a selective compression of its range.

THE MEANING OF THE LIFE-WORLD

How are we to understand the life-world? Can it be grasped as the object of a mental act? If not, how are we to apprehend it? By "life-world" we may understand the horizon of experience from which human meanings originate. But, since the life-world is prior to any theoretical or reflective attitude that we may hold and, in fact, makes such attitudes possible, it is particularly difficult to grasp conceptually. For once it is subjected to theoretical scrutiny, it ceases to be what it is, the whole of our prereflective experiential field, the point of intersection between what is constructed through our manner of being in the world and what is given:

This article originally appeared in *Centerpoint: A Journal of Interdisciplinary Studies* 1, no. 1 (Fall 1980): 32–42. It is reprinted here by permission of the author.

The life-world for us who wakingly live in it, is always already there, existing in advance for us the "ground" of all praxis. . . . The world is pre-given to us, the waking, always somehow practically interested subjects, not occasionally but always and necessarily as the universal field of all actual and possible praxis, as horizon. To live is always to live-in-certainty-of-the-world. Waking life is being awake to the world being constantly and directly "conscious" of the world and of oneself as living *in* the world.[2]

This view of the life-world does not leave our understanding of the human person unaffected. Human existence can no longer be interpreted as inserted into the world as an isolated subject, a consciousness that surveys the world from the privileged position of his or her own subjectivity; nor is the world a system of physical objects whose existence can be described as *partes extra partes* with the individual as only another entity in the world. In the latter case the existing individual is reduced to an object of physics, in the former to an isolated monad for whom the phenomenal world is the content of consciousness. Instead the person is a mode of activity that constitutes the phenomenal field in which he or she lives. The world toward which the person is directed offers itself as an existing or possible task. We may express this intersection of person and world as the "lived body."[3] The existent, the lived body, the person, inhabits a world of indeterminate horizons from which phenomena arise.

The life-world can be envisioned as a three-tiered field of experience: the inanimate world given in primary sensation; the vital world, what is given to us as living beings, self-motion, self-boundedness, and "inner" states experienced in their temporal flux; and an axiological or ethical dimension in which other persons are apprehended as centers of value.[4] These worlds are interlocking in the manner of concentric circles: The ethical world cannot emerge without the existence of anterior levels, that is, of the vital and the inanimate as its ontological ground. Nevertheless, the ethical is given in its immediacy even if it presents itself in a quite different manner from the inanimate and the vital. All sociocultural forms of existence "live on" or express this fundament although no *specific* pattern of culture is endemic to the life-world as such. It is the structure of experience that enables cultural forms to emerge. Prior to the appearance of the concentration camp it was possible to imagine the destruction of all human life, but it was not possible to imagine the paradox: Life perdures but the life-world ceases to exist.

METAPHYSICS OF THE "PURE" AND THE "IMPURE"

Perhaps the concentration camp signals the emergence of a new and barren life-world but does not after all, spell the end of the life-world. For if the latter is true how can it become a theme for discussion since all meaning arises in the life-world? How would this coming to an end manifest itself? At this stage we can only give a preliminary answer to these questions by bringing to light the aim or interest for which the camp provides the means. This end or interest is the ultimate death of every inmate. Even if documentary evidence were lacking, the existence of the means themselves attest to this. Conversely, if we suppose the means as our starting point, we see that they cannot exist as *mere* means, as "implements" of death. Because death itself is a terminus, these means can lead to no further ends, thus foreclosing the possibility that they are merely instrumental. The camps are ends in themselves, uniquely designed death-worlds. Means and ends are compressed into a single signification, death.

Is there any foredisclosure of this design? Or do the camps only come into being in a cumulative but ad hoc manner combining, for example, the idea of an imprisoning work space for political dissidents, the techniques of mass killing developed in Hitler's euthanasia program, and the political decision to implement the "Final Solution of the Jewish question" by killing all Jews? While these events play a role in the development of individual aspects of camp structure, the context from which the overall necessity of the structure itself will emerge is already disclosed in Hitler's declaration of aims. Without alluding to the idea of concentration camps, the perverse consciousness that intends the camps, envisages their necessity, is already fully revealed in *Mein Kampf*.[5] This statement of intent deserves attention not because of its programmatic character, but as bringing to light the bizarre world in which the concentration camp would assume centrality.

Three points are of interest to us. First, Hitler designates the ideological content of National Socialism as a "philosophy of life." Thus, for him, it is not a political doctrine.[6] For Hitler this entails a belief in its absolute truth as well as its absolute inclusivity. Not only the political or economic domains but the total sphere of existence lies within its purview. Second, all manifestations of social existence are interpreted as superstructure, the expression of a more primordial base: "race" or "blood." This ideology is elaborated in terms of a distinction between culture-founding and culture-bearing races. The culture-founding "Aryan" is destined to rule the multitude of races who are seen as the necessary but dispensable vehicles through which the stream of Aryan life may pass, but which, in the end, are fated to become extinct.[7] Hitler's racial doctrine demands a demonic double, a counterpart for the term "Aryan." He does not find this double in the "slave" races but in the Jew. He sees the Jew neither as a true nomad nor as a settled inhabitant, but as a perpetual anomaly whose existence is interpreted as thwarting the evolutionary design of a nature red in tooth and claw.[8] The metaphysical dualism of spirit and matter, mind and body is now reinterpreted in the hypostases of "pure" and "impure" races. Third, the principles of "humanitarianism and aesthetics" must be sacrificed in the interest of this putative "elite." Citing Moltke, Hitler asserts: "As for humanitarianism . . . in war it lies in the brevity of the operation and that means the most aggressive fighting technique is the most humane."[9]

The world of the Other (the non-Aryan) is in *Mein Kampf* a de jure world of death. It cannot, in accordance with Hitler's primitive understanding of the Hegelian conception of history, be mediated by symbolic structures but must be transformed into a sphere of death in actuality. The means for bringing this about are nowhere made explicit. Nevertheless, the existence of a "true" world is predicated from which the non-Aryan world is to be distinguished as that world that has no being of its own. Lacking significance, the being of inanimate nature is attributed to this non-Aryan sphere. "When [Aryan man] departs from the world, these concepts [humanitarianism and aesthetics] are again dissolved into nothingness, for Nature does not know them."[10] The non-Aryan world is at once feared by Hitler as the sinister obverse of the "true" world and thus as a threat to the "true" world's existence while, at the same time, it is interpreted as a nullity. This vacillation in meaning is ominous. For it portends an attempt to bring the world of fact, whatever the cost, into conformity with one of these meanings. Proceeding by degrees, Hitler will attempt to sublate the "sinister" existence of the non-Aryan world by stamping it out altogether thus confirming its lack of value, its nullity. Once these premises are laid down, the raison d'être, if not the ground plan for the concentration camps, is already in place.

In fact, this early world scheme compels the envisagement of an ever-widening sphere of death. It is always theoretically possible to subdivide an existing people into "pure" and "impure" components. The conceptual model presupposes an infinite divisibility of peoples as though this divisibility were analogous to the divisibility of space in Zeno's paradox. But, given a finite quantity, this policy must be self-defeating, for even if the elimination of mankind is envisaged, all division must come to an end when the null point is reached.[11] Of course this conclusion is never drawn when the camps are brought into being. In fact, Hitler's emphasis on efficiency, on the "brevity of the operation," led to an ever more frenetic search on the part of the camp bureaucracy for improving the means for carrying out this policy. Thus Höss, the commandant of Auschwitz, states in his autobiography: "I had only one end in view: to drive everyone and everything forward in my determination to improve the general conditions so that I could carry out the measures laid down."[12] What was to be achieved by these measures? In the rote language of Nazi official speech Höss writes: "By the will of the *Reichsführer SS,* Auschwitz became the greatest extermination center of all time."[13]

CONCENTRATION CAMPS AND THE EXPERIENCE OF THE VITAL

At the level of the vital, the existent experiences himself in his spatiotemporal orientation. Prior to a theoretical grasp of geometrical space, the existent encounters the world as oriented being: The body's motility is directional, movement is experienced as up or down, backward or forward, left or right, while distance is apprehended as near or far, and so on. As temporal being the existent lives the past as the sediment of his completed acts, the future as the field of his possibilities. Generally as the past lengthens the future is foreshortened but this process can, under special circumstances, be experienced quite differently. Thus, when some long-range project is undertaken, the foreshortening of the future can be arrested. On the other hand, its course can be accelerated in hedonic experience. The existent learns to depend upon this order modifying his activity in accordance with ongoing experience. Thus in describing the life-world John Wild writes:

> I know there will be a thread of continuity running through my disparate experiences. Each new occurrence, no matter how unique it may be, will be experienced by the same body seeking to satisfy its needs in the life-world. *There must be a minimum uniformity grounding my habits in this world, or it would not be habitable, and I could not survive.*[14]

We have already seen that the posited aim of the concentration camp is death. Even if the vestiges of life are permitted to subsist, this existence is a brief interim during which the inmate is expected to work until he dies of disease or drops from sheer exhaustion. In effect he is already reckoned as dead. The nugatory status of the groups whose existence is proscribed (particularly Jews, but also Gypsies and Jehovah's Witnesses) become, in effect, the living dead. Thus Alexander Donat, Jewish journalist from Poland, in his account of Maidanek writes:

We had arrived in the kingdom of death, in the Third Field of the
Maidanek concentration camp.

Maidanek was hell. Not the naive inferno of Dante, but a twentieth century hell where the art of cruelty was refined to perfection
and every facility of modern technology and psychology was combined to destroy men physically and spiritually.[15]

Gertrud Kolmar, a German-Jewish poet who perished at Auschwitz,
writes with prescience of the death-world:

Stiff, wounded, branded with official stamps,
They walk like slaughter cattle for the knife and still remember
dimly trough and herd.[16]

Even camp personnel are compelled to confront the omnipresence of
death. Thus Johann Paul Kremer, an SS medical doctor at Auschwitz,
writes:

This noon was present at a special action in the women's camp. . . .
Thilo, military surgeon is right when he said today to me we were
located in *"anus mundi."*[17]

How can the life-world which functions as a primordial system of
significations be altered? By what means is its sublation achieved? Such
a change cannot come about by trading old significations for new since
new meanings in the prereflective sphere of everyday existence can
often be accommodated even when an alteration in life circumstances is
profound. This is attested in the histories of persons who suffer physical
impairment, imprisonment, or the like. In the world of the concentration
camp, the process of sublation is quite different. Here, the system of old
significations is permitted to subsist while new and contradictory
meanings are added. These "additions" occur at the most primordial
levels of experience. In effect, a systematic effort is made to confound
accepted, taken-for-granted meanings by developing opposed meanings
in order to create the widest possible discrepancy between alleged and
actual significations.[18] Tadeusz Borowski, Polish poet, writer, and survivor of Auschwitz, illustrates the exercise of this technique by showing
how the meaning of food and death coalesce. Borowski depicts hunger
as the omnipresent background of camp life: No one could evade the
threat of its depradations. For those camp workers who unloaded the
human cargo that resulted from the mass deportations and was de-
posited at Auschwitz, access to food (often in quantity) was available.
But relief from hunger depended upon unloading this human freight
and hurrying the herded masses to their deaths in the gas chambers.
Thus, for example, when the narrator of one of Borowski's stories
expresses his fear of impending hunger, his cynical friend replies: "Stop

talking nonsense. They can't run out of people." While some anomalies occur fortuitously, most are systematically created. Thus Primo Levi, a Jewish chemist from Italy and survivor of Auschwitz, speaking of his arrival at the camp, remarks:

> A band begins to play, next to the entrance of the camp: it plays *Rosamunda*, the well-known sentimental song, and this seems so strange to us that we look sniggering at each other; we feel a shadow of relief, perhaps all these ceremonies are nothing but a colossal farce in Teutonic taste. But the band . . . continues to play . . . suddenly the squads of our comrades appear returning from work. They walk in columns of five with a strange, unnatural hard gait, like stiff puppets made of jointless bones; but they walk scrupulously in time to the band.[19]

The misalliance of meanings is particularly grotesque when the prisoners are unable to penetrate the disguised meaning and accept the world as it is presented. Thus Richard Glazar, one of the planners and executors of the revolt at Treblinka, when interviewed by Gitta Sereny, describes the unloading ramp at the camp as being disguised in the form of a provincial railroad complete with flowers. He adds: "We all crowded to look out the windows. I saw a green fence, barracks, and I heard what sounded like a farm tractor. I was delighted."[20] In order to maintain the credibility of some deceptions, elaborate stratagems were devised by the camp bureaucracy. Thus, Höss describes the lesser ruses designed to maintain the primary deception of Auschwitz:

> The "camouflage" of the gas chambers: Difficult individuals were picked out early on and most carefully supervised. At the first signs of unrest, those responsible were unobtrusively led behind the building and killed with a small-calibre gun, that was inaudible to the others. The presence and calm behavior of the Special Detachment served to reassure those who were worried or who suspected what was about to happen.[21]

This system of multiple contradictory significations is not merely a procedural matter, a technique used in the interest of some end extrinsic to the destruction of meaning itself. On the contrary this destruction of meaning *is* the end of the life-world at the vital level. An assured pattern of meaning is fundamental to the life-world. John Wild writes:

> As long as I exist, therefore, I can be sure that this general pattern will remain. . . . As long as we exist, we must believe in those objects and structures which constitute the world, and make it endurable. It is only under endurable condition that we can endure. What it

would be like for us to be enduring in an unendurable world is beyond our powers of imagination and comprehension.[22]

Is there any pattern that can be discerned in the multiple and contradictory system of significations such that it constitutes a "law" of experience in the concentration camp? If we consider first the life-world of ordinary experience in its ordinary operations as a field of language, of meanings that are bound up with one another, its structure can be described in terms of the relationship between a signifier, the term of the relationship which intends something else, and a signified, that which is meant or intended.[23] For example, if we consider the term "food" as a signifier, multiple concrete meanings may be attached to the signified, this dinner I am eating now, the shared conviviality of my friends, the taste, warmth, and satiety that together constitute the event of eating, and so on. In the life-world of ordinary experience it is clear that the signified (the multiple meanings of food) *surpasses* the signifier, "food."[24] But in the world of the concentration camp, a new and complex relationship governs linguistic behavior. On the one hand all the patterns of the life-world as we understand them persist (in the case of food, the concreteness of this bread, satiety, warmth, flavor, etc.). *But, at the same time the signified is also and always death.* The signifier "collapses" into the signified which is now no longer more extensive in range than the signifier. For each and every signifier the full range of obsolete meanings is retained together with their negation, the new signified, death.

Thus, a new concept of language must be learned by the camp inmate. Reading from each and every old signifier, he or she must learn to decipher the new meaning, death, as it applies in every situation and every instant. He or she must learn that at every instant his or her own death is intended. Thus Alexander Donat, describing the ordeal of his introduction to the Maidanek concentration camp, cites the advice of the Block Elder:

> With brutal frankness he told us what it was like there. "This is a K.L.," he said. "Remember those two initials K.L. . . . *Konzentration-slager*. This is a death camp, a *Vernichtungslager*. You've been brought here to be destroyed by hunger, beating, hard labor, and sickness. You'll be eaten by lice, you'll rot in your own excrement. . . . Forget who and what you were. . . . Everyone here is the same. . . . All are going to die.[25]

What possible responses could be made to this death-world? It was always fatal to lapse even for a moment into accepting the old significations at face value, for without utmost vigilance death was assured. On the other hand, anamnesis in regard to the old significations was equally fatal. For those who succumbed to the power of death became "*Mussel-manner*," the camp term for those who surrendered the will to live. Primo Levi writes:

> They crowd my memory with their faceless presences, and if I could enclose all the evil of our time in one image, I would choose this image which is familiar to me: an emaciated man, with head dropped and shoulders curved, on whose face and in whose eyes not a trace of thought is to be seen.[26]

At the vital level of the life-world, which arises as spontaneity and is expressed in motility, affective response, work, linguistic and gestural activity, the concentration camp succeeded in suppressing the primordial modes of man's being in the world. Furthermore, it is impossible to speak of the life-world of our own present experience as though it were comparable to that which existed before the advent of the concentration camp. For the life-world now and in the future includes in collective experience and shared history the death-world of the camp. *Once the death-world has existed it continues to exist, in the mode of eternity, as it were, for it becomes part of the sediment that is the irrevocable past.*[27]

How is the death-world lived by survivors? The point has often been made that survivors lived to bear witness to the existence of the death-world. What is more, this aim was appropriated by the camp inmates as an explicitly conscious motive for remaining alive. It thus became for them the manner in which they lived their futures. It impinged upon the present of camp existence as the most meaningful possibility of the prisoner functioning as that end for which a thousand small strategies for survival were devised. Donat, recounting a conversation in Maidanek, cites his friend Dr. Schippers, a journalist from Warsaw as saying:

> Should our murderers be victorious, should *they* write the history of this war . . . their every word will be taken for gospel. Or they may wipe out our memory altogether, as if we had never existed, as if there had never been a Polish Jewry, a Ghetto in Warsaw, a Maidanek. Not even a dog will howl for us. But if *we* write the history of this period . . . we'll have the thankless job of proving to a reluctant world that we are Abel, the murdered brother.[28]

THE ETHICAL LEVEL

Can we say that, at the axiological level, the life-world suffered the condensation of meaning that occurred at the vital level? This question is meaningful because we can understand the axiological as arising first out of the vital at a prereflective and pretheoretical level. The phenomenal aspect of values is first given as the distinction we make in immediate apprehension between persons and anything else, whatever that may be, given as a phenomenon. This distinction is experienced when, in apprehending another, we are aware that we are ourselves possible objects of apprehension for the other. Thus, for example, while *both* things and persons may be seen as beautiful or ugly, sturdy or fragile, and the like, only in the case of persons is reciprocal apprehension experienced. This difference also bears upon the way in which beauty and ugliness are ascribed to the object. We know that things are fragile, break, get used up, but the manner in which persons disintegrate is quite different; the person exists as corporeality, as a self-bounded vital being, as a spontaneity that expresses itself in motility, language, and the like. Moreover, included in our grasp of the others as vital being, is our apprehension of this being as imposing a demand upon us: the demand that we recognize him as corporeally vulnerable. He appears in this manner as a node of value.

How and in what way did the experience of other persons as nodes of value alter in the concentration camp? It is clear that the camp inmate was intended to take himself and others as reducible to a single signification, death, in all of the protean guises it assumed through camp existence. He was to know the human life of inmates as expendable while the life of the guards and camp bureaucrats was to be apprehended as inviolable. Thus he was intended not to see himself and other inmates as centers of value. Everything possible was done toward achieving this end.

Did the system succeed in bringing this change about? It would seem that the desire to bear witness expressed by many survivors would abet the destruction of the ethical since, in order to bear witness, one had to survive and survival appeared to necessitate purely self-serving behavior. But the contrary was in fact the case. One survived to tell of others who could not speak for themselves. Thus Leon Wells, a Jew from Poland and a survivor of the death brigade, a corps of workers forced to eradicate the traces of mass murder, writes upon his liberation: "Today the anguish for those who had been killed flooded over me."[29] What is more, once the desire to bear witness had been conceived as a hope, if only sporadically it began to irradiate behavior in the present. It became important to survive as an ethical being even if this meant stripping away sentiments that usually accompany ethical acts. Thus Donat writes:

> Yet how little sometimes suffices to save a perishing man: a glance, a word, a gesture. Once I gave a fellow prisoner a boiled potato and he never stopped thanking me for having saved his life. . . . Prisoners

helped one another as best they could, but they shied away from sentiment. Help, yes; compassion, no.[30]

A rough code developed among inmates. Donat writes: "In camp slang to organize meant to look after Number One. It was to steal soup from the kitchen, for example; but to steal bread from another inmate, however was to *really* steal."[31] Being for others guided survival even when this did not appear to be the case. Thus Richard Glazar remembers:

> If I speak of a thirst or talent for life as the qualities most needed for survival . . . I don't mean to say that these were deliberate acts or even feelings. They were, in fact, largely unconscious qualities. Another talent one needed was a gift for relationships. Of course there were people who survived who were loners. They will tell you now they survived *because* they relied on no one but themselves. But the truth is probably—and they may either know it, or not be willing to admit it to themselves or others—that they survived because they were carried by *someone*, someone who cared for them as much, or almost as much as for themselves.[32]

Sometimes the social act was expressed in a quite different manner. Primo Levi, carrying a vat of watery soup with his young French friend, the "pikolo" (a privileged adolescent who, because of personal beauty or charm, was excluded from the heaviest manual labor), writes:

> The canto of Ulysses. Who knows how or why it comes into my mind. . . .
> . . . Who is Dante? What is the Comedy? . . .
> Here, listen Pikolo, open your ears and your mind, you have to understand, for my sake:
>
> > "*Think of your breed; for brutish ignorance*
> > *Your mettle was not made; you were made men,*
> > *To follow after knowledge and excellence.*"
>
> As if I also was hearing it for the first time: like the blast of a trumpet, like the voice of God. For a moment I forget who I am and where I am.[33]

While the modes of significance were destroyed by the camp system at the vital level of existence, this collapse of meaning did not come about at the ethical level in the manner intended by the camp's executioners. Once survival in order to bear witness was conceived as a value, living for others, for the destroyed sociocultural community, came to the fore. A curious reversal of ordinary values took place: Remaining alive under odious conditions was more difficult than suicide, this rendering survival a self-sacrificial act in many instances. Even with the virtual destruction of the vital level, the apprehension of the other as a node of values was sustained. The strategies required for self-preservation more often than not forced the ethical motive into the background. But so long as and wherever the other is recognized as a node of value the ethical level of the life-world is continued. Unlike the vital level where the field of existence expands or shrinks as a whole, single ethical acts "irradiate" the larger field of existence since they take on paradigmatic quality. Thus a single ethical act attests the existence of an ethical field. While the camp system brutalized many, ethical acts emerge in the life-world in a "ripple" effect, which the camp system could not destroy.

NOTES

1. A distinction should be made between the "concentration camp" and the "extermination camp." The latter were designed solely for the extermination of Jews and Gypsies. There were four such camps set up toward the end of the war: Chelmo (Kulmhof) in December 1941, Belsec (March 1942), Sobibor (May 1942), and Treblinka (June 1942). All were located in relative proximity to Warsaw. "Concentration camps" were far more numerous and were scattered throughout Germany and occupied Europe. The latter formed a vast chain of slave labor. See Gitta Sereny, *Into That Darkness: From Mercy Killing to Mass Murder* (New York: McGraw-Hill, 1974), pp. 98ff. In this paper I use the term "concentration camp" since there is no point in speaking of a life-world in the extermination camps, where all were immediately killed. Where the report of a survivor of Treblinka is cited, I retain the term "concentration camp" for the sake of convenience.

2. Edmund Husserl, *The Crisis of European Sciences and Transcendental Phenomenology*, trans. David Carr (Evanston: Northwestern University Press, 1970), pp. 142–43. Of course the Nazi rationale for the death camps does not reflect a conscious attempt to negate the life-world. The relationship of the concept of the life-world to the rise of Nazism is, however, complex. Husserl himself felt compelled to grapple with what he saw as the crisis of European man. His response to this crisis included the development of the notion of the life-world. See pp. xviff of "Translator's Introduction." The matter is further complicated by the fact that the concept of *Lebenswelt* does not have a univocal meaning in Husserl's work. Maurice Natanson in "The Lebenswelt," in *Phenomenology: Pure and Applied: The First Lexington Conference*, ed. Erwin Straus (Pittsburgh: Duquesne University Press, 1964), p. 80, cites three meanings: "one, the lived world of individual experience; the locus for the phenomenological grounding of knowledge, science and history; a constituted intentional structure with a transcendental machinery." I confine my usage to a development of the first of these.

3. Maurice Merleau-Ponty, *The Phenomenology of Perception*, trans. Colin Smith (London: Routledge and Kegan Paul, 1962), p. 100.

4. For in-depth analyses of each of these stages respectively, see Erwin Straus, *The Primary World of the Senses*, trans. Jacob Needleman (Glencoe, Ill.: Free Press, 1963); Max Scheler, *Man's Place in Nature*, trans. Hans Meyerhoff (New York: Noonday Press, 1961); Alphonso Lingis, *Totality and Infinity*, trans. Emmanuel Levinas (Pittsburgh: Duquesne University Press, 1969).

5. Adolf Hitler, *Mein Kampf,* trans. Ralph Mannheim (Boston: Houghton Mifflin, 1943).

6. Ibid., p. 455.

7. Ibid. This view is expounded in the chapter "Nation and Race," and constitutes the underpinning of the entire structure.

8. Mary Douglas, *Purity and Danger* (London: Routledge and Kegan Paul, 1966) shows the role of "anomaly" in culture as threatening a culture's taxonomic structure. Avoidance of anomalous things was a technique often used to strengthen the original classification system. Anomalies could also be treated as dangerous or on the other hand incorporated into the symbol structure of a culture to enrich meaning. See chap. 7.

9. Hitler, *Mein Kampf,* p. 178.

10. Ibid.

11. The contemporary filmmaker Werner Herzog in *Aguirre, Zern des Gottes* contemplates this possibility in what may be interpreted as a metaphor for Hitler's dream of conquest. Aguirre, the mad Spanish conqueror, having lost all his followers ends by chattering to a band of monkeys, his last remaining subjects.

12. Rudolf Höss, "Autobiography of Höss," trans. Constantine Fitzgibbon, in *KL Auschwitz Seen by the SS: Höss, Broad, Kremer,* ed. Jadwiga Bezwińska and Danuta Czech (W. Oswiecimiu: Publications of Panstwowe Muzeum, 1972), p. 88.

13. Ibid.

14. John Wild, "Husserl's Life World and Lived Body," in Straus, *Phenomenology Pure and Applied,* p. 24; emphasis added.

15. Alexander Donat, *The Holocaust Kingdom* (New York: Holocaust Library, 1963), p. 167. George Steiner in *Bluebeard's Castle: Some Notes towards the Redefinition of Culture* (New Haven: Yale University Press, 1971) writes: "*L'univers concentrationnaire* has no true counterpart in the secular mode. Its analogue is hell. The camp embodies, often down to minutiae, the images and chronicles of Hell in European art and thought from the twelfth to the eighteenth century" (p. 53).

16. Gertrud Kolmar, *Dark Soliloquy,* trans. Henry A. Smith (New York: Seabury, 1975), p. 34.

17. Johann Paul Kremer, "Diary of Kremer," in Bezwińska and Czech, *KL Auschwitz,* p. 215. Kremer was involved in notorious medical experiments at Auschwitz.

18. Gregory Bateson in "Toward a Theory of Schizophrenia" in *Steps to an Ecology of Mind* (New York: Ballantine Books, 1972) describes the repetition of the traumatic experience of receiving a negative injunction, then a second and conflicting injunction while the victim is prevented from escaping this double bind. The aetiology of schizophrenia is explained in this fashion.

19. Primo Levi, *Survival in Auschwitz: The Nazi Assault on Humanity,* trans. Stuart Woolf (New York: Collier, 1959), p. 25.

20. Sereny, *Into That Darkness,* p. 148.

21. "Autobiography of Höss," *KL,* p. 96.

22. John Wild, "Husserl's Life World and Lived Body," in Straus, *Phenomenology Pure and Applied,* p. 24.

23. Maurice Merleau-Ponty, "On the Phenomenology of Language," in *Signs,* trans. Richard C. McCleary (Evanston: Northwestern University Press, 1964), pp. 89ff.

24. Ibid., p. 90.

25. Donat, *The Holocaust Kingdom,* p. 168.

26. Levi, *Survival in Auschwitz,* p. 82.

27. Merleau-Ponty, *Phenomenology of Perception,* p. 393, writes: "To say that an event *takes place* is to say that it will always be true that it has taken place," and p. 392, "The non-temporal is the acquired."

28. Donat, *The Holocaust Kingdom,* p. 211.

29. Leon Weliczker Wells, *The Death Brigade* (New York: Holocaust Library, 1963), p. 244.

30. Donat, *The Holocaust Kingdom,* p. 169. This view confirms that of Viktor E. Frankl, who emphasizes the affirmation of values, the primary value being love, as cited in Terrence Des Pres, *The Survivor* (New York: Oxford University Press, 1976), p. 219. Des Pres also stresses the role of the gift.

31. Donat, *The Holocaust Kingdom,* p. 169.

32. Sereny, *Into That Darkness,* p. 186.

33. Levi, *Survival in Auschwitz,* p. 103.

17

LANGUAGE AND GENOCIDE

Berel Lang

The explanation of a historical event inevitably bears the mark of artifice. If it did not omit or compress, it would be as extensive as the events it was intended to explain and would be no more coherent than they were individually. To be sure, it is not only because of the complexity of historical connections in general that even the most sustained attempts to identify the causes of the Nazi genocide against the Jews seem inadequate. The difficulties here add the extraordinary character of that occurrence to the unusual status of evil itself, which even in less extreme appearances seems always to leave a remainder after the apparent social, economic, or psychological factors have been named. Beyond these intrinsic constraints, moreover, we recognize the physical scale on which the Nazi genocide was set—crossing the boundaries of continents, involving as victims, agents, and bystanders scores of nations, tens of millions of people. Accounts of an event enlarged to these magnitudes must be hard put even to distinguish between causes and effects, let alone to determine the exact points at which they met; it would be a large accomplishment to have established a bare chronicle of the event—what *happened,* and this indeed remains the single most important task of all writing about that event.

Thus, too, the assertion made here of a connection between language and the Nazi genocide may seem hardly to move beyond the claim that language was at once a victim of the genocide and an agent causing it. But acknowledgment of even a connection between the two is significant; the violence done to language in the genocide—in a special sense, to the German language, in a larger sense, to language as such—provides a distinctive representation of what the intention to exterminate the Jews required of its perpetrators in the way of will and of artifice; it discloses how deeply set the design of genocide was and how fully developed a world view it became. The Nazi genocide, seen from the perspective of language, is unusual in another respect as

Copyright by Berel Lang 1987. A version of this essay will appear in the author's forthcoming book *Act and Idea: Aspects of the Nazi Genocide.*

well—since from that perspective, the victims are shown to include not just those against whom the work of genocide was directed, but those who shaped or used the language. The distortion of language is in this sense a more generalized violation than others that have more obviously terrible consequences and in which the distinction between agents and victims is explicit and constant. To escape the consequences of language, for worse or for better, would require an impossible step outside history not less for its speakers or writers than for its audience—and it has been a principal theme of the preceding pages that whatever else we discover about the Nazi genocide, the evidence is only too clear of its place *within* history, as motivated and embodied in historical cause as well as in effect.

The background to this claim of the significance of language is broader than the specific evidence of its role in the Nazi genocide. The existence of a causal relation between language and history, between linguistic practice and events in the social context, would be disputed only if one views language as a neutral and transparent medium, perhaps following certain formal rules of development, but even then serving as an incidental means for the prior and more "real" intentions of its speakers or writers. According to this view, the function of language is independent of its objects; thus the moral character of the events of which it provides a representation stands quite apart from anything in the detail of syntax and vocabulary by which the representation is constituted. In the terms made current by Ferdinand de Saussure, the "signifier" and the "signified" that constitute the linguistic transaction are arbitrarily related to each other—and also, beyond that, to the historical events that they are then, however mysteriously, understood to denote. Neither natural nor historical causality is seen to influence the structure or stylistic patterns of language; nor, conversely, do the forms of language, whether in actual usage or in formal structure, reflect in any significant way what is said by their means. *What* is said is thus held to be independent of *how* it is said; the same "thing" can be expressed in quite different ways and across what appear as quite different linguistic structures. It is linguistic content that has consequences: which descriptions or commands are to be given, which purposes are announced, and what evidence is credited—but not, in any event, the variations in the forms by which such utterances are expressed.

The narrowness of this view of language would be demonstrable even without the unusual evidence provided by the linguistic embodiment of the intentions directing the Nazi genocide. Testimony comes from many different sources of the history of language as "real" history, evolving in direct relation to features of the historical and social context.

Those features extend from the constraints imposed by human physiology to the effects of specific technological developments like the alphabet or the printing press—and then also, to the consequences of radical political change or upheaval that may affect not only specific linguistic usage but the concept of language as such. So de Maistre would write that "every individual or national degradation is immediately heralded by a strictly proportional degradation in the language itself"—and his words here, one infers, bear not only on "degradation" but, more generally, on all significant change.

The relation between linguistic practice and the causes that affect it, moreover, reflects the content of specific linguistic expressions as well as the social history external to language. Thus, a central issue in the history of literature has focused on the problem of genres—the relation between literary forms or means, on the one hand, and the content of the texts that have those forms, on the other. The difficulty that becomes evident from such analysis of sustaining a sharp distinction between form and content itself would suggest their interrelation, and that conclusion is further supported as instances of supposedly formal stylistic analysis tend to revert to the question of content: what a literary text is "about" or "of." As the corporate forms of expression—art, legal institutions, religious practice—reflect the varieties of purpose and moral agency at their origins, moreover, it is hardly surprising that this should also be the case for language which is another such form—one, in fact, on which each of the others depends. Indeed, as soon as discourse is conceived as a means of agency on the part of a speaker, this connection is made: *Some* understanding of origin and purpose becomes associated with meaning; because they are historical, those sources then affect the shape of expression.

On these general grounds, it is predictable that linguistic developments associated with the Nazi genocide would disclose analogous features to those that characterize the literal genocide itself; it would be difficult to understand how the latter might occur without such changes. The evidence of such a connection forms the basis of the discussion here—a connection that extends, moreover, to the *idea* of language as well as to specific patterns of usage. As individual features of language—syntax, grammar, figures of speech—come to be viewed in the Nazi vocabulary as mere instruments, to be subordinated in rhetoric or art or theoretical discourse to political ends, so in the role of language applied to the work of genocide, language as a whole is conceived as an instrument, entirely subordinated to ends determined independently of it. Language is in this process detached from history and nature and finally also from moral judgment, becoming only a means by which certain intentions, themselves independently defined and allegedly translinguistic, are to be implemented. It thus takes on the character of impersonal technique, to be applied to whatever ends its agents independently decide on and reflecting only as much of those ends as the agents determine that it should. Language, in other words, becomes entirely contrivance, mute with respect to its own voice, detached from all sense of its own origins or purposes.

This conception of language differs markedly from that more traditionally associated with it, according to which language is historically bound—caused by and expressive of the agent who speaks or writes it. On these terms, language is linked intrinsically to thought and social practice, reflecting or representing its agents and their purposes. To be sure, extreme versions of the latter view—where a particular language was identified with nature or with a mark of self-asserted authority (civil or religious)—could be as dogmatic in their consequences as the opposed claim that there are no such connections; such versions were no less common, moreover, than were the visions of a "universal," artificial language such as that proposed by Leibniz. What is historically decisive in the relation between genocide and language, however, is the displacement at the levels of both concept and practice of the view of language as a form of disclosure and expression. In that displacement, we find the willed re-creation of language entirely as an instrument or means, together with the conditions that accompany that change: the claim by political authority to authority also over social memory and history; the reconstruction of language as pervasively ideological and thus as independent of facts, on the one hand, or of human agency, on the other; the assertion of political power to fill the space that is left by the denial to language of any authority of its own.

These summary comments about the general relation between language and history do not depend only on the consequences for language of the Nazi genocide against the Jews or even, at a more general level than that, on the technological and totalitarian character of the Nazi state, which were conditions, and undoubtedly necessary conditions, of that genocide. It is evident, moreover, that aspects of what is alleged here to characterize the language of the Nazis can be found in other linguistic usage as well, certainly as a consequence of the Nazi's own precedent, but in some measure also prior to it. Yet as in other respects, the Nazis defined paradigmatically the essential features of the act of genocide, so too, through their explicit and methodical elaboration of that act—the *constancy* of their intentions—they provide an extraordinary view of the role that language both had and suffered in the phenomenon of genocide.[1]

One does not have to look for a significant instance of such usage beyond the single term by which the Nazis chose to designate their genocidal war against the Jews—that is, the *"Endlösung"* or "Final Solution," which after the Wannsee Conference of January 20, 1942, was adopted by Nazi officialdom as the code word meant at once to disguise and to refer to that plan of extermination. In this term appear the characteristic features of a complex inversion of language—a linguistic equivalent of the very phenomenon to which the term itself refers; in it, we also see the form of the general turn that the language of genocide was to take.

It is well to understand that *"Endlösung"* had a history prior to its adoption by the Nazis, not so much as a term of general usage (although it was so used, albeit infrequently) as in the sense that other terms, close in meaning, had been "tried out" before the choice of *"Endlösung"* itself was made. So, there is reference to *"Endziel"* ("final goal") in Reinhard Heydrich's order to the *Einsatzgruppen* (September 21, 1939); to *"Gesamtlösung"* ("total solution"), by Göring in his directive to Heydrich of July 31, 1941 (Göring in this same statement *also* uses *"Endlösung"*); and to the *"endgültige Lösung"* ("conclusive solution") in a statement by Himmler concerning the "Gypsy question" (December 8, 1939). We have mainly to speculate about the process by which these alternatives came to be rejected in favor of *"Endlösung"* (for which Adolf Eichmann, probably on the basis of the Wannsee Conference, was to claim pride of authorship)—although one reason might well be that it avoids the possible ambiguities in the others: *"Ziel"* ("goal") as something that may or may not be within reach; *"gesamt"* ("total" or "collective") referring to all the parts of a problem at a time but not necessarily to a historical end.[2]

In any event, it seems evident that the Wannsee Conference at which the *Endlösung* was ratified in name and intention took for granted that term's implication of *other* "solutions" that had been proposed to the same "problem" or "question" that was being addressed at the conference, but that were not, by contrast, "final." It was not the Nazis, moreover, who initiated the use of the complementary terms—"question" or "problem" on the one hand, and "solution," on the other—in connection with discussions of the status of the Jews. The "Jewish question" to which various solutions or answers *would* be sought is, in fact, a conventional locution, used by non-Jewish—and anti-Jewish—writers, but also by Jewish and philo-Jewish writers, however differently the latter defined the "question" or "problem."[3]

The first part of the agglutinative noun *"Endlösung"* as applied by the Nazis to the "Jewish question" does, of course, also refer to the prior efforts of the Nazis themselves—the earlier and "less than final" solutions which the Nazis had been proposing virtually from the moment they came to power in 1933. Those efforts included the sequence of racial legislation epitomized by the Nuremberg Laws of 1935 which, by imposing a combination of economic and social restrictions, had as their principal purpose the confiscation of property and the coercion of Jewish emigration from Germany—a policy that persisted with some variations until the edict of October 23, 1941, prohibiting Jewish emigration. (This policy included the scheme for resettling the Jews in Madagascar, a plan that seems never to have come close to implementation but was the occasion of speculation between 1938 and 1940, and was certainly consistent with the policy of forced emigration—mentioned, among others, in statements by Göring, November 12, 1938, by Hans Frank in January 1940, and perhaps for the last time, in February 1941 by Hitler himself.)[4] Measures such as these, directed in common to the goal of a *"judenrein"* Germany, were not "final solutions" for reasons that are only too evident. These measures had, it seems, become increasingly problematic for the Nazis by the time of the Wannsee Conference, undoubtedly because they were encouraged by the lack of resistance to their earlier policies, but of more importance, because of their military conquests. The partition of Poland between Germany and Russia on September 28, 1939, had itself brought almost two million additional Jews under Nazi control—and such developments afforded new temptation and new opportunity, including of course, the possibility that what the Nazis could think of doing to the Jews might now be done farther from the sight of the West (indeed farther from the sight of the Germans themselves) and with the aid of native populations whom the *Einsatzgruppen* discovered immediately after the invasion of Russia to be likely collaborators. It was, then, in this context that the *Endlösung* was proposed—to solve the now larger "Jewish question" in a plan of extermination that was to include *all* the Jews of Europe, those of Great Britain and of the neutral countries, Sweden and Switzerland, in addition to those in countries that the Nazis already held in their grip.[5]

The superficial intelligibility from the point of view of the Nazis that is in this way supplied by the historical background of the term *"Endlösung"* joins the persuasive connotation of the term itself. For viewed out of context, in its dictionary meaning, *"Endlösung"* is no less benign a concept than its partial root, *"Lösung."* Solutions are responses to problems which, by definition, are troublesome, hindering, things that *should* be overcome or solved. They also carry with them, in fact, the implied possibility of solution: To acknowledge something *as* a problem suggests that it is capable of being solved. Thus, phrases such as "the Jewish question" or "the Jewish problem," in their most benign or neutral formulations, anticipate responses in the form of "solutions." Given the reasonable corollary that if a problem is to be solved, it is best solved once and for all, an *"Endlösung"* is desirable in a way that provisional or incomplete solutions are not. Out of historical context, then, the prospect of a "Final Solution" offers a welcome convergence of discursive and affective content: Problems are meant to be solved—and the more fully or finally, the better.

And yet, of course, in the Nazi vocabulary *"Endlösung"* stands for the extermination of a people—not their deportation or their enslavement (although these also, as it happened), but their annihilation; this is the literal act to which the opposed connotation of the term was joined in the Nazi vocabulary. The blatant disparity between the normal connotation of the word, on the one hand, and its reference in that vocabulary, on the other, amounts to what in the usual conventions of linguistic meaning or social practice would be seen as a contradiction. Moreover, the fact that the Nazis themselves took the trouble to develop a set of "speech rules" explicitly intended to conceal literal meaning—among which the rule for the use of *"Endlösung"* occupied an important place—suggests that they themselves were well aware of this tension. It must not be supposed, moreover, that the use of speech rules or a code was intended entirely or only for an external audience, that the Nazis among themselves were ready to speak openly—that is, literally—of what the code concealed. For there is substantial evidence in support of the contention that the use of *"Endlösung"* (and some, although not all of the other terms to be discussed) was meant even mainly for internal use, as a conscious attempt to disguise or misrepresent something it would have been dangerous or morally wrong to address more directly. Like other attempts at concealment by the Nazis which lead naturally to the question of *why* they sought to conceal what they did, speech rules provide important evidence of what the act of genocide represented in terms of Nazi beliefs—what, beyond what they *did*, they *thought* they were doing.

In choosing and using the term *"Endlösung,"* in any event, the Nazis were attempting to add to the referential force of the word elements that go well beyond the purposes of reference. What results from this process is a term that has been "figured" or "turned" much in the way that figurative language of *any* kind originates, reflecting—as all such usage does—the intention to make a word mean more than it would in its literal appearance. There are, of course, various ways in which figurative discourse adds to the meaning of words, and it may seem perverse to suggest that an understanding of those ways will be informative about a word with the extraordinary history—much more immediately social and political, after all, than literary—that *"Endlösung"* has had. Yet the probability that the turns of language reflect or display the turns of history more generally is too evident to be ignored. Beyond the matter of the particular example, moreover, is a general issue of the relation between "normal" and "abnormal" discourse, and then of the historical status of language as such; it is an instance again—as for the act of genocide more generally—where extremity serves as a proof or test of the ordinary.

Considered then against the background of conventional figures of speech, "Endlösung" may seem to have been intended as ironical, implying, as irony characteristically does, the opposite or at least a reversal of what it superficially affirms: It denotes a solution to a problem by proposing the destruction of the problem. On this account, the term would be a form of gallows humor, initiated from the point of view of the builder rather than that of the victim—a joke meant to add to the larger aggression.[6] But both internal and external evidence suggest that it is not irony that is intended by the Nazi choice of the term, not even the less pointed equivocation we find in "Endlösung" as we recognize through it that not only the problem "to be solved" but also the *solutions* to the problem would have come to an end. The purpose of the Nazi speech rules was to *avoid* calling attention to themselves, and this policy was applied more stringently than was usual in the guarded references allowed even to the code words themselves. There are also general reasons for doubting that the purpose here was ironic: The characteristic feature in irony of "double vision," of language reiterating itself with a difference—and a negation at that, which the reader has to supply—makes irony an unlikely feature of totalitarian discourse at any time. In this role, irony thus typically underscores the possibility of nonliteral meaning and impels the reader beyond the apparent text (thus also beyond censorship)—both of these affording to both the writer and the reader a measure of freedom that would only be seen by totalitarianism as subversive.

In addition to such prima facie evidence, moreover, nothing in the appearances of "Endlösung" in Nazi documents hints at an intention to undermine its surface meaning. It is rather the literal denotation, the deliberate assertion that through it the Jewish "problem" will be solved once and for all, that is intended; and although for most instances of figurative language (metaphor, for example) the absence of apparent intention from the figure itself may be irrelevant or even an advantage, this is not the case for irony. A statement or term that we read as metaphorical will never have a meaning simply contradictory to the meaning of the same statement or term read literally or nonmetaphorically. Irony alone has that feature, and for it intention is crucial; there is no irony that does not itself disclose the will responsible for it, let alone irony that is simply unwilled.

For the audience who was "in" on the secret of the Nazi language

rules, the term *"Endlösung"* denoted the extermination of the Jews—
although even for it, the term was meant at once to affirm and to
obscure the referent. To the German public and the public outside
Germany, as they might subsequently encounter the term and half-
know, half-not-know what it referred to, it would, on one level in any
event, have the benign connotation of designating something that
ought to be done: tautologically, the resolution of a problem that should
be overcome because it was a problem, with the accompanying concealment that abstraction—"solution"—always provides when it replaces
the name or image of a concrete act—"extermination." No space remains
for irony at either end of this tandem of contradictory meanings.

The question thus persists, If *"Endlösung"* is not irony, what figure
or trope of speech is it? For the term is evidently contrived, turned,
figurative in *some* way; certainly it is not innocent or straightforward,
not matter of fact or literal in its overall force, despite—more accurately,
because of—the evident intention, which *is* part of it, that it should be
understood literally. This apparently academic question about figurative
discourse is not at all academic in its results. For among the four
classical figures of speech under which varieties of the linguistic turn
are often subsumed, irony has already been ruled out—and none of the
other three provides a more adequate account: not metaphor (the
"solution" is meant literally as a solution: Tenor and vehicle are one);
not metonymy (as "final," the solution is not a part substituted for a
whole); not synecdoche (again, *Endlösung* is a *denial* of the part–whole
relation). Related or similar objections block the appeal to more
restricted figures of speech. The suggestion often made that *"Endlösung"*
is an instance of euphemism, for example, although superficially
plausible is no more adequate than would be the suggestion that it is
hyperbole. To refer to someone as having "gone to sleep" rather than
as having died is to intend a euphemism (based on a metaphor). The
literal and euphemistic versions agree at least that the person referred
to is motionless and unconscious; the euphemistic connotation of sleep
adds the comforting possibility of peacefulness and perhaps of a later
awakening. But when the description of an act has a connotation added
to it that turns it into its opposite, we reasonably conclude that the
linguistic turn taken is no longer euphemism but a different figure
altogether.

It seems not too much to claim here, in fact, that with *"Endlösung"*
(and related terms that are mentioned below), the language of genocide
has contrived a distinctive literary figure. The characteristics of this
figure are that the denotation of the term, although logically consistent
with it (in principle, *any* act might be called a solution) substantively
contradicts it; that the term itself is abstract and general but designates

an event or object that is concrete and specific; and that the figurative term is meant to draw attention away both from this change and from the individual aspects of its referent, thus concealing what is denoted (and intending to conceal the fact of concealment as well). The figure of speech thus constituted diverges in each of these three respects from the common purpose of figurative language, which is both to bring into focus—to "figure"—certain concrete aspects of the referent and to call attention to itself (and to itself as figurative).

I propose, quite simply, to call this new figure by an old name, one that more usually would not be associated with *figures* of speech at all—that is, the lie. The reasons for invoking this term should, however, be clear: As the person who is a liar knowingly affirms what is false, so here a linguistic expression affirms what it "knows" to be false. Moral violation thus takes on the guise of literary form. Admittedly, one can anticipate objections to this (or any) claim for a linguistic version of ethical principle. For one thing, figurative language is usually viewed as distinguishable from the speaker's own—extralinguistic—purposes which can be understood literally and as the proper object of moral judgment. Thus, speakers or writers may use hyperbole and other literary figures for the *purpose* of lying but still avoid lying *within* those figures: It is the action the words serve that is in these cases subject to moral assessment. Moreover, when figurative language associated with poetry or fictional discourse is meant quite explicitly to be ornamental, an imaginative heightening of aspects of objects that would otherwise have only a nonfigurative or "literal" existence, this is not usually judged to be a lie or instance of deception. "Achilles is a lion" is not meant to be understood literally; if it were, the statement *might* be a lie as well as false. On the other hand, the distinction between figurative and moral discourse seems inadequate for understanding the figurative terms conceived by the Nazi speech rules: Their moral quality seems so fundamental as to be part of the expression itself, to be engaged in the *manner* of speaking. A person who denies having done something he knowingly did is lying—but it is not the language that then does the lying, it is the speaker. Calling the Nazi genocide a "Final Solution," by contrast turns the phrase itself into a lie—as calling Achilles a "lion" discloses the latter term to be a metaphor. The figurative lie links two contradictory literal references; it also attempts, in asserting the connection, both to deny the contradiction and to conceal it. (Oxymoron, although it includes the former feature, that of the contradiction, does not have the latter.) To be sure, a speaker or writer who employs the figure of the lie will often, perhaps even necessarily, be lying also in the moral sense: Language does not, after all, speak itself. But there is still the distinction to be made between the language and its user, where the language *itself* lies, asserting to be true what is false as language.[7]

To focus discussion of the language of genocide on the term applied by the Nazis to the act itself, is to cite only one example of many possible ones; there is, in fact, a more general "vocabulary" that provides much broader evidence of the role of the figurative lie. An important example among these is the lengthy list of words substituted in the Nazi vocabulary for "killing" or "execution." *"Sonderbehandlung"* ("special treatment") comes closest among these terms to repeating the linguistic conditions mentioned in connection with *"Endlösung,"*[8] but other "synonyms" have much the same character. So, for example: *"entsprechend behandelt"* ("treated appropriately"), *"Aussiedlung"* ("evacuation"), *"Umsiedlung"* ("resettlement"), *"Auflöckerung"* ("thinning out"—as in the removal of inhabitants from a ghetto), *"Befriedungsaktion"* ("pacification") and *"A.B. Aktion,"* that is, *"ausserordentliche Befriedungsaktion"* ("special pacification"), *"Ausschaltung"* ("removal"), *"Abwanderung"* ("having been migrated"), *"Säuberung"* ("cleansing"), *"sicherheitspolizeilich durchgearbeitet"* ("worked through in a Security Police manner") were all used in place of standard terms for killing or execution. Such usage occurred, moreover, not only in communications issued to the Jewish public when the intention of those issuing the communications was to deceive the Jews in order to minimize the likelihood of resistance, but also in addressing the outside world and, perhaps more significantly, for internal communications as well, among officials who unquestionably knew (who were themselves sometimes responsible for) the linguistic substitutions stipulated by the speech rules. (At times, of course, the standard and nonfigurative terms were used for each of these audiences, but the context then was usually an order concerning the execution of individuals who were named, or as a warning directed against specific acts; the orders for larger and more abstract plans of killing under the general edict of the Final Solution were almost always couched in the diffuse and abstract terms noted here.)

The list of such terms, moreover, does not stop with those that refer to killing: The apparatus that would make that act possible also required figurative elaboration. So, *"Hilfsmittel"* ("auxiliary equipment") designated the vans that had been turned into the mobile gas chambers that killed by recycling the carbon monoxide from the vans' engines and which continued to be used elsewhere even after the *"Badeanstalten"* ("bath arrangements"—i.e., gas chambers) had been constructed at Auschwitz. *"Briefaktion"* ("letter action") would refer to coercing new arrivals in the camps to write to relatives or friends in the ghettos or cities, reassuring them about the prospects of "resettlement." *"Gleichschaltung"* ("putting into the same gear") could range in meaning from the abolition of divergent political parties to the removal of individuals (although not usually their execution)—in effect the "evening out" of obstacles or impediments.

Such terms, moreover, were not left to the moment or to individual inventiveness; they were part of an official, although evolving code or set of rules (*"Sprachberegelungen"*) which identified the words that should not be used and the terms intended to replace them. An example of how these rules were made appears in a directive by which the use of *"Sonderbehandlung"* was announced. This order (dated September 26, 1939) reiterates "the stipulation of the rules in accordance with which the so-called delights of war are to be renamed," and then goes on specifically to designate the abbreviation *"Sb"* for *"Sonderbehandlung."*

To be sure, even the most persistent calculations of the "speech rules" would not anticipate all contingencies, and the requirements of a vocabulary consistent with the act of genocide would predictably run out of terms in a language that had not yet conceived of the act. The extraordinary phenomenon of the Nazi genocide discloses itself then also in the fact that for some of its features, there simply would be—perhaps even *could* be—no satisfactory terms, whether in the language available or by contrivance, whether literal or figurative. In order to arrive at such terms, the events themselves would first have to be fully imagined—and there were at the time features of the genocide (some remain even now, decades later) that posed substantial difficulties for the imagination. An important example of this difficulty is represented in the term "genocide" itself, which was coined by Rafael Lemkin in the early 1940s in his effort to give legal definition to the phenomenon of the Final Solution. That example, to be sure, is in the context not a neutral one and would hardly have been assimilated to the Nazi vocabulary, at least not as the term has since been applied to their war against the Jews. But other examples that are not "tendentious" in this way also indicate the difficulty *in principle* of finding words for features of the Nazi genocide.

Especially noticeable among these examples are the problematic terms meant to designate the Jews who had been brought to the death camps. The problem of giving a name to them in this role exactly mirrors the extraordinary nature of that role itself. Again: the Jews collectively had been condemned to death by the order to implement the Final Solution. (No single and explicit written order to this effect has been found, a fact that has led to arguments about whether such an order was ever given, or if it was, whether Hitler issued it, or more bizarrely still, whether Hitler was himself aware that the Final Solution was being implemented.)[9] On the other hand, for "practical" reasons, it was evident that any such order or series of orders could not be carried out instantly but required organization and time; and this, together with such other "practical" reasons as the need for skilled labor that the Jews might provide, sometimes argued for delaying the implementation of the order. Thus, distinctions were made on occasion even within the death camps and more often in the concentration camps among those to be killed immediately and those whose execution could be delayed. And when the genocidal sentence of death is combined with such gradations of treatment (however temporary), the problem of finding a specific name for the "victims" of such an act is evident. They were to be treated arbitrarily as a matter of principle, with death as the end, but not necessarily immediately; while they lived, they had no rights, not even the right to a specific "death sentence," although they might indeed receive that if they took some action that was not merely submissive. ("*Kadavergehorsam*" ["cadaver obedient"] was the ghoulish term—not a code word at all—that designated *this* requirement.) The Jews held in the camps in effect lacked the rights that even animals were assured in the Third Reich. What, then, could they be called? They were, obviously, "prisoners"—but that term would not distinguish between them and people held (and *maintained*) in custody for a specified length of time and possibly, then, to be released. For some of the same reasons, they would not be "inmates"—a term that adds the sense of protective custody to the possibility that rehabilitative measures might be part of the design. In the spring of 1945, when the camps still functioning (for example, Buchenwald and Bergen-Belsen) were overrun by the Allied armies, newspapers in the United States (see, e.g., the *New York Times*, April 18 and 19, 1945) typically spoke about the "slaves" who were found there—the dead as well as the living—building on the erroneous assumption, which in almost any other circumstance would have been reasonable, that the main function of the camps was to provide slave labor. But this, too, of course, skews the description, since although Jews in the camps were sometimes used as slave labor and although, like slaves in extreme settings, they lacked all legal rights of protection or care, the *main* purpose for which they were in the camps was not to work but to die.

"Victims" is sometimes used in reference to the Jews inside the camps (as well as to those killed outside them), but again, although obviously accurate in one sense, the conventional association of the term with people killed in individual acts of violence or even in accidents or natural catastrophes does not touch the rationale behind the death camps. (Even the reference to individual "victims" of premeditated murder misses the essential features of deliberation and organization that characterize genocide.) Nor could they be termed "captives" which might suggest both that they had been caught after having been freed and that the future awaiting them was contingent. Yet, although in the strict sense they were "condemned" to death, they were not exactly awaiting execution either, since this, again, suggests a definiteness about their status and the fate awaiting them that did not obtain except in the most general sense: Starvation, disease, and overwork were officially expected to kill many of the Jews in the camps, but that is not what is meant ordinarily, in judicial terms, by a death sentence. The term *"Häftling"* that the Nazis themselves usually applied comes close to the sense of "captive" or "prisoner" and is thus also something of a euphemism. (To the extent that *"Häftling"* implies captivity as part of a specific sentence or as awaiting sentence, it would be simply misleading; to *be* a Jew, as the Nazis had defined that, was itself to have sentence pronounced.) The Nazis had a variety of reasons, symbolic as well as practical, for tattooing numbers on the people in the camps, but one consequence of the practice was that the number itself would sometimes serve as a means of direct address or reference. The people in the camps devised for themselves the term "KZ-etnik" from the letters of *"Konzentration Lager,"* a neologism that suggested something novel in their situation, but was not descriptive. (The Nazis sometimes explicitly prohibited calling those who died "victims," or even "corpses," stipulating the term *"Figuren"* ["figures," "pieces," as in chess].) There seems in fact to be no term of common usage that meets the specific conditions imposed by the act of genocide on those subjected to the act, a problem that recurs, moreover, for the verb(s) to be associated with the act. "Killing," "execution," even "murder"—all miss the distinctive character of the act, although each, to be sure, is within limits accurate. Thus genocide as it evidently stretched the imagination in its own conception, forcing revision in the history of evildoing, also reaches the limits of language as it requires terms to describe *what* it intended and attempted.

It is evident, moreover, that the consequences of genocide for language were not confined to official documents or statements, nor even to explicit decisions about speech rules (although these, too, reached the public domain). So, for example, Goebbels (December 13, 1937) would stipulate that "from today the word *'Volkerbund'* ('League of Nations') will no longer be used in the German press. This word no longer exists." There was also, as might have been expected, and in some ways still more revealing linguistic "unconscious," the consequences of which appeared in standard usage even when the discussion did not refer to the Final Solution or to military or political matters at all. The inversion of language that results in the figure of the lie may not be as graphic in these more commonplace appearances as it is in terms like *"Endlösung,"* but the pattern of a general style disclosed by them is in some ways still more significant. For here it is the image of a general social and cultural order that we see, not only the conscious dictates of a political or military will. And here, too, there is evidence of the same general purpose at once to rationalize language and to subordinate it to authority, that is, to make it into a political instrument which within its own structure would incorporate the features of moral violation that otherwise constitute the lie.

The usage thus introduced reflects in language a genocidal society in its "everyday" life; the linguistic features that might be cited in this connection extend from some that apply to other aspects of culture as well as to language, to some that are quite specific in linguistic usage. The features of repetition and exaggeration or monumentality, for example, have often been cited as characteristic of totalitarian "style"—and these were indeed persistent features of Nazi rhetoric (thus, Kenneth Burke's association of Hitler's hold on his audience with the "power of endless repetition"),[10] as they were elsewhere also, for example, in Nazi architecture and in its drama, particularly in the giant Nazi rallies. Those same features, moreover, extended beyond the official language to common linguistic usage, in journalism and popular fiction as well as in school textbooks. There, too, the style of domination controls the expressive means; language appears as a technological instrument that can be made to serve purposes quite apart from, even in conflict with, the direct representation of events or objects.

The more specific means employed for this purpose cover a spectrum of changes that extend beyond the "style" of figurative discourse to semantic and syntactic alterations as well. Thus, for example, hyperbole is normalized with the common use of exaggerated terms like *"einmalig"* ("unique"), *"historisch"* ("historic"), *"total"* ("total"). *"Fanatisch"* ("fanatic"), which had the connotation of madness, would now in the Nazi vocabulary count as commendable (and expected, i.e., normal) dedication. The same pattern of repetition and hyperbole was further joined to a conscious effort at defamiliarization: Archaic or "folk" words were revived (e.g., *"Mädel"* for *"Mädchen"* ["girl"], *"Sippe"* for *"Familie"* ["family"]), and certain foreign words were adopted (e.g., *"Aktion"* for *"Unternehmung"*). It may seem that the last two impulses conflict—one attempting to reach back to German history, the other reaching outside, to alien sources—but in context, the two are quite consistent. The former is impelled by a mystique of the German past that served as an important ideological element in Nazi doctrine; the latter provides an aura of technological rationality and irrefutability that the Nazis wished now to extend to language as well: Thus, on the one hand, the sources offer the lure of the unfamiliar and so of novelty and power; on the other hand, they conspire to turn a history of ethnic origin into a promise of national destiny (once again, of power). Again, more generally we infer from this usage the intention to subject language itself to political authority to demonstrate that this common medium of exchange, which often appears in the guise of nature itself, is also subordinate to political authority. The Nazis would not only contrive a language *of* domination, they intended to demonstrate that language itself, as a whole, was subject to domination.

The means by which the theme of domination is given a linguistic form are designed in such a way as to leave the listener or reader only the option of submission to the spoken or written words that address him. The use of puns and alliteration in Nazi political slogans, for example, forcibly joins words and phrases that have little to do with each other except for the process of assertion itself. Thus: *"Die Liebe der SS das Leben der Führer umgürtet"* ("The love of the SS protects the life of the Führer"); or *"Das Leben des Führer bleibt nicht ein Wirklichkeit sondern wird zu einer Wahrheit"* ("The life of the Führer does not remain a reality but becomes a truth"). An analogous example is the use of conjunctive phrases in contexts the purpose of which is to assert the conjunction rather than to identify related meanings—in such redundant transitions, for instance, as *"und damit"* and *"und mit diesem"* ("and thereby" and "and therewith"). It is not only the *act* of conjunction that is intended in such usage, moreover, but the whole that is then constituted (*"organisch"* ["organic"] is itself a favorite term): The reader or listener was to see *himself* as part of a larger whole. Thus, as the conjunctions lead to larger and larger units, the alternatives left to the audience turn out to be those either of full acceptance or of an equally complete denial—the latter, from the point of view of language tantamount to an acceptance of silence and nonexistence. There are no gaps left in the discourse that might be claimed by the listener or reader for his alternatives or objections; the writer or speaker anticipates all the questions that arise or, more characteristically, denies their possibility: The implied audience is to be of one mind with the author.

The implication that things or events are not determinate or accessible unless they are brought together in a discursive whole is also emphasized by the practice of adding suffixes to nouns that attach a *state* of being to references that otherwise might be specific and active, not merely potentialities for action: so, for example, *"Volkheit"* ("people-ness") or *"Wehrheit"* ("defenseness"). These suffixes identify the thing named as itself indeterminate or tentative—and thus as requiring for "real" existence a state or condition shared with other would-be individuals and provided by a more general and abstract source of being. Thus, what more immediately would be a single and independent noun, standing for an individual referent or thing, turns out only to be part of a larger—by implication, of a single—whole. It requires no great imaginative leap to see in that whole the totalitarian will or its political embodiment in the state.

Again, the features thus identified recurred in popular and informal writing as well as in official documents. (To be sure, given the increasing control of censorship, at some point, certainly by 1940, virtually anything published in Nazi Germany, textbooks, newspapers, and the like, would have to be considered an official document.) Admittedly, sustained analysis of stylistic change at this level would require the study of personal correspondence and other informal writing that was not intended to be published, as well as of fiction or poetry that (for literary, not political reasons) moved as far as any publications officially sanctioned could from "normative" usage. The detailed analysis of these sources is not undertaken here, but superficially at least, the stylistic representation discerned in the Nazi vocabulary seems also to appear in these unofficial sources—in academic and literary prose and in personal and casual communications that were not intended for public inspection at all, in what might be called the "private" style. This corollary, it seems, is predictable if not inevitable: The distinctions that language makes or avoids would hardly be impervious to the context in which those distinctions had themselves arisen.

To be sure, like other figures of speech, the literary figure of the lie is accessible to analysis and even before that to the self-consciousness that enables a reader or listener to place it historically in a context of motives, intentions, and consequences. This is the sense in which all expression, however figurative, is also literal and truthful; willingly or not, it discloses its own means, art not quite concealing all of art. The "style" of common linguistic usage under the Nazis is subject to this disclosure no less than are the language rules officially adhered to more explicitly: One thing the will to domination cannot control is the appearance as seen from the outside—if only an "outside" remains—of the will to dominate. Viewed from that perspective, the language of genocide, even in its many and complex facets, reveals the singular intention to turn language itself into an instrument of domination and deceit, enabling in practice and principle an act that controverts the most basic ideals of moral life as it denies the social reality of language and then the reality of human experience beyond that. This is, as has been suggested earlier in these pages, exactly what the physical fact of genocide itself intends and accomplishes: the willing of evil for its own sake quite apart from the consideration of practical consequences. Language itself, moreover, may become a part of that intention, one of its agents—no less revealing of the mind that conceives of genocide as "desirable" than those more obvious instruments of which the will for genocide was to make use.

The assertion made here of a relation between genocide and

language does not claim that violence done to language, even on the scale of violence realized by the Nazis, leads inevitably to genocide. Nor does it claim that genocide would only be possible in a setting for which the inversion of values had been so complete as to include language—the currency of thought—as a whole. An alteration in language of the kind described is thus neither necessary nor sufficient as a cause—but again, there is nothing unusual in this limitation either for tracing historical causality in general or for attempting to identify the causes of the Nazi genocide in particular; indeed such limitations would be predictably more severe for an aspect of culture as subtle and diffuse as language. It might well be argued that the reason we become aware of the role of language as a feature of genocide at all is because we have before that been confronted with the physical act of genocide—although as soon as we hear this, we recognize also that even that first awareness may also include reference to the violation of language. It is the mind, together with bodies, that genocide acts to destroy; and as language is an essential element of mind, it would be extraordinary if an attack on the latter did not also involve the former, if the genocidal destruction of a people, directed against every level of its existence, could be envisioned without an accompanying assault on what is thought and said. Like other types of action, evildoing requires a means—and the more elaborate and profound the action, so too the means required for it. The fact that it was the German language that most immediately suffered this violence is an irony of the Nazi genocide, although this feature itself also bears on another more general and more familiar implication that evildoing claims among its victims the evildoer as well as the intended victims.

Thus, too, I have not been claiming that the role of language in the Nazi genocide is uniquely located either there or in the phenomenon of genocide as such. The forces contributing to the deformation of language did not begin or end with the Nazi genocide even though there is a connection, causal as well as conceptual, between the two. Both the idea and the practice of language that emerged to such coercive effect in the Nazi genocide seem, moreover, to have taken on a strange life of their own subsequently. Evidence of that development is as close at hand as almost any newspaper quotation of political rhetoric in the years since World War II: So the view of language as a technological and impersonal instrument, a view that at the level of political reality was not long ago a radical innovation, now becomes naturalized and familiar, something virtually assumed as native to political language and discourse, even for institutions professedly opposed to and in many other respects removed in intent from those of the Nazis.

It hardly needs to be said that compared to other aspects of the moral enormity constituted by the Nazi genocide, the inversion of language described here, in the elevation of the lie to a principle of discourse, does not constitute the most immediate or the greatest harm effected there. But since it does not appear by itself but as part of an effort at total destruction, there can be little comfort in this. As people live by representations in the present and by memory in the past, moreover, the role of language in the genocide remains a cogent representation of that event more generally. We find language, in this role, replete with evidence of the will to do evil, the power of the imagination to enlarge on that will, and capable of the violence that such impulses nourish inside language or out. These effects can be understood in the character of genocide itself and the requirements imposed by it on those who conceive and "do" it. If it is true that genocide implies the deliberate choice of evil as an end, assuming in the act of killing a conceptualization of the group and the choice of the group as its object, the violation of language in the act of genocide represents something more than only an analogy between language and genocide. It is not only, then, that language becomes morally culpable by its figurative device of the "lie"—but that elements of the lie are also themselves effective causes in the deliberate act of genocide: There is in both the denial of truth and history—a denial, we learn by way of the Nazi language rules, of which the Nazis themselves were aware. Furthermore, the "objects" of genocide—people and language—that are denied the right to exist are closely related to each other in their group or social character. It is not only individual parts or uses of language that are violated—but language as such, a corporate entity much like the corporate object, the *genos,* of genocide itself.

This is not meant to suggest that all evildoing turns out to be one, that any single act entails all others and the guilt for them—or more specifically, that genocide and the violation of language are intrinsically related. But it does mean that as evildoing involves always human agents and human victims, there will undoubtedly be more at issue in any single act than what the act itself explicitly designates. Especially in language do we recognize the figure and the moral spirit of its source; there is little to distinguish the linguistic representation from what it is a representation of or from the agent who intends it as a representation. Thus also, the language of genocide, long after the conditions that initially produced it, may persist still, as a challenge to the present as well as to the past. It would be a mistake to imagine that the history of the language of genocide, any more than other consequences of the genocide, ended with the conclusion of the physical act.

The relation between character—whether in the individual or in the group—and language becomes further evident in what started here as analogy but has disclosed itself as more than that: in the common feature of domination that in the name of principle engendered both the act of genocide and the instrumental role ascribed to language. On both sides of that analogy, distinctions based on evidence and moral principle are overridden; categories and distinctions devised and willed by the agent are made to seem natural and necessary, and this is itself part of the intention. Not only language but logic is brought inside history by these efforts, moreover; and not only the cultural appearances of these domains are brought into history, but so also are the "objects" they ostensively refer to. There is nothing in language, as in humanity more generally, that is exempt from the controlling intention. The will to do evil through the medium of genocide is in fact the will to transcend *all* limits or restrictions, and this intention which includes language among its objects, produces a lie of even a larger order than does the language specifically tied to the act of genocide itself. In this increasingly generalized consequence the moral lie comes close to being absolute, denying the figurative representation of truth in all its forms and even the possibility of truth itself; the moral lie chooses evil as its good on grounds of principle, and this means that no subordinate purpose is acknowledged or chosen by the agent of genocide that is not evil. For the *language* of genocide, the change is smaller but hardly less noticeable. In it, the lie becomes a figure of speech, when it had been the native purpose of figurative language, arguably of *all* language, to disclose and to enlarge, not to conceal or to diminish, much less to destroy, still less to destroy completely.

NOTES

1. Among the accounts given of the Nazi use of language, see especially Nachman Blumenthal, "On the Nazi Vocabulary," *Yad Vashem Studies* 1 (1957): 49–66; and "From the Nazi Vocabulary," *Yad Vashem Studies* 6 (1967): 69–82; Gordon A. Craig, *The Germans* (New York: G.P. Putnam's Sons, 1982), pp. 323–25; Shaul Esh, "Words and Their Meanings: Twenty-Five Examples of the Nazi-Idiom," *Yad Vashem Studies* 5 (1963): 133–67; Henry Friedlander, "The Manipulation of Language," in *The Holocaust: Ideology, Bureaucracy, and Genocide,* ed. Henry Friedlander and Sybil Milton (Millwood, N.Y.: Kraus International, 1980), pp. 103–14; Eugen Seidel and Ingeborg Seidel, *Sprachwandel im Dritten Reich: Ein critisches Untersuchung faschischten Einflüsse* (Halle: VEB, 1961); George Steiner, *Language and Silence* (New York: Atheneum, 1974), pp. 95–109.

2. Göring was to offer a version of this distinction in his own defense at Nuremberg. See G. Reitlinger, *The Final Solution* (South Brunswick, N.J.: Thomas Yoseloff, 1968), p. 85.

3. Perhaps the best-known use of the term is in Marx's *Zur Judenfrage* (1844), but see also, for examples: Ahad Haám, "The Jewish State and the Jewish Problem" (1897);

Theodore Herzl, *Der Judenstaat, Versuch einer modernen Lösung der Judenfrage* (1896); Louis Brandeis, "The Jewish Problem and How to Solve It" (1915).

4. See Raul Hilberg, *The Destruction of the European Jews,* abridged ed. (New York: Holmes and Meier, 1985), p. 161.

5. Such plans were not, as they might seem, matters of fantasy. Germany occupied England's Channel Islands at the end of June 1940. Legislation soon followed requiring the registration of the few Jews who lived on Jersey and Guernsey, and the sale of Jewish businesses to non-Jews; almost all the Jews identified were subsequently deported to concentration camps on the continent. (A concentration camp was also constructed on Alderney; a number of Jews who had been transported from the continent were killed there.) See, e.g., A. Wood and M. S. Wood, *Islands in Danger* (London: New English Library, 1965).

6. Hilberg cites a counterpart to the Nazi vocabulary in that of the victims (for example, the designation in Auschwitz of the crematorium as "the bakery"); see *Destruction of the European Jews,* rev. and definitive ed., 3 vols. (New York: Holmes and Meier, 1985), pp. 1041-42. But what might be irony from the point of view of the victim is something quite different in the Nazi vocabulary.

7. See, for an anticipation of this conception of the linguistic lie, Harold Weinrich, *Linguistik der Lüge* (Heidelberg: Lambert Schneider, 1966), pp. 34-41.

8. The first use of *"Sonderbehandlung"* in this sense is attributed to Heydrich in a letter of September 20, 1939—directed against Germans rather than Jews. See Joseph Wulf, *Aus dem Lexikon der Mörder: "Sonderbehandlung" und verwandte Worte in national-sozialistischen Dokumenten* (Gutersloh: Sigbert Mohn, 1963), p. 7.

9. For an assessment of these claims, see Gerald Fleming, *Hitler and the Final Solution* (Berkeley: University of California Press, 1984); and Eberhard Jäckel, *Hitler in History* (Hanover: University Press of New England, 1984), chap. 3.

10. Kenneth Burke, "The Rhetoric of Hitler's *Battle,*" in *The Philosophy of Literary Form* (Berkeley: University of California Press, 1973), pp. 217-18. See also Harold D. Lasswell, Nathan Leites, and Associates, *Language of Politics* (New York: G.W. Stewart, 1949), introduction; and Saul Friedländer, *Reflections of Nazism,* trans. T. Weyer (New York: Harper & Row, 1984), pp. 50-53.

PART FOUR
Challenges to the Understanding

18

SOCIAL SCIENCE TECHNIQUES AND THE STUDY OF CONCENTRATION CAMPS

Hannah Arendt

Every science is necessarily based upon a few inarticulate, elementary, and axiomatic assumptions which are exposed and exploded only when confronted with altogether unexpected phenomena which can no longer be understood within the framework of its categories. The social sciences and the techniques they have developed during the past hundred years are no exception to this rule. It is the contention of this paper that the institution of concentration and extermination camps, that is, the social conditions within them as well their function in the larger terror apparatus to totalitarian regimes, may very likely become that unexpected phenomenon, that stumbling block on the road toward the proper understanding of contemporary politics and society which must cause social scientists and historical scholars to reconsider their hitherto unquestioned fundamental preconceptions regarding the course of the world and human behavior.

Behind the obvious difficulties of dealing with a subject matter in which the mere enumeration of facts makes one sound "intemperate and unreliable"[1] and on which reports are written by people who during their very experience were "never wholly successful" in convincing "themselves that this was real, was really happening, and not just a nightmare,"[2] lies the more serious perplexity that within the framework of commonsense judgments neither the institution itself and what went on within its closely guarded barriers nor its political role make any sense whatsoever. If we assume that most of our actions are of a utilitarian nature and that our evil deeds spring from some "exaggeration" of self-interest, then we are forced to conclude that this particular institution of totalitarianism is beyond human understanding.

This article is reprinted here by permission of the editors of *Jewish Social Studies*, where it originally appeared in vol. 12, no. 1 (1950); 49–64.

If, on the other hand, we make an abstraction of every standard we usually live by and consider only the fantastic ideological claims of racism in its logical purity, then the extermination policy of the Nazis makes almost too much sense. Behind its horrors lies the same inflexible logic which is characteristic of certain systems of paranoiacs where everything follows with absolute necessity once the first insane premise is accepted. The insanity of such systems clearly does not lie only in their first premise but in their very logicality which proceeds regardless of all facts and regardless of reality, which teaches us that whatever we do we can't carry through with absolute perfection. In other words, it is not only the nonutilitarian character of the camps themselves; the senselessness of "punishing" completely innocent people, the failure to keep them in a condition so that profitable work might be extorted from them, the superfluousness of frightening a completely subdued population, which gives them their distinctive and disturbing qualities, but their antiutilitarian function, the fact that not even the supreme emergencies of military activities were allowed to interfere with these "demographic policies." It was as though the Nazis were convinced that it was of greater importance to run extermination factories than to win the war.[3]

It is in this context that the adjective "unprecedented"[4] as applied to totalitarian terror receives full significance. The road to total domination leads through many intermediary stages which are relatively normal and quite comprehensible. It is far from unprecedented to wage aggressive war; massacres of enemy populations or even of what one assumes to be a hostile people look like an everyday affair in the bloody record of history; extermination of natives in the process of colonization and the establishment of new settlements has happened in America, Australia, and Africa; slavery is one of the oldest institutions of mankind, and forced labor gangs, employed by the state for the performance of public works, were one of the mainstays of the Roman Empire. Even the claim to world rule, well known from the history of political dreams, is no monopoly of totalitarian governments and can still be explained by a fantastically exaggerated lust for power. All these aspects of totalitarian rule, hideous and criminal as they are, have one thing in common which separates them from the phenomenon with which we are dealing: In distinction from the concentration camps, they have a definite purpose and they benefit the rulers in much the same way as an ordinary burglary benefits the burglar. The motives are clear and the means to achieve the goal are utilitarian in the accepted sense of the term. The extraordinary difficulty we have in attempting to understand the institution of the concentration camp and to fit it into the record of human history is precisely the absence of such utilitarian criteria, an absence which is more than anything else responsible for the curious air of unreality that surrounds this institution and everything connected with it.

In order to understand more clearly the difference between the comprehensible and the incomprehensible, that is, between those data which respond to our commonly accepted research techniques and scientific concepts and those which explode this whole framework of reference, it may be useful to recall the various stages in which Nazi anti-Semitism unfolded from the moment of Hitler's rise to power in 1933 up to the establishment of the death factories in the midst of the war. Anti-Semitism by itself has such a long and bloody history that the very fact that the death factories were chiefly fed with Jewish "material" has somewhat obliterated the uniqueness of this "operation." Nazi anti-Semitism, moreover, showed an almost striking lack of originality; it did not contain a single element, either in its ideological expression or propagandistic application, which could not be traced back to earlier movements and which did not already constitute a cliché in the literature of Jew hatred before the Nazis ever existed. The anti-Jewish legislation in Hitler Germany during the thirties, culminating in the issuance of the Nuremberg Laws in 1935, was new in terms of nineteenth- and twentieth-century events; it was neither new as the avowed goal of anti-Semitic parties all over Europe nor new in terms of earlier Jewish history. The ruthless elimination of Jews from the German economy between 1936 and 1938 and the pogroms in November 1938 were still within the framework of what one would expect to happen if an anti-Semitic party seized the monopoly of power in a European country. The next step, the establishment of ghettos in Eastern Europe and the concentration of all Jews in them during the first years of the war, could hardly surprise any careful observer. All this appeared hideous and criminal but entirely rational. The anti-Jewish legislation in Germany aimed at satisfying popular demands, the elimination of Jews from the overcrowded professions seemed destined to make place for a seriously underemployed generation of intellectuals; forced emigration, with all its concomitants of plain robbery after 1938, was calculated to spread anti-Semitism throughout the world, as a memo of the German Foreign Office to all officials abroad succinctly pointed out;[5] the herding of the Jews into Eastern European ghettos followed by some distribution of their possessions among the native population seemed to be a marvelous political stratagem to win over the large anti-Semitic segments of Eastern European peoples, to console them for their loss of political independence and frighten them with the example of a people who suffered so far worse a fate. What could be expected in addition to these measures were starvation diets on the one hand and forced labor on the other during the war; in case of victory, all these measures seemed to be the preparation for the announced project of establishing a Jewish reservation in Madagascar.[6] As a matter of fact, such measures (and not death factories) were expected not only by the outside world and the Jewish people themselves but by the highest German officials in the administration of the Occupied Eastern Territories, by the military authorities, and even by high ranking officers in the Nazi party hierarchy.[7]

Neither the fate of European Jewry nor the establishment of death factories can be fully explained and grasped in terms of anti-Semitism. Both transcend anti-Semitic reasoning as well as the political, social, and economic motives behind the propaganda of anti-Semitic movements. Anti-Semitism only prepared the ground to make it easier to start the extermination of peoples with the Jewish people. We know now that this extermination program of Hitler did not stop short of planning the liquidation of large sections of the German people.[8]

The Nazis themselves, or rather that part of the Nazi party which, under the inspiration of Himmler and with the help of the SS troops, actually initiated extermination policies, were in no doubt as to the fact that they had entered an altogether different realm of activities, that they were doing something which not even their worst enemies expected them to do. They were quite convinced that one of the best chances for the success of this enterprise lay in the extreme improbability that anybody in the outside world would believe it to be true.[9] For the truth was that while all other anti-Jewish measures made some sense and were likely to benefit their authors in some way, the gas chambers did not benefit anybody. The deportations themselves, during a period of acute shortage of rolling stock, the establishment of costly factories, the manpower employed and badly needed for the war effort, the general demoralizing effect on the German military forces as well as on the population in the occupied territories—all this interfered disastrously with the war in the East, as the military authorities as well as Nazi officials, in protest against the SS troops, pointed out repeatedly.[10] Such considerations, however, were not simply overlooked by those who had put themselves in charge of extermination. Even Himmler knew that in a time of a critical shortage of labor, he was eliminating a large amount of workers who at least could have been worked to death instead of being killed without any productive purpose. And the office of Himmler issued one order after another warning the military commanders as well as the officials of the Nazi hierarchy that no economic or military considerations were to interfere with the extermination program.[11]

The extermination camps appear within the framework of totalitarian terror as the most extreme form of concentration camps. Extermination happens to human beings who for all practical purposes are already "dead." Concentration camps existed long before totalitarianism made them the central institution of government,[12] and it has always been characteristic of them that they were no penal institutions and that their inmates were accused of no crime, but that by and large they were destined to take care of "undesirable elements," that is, of people who for one reason or another were deprived of their judicial person and their rightful place within the legal framework of the country in which they happened to live. It is interesting to note that totalitarian concentration camps were first established for people who had committed a "crime," that is, the crime of opposition to the regime in power, but that they increased as political opposition decreased and that they expanded when the reservoir of people genuinely hostile to the regime was exhausted. The early Nazi camps were bad enough, but they were quite comprehensible: They were run by the SA with bestial methods and had the obvious aim to spread terror, kill outstanding politicians, deprive the opposition of its leaders, frighten would-be leaders into obscurity, and satisfy the SA men's desire to revenge themselves not only upon their immediate opponents but also upon members of the higher classes. In this respect, the SA terror clearly constituted a compromise between the regime, which at that time did not wish to lose its potent industrial protectors, and the movement which had been led to expect a real revolution. Complete pacification of the anti-Nazi opposition seems to have been achieved by January 1934; this at least was the opinion of the Gestapo itself and of high-ranking Nazi officials.[13] By 1936 the sympathies of the overwhelming majority of the people for the new regime had been won: Unemployment had been liquidated, the living standard of the lower classes was steadily rising, and the more potent sources of social resentment had all but dried out. Consequently the population of the concentration camps reached an all-time low for the simple reason that there no longer existed any active or even suspected opponents whom one could take into "protective custody."

It is after 1936, in other words, after the pacification of the country, that the Nazi movement became more radical and more aggressive on the domestic as well as on the international scene. The less enemies Nazism encountered within Germany and the more friends it gained abroad the more intolerant and the more extremist became "the revolutionary principle."[14] The concentration camps began their new increase in 1938 with the mass arrests of all male German Jews during the November pogroms; but this development had already been announced by Himmler in 1937 when, during a speech to the higher officer staff of the Reichswehr, he explained that one would have to reckon with a "fourth theater in case of war, internal Germany."[15] No reality whatsoever corresponded to these "fears," and the chief of the German police knew this better than anyone else. When war broke out a year later, he did not even bother to keep up the pretense and use his SS troops for police duties inside Germany but sent them at once to the eastern territories where they arrived when military actions had been successfully concluded in order to take over the occupation of the defeated countries. Later, when the party had decided to bring the whole army under its exclusive control, Himmler did not hesitate to send his SS companies to the front.

The main duty of the SS, however, was and remained even during the war the control and administration of concentration camps, from which the SA was completely eliminated. (Only during the last years of the war did the SA again play some minor role in the camp system, but then the SA troops were under the supervision of the SS.) It is this type of concentration camp rather than its earlier form which strikes us as a new and at first glance incomprehensible phenomenon.

Only a fraction of the inmates of these new camps, usually survivors from earlier years, could be regarded as opponents of the regime. Greater was the percentage of criminals, who were sent to the camps after they had served their normal prison terms, and of the so-called asocial element, homosexuals, vagabonds, work shirkers, and the like. The overwhelming majority of people who formed the bulk of the camp population was completely innocent from the point of view of the regime, quite harmless in every respect, guilty neither of political convictions nor of criminal actions.

A second characteristic of the camps, such as they were established by Himmler under SS rule, was their permanent character. Compared to Buchenwald, which in 1944 housed more than 80,000 prisoners, all earlier camps lose their significance.[16] Even more obvious is the permanent character of the gas chambers whose costly apparatus made the hunting for new "material" for the fabrication of corpses almost a necessity.

Of great importance for the development of the concentration-camp society was the new type of camp administration. The earlier cruelty of the SA troops who had been allowed to run wild and kill whomsoever they pleased, was replaced by a regulated death rate[17] and a strictly organized torture, calculated not so much to inflict death as to put the victim into a permanent status of dying. Large parts of the inner administration were given into the hands of the prisoners themselves who were forced to mistreat their fellow prisoners in much the same way the SS did. As time went on and the system became more established, torture and mistreatment became more and more the prerogative of the so-called *Kapos*. These measures were not accidental and hardly due to the growing size of the camps. In a number of instances, the SS was expressly ordered to have executions carried out only by prisoners. Similarly, mass murder not only in the form of gassing, but also in the form of mass execution in ordinary camps, became as mechanized as possible.[18] The result was that the population in the SS camps lived much longer than in the earlier camps; one has the impression that new waves of terror or deportation to extermination camps occurred only when new supplies were assured.

The administration was given into the hands of the criminals who formed the unchallenged camp aristocracy until, in the early forties, Himmler reluctantly yielded to outside pressure and allowed the camps to be exploited for productive labor. From then on, the political prisoners, mostly old-timers, were promoted to the position of the camp elite, because the SS soon found it impossible to have any work performed under the chaotic conditions of the former aristocracy of criminals. In no instance was the administration given into the hands of the largest and obviously least harmful group of completely innocent inmates. On the contrary, this category always belonged to the lowest level of the internal social hierarchy of the camps, suffered the heaviest losses through deportation, and was most exposed to cruelty. In other words, in a concentration camp it was by far safer to be a murderer or a Communist than simply a Jew, Pole, or Ukrainian.

As to the SS guards themselves, we must unfortunately discard the notion that they constituted a kind of negative elite of criminals, sadists, and half-insane persons—a notion that is largely true for the earlier SA troops who used to volunteer for concentration-camp duty. All evidence points to the fact that the SS men in charge were completely normal; their selection was achieved according to all kinds of fantastic principles,[19] none of which could possibly ensure the selection of especially cruel or sadistic men. Moreover, the administration of the camps was run in such a way that it appears to be beyond doubt that within this whole system the prisoners did not fail to fulfill the same "duties" as the guards themselves.

Most difficult to imagine and most gruesome to realize is perhaps the complete isolation which separated the camps from the surrounding world as if they and their inmates were no longer part of the world of the living. This isolation, already characteristic of all earlier forms of concentration camps, but carried to perfection only under totalitarian regimes, can hardly be compared to the isolation of prisons, ghettos, or forced labor camps. Prisons are never really removed from society, of which they are an important part and to whose laws and controls they are subject. Forced labor as well as other forms of slavery do not involve absolute segregation; laborers by the very fact of their work come constantly in contact with the surrounding world, and slaves were never really eliminated from the environment. Ghettos of the Nazi type have the closest similarity to the isolation of concentration camps; but in them families, and not individuals, were segregated so that they constituted a kind of closed society where an appearance of normal life was being carried on and sufficient social relationships existed to create at least an image of being and belonging together.

Nothing of this kind is true for concentration camps. From the moment of his arrest, nobody in the outside world was supposed to hear of the prisoner again; it is as if he had disappeared from the surface of the earth; he was not even pronounced dead. The earlier custom of the SA to inform the family of the death of a concentration-camp inmate by mailing to them the zinc coffin or an urn, was abolished and replaced by strict instructions to the effect that "third persons (are to be left) in uncertainty as to the whereabouts of prisoners.... This also includes the fact that the relatives may not learn anything when such prisoners die in concentration camps."[20]

The supreme goal of all totalitarian governments is not only the freely admitted, long-range ambition to global rule but also the never-admitted and immediately realized attempt at the total domination of man. The concentration camps are the laboratories in the experiment of total domination, for human nature being what it is, this goal can be achieved only under the extreme circumstances of a human-made hell. Total domination is achieved when the human person, who somehow is always a specific mixture of spontaneity and being conditioned, has been transformed into a completely conditioned being whose reactions can be calculated even when he is led to certain death. This disintegration of personality is carried through in different stages, the first being the moment of arbitrary arrest when the judicial person is being destroyed, not because of the injustice of the arrest but because the arrest stands in no connection whatsoever with the actions or opinions of the person. The second stage of destruction concerns the moral personality and is achieved through the separation of concentration camps from the rest of the world, a separation which makes martyrdom senseless, empty and ridiculous. The last stage is the destruction of individuality itself and is brought about through the permanence and institutionalizing of torture. The end result is the reduction of human beings to the lowest possible denominator of "identical reactions."

It is with a society of such human beings, each at a different stage on its way to becoming a bundle of reliable reactions, that the social sciences are called upon to deal when they try to investigate the social conditions of the camps. It is in this atmosphere that the amalgamation of criminals, political opponents, and "innocent" people takes place, that ruling classes rise and fall, that interior hierarchies emerge and disappear, that hostility against the SS guards or the camp administration gives way to complicity, that the inmates assimilate themselves to the outlook on life of their persecutors, although the latter rarely attempt to indoctrinate them.[21] The unreality which surrounds the hellish experiment, which is so strongly felt by the inmates themselves and makes the guards, but also the prisoners, forget that murder is being committed when somebody or many are killed, is as strong a handicap for a scientific approach as the nonutilitarian character of the institution. Only people who for one reason or another are no longer ruled by the common motives of self-interest and common sense could indulge in a fanaticism of pseudoscientific convictions (the laws of life or nature) which for all immediate practical purposes (winning the war or exploitation of labor) was quite obviously self-defeating. "Normal men do not know that everything is possible,"[22] said one of the survivors of Buchenwald. Social scientists, being normal men, will have great difficulties to understand that limitations which usually are thought to be inherent in the human condition could be transcended, that behavior patterns and motives which usually are identified, not with the psychology of some specific nation or class at some specific moment of its history, but with human psychology in general are abolished or play a quite secondary role, that objective necessities conceived as the ingredients of reality itself, adjustment to which seems a mere question of elementary sanity, could be neglected. Observed from the outside, victim and persecutor look as though they were both insane and the interior life of the camps reminds the onlooker of nothing so much as an insane asylum. Our common sense, trained in utilitarian thinking for which the good as well as the evil makes sense, is offended by nothing so much as by the complete senselessness of a world where punishment persecutes the innocent more than the criminal, where labor does not result and is not intended to result in products, where crimes do not benefit and are not even calculated to benefit their authors. For a benefit, expected to be realized in centuries,[23] can hardly be called an incentive, especially not in a situation of great military emergency.

The fact that due to an insane consistency this whole program of extermination and annihilation could be deduced from the premises of racism is even more perplexing, for the ideological supersense, enthroned, as it were, over a world of fabricated senselessness, explains "everything" and therefore nothing. Yet, there is very little doubt that the perpetrators of these unprecedented crimes committed them for the sake of their ideology which they believed to be proved by science, experience, and the laws of life.

Confronted with the numerous reports from survivors, which in remarkable monotony always "report but do not communicate" the same horrors and the same reactions,[24] one is almost tempted to draw up a list of phenomena which do not fit into the most general notions we have of human being and behavior. We do not know and can only guess why the criminals withstood the disintegrating influences of camp life longer than other categories and why the innocents in all instances were those who disintegrated most quickly.[25] It seems that in this extreme situation it was more important to an individual that his sufferings could be interpreted as punishment for some real crime or some real defiance against the ruling group than to have a so-called good conscience. The complete absence of even rudimentary regret on the side of the persecutors, on the other side, after the close of the war when some gesture of self-accusation might have been helpful in court, together with the ever-repeated assurances that responsibility for the crimes rested with some superior authorities, seem to indicate that fear of responsibility is not only stronger than conscience but even stronger, under certain circumstances, than fear of death. We know that the object of the concentration camps was to serve as laboratories in training people to become bundles of reactions, in making them behave like Pavlov's dog, in eliminating from the human psychology every trace of spontaneity; but we can only guess how far this is actually possible—and the terrible docility with which all people went to their certain death under camp conditions as well as the surprisingly small percentage of suicides are frightful indications[26]—and what happens to human social and individual behavior once this process has been carried to the limit of the possible. We know of the general atmosphere of unreality of which the survivors give such uniform accounts; but we can only guess in what forms human life is being lived when it is lived as though it took place on another planet.

While our common sense is perplexed when confronted with actions which are neither passion inspired nor utilitarian, our ethics is unable to cope with crimes which the Ten Commandments did not foresee. It is senseless to hang a man for murder who took part in the fabrication of corpses (although of course we hardly have any other course of action). These were crimes which no punishment seems to fit because all punishment is limited by the death penalty.

The greatest danger for a proper understanding of our recent history is the only too comprehensible tendency of the historian to draw analogies. The point is that Hitler was not like Jenghiz Khan and not worse than some other great criminal but entirely different. The unprecedented is neither the murder itself nor the number of victims and not even "the number of persons who united to perpetrate them."[27] It is much rather the ideological nonsense which caused them, the mechanization of their execution, and the careful and calculated establishment of a world of the dying in which nothing any longer made sense.

NOTES

1. "If I should recite these horrors in words of my own, you would think me intemperate and unreliable," Justice Robert H. Jackson in his opening address to the Nuremberg trials. See *Nazi Conspiracy and Aggression* (Washington, D.C.: U.S. Government Printing Office, 1946) vol. 1, p. 140.

2. See Bruno Bettelheim's report "On Dachau and Buchenwald" in ibid., vol. 7, p. 824.

3. Goebbels reports the following in his diaries for March 1943: "The Fuehrer is happy ... that the Jews have been ... evacuated from Berlin. He is right in saying that the war has made possible for us the solution of a whole series of problems that could never have been solved in normal times. The Jews will certainly be the losers in this war come what may." *The Goebbels Diaries 1942–1943*, ed. Louis P. Lochner (New York: Doubleday, 1948), p. 314.

4. Jackson, in *Nazi Conspiracy*, vol. 2, p. 3.

5. The circular letter of January 1939 from the Ministry of Foreign Affairs to all German authorities abroad on "The Jewish Question as a Factor in German Foreign Policy in the Year 1938" stated: "The emigration movement of only about 100,000 Jews has already sufficed to awaken the interest if not the understanding of many countries in the Jewish danger. We can estimate that here the Jewish question will extend to a problem of international politics when large numbers of Jews from Germany, Poland, Hungary, and Rumania are put on the move.... Germany is very interested in maintaining the dispersal of Jewry ... the influx of Jews in all parts of the world invokes the opposition of the native population and thereby forms the best propaganda for the German Jewish policy.... The poorer and therefore the more burdensome the immigrating Jew is to the country absorbing him, the stronger this country will react." See *Nazi Conspiracy*, vol. 6, pp. 87ff.

6. This project was propagated by the Nazis at the beginning of the war. Alfred Rosenberg announced in a speech of January 15, 1939, that the Nazis would demand that "those people who are friendly disposed to Jews, above all the Western democracies who have so much space ... place an area outside of Palestine for the Jews, of course in order to establish a Jewish reserve and not a Jewish State." Ibid., p. 93.

7. It is very interesting to see in the Nazi documents published in *Nazi Conspiracy* and the *Trial of the Major War Criminals* (Nuremberg, 1947), how few people in the Nazi party itself had been prepared for extermination policies. Extermination was always carried out by the SS troops, upon the initiative of Himmler and Hitler, against the protests from the civilian and military authorities. Alfred Rosenberg, in charge of the administration of Russian-occupied territories, complained in 1942 that "new plenipotentiaries-in-chief (i.e. SS officers) endeavored to carry out direct actions in the occupied eastern territories, overlooking those dignitaries who were appointed by the Fuehrer himself" (i.e., Nazi officials outside of the SS). See *Nazi Conspiracy*,

vol. 4, pp. 65ff. Reports about conditions in the Ukraine during the fall of 1942 (*Nazi Conspiracy*, vol. 3, pp. 83ff.) show clearly that neither the *Wehrmacht* nor Rosenberg was aware of the depopulation plans of Hitler and Himmler. Hans Frank, governor general of Poland dared even in September 1943, when most party officials had been frightened into submission, to say during a meeting of the *Kriegswirtschaftsstabes und des Verteidigungsausschusses:* "Sie kennen ja die toerichte Einstellung der Minderwertigkeit der uns unterworfenen Voelker, und zwar in einem Augenblick, in welchem die Arbeitskraft dieser Voelker eine der wesentlichsten Potenzen unseres Siegringens darstellt." *Trial of the Major War Criminals* (Nuremberg: International Military Tribunal, 1948), vol. 29, p. 672.

8. During a discussion in Hitler's headquarters about measures to be carried out after the conclusion of the war, Hitler proposed a National Health Bill: "After national X-ray examination, the Fuehrer is to be given a list of sick persons, particularly those with lung and heart diseases. On the basis of the new Reich Health Law . . . these families will no longer be able to remain among the public and can no longer be allowed to produce children. What will happen to these families will be the subject of further orders of the Fuehrer." *Nazi Conspiracy*, vol. 7, p. 175.

9. "Imagine only that these occurrences would become known to the other side and exploited by them. Most likely such propaganda would have no effect only because people who hear and read about it simply would not be ready to believe it." From a secret report concerning the killing of 5,000 Jews in June 1943, *Nazi Conspiracy*, vol. 1, p. 1001.

10. It is noteworthy that protests from military authorities were less frequent and less violent than those of old party members. In 1942, Hans Frank stated emphatically that the responsibility for the annihilation of the Jews came from "higher quarters." And he goes on to say: "I was able to prove the other day . . . that [the interruption of a big building program] would not have happened if the many thousands of Jews working at it had not been deported." In 1944, he complains again and adds: "Once we have won the war, then for all I care, mince-meat can be made of the Poles and the Ukrainians and all the others who run around here." *Nazi Conspiracy*, vol. 4, pp. 902, 917. During an official meeting in Warsaw in January 1943, State Secretary Krueger voiced the concern of the occupying forces: "The Poles say: After the Jews have been destroyed, then they will employ the same methods to get the Poles out of this territory and liquidate them just like the Jews." That this was indeed intended to be the next step is clear from a speech of Himmler in Cracow in March 1942. Ibid., vol. 4, p. 916 and vol. 3, pp. 640ff.

11. That "economic considerations should fundamentally remain unconsidered in the settlement of the (Jewish) problem" had to be repeated from 1941 onward. Ibid., vol. 6, p. 402.

12. Concentration camps made their first appearance during the Boer War, and the concept of "protective custody" was first used in India and South Africa.

13. In 1934, Reichsminister of the Interior, Wilhelm Frick, a party member of old standing, tried to issue a decree "stating that 'on the consideration' of the 'stabilizing of the national situation' and 'to reduce the abuses in connection with the infliction of protective custody,' 'the Reichsminister had decided' to place restrictions upon the exercise of protective custody." See *Nazi Conspiracy*, vol. 2, p. 259; cf. also vol. 7, p. 1099. This decree was never published and the practice of "protective custody" increased greatly in 1934.

According to a sworn affidavit of Rudolf Diels, former chief of the political police in Berlin and acting chief of the Gestapo in 1933, the political situation had become completely stabilized by January 1934. Ibid., vol. 5, p. 205.

14. In the words of Wilhelm Stuckart, state secretary of the Ministry of Interior. Ibid., vol. 8, p. 738.

15. See Heinrich Himmler, "On Organization and Obligation of the SS and the Police," in *National-politischer Lehrgang der Wehrmacht vom 15.–23. Januar 1937* (restricted for the Armed Forces). Translation in *Nazi Conspiracy*, vol. 4, pp. 616ff.

16. This table shows the numerical expansion and the death rate of the concentration camp Buchenwald during the years 1937–45. It was compiled from several lists, given in *Nazi Conspiracy*, vol. 4, pp. 800 *ff*.

Year	Arrivals	Camp Strength		Deceased[b]	Suicides
		High	Low		
1937	2,912	2,561	929	48	—
1938	20,122[a]	18,105	2,633	771	11
1939	9,553	12,775	5,392	1,235	3
1940	2,525	10,956	7,383	1,772	11
1941	5,896	7,911	6,785	1,522	17
1942	14,111[c]	10,075	7,601	2,898	3
1943	42,172	37,319	11,275[d]	3,516	2
1944	97,866	84,505	41,240	8,644	46
1945	42,823[e]	86,232	21,000[f]	13,056	16

[a] These were of course mostly Jews.
[b] The total of deceased is certainly higher and is estimated at 50,000.
[c] This figure shows the influx from the Eastern Occupied Territories.
[d] The difference between arrivals and camp strength, or between High and Low no longer indicates liberations but transports to other camps or to extermination camps.
[e] Only for the first three months of 1945.
[f] Camp strength at moment of liberation.

17. The following is an excerpt from a letter of December 1942 from the SS Main Office of Economic Administration to all camp commandants: "a compilation of the current arrivals and departures in all the concentration camps . . . discloses that out of 136,000 arrivals about 70,000 died. With such a high rate of death, the number of the prisoners can never be brought up to the figure as has been ordered by the Reichsfuehrer of the SS. . . . The Reichsfuehrer has ordered that the death rate absolutely must be reduced." Ibid., vol. 4, annex 2.

18. Ernest Feder in "Essai sur la psychologie de la terreur," in *Synthèses* (Brussels, 1946) reports an order of the SS to kill daily several hundred Russian prisoners of war by shooting through a hole without seeing the victim.

19. Himmler described his selection methods as follows: "I did not accept people under 1.7 m . . . because I know that people who have reached a certain height must possess the desired blood to some degree"; "On Organization." Translation in *Nazi Conspiracy*, vol. 4, p. 617. He also obtained photographs of the applicants who were asked to trace their ancestry back to 1750, to have no family members of ill political repute, to "acquire black trousers and boots from their own means," and, finally, to appear in person before a race commission.

20. *Nazi Conspiracy*, vol. 7, pp. 84ff. One of the many orders forbidding information on the whereabouts of prisoners, gave the following explanation: "The deterrent effect of these measures lies (a) in allowing the disappearance of the accused without a trace, (b) therein that no information whatsoever may be given about their whereabouts and their fate." Ibid., vol. 1, p. 146.

21. Under Himmler's regime, "any kind of instruction on an ideological basis" was expressly prohibited.

22. David Rousset, *The Other Kingdom* (New York: Reynal and Hitchcock, 1947).

23. It was Himmler's specialty to think in centuries. He expected the results of the war to be realized only "centuries later" in the form of "a Germanic World Empire" (see his speech at Kharkov, in April 1943; *Nazi Conspiracy*, vol. 4, pp. 572ff.); when confronted with the "deplorable loss of labor" caused by the death of "tens and hundreds" of prisoners, he insisted that this "thinking in terms of generations is not to be regretted." (See his speech at the meeting of the SS major generals at Posen, October 1943: ibid., vol. 4, pp. 558ff.) The SS troops were trained along similar lines. "Everyday problems do not interest us . . . we are only interested in ideological questions of importance for decades and centuries, so that the man . . . knows he is working for a great task which occurs but once in 2000 years." See his speech of 1937, in Himmler, "On Organization." Translation in *Nazi Conspiracy*, vol. 4, p. 626.

24. See *The Dark Side of the Moon* (New York: Scribner, 1947) a collection of reports from Polish survivors of Soviet concentration camps.

25. This fact is quite prominent in many published reports. It has been especially remarked and interpreted by Bruno Bettelheim, in his "Behavior in Extreme Situations," *Journal of Abnormal and Social Psychology* 38 (1943). Bettelheim speaks of the self-esteem of the criminals and the political prisoners as distinguished from the lack of self-respect in those who have not done anything. The latter "were least able to withstand the initial shock" and were the first to disintegrate. Bettelheim, however, is wrong when he thinks that this is due to the middle-class origin of the "innocents"— at his time mostly Jews; we know from other reports, especially also from the Soviet Union, that lower-class "innocents" disintegrate just as quickly.

26. This aspect is especially stressed in David Rousset, *Les Jours de Notre Mort* (Paris: Editions du Parois, 1947).

27. Jackson, in *Nazi Conspiracy*, vol. 2, p. 3.

19

THE CRISIS IN KNOWING AND UNDERSTANDING THE HOLOCAUST

Alan Rosenberg

> If we are to begin to understand ourselves we must somehow come to grips with the reality of Auschwitz.
>
> *Karl A. Schleunes, 1972*

> Humankind has very curiously and subtly, very ingeniously and systematically, prevented itself from reaching out to new types of reality. This is partly because we defend ourselves against a bolder type of extension of knowledge . . . man is forever at work keeping vast areas of unwelcome reality out of his view, trying especially to suppress knowledge of his own nature.
>
> *Gardner Murphy, 1975*

Holocaust studies are at a turning point. We know what happened; we are now challenged to *understand* this event, to move from recounting the facts to assimilating their *meanings*.[1]

The popular slogan "Never Again!" has captured the Jewish imagination. If we are to realize its intent, if we are to build a future in which another Holocaust will not happen, we shall have to generate understanding of what we know. We must pass beyond knowledge of the past as merely a matter of record to the point where the past becomes a moving principle of daily life, an existential commitment capable of effecting changes at every level of our social and political lives. We must take what George Santayana once called "the dead knowledge of what happens to have happened"[2] and transform it into an *understanding* capable of determining the future we hope for. To achieve understanding, I believe we must transcend the limits of the "Judeo-centric" approach to the Holocaust.[3] We must accept the challenge implicit in the words of the Protestant theologian, Robert McAfee Brown:

I think we are finally challenged by the Holocaust to the daring and frightening notion that an obscenity can be used as a way of forestalling other obscenities. If we can so affirm, then there is hope that the Holocaust, unredeemably evil in itself, could be a grotesque beacon, in the light of which we could gird ourselves against its repetition toward any people, in any time, in any place. And I believe that unless we can use it as such a beacon, the Nazis have finally won.[4]

Of course, it is true that nowadays we talk more about the Holocaust and the Nazi destruction of other people than we ever did before. It is also true that the Holocaust is being written about and taught about more than before. It is also a fact that approximately one hundred million people watched at least part of the television series "The Holocaust," and that across the world millions upon millions of others have seen it and other cinematic television treatments inspired by the same subject. But this astonishing upsurge of interest in the Holocaust (which may already be on the wane) does not mean that we have attempted to understand the significance of these events for our personal lives and for the societies in which we live.

Could an individual understand the significance of the Holocaust and have integrated it into his or her mental and moral world and yet remain an anti-Semite or a racist? The Holocaust would have been inconceivable without the "practice of social anti-Semitism," which undermined the ordinary Germans' ordinary decency and "their resistance . . . to the stigmatization and persecution to come."[5] Can ordinary Americans claim to have reflected seriously on the genocidal destruction that took place during the Second World War, and stand by while peoples once again are being destroyed?[6] Not only do we as a nation stand by while groups of people are being destroyed, we use the same language of indifference, as well as the same language of the empty gesture that was used by the onlooking nations during the Holocaust.

That is why I speak of a *crisis* that hinges on the difference between knowing and understanding the Holocaust. "It is not only true that the lessons of the Holocaust have not yet been learned, it is doubtful that they have been discovered."[7] As a result, we have yet to achieve the cultural integration of the meaning of the Holocaust, which is essential if the slogan "Never Again!" is to become a living reality. We must ask ourselves why we have failed. Is it because we are unwilling to face the meaning of the event? Are we so repelled by its sheer horror that we are unintentionally repressing the investigation of what it means in terms of the future of our civilization? Is it because we start with the a priori assumption that events of this sort are unintelligible? Have we so "mystified" the event itself that it seems somehow disconnected from our own age, something that happened on another planet entirely?[8] It seems clear to me that the crisis we face with regard to knowing and understanding the Holocaust is partly, if not largely, one of our own making.

Before I address those questions, I must comment on three specific issues relevant to my thesis. The first is the claim advanced by a number of writers, Elie Wiesel among them, that it is simply and finally *impossible* either to know or to understand the Holocaust. He could not be more succinct: "We shall never understand how Auschwitz was possible."[9] If this claim is correct, it would be futile even to attempt to discern what can be learned from the Holocaust. Its horrible facts would yield no understanding directed toward making the world free from genocide. However sympathetic I may be to Wiesel as a witness, I am compelled to reject his position. It is, in fact, possible for us to comprehend what the Holocaust uniquely shows us about the nature of human beings and the social conditions that made the Holocaust a historical fact. Not only is comprehension possible, it is necessary:

> It is the responsibility of the historian of modern history to prevent the isolation of Auschwitz from the mainstream of European history, to prevent the study of Auschwitz in an abstract void. It is the task of the historian, philosopher, thinker, theologian, and scholar, Christian and Jew alike, to anchor the Holocaust in European reality and culture.[10]

Clearly, there *are* factors that help make Auschwitz understandable. We can isolate institutional and political developments, as well as conceptual and ideological trends, that constituted enabling conditions for Hitler's enactment of his Final Solution. But we will never grasp them if we persist in the conviction that the Holocaust was an unintelligible anomaly, a historical aberration that "couldn't" happen. We must acknowledge the antecedent conditions of the Holocaust if we are to develop an understanding that will prevent them from ever prevailing again. We must acknowledge that the fact of Auschwitz implies a deep criticism of assumptions concerning the values of Western civilization, the nature of progress, and the impact of science and technology on human lives. Once we understand that criticism, we can begin to envisage how Western values and assumptions can be so transformed or reconstructed that another Auschwitz becomes impossible.[11] These are only first steps, however. For the *actual* transformation of values, of conceptual structures, and of institutions that implement those values, is an infinitely more complex and demanding task than merely identifying what went wrong in the past.[12]

My second preliminary point concerns the two key terms in the title of my essay: "knowing" and "understanding." The distinction that I make between them may already be apparent. Let me reinforce it by citing Saul Friedländer: "Three decades have increased our knowledge of the events as such, but not our understanding of them. There is no clearer perspective today, no deeper comprehension than immediately after the war."[13] We have increased our factual knowledge of the events that make up the Holocaust, Friedländer suggests, but we have still not grasped their significance for the world we live in. What Friedländer is pointing to is a difference between knowing and understanding.[14] *Knowing*, in this context, refers to factual information or the process by which it is gathered. *Understanding*, on the other hand, refers to systematically grasping the significance of an event in such a way that it becomes integrated into one's moral and intellectual life. Understanding the Holocaust in this sense would radically change how one experiences and acts in the world. The Holocaust would become a standard for evaluating both one's own behavior and that of one's society. One can know a great deal about the Holocaust without understanding it. Facts can be absorbed without their having any impact on the way we understand ourselves or the world we live in. Facts in themselves do not make a difference; it is the understanding of them that makes a difference. As Bruno Bettelheim states, "It is the most common reaction to the Holocaust—to remember it as a historical fact, but to deny or repress its psychological impact which would require a restructuring of one's personality and a different world view from that which one has heretofore embraced."[15] Those who integrate the Holocaust into consciousness find that their world becomes a different world and that they must generate a new way to be in the new world. Since each person's way of being in the world is relatively fixed—and serves as protection against the anxieties of the unknown—integration is extremely hard. To give up a world in which one's life makes sense means undergoing great loss. Yet, without the readiness to risk that loss we cannot hope to pursue understanding.[16]

My third preliminary consideration is this: The factors that tend to "mystify" the Holocaust—or otherwise block our understanding of its profound significance for the future of our civilization—must be identified and analyzed. These blocks must be challenged and removed, even if we may sometimes find the process a painful one, even if we may sometimes appear to be critical of Holocaust writers who have earned our respect and gratitude. For the very language that they use often stands in the way of deeper understanding.[17] Once again, I turn to Elie Wiesel to illustrate my point, not because his language is unique in this regard, but because it is typical. Here is Wiesel: "to substitute words, any words, for it [the Holocaust] is to distort it."[18] Now, either this claim is trivial since no historical event can be fully captured in language, or it raises a central issue. If it is impossible to express the Holocaust within language, how then can we understand it? And if we cannot know and understand it, how can we learn from it in order to make "Never Again!" a reality? Every formulation of an event opens as well as closes avenues of inquiry. Formulations that prevent us from moving forward in the pursuit of understanding block our efforts, by blocking our perception. Events emerge only in and through the formulations we use to articulate them. To know and understand the Holocaust we must analyze and criticize all formulations that block further inquiry. Unless we remove them, we cannot get on with the task at hand, preventing future genocides.

In sum, then, we must bear three things in mind as we approach the crisis in understanding the Holocaust. As we write about it, and teach about it, we must try to avoid presenting it in such a way that understanding is foreclosed at the outset. Without diminishing our revulsion at the facts, we must not suggest that the Holocaust is so inhuman, so horrible, that it is completely and forever beyond the grasp of human understanding. If what happened cannot be explained, if understanding cannot grapple with the significance of the Holocaust, we will be powerless to prevent it from happening again. Second, we must be clear that it is not enough simply to *know* what happened. We must strive for that deeper comprehension that will actually lead us, through critical analysis, to an understanding of how it was possible. Only then can we institute those changes that will prevent it from happening again. Finally, we must not be afraid to formulate the meaning of the event in terms that may take away some of its "uniqueness." Unless we are able to see the Holocaust in relation to other genocidal events, our efforts at preventing it from happening again will be blocked. In the end our understanding of the Holocaust is increased—not diminished—when we permit ourselves to grasp its generic relationship with other genocidal events, to see both how it resembles them and how it is genuinely unique.

Having made the decision that the Holocaust can and must be the object of our understanding, we must prepare ourselves to deal with a number of difficulties. First of all, there is the human tendency to forget. We repress traumas in our own lives and tragedies in the historical lives of others. The tendency to blot out the darkest pages of human history is nearly universal.[19] Yet we must want to remember them if we are to profit from them.[20] To remember, we must be willing to enter the anxiety and despair that the Holocaust evokes. The process is painful. The pain is inseparable from understanding. The road to understanding passes through anguish.[21] That anguish is particularly acute among survivors who struggle to forget at the same time that they want themselves and the world to remember and to understand.[22] So complex is the task of remembering that only recently has Israel required inclusion of the Holocaust as a regular part of its school curriculum.[23]

But these dimensions of the problem are not novel. The novelty stems from another source: A large part of the world *wants* to forget the Holocaust; it acts as if it never happened; it even resents being reminded of it. The novelist François Mauriac perceived the truth some thirty years ago: "We want to forget that we are implicated in the [Holocaust], all of us, simply because we are human beings: this is what man is capable of."[24] Or, as George M. Kren says:

> Study of the Holocaust creates new feelings of personal vulnerability, following from the knowledge that these things are possible. One learns that the victims and the executioners are not different from oneself, and that under the right circumstances one could become either a victim or an executioner.[25]

Our civilization on the whole would like to forget or minimize the event, not only because many of its major institutions actively or passively participated in it, but also because the Holocaust shakes the value structure of this civilization to its very core. When taken seriously, the Holocaust demands a thorough re-evaluation of most of the values that we in the West hold dear—certainly a process no culture likes to be forced to undergo.[26]

Ironically, the desire to forget, or to ignore, receives support from those formulations that claim that the Holocaust *cannot* be understood. By maintaining that the event cannot be represented by language, or that only the survivors can know and understand its meaning, we provide excuses for those who would rather forget than remember.

Another difficulty facing us is the relatively short span of time separating us from the actuality of the Holocaust. It took place only forty-three years ago, only yesterday on the scale of historical time. The full significance of such a momentous event cannot emerge overnight. The necessary "philosophical and historiosophical systems . . . require a long perspective to come into being and crystalize."[27]

Nevertheless, although forty-three years may be insufficient for the significant implications of the Holocaust to have penetrated our understanding, by now there ought to be some apparent signs of the recognition of its significance. Emil Fackenheim gives voice to that expectation: "The passage of time has brought the Holocaust closer rather than moving it farther away, disclosing that the world has thus far shied away from it but must at length confront it with unyielding realism and, if necessary, despair."[28]

Perhaps the world has shied away from trying to understand the Holocaust because of the way it has been presented. It is often portrayed, understandably enough, as a horror story. To overlook or to minimize its horror would certainly distort our knowledge and perception of the Holocaust. Such presentations, however, usually stop with horror. Limited to recounting atrocities and brutalities, attempting to extract no wider implications from the event, they assault and overwhelm our emotions—and in the end either suffocate us or cause us to turn away.[29] Alice L. and A. Roy Eckardt address this danger:

> There is the danger that the Holocaust will be appropriated only as a nightmare, a horrible episode that erupted within a brief span of years as part of a special ideological development or political tragedy or whim of an insane man, a nightmare from which we have long awakened. There is the temptation to reduce the Holocaust to an aberration, a kind of cultural-moral mutation. In consequence, a needed comprehension of the event as the logical and inevitable climax of a lengthy and indestructible ethos-tradition and theological obsession may be lost.[30]

The task in presenting the Holocaust is to do simultaneous justice to two contrarieties: Its inhuman horror versus its human creation:

> The description of the Holocaust must somehow incorporate the full horror of what happened rather than recasting it too rapidly as just another fact of history requiring explanation. And yet, at the same time, we must admit that that is all it is, just another fact, produced by humans under determinate conditions.[31]

A study of the NBC-TV's "Holocaust" program by the American-Jewish Committee gives some sense of how difficult this task may be. When viewers were polled on the question, "What are the main ideas or impressions that the Holocaust left with you?" the largest response (27 percent) was horror, the senselessness of the event. Nearly one-fifth (19 percent) said that the program has taught them a lesson—that it should not be allowed to happen again. Ironically, only 7 percent of the viewers were upset by the depictions of violence and brutality. And 11 percent—the same number that expressed sympathy with the victims—gave no answer whatsoever.[32]

The disparity between the number left with an impression of senseless horror after viewing the program and the low number of those upset by the actual depictions of violence and brutality is puzzling. But all too clear is the message of senseless horror that the program, despite good intentions, imparted to its audience.

Indeed, it can be argued that the actual experience of the horrors or knowing about the horrors lies at the center of a whole cluster of difficulties that hinder our ability to investigate the significance of the Holocaust.[33] The shock of experiencing Auschwitz or Warsaw, or even the awareness of what the Nazis had planned for the Jews and the non-Aryan peoples, was so overwhelming that in response, as mechanisms of defense, certain formulations of the events were generated. These formulations did serve a positive function, at least in the beginning, since they created a distance from the horror and made healing possible. But they also became serious obstacles to understanding.

To account for the need to develop defensive mechanisms to deal with the Holocaust, we may turn to Leon Festinger's theory of cognitive dissonance. Briefly stated, "this theory centers around the idea that if a person knows various things that are not psychologically consistent with each other, he will in a variety of ways try to make them consistent."[34] One of the ways of maintaining psychological consistence is to "actively avoid situations and information which would be likely to increase dissonance."[35] One way of not having to confront the massive psychological dislocations generated by the Holocaust, is to declare the event incomprehensible. As Bruno Bettelheim has pointed out, some people found that it was "better to declare the Holocaust unimaginable, unspeakable, because only then could one avoid facing the full horror of what happened in its details, which would be extremely upsetting, guilt-provoking and anxiety-creating."[36] Other claims have the same effect. For example:

1. The Holocaust transcends language, is beyond articulation.
2. The Holocaust is unique, a historical aberration.
3. The Holocaust is an irrational event, the product of *pathological* individuals.
4. The Holocaust is meaningless.
5. The Holocaust can only be known and understood by survivors.
6. The Holocaust is incomprehensible; it is beyond the *reach* of method.

Each assertion reduces anxiety but blocks inquiry.

Of particular importance here is the unintended block to understanding often erected by survivors' testimony. Elie Wiesel states that "whoever has not lived through it can never know it. And whoever has lived through it can never fully reveal it."[37] To those who are not survivors, he is emphatic:

You, who never lived under a sky of blood, will never know what it was like. Even if you read all the books ever written, even if you listen to all the testimonies ever given, you will remain on this side of the wall, you will view the agony and death of a people from afar, through the screen of a memory which is not your own.[38]

Those words are eloquent, in one sense true, and at the same time dangerous. Taken literally, they may discourage us from even trying to understand, and thus defeat Wiesel's very purpose. For Wiesel surely wants us to understand and to take all steps necessary to see that no future child or adult has to live through the agony he has known.

Moreover, the survivors' frequent reminder that we have failed them, that we have not made the world safe from another Holocaust, may perversely have the opposite of its intended effect: "Nothing has been learned: Auschwitz has not served as a warning," Wiesel laments. "For more details consult your daily newspaper."[39] Does such hyperbole serve its purpose? On the one hand we are told that we cannot understand the Holocaust if we have not lived through it, and on the other we are told that it is of the utmost importance that we learn the profound lesson implicit in the event and that our evident failure to do so is a bitter disappointment to the survivors.[40]

There is a fundamental confusion at the root of this dilemma. It is a confusion between knowledge by direct experience (which survivors alone can possess) and knowledge about something experienced indirectly. This second kind of knowledge, which philosophers often call "reflective," as opposed to "immediate," we *can* hope to achieve.[41] We cannot relive the experience of the survivors. We cannot have an immediate experience of the full and actual horror of the events. What the survivors are telling us, then, is that we cannot know Auschwitz or the Warsaw ghetto as an immediate experience.

This, however, does not mean that we cannot know about the Holocaust. There is no reason we should not try, as we do with other events of historical importance, to know and to understand the factors that gave rise to the context that made Auschwitz and Warsaw possible. Nor is there anything—except a lack of will and a desire for avoidance—that makes it impossible to understand the implications of the Holocaust for our civilization and time. The survivors have unintentionally presented us with a serious contradiction, which inhibits our ability to accomplish the task they demand from us, by not appreciating the crucial epistemological distinction between knowing by experience and knowing about.

In addition to this contradiction, the nature of survivors' accounts adds difficulties to attempts to understand the Holocaust. Both Lucy

Dawidowicz and Emil Fackenheim have pointed out that we cannot take for granted that survivors' accounts will be factually correct.[42] On many of the key issues concerning the Holocaust survivors radically disagree. One needs only to compare Bettelheim's portrayal of concentration-camp life with that of Alexander Donat to see how greatly accounts can differ. But accuracy is less vexing a problem than that suggested by Fackenheim:

> It is normally assumed that, with all due allowance for bias of perception and memory, the eyewitness is the most reliable source of "what actually happened." When the eyewitness is caught in a scheme of things systematically calculated to deceive him, subsequent reflection is necessary if truth is to be given to his testimony.[43]

Fackenheim's insight has not received the attention it deserves. During the Holocaust, the persecuted were purposefully deceived about the nature of what was happening.[44] As a result, the survivors' reports cannot be taken at face value. The survivor may have been fooled. Although the accounts of the survivors remain an invaluable source for knowing and understanding the Holocaust, we must nevertheless treat them as we would any other important historical record. We must evaluate their accuracy, but we must proceed with care.

To begin with, we must keep in mind that formulations of the meanings of the Holocaust, like all historical constructions, necessarily involve selectivity and judgments on three levels. The eyewitness judges the materials of his experience and selects from them what he chooses to preserve in memory and written record. That memory or record is then supplemented by what can be learned from the public record, from official documents, statistics, other eyewitness accounts. Once again selectivity and value judgments are present. Finally, we, as inquirers into the explanation and meaning of what happened, make our own selections and form our own judgments. These will inevitably reflect our own concerns and those of the age in which we live. The presence of all three levels of selection and judgment permits a simultaneous analysis of three different "presents." Coherence of explanation is reached when, through synthesis of these perspectives, a meaningful historical construction emerges. What results is never the event "as such—as it was in itself. For when an event is analyzed and explained, when it enters into history, it is not what it was before it was subjected to the scrutiny of inquiry. As John Dewey has pointed out concerning this problem of inquiry into the events of the human past:

> As soon as the event takes its place as an incident in a particular history, an act of judgment has loosened it from the total complex

of which it was a part, and has given it a place in a new context, the context and place both being determinations made in inquiry, not native properties of original existence.[45]

This, of course, is true of all subjects of inquiry, and applies not merely to historical events. For no subject matter emerges from inquiry untouched and unchanged. Meaning is elicited through the experience of inquiry; understanding is created and it is joined with the event. In the end, it is only through such processes of inquiry that the experiences of survivors can become joined with our own.

We can do justice to the witness of the survivors, I believe, only by approaching their testimony in this fashion. By conjoining contemporary accounts of others, of the persecutors as well as the persecuted, we may yet comprehend what has been termed incomprehensible. It may be objected that the Holocaust is different from all other historical events, including other genocidal catastrophes, that it is "unique" and therefore incomprehensible in a way that other apparently similar events are not. It may be objected that there is something about the Holocaust—perhaps the sheer size and extent of the destruction, perhaps the special nature of the target population, or perhaps the particular motives and intentions of the perpetrators—that sets the Holocaust apart from all other examples of genocide.[46]

We must evaluate in this light suggestions that we will never be able to comprehend what it was like to be a victim. It is in this light that we must try to understand Fackenheim's despair when he says that "despite all necessary attempts to comprehend it, the Nazi system in the end exceeds all comprehension. One cannot comprehend but only confront and object."[47] And it is in this same light that we must interpret the tragic implications of Nora Levin's view that "the Holocaust refuses to go the way of most history, not only because of the magnitude of the destruction . . . but because the events surrounding it are still in a very real sense humanly incomprehensible . . . indeed comprehensibility may never be possible."[48] But, at the same time, *we must not allow such statements to mystify the events.* We must take Andrew Greeley seriously when he warns that "if one is told often enough that one cannot understand one eventually stops trying."[49]

The only acceptable meaning we can give to the claim of incomprehensibility is the one that applies to every historical event of cataclysmic proportions. We begin by using the method at hand. We seek to understand by using categories that have worked in the past, the traditional presuppositions of the social scientist. Later, we may come to realize that because this event exceeds the usual categories of explanation, we must develop new categories. Such cataclysms may make our customary categories of explanation obsolete. For they are radically different events in that they are not merely continuations of the moral processes of civilization. They instead embody radical transformational implications, implications that go to the very roots of civilization itself, striking at the most fundamental values and beliefs upon which that civilization is founded. Such were the fall of the Roman Empire, the Reformation, and the French Revolution. By their nature they forced upon us the need to reevaluate the existing categories and modes of inquiry and explanation that had provided legitimation for the institutions and concepts that these events rendered null and void. Refinement and development in the modes of inquiry and explanation must be a continual process, for each new generation comes to terms with past historical events through reinterpretation tempered by its own particular social milieu, perspective, and concerns. As perspectives shift and interpretations change, our understanding is modified. Were this not the case, history would have been a dead end from the beginning. Saint Augustine wrote his *City of God* in response to the cataclysmic event of his time, the fall and sack of Rome by the barbarians. He tried to reinterpret human history and analyze the causes of this particular event in the light of the formulations he originated and developed from the perspectives and explanations of Christian revelation. Today his interpretation and explanation of the fall of Rome form one of a number of perspectives available to us. The worth of Augustine's original insights is not diminished because later interpretations have provided alternatives to them. It should be obvious that each new attempt to interpret and explain a cataclysmic event is an admission that no one perspective, no one mode of explanation, no single interpretation, is sufficient to exhaust understanding of the event. The meanings of such events emerge only as we open ourselves to new avenues of inquiry and reinterpretation, entirely new categories of understanding. It also requires that such efforts be continuous. It is not surprising, therefore, that Fackenheim should say of the Holocaust: "The event . . . resists explanation—the historical kind that seeks causes, and the theological kind that seeks meaning and purpose. . . . More precisely, the better the mind succeeds with the necessary task of explaining what can be explained, the more it is shattered by its ultimate failure."[50] For the task *is* formidable and does threaten to shatter the mind that attempts to grasp it in conventional terms. And yet Fackenheim cannot mean that we must give up the task, that we must not seek new and, perhaps, unconventional means of understanding what happened. For, if we give up the task, what are we to tell our children? What are we to teach our students? Are we simply to say that the Holocaust happened, and that we have no understanding of it? Are we to succumb to the mystification of the event?

We cannot allow ourselves to be deterred from the task of trying to understand the Holocaust by the claim that it is, in the end, utterly beyond our human power of comprehension. We must, I believe, approach the Holocaust as we would any other major historical event that has potential to transform the fundamental precepts and principles upon which the civilization in which it occurs are based. We must seek an understanding of that transformational potential within the arcana of the Holocaust itself if we are not to make a bitter mockery of the words "Never Again!" Michael Berenbaum writes: "We cannot begin the process of learning [about the Holocaust] with the statement that one will never know, nor can we allow mystery to obscure those dimensions of reality that are comprehensible and discernible through the tools of contemporary scholarship."[51] And who is to say that, as I have suggested, we may not be able to create new tools of scholarship even more suited to the task? Dan Magurshak is surely right when he draws the conclusion that "if the Holocaust is humanly incomprehensible, then the incentive to study the phenomenon, the commitment to spreading awareness . . . and the ability to prevent similar occurrences are seriously diminished."[52] It will not be easy, for the task requires a radical overhaul of our conceptual framework for understanding. The Holocaust cataclysm implies a deep and sweeping criticism of existing culture, of existing methods of cultural interpretation, of accepted value structures and cherished beliefs and institutions. There is indeed a sense in which we can assert that the Holocaust is unique: That uniqueness derives from our not yet having devised an adequate conceptual structure for comprehending it.

Stated in the simplest terms, we must find new ways of thinking about the Holocaust that will help us to make sense of what happened. We need to create what Lawrence Langer has called a "framework of insight without diminishing the sorrow of the event itself."[53] That we presently lack such a framework is painfully clear. I have tried to show some of the reasons why this is so, and to suggest how some of these obstacles may be overcome. We need, at a minimum, to place the Holocaust firmly in the context of its time, making clear how it is both a continuation of the customs and traditions of the West and, at the same time, a break with them. We must relate the Holocaust to other genocidal events. We must discover, through inquiry, how the Holocaust incorporates both common motives for destruction, and unique ones that are traits of the Holocaust alone. And if the methods of inquiry at our disposal prove inadequate to the task at hand, we must devise new and better ones until we have tools adequate to render the complex meanings of the Holocaust in clear and unmistakable terms.

If we can accomplish this we shall have met the crisis of knowing and understanding the Holocaust. It will then be possible for the slogan "Never Again!" to be a reality instead of a dream. Hope requires nothing less than that we make what has been alleged to be incomprehensible an object of our common understanding.

NOTES

1. As Emil Fackenheim states, "Only when [the facts] are assimilated by historical consciousness of succeeding generations are they capable of transforming the future." *The Jewish Return into History: Reflections in the Age of Auschwitz and a New Jerusalem* (New York: Schocken, 1978), p. 210.

2. Quoted by John Herman Randall, Jr., *Nature and Historical Experience* (New York: Columbia University Press, 1970), p. 15.

3. This remark should not be taken to mean that the Jews were not at the center of the Nazi reconstruction of the world, or that the Holocaust is not in important ways a unique event, but to indicate that Nazi plans went far beyond just being a "war against the Jews," and that it is necessary to understand the universal elements as well as the unique ones that comprise this transformational event. For a further elaboration of my position, see "The Genocidal Universe," *European Judaism* 13, no. 1 (Autumn 1979): 29-34; and "The Philosophical Implications of the Holocaust," in *Perspectives on the Holocaust*, ed. Randolph L. Braham (Boston: Kluwer/Nijhoff, 1983), pp. 1-18; and "Was the Holocaust Unique? A Peculiar Question," in *Genocide and the Modern Age: Ideology and Case Studies of Mass Death*, ed. Isidor Wallimann and Michael N. Dobkowski (Westport, Conn.: Greenwood Press, 1987), pp. 145-61.

4. Robert McAfee Brown, "The Holocaust as a Problem in Moral Choice," in *Dimensions of the Holocaust* (Evanston: Northwestern University Press, 1977), p. 62.

5. Milton Mayer, *They Thought They Were Free: The Germans 1933-45* (Chicago: University of Chicago Press, 1955), p. 55.

6. Elie Wiesel, "Now We Know," in *Genocide in Paraguay*, ed. Richard Arens (Philadelphia: Temple University Press, 1976), pp. 165-67. Also see Leo Kuper, *Genocide* (New Haven: Yale University Press, 1982).

7. Anson G. Rabinbach and Jack Zipes, "Lessons of the Holocaust," *New German Critique*, no. 19 (Winter 1980): 7.

8. Yehuda Bauer, *The Holocaust in Historical Perspective* (Seattle: University of Washington Press, 1978), pp. 43-49.

9. Elie Wiesel, *One Generation After* (New York: Avon, 1970), p. 167.

10. Yaffe Eliach, "Defining the Holocaust: Perspectives of a Jewish Historian," in *Jews and Christians after the Holocaust*, ed. Abraham J. Peck (Philadelphia: Fortress Press, 1982), p. 14. "The question for the social psychologist is what are the conditions under which normal people become capable of planning, ordering, committing or condoning acts of mass violence." Henry Kelman, "Violence without Moral Restraint," *Journal of Social Issues* 29, no. 4 (1973): 31. "The problem for students of the Holocaust is to discover the matrix of historical conditions which produce functionaries like Eichmann." Henry Feingold, "The Bureaucrat as Mass Killer: Arendt on Eichmann," *Response* 12, no. 3 (Summer 1980): 48.

11. See George Kren and Leon Rappoport, *The Holocaust and the Crisis of Human*

Behavior (New York: Holmes and Meier, 1980), pp. 125–43; and Rosenberg, "The Philosophical Implications," pp. 8–16; and Chapter 10 in this volume.

12. See Peter Manicas, "John Dewey and the Politics of Social Change," *Occasional Papers, University of Hawaii* 1, no. 1 (October 1980): 22–43; and Roy Bhaskar, "Emergence, Explanation and Emancipation," in *Explaining Behavior: Consciousness, Human Action and Structure*, ed. P. F. Secord (Beverly Hills, Calif.: Sage Publications, 1982), pp. 275–310.

13. Saul Friedländer, "Some Aspects of the Historical Significance of the Holocaust," *Jerusalem Quarterly* 1, no. 1 (Fall 1976): 36.

14. Many have pointed to the distinction between knowing and understanding, but its implications have been insufficiently developed. In "Another Aspect of War" (*Military Affairs* 30, no. 4 [December 1976]), George Kren points out that "although our knowledge of the events has increased substantially as the details of the *Endlösung der Judenfrage* have come to light, with numerous monographic studies, court records of the trials and even reminiscences of those who ran the camps, and memoirs of survivors— in short, although we know an infinite number of facts—this has by no means led to any greater comprehension or understanding of what has happened" (p. 194). Two decades earlier Raul Hilberg suggested that the focus on facts (knowing) had not been accompanied by any exploration of import (understanding): "Acknowledgement of a fact does not signify its acceptance. . . . Unprecedented occurrences of such magnitude are accepted academically only when they are studied as tests of existing conceptions about forces, about relations between cultures, about society as a whole." *The Destruction of the European Jews* (New York: Harper and Row, 1979), p. v.

15. Bruno Bettelheim, *Surviving and Other Essays* (New York: Knopf, 1979), p. 33.

16. For suggestive exploration of factors that stop us from developing a Holocaust consciousness, see Jack Zipes, "In Pursuit of a Holocaust Consciousness: Jews in West Germany," *Jewish Socialist Critique* 1, no. 3 (Spring–Summer 1980): 15–18.

17. According to John Dewey, the terminology used to discuss a subject is "always a very important matter because of the role of symbols in directing thought." *Philosophy and Civilization* (New York: Capricorn Books, 1963), p. 268. In addition, Erik Olin Wright points out, "terminological disputes are rarely innocent. It is generally the case that drawing the boundary criteria for a concept in one way or another opens up or closes off lines of theoretical inquiry." "'Giddens' Critique of Marxism," *New Left Review*, no. 138 (March–April 1983): 21.

18. Elie Wiesel, *A Jew Today* (New York: Random House, 1978), p. 197.

19. For a different perspective on this problem, cf. Roger S. Gottlieb, "Some Implications of the Holocaust for Ethics and Social Philosophy," *Philosophy and Social Criticism* 8, no. 3 (Autumn 1981): 309–10.

20. For a brilliant statement of the importance of memory for man's historical development, see John Dewey, *Reconstruction in Philosophy*, enlarged ed., (Boston: Beacon Press, 1948), pp. 1–3.

21. As George Kren remarks, "Confrontation with [the Holocaust] cannot fail to evoke anxieties." "Psychohistory and the Holocaust," *Journal of Psychohistory* 6, no. 3 (Winter 1979): 410. Elie Wiesel is even more succinct: "All questions pertaining to Auschwitz lead to anguish." *One Generation After*, p. 56. No matter how painful remembering is, Odd Hansen is correct when he states, "the worst crime you can commit today, against yourself and society, is to forget what happened [during the Nazi period] and slip back into indifference. . . . [Since] it was indifference of mankind that let it take place." *From Day to Day* (New York: G.P. Putnam's Sons, 1949), p. 485.

22. For a powerful dramatization of this problem, see Elie Wiesel, *The Oath* (New York: Random House, 1973).

23. Arye Carmon, "Holocaust Teaching in Israel," *Shoah* 3, nos. 2-3 (Fall-Winter 1982-83): 22-25.

24. Quoted by Jacques Maritain, "Breviary of Hate," *Social Research* 20, no. 2 (Summer 1953): 220.

25. Kren, "Psychohistory and the Holocaust," p. 410.

26. For the direction that such a re-evaluation must take, see Kren and Rappoport, *The Holocaust*, pp. 13-15, 125-43. Richard L. Rubenstein, *The Cunning of History: Mass Death and the American Future* (New York: Harper and Row, 1975), pp. 1-35, 48-67, 78-97; and Rosenberg, "The Philosophical Implications," pp. 8-16.

27. Philip Friedman, *Roads to Extinction: Essays on the Holocaust* (New York and Philadelphia: Jewish Publication Society of America and the Conference of Jewish Social Studies, 1980), p. 554. On the other hand, the passage of time, even the passage of a historical "day," hinders assimilation of the event. Memory dims, except perhaps among the survivors. The shock of the event loses its immediacy. The details blur, and disappear into the flux of other events, and in doing so deprive the event of its distinct identity. The world, though in a sense it may never be the same again, resumes its mundane continuity.

28. Fackenheim, *The Jewish Return*, pp. 106-7.

29. William Styron brilliantly sums up the problem when he says, "What troubled me when I read things about the Holocaust is that while they were terribly sincere, most of these novels and non-fictional accounts were so close to the event—in the way they described things—that they suffocated the reader with a sense of horror. All of which is important to record, but as art lacks, to me at least, ultimate impact because it does not distance itself enough to be moving. It's like going to an operating room—you're horrified when you're there, not moved. It takes distance in time and space to register tragic feelings about an event and for people to absorb the implications of things." Quoted in Michiko Kakutani, "40 Years After, Artists Still Struggle with the Holocaust," *New York Times*, December 5, 1982, sect. 2.

30. Alice L. and A. Roy Eckardt, "Studying the Holocaust's Impact Today: Some Dilemmas of Language and Method," *Judaism* 27, no. 2 (Spring 1978): 227. Reprinted here as Chapter 23.

31. Ronald Aronson, "Why? Towards a Theory of the Holocaust," *Socialist Review* 11, no. 4 (July-August 1981): 67-68.

32. *Americans Confront the Holocaust: A Study of Reactions to NBC-TV's Four-Part Drama on the Nazi Era* (New York: American Jewish Committee: Institute of Human Relations), p. 6.

33. See Claude Lanzmann, "From Holocaust to 'Holocaust,'" *Dissent* 28, no. 2 (Spring 1981): 190.

34. Quoted by Richard L. Rubenstein, *The Age of Triage: Fear and Hope in an Overcrowded World* (Boston: Beacon Press, 1983), p. 131.

35. Leon Festinger, *A Theory of Cognitive Dissonance* (Stanford: Stanford University Press, 1957), p. 3.

36. Bettelheim, *Surviving*, p. 91.

37. Wiesel, *A Jew Today*, pp. 197-98.

38. Elie Wiesel, "Why I Write," in *Confronting the Holocaust: The Impact of Elie Wiesel*, ed. Alvin Rosenfeld and Irving Greenberg (Bloomington: Indiana University Press, 1978), pp. 203-4.

39. Wiesel, *One Generation After*, p. 15.

40. Cf. Elie Wiesel, "Does the Holocaust Lie beyond the Reach of Art?" *New York Times*, April 17, 1983, sect. 2.

41. See William James, *The Principles of Psychology* (New York: Henry Holt, 1890),

vol. 1, pp. 221–23; and Bertrand Russell, *Mysticism and Logic: And Other Essays* (London: Allen and Unwin, 1949), pp. 209–32.

42. Lucy S. Dawidowicz, *The Holocaust and the Historians* (Cambridge, Mass.: Harvard University Press, 1981), pp. 126–30; Fackenheim, *The Jewish Return*, pp. 58–67.

43. Fackenheim, *The Jewish Return*, p. 58.

44. For a brief analysis of the ways Jews were deceived by the Nazis see Alex Grobman, "Attempts at Resistance in the Camps," in *Genocide, Critical Issues of the Holocaust: A Companion to the Film Genocide,* ed. Alex Grobman and Daniel Landes (Los Angeles: Simon Wiesenthal Center and Chappaqua, N.Y.: Rossel Books, 1983), pp. 245–48.

45. John Dewey, *Logic: The Theory of Inquiry* (New York: Henry Holt, 1938), p. 210.

46. See Rosenberg, "Was the Holocaust Unique?," pp. 145– 61.

47. Fackenheim, *The Jewish Return*, p. 93.

48. Nora Levin, *The Holocaust: The Destruction of European Jewry 1933–1945* (New York: Schocken, 1973), p. xi.

49. Andrew Greeley, "Listen to the Survivors," *New York Times Book Review,* January 21, 1979, p. 10.

50. Fackenheim, *The Jewish Return*, p. 279.

51. Michael Berenbaum, "Reflections on Teaching about the Holocaust," *Conservative Judaism* 34, no. 3 (January–February 1981): 43–44.

52. Dan Magurshak, "The 'Incomprehensibility' of the Holocaust: Tightening up Some Loose Usage," *Judaism* 29, no. 2 (Spring 1980): 234. Reprinted here as Chapter 22.

53. Lawrence L. Langer, *Versions of Survival: The Holocaust and the Human Spirit* (Albany: State University of New York Press, 1982), p. 185.

20

THE POLITICS OF SYMBOLIC EVASION: Germany and the Aftermath of the Holocaust

Manfred Henningsen

Was Hitler allowed to treat German Jews as prisoners of war and to intern them in camps? The prominent German historian Ernst Nolte thought so, and in the summer of 1986, his unusual thoughts provoked a public debate about the place and meaning of the Third Reich in the context of German history. Nolte's views were first published in a British volume on the Third Reich[1] and then revised for a public colloquium in Frankfurt. Whether Nolte had misunderstood the conditions of his invitation (as the organizers of the colloquium claimed) or whether he was disinvited (as Nolte charged), he published his speech in the leading conservative newspaper, the *Frankfurter Allgemeine Zeitung.*[2] This chapter in the British book and his speech in the newspaper were received by many intellectuals of the German left as the end of a post-Nazi consensus and the beginning of historical revisionism.

Jürgen Habermas, philosopher at the University of Frankfurt, articulated and summarized the thrust of these private and public reactions in a long article in the weekly newspaper *Die Zeit* under the headline "Some Kind of Damage Control."[3] The Habermas article triggered a series of responses by historians, many of them defending Nolte and attacking the philosopher for the distortion of historical arguments. Their support for Nolte was not only dictated by a collegiate code of protection; they were also acting in self-defense.[4] Habermas had included other candidates in his critical analysis of "apologetic tendencies" among prominent contemporary German historians.

However interested Habermas may have been in the political motivations of the historical revisionists in general, he was particularly intrigued by the arguments of Nolte. Nolte had raised what he called a "fundamental question" by asking whether "the history of the Third Reich, 40 years after the end of the war, [is] in need of revision." His positive answer suggests that we should look to the Bolsheviks as the originators of genocidal policies in the twentieth century. Their wholesale destruction of entire classes taught the Nazis memorable lessons. "He who does not want to see Hitler's annihilation of the Jews in this context," Nolte declares,

> is possibly led by very noble motives, but he falsifies history. In his legitimate search for the direct causes he overlooks the main precondition without which all those causes would have remained without effect. Auschwitz is not primarily a result of traditional anti-semitism. It was in its core not merely a "genocide" but was above all a reaction born out of the anxiety of the annihilating occurrences of the Russian Revolution.

Nolte concedes that the Nazis may have been more horrifying than the Bolsheviks because they carried out their terror "in a quasi-industrial manner." "It was more repulsive," he continues,

> than the original because it was based on mere assumptions, and almost free from ... mass hatred.... All this constitutes singularity but it does not alter the fact that the so-called annihilation of the Jews during the Third Reich was a reaction or distorted copy and not a first act or an original.[5]

As daring as this claim to historical originality may already sound when one notices such phrases as "merely a 'genocide,'" "a quasi-industrial manner," "the so-called annihilation of the Jews," Nolte tops his genocidal aetiology with a story that puts him in the company of British historian David Irving. When Irving could not find Hitler's orders for the mass extermination of European Jewry in a written document, he concluded, in *Hitler's War*, that Hitler had neither ordered nor planned or even known about the "Final Solution." While Irving failed to find his missing link and therefore, in tune with the positivist literalism of his impoverished art, had to exonerate Hitler, Nolte did find a Jewish connection. "But it can hardly be denied," he wrote in defense of Irving's general revisionist inclinations,

> that Hitler had good reasons to be convinced of his enemies' determination to annihilate him much earlier than when the first information about Auschwitz came to the knowledge of the world. The 1940 pamphlet "Germany must perish" by Theodore N. Kaufmann has often been mentioned in the literature, but I do not remember seeing it in any of the more important German books I have read about Chaim Weizmann's official declaration in the first days of September 1939, according to which Jews in the whole world would fight on the side of England.

Nolte's reading of the period culminates in the remark that the state-ment "might justify the consequential thesis that Hitler was allowed to treat the German Jews as prisoners of war and by this means to intern them."[6]

Forty years after the collapse of Nazi Germany and the dramatic opening of the concentration camps to public inspection a well-known German historian treats a Nazi argument as a serious justification for the beginning of the Holocaust on German territory. This intellectual per-formance becomes all the more extraordinary when Nolte's documen-tary evidence is confronted with a random sampling of Nazi statements in the twenties. After all, long before they came to power the Nazis were quite frank about their intentions toward Jews, German or not. Hitler left no doubts in his *Mein Kampf* about his terminal ideas and Goebbels proclaimed in a speech in 1926: "We have the enemy, the global enemy recognized: international Jewry." And: "We want to undertake the fight against this world enemy. We want to make a state out of Germany, a nation out of the German people. This people has to be prepared to drive the dagger into the heart of the enemy."[7] Election pamphlets of the Nazi party called for Jewish destruction as early as 1927. One leaflet, produced by the Propaganda Department of the party in Munich, advertised extermination on a grand scale. "Never forget," it said, "that our day of reckoning with the Jews will not come about as a result of some laughable single clash, but only when we have the power of the state in our hands to carry out a thorough extermination (*Vernichtung*) of this international racial parasite."[8]

How is it possible that a German historian who must know these and other passages from the Nazi discourse of murder, blamed the victims for having instigated their own destruction? Why was Nolte not shamed into silence by his fellow historians? Why did they come to his rescue, attacking the philosopher instead? Apart from exposing Nolte's collaborationist logic of reasoning, Habermas had bared the political interest of the profession. As he saw it, the historians were all working on the same ideological project, namely to relativize the importance of the twelve years of the Third Reich in the context of German history. They wanted to reactivate German historical imagination for the sym-bolic purpose of providing the Federal Republic of Germany with a cleansed German historical record. Instead of letting the Communist regime in East Germany exploit one thousand years of German history for its symbolic purposes, the West German historians were encouraged by conservative politicians like Chancellor Helmut Kohl to invest their professional energy in the enterprise of historical legitimation for the West German state. In fact, Kohl himself had provided some guidelines by his famous expedition to Bitburg cemetery in May 1985, using a naive but willing American president to fake global approval for his idea of the symbolic reconstruction of German identity. Kohl actually initiated plans and earmarked funds for the creation of two history museums and received support from many of the historians Habermas reviewed in his article. Currently the plans call for a "House of German History" in West Berlin and a "House of History of the Federal Republic of Germany" in Bonn. The division of symbolic labor would take care of the problem of the Holocaust. The Federal Republic, which was founded in 1949, could legitimately send all Holocaust visitors to Berlin. However, for wreath-laying ceremonies of visiting political dignitaries Kohl has plans for a huge memorial hall in Bonn under whose roof German war dead, German war criminals, and German victims will be proportionately represented.[9]

The politics of symbolic evasion which reached worldwide attention during the Bitburg incident and will be monumentalized in the historical museums and the hall of the dead has accompanied the history of the three successor states of the Third Reich: West Germany, East Germany, and Austria. The East German version of the symbolic evasion has been ideologically the most austere one: It negates all historical ties with the Nazi period, redirecting them all across the border to West Germany. Austria chose a somewhat less elegant but, until recently, equally successful version, namely to blame it all on the Germans and to claim the status of a victimized nation. The Waldheim affair has put an end to this version, reconnected the Austrians with their blurred German memory. The Austrian president Kurt Waldheim represents the mode of historical consciousness that has been characteristic of the politics of evasion in all three Germanies. His hollow language reveals the banality of those who carried out the evil orders of the Nazi empire. In an interview with the news magazine *Der Spiegel* he gave this classic answer of evasiveness: "I deeply regret the horrible tragedy the Hitler regime has caused, especially against the Jewish population, but I personally do not feel responsible for it."[10] Waldheim sounds like a figure out of Claude Lanzmann's *Shoah,* comparable to a bureaucrat like Dr. Franz Grassler, deputy of the Nazi commissioner of the Warsaw ghetto, or Walter Stier, former head of the Reichsbahn Department 33. Grassler responded to Lanzmann's question concerning his recollections of the Warsaw ghetto innocently: "Not much. I recall more clearly my prewar mountaineering trips than the entire war period and those days in Warsaw. All in all those were bad times. It's a fact: we tend to forget, thank God, the bad times more easily than the good. The bad times are repressed." Grassler's admission captures the will to evasion of a whole generation when Lanzmann is reading to him dates from the Jewish Council president's diary. Grassler responds with honest surprise to

Lanzmann's exact dates: "July 7, 1941? That's the first time I've relearned a date. May I take notes? After all, it interests me too. So in July I was already there."[11] Stier who was in charge of the death trains was shocked by Lanzmann's suggestion that he may actually have seen a train: "No, never. We had so much work, I never left my desk. We worked day and night" (p. 132; page references in this paragraph are to Lanzmann, *Shoah*). Asked about his knowledge of the extermination camp Treblinka he bristled: "Good God, no! How could we know? I never went to Treblinka. I stayed in Krakow, in Warsaw, glued to my desk. . . . I was strictly a bureaucrat" (p. 135). He finally admitted to some kind of knowledge: "Well, when the word got around. When it was whispered. It was never said outright. Good God, no! They'd have hauled you off at once! We heard things." Lanzmann asked encouragingly: "Rumors?" Stier: "That's it, rumors" (p. 136). Certainly, there is a qualitative difference between the will to evasion in people like Grassler and Stier and the politics of evasion represented by people like Waldheim. Grassler and Stier have worked hard to suppress the memories of personal guilt in the practice of evil. They have reached a vacuous emptiness at the core of their personality and want to be left alone. Waldheim, on the other hand, ran for and became president of Austria. The righteousness of his rhetoric indicates that he is not haunted by any memories but surprised by the memories of others.

This righteousness of the moral pretenders as well as the public support they have managed to generate has always struck a sensitive chord in younger people. Chancellor Kohl, when helping his friend Waldheim during his election campaign, attacked the young critics for being consumed by the "arrogance of those who were born late."[12] Kohl himself had used a slightly different phrase when he was on a state visit to Israel in January 1984 and tried to distance himself from a historical German responsibility for the Holocaust. He refered to the "grace" of his "late birth" to brush aside all moral questions. A delegation of the German Green party was caught in a Kohl-like posture during a tour of the Middle East at the turn of 1984–85 when its members used the grace of their birth certificates to deal with the Palestinian question in terms of the "victims of the [Holocaust] victims." They were denounced by Israelis for their brown [Nazi] roots and were reminded by other Greens that one may "inherit crimes one hasn't committed."[13]

A similar controversy surrounding a play by the late movie director Rainer Werner Fassbinder preoccupied the German culture scene between the Kohl-Reagan march to Bitburg in May 1985 and the Nolte debate in July 1986. Fassbinder's play, about urban renewal in Frankfurt, *Der Müll, die Stadt und der Tod* (*Trash, the City, and Death*), had remained unproduced since its publication in 1976. It had always been labeled

anti-Semitic because of its portrayal of a Jewish developer. The scheduled opening in November 1985 was stopped by Jewish protesters who
occupied the stage and threatened to repeat their protest at each
scheduled performance. This first exercise in civil disobedience by
German Jews became a national media event. Although it was hotly
discussed as a civil liberties issue the rights and limits of free artistic
expression and free speech were overshadowed by the question whether
the German post-Holocaust culture should tolerate the negative portrayal of a German Jew.[14] Fassbinder's play was not performed, but his
voice was added to a disturbing chorus. The play may have less to do
with a Jewish developer in contemporary Frankfurt than with Fassbinder's unsorted and convoluted ideas about the Third Reich. But like
the disturbing questions the Greens had raised about Israel's treatment
of the Palestinians, it reflects his generation's angry attempts to develop
a critical posture toward the world they are living in. The answers he
came up with were unsettling for a society that wants to forget a past it
has never completely understood.

One of the most extraordinary manifestations of the search for
answers that comes out of Fassbinder's generation is the autobiographical essay *Die Reise* (*The Trip*) by Bernward Vesper. Vesper was born in
1938, the son of Will Vesper, one of the more prominent poet laureates
of the Third Reich. Bernward Vesper had a son by Gudrun Ensslin, a
member of the inner circle of the Baader-Meinhof group who died on
October 18, 1977, together with other members under still mysterious
circumstances in prison. Vesper committed suicide in a mental hospital
in Hamburg in 1971. The more than seven hundred pages of Bernward
Vesper's essay–novel (posthumously published in 1977) revisit, interpret, and dissect the stages of his journey from the cultural top of the
Nazi world to the anarcho-terrorist underworld of the extreme left in
the early seventies. Vesper's *Reise* is the record of a trip he made
through European but especially German landscapes and cities while
being high on or looking for drugs. He describes his encounters with
the Baader-Meinhof group and the social scene that supported it. His
raging tirades against contemporary West German society, the left-
liberal government under Chancellor Willy Brandt, American imperialism, and the like make him an activist sympathizer of the radical
group. Yet the recollections of his childhood during and after the war
lend authenticity to his fury. His father and mother represent that
German culture milieu that provided Hitler with his strongest support
group and the bloated language of legitimation. The stories of his
upbringing retrace a history of destruction, the destruction of the
person as child. A boy who is growing up in an authoritarian household
par excellence learns in his twenties what had happened to him, and

he rebels. The rebellion takes place against those "who have crushed me. It isn't blind hate, a drive back into Nirvana before birth. But the rebellion against the twenty years in the parents' house, against the father, the manipulation, the seduction, the waste of youth, enthusiasm, elan, hope."[15]

Vesper's *Reise* is an existential self-analysis of Hitler's children or, at least, of those of them who never forgave their parents for what they had done to them. The rebellion against their upbringing becomes intensified by the anger about the record of destruction and extermination of the Nazi regime which their parents had supported or tolerated. Vesper presents the story of his father as that of a believer who was not shaken by the historical truth. On the contrary, the historical truth about the Nazis confirmed his belief in the reality construction of the Nazis. Bernward Vesper met a welter of professors, doctors, lawyers, teachers, small businessmen who shared his father's convictions (p. 488; page references here and in the following paragraph are to Vesper's *Reise*).

The young Vesper's report bears on the arguments of Nolte, for it was precisely the Nazi poet Vesper who refused to accept Nazi responsibility for the war. "The allies are guilty for the war," his son quotes him (p. 449). And he paraphrases his father's resentment about Jewish ingenuity to distract attention from the "revenge of Israel" as a cause of war. Vesper writes about the opinions of his father: "Chaim Weizmann has proclaimed in New York, Herr Hitler this is our war. Well, all right said the Führer, if you want it you can have it" (p. 451). "Hitler was forced into the war," Vesper quotes his father, "world Jewry had already declared war against him in 1933. He stated to Mr. Weizmann of New York: You wanted the war and now you have it" (p. 144). Vesper may have gone further than Nolte by constantly reiterating to his small son the whole range of Nazi arguments. But then, Will Vesper belonged to the intellectual collaborators of the Nazis whereas Nolte and his colleagues did not. The opinions, however, that they are suddenly expressing bode ill for the future portrayal of the Third Reich and the place its record will occupy in the symbolic memory of Germany.

The painless way in which some historians are proceeding in the transvaluation of the Nazi past conforms with patterns of memory loss that have established themselves or become perpetuated in other academic and intellectual disciplines. The geneticist Benno Müller-Hill, for example, tried to remind German scientists in anthropology, genetics, medicine, and other disciplines of their active participation in the conceptualization, planning, and realization of the extermination projects against Jews, Gypsies, and mental patients.[16] He became an outcast in his field. German psychoanalysts discovered only in 1982 that they had a Nazi past. Since the first publication of an article entitled "Psychoanalysis in Hitler-Germany" in the leading psychoanalytic journal *Psyche* in 1982, the discussion about the expulsion of Jews from the German psychoanalytic association and the systematic purge of the Freudian and other Jewish origins of the discipline has not come to an end. Academia in the Third Reich is the sad story of a few courageous men and women in an otherwise well adjusted, apolitical, and sometimes sympathetic environment.[17] Sheldon Wolin noticed in a review of Hans-Georg Gadamer's *Philosophical Apprenticeships* the language of concealment the German philosopher employed when writing about Martin Heidegger's years of Nazi collaboration and describing his own meetings with former Jewish colleagues who had fled to Paris.[18] This language of concealment was the impotent style of the German university and practiced in a masterful way by Heidegger himself, the teacher of Gadamer and, for that matter, Nolte.

Heidegger had always refused to respond to criticism about his initial public approval of the Third Reich. He remained silent until his death in 1976 when *Der Spiegel* published posthumously a long interview with him that had been taped in 1966 but could not be printed before his death. The interview brought no revelations but confirmed Hannah Arendt's surprising absolution of Heidegger in the *New York Review of Books* on the occasion of the philosopher's eightieth birthday in October 1971. In that famous birthday article Hannah Arendt absolved the philosopher of any historical responsibility for "the attraction to the tyrannical." Comparing his attraction with that of other great thinkers, she wrote about Heidegger: "It does not finally matter where the storms of their century may have driven them. For the wind that blows through Heidegger's thinking . . . does not spring from the century he happens to live in. It comes from the primeval."[19] Heidegger was pleased with this birthday article, as Elizabeth Young-Bruehl has indicated in her revealing Arendt biography. In the *Spiegel* interview he anticipated Arendt's "primeval" generosity when evading all charges of responsibility in the conventional way of his generation and darkly hinting: "Only a God can save us now."[20]

Whether Heidegger could have regained the integrity of his thinking after the war by going public is less interesting than why so few contemporary philosophers, inside and outside Germany, are concerned with this betrayal of the spirit in the first place. The New York philosopher Edith Wyschogrod, for example, has written a remarkable book about "the creation of death-worlds and the death-event" in the twentieth century.[21] She sees in these scenarios of mass destruction and human annihilation a qualitatively new experience in history. Especially in the death-worlds of Stalin's labor camps and Hitler's extermination camps she recognizes a "remythologizing response to the technological society."[22] She introduces Heidegger as one of the few authentic thinkers of our alienated century without ever asking why the philosopher of Being could fall for the *Daseins* projects of the Nazis. "The philosopher's task is to reclaim," she suggests, "the meaning of Being through thinking, to purify this history by peeling away its accretions and bringing Being into unconcealment. To put it otherwise, Heidegger undertakes a greening of metaphysics."[23] The complicity of the thinker Heidegger in the initial legitimation of the death-world of the Nazis, his confusing their deadly *Dasein* with Being, and his unwillingness to elucidate this concealment par excellence are not discussed in Wyschogrod's book. Although she does not excuse his endorsements of the Nazi revolution in 1933, she does not focus on the representative quality of his silence after 1945 either.

Heidegger's silence in the postwar years was colored by the same kind of defiant indifference that characterized the behavior of many culture Mandarins who had stayed behind in Nazi Germany. Some of these Mandarins had expected to be praised by the returning refugee Mandarins for their occasional gestures of contempt toward Nazi leaders and Nazi masses. Others had hoped that these gestures would be seen as courageous acts of resistance. When the expectations of the resident Mandarins were not honored, some refugee Mandarins, such as Thomas Mann, were attacked by resident Mandarins for their anti-Nazi activities during exile. Many of the resident Mandarins, however, retreated into their culture niches and resumed a life of the apolitical spirit. Their defiant evasiveness became institutionalized as a general style of behavior in the predominantly nonleft and nonrefugee culture of schools, universities, and the media of the 1950s and early 1960s. Whether the Mandarins could have initiated a process of public mourning and critique is uncertain. Yet their bad faith contributed to a climate of evasiveness that promoted as virtue the suppression of historical memory and responsibility. This climate did not last. It was profoundly changed by the student and culture rebels of the late sixties. Bernward Vesper's *Reise* documents the changes and, at the same time, connects the climate of evasiveness and the fury of rebellion. The fury of rebellion turned into the rage of terrorist destruction and provided the politicians of evasiveness in the seventies with still new arguments against reflective and moral inquiry.

The Hollywood television series "Holocaust" finally triggered a reaction against collective memory loss unheard of until then on this scale. The series was aired on German television in late January 1979. When German television officials had reluctantly agreed to show the series, they expected small audiences and a bad press; German journalists had ridiculed the series as a typical American soap opera. They were stunned when Hollywood's "Holocaust" generated the first nationwide debate about the Holocaust. The debate demonstrated, among other things, a generational divide between older Germans who wanted to forget and young Germans who wanted to know.[24] Later the young Germans' curiosity found an outlet in community projects that tried to recover the buried, hidden, or rundown structures of the Nazi world in their own countryside and cities. A kind of spontaneous archaeology movement began to spring up, focusing public attention on former Nazi concentration camps located in the Federal Republic of Germany. The author of a concentration-camp travelogue has confirmed what the amateur archaeologists discovered, namely, that the original refusal to acknowledge the criminal reality perpetuated itself in the forgetting of the camps.[25] The monuments in stone with their harmless inscriptions distract from the knowing complicity that prevailed in the surrounding German communities while those camps were executing the death event. The remembrance of that complicity became the focal point of the communal archaeologists. They had put life in the statistics of Nazi crimes which had rarely aroused the public conscience in the postwar decades. The statistics are always presented when questions are raised about the seriousness of Nazi crime prosecutions in West Germany. But the statistics of investigation, prosecution, and sentencing—in August 1986 the following data were published by the federal government: from the end of the war until January 1986, 90,921 investigations were opened, 6,479 sentences were pronounced, 83,140 cases were closed, and 1,302 cases are still pending[26]—create a clear impression of the rather mediocre success of the normal criminal justice system in dealing with the Holocaust. But then, the normal criminal justice system was not designed for that purpose. Successful resistance movements, culminating in the revolutionary overthrow of a regime, historically take care of such abnormal situations. The Third Reich, however, was overthrown by the Allies who established their own tribunals for a few years until Germans regained authority in the 1950s and were allowed to prosecute Nazi criminals. This delay in the German prosecution of Nazi criminals may have contributed to the lack of impact Nazi trials—including the well-publicized Auschwitz and Maidanek trials—had on the political culture of West Germany. These trials did not create enough public interest to launch a national debate. Hollywood, however, succeeded where the West German criminal justice system had failed.

The success of Hollywood was based on a simple aesthetic decision. Instead of overwhelming the audience with the statistics of the "death event," Hollywood chose the vehicle of a Jewish family to dramatize the obliteration of a people. This miniaturization of the Jewish march into the death-world made people participate in the death of a family and the responsibility of Germans for that death. The persuasive simplicity of this television reconstruction broke through the layers of concealment and confronted other Germans with experiences they had managed to suppress and cover up for the younger generation. The unwillingness of older Germans to join the younger Germans in a public process of mourning reaffirmed the experiential distance they had cultivated since the war. After all, their mourning would have touched upon their collaborationist and cowardly behavior throughout most of the Third Reich. They were the survivors of complicity, they were not surviving victims. Kohl's plans for Bitburg, therefore, were celebrated as a welcome end to an unwelcome remembrance of that past of complicity.

In 1985 the conservative West German president, Richard von Weizsäcker, added an unexpected note to the events. Immediately after the spectacle of Bitburg on May 8 of that year he delivered before the West German parliament a speech commemorating the fortieth anniversary of the collapse of the Third Reich. He pleaded for active memory recovery as political praxis. Condemning the politics of evasion, he urged Germans to accept the truth about themselves, the truth about their complicity. Weizsäcker's speech was hailed by the German Left, Social Democrats, and Greens alike. Social Democrats felt especially encouraged because they had been systematically attacked throughout the history of postwar Germany from the right, for having elected as party chairmen a KZ-inmate (Kurt Schumacher, 1945–52) and two refugees from Nazi Germany (Erich Ollenhauer, 1952–63, and Willy Brandt, 1964–87). The conservatives initially praised Weizsäcker's speech cautiously but have since distanced themselves from its tenor. They had difficulties with Weizsäcker's approach, probably because they lack his privileged experiences. Weizsäcker is the son of a German diplomat who had been the state secretary of the Nazi foreign minister Joachim von Ribbentrop. Weizsäcker's father was among the accused of the Nuremberg trials, and the young Richard von Weizsäcker had been a member of his father's legal defense team. Being on the Nuremberg rosters for war criminals and for lawyers, the Weizsäcker name was forever connected with the anti-Nazi tribunal. The Weizsäckers could not evade a past that had put their family in the history books; they had to face and accept the record of their involvement in the regime. The public character of Weizsäcker's personal history made it impossible for him to sanitize the historical memory or to relativize the importance of the Third Reich in a larger context of German history. He rejected the ideological strategy of Chancellor Kohl and carried the debate on authentic and false historical reconstruction into the center of the conservative block. Weizsäcker gave his speech in 1985, yet the historians began publicly discussing their new version of German history in 1986. Did Weizsäcker speak in vain?

The conservative politicians and the historians who are ideologically close to them have little understanding of the place of personal historical experience in Weizsäcker's framework of symbolic meaning. They seem to underestimate or disregard the intensity of the personally lived experience. But the experience of the trial of his father did not allow him to distance himself epistemologically from the historical record of the Third Reich. He could not detach himself from that record in the way of positivist historians who want to know *"wie es eigentlich gewesen"* (what actually happened). In order to defend his father in the trial he had not only to understand him, but also to reenact his father's story as well as the stories of the others. The stories of the others included the experiences of surviving inmates of the Nazi camps. When defending his father in Nuremberg he had to see him as a representative of the regime that had made victims out of the others. Their stories had become intimately connected with his father's story and, finally, his own. When he was called upon as president to speak on occasion of the fortieth anniversary of the collapse of Nazi Germany his personal story became identical with the history of his society. In a truly representative manner he had processed his father's and his country's criminal record for himself.

Weizsäcker's case represents an exceptional German career. Not even Willy Brandt, the returned emigrant and future West German chancellor, could match the potentially paradigmatic character of Weizsäcker's case. Brandt, after all, was proven right from the beginning when he left Germany in 1933. Just twenty years of age and not a Jew, he exemplified genuine political resistance. His case infuriated conservative Germans in the Federal Republic and made them attack him viciously throughout his political career. He personified "the other" Germany they had rejected, the Germany the Nazis had sent into exile, prison, concentration and death camps. He reminded conservative Germans of their historical failure. Weizsäcker, on the other hand, showed them a way to accept and, at the same time, overcome that failure. The behavior of conservative politicians and historians, however, seems to indicate how essential the processing of personal experiences is to initiate the constructive overcoming of an abstract syndrome of historical guilt.

The marginal presence of Jews in contemporary Germany as a consequence of the Holocaust has led to the macabre but truthful situation that the "new German consciousness is *judenrein* [free of Jews]."[27] The Jewish survivors have left the successor states of the Third

Reich and are not reminding Germans concretely of their historical guilt by their presence. A few young Jewish intellectuals actually emigrated from the Federal Republic to Israel and published their observations and sentiments in books like Lea Fleischmann's *Dies ist nicht mein Land* (1980; *This Is Not My Land*). The German survivors of the Holocaust, the perpetrators, collaborators, and bystanders of the death event, did everything to suppress its public remembrance and contributed to what Fleischmann recognized as the "gap" in the tradition of her students. She asked:

> And isn't their gap bigger than my own? My parents did not tell me anything about the war and about the prewar time. But when I rummage in the past I find nothing to be ashamed of. My parents did not remain silent out of shame but out of pain. But when my students begin to rummage in their history what will they find? They will discover that all words of virtue and morality, all high and ethical claims of German writers and philosophers, will fall apart over Auschwitz.[28]

Yet the perspective emerging from this total indictment of German culture amounts to collective cultural suicide. Instead of reflecting and overcoming the threat of the shadow, Germans would submit to it. Jews and Germans would commemorate forever the eternal recurrence of the death event.

Reading some witnesses of the death event, we can discern a different strategy. The literature of the survivors constitutes an existential hermeneutics of the death event. The survivors have interpreted the cruel journey of self-discovery they had to travel to understand fully what had happened to them. Yet not all witnesses who understood their situation survived. Etty Hillesum, for example, a member of the Jewish community in Amsterdam, was one of those who died in Auschwitz but left her diaries behind. *An Interrupted Life* allows us to participate in Hillesum's discovery of the non-Jewish world that is abandoning her— the German world that was planning to exterminate her—and the Jewish world that is making claims on her identity. Hillesum was raised and educated to live the life of an intellectually independent woman but had to realize late in life that she belonged to a category of people who were marked for death. She begins to live in anticipation of this end without becoming suffocated by it. In July 1942 she made these entries: "I must admit a new insight into my life and find a place for it: What is at stake is our impending destruction and annihilation, we can have no more illusions about it. They are out to destroy us completely, we must accept that and go on from here." "I shall not be bitter," she continued, "if others fail to grasp what is happening to us Jews. I work and continue to live with the same conviction and I find life meaningful— yes, meaningful—although I hardly dare say so in company these days." She is unsentimental in her recognition of the fate to come: "I have looked our destruction, our miserable end which has already begun in so many small ways in our daily life, straight in the eye and accepted it into my life, and my love of life has not been diminished."[29] She refuses to be saved, she wants to go to the camps, to all the camps in order to become a witness to the atrocities committed against her people. "As if it really mattered," she tells herself,

> which of us goes. Ours is now a common destiny and that is something we must not forget . . . I shall wield this slender fountain pen as if it were a hammer and my words will have to be so many hammer-strokes with which to beat out the story of our fate and of a piece of history as it is and never was before. Not in this totalitarian, massively organized form, spanning the whole of Europe. Still, a few people must survive if only to be the chroniclers of this age. (p. 147)

Her faith in a human future is not based on any external help: "I believe that we must rid ourselves of all expectations of help from the outside world" or an intervention by God: "But one thing is becoming increasingly clear to me; that You cannot help us, that we must help You to help ourselves. And that is all we can manage these days and also all that really matters: that we safeguard that little piece of You, God, in ourselves" (p. 151). Hillesum's Jewish spirituality is also Christian in its radical overcoming of hate: "Each of us must turn inwards and destroy in himself all that he thinks he ought to destroy in others. And remember that every atom of hate we add to this world makes it still more inhospitable" (p. 180). Hillesum's existential revisionism opens the only pattern for deconstructive thinking after the Holocaust: "How much I want to write. Somewhere deep inside me is a workshop in which Titans are forging a new world. I once wrote in despair: 'it is inside my little skull that this world must be rethought, that it must be given fresh clarity.'" And finally: "if you destroy the ideas behind which life lies imprisoned as behind bars then you liberate your true life, its real mainsprings, and then you will also have the strength to bear real suffering, your own and the world's" (pp. 186ff.).

Etty Hillesum's thinking became transformed by the anticipation of the death-world. Her memory will therefore always be connected with the Holocaust. Yet the impetus of her thinking went beyond the privileged commemoration of Jewish suffering and dying. She combined the rebellious anger about a murderous world of Sophocles' Antigone with Socrates' trust in the possibility of ethical and intellectual metanoia or mind reform. She determined the perimeters of discourse for all historical and contemporary post-Holocaust societies, the societies of surviving victims, perpetrators, and collaborators, and their children. The history of West Germany indicates how tempting it has always been to substitute the avoidance of the Holocaust for the discourse that tried to integrate this limiting experience in the creative revisioning of politics. However, the contemporary dynamics of social movements in the Federal Republic suggest that the syndrome of avoidance may have, in the long run, actually stimulated the process of rethinking Etty Hillesum was hoping for when facing the death-world of the camps.

NOTES

Acknowledgments: I want to thank Henry Kariel for critical advice. The article was completed in October 1986.

1. H. W. Koch, ed., *Aspects of the Third Reich* (London: Macmillan, 1985).

2. Ernst Nolte, "Vergangenheit, die nicht vergehen will: Eine Rede, die geschrieben, aber nicht gehalten werden konnte," *Frankfurter Allgemeine Zeitung,* June 6, 1986.

3. Jürgen Habermas, "Eine Art Schadensabwicklung: Die apologetischen Tendenzen in der deutschen Zeitgeschichtssreibüng," *Die Zeit,* July 11, 1986.

4. See Klaus Hildebrand, "Das Zeitalter der Tyrannen. Geschichte und Politik: Die Verwalter der Aufklärung, das Risiko der Wissenschaft und die Geborgenheit der Weltanschauung. Eine Entgegnung auf Jürgen Habermas," *Frankfurter Allgemeine Zeitung,* July 31, 1986.

5. Ernst Nolte, "Between Myth and Revisionism? The Third Reich in the Perspective of the 1980s," in Koch, *Aspects of the Third Reich,* pp. 35ff.

6. David Irving, *Hitler's War* (New York: Viking, 1977); Koch, *Aspects of the Third Reich,* pp. 27ff.

7. Joseph Goebbels, *Lenin oder Hitler? Eine Rede. Zwickau 1926,* quoted in C. E. Bärsch, "Die Geschichtsphilosophie des Joseph Goebbels," in *Von kommenden Zeiten,* ed. J. H. Knoll and J. H. Schoeps (Stuttgart and Bonn: Burg Verlag, 1985), pp. 174ff.

8. S. Taylor, *Prelude to Genocide: Nazi Ideology and the Struggle for Power* (New York: St. Martin's Press, 1985), p. 218.

9. *Der Spiegel,* April 14, 1986, pp. 42–46.

10. Ibid., p. 155.

11. Claude Lanzmann, *Shoah: An Oral History of the Holocaust* (New York: Pantheon, 1985), pp. 175ff.

12. "Die Spätgeborenen," *Die Zeit,* May 9, 1986.

13. *Der Spiegel,* February 11, 1985, pp. 23–27.

14. See H. Lichtenstein, ed., *Die Fassbinder-Kontroverse oder Das Ende der Schonzeit* (Königstein: Athenäum, 1986).

15. Bernward Vesper, *Die Reise: Romanessay. Ausgabe letzter Hand* (Hamburg: Rowohlt, 1983), p. 55.

16. Benno Müller-Hill, *Tödliche Wissenschaft: Die Aussonderung von Juden, Zigeunern und Geisteskranken 1933–1945* (Hamburg: Rowohlt, 1984).

17. See Peter Lundgren, ed., *Wissenschaft im Dritten Reich* (Frankfurt: Suhrkamp, 1985).

18. Sheldon Wolin, "Under Siege in the German Ivory Tower," *New York Times Book Review*, July 28, 1985, p. 12.

19. Hannah Arendt, "Martin Heidegger at Eighty," *New York Review of Books*, October 21, 1971, p. 54.

20. *Der Spiegel*, May 31, 1976, pp. 193-219.

21. Edith Wyschogrod, *Spirit in Ashes: Hegel, Heidegger and Man-Made Mass Death* (New Haven: Yale University Press, 1985), p. 15.

22. Ibid., p. 51.

23. Ibid., p. 176.

24. See "Holocaust—Die Vergangenheit kommt zurück," *Der Spiegel*, January 29, 1979, pp. 17-34; "Holocaust— Melodrama vom Massenmord," *Die Zeit*, January 26, 1979; "Auschwitz: Eine Generation fragt," *Der Spiegel*, February 5, 1979, pp. 28-65.

25. Bernd Eichmann, *Versteinert, Verharmlost, Vergessen: KZ-Gedenkstätten in der Bundesrepublik Deutschland* (Frankfurt: Fischer Taschenbuch, 1985).

26. "Bilanz der Ermittlungen wegen NS-Straftaten veröffentlicht," *Süddeutsche Zeitung*, August 5, 1986.

27. Y. M. Bodemann, "Die Überwölbung von Auschwitz: Der jüdische Faktor in der Mythologie der Wenderepublik," *Ästhetik und Kommunikation* (Berlin, November 1984), p. 45.

28. Lea Fleischmann, *Dies ist nicht mein Land: Eine Jüdin verlässt die Bundesrepublik* (Hamburg: Rowohlt, 1980), p. 189.

29. Etty Hillesum, *An Interrupted Life: The Diaries of Etty Hillesum, 1941-1943* (New York: Pantheon, 1984), p. 122.

21

THE ABUSE OF HOLOCAUST STUDIES: Mercy Killing and the Slippery Slope

Peter H. Hare

The magnitude of Holocaust literature (including films) in the last twenty-five years is difficult to grasp. Probably no other event in the history of humankind has been as intensively examined. Although every decent human being applauds the effort to record and understand the horrors of the Third Reich, this tidal wave of literature carries with it dangers as well as benefits. I share Alan Rosenberg's view that the Holocaust is "a transformational event"[1] that "implies a deep and sweeping criticism of existing culture,"[2] but we must be on our guard against the abuse of the cry "Never again!"

As much as we may dislike to think of it in terms of fashion, it cannot be fairly denied that the Holocaust has become a fashionable topic among intellectuals and to a lesser extent in the general population. We need not be cynical to be suspicious of the motives of persons attracted to this fashion. Emotional satisfaction can be gained by expressing horror of such an indisputable evil. In a world of ambiguities and dilemmas, it is gratifying to have something that no one denies our right to despise.

Caught up in this fashion, we naturally shrink in horror from any proposed action that people suggest might lead even indirectly to another Holocaust. If, for example, we are critical of Israel's foreign policy and are told that the abandonment of that policy will somehow start the world down a slippery slope at the bottom of which will be the destruction of Israel and another Holocaust, we are reluctant to press our criticism despite the paucity of evidence offered in support of this prediction. We are so overawed by the certainty and enormity of the evil of the original Holocaust, that mention of the *mere possibility* of another Holocaust is sufficient to dissuade us from pressing our criticism. "Never again" has paralyzed our critical faculties.

Although the Nazi analogy can be used almost anywhere in ethical or political debate, in this essay I want to limit my attention to its use in bioethics,[3] more particularly to its use in the slippery slope argument against mercy killing or active euthanasia. If readers come to understand the dangers of the analogy in the debate about mercy killing, they will have little difficulty understanding them in other debates.

I should first explain what I mean by "mercy killing." Mercy killing is the use by one person of active means (e.g., lethal injection, shooting) to end the life of another for that other person's sake. I focus on mercy killing instead of "letting die" (passive euthanasia) because if mercy killing can be shown to be defensible, then a fortiori passive euthanasia can be too.

In my usage, mercy killing may be of a *terminally* ill (e.g., cancer) or of a *chronically* ill (e.g., paralysis) patient; it may be *voluntary* (e.g., a cancer patient pleads for death) or *nonvoluntary* (e.g., a severely defective newborn or someone in an advanced stage of Alzheimer's); it may be done by a *health professional* (e.g., a physician) or by a *nonprofessional* (e.g., a family member).

I believe that there are circumstances in which such killing is morally permissible and even obligatory and that changes should be made in the law so that people can do their duty without severe legal sanctions.

Readers will all be familiar with cases, but perhaps I should mention two cases involving Alzheimer's disease that are illustrative of this profoundly disturbing problem.

John Kraai, a physician outside Rochester, New York, was charged with second-degree murder in the insulin overdose death of Frederick Wagner, eighty-one, the doctor's childhood friend and long-time patient. Kraai told police that he had given Wagner three injections of insulin in Wagner's room at a nursing home because he could not bear to see his friend suffer the degenerative effects of Alzheimer's disease. Three weeks later Kraai, seventy-six, was found dead in his driveway, the victim of an apparent suicide. He had delivered more than 5,000 babies in his career and still made house calls at the time of his arrest. Fifteen hundred mourners attended his funeral where he was eulogized as someone who had "lived and died a doctor above all."

Even more heartbreaking is the Roswell Gilbert case dramatized in "Mercy or Murder," a television film starring Robert Young. Gilbert shot his wife who was in an advanced stage of Alzheimer's, after she had pleaded for help in dying. He was convicted of first-degree murder and imprisoned with the first possibility of parole in twenty-five years when he would be one hundred years old. Especially tragic is that it is very likely that the jury would have acquitted him on grounds of temporary insanity if he had not been a person of exceptional integrity and self-respect. On the witness stand Gilbert refused to tell of the terrible anguish he had felt about his wife's suffering and about killing her. He was convinced that, if he once started to tell of his feelings, he would break down and the jury would be moved to acquit him out of pity, not out of a belief that he had done the right thing. When cross-examined by the prosecuting attorney, Gilbert insisted that he had done what he ought to have done. Though Gilbert readily conceded that his act was illegal, the prosecutor pressed him to concede that it was murder. Looking him straight in the eye, Gilbert evenly replied, "Yes, it was murder, and so what?" After the trial the jury foreman described Gilbert as "arrogant."

Why do I think that acts such as those of Kraai and Gilbert are ethically permissible and even obligatory? For the simple reason that there are circumstances in which life is not worth living. In my view life has value only when it makes possible experiences of positive value. If experiences are overwhelmingly of negative value or there are no experiences at all, an individual is better off dead. If that individual is not in a position to end his life by himself, then another person has the right and even sometimes the duty to end that life—where the individual either clearly expresses that wish or clearly is incompetent to express any wish about life or death. What arguments are offered against mercy killing and how can they be rebutted?

1. It is said that mercy killing is murder and should be condemned like any other homicide. But, call it what you will, it is radically different from what is normally called murder in that it is done for the sake of the person killed and in that the individual requests it or is not in a position to request anything.

2. Why not use only passive means (e.g., withdrawal of a feeding tube)? Because such means only entail more suffering (e.g., a defective newborn may take many days to die by starvation). However, in cases where mercy killing does not entail significantly less suffering than letting die the latter is, of course, preferable.

3. Can't today's sophisticated painkilling drugs eliminate suffering if properly used? Much suffering can be avoided but there remain many situations where it is medically impossible to avoid terrible suffering. Advanced emphysema where a patient must frantically gasp for breath is one example.

4. Why not suicide? Because we are speaking of situations in which it would be extremely difficult or impossible for the individual to take her own life.

5. In cases where the individual expresses the wish to die, how do we know that he would not change his mind if he stayed alive longer? There are few certainties in this world. We can establish *beyond a*

reasonable doubt that the person would not change his mind. If that standard of evidence is good enough in a court of criminal law, it should be sufficient here also.

6. How can we be sure it is *really* her wish—that trauma, pain, and social pressure have not clouded the person's judgment? Many fear, for example, that a patient will ask for death because she believes that family members wish to be relieved of the inconvenience and expense of her care. Especially alarming to many is the statement of former Governor Richard Lamm of Colorado that terminally ill elderly people have "a duty to die." Again, we can establish *beyond a reasonable doubt* that it is the person's own wish. It should also be noted that if we are inclined to be skeptical of the genuineness of any wish to be killed, we should for consistency's sake be skeptical of the genuineness of a wish to stay alive through terrible suffering without hope of relief. It may be that many terminally ill patients in terrible pain accept treatment because they believe others (their physician, family members, etc.) expect it of them. Do we think it is necessary that we be *certain* that a person is not being significantly influenced by others in her wish to be kept alive?

7. How do we know that if the individual were kept alive by aggressive treatment or even left without treatment, medical scientists would not find a cure soon enough to save him? This question betrays an ignorance of the history of medicine. Cures do not suddenly appear on the scene. Physicians learn well in advance what treatments are being explored as promising, and, of course, mercy killing would be inappropriate where a promising treatment might soon be available. However, when a person is, for example, in an advanced stage of Alzheimer's, nothing short of a brain transplant would do since so many brain cells have been destroyed.

8. How do we know that the patient has not been misdiagnosed? If we used only passive means, if we only withdrew treatment, there would be an opportunity to discover misdiagnosis, but mercy killing will irreversibly destroy any chance of discovering misdiagnosis. To be sure, we must limit mercy killing to cases where disease is so far advanced that there can be no reasonable doubt of the diagnosis. In the Gilbert case, for example, it would be absurd to suppose that there was a significant possibility of his wife not having advanced Alzheimer's.

9. Won't condoning mercy killing start our society down a slippery slope at the bottom of which will be another Holocaust? This is the objection to active euthanasia that I want to examine in some detail.

It is argued, for instance, that if we permit mercy killing of those who request it or are incapable of making requests, we will gradually come to believe it is acceptable to kill a person against her will. Or, if we permit *mercy* killing, we will gradually come to consider it acceptable to kill when the person killed is not being spared terrible suffering, when his death is only sparing the killer inconvenience, expense, and the like. If we condone Gilbert killing his suffering wife, we unintentionally move society—so the argument goes—closer to condoning killing when the spouse is not suffering but is a psychological or financial burden on the killer.

We must first distinguish between the logical and the psychological forms of the slippery slope argument. In its logical form it is claimed that any principle that makes the killing of Gilbert's wife morally acceptable will logically commit its user to accept, for example, killing a person against his will. In other words, it is argued that no clear conceptual differences can be found between the forms of killing. In the recent literature it has been shown that this form of the argument is quite implausible; it is a relatively simple matter to state the conceptual differences.[4] The *psychological* or *sociopsychological* form of the argument presents a more serious challenge, however. Many are persuaded that it is psychologically likely that society will move to acceptance of conceptually distinct acts without the movement being anyone's intention. This sort of prediction has led many to insist that it is best to leave intact laws that make mercy killing illegal while it is conceded that acquittal on grounds of temporary insanity would have been morally acceptable in Gilbert's case. An unrevised homicide law is thought to be a psychological brake which stops a slip pell-mell down the dreaded slope.

It must be granted that the psychological form of the slippery slope argument can sometimes have genuine force.[5] It would be unreasonable to deny that historical examples of such unintended slipping from one moral code to another can be found and unreasonable to claim that such slipping cannot occur in the future. Indeed, as will become clear, I think the most important "transformation" wrought by the Holocaust has been its making us aware of our abysmal ignorance of the ways that ordinary human beings slip into evil. What I am rejecting is not the slippery slope argument per se but rather its *uncritical* use. I reject its uncritical use with some vehemence because implausible slope claims are not harmless intellectual sins; when widely made, they can mean untold amounts of unnecessary suffering in the world. In this essay I am presenting their use in the euthanasia debate as an illustration of this dire result. That the slippery slope argument is used uncritically in the euthanasia debate can be shown in various ways.

As James Rachels has pointed out, we have much evidence that "the approval of killing in one context does not necessarily lead to killing in different circumstances."[6] Examples are the killing of defective infants in Greece, the sacrifice of infants and feeble old people in some Eskimo societies, and, most important, killing in self-defense in our own society. In none of these cases do we find a slipping from one kind of killing to another.

Lucy Dawidowicz, the distinguished Holocaust scholar, has another way of showing how uncritically the slippery slope argument is used. As she explains, euthanasia under the Nazis is irrelevant to the current debate about mercy killing.

> In none of the [Nazi] cases was death administered because of a sick or dying person's intolerable suffering or because of a patient's own feelings about the uselessness of his life. In no case did the patient ask for death.... "Euthanasia"... was the code name applied to the murder—negative eugenics—of persons of "Aryan" origin whose bioracial characteristics were regarded by the Nazis as harmful to the social health of the *Volk*... [consequently] I do not think we can usefully apply the Nazi experience to gain insight or clarity to help us resolve our problems and dilemmas.[7]

If what was introduced as "euthanasia" by the Nazis was so different, we cannot, she thinks, reasonably argue that what we call euthanasia today will lead to what Nazi euthanasia led to. However, in response to Dawidowicz, Laurence McCollough suggests that the analogy may hold up after all. He concedes that in our society we do not have the "racist attitudes already in place" that in German society made possible the slippery slope but suggests that in our society a commitment to an "economic rationale" (i.e., social utility) already in place might play the same role as racist attitudes did in Germany. "There, racism overrode personal autonomy; here, it might be an economic rationale—the attitude that we won't spend so much per year to keep somebody alive."[8] Although some have urged that our society take serious account of social utility in the allocation of resources to health care, surely the billions of federal dollars spent annually on kidney dialysis is enough to show that "an economic rationale" in the arena of health care has little influence in our society. By even the most generous standard, many of those on dialysis (e.g., drug addicts whose unsanitary needles led to infection and kidney failure) have no significant contribution to make to society, but the public (and its elected representatives) is horrified by the suggestion that such people be denied free dialysis.

Taking another tack, Milton Himmelfarb suggests that an argument

> could be made ... about a general coarsening of regard for life. There exists a kind of slippery slope in a certain kind of accountant's mentality or an engineer's mentality in dealing with the questions

of life. The bias of a quasi-religious awe toward life, which has been there all along, at least in principle, is now eliminated. In its place is a coarser and maybe even a cruel way of thinking about human beings and handling them like commodities. Someone might call this Nazi, if only for rhetorical purposes. While it has nothing to do necessarily with the specifics of Nazism, yet the Nazis too did not have the bias of awe toward life and dealt with life (certain kinds of life at any rate) as if they were dealing with mere things.[9]

However, insofar as such a generalization about attitudes in our society has clear meaning, it is challenged by such counterexamples as the federal dialysis program.

Enough examples have been given, I trust, to make plain how readily one can imagine slippery slopes down which our society might slide to another Holocaust. A little ingenuity and rhetorical imagination is enough to describe numerous dreadful slopes. But I want to argue that this speculative plethora of possible slopes has a significance very different from what is usually supposed. This significance can be seen if we look at the full range of imaginable slopes.

Let us imagine what might be called a "reverse" slippery slope. Just as one may argue that killing in specific circumstances will lead to generalized killing, one may argue that refusal to permit mercy killing is an expression of indifference to suffering in specific circumstances that may lead by a slippery slope to a general indifference to suffering in our society. One speculative slippery slope is as plausible (or implausible) as the other.

Another reverse slippery slope may be imagined. As I pointed out, Roswell Gilbert's exceptional integrity played a major role in his conviction. One may argue that the conviction for mercy killing of people of such character will lead our society via a slippery slope to a general disregard for personal integrity. My point is simply that, for every slippery slope that can be imagined as bringing another Holocaust from *permitting* mercy killing, there can be imagined another slope that will bring such consequences from *refusal to permit* mercy killing. These speculative predictions, in other words, cancel one another out.

This is not to suggest that we abandon slippery slope arguments altogether. As I said above, the psychological form of the argument can sometimes have merit. The argument has merit when it is based on adequate evidence in support of the prediction of disaster. At present such predictions are wildly speculative and uncritical uses of the argument abound.

A more responsible approach is found in the work of John Sabini and Maury Silver, who have looked carefully at the variety of empirical studies made by social scientists of the ways in which people slip into actions characteristic of the Holocaust.[10] Perhaps most famous are the studies by Stanley Milgram. In Milgram's classic experiments subjects of normal morality come to obey orders to give the experimenter's confederate what the subjects believe are severe shocks. Less well known are the prison studies in which normal college-age males were asked to play the roles of guards and prisoners and came to treat each other with shocking brutality. Other relevant empirical studies are those of peer influence on a subject's judgment.

As they explain, the purpose of Sabini and Silver's sociopsychology of the Holocaust is to

> bring the phenomena of the camps closer to home, to see how this horror, this inhumanity, could have been the product not only of deranged individuals but of "normal" people placed in deranged circumstances. We have attempted to draw links between what we know the artisans of the Holocaust did and what ordinary people have done in laboratory settings.[11]

Significantly, Sabini and Silver do not employ slippery slope arguments to condone or condemn disputed forms of behavior in our society. They recognize that their sociopsychology, though it is more scientific than the seminal work of Hannah Arendt, is much too sketchy to permit responsible predictions of the sort required in cogent slippery slope arguments.

Most important, the work of Sabini and Silver suggests the true significance of the Holocaust for our society. Holocaust studies benefit our society most when they are rigorous empirical investigations of how ordinary human beings can slip into actions characteristic of the Holocaust, when they are steps on the way to a fully adequate sociopsychology in which cogent slope predictions can be made. However, until an approximation of an adequate sociopsychology is achieved, the use of slippery slope arguments, as in the mercy-killing debate, is a dangerous abuse of Holocaust studies. Under cover of condemnation of the Third Reich, users of such arguments are adding to the sum of suffering in the world. Moreover, their irresponsible arguments are likely to discredit Holocaust studies in general. If Holocaust studies are discredited, the motivation to produce an adequate sociopsychology of evil will be lost and the transformation of our society in light of the meaning of the Holocaust will no longer be possible.

NOTES

1. Alan Rosenberg, "The Philosophical Implications of the Holocaust," in *Perspectives on the Holocaust*, ed. Randolph L. Braham (Boston: Kluwer Nijhoff, 1983), p. 4.

2. Alan Rosenberg, Chapter 19, "The Crisis in Knowing and Understanding the Holocaust."

3. "Biomedical Ethics and the Shadow of Nazism: A Conference on the Proper Use of the Nazi Analogy in Ethical Debate, April 8, 1976," *Hastings Center Report* 6, no. 4 (August 1976): 1–20. The *locus classicus* of the use of the slippery slope argument in the context of the euthanasia debate is Leo Alexander, "Medical Science under Dictatorship," *New England Journal of Medicine* 241, no. 2 (July 14, 1949): 39–47.

4. Tom L. Beauchamp and James F. Childress, *Principles of Biomedical Ethics*, 2d ed. (New York: Oxford University Press, 1982), pp. 120–22.

5. Gregory W. Trianosky, "Rule-Utilitarianism and the Slippery Slope," *Journal of Philosophy* 75 (1978): 414–24.

6. James Rachels, *The End of Life: Euthanasia and Morality* (New York: Oxford University Press, 1986), p. 174. In my view, Rachels's book is the most persuasive discussion of euthanasia to date. It would be pointless to try to summarize his arguments here. However, it should be noted that he recognizes that legalized mercy killing might be abused "just as there are abuses of virtually every social practice. . . . The crucial issue is whether the evil of the abuses would be so great as to outweigh the benefit of the practice" (p. 175). Although he concludes the benefits are not outweighed, he is careful to explain precisely what form the legalization should take: "My suggestion for legalizing euthanasia is that a plea of mercy-killing be acceptable as a defence against a charge of homocide in much the same way that a plea of self-defence is acceptable. . . . If this proposal were adopted, it would *not* mean that every time euthanasia was performed a court trial would follow. In clear cases of self-defence, prosecutors do not bring charges. . . . Similarly, in clear cases of mercy-killing, where there is no doubt about the patient's hopeless condition or desire to die, charges would not be brought for the same reasons" (pp. 185–86).

7. "Biomedical Ethics and the Shadow of Nazism," p.4.

8. Ibid., p. 15.

9. Ibid., p. 18.

10. John Sabini and Maury Silver, *Moralities of Everyday Life* (Oxford: Oxford University Press, 1982), pp. 55–87.

11. Ibid., pp. 86–87. Cf. Janice T. Gibson and Mika Haritos-Fatouros, "The Education of a Torturer: There Is Cruel Method in the Madness of Teaching People to Torture. Almost Anyone Can Learn It," *Psychology Today*, November 1986, pp. 50–58.

22

THE "INCOMPREHENSIBILITY" OF THE HOLOCAUST: Tightening up Some Loose Usage

Dan Magurshak

As scholarship concerning the destruction of European Jewry accelerates, articulate survivors and some well-informed scholars remind the researchers that, as an event that demands serious investigation, the Holocaust may be, nonetheless, uniquely incomprehensible. Nora Levin writes: "The Holocaust refuses to go the way of most history, not only because of the magnitude of the destruction . . . but because events surrounding it are still in a very real sense humanly incomprehensible. . . . Indeed, comprehensibility may never be possible."[1] In the same vein Elie Wiesel asserts that "Auschwitz cannot be explained" because "the Holocaust transcends history." Emphasizing his point, he soberly adds, "The dead are in possession of a secret that we, the living, are neither worthy of nor capable of recovering."[2] If Holocaust scholars accept these statements about the incomprehensibility, the inexplicability, and the historical transcendence of their subject matter as true, they find themselves in the bind of secular Aquinases. Committed to complete understanding and explication of an inexplicable, they can hope only to make the darkness a little brighter. Convinced that the horror of systematic genocide must be comprehended, they must still admit that their subject, like Thomas's Trinity, is theoretically incomprehensible in principle.

As Levin and Wiesel use the notion, incomprehensibility, at the very least, means the impossibility of understanding fully and adequately the "jointly sufficient," or the necessary, conditions for the Holocaust's occurrence. It means that even after ideally exhaustive historical, psychological, and sociological analyses, the researchers would still have failed to penetrate the essence of this event. It also implies that, since control and prevention of such outrages presuppose some under-

This article is reprinted from *Judaism* 29, no. 2 (Spring 1980): 233–42, with permission.

standing of their essential components, a generation whose scholars remember the past may, because of its incomprehensibility, still be doomed to repeat it. Indeed, some would-be investigators might even conclude that, since a "historically transcendent" phenomenon is inexplicable, scholarly "remembrance," except for honoring the dead, is rather fruitless.

If the Holocaust is humanly incomprehensible, then the incentive to study the phenomenon, the commitment to spreading an awareness of it beyond academic circles, and the ability to prevent a similar occurrence are seriously diminished. And, since these implications are not inconsequential for humankind's appropriation of the past in constructive self-knowledge, I intend to examine this notion of incomprehensibility to show in what legitimate sense the Holocaust may be considered incomprehensible. Distinguishing the various important meaning variations of this term one from another, I suggest that, except in the case of "affective comprehension" and for the "theological" and religiously neutral "cosmic" ways of asking why the Holocaust occurred, the Holocaust is, in principle, as comprehensible and as amenable to disciplined study as any complex human phenomenon. And where it is incomprehensible I suggest that it is not uniquely so.

THE HOLOCAUST AS INCOMPREHENSIBLE

"Holistic" and Empathetic Incomprehensibility

In standard usage, to comprehend is "to grasp with the mind, conceive fully or adequately, understand, 'take in.'"[3] To call an event "incomprehensible," then, is to assert that one cannot fully or adequately understand it; in this sense, one may find modern physics incomprehensible. There is, however, an extended use of this term not unfamiliar to students of the Holocaust. After watching *Night and Fog,* listening to a survivor soberly recalling an "average" day in Auschwitz, or reading Elie Wiesel's *Night,* one is often overwhelmed as an affective, intelligent, and articulate being. Consider the following passage from *Night:*

> Not far from us, flames were leaping up from a ditch, gigantic flames. They were burning something. A lorry drew up at the pit and delivered its load—little children. Babies! Yes, I saw it with my own eyes . . . those children in the flames. (Is it surprising that I could not sleep after that? Sleep had fled from my eyes.)[4]

Having entered the kingdom of darkness through such testimony, one seems to collapse; a benumbed mind is unable to reflect as one dumbfoundedly sits in a silent unreality. A mixture of moral outrage, frustration, and profound sorrow churns in the pit of one's stomach. One is unable to speak, one does not know how to respond to children burning alive for the sake of saving two-fifths of a pfennig on poison gas. The occurrence is "unimaginable," "unbelievable," "incomprehensible." And even after one has analyzed such an atrocity historically, psychologically, and from other perspectives, a rereading of the account can plunge one back into the same experience. Somehow, the fact of burning children is irreducible to a complete explanation.

Nonetheless, the terms used in this context do not assert that this typical Holocaust atrocity is actually beyond the bounds of human imagination, unworthy of epistemic belief, or unintelligible in principle. They simply express a sense of being completely overwhelmed, a sense that is not unique to the horror of the Holocaust either in its occurrence or in its reoccurrence after explanations of the horrifying event have been given. One can, in fact, have the same experience with beauty.

Take, for example, the comparatively trivial phenomenon of a sunset. The explanation of this occurrence is quite complete; the earth orbiting around the sun and rotating on its axis has an atmosphere of a certain composition which refracts and diffuses light rays in ways determined by the angle of incidence and other physical considerations. Even the human interest in the sun is fairly explicable; we are a diurnal species whose survival depends upon the light, heat, and relative position of this star. In spite of such comprehension, however, we are still overwhelmed by a sunset and we still call it "mysterious" or "unbelievably beautiful" to express our aesthetic wonder. Such expressions do not assert that a sunset is theoretically impenetrable, since we already understand it; they simply call attention to two different human modes of encountering the phenomenon, modes (a theoretical one and an affective or aesthetic one) whose relation to one another and whose relative importance to human beings are still much debated. Analogously, an investigator can comprehend rather completely the course of political, social, and economic events that led to modern German anti-Semitism and to the adoption of a policy that exterminated the Jew like vermin. Yet, when the investigator rereads the passage quoted above, he or she may still numbly ask how it could have happened. From a perspective importantly similar to that in which one experiences the majesty of a sunset, the Holocaust as a totality and in its particular atrocities may be called "incomprehensible." Such incomprehensibility, however, does not entail the conclusion that the Holocaust is theoretically incomprehensible, an impenetrable mystery that remains in principle beyond the grasp of human understanding. Like other instances of overpowering beauty or horror, it is overwhelming without necessarily being incomprehensible. One may still conceive of it adequately, understand it, "take it in."

One can also speak of the incomprehensibility of the Holocaust in a related but narrower sense when one notes the difficulty that a sympathetic nonparticipant might have in empathizing with survivors. As Wiesel asserts, "Only those who were there know what it was; the others will never know."[5] Levin concurs when she writes: "Ordinary human beings simply cannot rethink themselves into such a world and ordinary ways to achieve empathy fail, for all of the recognizable attributes of human reaction are balked at the Nazi divide; the world of Auschwitz was, in truth, a new planet."[6] Both writers state that even sympathetic readers are unable to identify intellectually or to experience vicariously the feelings, thoughts, and attitudes of the victims. And anyone who has read Holocaust literature extensively would have no difficulty extending this claim to the experiences of the executioners and the bystanders as well. When one reads about Warsaw Christians apparently enjoying the infernal spectacle of the ghetto's destruction on Easter Sunday, one finds it sickeningly difficult to empathize with these spectators, some of whom were more than willing to call the Nazis' attention to burning people as they leaped from the blazing buildings.[7] Nor can one easily "think oneself back" to experience the world as did Adolf Eichmann in Vienna. If the term "incomprehensible" refers to this overtaxing of one's capacity for empathy, then, perhaps, the Holocaust is incomprehensible.

Upon careful consideration, however, one sees that such incomprehensibility is again neither unique to the Holocaust nor unquestionably absolute. For example, no matter how much one reads about men in battle or steeps oneself in war films and documentaries, one still remains an observer rather than a participant if one has never been in combat. Even if one successfully empathizes with the young soldier in *All Quiet on the Western Front*, one still has not lived that experience which belongs to the veteran. Given any possible experience, one who has lived through it has, in some sense, a jump on those who have experienced it only vicariously, at least in terms of "knowing" what that experience is like. Of course Wiesel and Levin assert that one cannot even empathize with the people of the Holocaust, that a gulf exists between one's total experience and that of the survivors which makes it nearly impossible to experience even vicariously the world of gas chambers and incinerators. The same thing might be said, however, of the attempt to empathize with a combat soldier if one lacks any experience of a combat situation. At first, both kinds of experience are relatively incomprehensible; but as one begins to identify feelings, attitudes, and thoughts in one's own experience that appear analogous to those described by soldiers, inmates, or SS guards, one may piece together a fairly accurate sense of what it must have been like to live through some aspects of battle or some episodes of the Holocaust. For example, a person who has been subject to military induction or some other impersonal processing might well imagine what deportation might have been like. And if one is honest about one's own feelings of prejudice, one might begin to understand how such emotions, combined with the proper circumstances and ideology, could become murderous. The more one reflects upon and analyzes the experiences in question, the more one is able to explore that "new planet" which first seemed inaccessible to "ordinary people." The difference between the experiences of a participant and a spectator is undeniable; nonetheless, the initial inability to empathize with the Holocaust people may be overcome asymptotically as one studies, reflects, and steeps oneself in the vivid testimony of that time. It is, after all, precisely one of the functions of literature and film to allow us to enter into a new world and to experience it as if we had lived through it ourselves.

Theoretical Incomprehensibility

In addition to speaking about the "holistic" and empathetic incomprehensibility of the Holocaust, one can also refer to its "cosmic" incomprehensibility.[8] That is, when one asks the theoretical question, Why did, or how could, the Holocaust occur? from either a theological or religiously neutral perspective, one can offer no empirically verifiable answer. As is the case with any event, one cannot fully grasp or adequately understand why God would let such an atrocity occur or why the cosmos is such that it could have happened.

Believers in Israel's God of history or in the Christian God of the resurrection have often asked how God—omnipotent, omniscient, benevolent—could let the children burn under the blue and empty sky. The event demands a rethinking of speculations about God's nature, its relationship to humankind, the plausibility of its existence, and its purpose in at least allowing, if not willing, such carnage. Whether it is proper or not, some troubled believers, in Eliezer Berkowitz's words, would like "to steal a glance at 'the hand' of the Almighty in order to be able to appreciate what meaning the senseless destruction of European Israel might have in the divine scheme."[9] But, given the nature of theological questions, no complete and totally satisfying answers will be forthcoming; at best, believers can hope only for disciplined speculation consistent with a certain set of theological assertions perhaps rationally supported and made within a context of a particular faith. And if theologians accept Irving Greenberg's injunction not to present any insights that would mock the reality of the burning children, they are constantly reminded of the difficulty of reconciling traditional notions of God with the technological mass murder of the chosen people.[10] In the context of traditional theistic theology, the Holocaust seems theoretically incomprehensible; as such, however, it is only another case of theological puzzlement familiar to every theologian, a case not unlike that of the Lisbon earthquake which dominated philosophical theology for a century. The problem of evil and the purposes of the intelligent God of theism have always taxed human comprehension.

A similar incomprehensibility appears when one asks the "ultimate" cosmic questions. Paul Edwards correctly observes that "when we ask of anything, x, why it happened or why it is what it is ... we assume that there is something or some set of conditions, other than x, in terms of which it can be explained."[11] But once one has investigated the historical, socioeconomic, and psychological conditions that made the Holocaust possible, one often has a not uncommon tendency to ask why the universe could not have been such that a technologically simplified program of genocide would have been impossible. Could there not have been a universe with all of the advantages of this one but with none of its disadvantages, particularly moral evil? If confronted with a theological response to this question, the inquirer could simply ask why the God that does exist should exist, rather than another. The question is ultimate insofar as the questioner accepts no set of conditions as an adequate response; he or she simply asks why these conditions, rather than others, should obtain and, therefore, rules out, a priori, any answer to the inquiry. If this is the case, then the Holocaust is also "ultimately" incomprehensible, but no more so than any other event in human or natural history. Any time one presses an inquiry to the ultimate "why," one places oneself within a realm where self-consistent speculation lacking cogency and compellingness is all that one can achieve. For some thinkers, unanswerable ultimate questions are, in some sense, the most meaningful and most important inquiries; hence, to say that the Holocaust is incomprehensible in this sense is, for them, to say that, in the way that really matters the event is, indeed, an impenetrable mystery. But this means only that the destruction of European Jewry, like any event in the cosmos, is not "ultimately" explicable.

THE HOLOCAUST AS COMPREHENSIBLE

Once one has noted that confronting the Holocaust is overwhelming, empathetically taxing, and both theologically and ultimately incomprehensible, one is free to investigate it simply as a tragic but, nonetheless, human phenomenon. One can take the general question, Why, or how, did the Holocaust occur? and break it down to the following concerns:

1. How was it possible for a modern state to carry out the systematic murder of a whole people for no other reason than that they were Jews?
2. How was it possible for a whole people to allow itself to be destroyed?
3. How was it possible for a world to stand by without halting this destruction?[12]

And, in asking these questions, one assumes that one can discover the jointly sufficient or the necessary conditions—depending upon one's theory of explanation—that make aspects of the phenomenon intelligible. One expects that the event will yield to the analytical efforts of the various disciplines, and nothing that has been said about its incomprehensibility entails a contrary expectation. At present the Holocaust may be, in large measure, uncomprehended, but this in no way entails or even plausibly suggests that disciplined study is incapable of comprehending it. There is no good reason to deny that careful, exhaustive, historical, cultural, and psychological studies will not, at least ideally, yield a complete and coherent account that traces the course of events and the play of factors by which the atrocity came about. Like any event of similar magnitude, the mass annihilation of Jews, Gypsies, and other enemies of the Reich rests upon a complex foundation of conditions which may never be completely excavated because of time limitations, lack of information, and a dearth of investigative insights; nonetheless, the investigator aims at an ideal completeness that indicates at least the possibility that more time, more information, and new theories will gradually diminish the relative incomprehensibility of this event. One can see the plausibility of this approach in a brief summary of two analyses, one historical and the other psychological, [which makes partially intelligible] what some thinkers might have once relegated to the realm of impenetrable mystery.

Breaking down the first question quoted above, one can ask how anti-Semitism in modern Germany developed; more important, one might ask how anti-Semitism became politically acceptable. In the second chapter of The War against the Jews,[13] Dawidowicz sheds a good deal of light upon the conditions that made this acceptance possible. As she explains it, the German peoples of the nineteenth century inherited a Christian-inspired popular and intellectual anti-Semitism that depicted Jews as foreigners—a state within a state—killers of Christ, well poisoners, and the cause of every misfortune, whether natural, economic, or political. The forces of nationalism, *Volkist* theory, bogus racial science, and fear of modernity reinforced and built upon this foundation. The religious outcast and transmitter of plague now became politically dangerous, a threat to national unity, a defiler of the transcendental essence of the German peoples, and the capitalistic cause of the urbanism and industrialism that threatened the peasant, the small merchant, and the *Volkist* ideal of the simple life rooted in the soil of the homeland. Involved in the expanding money economy, the Jews became the scapegoat for the depression of 1873. Soon, politicians campaigned on explicit anti-Semitic platforms, and, in 1887, Böckel was elected to the Reichstag by a peasant constituency that agreed with his message that Jews were, by nature, alien to Germany. In 1892, the Conservative party, the most prestigious party of its day, adopted an explicit anti-Semitic plank. In this account, Dawidowicz weaves the various forces and influences into a coherent narrative that allows one to comprehend how an important segment of the German voting population could live with, and support in good conscience, the apparently self-evident truth that the Jew was, and always would be, a troublemaking, alien inferior. She also helps one to understand that when such an unquestioned assumption was reinforced by intellectuals, "scientists," and politicians, an upstanding German might consider himself bound to seek a "final solution" of some sort to the "Jewish question." On the basis of this account, one can comprehend, perhaps with a shudder, how insidiously subtle and unnoticed the development of a catastrophe might be, particularly for those involved in it.

But once the murder began, how could an upstanding German participate in any of its phases? Stanley Milgram's by now classic experiments on obedience to authority contribute much to comprehending this aspect of the general question, an aspect that initially strained the understanding of both lay people and social scientists.

Milgram introduces his investigation by placing it in the following context:

> From 1933 to 1945 millions of innocent people were systematically slaughtered on command. Gas chambers were built, death camps were guarded, daily quotas of corpses were produced with the same efficiency as the manufacture of appliances. These inhumane policies may have originated in the mind of a single person, but they could only have been carried out on a massive scale if a very large number of people obeyed orders.[14]

To find out whether or not ordinary people would act against their own moral standards in obeying the commands of one perceived as a legitimate authority, Milgram devised an experimental situation in which subjects agreed to perform a task that, they believed, inflicted pain upon another person whenever the latter failed to respond correctly. Milgram's findings were as follows:

> It is the extreme willingness of adults to go to almost any lengths on the command of an authority that constitutes the chief finding of the study and the fact most urgently demanding explanation. . . . Ordinary people, simply doing their jobs, and without any particular hostility on their part, can become agents in a terrible destructive process. Moreover, even when the destructive effects of their work become patently clear, and they are asked to carry out actions incompatible with fundamental standards of morality, relatively few people have the resources needed to resist authority.[15]

Milgram explains these phenomena in terms of antecedent conditions, the nature of the "agentic state," and the factors that bind one to submissive obedience. According to him, human beings manifest a tendency to obey which functions adaptively in communal life and which all types of social groups strongly reinforce. One develops a habit of obedience to authority and although one may intellectually decide not to obey a particular order in a situation like Milgram's experiment, one is "frequently unable to transform this conviction into action."[16] One is tightly bound to the task by the recurrent nature of the action (to quit now is to admit that it was wrong to do until now), the initial agreement with the experimenter, and anticipated embarrassment of breaking up a well-defined social situation. Furthermore, one sees the entire project with reference to one's relationship to the experimenter; wishing to perform competently, one attends to instruction, focuses almost exclusively on the authority while tuning out the victim, and endows the authority with an almost superhuman character. One also tends to accept the definition and interpretation of the situation provided by authority, for example, that this experiment is a noble pursuit of knowledge. But, perhaps most important, once a person submits to authority, then a superego function shift occurs; that is,

> A man feels responsible *to* the authority directing him but feels no responsibility *for* the content of the actions that the authority prescribes. Morality does not disappear, but acquires a radically different focus: the subordinate person feels shame or pride depending on how adequately he has performed the actions called for by authority.[17]

Milgram's findings apply to people acting in a freely accepted situation. When conditions such as a totalitarian state, the dehumanization of the victim, and the threat of capital punishment for disobedience are added, then one comprehends even better how decent people could participate in the task of mass murder.

Neither Milgram nor Dawidowicz answers all questions about the respective problems, but such incompleteness is neither absolute nor unique; given access to all relevant information, an investigator can, at least in principle, fill in the picture up to the boundaries of the cosmic questions already discussed. Practically speaking, the Holocaust, like the French Revolution, the Second World War, or any complex human phenomenon provides the various disciplines with an almost endless field of investigation which is, nonetheless, always open to further comprehension.

CONCLUSION

The argument of this essay has not intended to minimize the overwhelming importance of the mass murder of six million Jews, five hundred thousand Gypsies, and millions of other people. It denies neither the awesome horror of this event nor the harsh challenge with which it confronts the contemporary generation of scholars and thoughtful laypersons. It simply clarifies the senses in which the Holocaust may be properly called incomprehensible and, thus, clears the way for the unimpeded investigation of this event. The calculated extermination of human beings, pursued for its own sake, must not be forgotten, but neither should it only be remembered; it must be critically and compassionately analyzed, explained, and comprehended. Only in this way might the fires of Auschwitz "illumine otherwise dark corners of our moral landscape, making us aware of present acts of human demonry we would not otherwise see."[18] Through the study of the Holocaust, human beings can gain a brutally harsh knowledge of their capabilities and tendencies, a self-knowledge that is a necessary condition for the prevention of the actualization of their worst possibilities.

NOTES

1. Nora Levin, *The Holocaust: The Destruction of European Jewry 1933–1945* (New York: Thomas Y. Crowell, 1968), p. xi.

2. Elie Wiesel, "Trivializing the Holocaust: Semi-Fact and Semi-Fiction," *New York Times*, April 16, 1978, sect. 2.

3. *Oxford English Dictionary* (Oxford: Clarendon Press, 1961), vol. 2, p. 741.

4. Elie Wiesel, *Night*, trans. Stella Rodway (New York: Avon, 1960), p. 42.

5. Wiesel, "Trivializing the Holocaust," p. 29.

6. Levin, *The Holocaust*, p. xii.

7. Alexander Donat, *The Holocaust Kingdom* (New York: Holocaust Library, 1978), pp. 152–53.

8. The notion of cosmic questions, with its distinction between theological and ultimate questions, is used by Paul Edwards in his article, "Why," in the *Encyclopedia of Philosophy* (New York: Macmillan, 1967), vol. 8, pp. 296-302.

9. Eliezer Berkovits, *Faith after the Holocaust* (New York: KTAV, 1973), p. 69.

10. Irving Greenberg, "Cloud of Smoke, Pillar of Fire: Judaism, Christianity, and Modernity after the Holocaust," in *Auschwitz: Beginning of a New Era? Reflections on the Holocaust,* ed. Eva Fleischer (New York: KTAV, 1977), pp. 23, 26, and 34.

11. Edwards, "Why," p. 301.

12. Lucy S. Dawidowicz, *The War against the Jews, 1933-1945* (New York: Bantam Books, 1976), p. xxi.

13. Ibid., pp. 29-62.

14. Stanley Milgram, *Obedience to Authority: An Experimental View* (New York: Harper Colophon Books, 1975), p. 1.

15. Ibid., pp. 5-6.

16. Ibid., p. 148.

17. Ibid., pp. 145-46.

18. Robert McAfee Brown, "The Holocaust as a Problem in Moral Choice," in *Dimensions of the Holocaust* (Evanston: Northwestern University Press, 1977), p. 62.

23

STUDYING THE HOLOCAUST'S IMPACT TODAY: Some Dilemmas of Language and Method

Alice L. and A. Roy Eckardt

While studying certain aspects of the aftermath of the Holocaust in Germany and other parts of Europe, as well as in Israel, during the latter half of the 1970s—especially that event's continuing interpretations and reputed lessons in our time—we became aware that some basic conceptual and procedural problems face all those engaged in such study. The present discussion represents our tentative consideration of these issues.

"DIE ENDLÖSUNG"

Although we are not dealing with the event of the Holocaust as such, we can hardly escape or ignore divergent views of the nature and meaning of that reality.

The German Nazis determined upon *die Endlösung der Judenfrage in Europa* ("the final solution of the Jewish question in Europe"). This formulation was officially put forth on January 20, 1942, at a conference at Gross-Wannsee, although the actual decision had probably been made earlier.[1] The Wannsee agreement was simply the logical consummation, or merely gave expression to, a resolve whose roots are traceable to 1919, when Adolf Hitler declared that his ultimate objective was "the removal of the Jews altogether." According to the minutes of the Wannsee Conference, the eleven million Jews of all Europe were marked for death.[2] Yet it is misleading to comprehend the Holocaust solely within the *Aktion* of killing.

The *Endlösung* means that everything is permitted, that any and every method is to be used in the struggle—indeed, in the *enjoying* of the struggle[3]—to obliterate the single pestilence that is destroying the

This article is reprinted from *Judaism* 27, no. 2 (Spring 1978): 222-32, with permission.

entire world: the Jew. The German Nazis taught that the Jew is the *Untermensch*, the contaminator from below. Accordingly, his "name" is taken away; he does not deserve one; he is only the number tattooed into his flesh.

The *Endlösung* is the competitive "race of the dead" at the killing center of Treblinka and elsewhere, a physiological competition that makes one man's survival absolutely dependent upon the next man's extinction. For the "race of the dead" decreed which prisoners would be murdered and which ones "spared."

At the heart of the *Endlösung* is the use of Jews as officially determined agents to revile and torture their fellow Jews. The Jew is turned into the accomplice of his executioners. The *Endlösung* is ultimate degradation. It is the attempted dehumanization of the Jew and the torture process that makes it possible. The *Endlösung* is total mental, physical, and spiritual breakdown. It is the ontic separation of children and parents, wives and husbands. Child, parent, wife, husband—all are enforced witnesses to the suffering and annihilation of their loved ones.

The chronology of *das perfide System* (Jan Bastiaans) was: Declare the Jew to be the *Untermensch*; then make certain he is this, thereby vindicating your major premise; and only then, kill him. In this respect, the *Endlösung* had nothing to do with the specific advent of death, for the ultimate shamefulness lay in staying alive. Objectively speaking, death was transfigured into a form of mercy. Death became salvation—although, of course, the *manner* of death incarnated the dehumanization and was the mirror image of the terror. It is often said that the nightmares of the captives were perhaps more frightening than their encounter with death.

Speaking of life in the Vilna ghetto, Abba Kovner (who helped to lead the uprising there) attests that the most appalling thing was not death but being defiled to the depths of one's soul every hour of the day.[4] Perhaps the ultimate in attempted dehumanization was the Nazi effort to obliterate the Jews and Jewishness from all human memory. At the same time, we are not allowed to forget the complicity of those people and nations other than the persecutors themselves. There is much truth in Elie Wiesel's judgment that the victims suffered more "from the indifference of the onlookers than from the brutality of the executioner."[5] Cynthia Haft writes that the futility of the agony is contained in the words *et ils savaient que vous ne pleureriez pas* ("and they knew that you would not weep").[6]

Again, the *Endlösung* reached out even to those who gave the appearance of surviving it. Many could not endure the shock of "liberation." They died. For vast numbers of those who lived, the years after liberation were as dreadful as, or worse than, the horror of the camps.

Most sadly, some no longer retained the strength that human beings are required to muster if they are to be happy.[7] Thus, to be freed was, in many cases, not to be freed. How could these people adapt to a life that they had lost? Many lacked the power to retrieve their former world, a fight that would demand enormous inner resources. Even those with some strength left found that the old world was gone. Their loved ones and friends, their homes and their countries—all these had been destroyed.

There is the valley of the shadow of death. And there is the *Endlösung*: the valley of the historical dehumanization, terror, agony, and final murder of the Jew, only because he is a Jew. But we cannot exclude, and we are not permitted to forget, the historic resistance of the Jew to the war against him. For a light burns within the shadows: The German Nazi campaign to dehumanize the Jewish people failed. Jewry as a whole refused to fall to the level of the *Untermensch*. Only the real *Untermenschen* did that, the enemies of the Jews.

"HOLOCAUST": ACCEPTED BUT QUESTIONED CONCEPT

In various countries the term "Holocaust," with its counterparts in different languages, has not gained total recognition as a means of identifying the reality whose aftermath occupies us, although that word is being used more and more. A major objection to it is that, within its historically original frame of reference, the concept designated a totally burnt or consumed offering. (Some victims of the Nazis were, of course, burned, but most were murdered by other means). It would be infamous to identify these human beings as offerings or sacrifices. This is not to ignore the sublime fact that many Jews did sacrifice themselves for the sake of others (as did some non-Jews).

A further objection is the imprecision of "Holocaust," in partial contrast, for example, to a term often employed in Germany: *Judenvernichtung*, the annihilation of the Jews. Imprecision is found as well in the Hebrew concept of *Shoah* (destruction, catastrophe), although in Jewish circles and in Israel that term is widely applied to the Holocaust. The major difficulty with it is its implication of a kind of impersonal fatality. (English-using scholars in Israel and elsewhere now customarily employ "Holocaust.")

Imprecision also appears in certain other Hebrew words sometimes used to stand for the Holocaust. The French scholar Bernard Dupuy refers to the habitual word *Shoq*, which evokes the idea of catastrophe or cataclysm. Again, there is *Hurban*, which, like *Shoah*, signifies destruction or ruin, although in this case a specific application has traditionally been made to the destruction of the Temple in 70 C.E. Various French terms involve the same difficulty of imprecision, and there is an added problem. Two words that appear in French and correspond to the customary meaning of *l'holocauste* are *olah* and *qorban*. (These are simply transliterations from the Hebrew originals.) We indicated the problem above: Both concepts connote, in varying ways, the idea of a sacrificial offering. Dupuy concludes that some Christian authors manifest an excessive tendency to comprehend *"la Shoa"* (*Ha'Shoah*) in a sacrifical sense.[8]

Although *holocauste* is a French word, many French interpreters (with others) use the improperly selective, though powerful, symbol, "Auschwitz." The Nazi concept, *die Endlösung*, as used above, is justified only in the interest of grappling, as though from inside Nazi demonry itself, with the total, eschatological nature of the *Judenvernichtung*.

Among Germans, the word "Holocaust" is still unfamiliar, and there is no specific counterpart in the German language. However, in *Christen und Juden*, a 1975 study officially adopted by the Council of the Evangelische Kirche in Deutschland (EKD, the Protestant church in Germany), recognition is afforded the term, and a discriminate definition is supplied: "the annihilation of a great part of European Jewry through National Socialism."[9]

Because of the wide and increasing acceptance of the wording "the Holocaust," there appears to be little choice but to use it, although always with a certain unease. The EKD definition is not perfect: It communicates nothing of the systematic, technological, and official character of the *Judenvernichtung*. Again, as pointed out above, the *Endlösung* means infinitely more than "killing." "Annihilation" must be taken to encompass the total process of the war against the Jewish people. And the concept of the Holocaust must always be extended to the great acts and spirit of resistance to that would-be destruction.

The imprecision of the various words previously enumerated is partially relieved when the definite article is attached as in *Ha'Shoah*, *the* destruction; *the* Holocaust, *the* burning or annihilation. Capitalization is of further help; we are not here concerned with "holocausts" (a word often applied to such acts as the thermonuclear burnings at Hiroshima and Nagasaki). In belles lettres, as elsewhere, the word "holocaust" has come to be employed loosely and, thereby, somewhat misleadingly.[10]

It must be stressed that, behind any seeming pedantry of the foregoing paragraphs, there loom momentous human questions. For example, what is the relation of *the* Holocaust to different "holocausts," to other acts of human destruction? *This* Holocaust—in what ways is it unique?

DILEMMAS FOR THE ANALYST

A student of the Holocaust and its aftermath may exhibit a form of clinical, detached objectivity.[11] In contrast, there is the approach of a participant, *un homme engagé*, an interpreter who insists that detachment is the adversary of human obligation. Along which path is the investigator of today to make his journey? Or may he succeed in traveling both of the roads? Perhaps it is useful to include an autobiographical note, not for personal reasons, but because it bears upon the methodological dilemmas that pervade our subject and, also, because of the requirement of fairness.

It was in an intellectual–experiential way that we came to the particular issue of the Holocaust, its meaning and its consequences. This occurred after having attended, for a number of years, to the historical, ideational, and moral relationships between Christianity and Judaism, between Christians and Jews. Although it is the case that a beginning study in the latter general realm was prepared back in the immediate post-Holocaust time (1945–47), the effort was not primarily a response to the Nazi *Endlösung*, even though it did deal somewhat with that reality and it sought to grapple with antisemitism, especially Christian theological antisemitism.[12] The bare truth is that we did not come to the subject of the Holocaust, nor earlier to that of Christian–Jewish relations, through any traumatic personal encounters within, or even outside, the Europe of 1933–45. Rather, it was the anti-Jewish problematic within Christian teaching and the history of Christianity that finally led us, perhaps inexorably, to the Holocaust.

The last thing we should ever imply is that direct participation in, or victimization by, the *Endlösung* makes the survivor incapable of comprehending and of placing the evil within a broad and deep frame of reference. On the contrary, such direct confrontation may be of crucial aid in the achievement of a "theory" of the event, in the highest sense of that term. Jacob Robinson points out that the judgments of some authors are weakened by the fact that they never experienced the Holocaust (or any other mass disaster). Many writers did not even follow closely the development of the *Endlösung*.[13] Many who suffered in the Holocaust but who somehow managed, or were enabled, to survive it have attained, especially with the distancing years, a kind of creative objectivity in their very descriptions and assessments of Nazism.

Wherein, then, lies the relevance of our own accounting? There is the danger that the Holocaust will be appropriated only as a nightmare, a horrible episode that erupted within a brief span of years as part of a special ideological development or political tragedy or whim of an insane man, a nightmare from which we have long since awakened. There is the temptation to reduce the *Endlösung* to an aberration, a kind of cultural–moral mutation. In consequence, a needed comprehension of the event as the logical and even inevitable climax of a lengthy and indestructible ethos tradition and theological obsessiveness may be lost. Against this, we must root ourselves in the fateful past—a possibility that has only of late gained a foothold within scholarly circles, and within and beyond the Christian church. We seek for the grace that may derive from a certain historical perspective, from a kind of distancing that is, at the same time, nearness. Captivation by, and concern for, the centuries-long story of antisemitism and particularly the anti-semitism that is fatefully linked to one's own religious tradition, will produce, it is hoped, at least three results: It will aid us in avoiding a facile approach; it will help to foster a concerned objectivity; and it may offset, a little, the personal condition of having passed the Holocaust years at a protected distance.

Those who contend that one must have been a part of the horror in order to write of it face the difficulty that no written word can equal the experience itself. It is a Holocaust survivor, and not some mere onlooker, who has written: "Perhaps, what we tell about what happened and what really happened have nothing to do one with the other."[14] True, the nonparticipant's writing is at least twice removed from the reality. However, the participant's writing remains once removed. In both cases there is a break with noumenal truth.[15] This is not to disagree that, in principle, a qualitative difference obtains between literature that is once removed and writings that are twice removed.

To those who say that you must have been within the inferno in order to approach it and write of it, we can only respond, with Cynthia Haft, that "we too want this event, so unique, never to be forgotten, that we too feel obliged to join with them in their efforts to remind others and to bear witness, without in any way violating the sanctity of the subject matter.[16]

We trust that the struggle against false objectivity is carried forward in some measure through the elements of personal encounter upon which our own studies are grounded. There is no way to separate one's acts as a human being from one's work (without falling into a certain personality split). The two elements are bound together within the larger category of "calling" (*vocatio*). Objectivity without commitment contains temptations—most lamentably, those of neutrality and coldness. This condition must be fought. The objectivization of the Holocaust, that is, the removal of, or the refusal to make, evaluative judgments about the event, constitutes, in effect, a justification of the

German Nazi program. One either opposes Nazism or supports it; the bystander, by default, ranges himself on the side of the supporter.

It is a fact that the very study of the Holocaust's aftermath becomes, inevitably, part of that aftermath, part of *Existenz*. There is objectivity for the sake of truth, and subjectivity for the sake of goodness. Truth and goodness are not separable.

A further moral complexity appears. Allusion is made above to the German Nazi device of setting camp inmates in competition for their very survival. We ourselves do not totally escape a related kind of evil whenever we call attention to the testimonies and records of certain sufferers but not to those of others. For all representations of the testimonial literature[17]—not excepting those made by compilers or interpreters who are themselves survivors—are inevitably caught up in judgments of value: This piece is "better" than that piece, or is at least "more memorable" than that one, or at least this one is to be called to public attention instead of that one. Cynthia Haft observes that, unfortunately, the mere fact of having been in a concentration camp, or of having learned what happened to others there, does not necessarily bestow literary talent on a writer or create a work of art. In her study, *The Theme of Nazi Concentration Camps in French Literature*, she dwells upon those writings "whose extraordinary literary value distinguishes them from the mass." Why are value judgments and acts of selection essential respecting the mass of writings? Because, so Haft argues, the phenomenon of the concentration camps can penetrate the individual and collective consciousness of our time only through the vehicle of outstanding literature. "Only when this phenomenon has become a literary theme, a poetic theme, will its intense ramifications be felt. The power of language is to contain and transmute all passions, all human experiences of men."[18] Only great literature will truly give expression to this power. (We may anticipate that some of the Holocaust writings will become part of the torah, and perhaps even the Torah, of tomorrow.)

The literary scholar Lawrence L. Langer apologizes for having regretfully omitted from consideration such works of unusual distinction as Piotr Rawicz's *Blood From the Sky* and Charlotte Delbo's *None of Us Will Return*.[19] This apology is as essential as the one we ourselves are obliged to make in conjunction with our own work—and it fails to meet the moral problem just as surely as any explanation that we could marshall. All of us act in a way that keeps the memory of one witness alive and lets another's die. Insofar as the nonparticipant in the Holocaust cites this witness and not that one, he shares the same fault as we, who, with Haft and Langer, are not survivors. The only person who does not enter into this fault is the death-camp inmate who wrote in a purely testimonial way and not in a competitive way, and then died or removed himself from literary effort. Once an individual who has survived engages in literary effort, he has become a part of the dubious arena of competition, of the battle that every "writer for publication" knows, of the fierce world of author egos.

In sum, none of us is devoid of sin. The only question is, Which sin is peculiarly ours? We who write about the Holocaust today are all, in a sense, the profiteers of torment.

A further word is in order respecting the testimonial literature. These writings tend to fixate themselves, properly and understandably, upon death and victimization. But, as we have said, the terrible world of the Holocaust also encompasses acts of resistance to the terror. Here is one important reason why concentration upon great portions of the testimonial literature must be balanced by attention to historical analyses and, especially, to more recent historiography with its important finding of spiritual and moral resistance, and of armed Jewish struggle against the Nazi foes.[20] However, any differentiation between the testimonies of helpless sufferers and the accounts of resistance and resistance heroes is a highly relative one. The line is thin. Considerable testimonial literature recounts acts of resistance, while, on the other side, honest historiography is called upon to chronicle the powerless suffering and the annihilation.

An additional problem is tied to the bafflement that many have confessed before the *Judenvernichtung*. They ask, How is the unspeakable to be spoken about? Certainly, we ought to speak of it, but how can we ever do so? Again, how are we to engage in scholarly work on a subject that staggers the mind and stabs the soul, or ought to do so: the human effects of *this* crusading political technological annihilation of an infinity of children, women, and men? Irving Greenberg once said in our hearing that the basic lesson of the Holocaust is that there are no lessons.[21] From this standpoint, the *Endlösung* is too shattering for us to learn anything from it and, accordingly, even to reckon with it.

Are we bereft of a means for coming to terms with the Holocaust? Many interpreters have concentrated upon what is, for them, the incomprehensibility and total irrationality of the event, as against the claim that it is somehow meaningful, or at least that something can be learned from it. We do no prejudice to Greenberg's conclusion when we point out that the noumenal or ostensibly mysterious character of the Holocaust is one thing, while the consequences that the event has had and is having within human life and thought are quite something else. Greenberg's own asserted bafflement exemplifies the second of these categories. We allude now to the phenomenal impact of the Holocaust, noting the aptness of the ambiguity in the concept "phenomenal": The word has come to mean "powerful" and "decisive" while also retaining its philosophical connotations of "empirical" and "observable."

The available or parsimonious way to judge what the impact of the *Endlösung* may be upon an individual or a collectivity is through empirical availability or nonavailability. (Nonimpact is as much a part of the historical and scientific question of the Holocaust's aftermath as is positive impact.) We simply study the evidence. The phenomena may be exhibited either volitionally or nonvolitionally, directly or indirectly. In many cases we have to probe for meanings and implications that lie below the surface.

The fine novelist Cynthia Ozick has declared that the Holocaust is already dangerously literary, dangerously legendary, dangerously trivialized to pity, and the pity to poetry.[22] She properly reminds us of the embarrassment of available literary and documentary riches on our subject. On the matter of legend, it is true that the human proclivity to mythologize the past is universal and sometimes dominating. But we do not believe that pity trivializes the Holocaust, unless, or until, it becomes the exclusive response. (Whether pity is trivialized in poetry, we do not have the capacity to judge.) However, the real stumbling block to agreement with Ozick is that we are forced into literature, legend, pity, and poetry in the very acts of observing and guarding against the dangers in these and other pursuits.

The imponderability and *mysterium tremendum* of the Holocaust, together with varied calls for silence before its unspeakableness, have not prevented the production of a multiplicity of materials on the subject. In this respect, our problem is not so much how to speak of the unspeakable, but, instead, how to confront and reasonably assimilate an incredibly large body of published literature, documents, and testimonies as, at the same time, we seek out living people and fresh interpretations and dare to venture interpretations of our own.

As with any powerful historical development, data that reflect the continuing impact of the Holocaust are mediated to the scholar through varied ways of understanding. If this state of affairs makes for a pluralistic coloring in much of our own work, and if it suggests findings and judgments that are at best tentative and uncertain, these results are made necessary by the vastness of the subject, its severely controversial aspects, and its many impalpable elements. Pluralistic understanding is associated as well with the kinds of questions that an investigator resolves to ask. Insofar as his interests center in problems of causation and social conditioning, he will turn to sociohistorical or psychohistorical materials. If he is concerned with questions of meaning and value, he will turn to literary creations or to philosophic and theological sources. Yet the lines are always crossing, for the latter kinds of source are inevitably influenced by given social milieus, just as the former kinds of source are always conditioned by existential and moral experience. To set one type of approach qualitatively above the other is never very convincing.[23]

This brief discussion of linguistic and methodological dilemmas suggests the concept "phenomenology," a term that epitomizes the overall approach we are following in our research. All ways of apprehending phenomena are fallible. We must strive for representativeness of an ideational, factual, and geographical kind. Yet it is impossible wholly to escape impressionism or to elude Alfred North Whitehead's dictum that all life proceeds by simplification. The work of any analyst of the Holocaust and its consequences entails an apprehension of selected data from varied standpoints, not excepting his own. The ambiguity in the word "apprehension"—standing, as it does, for both the claimed receiving of truth and a certain anxiety respecting the future, including in the present instance the anxiety over harming human beings through one's research and writing—invests that word with a certain fearful propriety.

NOTES

1. So Gerald Reitlinger argues: see his *The Final Solution: The Attempt to Exterminate the Jews of Europe 1939-1945* (New York: A.S. Barnes, 1961), p. 102. Raul Hilberg speaks of the fateful step across the "dividing line" that inaugurated the "killing phase," and he refers to two all-decisive orders by Hitler in 1941 that were to doom all European Jewry. *The Destruction of the European Jews* rev. ed. (Chicago: Quadrangle Books, 1967), pp. 177ff.

2. Of these, the Nazis succeeded in destroying about 6,000,000. It is not possible to furnish exact figures. The *Encyclopaedia Judaica* (Jerusalem) estimates the number at 5,820,960.

3. Abel J. Herzberg illustrates this aspect of the truth in his essays on Bergen-Belsen, *Amor Fati, Zeven opstellen over Bergen-Belsen* (Amsterdam: Moussault's Uitgeverij, 1950).

4. Abba Kovner, "A First Attempt to Tell," unpublished preparatory paper for International Scholars Conference on the Holocaust, New York, March 3-6, 1975.

5. Elie Wiesel, *Legends of Our Time* (New York: Avon, 1968), p. 229.

6. Cynthia Haft, *The Theme of Nazi Concentration Camps in French Literature* (The Hague: Mouton, 1973), p. 133.

7. Ibid., p. 153.

8. Bernard Dupuy, "Un théologien juif de l'Holocauste, Emil Fackenheim," *Foi et Vie* (Paris) 73, no. 4 (September 1974): 12n. Dupuy is secretary of the French Bishops' Committee for Relations with Judaism.

9. *Christen und Juden, Eine Studie des Rates der Evangelischen Kirche in Deutschland* (Gütersloh: Gerd Möhn, 1975), p. 53. The word "annihilation" (*Vernischtung*) in the EKD statement is particularly apt, in contradistinction to the oft-used "extermina-

tion." A colleague in the United States, Bernard Mikofsky, properly objects to "extermination" because of its implied or unconscious sanctioning of the German Nazi contention that Jews are subhuman: We speak, for example, of exterminating rodents and roaches. "Annihilation" is the more objective word.

10. The novelist R. F. Delderfield uses the lower-case form of the word simply to epitomize the Second Great War. *To Serve Them All My Days*, bk. 2 (London: Coronet Books, 1973), p. 370. Martin Middlebrook reads back the concept "holocaust" into the First Great War, as cited in Paul Fussell, *The Great War and Modern Memory* (New York: Oxford University Press, 1975), p. 82.

11. Hilberg's *The Destruction of the European Jews*, which restricts itself to the Holocaust as such, is often singled out as an illustration par excellence of this outlook. Not unrelated to the point is the fact that Hilberg comes to the *Endlösung* as though from the standpoint of its perpetrators rather than of its victims. We say "as though" because Hilberg is the foe of everything Nazi. His work remains authoritative.

12. A. Roy Eckardt, *Christianity and the Children of Israel* (New York: King's Crown Press, 1948). The volume was based on a doctoral dissertation composed under the supervision of Reinhold Niebuhr.

13. Jacob Robinson, assisted by Mrs. Philip Friedman, *The Holocaust and After: Sources and Literature in English*, Yad Vashem Martyrs' and Heroes' Memorial Authority, Jerusalem, and Yivo Institute for Jewish Research, New York, Joint Documentary Projects, Bibliographical Series, no. 12 (Jerusalem: Israel Universities Press, 1973), p. 323.

14. Elie Wiesel, "Jewish Values in the Post-Holocaust Future," *Judaism* 16, no. 3 (Summer 1967): 283.

15. Cf. Immanuel Kant's teaching that the noumenal world forever eludes us, in contrast to the world of phenomena.

16. Haft, *The Theme*, p. 11.

17. The phrase "testimonial literature" is used to cover writings of those who met their death under the German Nazi persecutors and also of those who suffered but survived. The term extends to memoirs, poetry, diaries, stories, lamentations, contemplative writing, calls for help, and eyewitness accounts.

18. Haft, *The Theme*, pp. 10-11, 189. Haft identifies these works as "masterpieces of the deportation": Elie Wiesel, *Night* (New York: Avon Books, 1960); Charlotte Delbo, *Aucun de nous ne reviendra* (*None of Us Will Return*) (Paris: Editions de Minuit, 1970); and Jorge Semprun, *Le grand voyage* (*The Great Journey*) (Paris: Gallimard, 1963).

19. Lawrence L. Langer, *The Holocaust and the Literary Imagination* (New Haven: Yale University Press, 1975), p. xiii.

20. Cf., e.g., Yehuda Bauer, *They Chose Life: Jewish Resistance in the Holocaust* (New York: Institute of Human Relations, American Jewish Committee; Jerusalem: Institute of Contemporary Jewry, The Hebrew University, 1973); Yuri Suhl, *They Fought Back: The Story of the Jewish Resistance in Nazi Europe* (London: MacGibbon & Kee, 1968); Reuben Ainsztein, *Jewish Resistance in Nazi-Occupied Eastern Europe* (London: Elek, 1974).

21. Irving Greenberg, "Lessons to Be Learned from the Holocaust" (Paper prepared for the Hamburg Holocaust Conference, June 8-11, 1975).

22. Cynthia Ozick, "The Uses of Legend: Elie Wiesel as Tsaddik," *Congress Bi-Weekly* 36, no. 9 (June 9, 1969): 19. Cf. Wilfred Owen, referring to the First Great War: "My subject is war, and the pity of war. The poetry is in the pity."

23. Cf. the discussion by Laurence J. Silberstein in Moshe Davis, *Contemporary Jewish Civilization on the American Campus: Research and Teaching* (Jerusalem: Institute of Contemporary Jewry, The Hebrew University, 1974), pp. 70-71.

THE CONTRIBUTORS

HANNAH ARENDT before her death in 1975 was a fellow of the Committee of Social Thought at the University of Chicago and University Professor of Political Philosophy at the New School for Social Research. She was the author of many articles and books, including *Eichmann in Jerusalem*, *The Human Condition*, and *The Life of the Mind*.

RONALD ARONSON is Professor of Humanities in the University Studies/Weekend College Program at Wayne State University, Detroit. He is the author of *Jean-Paul Sartre: Philosophy in the World* and *The Dialectics of Disaster: A Preface to Hope*. He is currently working on a book entitled *After Progress*.

RAINER C. BAUM is Professor of Sociology at the University of Pittsburgh. He wrote *The Holocaust and the German Elite: Genocide and National Suicide in Germany, 1871-1945*, coedited *Explorations in General Theory in Social Science*, and wrote, with Martha Baum, *Growing Old: A Societal Perspective*.

ALICE L. ECKARDT is Professor of Religion at Lehigh University. She is the editor of and a contributor to *Jerusalem: City of the Ages* and co-author of *Long Night's Journey into Day*, which will be issued in a revised edition in 1988. She and A. Roy Eckardt will be Visiting Fellows at the Centre for Hebrew Studies, Oxford University, for the academic year 1988-89.

A. ROY ECKARDT is Professor Emeritus, Department of Religion Studies, Lehigh University. He is the author of *For Righteousness' Sake: Contemporary Moral Philosophies; Elder and Younger Brothers: The Encounter of Jews and Christians*; and, with Alice L. Eckardt, of *Long Night's Journey into Day*, a revised edition of which will be published in 1988.

MARTIN P. GOLDING is Professor of Philosophy and Law at Duke University. He is the author of *Philosophy of Law* and *Legal Reasoning*, and is the editor of *The Nature of Law*. He has also published articles on legal and moral philosophy and bioethics in a number of journals and books.

443

PETER H. HARE is Professor of Philosophy and Chairperson of the Department of Philosophy at the State University of New York at Buffalo. He is co-author of *Evil and the Concept of God* and of *Causing, Perceiving and Believing: An Examination of the Philosophy of C. J. Ducasse.* He is co-editor of *History, Religion and Spiritual Democracy: Essays in Honor of Joseph L. Blau* and of *Naturalism and Rationality.* Since 1974 he has edited the *Transactions of the C.S. Peirce Society: A Quarterly Journal in American Philosophy.*

MANFRED HENNINGSEN is Professor of Political Science at the University of Hawaii at Manoa. He has published books, essays, and articles, mostly in German, on Toynbee's philosophy of history, the European images of America from the eighteenth to the twentieth century, and social science epistemology.

HANS JONAS is Alvin Johnson Professor Emeritus of Philosophy at the New School for Social Research. He has written many articles on ancient gnosticism, the philosophy of biology, and the ethics of technology. He is the author of *The Gnostic Religion; The Phenomenon of Life; Philosophical Essays;* and *The Imperative of Responsibility.*

STEVEN T. KATZ is Professor of Jewish History and Religion and Chairman of the Department of Near Eastern Studies at Cornell University. His published works include *Jewish Philosophers; Jewish Ideas and Concepts; Mysticism and Philosophical Analysis; Mysticism and Religious Traditions;* and *Post-Holocaust Dialogues: Studies in Modern Jewish Thought.*

GEORGE M. KREN is Professor of History at Kansas State University. He is the author of many articles on psychohistory and the Holocaust. He is co-author of *The Holocaust and the Crisis of Human Behavior* and co-editor of *Varieties of Psychohistory.*

BEREL LANG is Professor of Philosophy and Humanistic Studies, and Director of the Center for Humanities at the State University of New York at Albany. He is the author of many articles and books, among them *Philosophy and the Art of Writing* and *Faces, and Other Ironies.* He is the editor of *Philosophical Style* and of a special issue of the *Philosophical Forum,* which was devoted to the Holocaust.

LAWRENCE L. LANGER is Alumnae Professor of English at Simmons College, Boston. He is the author of many articles and books that deal with the Holocaust, among them *The Holocaust and the Literary Imagination; The Age of Atrocity: Death in Modern Literature;* and *Versions of Survival: The*

Holocaust and the Human Spirit. He is presently analyzing recurrent themes in survivor testimonies gathered in the Video Archive for Holocaust Testimonies at Yale.

DAN MAGURSHAK is Professor of Philosophy at Carthage College in Kenosha, Wisconsin. He is the author of several articles on topics in recent continental philosophy. He has cotranslated the English edition of Otto Pöggeler's *Der Denkweg Martin Heidegger's. (Martin Heidegger's Path of Thinking).* He is currently at work on a book concerning the analysis of everydayness in the works of Kierkegaard and Heidegger.

PAUL MARCUS is a clinical psychologist in private practice. He has written a number of articles which have appeared in the *Journal of the American Academy of Psychoanalysis, Psychoanalytic Inquiry,* and the *British Journal of Plastic Surgery.* He also has co-edited *Psychoanalytic Reflections of the Holocaust: Selected Essays.* He is currently under contract to write a book with Alan Rosenberg entitled *The Faith of Holocaust Survivors: A Psychological Inquiry.*

GERALD E. MYERS is Professor of Philosophy at Queens College and the City University of New York Ph.D. program in philosophy. He has written many articles on aesthetics, the philosophy of mind, and American philosophy. He is the author of *William James: His Life and Thought.*

ALAN ROSENBERG is a Lecturer in the Department of Philosophy at Queens College, the City University of New York. He is the author and co-author of a number of articles and reviews that have appeared in a variety of journals and books, including *Modern Judaism, Cross Currents, European Judaism, Journal for the Theory of Social Behaviour, Simon Wiesenthal Center Annual, Holocaust and Genocide Studies,* and *SHOAH.* He is currently under contract to write a book with Paul Marcus entitled *The Faith of Holocaust Survivors: A Psychological Inquiry.*

ABIGAIL L. ROSENTHAL is Professor of Philosophy at Brooklyn College of the City University of New York. She is the author of *A Good Look at Evil* (Temple University Press, 1987) as well as a number of articles that have appeared in a variety of journals, including *Clio, Journal of Applied Philosophy, Journal of the History of Philosophy,* and *The Monist.*

JOHN K. ROTH is the Russell K. Pitzer Professor of Philosophy at Claremont McKenna College, California. In addition to serving as a Special Adviser to the chairman of the United States Holocaust Memorial Council, Washington, D.C., he has been Visiting Professor of Holocaust

Studies at the University of Haifa, Israel. Presently the book review editor for *Holocaust and Genocide Studies*, Roth is the author of numerous articles on the Holocaust. He has also published ten books, including *A Consuming Fire: Encounters with Elie Wiesel and the Holocaust*. His most recent book, written with Richard L. Rubenstein, is *Approaches to Auschwitz: The Holocaust and Its Legacy*, published in 1987 by John Knox Press.

KENNETH SEESKIN is Professor of Philosophy and Chairperson of the Department of Philosophy at Northwestern University. He is the author of a number of articles on Greek philosophy, the history of philosophy, and the philosophy of religion. He is also the author of *Dialogue and Discovery: A Study in Socratic Method*.

LAURENCE THOMAS is Professor of Philosophy at Oberlin College. He is the author of a number of articles that have appeared in a variety of journals and books, including *Synthèse*, the *Canadian Journal of Philosophy*, the *American Philosophical Quarterly*, and *Epistemology and Sociobiology*, edited by James Fetzer. He is presently completing *A Psychology of Moral Character*.

WARREN K. THOMPSON is Professor of Philosophy and director of the Leadership Studies Program at Lebanon Valley College in Annville, Pennsylvania. His major interests are social and political ethics and ethical issues in the professions.

EDITH WYSCHOGROD is Professor of Philosophy at Queens College of the City University of New York. She is the author of many articles and books. Her latest book is *Spirit in Ashes: Hegel, Heidegger and Man-Made Mass Death*.

INDEX